PETER IN ROME

Daniel Wm. O'Connor is Professor of
Religion at St. Lawrence University in
Canton, New York.

PETER IN ROME

The Literary, Liturgical, and Archeological Evidence

by Daniel Wm. O'Connor

COLUMBIA UNIVERSITY PRESS

New York *and* London 1969

Daniel Wm. O'Connor is Professor of Religion
at St. Lawrence University

To Carolyn,
Kathlyn,
and
Dan

Foreword

THE first scholar to question the tradition of Peter's residence in Rome, his martyrdom, and burial there, was Marsilius of Padua, rector of the University of Paris in the fourteenth century and author of the famous *Defensor Pacis* (1324). Somewhat earlier, the Waldensians in northern Italy had opened the issue when they limited the data of Christian doctrine exclusively to the Holy Scriptures—for the New Testament has nothing explicit to say about the latter years of Peter. The *Defensor Pacis* was not published until 1522, when it became an influential document in the theological debates inspired by the Reformation, especially those concerned with church authority and the historical foundations underlying the Church's teaching, especially the beginnings of the papacy. From the early sixteenth century to the present day, the question of Peter's residence in Rome, his martyrdom, and burial there, has been continually examined and debated, with the fullest possible examination of the literary and liturgical data and, most recently, the search for archeological evidence.

The fundamental problem is set by the fact that the New Testament says nothing affirmatively on the subject, nor do the earliest Christian writings outside the New Testament say more. The absence of evidence in Jewish, Greek, or Latin writings is not significant, as their authors had no occasion to mention Peter. The positive testimony to Peter's residence in Rome, his death, and burial there, begins as late as the end of the second century. What went before—that is, what has survived—including the New Testament writings with a mere handful of brief mentions, are only hints, innuendoes, shy and obscure references that could be interpreted as assuming his leadership in the Christian community at Rome, his martyrdom at the hands of the Roman authorities, and a secret burial the location of which only the Christians knew and may more or less have forgotten. It is no wonder that the state of this study is hedged about with problems and that one of these, at the very outset, is to explain why these obscurities exist. Only a skilled master in this area of historical research can hope to shed any light on the complicated, intricate, faintly traced ancient data.

Dr. O'Connor is such a master, and his book is one of the three best works on the subject in the past hundred years—and the very best ever produced on this side of the Atlantic. He is perfectly familiar with the literature of the subject—his "Selected Bibliography" lists more than five hundred titles; but he does not merely survey the problems and outline the efforts at their solution—he positively undertakes their solution, with sound judgment and full awareness of the background and implications involved in his solutions. Not only are the major problems examined, but the ancillary, minor ones: Why did Clement of Rome say that the pillars of the Church were persecuted "through jealousy and envy"? What was the tropaeum erected at Peter's (?) tomb? And, what was it doing in a cemetery? And how did it get there? What was the basis of the theory of a removal from one tomb to another? Every step on the way of this research is full of questions—even long before the master problem is undertaken, namely, the burials underneath the Basilica of St. Peter on the Vatican Hill.

This book will interest every person to whom the origins of Christianity are important. It pours the clear, cold light of modern historical research upon the traditions and legends of the past, and recognizes the possibilities, even the probabilities, that lie within the elaborate hull of fancy and devotion. For those whose faith depends upon the historicity of Peter's residence in Rome, his headship of the Church there and elsewhere, his martyrdom, and burial on the Vatican Hill, it may be difficult to accept the negative results of modern historical and archeological research. But the great *fundamenta* upon which the Catholic Church rests must surely be firmer than legend or even tradition. It is the ontological reality of the institution itself that is self-evident. For those whose faith does not depend upon historical dates and events or their various records, the story of Peter's last years and days is an heroic tale brought down from the heroic age of the martyrs. We do not have all the details we would like. But this is often the way with religious origins, always and everywhere. It is the spirit of that age that is most important, and still speaks to all ages.

FREDERICK C. GRANT

Gwynedd, Pensylvania
January, 1968

Preface

ANY attempt to verify the tradition that Peter resided in Rome and that he was martyred and buried there is immediately involved in few answers and many questions. Some questions are extremely difficult to answer; others are unanswerable. This book does not pretend to solve the intricate problems but attempts to raise the important questions, to present fairly the various solutions proposed, and to decide among them when it appears that sufficient evidence is available. Very often the choice is not between one theory that is correct and another that is false, but between one that appears to be more possible or probable than another; that is, often the choice is not between black and white but between shades of gray.

The author endeavors through the text and especially through the footnotes to present material and sources that will be helpful in enabling others to continue this research. The relevant literature is vast. Over 525 titles have been entered in the bibliography at the end of the book which hopefully includes all significant contributions. Numerous reviews and translations of books listed, as well as a number of brief critical notes, have been omitted.

Grateful acknowledgment is made to the following for their permission to use copyrighted material: Aschendorffschen Verlagsbuchhandlung for figure 18 in *Die Cathedra im Totenkult der heidnischen und christlichen Antike* (Liturgiegeschichtliche Forschungen, Heft 9, 1927); editors of *Capitolium* for two figures included on pages 62 and 65 of the 1950 issue (Volume XXV) of *Capitolium* in which appeared the article "L'Obelisco Vaticana" by Carlo Cecchelli; Desclée and Co. for figure 4 in *Roma sotterranea; le Pitture delle Catacombe* (1903) by Josef Wilpert; Margherita Guarducci for figures 17 and 44 in *Cristo e San Pietro in un Documento precostantiniano della Necropoli Vaticana* (1953) published by "L'Erma" di E.e.G. Bretschneider; La Pontificia Accademia romana di Archeologia for one figure which appeared in "Sulla Ricostruzione della 'mensa martyrum' nella Memoria Apostolorum in Catacumbas," by Adriano Prandi in the *Atti della Pontificia Accademia romana di Archeologia: Rendiconti*, Vol. XIX (1943); Libreria Editrice Vaticana for figures 4 and 5 in *Le Reliquie di Pietro sotto La Confessione della Basilica Vaticana* (1965) by Margherita Guarducci; Libreria editrice Vaticana for figures 54, 65, 75, 79, 80, 81, 84, 87, 88, 89, 90a and b, 91, 98, 100, 101, F and G in Volume I and figure CIV in Volume II in *Esplorazioni sotto la Confessione di San Pietro*

ix

in Vaticano by B. M. Appollonj-Ghetti, Antonio Ferrua, Enrico Josi, and Englebert Kirschbaum (1951); Munksgaard International Boghandel og Forlag Akticselskab for figures 15 and 52 in 1953 (Volume XXIV) issue of *Acta Archaeologica* in which appeared the article, "The Vatican Excavations and the Cult of St. Peter" by Hjalmar Torp; Pantheon Books for figure 3 in *The Shrine of St. Peter and the Vatican Excavations* by Jocelyn Toynbee and John Ward Perkins; Pontificio Istituto di Archeologia cristiana for figure 5 in the 1954 (Volume XXX) issue of *Rivista di Archeologia cristiana* in which appeared the article, "Noterelle sulla 'Memoria Apostolorum' in Catacumbas" by Pasquale Testini; Società "Amici delle Catacombe" for figures I, IIIa, IIIb, IV, V and XLIII in *Memorie degli Apostoli in Catacumbas* (1953) by Francesco Tolotti; Società "Amici delle Catacombe" for figures 20 and 21 in *Le Tombe apostoliche nell'età paleocristiana* (1948) by Giulio Belvederi; Verlag Herder Freiburg for figures II and IIIa in the 1915 (Volume XXIX) issue of *Römische Quartalschrift* in which appeared the article "Scavi a San Sebastiano" by Paul Styger.

I am indebted to Professors Cyril C. Richardson of Union Theological Seminary and Morton Smith of Columbia University for their valuable advice and help in the early stages of research and writing; to Professor Frederick C. Grant, retired from Union Theological Seminary, for his suggestion a number of years ago that this study be undertaken, for his counsel and guidance, and writing of the Foreword; to Mrs. Hugh Foster, Research Librarian and retired from Union Theological Seminary, and Mrs. John Mentley, Research Librarian, St. Lawrence University, for their help in locating and securing a great number of periodicals and books; to Mrs. Ruth Stokes for her care in typing revisions of the manuscript for publication; to my friend and colleague Professor J. Calvin Keene of St. Lawrence University, for his support, suggestions, and patient reading of the manuscript and proof; and to my wife, Carolyn, for her constant encouragement and the hundreds of hours devoted to preparation of the original typescript. Finally, I am indebted to St. Lawrence University which cooperated with Columbia University Press in making possible the publication of this book.

DANIEL WM. O'CONNOR

St. Lawrence University
June, 1968

Contents

LIST OF PLATES

Introduction

MOST authorities will readily acknowledge that within the New Testament Peter is recognized as the spokesman of the disciples, and to deny that Peter held a special place of prominence among the Twelve is impossible. The Scriptures inform us that Peter was often timid and uncertain, lacking in determination and courage. At times he is depicted as hasty and rash, irritable and capable of great anger. At other times he is described as gentle and, as in his protestations to Jesus, capable of great loyalty and love. He could be vacillating and unsure, as in his relations with the church at Antioch; but he could also be resolute, as after Pentecost.

The New Testament reports that Peter was uneducated in the sense of being untrained in the Law; and that he knew Greek is very doubtful. It appears that he learned slowly and erred time and time again in the same manner, but later, entrusted with responsibility, he demonstrated that he was not unintelligent. Peter was a "rock," and yet he was not; he was courageous, but not all the time. He was, like most men, a paradox, neither good nor bad, neither strong nor weak, largely governed by the circumstances in which he found himself and all too prone to be subject to the pressures which were exerted upon him.

All this may be gleaned from the pages of the New Testament—explicitly, from the statements concerning Peter, or implicitly, from his actions and reactions as revealed by a number of episodes in which he figures prominently.

What does the New Testament have to say of Peter's alleged sojourn in Rome, his martyrdom and burial there? There is the vague reference to his martyrdom in the disputed passage of John 21,[1] but it contains no indication of place. The only verse which implies that Peter did visit Rome is 1 Peter 5:13.[2]

Despite the almost complete silence in the New Testament concerning this question, there has been since the earliest period of Christian history a persistent tradition that Peter did visit Rome, suffered martyrdom there, and was buried in the vicinity of the city outside its walls. The problem of this study is to weigh carefully all the literary, liturgical, and archeological evidence, and if possible to determine, especially in light of the recent excavations beneath the Church of St. Peter in the Vatican, whether these claims of ancient tradition are reasonably valid.

The word "reasonably" is used advisedly, since in none of the earliest authentic documents do we find an unequivocal statement to corroborate the tradition in such a way as to make further investigation superfluous. Nor, it might be said at the outset, has the archeological investigation produced any evidence so conclusive as to render unnecessary careful examination of all relevant testimony.

There are no firsthand accounts of a Roman visit written by a companion of Peter who journeyed with him. Nor are we so fortunate as to possess contemporary accounts of his martyrdom or burial. We must therefore be content to work in the realm of possibilities and probabilities. I shall attempt to evaluate the evidence as to its importance for or against the tradition.

The importance of this study does not lie simply in the fact that we wish to learn as much as possible about those first disciples, who listened to the words of Christ and were charged with the responsibility of preaching the Gospel to all the world. It is not curiosity concerning the latter part of Peter's life, his death and his burial, that prompts this work. In fact, if these were the only elements of interest, it is most probable that the tradition would never have been questioned in the first instance. One point of importance in the problem lies in the relationship which exists between the coming of Peter to Rome, his martyrdom and burial there, and the

---

1. See below, pp. 61–64.
2. See below, pp. 15–18.

question of the supremacy of the Roman See and the Roman pontiff. Roman Catholic tradition claims that the Roman pontiff is the legitimate successor to St. Peter and undisputed heir to his prerogatives and privileges, by virtue of the traditional interpretation of the statements to Peter found in Matthew 16:17–19 and John 21. However, even if it should be found that there is sufficient evidence to substantiate the claim that Peter did visit Rome, was martyred, and buried there, this does not mean that *ipso facto* the claims of the Roman See or the Roman pontiff are justified, that is, that the powers and privileges were intended, by Him who allegedly conferred them upon Peter, to be handed down to successors, "non solum pro seipso, sed pro omnibus successoribus suis."[3] On the other hand, were it disproved that Peter visited Rome and was martyred and buried there, this would not destroy the foundations of the Papacy. Most defenders of the Roman Catholic position emphasize that the Papacy rests upon faith and not upon facts of history,[4] although assumptions based upon supposed facts most assuredly contributed in the beginning to the foundation of such faith.

This study is undertaken neither to satisfy simply the demands of Christian curiosity concerning one of its earliest and most important figures nor to validate or to undermine the claims of the Roman Catholic Church.

The purpose is not to plead a cause but, as critically and scientifically as possible, to examine a tradition, to determine insofar as possible its validity, without thought for the possible ramifications for theology. This book is limited to the questions of Peter's presence in Rome, his martyrdom, and his burial. I do not attempt to discuss the relationship of the findings to the question of Roman primacy, nor to carry the discussion of the literary and liturgical sources beyond that date when the tradition is so widely known and accepted that additional material would be nothing more than a reflection and interpretation of such tradition.

After a brief introduction and examination of the history of the problem to the moment of writing, Part I continues with a discussion of the sojourn of Peter in Rome; here the relevant literary and liturgical material is considered chronologically. Following the same procedure, Part II deals with the question of the martyrdom of Peter in Rome. The subject of Part III is the tradition of the burial of the apostle in Rome. In addition to the literary and liturgical evidence, extensive account is taken of the excavations at San Sebastiano and in the Sacred Grotto of St. Peter's in the Vatican. A chronological chart is provided in the Appendix which lists and evaluates the sources concerning the Roman tradition of Peter.

---

3. "Not for himself alone, but for all his successors," Cajetan, *De Comparatione Auctoritatis Papae et Concilii*, p. 28.

4. "The indissoluble union of the office of the bishop of Rome and the universal transapostolic pontifical office and authority is a dogmatic fact for us [the Roman Catholic Church] which history of course can never contradict, but which at the same time it can never establish, and which depends upon a certitude higher than that of history," Journet, *The Primacy of Peter*, p. 106. This view is shared by Campiche, "Saint Pierre et son Martyre," p. 251: Fundamentally if we could prove that Peter never set foot in Rome nor died there,

---

still Pope Pius XII would be "pour nous le successeur de Pierre comme pasteur de tout le troupeau. . . . Il est donc bien vain de nier la venue de Pierre à Rome si c'est l'espoir de ruiner l'Église catholique." But the facts of history are not *totally* unrelated to the foundation and validity of the Roman Papacy, as Corte, *Saint Pierre est-il au Vatican?* p. 9, indicates. The question of the Papacy is not "entirely distinct" from the problem of the coming of Peter to Rome. Actually the Pope is bishop of Rome *because* Peter came to Rome, and after him in that See there was an uninterrupted succession of bishops. See also for the same view Burger, *La Tombe*, p. 5.

PART I

A Brief Historical Survey
of the Problem and the Literary
Evidence for the Tradition
of the Residence of Peter
in Rome

CHAPTER 1

The Debate Concerning
the Roman Tradition of Peter[1]

IT IS A fairly common opinion even shared by some historians[2] that the debate over the coming of Peter to Rome began in the heat of controversy during the Reformation. In reality, it was not the Protestants of this period who first voiced doubts, but the Waldensians, as early as the beginning of the thirteenth century. This sect, living in the valleys of the Alps, was convinced that the only standard of the Christian faith was the Holy Scriptures. Therefore, since the Bible contained no explicit reference to the residence of Peter in Rome, the silence of Scripture was sufficient evidence to disprove the tradition. This argument from silence was continued by Marsilius of Padua in his *Defensor Pacis* (1326).

Aside from the doubts expressed by Martin Luther[3] and a few others, there was little interest in the question from the middle of the sixteenth to the early nineteenth century.[4] The period of cautious scepticism was at an end, however, when F. Christian Baur leveled his unprecedented frontal attack upon the tradition, an exaggeration which was debated and for the most part rejected.[5] What was more important than the particular views expressed by Baur and his critics was the immediate unfortunate divisive effect of the debate.

When T. C. Simon wrote in the mid-nineteenth century,[6] it was considered incumbent upon a Protestant that he attack every stand taken by the Roman Catholic Church concerning the primacy of Peter, lest by some small concession or admission the position of Protestantism be compromised. Simon examined the available evidence carefully and came to the conclusion that none of the documents gave reliable support to the tradition that Peter had ever lived in Rome or that he died there.

By the end of the century "the denial of the Roman tradition about Peter was almost universally abandoned,"[7] perhaps because of the violent reaction to and the continuing discussion over Baur's exaggerated attack upon the tradition.

Despite some doubts expressed in the last part of the nineteenth century, at this time there was virtual agreement concerning Peter's stay in Rome. Even Ernest Renan, not noted for his conservatism, took it completely for granted when he stated without qualification that "this party [Jewish Christians] which had always been strong at Rome, no doubt was much reinforced by the coming of Peter who became its head, and head of the Church there."[8] Such a positive attitude was continued by the eminent Protestant scholars, J. B. Lightfoot[9] and A. C. McGiffert.[10] Adolf

---

1. In view of the excellent survey of the early debate which is readily available in the recent work by Cullmann, *Peter*, pp. 71–75, only a brief statement concerning that debate will be made here.

2. For example, André Siegfried, *Tu es Petrus*, p. 71, cited by Corte, *Saint Pierre est-il au Vatican?* p. 9.

3. "Das ich den Wahn habe friegt, dass weder S. Petrus noch S. Paulus habe den ersten Stein an der Kirchen zu Rom gelegt." "Wider das Papsttum zu Rom, vom Teufel gestiftet," *D. Martin Luthers Werke*, LIV, 256. See also pp. 254, 255, and 293.

4. Cullmann, *Peter*, p. 74.

5. Baur, "Die Christuspartei," pp. 137 ff.

6. Simon, *The Mission and Martyrdom of St. Peter*.

7. Cullmann, *Peter*, p. 74.

8. Renan, *The Antichrist*, p. 53.

9. Lightfoot, *Apostolic Fathers*, Part I, Vol. I, affirms in a number of instances that Peter lived for a while in Rome and died there. For example, see p. 73; "The visit of Paul [to Rome] was followed after an interval . . . by a visit of Peter." See also pp. 351 f.

10. McGiffert, *A History of Christianity*, p. 591: "There can

Harnack wrote in 1897 that "der Martyrtod des Petrus in Rom ist einst aus tendentiös-protestantischen, dann aus tendenzkritischen Vorurteilen bestritten worden" and that the fact clearly "liegt heute für jeden Forscher, der sich nicht verblendet, am Tage."[11] Although convinced that Peter had visted Rome and had died there, Harnack did deny that Peter had founded the church or was the first bishop, or even that he had spent a great deal of time in Rome.[12] For many it seemed that the last word had been spoken and that the debate was closed, but this proved to be but the calm before the storm. The comparative unanimity of the last part of the nineteenth century was ended, and a second period of debate began.

In 1903 P. W. Schmiedel summed up his findings in an article in the *Encyclopedia Biblica* by saying, "our decision must therefore decidedly be that Peter never was in Rome at all."[13] The considered opinion, which included doubts, of the great Roman Catholic scholar Louis Duchesne may have provided some fuel for the fire.[14] In 1909 almost at the same time that the Protestant Charles Guignebert completely denied the tradition,[15] the Roman Catholic author J. B. Kirsch was writing that the Roman sojourn of Peter was an established fact, with the one reservation that "the duration of the sojourn is not known."[16] In this period the conservative Protestant biblical scholar Theodor Zahn sought to stem the tide of the debate and declared himself in

support of the tradition, disputing forcefully the negative conclusions of F. Christian Baur and Richard Lipsius that the traditions of the ministry and the death of Peter in Rome were derived from material contained in the Clementine Romances.[17] Paul Monceaux, in 1910, raised a calm and nonpolemic voice in defense of the Roman tradition, not blindly defending every position, but making a fair appraisal of the evidence which was then available.[18] He correctly challenged Guignebert's thesis that Peter was adopted by the Judeo-Christian group at Rome to counteract the influence of Paul, and he concluded that "the tradition concerning the Roman episcopate of Peter is earlier than the Roman pretensions . . . not manifested clearly before the end of the second century with Pope Victor . . . the tradition of the Apostolate is independent of the ambition of the Popes."[19] Although voices such as that of Guignebert had been raised in protest, the position as enunciated by Harnack appeared in the beginning of the century to be reasonably secure.

In 1915 Hans Lietzmann wrote his first edition of *Petrus und Paulus in Rom* which was destined to start the third chain reaction debate lasting virtually until the present time. Lietzmann examined not only the literary sources but, especially, the liturgical and the archeological sources, insofar as the latter were available in his day. He ended his scientific study with a conclusion which is almost poetic: "Es löst sich jede Schwierigkeit, wenn Petrus wirklich dort begraben wurde, wo sich jetzt Bramantes Kuppel wölbt, und Paulus seine letzte Ruhe fand, wo sich die Halle der drei Kaiser dehnt."[20] Lietzmann's excellent work, however, was not to go unchallenged. In 1916 Adolf Bauer wrote his answer, "Die Legende von dem Martyrium des Petrus und Paulus in Rom,"[21] to which Lietzmann

---

be no doubt that he [Peter] made his way to Rome before the end of his life and labored for some time there."

11. Harnack, *Die Chronologie*, I, 244n2.

12. *Ibid.*, pp. 703–7.

13. *Encyclopedia Biblica*, IV, 460.

14. *Histoire ancienne de l'Église*. Duchesne affirms the Roman tradition in principle, even if he does take exception to certain parts of it. Such cautious statements as the following earned for him censure within his own Church: The coming of Peter to Rome under Claudius "lacks sufficient foundation to win the assent of history," p. 55. See also p. 61. Because of Duchesne's opinions concerning the place of Peter in the founding of the Roman Church, his book, mentioned above, was placed on the Index by a decree of January 24, 1912. After this on March 1, Duchesne stated that his views had not changed.

15. *La Primauté de Pierre*.

16. *The Catholic Encyclopedia*, II, 748.

17. Zahn, *Introduction*, II, 166–71.

18. Monceaux, "L'Apostolat de Saint Pierre à Rome," pp. 216–40. See also Talmont, *Revue Augustinienne*, XVII (1910), 329–36.

19. *Ibid.*, XVII, 329. This view is contrary to the main contentions of the critics of the Roman tradition. For example, see Goguel, *L'Église primitive*, p. 231.

20. *Petrus und Paulus in Rom*, p. 177.

21. *Wiener Studien: Zeitschrift für klassische Philologie*, XXXVIII, 270 ff.

countered with a second edition of his *Petrus und Paulus in Rom* that included a long archeological appendix by Armin von Gerkan.[22] To the positive conclusions of Lietzmann were added at this time those of Oscar Cullmann,[23] various Roman Catholic scholars of the period[24] and E. Molland.[25] But there were also notes of protest amid the general acclaim for Lietzmann's positive results such as those sounded by Charles Guignebert in his article, "La Sépulture de Pierre."[26] A year later a critical article by Heinrich Dannenbauer appeared,[27] which was followed by the attack on tradition by Johannes Haller.[28] Between the two editions of Lietzmann's book, appeared the posthumous work of Louis Duchesne, in which he insists that "we have enough information to be able to affirm that they [Peter and Paul] came to Rome . . . and that both died there as martyrs."[29] A few years later an article favorable to the tradition was written by the Protestant scholar, F. J. Foakes-Jackson.[30]

In 1933 appeared the fourth edition of the *Manual of Christian Archeology* of Orazio Marucchi, the eminent Roman Catholic archeologist, author of over fifty-five books and articles related to the subject of Peter and Paul in Rome.[31] In it he claims that all the evidence combined permits the opinion not only that Peter did live in Rome, but also that he most likely arrived during the reign of Claudius, between A.D. 41 and 44, left after the edict of Claudius A.D. 49 and did not return again until the year of his death. This overconfident position is somewhat qualified when he adds that "these particular dates are not incontestable; but the principal fact of St. Peter's coming to Rome is historical, and capable of the most rigorous and scientific proof."[32] In 1936 Karl Heussi, critical of such acceptance, wrote the first of a number of articles which marshaled all available evidence against the Roman tradition of Peter.[33] Many were not at all convinced and he was answered in the same year by Hans Lietzmann,[34] and a year later by Berthold Altaner.[35] In this debate Heussi calls into question the usual "proof texts" cited in support of the Roman position; in particular he excluded the most important evidence of 1 Clement as completely without force in the attempt to prove the residence of Peter, or his martyrdom, in Rome. Lietzmann again answered Heussi sharply and sought, in his last attempt, to prove that the literary, liturgical, and archeological evidence was in complete agreement in favor of the tradition and that any other opinion would only meet with "insurmountable difficulties." In spite of this effort Heussi concludes that "Peter never came to the city of the Tiber, and the cupola of Michael Angelo does not vault over the grave of the Apostle of Jesus."[36] His views persist virtually unchanged in his many articles and one book which have appeared since 1939. One important article deals with the evidence concerning the date of the death of Peter implied in Paul's letter to

---

22. *Petrus und Paulus in Rom*, pp. 248–315.

23. "Les Causes de la Mort de Pierre et de Paul d'après le Témoignage de Clément Romain," pp. 294–300.

24. Jacquin, *Histoire de L'Église*, pp. 61–67; O'Hare, "St. Peter in Rome," pp. 337–54; Marucchi, *Pietro e Paolo a Roma*, p. 14. The beautifully illustrated work of Besson, should not be omitted from the list. He ends his study (p. 94) on a note no less positive than a statement contained in Hans Lietzmann's *Petrus und Paulus in Rom*, p. 238: "All the ancient sources leave one clearly to understand that St. Peter sojourned in Rome and died there."

25. "Petrus in Rom," pp. 439–44.

26. *Revue historique*, CLXVIII, 225–53.

27. "Nochmals die römische Petruslegende," Dannenbauer was convinced that "every small village in Palestine could raise up with more right a claim to be the place of the death of Peter than the capital of the Empire."

28. *Das Papsttum, Idee und Wirklichkeit*, I, 15. "Whoever keeps the sobriety of judgment, which after all is the first order of investigation, for him the legend of Peter remains, as the founder and first bishop of the Roman church, a saga without historical basis, poetry without truth."

29. "La Memoria Apostolorum de la Via Appia," p. 7.

30. "Evidence for the Martyrdom of Peter and Paul in Rome," pp. 74–78.

31. See also *Pietro e Paolo a Roma*, pp. xvii–xxi.

32. *Manual of Christian Archeology*, p. 22.

33. *War Petrus in Rom?* (1936).

34. "Petrus römischer Märtyrer," pp. 391–410. This article was then answered in a second article by Karl Heussi, "War Petrus wirklich römischer Märtyrer?," pp. 162–71.

35. "War Petrus in Rom?" pp. 177–88.

36. Xavier, pp. 456 ff. The last sentence is a critical paraphrase of the concluding sentence in both the first (1915) and the second (1927) editions of Lietzmann's *Petrus und Paulus in Rom*.

the Galatians.[37] Another discusses the origin of the Petrine tradition.[38] His book, while containing some new material, summarizes his previously published views.[39]

A study by Martin Dibelius, published in 1942, favors the traditional view and deals at length with 1 Clement, the basic literary passage quoted in defense of the Roman martyrdom of Peter, giving it a new interpretation which will be considered in Part II.[40] There appeared a year later a work by Maurice Goguel, in which he neither affirms nor denies that Peter came to Rome and was martyred there. He concludes by saying that

le développement de la tradition du Pierre à Rome et, plus encore, l'importance qu'on lui a donnée et les conséquences qu'on en a tirées ont été si exactement parallèles au développement du rôle de l'Église de Rome et la croissance de son autorité qu'on est obligé de conclure à une rélation organique.[41]

This is exactly the position attacked by Monceaux in 1910. Goguel continues by saying that if Peter ever did come to Rome, he certainly did not spend enough time there to found the Church nor to influence its development. By the middle of the second century the Roman Church, rightly or wrongly, certainly affirmed that Peter had come to Rome and that he was the founder and first bishop of the Church. In 1960 appeared the second edition of a very important work by Oscar Cullmann, published originally in 1952. In the second edition he devotes eighty-six pages to the literary, liturgical, and archeological sources relative to the sojourn, martyrdom, and burial of Peter in Rome and arrives at the position that at the end of his life Peter "came to Rome and there, after a very short work, died as a martyr under Nero."[42] Upon the publication of the first edition of Cullmann's book, a discussion

followed which, being theological in nature and for the most part concerned with the meaning, historicity, and implications of Matthew 16:17-19,[43] is not related to this study. There was general acceptance of his historical conclusions (with the outstanding exception of Karl Heussi), but comments and criticisms of his position concerning the Roman residence, martyrdom, and burial of Peter will be noted in the course of the discussion.[44] In a careful study of the subject of Peter in Rome, Theodor Klauser, after briefly examining the literary and liturgical evidence in light of the new excavations, asserts that "Petrus, wie die Überlieferung will, gegen Ende seines Lebens in Rom tätig gewesen und dort unter Nero im Jahre 64 als Märtyrer gestorben ist, und zwar in den vatikanischen Gärten."[45] An excellent book by Jocelyn Toynbee and John Ward Perkins, *The Shrine of St. Peter*,[46] provides a detailed interpretation of the recent excavations beneath St. Peter's. In the past decade a great number of articles and books have been written which deal almost entirely with the archeological evidence—the excavations at either San Sebastiano or the Vatican. Since most of them are mentioned in Part III and all appear in the bibliography, these have not been included in this brief historical survey. It must be mentioned, however, that an exhaustive annotated bibliography, including 870 titles and brief summaries of the more important articles and books on the subject of the tradition of Peter in Rome, has been prepared by Angelus De Marco.[47]

---

37. "Gal. 2 und der Lebensausgang der jerusalemischen Urapostel," pp. 67–72.

38. "Die Entstehung der römische Petrustradition," pp. 82 f., 301 f., 501–4.

39. *Die römische Petrustradition.*

40. "Rom und die Christen im ersten Jahrhundert," pp. 25–29.

41. Goguel, *L'Église primitive*, p. 231.

42. Cullmann, *Peter*, p. 157.

43. For example, see Journet, *The Primacy of Peter.*

44. For an extensive bibliography of reviews of Cullmann's, *Peter*, see De Marco, *The Tomb of St. Peter*, pp. 16–19.

45. *Die römische Petrustradition*, p. 16. The same position is reached by Kurt Aland in his article, "Wann Starb Petrus? Eine Bemerkung zu Gal. 2:6," pp. 267–75, in which he attacks the work of Karl Heussi, *Die römische Petrustradition in kritischer Sicht.*

46. *The Shrine of St. Peter and the Vatican Excavations.* See especially the conclusion concerning the Roman tradition; "The evidence of the texts, taken in conjunction with the new discovery of the mid-second century Vatican shrine and with the absence of any rival tradition, justifies us in accepting the Roman tradition as being far more likely to be factual than legendary," p. 133.

47. *The Tomb of Saint Peter*, pp. 1–256.

It is my conviction that there is need for a new treatment of the entire question. The large majority of books and articles have dealt with only one phase of the problem, or with the entire problem in a summary fashion. The archeological sections, even in such important works as those of Hans Lietzmann, are out of date as a result of the new information derived from the excavations at San Sebastiano since 1927 and the excavations beneath the Vatican since 1939. The recent work of Cullmann on the subject of Peter is excellent; but it treats of the problem of Peter's relationship to Rome only as a part of a larger work dealing mainly with the question of the important Petrine passage in Matthew 16:17–19. In this more general volume Cullmann was able to devote only about one third to the history of the debate and the literary, liturgical, and archeological evidence, as well as his own conclusions. This same remark concerning brevity can also be made in reference to Klauser's book in which he allows only twenty-three pages for discussion of the literary and liturgical evidence.

Jérôme Carcopino's works, *Études d'Histoire chrétienne* and *De Pythagore aux Apôtres* deal in the main with the archeological material and, apart from this limitation, support the tradition so completely and uncritically that many within the Roman Catholic Church find it difficult to accept a number of their conclusions. The articles, "Saint Pierre" and "Vatican," by Leclercq and Marrou in the *Dictionnaire d'Archéologie chrétienne et de Liturgie*[48] are excellent sources for a modern review of the entire problem. However, a number of conclusions, in particular those relating to the modern archeological evidence, are unacceptable. The work by Toynbee and Perkins, will be a standard work in English for many years to come. Like the works of Carcopino, however, this study is not limited to the archeological material directly related to the shrine itself and, therefore, is not able to concentrate on the area of the alleged tomb of Peter. Furthermore, except in occasional footnotes, it does not deal with the literary and liturgical documents.

The debate, as outlined, points to a need for an extended study which undertakes to interpret the various literary and liturgical sources and to offer an evaluation of each source as it bears upon the one particular problem of the relationship of Peter to Rome. This study must also deal with the recent excavations at San Sebastiano and must include a discussion and evaluation of the complicated Translation Theory which has found much support even to this day. Lastly, the study must examine briefly and in general all the excavations under St. Peter's and deal carefully with the Aedicula itself. It must take into account the various interpretations that have been made concerning this monument and be careful to relate all of the important conclusions to the literary and liturgical evidence.

---

48. Leclercq, *Dictionnaire d'Archéologie chrétienne et de Liturgie* (hereafter referred to as *DACL*), Vol. XIV, Part I, Cols. 822–981; Marrou, *DACL*, Vol. XV, Part II, Cols. 3291–346.

CHAPTER 2

The Literary Evidence
for the Residence of Peter in Rome

Now THAT the history of the debate has been traced briefly to the present, it is necessary to turn to the evidence itself with which the debate has been concerned. The information provided by each document may be placed in one or more of the following categories: 1) the supposition that Peter did visit Rome, 2) details concerning his founding of the Church there and of his being its first bishop, 3) the length of his stay in the capital city.

THE SILENCE OF THE LETTERS
OF PAUL AND THE BOOK OF ACTS

The argument from silence is often used in an attempt to show that an author of a certain writing was unacquainted with a specific idea or detail, or that the material of which he is ignorant originated later than his writing. This type of argument is only effective if it can be proved that the information in question, if known, would have had to have been used in order to validate or strengthen the argument of the writer. If this necessity cannot be demonstrated satisfactorily, then the silence of the writer is not conclusive evidence against the existence, validity, or date of origin of the idea or detail. For example, a modern author who refers to the Aedicula beneath the Vatican as the tomb of Peter must mention the literary documents which make such a conclusion reasonable. If the author fails to mention such documents, it can be accepted as most probable that he does not know of their existence, for their inclusion is not only strengthening but necessary to his argument.

If this reasoning is valid, how may we interpret the absence of any direct statement or any allusion to Peter's residence in Rome in the letters of Paul? Is there any situation dealt with in these letters in which the inclusion of such a fact would have been necessary or decisively strengthening? If 2 Timothy was written by Paul and if Peter was in Rome when the letter was written, Peter's presence would most probably have been mentioned in 4:21.[1] But it cannot be said that such mention was necessary.[2]

The silence of Romans is more serious. The letter was most likely written A.D. 56 or 57 from Corinth.[3] Paul was addressing a Church which had been founded for some time (1:8)—a Church, moreover, which he had not helped to found (15:20). If this Church were already established and not founded by Paul, is there any evidence in this passage that the Church must have been founded by Peter?[4] There is not a single clue which points in this direction.

---

1. See Campiche, "Saint Pierre," p. 268.
2. The same claim might also be made for the list found in Colossians 4:10–18.
3. See Knox, "Epistle to the Romans," p. 362. Romans was probably written "in A.D. 53 and certainly before A.D. 58."
4. Campiche, "Saint Pierre," p. 270, is inclined to accept the position that the Church *must* have been founded "by an apostle."

Although it is not necessary, as necessity is defined above, that Paul should have mentioned Peter in the last chapter of Romans, it is a stumbling block for the traditional view unless this chapter is in reality not a part of the original letter to the Romans at all but a short letter to Ephesus with an introduction for Phoebe.[5] A number of ingenious explanations have been offered to explain Paul's silence in an effort to preserve the tradition. It is possible, although petty and hardly worthy of Paul, that he purposely omitted the name of Peter because of the difference of opinion that had divided them at Antioch (Gal. 2:11-14). Also it is unlikely that Paul's express purpose in writing to the Romans was to neutralize the Judaizing doctrine which he believed had been taught there by Peter. The only justification for such an hypothesis is a further hypothesis that information of which we know nothing was available to Paul or that after Antioch Paul was anxious concerning the motives and activities of Peter.[6]

A weak argument which attempts to explain why Peter is not mentioned in Romans 16 is derived from the make-up and history of the Roman Christian community itself. If it may be assumed that there were in Rome in this period 30,000 to 40,000 Jews,[7] it is not unreasonable to suppose that Peter, the appointed apostle to the circumcision (Gal. 2:7), presided over the Jewish Christians, many of whom surely had been converted from the large Jewish population. A

successful proselytizing campaign by a highly popular Christian leader naturally would have led to friction between the Jewish and Christian communities.[8] This friction may have caused the Roman government in the interests of public order to interfere in what they considered to be a religious interparty quarrel. Such a state of affairs may serve to explain the Edict of Claudius, published A.D. 49,[9] by which the Jews were expelled

---

5. As the papyrus text P[46] would seem to indicate. This view is taken by Moffatt, *Introduction*, pp. 134-39; Goodspeed, *An Introduction*, pp. 85-87; Manson, "St. Paul's Letter," pp. 3 ff.; Knox considers this as a possibility ("Epistle to the Romans," pp. 365-68, 654) but is more inclined to see in chapter 16 a second-century addition which sought to bind the Roman Church closer to Paul, thus aiding that Church in its contest with the Gnostics.

6. The position of Lietzmann was justly challenged in the same year (1930) by Emmanuel Hirsch, pp. 63-76, especially pp. 70, 74-76, who claimed that Peter was not to be labeled a Judaizer because: 1) the person mentioned in Gal. 5:10 ("he who is troubling you") was not Peter (against Lietzmann and E. Meyer); 2) the conduct of Peter at Antioch, though weak and vacillating, was not that of a Judaizer.

7. Cullmann, *Peter*, p. 80. Juster, in *Les Juifs*, I, 209-10, argues that the Jews did form an important part of the Empire from the standpoint of population. He estimates that at Rome in the reign of Tiberius there were between 50,000 and 60,000 Jews out of the approximate total Roman population of

800,000. The figure is based upon the statement in Suetonius, *Tiberius* XXXVI, that Tiberius enrolled 4,000 Jews—young men. "This proportion is not possible except as based upon a Jewish population of 50-60,000. A figure corroborated by Josephus, *Antiquities* 17.11.1" (p. 209n12).

It is understandable that Peter would have visited a community of this size in spite of the fact that other cities such as Alexandria could claim a much higher concentration of Jews in this period. Rome was the capital of the Empire, and as such there was hope that missionary activity in this area would have great potential influence. It is necessary to call attention also to the probability that Rome was not the scene of extended missionary activity on the part of Peter. He may only have carried on a ministry in that city at the end of his life.

8. This is surely not the source of the "jealousy" to which Clement refers in 1 Clem. 5.

9. Compare the views of Goguel, *The Birth of Christianity*, p. 159, and Lewin, *Fasti Sacri*, pp. 295-96. The opposite point of view is found in Harris, "Hadrian's Decree," p. 199.

Jean Juster, *Les Juifs*, I, 411n2; II, 171n2, suggests that the Edict of Claudius, which is mentioned in Suetonius, *Claudius* XXV.4 ff. and Acts 18:2, is an error. Perhaps there was no such edict promulgated under Claudius. Neither Josephus nor Tacitus mention the edict, and Dio Cassius LX.6:6 says only that Claudius forbade the Jews the privilege of assembly. Juster is of the opinion that Suetonius, *Claudius* XXV and other references such as Orosius VII.6:15 are dependent upon Acts 18:2. He believes that the Edict of Claudius probably was published early A.D. 41 (for A.D. 41-42 Claudius published an Edict of Tolerance for the Jews of the whole Empire) rather than A.D. 49, as Orosius maintains.

Foakes-Jackson and Lake, *The Beginnings*, V, 295-96 accept the date A.D. 49 assigned by Orosius, but mention (p. 295n4) that W. M. Ramsey prefers A.D. 50. Foakes-Jackson and Lake point out that Claudius in this period (A.D. 47-52) was engaged in putting down foreign cults. Moses Hadas in the translator's postscript to F. Gregorovius, *The Ghetto and the Jews of Rome* assigns the edict to the period A.D. 49-51. If the edict was published in the early forties, then the suggestion is weak that Peter was not in Rome because of the expulsion of the Jews occasioned by that edict. If the date of the edict was A.D. 49, as proposed by Orosius, then the suggestion may have some validity.

from the City of Rome.[10] If such had been the case, then surely Peter, because of his prominent place within the Christian group (still considered by the Romans to be part of the Jewish community), would have found it necessary to leave Rome. If such absence were of long duration, when the apostle may have been fulfilling the missionary charge laid upon him in Luke 22:32 ("strengthen thy brethren"), this might explain why Peter was not mentioned in Romans 16. Furthermore, in the event that it could be shown that chapter 16 is not an original part of Paul's letter to the Romans the case still could rest upon the statement in 15:20. Peter was not in Rome when Paul wrote and probably had not been there previous to the writing of the Epistle, or Paul would have been building where he said he would not build—"on another man's foundation."

On the other hand, after a consideration of Romans 1:5–15, it hardly seems probable that Paul is addressing a group which had been founded by an apostle. If we assume that Paul is faithful to the decisions of the Council of Jerusalem (Gal. 2:7–10), it is difficult to justify the view that the community had been founded by Peter. In spite of Romans 15:20, Paul appears to consider Rome as a part of his province (1:9–15).

If the implication of Romans is correct, that no apostle had worked with the Christian community at Rome prior to Paul, then the statements in Ambrosiaster of the fourth century faithfully reflect the tradition. He claims that the Jews living in Rome, not the apostles, "passed on to the Romans the tradition that they ought to profess Christ, but keep the Law."[11] The relation of Peter to the founding of such a community would be then little more than the giving of the apostolic blessing to what had already taken place.

The most that can be said safely when confronted by the silence of Romans is that Peter was not in Rome when Paul wrote his letter. To conclude, however, from this silence in Paul's letter that Peter had not been in Rome previously is poor exegesis and unwarranted assumption.

There is only one statement found in the letters of Paul concerning the later life of Peter, and this is only a passing reference to the fact that his wife was with him on a missionary journey: "Do we not have the right to be accompanied by a wife as the other Apostles . . . and Cephas?" (1 Cor. 9:5).[12]

The Book of Acts has nothing at all to say concerning the Roman residence of Peter and, more surprisingly, also neglects this period in the life of Paul. In 12:17, after Peter's release from prison, it is mentioned that he went to "another place."[13] The place is not named, however, and while there is no internal evidence whatsoever to suggest that Rome is indicated, the possibility is not eliminated.[14] The term "another place" could simply mean a different house in the same area where the apostle might hide for a while until the authorities ceased looking for him. The word "place" in Acts 4:31 most probably refers to a place in a house or part of a house, and such may be the case here. The vagueness in the description might be explained as a security measure. The family who shielded Peter would have been endangered by any publicity, and in the period when Acts was written the house might still have been in use as a place of refuge for those Christians

---

10. Suetonius, *Claudius* XXV, trans. Rolfe, II, 52–53: "Judaeos, impulsore Chresto assidue tumultuantes Roma expulit."

11. *Preface to the Commentary on the Epistle to the Romans* (*Patrologiae Cursus Completus*, MPL, XVII, 45, 46. Below, this work will be abbreviated MPL for the Latin Fathers and MPG for the Greek Fathers). Ambrosiaster confirms this by saying, "Nulla insignia virtuum videntes nec aliquem apostolorum susceperunt fidem Christi" [Having seen no miracles, and not having seen any of the Apostles, they accepted faith in Christ]. See Knox, "Epistle to the Romans," p. 362.

---

12. Even here, in the use of the name "Cephas" I assume that this refers to Peter, but this is not a certainty. Later legends were built upon this reference, declaring that the wife of Peter attended his crucifixion, that he had a daughter named Petronilla, and so on. For a review of this problem and a view that Peter and Cephas are *not* the same person see Lake, "Simon Cephas, Peter," pp. 95–97, and La Piana, "The Tombs of Peter and Paul," pp. 94–97.

13. "εἰς ἕτερον τόπον." Robinson, "Where and When Did Peter Die?" pp. 255 ff. and Smaltz, "Did Peter Die in Jerusalem?" p. 214, interpret "εἰς ἕτερον τόπον" as a periphrasis for "into glory." The term "πορεύειν" is also seen as a euphemism for "to die" (Acts 1:25 and 1 Clem. 5:4). See הָלַךְ in Ps. 39:14 (πορεύειν in LXX).

14. Harnack, *Die Chronologie*, I, 244. Cullmann, *Peter*, pp. 80–82.

pursued by the authorities. If Antioch were the "other place," the name may have been left out purposely because of the previous difficulty between Peter and Paul in that city. The traditional view is that Rome is meant here, which satisfies the early assumption that Peter arrived in the city during the reign of Claudius,[15] a tradition connected with the Simon Magus legend which may have received its first impetus from the material in Acts 8:9–25.[16]

Among the explanations for the silence of Acts are those which argue that the book was written: 1) early, after Paul's arrival in Rome but before Peter's (if it can be accepted that Peter did not spend the traditional twenty-five years in Rome); 2) at a later time, but the author knew nothing of a Roman residence of Peter. It is also possible that 3) the author of Acts planned a third book to supplement the Gospel of Luke and the Book of Acts, which would have included the later work of Peter and Paul and an account of their martyrdom in Rome or elsewhere,[17] or 4) for some reason the author of Acts did not wish to mention these last days of the apostles because the account contained unedifying material, such as the internal jealousy perhaps alluded to in 1 Clement 4–6.[18] Finally, 5) the author may have been prevented from completing his work by sickness or death.

The first possibility, that the Book of Acts was written after the coming of Paul and before that of Peter, is very unlikely. Harnack in a later work suggests A.D. 63 or 64[19] in order to explain the lack of information concerning the later activity and the death of Peter and Paul. This is not a necessary stipulation, however, as Harnack demonstrated earlier[20] when he urged

a more realistic date between A.D. 80 and 93.[21] The second hypothesis is perfectly possible, but even those who are most opposed to the belief that Peter lived for a time in Rome and died there, decline to use the silence of Acts as evidence.[22] Concerning the third view nothing can be said, for there is no evidence whatsoever that a third book was contemplated and only silence as evidence that there was not. The fifth hypothesis is also undemonstrable, but the fourth, urged by Cullmann, may very well be the answer. The author of Acts declined to make public facts which were not apt to draw others to the Christian Church. More seriously, he sought to deemphasize material which might annoy the public officials whose government had previously acted as a result of such internal disturbances.[23]

If we could accept an early date for Acts, before the death of Peter and Paul, it might also be urged that this last episode in the lives of the apostles was omitted for security reasons, which reasons, however, would not in the least explain why there is no mention of Peter's missionary journeys.

It has also been suggested that Acts is a "selective" history, a fragmentary history, which simply did not include the facts pertaining to the last days and martyrdom of Peter and Paul. This is not acceptable, for such information would have been of great moment in the Early Church,[24] which a century and a half before the rise of the cult of martyrs, only thirty-two years after the death of the apostles, remembered their martyrdom vividly (1 Clement 5). The Early Church was so eager for details that within another century it created the full accounts which are found in the apocryphal Acts.

Whatever is the conscious or unconscious reason for the silence of the canonical Acts, the fact remains that nothing can be learned of a Roman residence or martyrdom of Peter from the one book of the New Testament in which we would most expect to find such information.

---

15. See below p. 35 n 229.

16. See Zahn, *Introduction*, II, 168.

17. *Ibid.*, III, 57 ff.; Macgregor, "The Acts," pp. 351 f.

18. See Cullmann, *Peter*, p. 104; "The Christians who had caused the death of other Christians did not offer an edifying example for others. Moreover, it is possible that the abrupt ending of the Book of Acts may be explained in this way."

19. *The Date of Acts*, trans. J. R. Wilkinson, pp. 90–125. Cited by Macgregor, "The Acts," p. 351.

20. *Die Chronologie*, I, 246–50.

---

21. See Macgregor, "The Acts," p. 21.

22. Heussi, *War Petrus in Rom?* p. 17.

23. See above, pp. 9–10.

24. Campiche, "Saint Pierre," p. 268.

THE RELATION OF GALATIANS 2:6 TO THE PROBLEM

It is necessary to analyze the verse in order to understand the hypothesis of Karl Heussi that Galatians 2:6 gives vital information concerning the date of Peter's death and is therefore pertinent to the question of his residence and death in Rome.[25] In the Revised Standard Version Galatians 2:6 is rendered: "And from those who were reputed to be something . . . what they were makes no difference to me . . . those, I say, who were of repute added nothing to me." Heussi suggests "qualis aliquando" [what once] as a translation for "ποτε" in this verse, against the opinion of Lietzmann, Zahn, and Meyer who favor "qualiscumque" [whatsoever, of whatever kind]. He argues that twice in the preceding passage of Galatians Paul has used "ποτε" in this way (Gal. 1:13, 23). The important part of his argument follows. In the usual interpretation of this verse, "ἦσαν" is unimportant. However, that the past tense in this case is not stylistic but conveys an important fact is emphasized by the Vulgate which translates "ἦσαν" correctly by "fuerint."[26] Paul used this form of the verb "εἰμί" for one of two reasons: he wished to convey either that Peter was no longer a "pillar" or that the apostle was "nicht mehr unter lebenden weilten." This evidence, Heussi is convinced, is older and more accurate than the later traditions which place the death of Peter in Rome under Nero and that of John in Ephesus under Trajan. Galatians 2:9, he maintains, refers to James, the son of Zebedee (who died according to tradition at the time of the Passover A.D. 44), rather than to James, the "brother of the Lord" (who according to tradition died a martyr's death A.D. 62). In other words, Heussi wishes to establish that, when the letter to the Galatians was written, the James in question had been dead for twelve years. Therefore, Peter who is mentioned with

this James is dead also. This conclusion is emphasized strongly even in spite of the fact that the James to whom Paul intended to refer three verses later (2:12) was obviously James, "the brother of the Lord"—the same James who was named expressly in 1:19. Heussi argues forcefully that James, the son of Zebedee, was the only James ever included in the "στύλοι" and that any member of the primitive community would be conscious of this fact. In like manner, the descriptive material in 2:12 would identify immediately that James as the "brother of the Lord." He suggests that confusion only arose in the minds of later readers of the epistle for whom the identity was not obvious through the description. Furthermore, if it were known that James, the son of Zebedee, was dead at the time of the events recounted in 2:11 f., it would not be necessary again to identify the James in 2:12. This theory incidentally gives support to the contention of Eduard Meyer, Eduard Schwartz, Alfred Loisy, and others that the Council of Jerusalem was held A.D. 43 or 44. At this early date it was still possible that James, the son of Zebedee, attended and gave the right hand of fellowship to Paul.

In 1 Corinthians 9:5, Peter is spoken of as still living; therefore, he must have died between the writing of 1 Corinthians and the writing of Galatians, that is, between A.D. 55 and 56.[27] We are not told whether his death was natural or violent.

The hypothesis of Heussi, if true, would be valuable in explaining the silence of Romans, for Peter would have been dead a short while when it was written. This hypothesis, however, comes into direct conflict with the testimony of Dionysius of Corinth that Peter and Paul had been in Italy together.[28] The theory of his early death would cancel the entire Roman tradition of Peter, unless perhaps it could be said that he had been

---

25. "ἀπὸ δὲ τῶν δοκούντων εἶναί τι, — ὁποῖοί ποτε ἦσαν οὐδέν μοι διαφέρει· πρόσωπον [ὁ] Θεὸς ἀνθρώπου οὐ λαμβάνει — ἐμοὶ γὰρ οἱ δοκοῦντες οὐδὲν προσανέθεντο...."

26. "Ab iis autem, qui videbantur esse aliquid (quales aliquando fuerint nihil mea interest. Deus personam hominis non accipit) mihi enim qui videbantur esse aliquid, nihil contulerant."

---

27. These dates are disputed, and there are those who would rather set this interval at A.D. 54–55. See Craig, "I Corinthians," p. 13 and Stamm, "Epistle to the Galatians," p. 441.

28. See below p. 24.

in Rome during the reign of Claudius and had left A.D. 49,[29] never to return to that city.

In spite of the value of this hypothesis to those who would attempt to show that the Roman tradition of Peter is unwarranted, there are a number of weak points in the argument.[30] If Peter is presumed dead, it is difficult to reconcile this assumption with the fact that he is mentioned three times in two chapters (1:18, 2:6–10, 2:11–21). More difficult to reconcile are the extremely harsh words of Paul in reference to Peter in Gal. 2:11–14.[31] Unless Peter was still alive, it is hard to imagine that Paul would use such language, even if he were frustrated and annoyed over the divisions within the Galatian church and even if Peter were guilty as charged.[32]

Heussi himself recognized the weakness in his argument to prove the identity of the James in Galatians 2:9, and this recognition is revealed in his choice of the expedient of maintaining that the identity of the James in 1:19 is a later addition reflecting a tendency toward specificity. This is hardly the case. The references to a James in 1:19, 2:9, and 2:12 all seem to refer to the same person who was identified in 1:19 as "the brother of the Lord."

It is necessary to accept that the "στύλοι" (2:9) are Peter, James (the brother of the Lord), and John, although there is some weight in Heussi's argument concerning this point. It may also be argued further that Heussi is in error when he suggests that a later redactor has tampered with Acts 15 by placing James in the center of the community since Acts 21:18–26 seems to assume that James is still in a strong central position. If Acts 12 is reliable tradition, as Heussi insists, then it is also a "guter Überlieferung" which reports in addition to the death of James, the son of Zebedee, the imprisonment of Peter and his miraculous escape and activity at the house of Mary, mother of Mark. Acts 12:12 "ἀπαγγείλατε Ἰακώβῳ καὶ τοῖς ἀδελφοῖς ταῦτα" indicates that the Lord's brother is in an important position even during the lifetime of James, the son of Zebedee,

unless chapter 12 covers a greater amount of time than is generally supposed. Nowhere is it mentioned that the leadership of James, hinted at in 12:17, is a recent event following upon the death of James, the son of Zebedee, as recorded in 12:2. If then, as Aland points out, James, the "brother of the Lord," is a member of the στύλοι, the argument which Heussi builds upon the denial of this fact is groundless. Furthermore, if one of the στύλοι was still living at the time that Galatians 2:9 was written, then the ἦσαν which is the cornerstone of his argument, is without significance and tells us nothing whatsoever concerning the time of the death of Peter.

The supposition that 1 Corinthians 9:5, where Peter is mentioned as still living, was written a year before Galatians is used by Heussi to locate the death of Peter between the writing of these two Epistles. Although Aland is correct in challenging the general thesis of Heussi, his argument is not justified when he definitely dates 1 Corinthians a year later than Galatians. Because the dating of these two Epistles is uncertain, an argument based upon their order is precarious. It has been emphasized also that ποτε is equivalent to "then" in Galatians 2:6 and that ἦν and ἐστίν are at times interchangeable in the New Testament, that is, John 5:13 and Acts 27:8.[33] Therefore, the ἦσαν does not necessarily refer to an event in the past, but could as defensibly refer to an action continuing into the present.

This recent dispute necessitates the above discussion, for if the arguments of Heussi were defensible all further investigation of the residence of Peter in Rome, his martyrdom under Nero, and his burial beneath the Vatican would be superfluous. Instead of making further investigation valueless, Heussi has led others to restudy the Epistle and to affirm with conviction that Peter did not die until after Galatians was written.[34]

---

29. A.D. 52, according to Lewin.

30. See the important criticisms of Heussi's argument in Aland, "Wann starb Petrus?" pp. 267–75 outlined below, and Barrett, "Paul and 'Pillar' Apostles," in which he argues that the argument of Heussi is incorrect since it presupposes that ἦσαν is related not to δοκοῦντες but to διαφέρει. See a brief review of this in Winter, St. Peter and the Popes, p. 85.

31. "ὅτι κατεγνωσμένος ἦν."

32. Aland, "Wann starb Petrus?" p. 270. "Sogar der moderne Mensch pflegte bei einer Polemik dem toten Gegner gegenüber irgendeine Reverenz zu machen."

33. Aland, "Wann starb Petrus?" p. 274. See also Aland, "Petrus in Rome," pp. 506–7.

34. Aland, "Wann starb Petrus?" p. 275. "Concerning the method of Heussi's essay, that is concerning the passage of Gal. 2, it can only be said that it indicates an extraordinary boldness, to build up one so far reaching conclusion on the interpretation of a single isolated ἦσαν." See Burger, La Tombe, p. 6.

THE FIRST EPISTLE OF PETER

Three aspects in the study of this Epistle are important to the question of Peter's residence in Rome: authorship, date, and the meaning of "ἐν βαβυλῶνι" in 1 Peter 5:13. We are concerned with the first only insofar as it is related to the second. Similarly, the second is directly relevant to this study only to the degree that it is an important factor in the evaluation of the evidence derived from 1 Peter 5:13. Only if one of three possible interpretations of a single word of that verse is adopted is the entire matter of interest at all.

The question as to whether Peter was the author of the First Epistle which bears his name did not arise until a relatively recent period. Before the Council of Nicaea it was accepted as a work of Peter. Eusebius states that Papias or Clement quoted from the Epistle, considering it to be authentic,[35] and we find parallels to 1 Peter in Polycarp.[36] Eusebius numbers the work among his ὁμολογούμενα,[37] while rejecting in this category: 2 Peter, the *Acts of Peter*, the *Preaching of Peter*, the *Apocalypse of Peter*, and the *Gospel of Peter*. Irenaeus refers to the material contained in 1 Peter as "what Peter taught the people in Pontus." Tertullian, Clement of Alexandria, Origen, and Cyprian also claimed its authenticity. Opposition to the assumption of Petrine authorship appeared in the nineteenth and early twentieth centuries in various works, including those by Hans von Soden, Hermann Gunkel, R. Knopf, Alfred Loisy, Hans Windisch, Ernest Renan, and Adolf Harnack. Among those who supported the traditional view were Bernhard Weiss, Theodore Zahn, Joseph B. Lightfoot,

Fenton J. A. Hort, Edwin Hatch, and James Moffatt.

Although we need not enter here into this very involved and controversial question, it is necessary to mention that the chief arguments against Petrine authorship relate to: 1) the supposed indebtedness to Paulinism, 2) the "good Greek" in which the Epistle is written, and 3) the implication that at the time when the Epistle appeared the mere profession of the "Name" was an offense.[38] The first objection is answered by saying that Peter may have had Silvanus write the letter for him as is indicated in 5:12. The second objection was urged by Harnack,[39] but it proves nonconclusive when one attempts to establish exactly what is meant by a Paulinism. The last point involves a discussion of which persecution is reflected in 1 Peter and whether that persecution involved punishment for the very profession of the "Name." The evidence is not at all conclusive, as may be gathered from the continued and sharp differences of opinion.

In the mid-twentieth century the question is still unsolved. Such eminent Protestant scholars as Edward G. Selwyn, A. H. McNeile, Charles Bigg, Vincent Taylor, D. S. Wohlenberg, and Jocelyn Toynbee as well as all Roman Catholic authors, including Jules Lebreton, Jacques Zeiller, and Enrico Josi support the traditional view. Oscar Cullmann[40] and Frank L. Cross[41] avoid taking a stand, while the Petrine authorship is doubted or denied by Maurice Goguel, Charles C. Torrey, Kurt Aland, Charles Guignebert, Hans Lietzmann, John Lowe, and Karl Heussi, to name only a few.

---

35. *Eusebius, The Ecclesiastical History* II.15:2 (trans. Lake, I, 144). [Below, this work will be abbreviated E.H.] Κλήμης ἐν ἕκτῳ τῶν Ὑποτυπώσεων παρατέθειται τὴν ἱστορίαν, συνεπιμαρτυρεῖ δὲ αὐτῷ καὶ ὁ Ἱεραπολίτης ἐπίσκοπος ὀνόματι Παπίας, τοῦ δὲ Μάρκου μνημονεύειν τὸν Πέτρον ἐν τῇ προτέρᾳ ἐπιστολῇ· ἣν καὶ συντάξαι φασὶν ἐπ' αὐτῆς Ῥώμης, σημαίνειν τε τοῦτ' αὐτόν, τὴν πόλιν προπικώτερον βαβυλῶνα προσειπόντα διὰ τούτων "ἀσπάζεται ὑμᾶς ἡ ἐν Βαβυλῶνι συνεκλεκτὴ καὶ Μάρκος ὁ υἱός μου." See Torrey, *Documents of the Primitive Church*, p. 10.

36. *Philippians* 1:3, 8:1 (*MPG*, V, 1005–6; 1011–2).

37. *E.H.* III.25:3 (Lake, I, 256–57).

38. See Hunter, "The First Epistle of Peter," pp. 77–80. See below pp. 53–55.

39. *Die Chronologie*, I, 164; II, 455 ff.

40. *Peter*, pp. 83, 86.

41. *I Peter, A Paschal Liturgy*, p. 44. While doubtful as to the authenticity, he mentions that the Epistle does display certain characteristics which mark it as a primitive work: 1) the undeveloped idea of the trinity, 2) primitive ordering of the ministry, 3) an eschatological stream of thought that has confidence both in "present realization" and the "future hope," 4) a suggestion that we are "still in the atmosphere of last things."

Whether Peter wrote the First Epistle bearing his name, while not crucial, makes some difference in the evaluation of the evidence. If it could be established that he was the author, then with confidence 1 Peter could be dated earlier than A.D. 64.[42] Opinions about the date vary considerably among those who doubt the Petrine authorship of the Epistle. Goguel, in agreement with Bornemann, suggests that the Epistle may have been written in two sections: the main body appeared around A.D. 80, and then around A.D. 110 the beginning and end of the letter were written so as to place the Epistle "under the patronage of Peter."[43] This may be an attractive way to settle a difficult problem, but there is no external evidence to warrant this conclusion. Although Kurt Aland accepts the Petrine authorship, he prudently treats the evidence for the Roman sojourn of Peter, which appears in the Epistle, only in the indefinite period prior to Dionysius of Corinth (A.D. c. 170). While denying the authenticity, Guignebert admits that the Epistle appeared before 1 Clement (A.D. c. 96).[44] Lietzmann agrees in the matter of authorship, but is confident that the Epistle indicates "the early existence of a firm tradition of a Roman residence of Peter."[45] Having affirmed that the apostle did write 1 Peter (for there is "no sufficient motive to refuse to Peter the paternity of his First Epistle"), Burger adds that "were it not authentic it is nonetheless a document of the first century which affirms the coming of Peter to Rome."[46]

One is reminded that even if the Epistle is not the work of Peter, it was most probably not written later than A.D. 110, for Polycarp (A.D. c. 115) quotes more frequently from it than from any other book of the New Testament.[47] If we cannot take a definite position concerning authorship, we must be cautious in setting a *terminus a quo*. On the other hand, since the Epistle was definitely used by Polycarp in such a confident manner (he considered it apostolic), we may set the *terminus ad quem* before A.D. 115. On the basis of the parallels found between 1 Peter and 1 Clement (Harnack numbers twenty and Lightfoot, twelve), we may safely say that it belongs to a period before A.D. 95. It would be reasonable to suggest in light of these considerations that 1 Peter should not be considered as evidence for a tradition of the Roman sojourn of Peter before the period A.D. 80 to 92.[48]

In 1 Peter 5:13 it is mentioned that "she who is at Babylon, who is likewise chosen, sends you greetings." Up until the time of the Reformation it was taken for granted that by "Babylon" the author intended a cryptic reference to Rome. Erasmus and Calvin in the sixteenth century were the first to suggest that Peter had come to Babylon in Mesopotamia on a missionary journey and there wrote the letter. Such an opinion was destined to be debated down into the twentieth century. However, before discussing this possible solution and the more probable traditional view, it is necessary to evaluate briefly the suggestion by Reinach that Babylon in 1 Peter 5:13 was intended to indicate the "military station" in the Nile delta near Memphis. Since there is no clear evidence tending in this direction, it is not to be

---

42. Selwyn, *The First Epistle of St. Peter*, p. 56, and more specifically, p. 60: "If the death of James in the year A.D. 62 gives us a *terminus a quo* and the Neronian persecution in the summer of A.D. 64, a *terminus ad quem*, we arrive at a period of a year and eighteen months which in no way is discordant with anything we know of the movements of St. Peter, St. Mark and of Silvanus."

43. Goguel, *The Birth of Christianity*, pp. 153, 339n1.

44. *La Primauté de Pierre*, p. 191.

45. *Petrus und Paulus in Rom*, 2d ed., p. 237.

46. *La Tombe*, p. 8.

47. If the thesis of P. N. Harrison, *Polycarp's Two Epistles*, is accepted, that chapters 1 through 12 were written A.D. c. 135 and only chapters 13 and possibly 14 are of the second decade of the second century, the witness of Polycarp only guarantees that 1 Peter was written before A.D. c. 130. Harrison's thesis, however, is open to criticism. See Headlam, "The Epistle of Polycarp," pp. 1–25 and *Early Christian Fathers*, ed. Richardson, pp. 124–25, 129. In view of the strong probability that chapter 13 and the rest of the letter were written at the same time and in view of the assumption that "not long after Ignatius' departure from the Middle East . . . Polycarp penned his letter to the Philippians" (*Early Christian Fathers*, ed. Richardson, p. 122), the traditional date of A.D. 115 is to be preferred.

48. Cullmann, *Peter*, p. 83, states that whether the epistle is genuine or not has little effect upon the discussion of the Roman sojourn because either Peter or someone else of the same period saw that apostle as having lived and died in Rome.

taken seriously.[49] There is only the vaguest possibility suggested by the use of "ἀρχιπάμην" in 5:4. This Greek word, meaning "sovereign shepherd" or "head shepherd," appeared on an Egyptian mummy case and in a late papyrus fragment dating from A.D. 338.[50]

Also, no tradition exists which indicates any relationship between Peter and the Babylon of the Euphrates except for the highly suspect *Acts of Philip* written A.D. c. 400. Here Philip is reported to have gone to the region of the Parthians and to have come upon Peter there. According to the oldest tradition, however, the apostle to the Parthians is Thomas.[51] Further doubt is cast upon the report of the apocryphal *Acts of Philip* by Pausanias, who mentions that of the Babylon in the Euphrates valley "there is no more than walls."[52] The report of Pliny is the same; the settlement "has returned to solitude."[53] "Babylon is . . . surrounded by walls," says Lucian (d. A.D. c. 200), "and extends over an immense area; soon one will seek it in its ruins as Nineveh."[54] Strabo agrees with such a description when he says that Babylon "has for the most part been deserted."[55]

Despite the report of the above authors, during the time of Artaban III (A.D. 12–42), Babylon was still the chief place of the satrapy; and perhaps the account of

desolation and ruin is only a semipoetic description of the area in comparison with its former glory. Even though it appears that a number of anti-Semitic riots had compelled the Jews to flee to Seleucia, it is inferred from statements in the works of Josephus[56] and Philo[57] that the area was still inhabited. The evidence indicates that it is very doubtful whether Peter worked in this area, especially in light of the notation in the Talmud to the effect that Christians did not live in the vicinity until the third century.[58]

As identification of the Babylon in I Peter 5:13 with the Babylon in Mesopotamia or that in Egypt has been discarded for lack of evidence, for the same reason the suggestion of Harnack[59] and Erbes[60] that the word stands for Jerusalem must also be eliminated.[61]

Convinced that Babylon does not stand for Rome, Karl Heussi suggest that, since I Peter 1:1 uses the metaphorical expression διασπορᾶς, therefore βαβυλῶν in 5:13 stands for the Diaspora, "the earthly world filled with homeless Christians."[62] He offers in this connection his own paraphrase of the verse which is singularly unconvincing: "the community which was chosen [elected] with you greets you, [a community] which like yours lives in homelessness." Thus the Babylon of this verse has nothing to do with the historical Peter nor with Rome.[63] If the identification of Babylon with Rome is to be made, Heussi claims that I Peter must have moved from east to west and was caught up in a misunderstanding of I Clement 5—a misunderstanding

---

49. See Strabo XVII:30, *The Geography of Strabo*, ed. Horace Jones, VIII, 84. Strabo, a geographer, in A.D. 18 reported that the Egyptian Babylon was a fortress founded by refugees from the Mesopotamian Babylon. However, later in the first century this fortress was only a military camp.

50. Goguel, *The Birth of Christianity*, pp. 155–56.

51. *E. H.* III.1:1 (Lake, I, 190–91).

52. Pausanias, *Description of Greece*, VIII.33:3, trans. Frazer, p. 417: "At Babylon, the sanctuary of Bel remains, but of that Babylon which was once the greatest city that the sun beheld, nothing is left but the walls." ("οὐδέν τι ἦν εἰμὴ τεῖχος.")

53. "Ad solitudinem rediit," Pliny the Younger, *Historiae Naturalis* VI.30:15, ed. Brotier, II, 1165.

54. "ἡ βαβυλῶν δὲ . . . ἐκείνη ἐστὶν ἡ εὔπυργος ἡ τὸν μέγαν περίβολον οὐ μετὰ πόλυ καὶ αὐτὴ ζητηθησομένη ὥσπερ ἡ Νίνος" Lucian, *Charon* XXIII, trans. A. M. Harmont, II, 442, 443.

55. Strabo, "ἡ δ' ἔρημος ἡ πολλή," *Strabo* XVI. 1:5, ed. Horace Jones, VII, 200. This view is confirmed by Diodorus III.22:1, ed. C. H. Oldfather, II, 145, who adds, however, that some people still live there.

56. Josephus, *Antiquities* XV.2:2, XVIII.9:8 in *Works of Flavius Josephus*, trans. C. Wilson, III, 80, 323.

57. Philo, *Legatio ad Caium*, p. 282, in *Philonis Alexandrini*, ed. L. Cohn, V, 207.

58. For this information see Cullmann, *Peter*, p. 86.

59. *Die Chronologie*, I, 459. Since Harnack believes that I Peter 1:1, 2 and 5:12–14 are late additions, the problem concerning the meaning of Babylon in 5:13 becomes academic for him. He suggests that it could stand for Jerusalem which had been destroyed A.D. 70 by God's justice, even as Sodom.

60. "Petrus nicht in Rom, sondern in Jerusalem gestorben," pp. 18 f. This assumption by Erbes is dismissed by Zahn, *Introduction*, II, 165, as a "desperate assumption."

61. This possibility is suggested in Photius, *Bibliotheca* 273 (*MPG*, CIV, 233).

62. *Die römische Petrustradition*, p. 39.

63. *Ibid.*, pp. 39–40.

which developed the tradition of a martyr-death of Peter in Rome from the knowledge of the martyr-death of Paul in that City.[64]

The last possibility to be considered is Babylon as a cryptic term indicating Rome. Such is surely the understanding in Revelation 14:8, 16:19 and especially 17:5, 6,[65] the *Sibylline Oracles* V:158 (see also V:143),[66] the Apocalypse of Baruch XI:1[67] and 4 Esdras 3:1 ff., 28, 31.[68] These instances prove nothing definite for they are of the same period or later than 1 Peter. In one minuscule the identification of Babylon with Rome is entered in the text;[69] and, as is pointed out in Kittel's *Wörterbuch*, this is the opinion of the Primitive Church

"mit verschwindend wenigen Ausnahmen."[70] That this identification was commonly made by the time of Papias (or Clement) is unmistakable, as the quotation of Eusebius suggests by offering an explanation in order to avoid any confusion.[71] Rome is also referred to cryptically as Babylon by Jerome in a passage involving Mark.[72] Most modern authors assume the identification whether or not they believe that Peter wrote the Epistle.[73] Before commenting upon the few difficulties associated with this identification it should be mentioned that, especially in Revelation, $\beta\alpha\beta\upsilon\lambda\hat{\omega}\nu$ is surely the technical term representing the chief city of the Empire in each succeeding age; at the time of the writing of that book the chief city was Rome.[74]

There are certain problems in identifying Babylon with Rome.[75] 1) If this term had been used in a cryptic way by Peter or the author of the Epistle, the precaution would have been useless if the meaning were as well known as is consistently pointed out in the attempt to establish the identification. 2) 1 Peter 2:13–17 recommends that the Christian be "subject for the Lord's sake to every human institution. . . . Honor all men. . . . Fear God. Love the Emperor." The identification of Rome with Babylon, in the face of all that the word Babylon would call to mind in its association with Jewish history, is not at all in keeping with the admonition to be subject and to honor. Therefore, unless 1 Peter 2:13–17 and 1 Peter 5:13 are derived from separate strata of tradition, there is difficulty in their reconciliation. Furthermore, in no other case in an

---

64. "War Petrus wirklich römischer Märtyrer?" pp. 168, 169.

65. "And on her forehead was written a name of mystery: 'Babylon the great, mother of harlots and of earth's abominations.' And I saw the woman, drunk with the blood of the saints and the blood of the martyrs of Jesus." Such a passage would be convincing early evidence except that Guignebert is probably right in placing it well after the destruction of Jerusalem A.D. 70. See *La Primauté de Pierre*, p. 184.

66. *Oracula Sibyllina*, pp. 164, 165. See Lightfoot, *Apostolic Fathers*, Part II, Vol. II, p. 492. This passage also is assigned to a period later than the destruction of the Temple. Goguel, *The Birth of Christianity*, p. 157, gives second or third century.

67. Charles, *Apocalypse*, pp. xxii, 41, assigns this passage to the period between A.D. 70 and 90. Bigg, *Epistles of St. Peter and St. Jude*, p. 76, sees no reason why an identification of Rome with Babylon could not have been made before the Fall of Jerusalem.

68. For these references see Lietzmann, "Petrus römische Märtyrer," p. 11; Cullmann, *Peter*, p. 85; Heussi, *Die römische Petrustradition*, p. 37, Winter, *Saint Peter and the Popes*, p. 84.

69. The minuscule 2138 would settle the question neatly by entering $P\acute{\omega}\mu\eta$ into the text in place of $\beta\alpha\beta\upsilon\lambda\hat{\omega}\nu$. See *Novum Testamentum Graece*, 23d Ed., eds. Nestle and Aland, p. 591. However, this weak evidence is late and of no value. The identification of Babylon with Rome is accepted unquestioningly by Zahn, *Introduction*, II, 165; Lietzmann, *Petrus und Paulus in Rom*, 2d ed., pp. 236, 237; Kuhn, "$\beta\alpha\beta\upsilon\lambda\hat{\omega}\nu$," I, 514; Bigg, *Epistles of St. Peter and St. Jude*, p. 87; Wohlenberg, "Der erste und zweite Petrusbrief und der Judasbrief," pp. xx, 162; Renan, *The Antichrist*, p. 54; Burger, *La Tombe*, p. 7; Selwyn, *The First Epistle of St. Peter*, pp. 243-44, 303-5; Marucchi, *Pietro e Paolo a Roma*, 4th ed., pp. 14,15; Lowe, *Saint Peter*, p. 29; Aland, "Petrus in Rom," p. 509. Guignebert, *La Primauté de Pierre*, p. 191, is not convinced but speaks of Rome as a possibility. Goguel, *The Birth of*

Christianity, pp. 339n1, 524n4, believes the last verses are those of a redactor who is responsible for the identification. Torrey, *Documents of the Primitive Church*, p. 9, asserts that the word "Babylon" did not refer to a known tradition of Peter in Rome but was used in order to create the belief without mentioning the imperial city.

70. Kuhn, "$\beta\alpha\beta\upsilon\lambda\hat{\omega}\nu$," p. 514.

71. *E. H.* II.15:2 (Lake, I, 144-45).

72. *De viris illustribus* 8 (MPL, XXIII, 638, 639).

73. For example, Renan, *The Antichrist*, p. 54; Lietzmann, *Petrus und Paulus in Rom*, 2d ed., pp. 236-37, and "Petrus römischer Märtyrer," p. 399; Goguel, *The Birth of Christianity*, p. 158; Cullmann, *Peter*, p. 86.

74. Zahn, *Introduction*, II, 165, Guarducci, *The Tomb of St. Peter*, pp. 27-28.

75. See Heussi, *Die römische Petrustradition*, pp. 37 ff.

epistle of the New Testament do we find the place of composition expressed in apocalyptic terms, although, of course, such terms in other connections are not unknown to the New Testament. In Galatians 4:26 we note that the Church eternal is called "the Jerusalem above,"[76] and Hebrews 12:22 and Revelation 3:12, 21:2, 10 refer to the "heavenly Jerusalem." 3) In the canonical letters the address of the sender is generally unexpressed, assuming a knowledge on the part of the hearer or reader of the whereabouts of the author (no doubt information imparted by the bearer).[77] Only when Paul or another greets several communities in a province does he name the province from which the letter was written.[78]

The "$\acute{\eta}$" in 1 Peter 5:13 has also been a stumbling block for a few, including Bengel, who insist that the article refers to the wife of Peter. The Vulgate avoids the difficulty by rendering the verse: "ecclesia quae est in Babylone. . . ." The ms $\aleph$ has entered "$\acute{\epsilon}\kappa\kappa\lambda\eta\sigma\acute{\iota}\alpha$" after "$\acute{\epsilon}\nu\ \beta\alpha\beta\upsilon\lambda\tilde{\omega}\nu\iota$" which also eliminates the problem. The same understanding is also reflected in the Armenian, Peshitto, and Oecumenius. It is certain that the "$\acute{\eta}$" was uninterpreted in the original, and the understanding of "$\acute{\epsilon}\kappa\kappa\lambda\eta\sigma\acute{\iota}\alpha$" as being in apposition was unquestioned.

Although it is precarious to insist upon the Petrine authorship of 1 Peter, it is tendentious to eliminate such a possibility. In any case it may be accepted that the Epistle was written before the end of the first Christian century. Whatever information it contains therefore is relevant and extremely valuable to the discussion at hand.

The letter is silent concerning the question of whether Peter founded the Church in Rome and was its first bishop. Furthermore, it lacks any indication as to his length of stay in that city. Since it is fairly obvious, however, that "Babylon" in 5:13 is a cryptic term for Rome, it may be said with confidence that by the end of the first century the tradition existed that Peter had lived in Rome and that he had written an epistle while there. Any further statement concerning the Roman residence of Peter as derived from this letter is mere guesswork.

From a purely chronological point of view it would be natural at this juncture to deal with the First Epistle of Clement to the Corinthians. However, following the plan of this book to deal with the Roman residence, martyrdom, and burial of Peter separately, this evidence will be analyzed carefully in a later chapter. It is not necessary to emphasize that any witness to the martyrdom of Peter in Rome is also indirectly a witness to his residence there—if only for a brief period at the end of his life.

THE EPISTLE OF IGNATIUS TO THE ROMANS

Since Roberto F. Bellarmino (1542–1621) wrote on Ignatius' Epistle to the Romans 4:3, this verse has been considered as an important support for the tradition of Peter's residence in Rome. Before discussing this verse in detail, it is necessary to mention briefly the lack of agreement concerning the authorship and date of the letter. As in the case of 1 Peter, the question of authorship is important only insofar as it is related to the problem of date, which in turn is important only to the degree that it is a factor in determining the value of the evidence in 4:3.

In the skeptical nineteenth century the authenticity of the Epistle was widely contested. Most scholars today, supported by the positive results of the research of Joseph B. Lightfoot, Adolf Harnack, and Theodor Zahn, agree that the Epistle was written by Ignatius, Bishop of Antioch, who died in the reign of Trajan (A.D. 98–117). The verdict is not unanimous, however. Dissenting voices are raised by Adolf Bauer,[79] Paul

---

76. Burton, *The Epistle to the Galatians*, p. 263; Cullmann, *Peter*, p. 84.

77. See Romans 16:21–23; 2 Cor. 13:12; Phil. 4:21 f.; Col. 4:10 ff.; Philemon 23; 2 Timothy 4:21; Titus 3:15; 2 John 5:13; and 3 John 5:15.

78. As in 1 Cor. 16:19 and Hebrews 13:24.

79. "Die Legende von dem Martyrium des Petrus und Paulus in Rom," p. 293. Bauer claims that the letter was written around A.D. 150 and that the notice in the letter to

Schmiedel, Alfred Loisy, and more recently by Karl Heussi.[80] Heussi claims that the letter is not from the period of Trajan but is roughly contemporary with the Letter written by Polycarp, who was born A.D. c. 70 and died (in the opinion of most) A.D. c. 155.[81] Heussi continues that, when he was approximately forty years of age, Ignatius came to Rome during the reign of Trajan. It was here that he wrote the letter to the Philippians when he was presumably a very old man.

Since Polycarp 7:1 is believed by many to be a particularly strong outburst against Marcion, the letter is dated at least after Marcion's coming to Rome A.D. 150. Polycarp in 13:2 mentions that he is sending letters of Ignatius, "those addressed to us and any others we had by us" and further requests that ". . . of Ignatius himself and those who are with him, let us have any reliable information that you know." On the basis of this, Heussi believes that he is justified in determining that the Epistle of Ignatius to the Romans was written shortly before the Epistle of Polycarp to the Philippians, that is, shortly before A.D. 150. This is not necessarily evidence for: 1) Polycarp 13 is considered by some to have been written after Ignatius left Philippi and before he met his martyrdom in Rome.[82] 2) The reference to Ignatius in Polycarp 9:1 implies that Ignatius had been dead for a long period. If these assumptions are true, then the supposition of Heussi (that on the basis of the Letter of Polycarp the letters of Ignatius are late) is weak. It is also argued by Heussi that if any man so close (A.D. c. 110–115) to apostolic times

and of such high rank in one of the apostolic communities had written a letter, then this would at least have been considered for a place in the Canon. In contrast to the cases of the Shepherd of Hermas and First Clement, no such consideration was given to the letters of Ignatius. Furthermore, Heussi claims that Irenaeus did not seem to know of a bishop of Antioch named Ignatius or he would have named him in *Against Heresies* V. 28:4 instead of saying "As one of ours says."[83] These arguments are weak, as any argument from silence is inclined to be. To make this one valid, it would be necessary to prove that Irenaeus would have had to have mentioned Ignatius in this instance, which is not the case. Furthermore, it may be countered that Irenaeus did not mention Ignatius simply because the latter was so well known that mention was unnecessary.

It is argued by Heussi that we cannot establish that Ignatius was a bishop of Antioch by resorting to the episcopal list of Julius Africanus, for any information contained in it concerning the period prior to A.D. 150 is "pure fiction." That an Ignatius does appear there may mean merely that the name was entered in response to some oral tradition. Eusebius in the *Chronicle* and the *Ecclesiastical History* reported no more than what he received from the Antiochean bishop's list, except that he accepted A.D. 107 as the date of the death of Ignatius which, before Heussi, was also recognized as arbitrary by Lightfoot.[84] Heussi's criticism would be valid if one could be sure that 1) the Antiochean bishop's list was derived from oral tradition and 2) such oral tradition was inaccurate. Without such proof we cannot take the objection seriously. Since Heussi's arguments

the Romans in which we are interested is a "primitive stage in the development of the Peter and Paul legend and its early localization in Rome." The arguments adduced by Bauer for this late date are considered by Lietzmann to be very weak (*Petrus und Paulus in Rom*, 2d ed., p. 237n5).

80. *Die römische Petrustradition*, pp. 30–35. Recently Henri Grégoire and Paul Orgels ("La véritable date du martyre de S. Polycarpe (23 février 177) et le 'Corpus Polycarpianum,'" pp. 1–38) have claimed a late date for the Letter of Polycarp. This argument was answered by Griffe. *Bull. de Litt. ecclés.*, (1951), pp. 170–77. See above p. 15n47.

81. In spite of the fact that Harnack, *Die Chronologie*, I, 382 ff., 719, suggests the Letter of Polycarp was written shortly before the end of Trajan's reign.

82. *Early Christian Fathers*, ed. Richardson, p. 124.

83. *MPG*, VII, 1187. *The Epistle to the Romans* is quoted by Irenaeus in *Against Heresies* V.28:4 (*MPG*, VII, 1199). See *The Ante-Nicene Fathers*, I, 557n8.

84. *Apostolic Fathers*, Part II, Vol. II, p. 449. "Trajano adversus christianos persecutionem movente. . . . Itidem [Ignatius] Antiochensium episcopus martyrium passus est, post quem iii antiochensium episcopus constitutus est Eron," see Eusebius, *E.H.* III, 36. Many dates are offered by modern scholars for the death of Ignatius: A.D. 107, 112, and 115; most still consider seriously that he died "under Trajan." See *Early Christian Fathers*, ed. Richardson, p. 75.

Harnack, *Die Chronologie*, I, 123, suggested that Eusebius himself had some reservations concerning the Antiochean bishop's list.

are not compelling, it can be agreed that Ignatius' Epistle to the Romans belongs to the second decade of the second century or, in the event that it is not the work of Ignatius, at least to the first half of the second century.

In the fourth chapter Ignatius appeals to the old traditions of the Roman Church concerning its relationship with the apostles Peter and Paul: "I do not give you orders like Peter and Paul. They [were] apostles: I [am] a convict. They [were] at liberty: I [am] a slave."[85] Since Ignatius is addressing the Church at Rome, it is possible, although not beyond dispute, that in his time Peter and Paul were considered as "the traditional legislators of the Roman community."[86] It is unreasonable for Dannenbauer to consider that 1) the reference to Peter and Paul together is of no greater import than that the two were known by Ignatius to have been together at Antioch and 2) their mention has no relationship to the Church at Rome.[87] In order to prove the last point Heussi explains that the verse can also be translated "I Ignatius . . . command you not as *if* I were Peter and Paul," and defends his translation by reference to two other passages: Ignatius' Epistle to the Ephesians 3:1, "I do not command you as *if* I were anyone special";[89] and the Epistle to the Trallians 3:3, "I have not valued myself so high, who am a slave, to command you as an apostle."[89] The last two instances refer implicitly to Peter and Paul and further demonstrate, he claims, that there is no greater relationship between Peter and Paul and the Church at Rome than between the two great apostles and the Churches at Ephesus and Tralles.[90] Why, then, are Peter and Paul named specifically in the letter to the Church of Rome?

Heussi's suggestion that the two names together, "Peter and Paul," were for Ignatius only a "familiar formula" is sufficient.[91] It is far more reasonable to suppose that the two apostles are mentioned in this *one* instance because there did exist a definite relationship to the Roman community, a relationship similar to that of Paul to the Church at Ephesus, in which letter that apostle alone is specifically named: "You have been initiated into the [Christian] mysteries with Paul."[92] No one will claim that either Peter or Paul had a special relationship to the Church at Tralles, and neither Peter nor Paul is mentioned by name in that letter. Ignatius simply says, "I have not valued myself so high . . . as to command you as an apostle." For the same reason (the absence of any specific relationship), the two apostles are not mentioned in the letters to Magnesia, Philadelphia, or Smyrna. Therefore it is justifiable for Lietzmann to insist that those who would seek to explain away the reference to Peter and Paul in this instance must explain not only why the two apostles are mentioned together but also, if no specific relationship existed between them and the Church at Rome, why Peter and Paul are mentioned here and nowhere else.[93] Such an explanation has not been satisfactorily given thus far by any critic of the tradition. The attempt by Heussi to discredit the Ignatian testimony is weak when he asserts that 1) the only reason for the mention of Paul in the letter to Ephesus is that Ignatius knew of a letter of Paul to that city and 2) the mention of Peter and Paul in the letter to the Romans can be explained by saying that "Ignatius opposed the highest aspects of this Christian community with highest aspects of both Apostles."[94] In another instance this same author urges that the use of the apostles' names in Romans 4:3 is simply to emphasize the unworthiness of Ignatius in contrast with the worthiness of the apostles.

---

85. "οὐχ ὡς Πέτρος καὶ Παῦλος διατάσσομαι ὑμῖν. ἐκεῖνοι ἀπόστολοι, ἐγὼ κατάκριτος· ἐκεῖνοι ἐλεύθεροι, ἐγὼ δὲ μέχρι νῦν δοῦλος.." (MPG, V, 809).

86. Lietzmann, *Petrus und Paulus in Rom*, 2d ed., p. 237; Peter and Paul are also mentioned together in 1 Clement V (A.D. c. 96).

87. "Nochmals die römische Petruslegende," p. 258.

88. "οὐ διατάσσομαι ὑμῖν, ὡς ὤν τι" (MPG, V, 733).

89. "ἀλλ' οὐχ ἱκανὸν ἐμαυτὸν εἰς τοῦτο ᾠήθην ἵνα ὢν κατάκριτος ὡς ἀπόστολος ὑμῖν διατάσσομαι" (MPG, V, 780). For the restoration of the text see Lightfoot, *Apostolic Fathers*, Part II, Vol. II, p. 160.

90. Munck, *Petrus und Paulus in der Offenbarung Johannis*, pp. 69, 70, takes this same view.

91. "War Petrus wirklich römischer Märtyrer," p. 170.

92. *Early Christian Fathers*, ed. Richarson, p. 91. Ignatius, Ephesians 12:1, 2: "οἶδα τίς εἰμι καὶ τίσιν γράφω. ἐγὼ κατάκριτος, ὑμεῖς ἠλεημένοι· ἐγὼ ὑπὸ κίνδυνον, ὑμεῖς ἐστηριγμένοι. πάροδός ἐστε τῶν εἰς Θεὸν ἀναιρουμένων, Παύλου συμμύσται τοῦ ἡγιασμένου τοῦ μεμαρτυρημένου, ἄξιο μακαρίστου" (MPG, 5, 745).

93. "Petrus römischer Märtyrer," p. 402. See also Altaner, "War Petrus in Rom?" pp. 184 ff.

94. Heussi "War Petrus wirklich römischer Märtyrer," p. 170.

This still leaves to be explained, however, why he emphasizes his unworthiness so much less specifically in the letters to Ephesus and Tralles than in the letter to Rome. Weary of the numerous criticisms of his former explanations,[95] Heussi arrived at the convenient conclusion that Romans 4:3 was a later addition. Perhaps all the letters were indeed later than previously supposed.[96] In an effort to discredit the testimony of Romans 4:3 altogether, this last point is amplified in a later work.[97]

Granted that the complete positiveness of Monceaux was unwarranted when he said that the passage is completely incomprehensible if one does not take the apostles here to be the founders of the Roman Church, the question still remains: Why were Peter and Paul mentioned together if not as cofounders of the Church at Rome? Surely the answer is not to be found in the New Testament. Peter and Paul are mentioned in Galatians 2; however, the conditions under which they there appear at Antioch would hardly be conducive to the placing of them together as cofounders of the Church at Rome. Such a function would have necessitated co-operation and a settlement of former differences, but the New Testament does not speak of reconciliation. There is the possibility that the two names were linked, not because of a Roman residence of Peter and Paul but because these two apostles had written to (given orders to) the Church of Rome. The letter of Paul to the Romans would explain the reference to this apostle, but why was Peter mentioned? Had he also written to Rome? Ignatius could not have had in mind 2 Peter. This Epistle had been ignored by Iranaeus,[98] placed among the disputed writings by Clement of Alexandria[99] and Eusebius,[100] and while it was accepted as canonical by later authors such as Augustine, he did not say it was authentic.[101] Furthermore, 2 Peter is not addressed to Rome or any other particular Church, it was sent by its anonymous author to all the Churches; and it is late, mid-second century, as 1:14–18 and 3:16 seem to indicate. The allusion to previous correspondence (3:1) and to a possible collaboration with Paul in writing to the Churches (3:15) does not make it necessary to accept the thesis that Ignatius in Romans 4:3 refers to letters written by Peter as well as by Paul to the Romans, but, on the contrary, these verses suggest that the author of 2 Peter knew Romans 4:2 f. and perhaps accepted this interpretation of διατάσσομαι himself. In addition, the high probability that the Epistle was written *at* Rome makes it less believable that it was written *to* Rome. In the absence of any other writing early attributed to Peter, which might have been addressed to Rome, we must look elsewhere for an explanation to account for the inclusion of his name in Romans 4:3. Since Peter is not mentioned in the letters of Paul, and Paul is not mentioned in 1 Peter, we derive no help from these quarters. It is possible that Ignatius was acquainted with 1 Clement or another tradition which linked the two apostles in Rome.

Defensible, but still far from certain, is Cullmann's conclusion that from the word διατάσσομαι in Romans 4:3 we may gather something of the tradition of Peter's ministry in Rome. If the verb refers to Paul's letter to the Romans, however, this would give us no information as to the work of Peter.[102] Equally plausible is the suggestion that διατάσσομαι recalls commands given in the course of a missionary journey. It is

---

95. Lietzmann, "Petrus römischer Märtyrer"; Altaner, "War Petrus in Rom?" p. 186; Goguel, *L'Église primitive*, p. 212; Cullmann, *Peter*, p. 111; Aland, "Petrus in Rom," p. 510.

96. *Neues zur Petrusfrage*, pp. 24 f.

97. *Die römische Petrustradition*, p. 73. It is helpful along with these attempts by Heussi to discredit the entire testimony of Ignatius, to read Aland, "Petrus in Rom," pp. 509 ff. Certain of the arguments appear below.

98. *Against Heresies* IV.9:2, "et Petrus ait in epistola sua" (note the singular "epistola"), quotes 1 Peter 1:8 (*MPG*, VII, 998; *The Ante-Nicene Fathers*, I, 472.

Against Heresies IV.16:5, "et propter hoc Petrus ait. . . ." quotes 1 Peter 2:16 (*MPG*, VII, 1019; *The Ante-Nicene Fathers*, I, 482.

99. *E. H.* VI.14:1 (Lake, II, 47).

100. *E. H.* III.3:1, 4 (Lake, I, 193) and III.25:3 (Lake, I, 257).

101. Augustine, *On Christian Doctrine* II.8:13 (*MPL*, XXXIV, 41; *The Nicene and Post-Nicene Fathers*, II, 538–39.) "Now the whole canon of Scripture on which this judgment is to be exercised is contained in the following books: . . . two of Peter [Petri duabus]."

102. James Kleist, "The Epistles of St. Clement of Rome and St. Ignatius of Antioch," in *Ancient Christian Writers*, I, 136, includes a note calling the attention of the reader at this point to 1 Cor.9:1 and 7:22. As a Roman Catholic author, however, he admits the important relationship of Peter to the Roman Church.

possible, but by no means demonstrable that, because of the parallelism in the context (see 4:1: ἐντέλλομαι, "give command"), the word may refer specifically to orders given in reference to martyrdom, that is, the people of Rome must not interfere.[103]

It is learned indirectly from the other letters of Ignatius and directly from Romans 4:3 that by the end of the first decade of the second century there was a tradition known even in Asia Minor that Peter and Paul had been to Rome and that they had enjoyed some position of authority in that church.[104] There is, however, no *explicit* reference in the letter to the Romans that Peter or Paul or both had lived or were martyred in Rome nor that they founded the Church there. There is no hint whatsoever that either apostle served as bishop in Rome unless it could be argued, in a tentative way, that since Ignatius himself was a bishop, he chose his examples from those who had filled the same office.[105]

THE FRAGMENTS OF PAPIAS

We have none of the works of Papias of Hierapolis (in Phrygia), and all that we know of this early Christian is derived from Irenaeus, the *Ecclesiastical History of* Eusebius, the *Scholia* of Maximus, Oecumenius, and Andreas Caesariensis. It is not known when he was born, and guesses range within the third and fourth quarters of the first century.[106] Irenaeus[107] and Eusebius[108] report that he "was a hearer of John and an associate of Polycarp." If what was written about Papias could be accepted as trustworthy tradition, we should possess important information concerning the Primitive Church.[109] Unfortunately, such is not the case; his "interpretations" are often bizarre and reveal either an overvivid imagination or an uncritical nature.[110] He is accused by Eusebius of being a man of "very mediocre intelligence," perhaps because of his chiliasm,[111] a belief which Eusebius hotly opposed. Despite Lightfoot's statement that it is "a tolerably safe inference . . . that Papias represents Saint Peter as being in Rome,"[112] the fragments cannot be accepted as overly important: 1) The fragments of Papias appear only secondhand in the works of Irenaeus and Eusebius and others. 2) Another fragment which seemingly contains a statement to the effect that 1 Peter was written in Rome by Peter is of little value, since it is not clear whether it is Papias or Clement who speaks of the tradition.[113] 3) If Papias could report tradition so uncritically as in the case of the fate of Judas, what he wrote concerning Mark is at least suspect. If, on the other hand, it is true that Papias was "a hearer of John and a companion of Polycarp," then, since we know that Polycarp used the Letter of Ignatius to the Romans,[114] it is at least reasonable that Papias had read Romans 4:3 and was acquainted with the tradition.[115] However, since Papias makes no reliable statement concerning such tradition, the available fragments of his work cannot be used as evidence in this book.[116]

---

103. Compare Cullmann, *Peter*, p. 111. See also Munck, *Petrus und Paulus in der Offenbarung Johannis*, pp. 64–65, 68, who, while rejecting a reference here to Paul's letters or a previous residence and work of Peter and Paul in Rome, accepts the interpretation mentioned also by Cullmann of the possibility of directives having been given by the prisoners Peter and Paul before their martyrdom.

104. Some, however, will admit no more than that there was a tradition known in the first decade of the second century that Peter and Paul had given directives *to* the Roman Church.

105. Lightfoot, *Apostolic Fathers*, Part II, Vol. II, p. 186; "Indeed we might read the epistle from beginning to end without a suspicion that the episcopal office existed in Rome at this time, if we had no other grounds for the belief."

106. Harnack, *Die Chronologie*, I, 357, suggests an acceptable date for Papias' fragments between A.D. 140 and 160.

107. *Against Heresies* V. 33:4 (*MPG*, VII, 1213).

108. *E. H.* III.39:1 (Lake, I, 291).

109. For example, see *E. H.* III.39:15 (Lake, I, 297).

110. See the passage in Apollinaris of Laodicea, in which Papias describes the gruesome death of Judas: *Ancient Christian Writers*, trans. Kleist, VI, 119.

111. See *Against Heresies*, V.33:4.

112. *Apostolic Fathers*, Part I, Vol. II, p. 494.

113. *E. H.* II.15:2 (Lake, I, 145); Cullmann, *Peter*, p. 113n71.

114. Lightfoot, *Apostolic Fathers*, Part II, Vol. II, p. 187.

115. If the accepted interpretation of that verse is correct: that Peter and Paul had been in Rome and that they both in some way had been related to that Church.

116. Heussi, *Die römische Petrustradition*, p. 44, is justified in disregarding the evidence of Papias.

THE LETTER OF DIONYSIUS, BISHOP OF CORINTH, TO THE ROMANS

Information gathered from the works of Eusebius helps in the dating of Dionysius' letter to Rome. We are told that Hegesippus visited Corinth (on his way to Rome) around A.D. 150 when Primus was bishop[117] and that during the Easter controversy (A.D. c. 190), involving Victor of Rome and the Churches of Asia, Bacchylus held the episcopate at Corinth.[118] From Eusebius' *Ecclesiastical History* it is also learned that Dionysius, whose episcopate came between Primus and Bacchylus, corresponded with the Roman Church during the episcopate of Soter (A.D. 166–74).[119] The *Chronicle* narrows down the interval further to 171 or A.D. 172. Therefore, it would not be very wrong to date the letter, as is commonly done, plus or minus A.D. 170.[120]

Important information is contributed by the fragments of the lost letters of Dionysius. In them we find the oldest witness to the Book of Acts,[121] the persecution in Athens, the theory that Dionysius the Areopagite was converted by Paul, and finally that 1 Clement was read during this period in the services of worship at Corinth.[122]

Those who deny that Peter helped found the Church of Rome see the indication that he did given by Dionysius, in his Epistle to the Romans:[123] 1) as an

error—Dionysius' claim that Peter as well as Paul founded the Church at Corinth (see 1 Cor. 3:6, 4:5; compare 1 Cor. 1:11–12) is simply popular tradition found in both Rome and Corinth,[124] 2) as the first witness to the legend that Peter founded the Church at Rome with Paul and was martyred and buried in that city—a legend which may have begun with Hegesippus who knew and falsely interpreted 1 Clement 5,[125] 3) as an attempt to bolster the prestige of the Church of Corinth by claiming that Peter and Paul founded that Church as well as the Church of Rome,[126] 4) as fiction written to magnify the Church of Rome and to institute an heir to the prerogatives supposedly given to Peter by Christ in Matthew 16:17–19 and John 21:18–19.[127] These critics recall that Marcion (A.D. c. 150), who had discarded Peter and the Twelve in favor of Paul, held that Paul alone had received the revelations from Christ and upon him alone was conferred the government of the Church. In order to protect Peter and the Twelve, Matthew 16:17–19 and John 21:18–19 were added later to the Gospels. Dionysius of Corinth continued this trend and only admitted the relationship of Paul to Rome because of the weight of the tradition. From this time forward the names of Peter and Paul are bound together; Paul, however, is in a subservient position.[128]

At this point it is necessary to turn to a study of the text itself. Attempts have been made to demonstrate

---

117. *E. H.* IV.22:2 (Lake, I, 375).

118. *E. H.* V.23:4 (Lake, I, 505).

119. *E. H.* IV.23:9–12 (Lake, I, 381, 383).

120. See Harnack, *Die Chronologie*, I, 30, 313.

121. *E. H.* IV.23:3 (Lake, I, 379).

122. *E. H.* IV.23:11 (Lake, I, 383).

123. *E. H.* II.25:8 (Lake, I, 182, 183). "By so great an admonition you bound together the foundations of the Romans and Corinthians by Peter and Paul, for both of them taught together in our Corinth and were our founders, and together also in Italy in the same place [or together] and were martyred at the same time."

"ταῦτα καὶ ὑμεῖς διὰ τῆς τοσαύτης νουθεσίας τὴν ἀπὸ Πέτρου καὶ Παύλου φυτείαν γενηθεῖσαν Ῥωμαίων τε καὶ Κορινθίων συνεκεράσατε. καὶ γὰρ ἄμφω καὶ εἰς τὴν ἡμετέραν Κόρινθον φυτεύσαντες ἡμᾶς ὁμοίως ἐδίδαξαν, ὁμοίως δὲ καὶ εἰς τὴν Ἰταλίαν ὁμόσε διδάξαντες ἐμαρτύρησαν κατὰ τὸν αὐτὸν καιρόν."

124. See Dannenbauer, "Die Petruslegende," p. 259 and Heussi, *War Petrus in Rom?* p. 54.

125. Heussi, *War Petrus in Rom?* p. 55.

126. Heussi, *Die römische Petrustradition*, p. 45.

127. Goguel, *L'Église primitive*, p. 213, concerning the period of Dionysius of Corinth, writes: "la tradition sur Pierre et Paul était invoquée pour fonder l'autorité particulière de l'Église de Rome."

128. See Henri Delafosse, "La Lettre de Clément," p. 80: "Denys qui nous sert cette histoire vers 170, n'est documenté. Il répète la leçon qu'on lui a apprise."

See also Grégoire, "Les Persécutions dans l'Empire romain," p. 101.

certain historical errors in order to discredit the state-ments concerning Peter. It is said that the passage of Dionysius, having been constructed upon 1 Corinthians 1:2 and 3:22, contradicts: 1) Acts 1:1–18—If Peter had been a founder of the Church at Corinth with Paul, the fact surely would have been mentioned; 2) 1 Corin-thians 3:10–15—There is no mention of Peter. Paul says plainly, "*I have laid the foundation*"; 3) 1 Corin-thians 4:15—Paul again emphasizes "*I have begotten you.*" If Paul had founded the Church with Peter, he would have mentioned the fact in some manner and surely would have avoided the first person singular. Whether the reasoning is sound or not, the criticism is valid. It is highly improbable that Peter had any hand in the founding of the Church at Corinth or had played any role in its early history.[129]

If it can also be shown that Dionysius claims that Peter and Paul were in Rome at the same time, then a second historical unlikelihood has been handed down as fact by that author. This question centers on the meaning of the word "ὁμόσε." Those who wish to discredit the historical reliability of the passage interpret it as having a temporal meaning which testifies that Peter and Paul "taught together in Italy at the same time."[130] Supporters of the tradition are as confident that what is meant is not that Peter and Paul were in Italy teaching at the same time but that they were "in the same place" in Italy, specifically Rome, at different times.[131]

If we admit that "ὁμοίως" in both places must have the same meaning, then ὁμόσε cannot repeat the second ὁμοίως, but reinforces εἰς τὴν Ἰταλίαν and means "in the same place," that is, Rome. It must be asked if the important fact which Dionysius seeks to convey is that Peter and Paul died together in Rome (emphasizing the place) or that they worked together in that city for a while (emphasizing time). Both inter-pretations present problems. If the author wished to emphasize place, then why would he not have said simply "Rome" instead of using the circumlocution "ὁμοίως δὲ καὶ εἰς τὴν Ἰταλίαν ὁμόσε διδάξαντες"?[132] On the other hand, if he sought to emphasize time, there remains the duplication of ὁμοίως and ὁμόσε, which results in the awkward, "and together also taught in Italy together." In spite of the difficulty involved, the emphasis upon place rather than time is the more acceptable.

The information in Dionysius concerning the time of the martyrdom of Peter and Paul is vague. Is the phrase, "κατὰ τὸν αὐτόν καιρόν" definite or indefi-nite? Does it indicate a period of a day, a year, or a generation? Harnack, no doubt influenced too greatly by the tradition, stated that the phrase means "in the same year."[133] This may well be the meaning suggested by tradition, and such meaning may be correct. It is not beyond dispute, however, that this is what Dionysius has written.

The statement of Dionysius concerning the partici-pation of the two apostles in the founding of the Chur-ches at Corinth and Rome is questionable. Since his most grievous error is in regard to the founding of the Church at Corinth by Peter and Paul, one is naturally suspicious about his parallel statement relative to the founding of the Church of Rome. He has, however, contributed some valuable information concerning the level of development of the tradition in the late second century.[134]

---

129. For a bibliography on and discussion of the question of Peter's relationship to the Church at Corinth, see Goguel, "L'Apôtre Pierre a-t-il joué un Rôle personnel dans les Crises de Grèce et de Galatie?" pp. 461–500. Goguel is skeptical that Peter went to Corinth or founded the Church there. Bernhard Weiss and Adolf Harnack are more favorably inclined toward the proposition.

130. See Cullmann, *Peter*, p. 116n67; and Toynbee and Perkins, *The Shrine of St. Peter*, p. 130. Heussi, *Die römische Petrustradition*, p. 45: "in gleicher Weise haben sie aber auch in Italien (= in Rom) *gemeinsam gelehrt* und zu der gleichen Zeit Zeugnis abgelegt."

131. Zahn, *Introduction*, II, 75, 76, holds this view as do most Roman Catholic scholars including Campiche, "Saint Pierre et son Martyre," p. 259, and Henri Leclercq, *DACL*, Vol. XIV, Part I, p. 840, who admits that if Dionysius had meant that Peter and Paul taught in Italy together he was in error. However, ὁμόσε must be taken in the sense of the "same place."

132. See Lake, I, 183, in his translation of *E. H.* II.25:8 "and together also taught in Italy in the same place."

133. *Die Chronologie*, I, 709.

134. *E. H.* IV.23:9–12 (Lake, I, 381, 383) and II.25:8 (Lake, I, 183).

THE SILENCE OF VICTOR IN THE EASTER CONTROVERSY
WITH POLYCRATES

Victor (A.D. 189–98) followed Eleutherus (A.D. 174–89) as bishop of Rome in the tenth year of Commodus (A.D. 189). At this time, and perhaps related to the election of Victor, there arose a controversy (A.D. c. 190) with Polycrates of Ephesus over the Easter celebration. It is not necessary to rehearse the debate here,[135] for what is important in this study is not what was said but what was not said. In an argument of this type, in which it would seem natural for both sides to appeal to all available authorities for support of their position, Victor makes no mention of the practice of Peter and Paul concerning Easter. Polycrates, on the other hand, recalls that both Philip and John as well as Polycarp[136] observed the season in such a way as to support his position. Instead of appealing to the apostles in general or to Peter in particular, as might be expected, Victor answers Polycrates with excommunication of the Eastern Churches.[137]

An argument from silence is dangerous and often leads to false conclusions, as was explained above in the discussion of Acts and Romans. Once again an argument from silence could prove to be extremely misleading. It is true that an appeal to the authority of Peter in this matter might have been decisive. An appeal to the practice of Peter could perhaps have made unnecessary the drastic action of excommunication. Granted that Victor did not mention Peter, is it therefore inevitable that Victor did not know of the tradition that Peter had lived in Rome, founded the Church there, and became its first bishop? This is possible, but by no means the only explanation of the silence.

Perhaps Victor did not wish to settle the question by a simple appeal to authority when there was the possibility of making a "test case" for the supremacy of the Roman See. It may be that the custom of the two apostles, or of Peter alone, differed from the Roman practice of the late second century, and mention of this fact would have weakened his position. There remains the third possibility, of course, that Victor was ignorant concerning the relationship of Peter to Rome.[138]

The first and second suggestions are possible, but not probable. If the custom of Peter were known at all in the tradition, it surely would have been known to Irenaeus, who, if such custom were unfavorable to the Roman position, certainly would have mentioned the fact in his letter to Victor. Conversely, if he had known of such tradition and it was favorable to Victor, he probably would have written not to him at all but rather to the Eastern bishops who challenged the Roman practice.

The third suggestion is also possible, but puzzling. That the Roman sojourn of Peter was unknown to Victor in A.D. 190 is indeed unlikely in view of the writings of Clement, Ignatius, Dionysius of Corinth, and, above all, Irenaeus with whom he now corresponded[139] and who had written so explicitly on the relationship of Peter and Paul to the Roman Church.[140]

In view of these considerations it is an extremely weak argument to infer from Victor's silence that he necessarily was ignorant concerning the tradition of Peter's residence in Rome. Since the silence of Victor may be interpreted in a number of ways, the Easter controversy cannot serve effectively as either a negative or a positive argument.

---

135. See Goguel, *L'Église primitive*, pp. 417–31, for a detailed discussion.

136. *E. H.* V.24:3–4 (Lake, I, 507).

137. *E. H.* V.24:9 (Lake, I, 509).

138. Lietzmann, "Petrus römischer Märtyrer," p. 403, is of the opinion that in the period A.D. 154–90 the Roman bishops were not in the habit of calling upon predecessors, even Peter and Paul, to support their views. Diekmann, "Das Zeugnis," pp. 627–34, suggests that the testimony of the Easter controversy contains possible references to the Roman graves of Peter and Paul.

139. *E. H.* V.24:11–17 (Lake, I, 509–13).

140. *Against Heresies*, III.3:1 ff. (*MPG*, VII, 849).

THE EVIDENCE OF JUSTIN, HIPPOLYTUS, TERTULLIAN,
AND CLEMENT OF ALEXANDRIA

One naturally would look in the works of Justin Martyr (d. A.D. 165?) for the first of the later testimonies. A search in the *Apologies* and in the *Dialogue with Trypho*, however, is rewarded only by a surprising silence on the subject of Peter's stay in Rome.[141] The absence of any reference is particularly strange when it is remembered that Justin refers to Simon Magus on three separate occasions.[142] In the mid-second century this thaumaturge was considered to be the arch foe of Peter, as is demonstrated by the extensive treatment of their conflicts in the *Acts of Peter* and the Pseudo-Clementine literature.

It has been explained by some that the original tradition of Simon Magus' activity in Rome, which appears in the works of Justin, rests upon a misunderstanding. They claim that Justin came upon an inscription which, if correctly read, referred to the ancient Sabine deity, Semo Sancus (who was associated by the Romans with Hercules). Justin was confident that the inscription read "semoni Deo Sancto" which he took to be a reference to "Simon the Holy God."[143] The inscription, however, which was rediscovered in 1574, actually contained the words, "Semoni Sanco Deo Fideo Sacrum" which has nothing at all to do with Simon Magus.[144] There is another explanation which would better fit the case. Justin *already* knew of a tradition of Simon Magus' residence in Rome; and the inscription "Semoni Sanco Deo Fidem Sacrum," although originally indicating a Sabine deity, in the late second and early third centuries may have been associated with Simon Magus. There seems to be some indication that Simon was deified. As Frederick C. Grant emphasizes,

The main characteristic feature of Hellenistic religion was syncretism: the tendency to identify the deities of various peoples and to combine their cults. Thus the Greek Zeus becomes Zeus-Amon-Re in Egypt. . . The Greek Artemis is identified with the old Italian goddess Diana of Aricia and elsewhere; Demeter is Ceres, Hephaestus is Vulcan, and so on. . . . Indeed, the religions of the Hellenistic age are like a large lake with many tributaries, uniting their waters into one.[145]

The simple fact that Justin makes no reference to Peter's being in Rome is not sufficient to establish that he was ignorant of such a tradition. This is admitted by even the most staunch critic.[146]

In the *Philosophumena* Hippolytus[147] mentions the coming of Simon Magus to Rome and says that there "he withstood the apostles [Peter and Paul]. [It was Simon Magus] whom Peter opposed when he [Simon Magus] was deceiving many by sorceries."[148] The reference to Simon Magus by Hippolytus rests ultimately upon Acts 8:9–25 but more immediately upon the information found in Justin Martyr,[149] the sources of the *Clementine Homilies* or the *Acts of Peter* and the Simonian tradition.

In a fragment by the same author it is learned that "Peter preached the Gospel in Pontus, Galatia, and Cappadocia, and Betania, and Italy, and Asia, and was afterwards crucified by Nero head downward, as he had himself desired to suffer in this manner."[150] This

---

141. Brief mention of this silence is made in Cullmann, *Peter*, p. 116, and Heussi, *Die römische Petrustradition*, p. 44.

142. *First Apology of Justin*, Vols. XXVI, LVI, and *Second Apology of Justin*, Vol. XV in *The Ante-Nicene Fathers*, I, 171–72, 182, 193.

143. *First Apology*, Vol. XXVI.

144. But see *The Ante-Nicene Fathers*, I, 171n4.

145. Grant, *Hellenistic Religions*, p. xiii.

146. Heussi, *Die römische Petrustradition*, p. 44. It must also be admitted that there is a possibility that the traditions concerning Simon Magus and those concerning Peter had not been combined in the period when Justin wrote.

147. For a discussion of the authorship see *The Philosophumena*, trans. Legge, I, 6.

148. *Ibid.*, VI, 1.267, in trans. II, 17.

149. *First Apology*, Vol. XXVI, in *The Ante-Nicene Fathers*, I, 171–72.

150. "Hippolytus on the Twelve Apostles," a fragment found in *The Ante-Nicene Christian Library*, eds. Roberts and Donaldson, Vol. II, Part II, p. 130.

must be considered as secondary information based upon the developing tradition. His last statement is most probably derived from the *Acts of Peter* XXXVII, or its source.

The writings of Tertullian, Clement of Alexandria, and Origen do not contribute greatly to my study of the Roman residence of Peter, but are considered to some extent below in Part II, the discussion of the martyrdom.

Apropos of the present discussion Tertullian (A.D. 200) reports that Clement was ordained by Peter,[151] a detail found also in the spurious *Epistle of Clement to James* which appears as the introduction to the *Clementine Homilies*. There is also one enigmatic passage which,

if interpreted in the manner of Giles, does suggest the Petrine origin of the Church of Rome. In the *De pudicitia* Tertullian aims his barbs at either Zephyrinus or Callistus and accuses the Roman bishop of claiming for himself the prerogatives of the Church. He asks, "do you presume for that reason [Matt. 16:17–19] to have diverted the power of binding and loosing to yourself, that is to every sister church of Petrine origin?" ("id est ad omnem ecclesiam Petri propinquam.")[152]

Clement of Alexandria (d. A.D. c. 220) in the sixth book of *Hypotyposes*, quoted twice by Eusebius,[153] mentions that Peter wrote his Gospel from Rome,[154] a tradition which may be independent or derived from a statement of Papias.[155]

THE PAPAL LISTS OF HEGESIPPUS, IRENAEUS, EPIPHANIUS, JULIUS AFRICANUS, AND EUSEBIUS

There are a number of lists containing information about the succession of Roman bishops. These lists are found in the works of 1) Hegesippus, 2) Irenaeus, 3) Hippolytus, 4) Julius Africanus, and 5) Philocalus. There is also a list in the *Liber Pontificalis*.

Hegesippus came to Rome during the bishopric of Anicetus (A.D. 157–68), or before, and he either left Rome or died when Eleutherus (A.D. 175–89) was bishop. What is known of his work πέντε ὑπομνήματα

ἐκκλησιαστικῶν πραξέων [Five Treatises on the Acts of the Church] is derived from Eusebius.[156] It is not certain whether the ὑπομνήματα, as the work is usually known, was a detailed history or a collection of miscellaneous matter. The passage which is of interest in this study contains a list of the bishops of Rome, which Hegesippus claims to have compiled himself.[157] That there was no list available when he came to Rome is obvious in his explicit use of the verb "ἐποιησάμην," if the reading in Eusebius is to be trusted.[158] The first

---

151. *De praescriptione haereticorum* XXXII (*MPL*, II, 45).

152. *De pudicitia* XXI (*MPL*, II, 1024). A few have recently attempted to see here a reference to the relics of Peter: "to every church near the grave [relics] of Peter." Actually the verse is quite vague and cannot be interpreted with certainty. The rendering of Giles could be rightfully accused of "begging the question." See also Heussi, *Die römische Petrustradition*, p. 47n1, W. Köhler, "Omnis ecclesia Petri propinqua," *Sitzungsberichte Heidelberg Akademie, 1937–38* (Heidelberg: C. Winter's Universitätsbuchhandlung, 1938), III, 1–38; Altaner, "Omnis ecclesia Petri propinqua," 130–38; P. Galatier, "Le véritable édit de Calliste," *Revue d'Histoire Ecclésiastique*, XXIII (1927), 464–88 and XXIV (1928), 41–51; H. Stoeckius, "Ecclesia Petri propria," *Archiv für katholisches Kirchenrecht*, CXVII (1937), 24–126; Harnack "Ecclesia Petri propinqua. Zur Geschichte der Anfänge des Primats des römischen Bishofs," *Sitzungsberichte der Preussischen Akademie der Wissenchaften, Phil. hist. Klasse, Berlin*, XX (1927), 139–52.

153. *E. H.* II.15:2; VI.14:6 (Lake, I, 145; II, 49, 51).

154. This quotation is discussed above, pp. 16–18.

155. *E. H.* III.39:15 (Lake, I, 297). See above, p. 22.

156. *E. H.* IV.22:1 (Lake, I, 375).

157. *E. H.* IV. 22:3 (Lake, I, 375) ". . . γενόμενος δὲ ἐν Ῥώμῃ, διαδοχὴν ἐποιησάμην μέχρις Ἀνικήτου· οὗ διάκονος ἦν Ἐλεύθερος, καὶ παρὰ Ἀνικήτου διαδέχεται Σωτήρ, μεθ' ὃν Ἐλεύθερος."

158. Lake, I, 375, and Harnack, *Die Chronologie*, I, 180 ff., agree in their translation of the passage: "When I was in Rome I recovered the list of succession until Anicetus." The verb "ἐποιησάμην" translated as "recovered" is influenced by the belief that there was a list available when Hegesippus came to Rome. If this were the case, we would expect to find a verb such as "ἀναλαμβάνω" or "ἀνακομίζω." The verb "ἐποιησάμην" should be translated "drew up." Even Heussi admits that Hegesippus made up his own list at this time.

list of Roman bishops was not composed, therefore, until approximately sixty years after the time of Clement and a hundred years after the martyrdom of Peter. The list of which Hegesippus speaks is not extant, but it may be recoverable from that list found in Epiphanius. Cuthbert H. Turner marshals convincing evidence to support this point: 1) The list of Epiphanius ends with Anicetus, which also would have been true in the case of Hegesippus who was in Rome during this pontificate. 2) It is reasonable to suppose that the list is not dependent upon that of Eusebius or Irenaeus since the name of the second pope is given as κλῆτος instead of 'Ανέγκλητος. 3) The basis of the document appears to have been Roman.[159] 4) Especially important is that ὑπομνηματισμοί is mentioned in the context, a word which Eusebius uses in various forms (ὑπομνήματα. ὑπομνηματίζεσθαι) in referring to the work of Hegesippus.[160]

The purpose of Hegesippus list was not historical. There was still no compulsion at this time in the Church to preserve the memories of the past. The intent was purely practical. Hegesippus mentions that while he was at Corinth he noticed that the Corinthians had remained in the true doctrine until Primus. Heresy was widespread at Rome, however, under Marcion, Basilides, and Valentinus. Therefore, Hegesippus wished to draw up a bishops' list to be used in combating these heresies. By demonstrating the authorized channel through which the true doctrine had come down to the present (probably to the period of Eleutherus) from Peter and Paul, he hoped the Roman succession would serve as "a guarantee of the unbroken transmission of the original faith."[161] If there were no bishops' list before this period, which is most likely the case, the memory of those living could still supply the needed information with reasonable accuracy. The problem is to ascertain what information was supplied. Did the list begin with Peter and Paul as the first bishops, or with Linus? Were Peter and Paul mentioned rather as "founders?" Did the list contain details such as the length of the various episcopates, and the like? These questions cannot be answered definitely since all that is known is what can be deduced from the various references to the words of Hegesippus in other sources. Lightfoot believes that the list did contain the length of office and did mention Peter and Paul at the beginning as the first bishops since the list of Epiphanius contains that data.[162] If this information appeared in the work of Hegesippus, it was isolated material gathered by him as "bearing on the question of the relation of Clement, third Bishop to the Apostles, with which context Epiphanius is as a matter of fact concerned."[163] Whether or not the list of Hegesippus contained the length of office of the early bishops, the basic observation of Turner and Lightfoot is acceptable that this is the earliest (between A.D. 157 and 189) *explicit* statement that Peter and Paul were jointly the first bishops of Rome.

The passage in the works of Irenaeus which is of interest in this discussion of the early lists of the Roman bishops is found in *Against Heresies*, written during

---

Dannenbauer mistakenly attributes to him the view, seemingly shared by Harnack, Lake, and Altaner, that Hegesippus found the list at Rome. The thought of Heussi is correctly interpreted by Altaner, "War Petrus in Rom?" p. 185, and Goguel, *L'Église primitive*, p. 213.

Lietzmann, *Petrus und Paulus in Rom*, 2d ed., p. 28, as well as Turner, "St. Peter in the New Testament and the Early Church," p. 198, see the list of Hegesippus as relatively unimportant. Pierre Batiffol, *Cathedra Petri*, p. 170, is not convinced of the relationship between Hegesippus and the list and says it is "not clear," while Lietzmann, p. 28, says that the words "γενόμενος δὲ ἐν Ῥώμῃ διαδοχὴν ἐποιησάμην μέχρις 'Ανικήτου are "hoffnungslos verdorben."

159. *Panarium* XXVII.6 (*MPG*, XLI, 371. See also Migne's note 87 on the same page.): "ἐν Ῥώμῃ γεγόνασι πρῶτοι Πέτρος καὶ Παῦλος ἀπόστολοι καὶ ἐπίσκοποι . . . ἦλθεν δὲ εἰς ἡμᾶς ἤδη πως μαρκελλίνα τις . . . ἢ πόλλους ἐλυμήνατο ἐν χρόνοις 'Ανικήτου ἐπισκόπου Ῥώμης. . . ."

See Lietzmann, *Petrus und Paulus in Rom*, 2d ed., p. 23. Lightfoot, *Apostolic Fathers*, Part I, Vol. I, p. 327, presents a theory convincingly (originally put forward in *Academy*, May 21, 1887, pp. 362 f.) that this passage continues the original list of Hegesippus. A more cautious attitude is maintained by Streeter, *The Primitive Church*, pp. 187, 295 ff.

160. See Turner, in *Theology*, XIII (1926), 198.

161. Lightfoot, *Apostolic Fathers*, Part I, Vol. I, p. 203.

162. This is by no means certain, as Harnack, *Die Chronologie*, I, 180, indicates. Lietzmann, *Petrus und Paulus in Rom*, 2d ed., p. 28, sees the list of Julius Africanus as the first of this type.

163. Turner, "The Early Episcopal Lists," *Journal of Theological Studies*, XVIII (1917), 120.

the pontificate of Eleutherus (A.D. 175–90). The purpose of Irenaeus, like that of Hegesippus, in presenting an episcopal list, is not historical but apologetic. As in the case of Hegesippus, his aim is to demonstrate that the heresies are not derived from the apostolic past, whereas the doctrine which he teaches is guaranteed by an unbroken line of authority from the very apostle-founders who appointed the first Roman bishop.[164]

After founding the Church at Rome, Irenaeus states that Peter and Paul "entrusted the office of the episcopate to Linus."[165] Later he adds that "third in order"[166] from the apostle, Clement is appointed to the episcopate. The list ends with Eleutherus, a contemporary of Irenaeus.

This list begins with Linus, not with Peter and Paul, as in the case of Epiphanius (that is, Hegesippus). Peter and Paul are founders, not bishops. When the complete document is checked carefully, however, Irenaeus is not entirely consistent. He opposes the plan of Hegesippus, by mentioning Anicetus as the tenth bishop.[167] In speaking of Cerdon, however, he relates that this heretic appeared in Rome during the pontificate of Hyginus who was "ninth in the episcopal succession from the apostles" (in which calculation Peter would be counted as the first bishop and Anicetus would stand not tenth but eleventh).[168] It must be admitted that "if the readings be correct, either the apostolic founder or founders must have been included in the enumeration, so that Linus would be the second bishop, or there must

be some accidental tripping in the number."[169] As Lightfoot points out, it is certain that Irenaeus did not adopt a different system of enumeration in the second case which is only one chapter removed from his own careful listing of the Roman bishops. It is most reasonable to accept the notion that a later hand changed the original listing from "eight" to "nine"[170] to account for the episcopacy of Peter as required by the emerging Roman tradition.

What is the source for Irenaeus' list of bishops?[171] Perhaps Irenaeus used either the *Syntagma* of Justin (which may have contained a list of bishops),[172] or the same oral or written materials used by Hegesippus or the work of Hegesippus himself. That the last possibility is definitely correct is the main thesis of a discussion of the episcopal lists by Streeter, in which he gives support to the original suggestion by Lightfoot.[173] In the original document of Hegesippus, we are told by Eusebius,[174] the passage containing the list of succession came after a discussion of 1 Clement. In the midst of his list of bishops,[175] after the mention of Clement, Irenaeus also begins a long digression that Streeter indicates is comparable to the argument which Hegesippus originally directed against the Gnostics at this point in his document. This digression in Irenaeus, Streeter urges, is clumsy and is to be explained only by the fact that it appeared in the document of Hegesippus which Irenaeus was copying.[176]

In the same place in his catalogue, Epiphanius also digresses after mentioning Clement. He does not quote directly from 1 Clement, however, but from certain

---

164. Cullmann, *Peter*, p. 116, and Streeter, *The Primitive Church*, p. 194, argue that the tradition found in *Against Heresies* III.1:1 (*MPG*, VII, 848), that Peter and Paul preached in Rome and founded the Church there, goes back to Papias.

Founding the Church and being its first bishop are not one and the same thing; using one term to mean the other is an error to be avoided. The ancient writers made a marked distinction; Marius Besson, *Saint Pierre et les Origines de la Primauté romaine*, p. 101, is misled in considering it inconsequential whether Irenaeus said Peter founded the Church of Rome or was the first bishop of Rome.

165. *Against Heresies* III.3:3 (*MPG*, VII, 849): "τὴν τῆς ἐπισκοπῆς λειτουργίαν ενεχείρισαν."

166. *Ibid.*, "ἐν τρίτῳ τόπῳ."

167. *Ibid.*, III.4:3 (*MPG*, VII, 857).

168. *Ibid.*, I.27:1, 3 (*MPG*, VII, 687): ἔνατον κλῆρον τῆς ἐπισκοπικῆς διαδοχῆς ἀπὸ τῶν ἀποστολῶν ἔχοντος . . . ὃς ἦν ἔνατος ἐπίσκοπος." See III.4:3 (*MPG*, VII, 857).

169. Lightfoot, *Apostolic Fathers*, Part I, Vol. I, p. 204.

170. *Against Heresies*, I.27:3 (*MPG*, VII, 687).

171. Batiffol, *Cathedra Petri*, p. 169; "La plus ancienne liste des évêques de Rome dont il y ait tracé est celle que produit saint Irénée." See Caspar, *Die älteste römische Bischofliste*, p. 185.

172. Lietzmann, *Petrus und Paulus in Rom*, 2d ed., p. 27.

173. Streeter, *The Primitive Church*, pp. 295–303. Compare the discussion of the problem in Lietzmann, *Petrus und Paulus in Rom*, 2d ed., pp. 21–28.

174. *E. H.* IV.22:1 (Lake, I, 375).

175. *Against Heresies* III.3 (*MPG*, VII, 849).

176. The statement by Harnack and Lightfoot that 1 Clement was not known at an early date in the West, and that this is the first mention of it, does much to strengthen the contention of Streeter. It should be added also that nowhere else does Irenaeus allude to 1 Clement.

ὑπομνήματα.[177] If Epiphanius derives his episcopal list from Hegesippus, it is reasonable to suppose that he also derives his digression from the same source.

Both Irenaeus and Epiphanius, Streeter continues: 1) quote from 1 Clement here and nowhere else, 2) digress at the same point in their catalogues of the bishops of Rome to quote from 1 Clement, and 3) quote in such a way as to betray an earlier identical or similar digression in their source (although this digression is used by each in a different way and for a different purpose).

Epiphanius in the *Panarium* refers to Clement "whom Paul mentions in the Epistle to the Romans." This is an error, for Paul mentions Clement not in Romans but in Philippians 4:3. Irenaeus avoids this error and after naming Linus, correctly adds that this is the one "whom Paul mentions in his Epistle to Timothy." According to Streeter, the error found in Epiphanius and avoided by Irenaeus may go back to Hegesippus.

Another interesting comparison is possible. Irenaeus in *Against Heresies* I. 25 mentions the Carpocratians and Marcellina who spread false doctrine under Anicetus.[178] Epiphanius gives the same account, except that his appears within his catalogue of the bishops of Rome.[179] The two allusions agree almost completely. Therefore, since Epiphanius does not derive his account from Irenaeus,[180] it is probable that both accounts depend upon a common source.[181] Curiously, in *Panarium* XXVII.6:1, Epiphanius states, "Anicetus, whom shortly before I have named in the Catalogue." This reveals careless copying, for in the *Panarium* the catalogue comes *after*, not *before*, this point.

Epiphanius mentions the Marcellina episode twice; the first time in words similar to those of Irenaeus, the second time in his "own vituperative paraphrase."[182] In Hegesippus the Marcellina episode no doubt was located in the latter instance at the point where Epiphanius had paraphrased it. Therefore, the words,

"Anicetus, whom shortly before I have named in the Catalogue," appeared in the original after the name of Anicetus had been mentioned.

In summary, Streeter concludes that Irenaeus and Epiphanius have used the same source in the preparation of their lists of Roman bishops and for their account of 1 Clement and Marcellina. They differ only to the extent that Irenaeus uses the longer form Ἀνέγκλητος and Epiphanius, the shorter κλήτος. Streeter claims that this difference is unimportant since the name Ἀνέγκλητος had been shortened in the course of time because of its constant repetition in the liturgies. There is one difference between the two lists which Streeter does *not* emphasize—a crucially important point for this study. While Irenaeus begins his list in *Against Heresies* III.3:3 with Linus as the first bishop, naming Peter and Paul as the founders, Epiphanius mentions the two apostles as the first bishops. Streeter's thesis may still be retained,[183] but it must be added that the development of the tradition has resulted in this alteration in the status of Peter and Paul.

There is still one remaining observation to be made. Epiphanius (A.D. c. 380) retains the name of Paul in the capacity of bishop even in a period (A.D. c. 380) when Paul had long since been most effectively eclipsed by Peter. The more common tendency is reflected in the *Liberian Catalogue*[184] (which is dealt with at length in Part III, chapter 8), written almost a half-century before Epiphanius. While carefully noting the duration of the episcopate of Peter, it makes no mention of an episcopate of Paul.[185] An additional bit of information in

---

177. See Eusebius' discussion of Hegesippus, *E. H.* IV.22 (Lake, I, 375–79).

178. This comparison is also pointed out by Lietzmann, *Petrus und Paulus in Rom*, 2d ed., p. 23.

179. *Panarium* XXVII.6:1 (*MPG*, XLI, 371).

180. See also Batiffol, *Cathedra Petri*, p. 171.

181. See Streeter, *The Primitive Church*, pp. 299, 300, for his arguments in support of this position.

182. *Ibid.*, p. 300.

183. There is also the possibility, suggested by Mommsen and followed by Lietzmann and Caspar, that behind Epiphanius there is a Roman document related to that which they call the "Index." See Lietzmann, *Petrus und Paulus in Rom*, 2d ed., p. 25.

184. Which shows the "contamination" of both types of list; that followed by Irenaeus having Ἀνέγκλητος and that of Epiphanius which reads κλήτος (unless we accept Streeter's explanation of the abbreviation of the name). Lightfoot, *Apostolic Fathers*, Part I, Vol. I, p. 64, indicates that the *Catalogue* may have been the work of Hippolytus.

185. See Lightfoot, pp. 252–61. The notice in the *Liberian Catalogue* stands, "Passus est Dominus noster Iesus Christus duobus Gemines coss. viii Kal. Apr., et post ascensum eius beatissimus Petrus episcopatum suscepit . . . Petrus ann. xxv, mens, i, d. viiii . . . passus autem cum Paulo."

Epiphanius, that Clement was ordained by Peter,[186] is ultimately dependent upon the apocryphal *Letter of Clement to James*, which serves as a preface to the *Clementine Homilies*.[187]

The author of *Against the Heresy of Artemon*, who may have been Hippolytus, writing at the time of Zephyrinus (A.D. c. 211),[188] informs us that Victor is the "thirteenth bishop of Rome after Peter." This reckoning implies that Linus, not Peter, is the first bishop, which view agrees with the list of Irenaeus, except that the name of Paul (in this short interval of a generation at most) has been dropped. As noted above, this trend is carried on in the *Liberian Catalogue* (A.D. c. 336), and by the time of Cyprian (d. A.D. 258), Paul has completely dropped out of the picture. Peter alone is named as the first bishop of Rome. In the interval between Hegesippus (A.D. c. 150) and Cyprian (A.D. c. 250), the idea of the monarchical episcopate evolved. Whereas the mention of Peter and Paul as first bishops was possible in the former time, the concept of Church government accepted in the mid-third century precluded such duality of leadership. The decision was made to eliminate Paul, probably not (as some have suggested) because he was supported by the despised Marcion,[189] but more logically because 1) common sense would dictate that he could not have been a first bishop if he were only in Rome as a prisoner and 2) greater stress was being laid upon Matthew 16:17–19 and the alleged prerogatives granted to Peter alone by Christ.[190]

The first *certain* trace of a Roman papal list, now lost, which indicated the length of the various episcopates was that of Sextus Julius Africanus (A.D. c. 220–35).[191] All the later lists, and that of Africanus is no exception, had as their point of departure the twenty-five-year episcopate of Peter. Africanus may also be responsible for the characterization of the Roman bishops as "ἡ κατὰ Ῥώμην πέτρου διαδοχή" and the claim of the Antiochean bishops that their office was derived from Peter (ἀπὸ Πέτρου).[192] The term "bishop" (ἐπίσκοπος) was not used by Africanus in connection with the name of Peter, but appears only later in the tradition of Jerome.

Hippolytus (A.D. c. 235) compiled a papal list up to his own time (Pope Pontianus, A.D. 230–35). His purpose was different from that of Hegesippus and Irenaeus. His interests were ecclesiastical history and chronography as well as theology. Besides containing a chronicle from the foundation of the world up to his own time including the Roman emperors, kings of Macedon, and the like, his work naturally included a papal list. The list itself has been lost, but it served as a source for a number of later lists.[193]

In the *Ecclesiastical History* (A.D. c. 326) of Eusebius there is no mention of Peter without Paul in the role of founder of the Church at Rome, and there is no date given for his "episcopate." A number of references, however, to later episcopal succession in Rome are found in this work.[194] In III.2:1 Eusebius seems to place the two apostles at the beginning of the line of episcopal succession, but interestingly he reverses the usual order as found in Epiphanius and others by naming Paul first. Linus is mentioned in III.4:8 as the first

---

186. *De praescriptione* XXXII.2 (*MPL*, II, 14). See Goguel *L'Église primitive*, p. 215. This information is also found in Tertullian, *De pudicitia* XXI (A.D. c. 200).

187. See Batiffol, *Cathedra Petri*, p. 173, and the *Epistle of Clement to James* in *The Ante-Nicene Fathers*, VII, 218.

188. This is the opinion of Lightfoot, *Apostolic Fathers*, Part I, Vol. II, pp. 377–80; Harnack, *Die Chronologie*, II, 224–26; Turner, in *Theology* (1926); and Connolly,"Eusebius *H. E.* V.28," pp. 73–79. (Lake, I, lvi), expresses doubts. This passage which appears in Eusebius, *E. H.* V.28:3, is called, according to Theodoret, *The Little Labyrinth*.

189. Heussi, *War Petrus in Rom?* p. 56.

190. See the remarks of Tertullian in *De pudicitia* XXI (*MPL*, II, 980).

191. Harnack, *Die Chronologie*, I, 123; Caspar, *Die älteste römische Bischofliste*, pp. 292, 398 f.; Lietzmann, *Petrus und Paulus in Rom*, 2d ed., p. 28.

192. Harnack, *Die Chronologie*, I, 705.

193. Duchesne is convinced that this list is to be found in the *Liber generationis*. See below, p. 35. See *The Book of the Popes (Liber Pontificalis)*, trans. Loomis, p. xii, and Lietzmann, *Petrus und Paulus in Rom*, 2d ed., p. 28. Peter is counted as the first bishop by Hippolytus (if *E. H.* V.28:3 is correctly atrributed to this author).

194. *E. H.* III.2:1, 4:8, 13:1, 15:1, 21:1, 34:1; IV.1:1, 4:1, 5:5, 10:1, 11:1, 2, 6–8, 19:1, 30:3; V.22:1, 28:3, 7; VI.21:1, 2, 23:3, 29:1–3, 39:13; VII.2:1, 5:3, 27:1, 30:23, 32:1 (Lake, Vols. I, II). See Lightfoot, *Apostolic Fathers*, Part I, Vol. I, pp. 206–7.

bishop *after* Peter, but when referring to various bishops by number, supposedly based upon his understanding of succession, Eusebius consistently omits Peter and Paul and starts with Linus.[195]

The so-called *Chronicle* (A.D. c. 325) of Eusebius[196] is preserved in three versions: the Armenian, Latin, and Syriac. The Armenian version, written according to Lightfoot in the fifth century and based upon the Greek or Syriac, contains the names of the bishops and the year of their accession.[197] Peter, unaccompanied by Paul, is neither included in the enumeration of the bishops nor called bishop. The Latin version of Jerome[198] in the section of the list with which we are concerned agrees with the Armenian version, aside from the fact that the Roman primacy of Peter, as might be expected, is more emphasized than it is in the Armenian version or the original of Eusebius. Peter is unequivocally named as the first bishop of Rome.[199] Oddly enough, however, in various references to bishops by number, Jerome's version follows what was probably the original plan of Eusebius—Peter is omitted.[200] The common opinion is that the Armenian version is the more accurate and that Jerome altered various of the later dates according to an unknown catalogue which was used also by Eusebius as a source for the *Ecclesiastical History*. Lightfoot disagrees with this conclusion owing to the fact that 1) there is only an interval of a few months between the writing of the *Chronicle* (A.D. 325) and the *Ecclesiastical History* (A.D. 326) and 2) there is no record of a boast by Jerome that he corrected the Eusebian list. Lightfoot takes the defensible position that whatever source had been used by Eusebius in the writing of one work was also used in the other.[201] No matter what differences are found among the lists contained in the *Ecclesiastical History* and those in the *Chronicle*, it must be pointed out that they do agree in the names of the bishops, in the order, and in the sum total of the years from Peter to Urbanus (d. A.D. 230).

If it is to be accepted that Eusebius used the same source for and adopted one position concerning the place of Peter in the episcopal list, it is only reasonable to suppose in light of the obvious differences between the lists found in the *Chronicle* and the *Ecclesiastical History* that he had a different purpose in view for each work. In the *Chronicle*, Eusebius desired a continuous chronology and chose to include the single apostle-founder and his length of pastorate. In the *Ecclesiastical History* he preferred "to emphasize the credit accrued to the Roman succession through its common descent from both Peter and Paul."[202] Another possible suggestion, rejected by Lightfoot for lack of evidence, is that Irenaeus was a source for the *Ecclesiastical History*[203] and Julius Africanus for the *Chronicle*.

Cyprian (d. A.D. 258) indirectly refers to Peter as the first bishop and Linus as the second when he names Hyginus as the ninth bishop.[204] Jerome (d. A.D. 420) in noting Clement as the fourth bishop after Peter[205] follows the same principle.

The writer of the *Liber Pontificalis* (between A.D. 514 and 530) used the material of the *Liberian Catalogue* in a body. The *Catalogue*, as mentioned above, is itself a composite document utilizing material from various traditions. This is illustrated by its use of both κλῆτος and Ἀνέγκλητος. Having found both names in a different source, the author of the *Catalogue* read them as separate popes not as variant spellings of the name of a single pope.[206]

By his uncritical appropriation of the *Liberian Catalogue*, the author of the *Liber Pontificalis* reveals

---

195. For example, IV.1:1: "καὶ Ἀλέξανδρος..., πέμπτην ἀπὸ πέτρου καὶ παύλου."

196. The actual name is unknown, but was most probably χρονικόν or χρονικά.

197. See Lightfoot, *Apostolic Fathers*, Part I, Vol. I, pp. 212–16.

198. *MPL*, XXVII, 1–651.

199. "Roman mittitur, ubi evangelium praedicans xxv annis ejusdem urbis episcopus perseverat." Cited by Lightfoot, *Apostolic Fathers*, Part I, Vol. I, p. 217.

200. "Post Petrum primus Romanam ecclesiam tenuit Linus . . . Romanae ecclesiae secundus constituitur episcopus Anacletus." *Ibid.*

201. *Ibid.*, p. 231, see also pp. 232–33.

202. Turner, "The Early Episcopal Lists," p. 115.

203. See *E. H.* III.23:3 (Lake, I, 243).

204. Epistle LXXIV written in A.D. 256, *Corpus Scriptorum Ecclesiasticorum Latinorum*, III, 799. (Hereafter this work will be identified as *CSEL*.)

205. *De viris illustribus* XV, written A.D. 392 (*MPL*, XXIII, 657).

206. Duchesne, *Le Liber Pontificalis*, Vol. I, Part I, pp. viii, ix, 2, 3. See Heussi, *Die römische Petrustradition*, pp. 74, 75.

that he either did not bother to consult other lists or did not know of their existence. Much of the author's material concerning the life of Peter is derived from Jerome's *De viris illustribus* I.[207]

Unfortunately, we do not have the original of the *Liber Pontificalis* and must be satisfied with the Felician (the list breaks off at the time of Felix) recension of A.D. 530 and the Cononian (continued to Pope Conon) in A.D. 687.[208] Mommsen disagrees with the majority of authorities, including Duchesne, and maintains that these recensions are based upon the original seventh-century text, being roughly contemporary with the recensions available to us.[209]

In comparison with the meagerness of the information offered by the earlier documents and lists, there is a marked increase in specificity and a comparatively large amount of material given to the notice of Peter as found in the *Liber Pontificalis*. The importance of the notice for the later tradition warrants its being quoted as follows:[210]

Blessed Peter, the Antiochene, son of John, of the province of Galilee and the town of Bethsaida, brother of Andrew and

chief of the Apostles, first occupied the seat of the bishop in Antiochia for seven years. This Peter entered the city of Rome when Nero was Caesar and there occupied the seat of bishop for 25 years, 1 month and 8 days [2 months and 3 days]. He was bishop in the time of Tiberius Caesar, and Gaius and Tiberius Claudius and of Nero.[211] He wrote two epistles which are called Catholic and the Gospel of Mark, for Mark was his disciple and son by baptism. . . .[212] He ordained two bishops, Linus and Cletus, who in person fulfilled all the services of the priest of the city of Rome for the inhabitants and for strangers; then the blessed Peter gave himself to prayer and preaching and instructing the people. . . .[213] He consecrated blessed Clement as bishop and committed to him the government of the See and all the Church.[214]

Errors in copying by the scribes of the following centuries account for the variation in Peter's length of episcopate. As in the case of the earlier recensions, the second edition of the *Liber Pontificalis* included the usual twenty-five years, but then proceeded to stipulate "two months three days" in place of the original "one month eight days." Later MSS vary considerably, but many differences may be accounted for by the addition or subtraction of an "X" (that is, ann. XXXV or XV for XXV or the like) or an "i."[215]

---

207. *MPL*, XXIII, 638–39. In addition to some relatively unimportant and unknown sources, such as that which speaks of the placing of Peter's body in a bronze coffin, Jerome, in *De viris illustribus*, makes use of the apocryphal *Letter of Clement to James*, which was used also by Tertullian, Epiphanius, and Hippolytus.

208. Duchesne, *Le Liber Pontificalis*, Vol. I, Part I, pp. xlix–lxvii.

209. *The Book of the Popes*, trans. Loomis, I, xx f. See Heussi, *Die römische Petrustradition*, p. 72.

210. In the following text as found in Duchesne, *Le Liber Pontificalis*, Vol. I, Part I, pp. 50 f. (cf. p. 118), the italicized words appear in the Felician and not the Cononian recensions or vice versa; the words in small caps appear only in the second edition and manifest retouching.

"Beatus Petrus, *Antiochenus*, filius Iohannis, provinciae Gallileae, vico Bethsaida, *frater Andreae et* PRINCEPS APOSTO-LORUM primum sedit cathedra episcopatus in Antiochia ann. VII. *Hic Petrus ingressus in urbe Roma Nerone Caesare ibique sedit cathedra(m) episcopatus* ann. XXV, mens. II, dies III [oldest texts: mens. I, dies viii]. Fuit temporibus Tiberii Caesaris et Gaii et Tiberii Claudi et Neronis. Hic scripsit duas epistulas quae CANONICAE [2d ed., "catholicae"] nominantur et evangelium Marci, quia Marcus auditor eius fuit et filius de baptismo. . . ."

In the second edition appears the following concerning Linus, Cletus, and Clement, *Ibid.*, p. 118: "HIC ORDINAVIT DUOS EPISCOPES LINUM ET CLETUM QUI PRAESENTILATER OMNE MINISTERIUM SACERDOTAE IN URBE ROMA POPULO VEL SUPER-VENIENTIUM EXHIBERENT; BEATUS AUTEM PETRUS AD ORATIONEM ET PRAEDICATIONEM POPULUM ERUDIENS, VOCABAT . . . HIC BEATUM CLEMENTUM EPISCOPUM CONSECRAVIT, EIQUE CATHE-DRAM VEL ECCLESIAM OMNEM DISPONENDAM COMMISIT. . . ." For the English translation, see *The Book of the Popes*, trans. Loomis, p. 4.

211. An admixture of two independent traditions may be noted at this point: 1) the *Acts of Peter and Paul*, that Peter did not come to Rome until the reign of Nero and 2) Jerome, that after he had reigned for twenty-five years he was put to death by Nero.

212. See the fragment of Papias, *E. H.* III.39:15 (Lake I, 297).

213. This material is derived from the *Preface to the Clementine Homilies* erroneously attributed to Clement and translated into Latin by Rufinus.

214. From the *Epistle of Clement to James* II, V, prefixed to the *Clementine Homilies*. See Duchesne, *Le Liber Pontificalis*, Vol. I, Part I, p. 118, line 8, and p. 119n8 and *The Ante-Nicene Fathers*, VIII, 218.

215. Duchesne, *Le Liber Pontificalis*, Vol. I, Part I, pp. 14–40.

The seven years that Peter is said to have resided as bishop of Antioch are not mentioned by any other author except Gregory the Great.[216] Also the *Liber Pontificalis* alleges that Peter came to Rome under Nero (A.D. 54–68) and died under the same emperor. In the interval Peter supposedly served as bishop for twenty-five years. This is an impossibility since Nero reigned for only thirteen years. A further difficulty is raised by the assumption of the author of the *Liber Pontificalis* that Peter resided as bishop in Rome from A.D. 30–55.[217] This requires the acceptance of two unlikely conclusions: 1) Peter arrived in Rome in the same year or in the year after the death of Christ. 2) He died in Rome very early in the reign of Nero. Furthermore, the author suppressed the doubts of Jerome as expressed in *De viris illustribus*,[218] concerning the Petrine authorship of the Second Epistle; and surely his mention of Mark as "filius de baptismo" is a development from 1 Peter 5:13.[219]

In addition to the growing awareness of the importance of the statements in Matthew 16:17–19 and John 21:18, 19 and of the fact that Paul's residence in Rome was only while a prisoner (even if he was given some degree of freedom), are there any other explanations to account for the deemphasis of Paul as noted in the episcopal lists?

In Dionysius of Corinth and possibly also in Ignatius' Epistle to the Romans, Peter and Paul share a common role as founders of the Church of Rome. This belief in the importance of both apostles is also reflected in the graffiti found at San Sebastiano and in the character of the liturgical celebration held on June 29.[220]

The point is well taken by Batiffol that between the mid-second and the mid-third century a change took place in the function of the bishops' list.[221] In the earliest period the κήρυγμα of the apostles was guaranteed by the διαδοχή or succession of the bishops. By the beginning or the middle of the third century, certainly by the time of Cyprian, another factor became singularly important, the legitimization of the Roman episcopacy by means of this same διαδοχή. While the earlier interest was served in retaining both Peter and Paul, the later was served by the exclusive presence of Peter as bishop.[222] Naturally, in the evolution of a monarchical episcopacy there was room for only one bishop at any given time.[223] Therefore, Paul had to be sacrificed. The See of Rome became the "Cathedra Petri."

The expressions of confidence concerning the length of the episcopacy of Peter, like those concerning the exclusive episcopacy of Peter itself, are phenomena of the third century.[224] It is not valid to dismiss the claim as a side manifestation of the development of the papal claims. More probably it evolved out of the desire for further details on the part of the early Roman ecclesiastics. As the list grew longer, the inclusion of the dates of accession for the various bishops made it more clear and obvious to the reader or hearer that no name had been lost from the list and that points of doctrine had

---

216. "Ipse [Petrus] firmavit sedem [Antiochia] in qua septem annis, quamvis discessurus sedit," *Epistle* VII.40 (*MPL*, LXXVII, 899).

217. Eusebius, as has been mentioned above, placed Peter's arrival in Rome A.D. 42, and his death A.D. 67. However, the *Acts of Peter and Paul* and Lactantius in *De Mortibus persecutorum* II (*MPL*, VII, 195, see note at the bottom of the page under "et per annos quinque et viginti"), retain the idea that Nero was in power when Peter came to Rome: "They scattered through the earth to preach the Gospel, and during twenty-five years, until the beginning of the reign of Nero, they laid the foundations of the Church throughout the provinces and cities. Nero was already in power when Peter came to Rome." ("Cumque jam Nero imperaret Petrus Romam advenit.") The twenty-five years were not spent *at* Rome; the period was spent in preaching the Gospel, an activity which ended at Rome in the reign of Nero.

218. And Eusebius in *E. H.* III.3:1 (Lake, I, 193).

219. Duchesne, *Le Liber Pontificalis*, Vol. I, Part I, p. 119n6.

---

220. Both subjects are discussed in Part III.

221. *Cathedra Petri*, p. 173.

222. See the opinion of Tertullian in *De pudicitia* XIII (*MPL*, II, 980) and especially XXI (*MPL*, II, 1024). The latter passage is obscure. The words "id est ad omnem ecclesiam Petri propinquam" have been variously interpreted. It is not acceptable to see a reference here to the relics of Peter. We may accept the Giles translation, *Documents Illustrating Papal Authority*, p. 27, "that is to every sister Church of Petrine origin." Another translation might be, "to all Churches related to the Church which Peter founded."

223. As, for example, the dispute between Novatian and Cornelius will confirm.

224. See McGiffert, *A History of Christianity*, p. 591. and Schmidt, *Studien zu den Pseudo-Clementinen*, pp. 357 ff.

been handed down in an unbroken line from the time of the apostles themselves.[225] The proposal of exactly twenty-five years for the episcopate of Peter suggests that there was confusion in the minds of those who composed the early episcopal lists.[226] For example, Hippolytus' chronology contains two persons as "successors" to Peter—Linus and Anencletus—who governed *during* the period of Peter, by his leave and under his authority.[227] To each of these men Hippolytus assigns twelve years.[228] Clement comes next in the list and is named as Peter's immediate successor. Thus if we include the "episcopates" of Linus and Cletus under Peter, Peter's reign is then approximately twenty-five years (twenty-four years to be precise).[229]

Another possibility to account for the growth of the legend of the long episcopate of Peter is its relationship with the legend of Simon Magus, who is said to have come to Rome during the reign of Claudius. The apocryphal *Acts* and Eusebius claim that Peter came to Rome and conducted a ministry there "against the pest of all mankind."[230] If we reckon from early in the reign of Claudius (A.D. 41–54) until late in the reign of Nero (A.D. 54–68), we allow for an interval of twenty-five years.

According to Harnack the "official" establishment of the twenty-five-year episcopate of Peter, for whatever reason, is to be recognized as roughly coincident with the supplanting of Paul in the tradition.[231]

THE APOCRYPHAL LITERATURE

The apocryphal material is, without exception, too untrustworthy and too late to offer any information which might be considered as reliable and independent.[232] Interest in the apocryphal details is justified only to the extent that they indicate a trend in the development of the tradition.

The following documents are the earliest of those which take into consideration the Roman residence and activity of Peter. Their relationship to the matter of martyrdom and burial is examined in Parts II and III.

The Acts of Peter

The *Acts of Peter* contains information concerning Peter which must be evaluated in light of the date when the *Acts* appeared, their authorship, the type of material and the context. Since there is no specific date given within the document and no certain historical allusion which would be of help, it is necessary to resort for the *terminus a quo* to the question of the sources used.

Lipsius proposes an early date for the *Acts of Peter*. Since he believes that the author was influenced by the *Gospel of Thomas*, which he is convinced is very early, he suggests around A.D. 160. Because Zahn sees a resemblance between the document and the *Acts of John* (A.D. c. 150), he is more inclined toward a date around A.D. 170. Later dates, A.D. 200 to 250, are

---

225. Marucchi, *Pietro a Paolo a Roma*, p. 19, rightly points out that "Ma è bene notare che la questione dei venticinque anni non è di capitale importanza e del resto dipende da dati cronologici troppo vaghi ed incerti perchè qui ce né possiamo occupare."

226. Lebreton and Zeiller, *The History of the Primitive Church*, trans. Messenger, I, 239*n*1. See also the text in Duchesne, *Le Liber Pontificalis*, Vol. I, Part I, p. 118.

227. The *Liberian Catalogue* has Linus and Clement, and the *Liber Pontificalis*, Linus and Cletus.

228. See Lietzmann, *Petrus und Paulus in Rom*, 2d ed., p. 28, and Caspar, *Die älteste römische Bischofliste*, pp. 175, 176, with Lightfoot, *Apostolic Fathers*, Part I, Vol. I, p. 261.

229. Given the two traditions of a twenty-five-year episcopate and the belief that by the command of Christ the apostles were not to leave Jerusalem until twelve years after the crucifixion (*Acts of Peter* V.1, M. R. James, *The Apocryphal*

New Testament, p. 307), we have a possible explanation for the position of Eusebius that Peter died A.D. 67 (A.D. 67 − 25 = 42; A.D. 42 − 12 = 30).

230. *E. H.* II.14:6 (Lake, I, 143). See also Harnack, *Die Chronologie*, I, 705, and *Acts of Peter* IV–XXXII, James, *The Apocryphal New Testament*, pp. 306–32.

231. Which he estimates happened between A.D. 190 and 217 in the pontificate of Zephyrinus. Harnack, *Die Chronologie*, I, 703–4.

232. See A. Rimoldi "L'Apostolo S. Pietro nella letteratura apocrifa," pp. 196–224.

proposed by Harnack, Vouaux, Schmidt, James, and Menzies.[233]

There has been a similar degree of disagreement concerning the place of origin. Lipsius[234] is in favor of Rome, a view which is at least considered by Harnack, although he is not inclined to accept it. Taking another position, Zahn states that since he sees no trace of any ancient tradition of the martyrdom and burial of Peter in Rome, this view—that the document emanates from Rome—must be rejected. He proposes instead the region of Asia Minor. It would be safe to say in approximate agreement with Leclercq that the *Acts of Peter* is not earlier than A.D. 200 nor later than A.D. 225, and the place of origin would be only a guess.[235]

The original was written in Greek, the text of which may be at least approximated in the MS of Athos, given the symbol *A*. The Latin versions appear in two recensions: one written in the seventh century at Vercelli and often called the *Acta Vercelli*, *V*; the second, Pseudo-Linus, *L* (preferred by Lipsius but now abandoned by most scholars). A Greek retranslation from the *Acta Vercelli* is found in the late MS of Patmos, *P*. That the work was originally written in Greek can be seen especially in chapter 38 of *V*, where a number of passages are unreadable in the Latin and show the marks of a poor translation from the Greek.[236] There are a number of other recensions in Syriac, Ethiopic, and Armenian, which need not be mentioned here.

Important, but not relevant to this discussion, is the accusation made by some, including Lipsius, that the *Acts of Peter* is Gnostic in origin. More important here

is the fact that the document reflects popular notions and not orthodox opinion, even if at a later date material which it contains was used by various writers.[237]

The author of the *Acts of Peter* is convinced that Peter did reside in Rome after the departure of Paul for Spain; but as in the case of all the apocryphal *Acts*, he is indifferent to the question of chronology. The only indication which is beyond dispute is that the author is of the opinion that Peter entered Rome shortly before his martyrdom. This indicates that he does not share the view current in his time that Peter had been bishop of Rome for twenty-five years.

Granted that the view of the late arrival of Peter in Rome is more in accord with the lack of information on the subject found in the earliest sources, it is not justifiable to say, therefore, that there is behind it some independent and trustworthy tradition.[238] One cannot say that in the *Acts of Peter* we possess reliable evidence that Peter left Jerusalem twelve years after the crucifixion of Christ,[239] or that Peter's stay in Rome was limited to less than a year.

---

233. Harnack, *Die Chronologie*, I, 553 ff., sets the date A.D. 190 slightly earlier than the others; Vouaux, *Les Actes de Pierre*, p. 207; Schmidt, *Die alten Petrusakten*, pp. 99–111, especially p. 104; James, *The Apocryphal New Testament*, p. 300; Menzies, "Acts of Peter," *Expository Times*, XIV (1903), 399.

234. *Die apokryphen Apostelgeschichten*, Vol. II, Part I, p. 274.

235. Leclercq, *DACL*, Vol. XIV, Part I, p. 932. Erbes, "Petrus nicht in Rom," p. 164, also supports Rome for various reasons including the seeming acquaintance of the author with Roman topography and the common Roman tendency to deemphasize Paul and to give all honor to Peter.

236. For a discussion of this view see Vouaux, *Les Actes de Pierre*, pp. 232–4.

237. *The Acts of Peter* appears in Origen, as quoted in *E. H.* III.1:2 (Lake, I, 193); in *The Muratorian Canon* 37; and especially in Jerome, *Sermon* XXVIII which states that Peter, after being bishop of Antioch, came to Rome in the second year of Claudius to oppose Simon Magus. Cyril of Jerusalem has an account of the end of Simon Magus, and Theodoret knows of the tradition that Peter was martyred head downward (see *E. H.* III.25:7, Lake, I, 259). Porphyry (Schmidt, *Die alten Petrusakten*, pp. 167–71) witnesses to the use of the *Acts of Peter* in a work of Macarius Magnus III.2 (A.D. c. 250) (Μακαρίου Μάγνητος Ἀποκρίτικος ἡ μονογένης), in which a follower of Plotinus reproaches Peter for his escape which cost the lives of his jailers, even though Christ had predicted that the gates of Hell could not prevail against him (Peter). The *Acts of Peter* was also used in such works as the *Didascalia* (Syrian, A.D. c. 225), *Didascalia Apostolorum*, trans. Connolly, pp. 200–3, especially p. 200, lines 24, 25.

238. The position of Leclercq, *DACL*, Vol. XIV, Part I, p. 932, that certain statements (such as Peter's having entered Rome after the departure of Paul for Spain) reveal some "historical traces," is not to be accepted without caution.

239. "Adimpletis duodecim annis, quod illi praeceperat dominus." ("the twelve years which the Lord Christ had enjoined upon him were fulfilled.") See *Acta Apostolorum apocrypha*, eds. Lipsius and Bonnet, p. 49:21 and James, *The Apocryphal New Testament*, p. 307.

Despite terms which suggest definite knowledge, such as, "Sunday," "the following Sunday," "next day," "the day before," "some days after,"[240] the apostolic legends contain little or no actual knowledge of the events. Eusebius lists the *Acts of Peter* among the early spurious writings and declaims them as "altogether wicked and impious."[241]

The Acts of Paul

The *Acts of Paul* was written in the second half of the second century by an orthodox Christian. Specific dates vary, but it is likely that it may be placed between A.D. 160 and 175.[242] Tertullian informs us that the work is a recent product of a presbyter of Asia who had prepared it in honor of Paul. The one sentence which is of interest in this study appears in what James calls "Detached Fragments" and, therefore, may or may not have appeared in the original document. In this fragment, which also contains a reference to the unknown *Preaching of Paul*, it is said that Jesus "also revealed all things to come which Peter and Paul preached at Rome, and that preaching continues in writing for a memorial."[243]

Acts of Andrew and Paul

In the minor *Acts of Andrew and Paul*, which are late, of uncertain date, and found only in fragmentary

Coptic texts or Ethiopic and Arabic texts taken from the Coptic, there is mention of the journey of Peter to Rome. A child, who is actually Jesus in disguise, tells Peter that a ship will take him to Rome. On the way Peter calms a storm and baptizes a certain Michel who sells the child (whom he does not recognize) to Peter. When the party arrives at Rome Peter orders the child to fish; an hour later the child has caught 12,000 fish. The story continues with the arrest and martyrdom of Peter and includes the detail known to Origen that Peter was crucified head downward.[244]

The Death and Assumption of the Virgin

The nucleus of the apocryphal tale of the *Death and Assumption of the Virgin* may belong to the third century, but the details and the text itself are certainly not earlier than the fourth. The Greek fragment, supposedly a discourse of John on the death of Mary, was edited by Tischendorf from five MSS of the eleventh to the fourteenth centuries; it has been translated by James. In it we find: "And thereupon I, John, fell to prayer. And the Holy Ghost said to the Apostles: All of you together mount up upon clouds from the ends of the world and gather yourselves together at Bethlehem the holy city of the mother of our Lord Jesus Christ, in a moment of time; Peter from Rome, Paul from Tiberia. . . ."[245]

The Clementine Homilies and Recognitions

The Clementine Literature,[246] or *Clementina* as it is popularly known, is a Judeo-Christian work consisting of five parts, all falsely attributed to Clemens Romanus: 1) the *Second Epistle*, 2) the two *Epistles on Virginity*, 3) the *Homilies* and *Recognitions*, including the *Epistle of Clement to James*, 4) the *Apostolic Constitutions*, and 5) the *Forged Decretals*. Usually the term "Clementine Literature" is applied to the third category which is the main interest of this study in this literature.

The so-called *Second Epistle* does not go back before about A.D. 150, and the *Epistles on Virginity*, before the

---

240. *Acta Apostolorum apocrypha*, eds. Lipsius and Bonnet, pp. 48:19, 50:10, 81:17. See the English translation of these terms in James, *The Apocryphal New Testament*, p. 308, line 15; p. 317, line 38; p. 318, line 22.

241. *E. H.* III.25:7 (Lake, I, 259). Earlier in the chapter Eusebius claims that "of the Acts bearing his [Peter's] name . . . we have no knowledge at all in the Catholic tradition, for no orthodox [ἐκκλησιαστικός] writer of the ancient time or of our own has used their testimonies." *E. H.* III.3:2 (Lake, I, 193). For nonorthodox use of the *Acts of Peter*, see above p. 36n237.

242. Since the *Acts of Paul* was used by Hippolytus, mentioned by Tertullian, quoted by Origen, and was known and held in great respect in Alexandria in the third century, it is presumed by Harnack, *Die Chronologie*, I, 492, to have been written "gewiss nicht nach c. 170."

James, *The Apocryphal New Testament*, p. 270, suggests a date of "about A.D. 160."

243. *Ibid.*, p. 298.

---

244. *Ibid.*, p. 474.

245. See *ibid.*, pp. xix, 194, 202-3.

246. For a concise discussion of this literature see McGuire, "Clementine Literature," pp. 797-99.

mid-third century. The common source of the *Homilies* and *Recognitions* (the *Circuits of Peter*, or *Periodoi*, περίοδοι) belongs to a period probably before Eusebius and certainly before Epiphanius.[247] The passage of Eusebius which refers to this literature mentions that "some have also quite recently put forward other verbose and long treatises purporting to be Clement's, containing dialogues with Peter and Apion [*Homilies*] but there is absolutely no mention of them among the ancient writers nor do they preserve the pure type of apostolic orthodoxy."[248] On the basis of this passage and other considerations, the date of the common source (perhaps Syrian in origin) of the *Homilies* and *Recognitions* is placed tentatively not earlier than A.D. 225.[249] It is also considered that the common source itself, the *Circuits of Peter*, or the *Periodoi* (περίοδοι) was based upon the *Kerygmata of Peter* (κηρύγματα πέτρου), written perhaps as early as the first third of the second century,[250] and the *Acta Vercelli*.

The *Homilies* are considered a second edition and abridgment of the common source and less orthodox than the *Recognitions*. The recensions of both works in the form in which they are known today probably do not go back further than A.D. 300 to 350,[251] and also most likely were written in Syria.[252]

After this brief introduction it is necessary to turn to the text of the *Homilies* itself. The story reveals that Peter visits and works in Caesarea Tripolis, Syrian Laodicea, and Antioch. Neither the *Recognitions* nor the

Homilies makes any specific statement to the effect that Peter ever reached Rome. In the *First Homily*, however, there is a hint that he did. After Clement is introduced to Peter, the latter invites him "to travel with us . . . from city to city, as far as Rome itself."[253] The statement, which shows the apostle's *intent*, presupposes some knowledge of Peter's having visited that city. The same tradition may be reflected indirectly in the mention by Peter of a certain merchant as "having sojourned *here* in Rome."[254]

In addition to a passage parallel to the above, noted in chapter XIII of the *Recognitions*, there are two possible references to Peter's intention to enter Rome in chapters LXIII and LXV. After a former disciple of Simon Magus had deserted and informed Peter of Simon's purpose to go to Rome (where the latter thought he would be accorded the honors of a God),[255] Peter ordained Zacchaeus as the pastor over the Church at Caesarea. He added, however, that he thought it good to remain with them "for three months; and so to go to the Gentiles, lest through our delaying longer, and the crimes of Simon stalking in every direction, they should become incurable."[256] It is possible to infer from this passage, in view of the words of the servant of Simon Magus in chapter LXIII, that Peter *eventually* intended to follow Simon Magus to Rome.[257]

The Epistle of Clement to James is most definite on the subject of Peter in Rome. Chapter I is devoted to the martyrdom of Peter there, and chapter II, to his ordination of Clement.[258] This Epistle accepts the

---

247. See *Panarium* XXX.15 (*MPG*, XLI, 429–32).

248. *E. H.* III.38:5 (Lake, I, 291).

249. Bigg, "The Clementine Homilies," p. 188, suggests A.D. c. 200. See also pp. 188–93. Cullmann, *Le Problème littéraire*, p. 157, says, "Nous admettrons donc que l'écrit fondamental a été composé entre les années 220 à 230." Rehm, "Zur Enstehung," p. 156, estimates that G (Grundschrift), the περίοδοι πέτρου, originated in Syria between A.D. 220 and 230, and McGuire, "Clementine Literature," p. 798, agrees.

250. Cullmann, *Le Problème littéraire*, p. 98, "du début du IIᵉ siècle"; McGuire, "Clementine Literature," p. 798; Rehm, "Zur Enstehung," p. 163.

251. *Ibid.*, p. 163. But Cullmann, *Le Problème littéraire*, p. 161, sees no reason why the *Homilies* should be dated "après le Concile, de Nicée," and he believes (p. 164) that the author of the ἀναγνωρισμοί "probablement vécu à la fin du IIIᵉ siècle."

252. Bigg, "The Clementine Homilies," p. 161.

253. "μέχρι Ῥώμης αὐτῆς' First Homily,', Book I.16 (See *Recognitions* I.13). See *Clementis Romani, Homiliae*, ed. Schwegler, p. 41, and "Clementine Homilies," *The Ante-Nicene Fathers*, VIII, 227.

254. "ἐνταῦθα τῇ Ῥώμη," Schwegler, *Clementis Romani*, p. 163; "Clementine Homilies," *The Ante-Nicene Fathers*, VIII, 261. It must be pointed out, however, that "ἐνταῦθα" more frequently means "there."

255. The servant mentions that Simon intended to go to Rome and quotes him as saying, "You will be sorry when you hear that glory I shall get in the City of Rome." (*The Ante-Nicene Fathers*, VIII, 131.)

256. *Ibid.*

257. Even though the *Recognitions* end (*The Ante-Nicene Fathers*, VIII, 209, 210) with Peter's arrival in Antioch.

258. "Epistle of Clement to James," *ibid.*, p. 218.

tradition, not found in any other source until Tertullian,[259] that Clement succeeded Peter immediately as the bishop of Rome. No mention is made of Linus, or Cletus (or Anencletus). The Epistle follows Justin Martyr in the identification of Simon Magus with the Sabine deity, Semo Sancus.[260] It may also be said of this Epistle that it presupposes the tradition of Peter as the first bishop of Rome; the same cannot definitely be said for the *Homilies* or *Recognitions*. The source of these works could not have been considered too unorthodox if Jerome refers to it in *Against Jovinian* XV[261] and the *Commentary on Galatians* I:18.[262]

The Apostolic Constitutions

The *Apostolic Constitutions* was unknown in the West until the Middle Ages. A Latin copy, found and published by Carolus Capellus in 1546, was followed seventeen years later by a Greek text edited by Franciscus Turrianus and another Latin translation by Bovius. Both Capellus and Bovius considered the *Apostolic Constitutions* to be authentic.

The *Didascalia* (the name given to the Syriac, Arabic, and Ethiopic versions as well as the Greek) in its present form dates from the third or fourth century.[263] While the original may belong to the early third century,[264] the Syriac is dated by R. H. Connolly between A.D. 300 and 330, and the Latin, as late as A.D. 385. The Syriac is certainly the earliest version of which we have any record; the Ethiopic and Arabic are allied, and both correspond closely to the Syriac. The Latin is derived from a Greek original which also closely approximates the extant Syriac text.

In the Syriac version there is one passage which relates to this study. This reference to Peter's being in Rome is derived from the *Acts of Peter* and deals with the activities of Simon Magus: "Then Peter looked upon Satan who was dwelling in Simon. . . . Now the party of Simon followed hard upon me [Peter], and came to corrupt the word, and when he [Simon Magus] was in Rome he disturbed the Church much and subverted many."[265]

The Ethiopic version is more elaborate and specific. While at Rome Peter says, "But I, Peter, stood, and prayed, and beheld him [Simon Magus] flying in the air."[266] This version also contains a list of those ordained by the apostles: "First in Jerusalem, James. . . . And in Antioch, first, Evodius [ordained] by Peter; and after him Ignatius, by Paul. . . . And in the Church of Rome, first, Linus [ordained] by Paul; and after him Clement, who was ordained by Peter."[267]

The Ethiopic version, preserved by the Monophysite Church of Abyssinia, thus protected the traditional place of Paul in the Roman Church, which had been deemphasized since the beginning of the third century. The tradition of these ordinations by Peter is peculiar to the *Didascalia*,[268] while the mention of the ordination of Clement by Peter is derived from the earlier *Acts of Peter*. Curiously there is no mention of Cletus or Anencletus.

The *Didascalia* reveals some knowledge of a relationship of both Peter and Paul to the Roman Church, but is not specific as to the character of such relationship. The two apostles are not mentioned specifically as either founders or bishops, but simply as apostles. The Ethiopic version claims that Peter and Paul together have some relationship to the Church at Antioch; separately Paul is related to the Churches of Ephesus and Cenchreae, and Peter, to the Church of Philadelphia.

While the document is late and reflects use of the *Acts of Peter*, the dual, undefined leadership of both Peter and Paul in Rome seems to be an echo of a second-century tradition such as is found in Clement of Rome and Ignatius.

---

259. *De praescriptione* XXXII.

260. See above pp. 26–27.

261. *MPL*, XXIII, 245.

262. *MPL*, XXVI, 354.

263. *Didascalia Apostolorum*, trans. Connolly, pp. xi–xxviii; lxxxvii–xci.

264. *Ibid.*, pp. lxxxix–xc. Connolly is completely undecided as to the exact date. The best that can be said is that it is a work of the third century.

265. *Syriac Didascalia*, XXIII (VI:7 and VI:8).

266. *The Ethiopic Didascalia* VI:9 (XXXII), trans. Harden, p. 144.

267. *Ibid.*, VII:46 (XLIII), p. 186.

268. See, however, the later *Liber Pontificalis*. Duchesne, *Le Liber Pontificalis*, Vol. I, Part I, pp. 50, 51, 118; *The Book of the Popes*, trans. Loomis, p. 6.

Late Legends

Among the late legends which appear to contain information relative to this study is the alleged stay of Peter in the Mamertine prison. In the late *Pseudo-Linus* text, which is little more than a detailed account of the *Martyrdom of Peter*, we find mention of Processus and Martinian, who supposedly were the jailers at this prison. The mere mention of their names in the *Pseudo-Linus* text is elaborated upon in the sixth-century *Acts of Processus and Martinian*. This prison in which Peter was allegedly held was at first called the Tullianum. (One may still enter it by rope or ladder to the place where once the accomplices of Catiline died of hunger.) The story mentions that the jailers, Processus and Martinian, were converted by Peter along with forty-seven other prisoners.[269] This one statement would be sufficient to discredit the tradition. A cell of 18 by 9 feet could hardly contain this number for any amount of time. However, Duchesne believes that some martyrs must have died here, in order to give rise to the tradition which later came to include Peter.[270]

How do such legends begin and develop? Delehaye convincingly answers this:

To show the extent to which material things dominate the intelligence and stifle the powers of reflection, people have pretended to have seen the "cornerstone which the builders rejected" and have begged for relics of "de lignis trium tabernaculorum," those three tabernacles which Saint Peter proposed to erect on the mountain of transfiguration. . . . In a similar way the names of the saints are linked with monuments or remarkable places which appeal to the popular imagination. Thus it is quite natural that in Rome the Mamertine prison should be selected as the scene of Peter's imprisonment, and

that men should be enabled to point out the precise spot where Simon Magus fell.[271]

Another instance in late apocryphal literature will serve as an illustration of the development of legend from the mere existence of an obscure name. The location in which we find today the Church of St. Nereus and St. Achilleus was called at one time the Fasciola, which in Italian means "bandage." No one was sure of the original reason why this name had been given to the church; and the tradition evolved that it had some relationship to Peter. A legend developed that the leg of the apostle, having been injured by the heavy chains which bound him, was wrapped in a bandage. As he was led to his execution, the bandage fell along the way. The place where it allegedly fell later became known as the Titulus of the Fasciola.

Kernels of truth often, but by no means always, lie behind traditions and legends. The factual nuclei in time are amplified by mistranslations, suggestions from monuments, conscious expansions of original documents, pure romance to give pleasure or edification, and even polemics by or against heretics.[272] One or more of these will serve to explain the origin of many traditions in the orthodox and apocryphal literature including those which refer to the long stay of Peter in Rome, the Mamertine prison, and the story of Simon Magus. Other legends appear relative to the activity and residence of Peter in Rome; one mentions that Peter lived for a time in the house of Senator Pudens and another indicates the place "where once Peter baptized." However, these are so late and so clearly devoid of any reliable information that they need not be considered in this book.

---

269. See Lipsius, *Die apokryphen Apostelgeschichten*, p. 6, line 26. Duchesne, *Le Liber Pontificalis*, Vol. 1, Part II, p. 419, mentions the "basilice sanctorum Processi et Martiniani" in the notice of Gregory III (A.D. 731–41).

270. Barnes, *The Martyrdom of St. Peter and St. Paul*, p. 96, gives some credence to the tale of the Mamertine prison.
271. Delehaye, *Legends of the Saints*, trans. Crawford, p. 42.
272. *Ibid.*, p. 53.

CHAPTER 3

The Liturgical Evidence
for the Residence of Peter in Rome

IN ADDITION TO the literary documents it is also necessary to examine the liturgical evidence which relates specifically to the Roman residence of Peter. The greater part of this material is concerned with the subject of burial. The liturgical festivals of February 22 and January 18, however, are related to the question of the Roman episcopate of Peter.

The most important liturgical evidence is found in the so-called *Chronograph of 354*,[1] compiled by Furius Dionysius Philocalus, a Christian who was interested in all types of chronology and who later became secretary to Pope Damasus (A.D. 366–84). The *Chronograph* is divided into three main parts. The third has no relation to this study. The second contains the *Liber Generationis* which Duchesne attributes to Hippolytus (A.D. 235).[2] The first part, made up of six subdivisions, contains three documents which are of varying degrees of importance to the question of the tradition of Peter in Rome.

The first of these documents is known as the *Depositio Episcoporum*, which contains the dates of death and burial of the Roman bishops from A.D. 254 (the year of the death of Lucius) to 335 (the year of the death of Sylvester). Philocalus also included a second document which is known as the *Liberian Catalogue* or the *Philocalian Catalogue*. (It is sometimes called the *Bucherian Catalogue* after Bucher, who first printed the list in Antwerp in 1633 in his *De Doctrina Temporum*.) The *Catalogue*, briefly mentioned above in connection with the long episcopate of Peter, includes a list of the popes from the time of Peter to Liberius (A.D. 352–66).

The *Depositio Martyrum*, which is the most important of the three documents pertaining to the residence of Peter in Rome, consists of a list containing the dates of the fixed festivals of the Christian year and, in addition, a list of the various festivals of the martyrs. The notice in the *Depositio Martyrum* for February 22 appears as follows: "viii Kal. Mart. Natale Petri de Cathedra." In connection with this notice there are six pertinent questions: 1) What is the origin and meaning of the festival? 2) When was it first initiated? 3) Where was it celebrated? 4) What is the relationship between this notice and the fuller one which appears in the *Martyrologium Hieronymianum*? 5) How is the celebration of February 22 related to that held on January 18? and 6) What is the value for this study of the information supplied?

As the notice stands, it appears plausible to agree with Duchesne that the festival is nothing more than the commemoration of the day on which Peter entered upon his episcopal office.[3] Further study reveals, however, that even if this statement is undoubtedly true for the fourth century and later, the matter is not so simply settled for the period before A.D. 300.

---

1. Duchesne, *Le Liber Pontificalis*, Vol. I, Part I, pp. vi–viii; Lightfoot, *Apostolic Fathers*, Part I, Vol. I, p. 65.

2. Duchesne, *Le Liber Pontificalis*, Vol. I, Part I, p. vii.

3. *Origines du Culte chrétien* (10th ed.) p. 268. See also Batiffol, "Natale Petri de Cathedra," pp. 401 f. Johann Peter Kirsch, "Le Feste degli Apostoli," pp. 62–71, admits that such is the understanding at least in the fourth century.

Carcopino, *De Pythagore*, pp. 265 ff., suggests that "natale" stands for a date of inhumation, not to be confused with the date of martyrdom. Thus prior to A.D. 336 and the *Depositio Martyrum*, two "natales" were celebrated for the two inhumations of Peter. This aspect of the Translation Theory will be considered along with others in Part III. The definition of Toynbee in *Gnomon*, (1957), p. 266, is better: "natale" does not refer to a Translation but to a birthday in a funerary Christian context. It can also mean a "heavenly birthday," that is, martyrdom or possibly a burial immediately after death.

The word "natale" may stand for the day when a person or a fact is recalled to memory. It is thus used, for example, in "natalis Constantini" which appears in the Calendar of Polemius Silvius (A.D. 448) for the "viii Kal. Aug.," the day when Constantine ascended to the throne. The same Calendar provides an illustration of a second meaning of the word. In the case of the "natalis Virgilii" it refers to a "birthday." A sermon dating from the fifth century, most probably preached on February 22 and falsely attributed to Augustine, seems to favor the former meaning.[4] On this day Peter allegedly ascended to the chair of his episcopate, or the apostolate as Duchesne prefers; it was the anniversary of the "Tu es Petrus." In another sermon, also incorrectly attributed to Augustine, the author refers to this date in connection with an honor paid to Peter, adding that while the day had been one of intemperance when it was known as the "cara cognatio," now it was a sober holiday.[5]

Some of the same nomenclature is recognized also in the Gallic *Bobbio Sacramentary*[6] and the *Missale Gothicum*.[7] In Rome, then, around A.D. 330–500 and in Gaul in the seventh century, the feast of the "Cathedra Petri" was celebrated and understood to commemorate the ascent of Peter to the episcopacy in Rome.

One serious problem in the recognition of this as the original interpretation of the festival is indicated by Goguel; the custom of commemorating the beginning of episcopates began only A.D. 282.[8] This observation indicates the possibility that the festival had an earlier meaning. The truth may be that in the beginning the date had one significance, and then through the effect of developments within the Church the significance changed. As suggested in the Pseudo-Augustinian sermons referred to above, it cannot be disputed that by the fifth century the festival definitely was related to the beginning of the episcopate of Peter. The information is contained in the *Sacramentarium Gelasianum* (fifth century?) that Felix III in A.D. 487 held a council on March 13, the fourth anniversary of his ordination. Four sermons attributed to Leo the Great were supposedly delivered on the anniversary of his ascent to the episcopacy.[9] Xystus III wrote to Clement of Alexandria and expressed the joy of the holy and venerable synod "quam natalis mihi dies favente Domino congregat." Paul of Nola explains that when he was but a presbyter he was invited by Anastasius (A.D. c. 400) to the "birthday," that is to the celebration of the anniversary of the latter's ordination.[10]

The word "cathedra" in the notice of the *Depositio Martyrum* may hold the key to the early character of the

---

4. *Sermon* CXC.1 (*MPL*, XXXIX, 2100): "Institutio solemnitatis hodiernae a senioribus nostris Cathedrae nomen accepit, ideo quod primus Apostolorum Petrus hodie episcopatus cathedram suscepisse referatur. Recte ergo Ecclesiae Natalem sedis illius colunt, quam Apostolus pro Ecclesiarum salute suscepit; dicente Domino: 'Tu es Petrus. . . .' Quod natalis ergo cathedrae hodie colitur, sacerdotale honoratur officium. Sibi hoc Ecclesiae praestant quibus necesse est ut tanto plus habeant dignitatis, quanto sacerdotale officium plus honoris." [The solemnity of the day was received from the forefathers (a senioribus nostris), the name of 'cathedra' because it is reported that on this day the first of the apostles, Peter, ascended to the chair of his episcopate. Therefore it is right that the Churches celebrate the anniversary of the birth (birthday, or natalis) of this See, that the apostle assumed for the health of all Churches. . . .] The fact that the festival is not of great antiquity may be derived from the use here of "seniores" [parents, forefathers] instead of "maiores" [ancestors]. The "seniores" could well be members of the last generation—the last part of the fourth century or at most a generation or two before.

5. *Sermon* CXCI.1 (*MPL*, XXXIX, 2101). The author adds "quia dum Natalem Cathedrae colimus episcopatum Petri Apostoli veneramur" [When we celebrate the "natalis cathedrae" we honor the episcopate of the apostle Peter].

6. *MPL*, LXXII, 473. Batiffol, *Cathedra Petri*, p. 127, mentions that the *Bobbio Sacramentary* is from the fifth century. This is at least a century early.

7. *MPL*, LXXII, 256–57: "The festival of the chair of St. Peter is the anniversary of the day on which the apostle received his powers over the Gentiles as over the Jews . . . when he received from the Saviour the keys of heaven . . . the day when was established for him the "cathedra episcopatus." The information derived from this source is not older than the seventh century and is related to the festival held on January 18, which is discussed below.

8. *L'Église primitive*, p. 225, and Lietzmann, *Petrus und Paulus in Rom*, 2d ed., p. 18.

9. *MPL*, LIV, 505–8. The authenticity is correctly contested by Lietzmann, *Petrus und Paulus in Rom*, 1st ed., p. 73, and Batiffol, "Natale Petri de Cathedra," p. 401, that the sermons were written as late as the eleventh century. But others such as G. Morin place them as early as the fifth century.

10. See Turner, "The Papal Chronology of the Third Century," p. 338.

PLATE I   Cathedrae in the Coemeterium Maius in Rome (photographs by Paul Styger).

festival.[11] The meaning of cathedra in Latin is "chair." On occasion it may mean also "locale," or "center of operations." In the mid-third century, however, when this festival was instituted, Latin had not yet been introduced generally into formal Church usage. It is therefore necessary to remember that the Greek "καθέδρα" may suggest a "place of rest." Although Photius rejects this definition as now (ninth century) abolished, he does list among the meanings of καθέδρα the festival which was held at the tomb on the thirtieth day after death by the family and friends of the deceased.[12] This meaning is reflected in the notice for February 22 found in the Calendar of Polemius Silvius (A.D. 448): "viii Kal. Mart. depositio sancti Petri et Pauli. cara cognatio, ideo dicta, quia tunc etsi fuerint vivorum parentum odia, tempore obitus, deponantur."[13] The definition of the term by Photius together with the illustration of this meaning

in Polemius Silvius may give us a clue to the early character of the festival held on February 22. The "cara cognatio" was celebrated on this day, which was in the last month of the pagan year. On February 13 the celebration of the nine-day long Parentalia (a pagan "All Souls' Day") began and ended on February 22. At this time the friends and families of the dead gathered in the vicinity of the grave and shared a meal.[14] All family disunity and disharmony was set aside;[15] hence the alternate title "caristia,"[16] which was also given to the pagan festival. At such meals there was usually a stone chair left vacant for the dead relative or friend in whose honor the feast was being held.[17] These meals and their settings are discussed at length in Part III in connection with the celebrations once held in the Triclia beneath the present Church of San Sebastiano. The Greek

11. See Balboni, "Natale Petri de Cathedra," pp. 97–126.

12. Lexicon "καθέδρα: τῇ τριακοστῇ γὰρ ἡμέρα τοῦ ἀποθανόντος οἱ προσήκοντες ἅπαντες καὶ ἀναγκαῖοι συνελθόντες κοινῇ ἐδείπνουν ἐπὶ τῷ ἀποθανόντι. καὶ τοῦ καθέδρα ἐκαλεῖτο." (Cited by Lietzmann, Petrus und Paulus in Rom, 2d ed., p. 19n3; Carcopino, De Pythagore, p. 267n48, and Guignebert, in Revue historique, CLXVIII (1931), 249, and mentioned by de Rossi, in Bullettino di Archeologia cristiana, Vol. V, No. 3 (1867), p. 41, col. 2n3.

13. Corpus Inscriptionum Latinarum, I, 337. Lietzmann, Petrus und Paulus in Rom, 2d ed., p. 100, and de Rossi, in Bullettino di Archeologia cristiana, Vol. V, No. 3 (1867), p. 41.

14. Tertullian, De idolatria X, points disapprovingly at the "cara cognatio." (MPL, I, 751; The Ante-Nicene Fathers, III, 66.)

15. See Valerius Maximus II.1:8, Valerii Maximi, ed. Kempf, p. 60.

16. See Cassell's Latin Dictionary, rev. Marchant and Charles, pp. 85, 93.

17. Similar to those illustrated in Plate I.

meal festival for Peter and Paul may have been called the καθέδρα τοῦ Πέτρου καὶ Παύλου and later abbreviated to καθέδρα, especially after the deemphasis of Paul.

The development of the idea of a feast in honor of the dead to the thought of a feast in honor of the "chair" of instruction or authority, that is, episcopal chair of Peter, is not difficult to imagine.[18] The idea that the καθέδρα has any relationship whatsoever to the relic venerated today in Rome under the name of the chair of Peter is to be rejected.[19] The cult of this relic only emerged at the time of Gregory the Great.

It is a plausible interpretation that the later Christian changes in the primitive pagan festival were in no small part due to the displeasure of the hierarchy over certain phases of the celebration adopted by the Christians in their cemetery observances. The family and friends of the deceased brought food and drink with them to share with the dead. The obvious corruption of this portion of the festival eventually brought down the wrath of certain of the Church Fathers, including Zeno of Verona, Ambrose, Chrysostom, Paulinus of Nola, and especially Augustine, as is evident in the *Confessions*.[20] Earlier such meals had been permitted, and numerous signs of such observances have been discovered in old Roman cemeteries. Because of greater rigor in the Church or greater excesses in the celebration, by A.D. 300 the strong ecclesiastical pressure, mentioned above, had been exerted and was successful in suppressing the feasts for the dead in the cemeteries.

This is one explanation of the early character of the celebration, but could it also be that February 22 was remembered in some early reliable tradition as the actual date of Peter's death?[21] Most probably not. It was more likely a day of veneration of the apostle on a date which was chosen for no other reason than that it had already been set aside by the pagan community for the veneration of ancestors, which statement implies that the Church did not have any memory of the actual date. Similar appropriation of the date of a pagan festival will be noticed later in the discussion of the celebration held on June 29, which is associated with traditions of burial or translation or both. If we consider seriously the Calendar of Polemius Silvius (A.D. 448), it is possible that one very early interpretation of the festival held on February 22 was as a feast in honor of the dead, that is, a feast in memory of Peter and Paul. Some have seriously questioned, however, whether the interpretation of Polemius is at all accurate for the fifth century.[22] This doubt arises as a result of information concerning fifth-century liturgical practices in his native Gaul which were derived from sources such as a Calendar of the Church of Tours (A.D. 490) used by Perpetuas, a contemporary of Silvius, and from a Canon of the Council of Tours (A.D. 567). This Canon inveighed against the funerary practices connected with the feast: "qui in festivitate cathedrae S. Petri apostoli cibos mortuis offerunt et post missas redeuntes ad domos proprias ad gentilium revertuntur errores et post Domini sacratas daemoni escas accipiunt."[23] Both sources mention that February 22 was primitively "festivitatis cathedrae Domini Petri," a festival relative to Peter's episcopal

---

18. Such a possibility has been urged by Guignebert, "La Sépulture de Pierre," p. 249: Klauser, *Die Cathedra im Totenkult*, pp. 172 ff.; Lietzmann, *Petrus und Paulus in Rom*, 2d ed., pp. 19 ff.; Duchesne, *Origines du Culte chrétien*, pp. 266, 267.

Klauser, *Die Cathedra im Totenkult*, p. 153, mentions that the first to allude to this possible derivation was Fedor Schneider, "Über Kalendae Januariae und Martiae im Mittelalter," p. 386; and, independently, F. J. Dolger reached the same conclusion in his 1919–20 Religionswissenschaftlichen Seminar at Münster.

19. See Marucchi, *Pietro e Paolo a Roma*, illustration VIII (after p. 206).

20. VI.2. The mother of Augustine took part in meals held in honor of the martyrs "as had been her custom in Africa—and she was forbidden to do so by the doorkeeper. And as soon as she learned that it was the bishop [Ambrose] who had forbidden it, she acquiesced so devoutly and obediently that I [Augustine] myself marveled how readily she could bring

herself to turn critic of her own customs, rather than question his prohibition." *Augustine: Confessions and Enchiridion*, trans. Outler, p. 114.

21. Erbes, *Die Todestage*, p. 44. Klauser, *Die Cathedra im Totenkult*, p. 172, disagrees.

22. Duchesne, *Origines du Culte chrétien*, pp. 268, 294–96, dismisses the suggestion of Polemius Silvius, that this festival has any relationship to a "depositio" of Peter and Paul, as a "lapsus," that is, error. So also Leclercq, *DACL*, Vol. XIV, Part I, p. 977.

23. *Corpus Inscriptionum Latinarum*, I, 386; de Rossi, in *Bullettino di Archeologia cristiana*, Vol. V, No. 3 (June, 1867), p. 41. See Griffe, in *Bull. de Litt. ecclés.* (1953), p. 141.

throne.[24] It is true and cannot be disputed that this is the significance of the later celebration, but the notice of Polemius Silvius may still contribute to our understanding of the character of the more primitive festival.[25]

If we grant that there was an original pagan character to the festival, it happened either that the Christians assimilated the pagan festival and continued it with some minor changes (that is, the commemoration of Peter on February 22 was originally funerary in character) or that the date was appropriated by the Church and at that moment, or soon thereafter, the character of the festival was completely changed (that is, the original Christian celebration commemorated the chair of Peter—his entrance upon episcopal office). There is also the possbility that there were two separate and distinct stages in the Christianization of the festival. On the strength of the evidence found in 1) the Triclia at San Sebastiano, 2) the later polemics against such funerary meals (which bespeak the prior existence of a fairly common custom), and 3) Goguel's interesting suggestion[26] that the character of the festival may have been changed in its competition with June 29, it is possible to see a series of steps in such Christianization. If the two festivals (February 22 and June 29) vied in the beginning for supremacy in commemorating the death or burial or both of Peter and Paul,[27] and February 22 was defeated in this competition, an explanation can be found for the facts that no other episcopate was commemorated before A.D. 282 and that February 22 was not celebrated at Rome after the fifth century (the old significance of the date was still remembered at Rome,

but in Gaul, Spain, and Africa the date may have been newly defined).[28] Another possibility to explain the development may lie in the confusion which logically could have arisen because of the various meanings of the word "καθέδρα," especially in the period of the transition from Greek to Latin in Rome. This factor, together with the increasing importance of the date of ordination or consecration (which, of course, no longer involved Paul), may serve to explain why the festival originally consecrated to the dead slowly evolved in the direction of the "removal of the episcopal chair to Rome by Peter."[29]

Therefore, while it is true, as Duchesne and others point out,[30] that the "Natale de Cathedra" found in the *Depositio Martyrum* (A.D. 335) refers to the day when Peter entered upon his episcopal office, it is by no means equally certain that this meaning was attached to the festival a century or so before this date. The festival in Rome cannot be traced back through literary documents before the third decade of the fourth century with any degree of certainty.[31] Since it cannot be found in the *Ambrosian Mass*, the Vatican *Gelasianum* or the Roman *Gregorianum*, it is plausible to agree with J. P. Kirsch, P. Batiffol, and others that by the sixth century the festival had fallen into disuse in Rome.[32] A letter allegedly written by Gregory the Great, seems to refer to it, but its authenticity has been called seriously into

---

24. Mentioned by de Rossi, *Bullettino di Archeologia cristiana*, Vol. V, No. 3 (1867), pp. 40 ff.; and Carcopino, *De Pythagore*, p. 268n51.

25. Leclercq, *DACL*, Vol. XIV, Part I, p. 977, confesses that all suggestions are actually guesses as to the original meaning of the festival of February 22 in Rome and the truth may never be known for certain. Carcopino, *De Pythagore*, p. 280, is not so pessimistic.

26. See Goguel, *L'Église primitive*, p. 225.

27. Lietzmann, *Petrus und Paulus in Rom*, 2d ed., p. 19, against Erbes, *Die Todestage*, p. 44, and Torp, "The Vatican Excavations," p. 64, rejects the possibility that the festival was ever celebrated by the Christians as a "Totenfeier" to Peter—for him February 22 was *from the beginning* a feast of the episcopate of Peter. See Klauser, *Die römische Petrustradition*, pp. 27, 28.

28. Goguel, *L'Église Primitive*, p. 225. See also Erbes, *Die Todestage*, p. 44.

29. Klauser, *Die Cathedra im Totenkult*, p. 183; or toward the "Ideal" Bishop's Chair which Christ bestowed upon Peter, Bishop of the "Welthaupstadt," Lietzmann, *Petrus und Paulus in Rom*, 2d ed., p. 211n1. The author further suggests that the bishop who officiated at the festival of February 22 may have instructed his flock in the manner of celebration somewhat as follows: "Non mortuorum cathedra hodie celebratur, sed Petri Apostoli cathedra, quam dominus fundavit super petram cum diceret 'Tu es Petrus.'"

30. See above, p. 41n3.

31. See the discussion of this point in Lietzmann, *Petrus und Paulus in Rom*, 2d ed., pp. 19–21, "Die liturgische Parallele wie die sonstigen chronologischen Daten lassen demnach auf eine Entstehung dieses Festes um 300 schliessen." Griffe, in *Bull. de Litt. ecclés.* (1953), p. 141, admits to the fourth century or early fifth, and mentions especially the "Natale" of Pope Anastasius mentioned in the letter of A.D. 400 (*MPL*, LXI, 248).

32. A bibliography to support this contention is to be found in Klauser, *Die Cathedra im Totenkult*, p. 153n8. See also Lietzmann, *Petrus und Paulus in Rom*, 2d ed., pp. 72–83.

question.[33] The probable reason for the disappearance of the festival in Rome may be that February 22 often fell in the Lenten season in some areas and festivals which had been held in antiquity during this period were no longer observed. The celebrations at the tombs would have continued, but without the participation of the pope. Since the Roman Sacramentaries, at least, may have included *only* those festivals in which the pope himself participated, the celebration of February 22 may for this reason have disappeared from these documents. Torp has more recently suggested that the festival of February 22, dating from about A.D. 300, is directly related to the establishment of the Aedicula found recently beneath the Vatican. He is convinced that the veneration of Peter at the Aedicula began in response to the liturgical development. Unfortunately, his theory is dependent upon the assumption that this monument is not to be associated with the cult of Peter before the beginning of the fourth century. That Torp's theory suggests a date which is at least a century and a quarter too late is demonstrated in Part III.[34]

There are literary indications that the celebration held on February 22 began in the fourth century.[35] By A.D. 500, however, it had been dropped in Rome, only to be continued in the Gallican Sacramentaries of the seventh to the ninth centuries which were compiled with the aid of the Roman liturgy. These included: 1) the *Missale Gothicum*, 2) the *Sacramentarium Gelasianum* in the Gallic redaction (not the primitive *Gelasianum*) made after the introduction of the *Gregorianum* by the effort of Charlemagne, and 3) the *Sacramentarium Gregorianum* (not the primitive *Gregorianum*) sent to Charlemagne by Pope Adrian. Thus it is seen that in an era when the festival was unknown in Rome, it was very popular in Gaul.[36] The festival of February 22 also appears in the *Sacramentarium Mozarabicum* preserved in the Codex of Toledo of the tenth or eleventh century. The *Sacramentarium Leonianum* cannot be summoned as evidence for the presence or absence of the festival in Rome, since it lacks the material for the first three months of the year.

After the festival of February 22 was reintroduced in Rome in the ninth century, this date for the festival of the chair of St. Peter remained until the sixteenth century, when the date of the celebration was changed to January 18, February 22 being reserved for the celebration of Peter's chair at Antioch. It is interesting that, while popular in Gaul and existing in both an early and later phase in Rome, the festival was never adopted in Carthage or the East.[37]

Before turning to an evaluation of this liturgical material relative to its importance in the solution of the question of Peter's Roman residence and alleged episcopate, it is necessary to examine the notice of February 22 preserved in the *Martyrologium Hieronymianum*.

Since there is no concrete evidence to the contrary it may be supposed that the first liturgical calendars were composed by individual churches, each according to its own custom. Approximately at the time of the "Peace of the Church" (A.D. 312), the first Roman and African Martyrologies were compiled; these in turn were later combined. Subsequent editors derived additional information from the *Gesta Martyrum*.

The *Martyrologium Hieronymianum* gathered facts from the early martyrologies.[38] Duchesne, followed by Burgher and Kirsch,[39] takes it for granted that the author knew and "corrected" the notices of the *Depositio Martyrum*. Duchesne maintains also that,[40] although

33. *Epistle* LV (*MPL*, LIV, 858 f.).

34. Torp, "The Vatican Excavations," p. 64.

35. See Klauser, *Die Cathedra im Totenkult*, p. 157, who mentions that "it is as good as sure that A.D. c. 450–67 the feast of 'Cathedra Petri' had been begun by the Romans." On page 170 of the same work he admits the possibility that the festival may go back even to the third century, especially if it is reasonable to assume that the commemoration had any causal effect upon the keeping of the dates of accession by Roman bishops. The first recorded date of accession is A.D. 282.

36. Johann Peter Kirsch, "Le Feste degli Apostoli," p. 64.

37. Leclercq, *DACL*, Vol. VIII, Part I, p. 642.

38. The definitive text is the *Martyrologium Hieronymianum ad Fidem Codicum*, eds. de Rossi and Duchesne, *Acta Sanctorum Bollandiana*, Vol. II; *MPL*, XXX, 433–86, especially 435, 440, 444, 464.

Among the best articles are those by: L. Duchesne, "Les Sources du Martyrologe hieronymien," pp. 120–60; Delehaye, "Le Témoignage des Martyrologes," pp. 78–99; Johann Peter Kirsch, "Le Feste degli Apostoli," pp. 62–71, and "Das 'Martyrologium Hieronymianum,'" pp. 253–72.

39. Burger, *La Tombe*, p. 17. Johann Peter Kirsch, "Das 'Martyrologium Hieronymianum,'" p. 255.

40. "La Memoria Apostolorum de la Via Appia," p. 2.

the document did not appear in its present form before around A.D. 590 to 600, the first elaboration of the text which presumably included a Roman calendar, goes back at least to A.D. 420.[41] Thus between A.D. 420 (when according to Duchesne the first Roman calendar was used in the preparation of the document under discussion) and about 592 (when the *Martyrologium Hieronymianum* appeared in the approximate form in which it is known today), there is a span of 170 years—a long period in which a great deal of alteration and elaboration could and no doubt did take place.

Duchesne and de Rossi are agreed that the prototype of the *Martyrologium Hieronymianum* was written at Auxerre (Kirsch suggests Luxeuil). This text was the basis for the MSS known as the Codices Epternacensis, Bernensis, and Wissemburgensis, all of which were used in the edition of Duchesne and de Rossi. Kirsch used principally the first two Codices, but he utilized the third when there was a lacuna in the text of the others.

A clue to the Gallic origin of the document is found in the use of Rome as a place name by the editor of the *Martyrologium Hieronymianum* when it did not appear in his source. For example, the *Depositio Martyrum*, which was a Roman document, had no need to enter this topographical detail in the notice of February 22, but in the *Martyrologium Hieronymianum* (for January 18) such a detail was deemed necessary.

With this introduction let us examine the notices relative to the festival of February 22.

Codex Bernensis (eighth century)

"viii Kal. Mar. Cathedrae [The MS reveals that it was first written 'Natale Cathedra' and later erased.] sancti Petri apostoli quam sedit apud Antiochiam. . . ."

---

41. Dom Quentin, "Per la Critica del Martirologio Gerolimiano," p. 103, agrees with Duchesne and places the date A.D. c. 425, but he also suggests that the Roman notices did not go back before the edition of A.D. 592. They appeared first in the marginal notes and only later were included in the text proper. The sources for these marginal notes were itineraries and hagiographic literature. He adds that only when a notice appears in the same place and in the same terms in two families of MSS can one be sure that the notice stems from the early stratum of the *Martyrologium Hieronymianum* of the fifth century. (See p. 108.)

Codex Epternacensis (A.D. 710)

"viii K(a)l(endas) M(artias) Cathedra Petri in Antioch-(ia)" ["et Romae" in some MSS].

Codex Wissemburgensis (A.D. 772)

"Natale S. Petri Apostoli cathedra(e) quam sedit apud Antiochia."

It is noticed immediately that the three MSS agree in the main, but whereas the *Depositio Martyrum* claimed that this date marked the consecration of Peter as bishop of Rome, these MSS mention Antioch. Compare now the notice for January 18 as found in the same MSS. Codex Bernensis has a lacuna at this point.

Codex Epternacensis

"XV K(a)l(endas) Feb(ruarias) depos(itio) S(an)c(tae) Mariae et cath(edra) Petri in Roma."

Codex Wissemburgensis

"XV K(a)l(endas) Febro(arias) [*sic*] dedicatio cattedras s(an)c(t)i Petri apostoli qua primo Romae Petrus apostolus sedit."

Two important questions are suggested by these texts: 1) Why are there two dates given in the *Martyrologium Hieronymianum* for the "Cathedra Petri," one which appears to be related to Rome and the other to Antioch? and 2) Why was the date of February 22 changed to January 18 for the festival in Rome?

The Gallic Sacramentaries, under Roman influence,[42] continue to mention the festival of the chair of Peter on February 22, but the *Martyrologium Hieronymianum* and others list this festival on January 18. Most agree that the explanation lies in the fact that February 22 often fell within the Lenten period.[43] To avoid a celebration, the nature of which was conceived to be incompatible with the solemnity of the season, the date was transferred to January 18—a date much too early ever to fall within the limits of Lent. While it is not supported by textual evidence and therefore by no means certain, this explanation is logical and attractive.

---

42. See above, p. 46.

43. Lietzmann, *Petrus und Paulus in Rom*, 2d ed., p. 94; Duchesne, *Origines du Culte chrétien*, p. 297; Batiffol, *Cathedra Petri*, p. 129.

So very little in fact is known about the ancient Gallic festival customs that Johann Peter Kirsch feels justified in at least offering the alternative interpretation that the two festivals are not interdependent but independent.[44] He suggests that January 18 is not related in any way to the festival of the chair of Peter but rather to the establishment of the Papacy. February 22, on the other hand, commemorates Peter's ascent to the episcopacy in Antioch, a tradition which may go back to Galatians 2:11 or even to the apocryphal *Clementine Recognitions*. Kirsch's alternative explanation may be true, but since it also has no textual support, the suggestion of Duchesne and Lietzmann, which is the most convincing, is to be accepted.[45]

There remains another thorny question. Why was January 18 chosen—a date so long before the earliest possible beginning of Lent (February 4)? Why not January 16 or 19? Lietzmann suggests that "der 18 Januar ein älterer gallikanischer Festtag ist: . . . Wir werden daraus folgern dürfen—oder müssen—dass am 18 Januar ein altes keltisches Fest gefeiert wurde, vielleicht auch ein Totenfest—."[46] It may be agreed that such is probable, but it is not *necessary* to accept it, as Lietzmann suggests. If such a festival did exist, perhaps it was similar to the Roman "cara cognatio" which had been held in Rome on February 22.

The double festival of the chair of Peter on January 18 and February 22 caused confusion in some quarters. The *Sacramentarium Gellone*, written in the eighth or ninth century, demonstrates this when it adds the explanation "secundum Gallos" in connection with the notice of January 18.

Carcopino proposes the following solution: 1) February 22 commemorates the translation of the relics of Peter from the Vatican to Catacumbas. 2) January 18 commemorates neither the chair of Peter nor, as Kirsch believes, a festival celebrating the inauguration of the Papacy but another translation of the relics of Peter, this time from Catacumbas to the Vatican. 3) January 25 is presumably the parallel festival

for the translation of Paul from Catacumbas to the Basilica on the Via Ostia.[47]

In actuality the work of the editor of the *Martyrologium Hieronymianum*, in his combination of the liturgical customs of the Roman and Gallic churches, is without any historical or liturgical value.[48]

Klauser mentions the earlier view of de Rossi and Grisar that the festivals of January 18 and February 22 commemorate the two traditions of the coming of Peter to Rome under Claudius and under Nero. The January 18 festival celebrates the inauguration of Peter's "Lehrstuhl" in the Coemeterium Maius; the February 22 festival, the same at the Vatican. January 18 is therefore conceived to be the celebration of Peter's first entrance into Rome, and February 22, the commemoration of his elevation to the pontificate.[49] This hypothesis can be safely set aside, since it lacks any reputable support. The tradition of Peter in the Coemeterium Maius rests solely upon the witness of a "longbardischen" Pilgrim around A.D. 600. Furthermore, there is no evidence that the January 18 festival of the chair of Peter was celebrated in Rome until the time of Paul IV (1555-59) as a result of the Papal Bull of 1558.

An ingenious suggestion made by Erbes to explain the choice of January 18 involved the assumption that February 22, A.D. 63 marked the end of the two-year sojourn of Paul in Rome (Acts 8:30) which terminated in his death. If Peter died at the same time as Paul, then, when the length of the alleged episcopate of Peter in Rome (precisely twenty-five years, one month, and eight days) is subtracted from February 22, A.D. 63, one arrives at the date, January 18, A.D. 38.[50] This latter date supposedly marks the celebration of the ascent of

---

44. In *Jahrbuch für Liturgiewissenschaft*, IV (1924), 48–58 and *Rivista di Archeologia cristiana*, II (1925), 62–71.

45. Lietzmann, *Petrus und Paulus in Rom*, 2d ed., p. 97, dismisses Kirsch's view as "very improbable."

46. *Ibid.*

47. Carcopino, *De Pythagore*, pp. 277–80. Piganiol, *L'Empereur Constantin*, p. 211, agrees. Compare Seston, "Hypothèse sur la date de la basilique constantinienne," pp. 153–59. The liturgical and archeological evidence for a possible translation of the relics of Peter and Paul are carefully considered in Part III.

48. Lietzmann, "Petrus römische Märtyrer," p. 409.

49. Klauser, *Die Cathedra im Totenkult*, pp. 158, 159.

50. Erbes, *Die Todestage*, pp. 43 ff., and "Die geschichtlichen Verhältnisse der Apostelgräber in Rom," pp. 59 ff. Both references are mentioned by Klauser, *Die Cathedra im Totenkult*, p. 160.

Peter to his Roman episcopate. Granted that the coincidence is interesting, the explanation of the appropriation of the date as a result of a pagan Celtic feast held on this day is more convincing, especially in light of the similar practice of the Church in appropriating the pagan festivals of December 25, February 22, and June 29.

A recent attempt at a solution to this problem was made by Toynbee, who explains that upon the authority of Henry Chadwick, she is now of the opinion that February 22 commemorates the date of the death and burial of Peter at the Vatican according to an alternative tradition that the deaths and burials of Peter and Paul took place on different days and in different years. The word "cathedra" in the familiar notice of the *Depositio Martyrum* was added later to mark him out as the founder of the line of popes. January 25 commemorated the death and burial of Paul in the Via Ostia. The word "conversio" was added to the notice of January 25 since this is the most spectacular event in the life of Paul. January 18 is a later and "less official commemoration of Peter's 'chair' in Rome," corresponding to the later and also less official commemoration of the "chair" at Antioch on February 22.[51]

There is no certain solution to the problem of the origin of this date; and it stands today as Klauser says, "ein schwieriges, vielleicht zur Zeit noch unlösbares Problem für sich."[52]

The present *Martyrologium* of the Roman Catholic Church contains the following notice for February 22: "Antiochiae cathedra sancti Petri Apostoli, ubi primum discipuli cognominati sunt Christiani," and for January 18: "Cathedra sancti Petri Apostoli, qua primum Romae sedit."

It was necessary to discuss at some length the liturgical evidence for the assumption that Peter had occupied the office of bishop in Rome, since in all treatments of the subject the festivals of January 18 and February 22 are at least mentioned. It has been ascertained, however, that there is no evidence whatsoever that the liturgical festival held on February 22 (January 18 is much later) antedated the beginning of the fourth century at the very earliest. Furthermore, evidence which appears in this period is worthless unless it can be proved that it rests upon very early, reputable, and independent tradition; for by about A.D. 300 literary documents containing well-elaborated traditions concerning Peter's role in the earliest development of the Roman Church had already circulated for at least a century and a quarter.

The information contained in the *Martyrologium Hieronymianum* could easily have been derived, in addition to the *Depositio Martyrum*, from Galatians 2 or from the works of Tertullian, Dionysius of Corinth, Gaius, Cyprian, Eusebius, or even from such apocryphal material as the *Acts of Peter*, the *Didascalia Apostolorum*, or the *Epistle of Clement to James*. Therefore since this information is not demonstrably ancient or independent, it cannot be accepted as authentic.

The second of the two important liturgical festivals which involve Peter, that held on June 29, is considered in Part III in relation to the question of the translation and the burial of Peter in Rome.

A BRIEF SUMMARY OF THE LITERARY AND LITURGICAL EVIDENCE FOR THE ROMAN RESIDENCE OF PETER

The silence of the New Testament, in particular Paul's Epistle to the Romans and the Book of Acts, is not decisive for or against the tradition that Peter had lived in Rome, except for the reasonable assumption that if he had ever been there at all, he was not in that city when Paul wrote his letter to Rome. Despite arguments to the contrary there is no evidence to be derived from Galatians 2.

---

51. "A Review of Jérôme Carcopino's *De Pythagore aux Apôtres*," *Gnomon*, XXIX (1957), 267.

52. Klauser, *Die Cathedra im Totenkult*, p. 161n44. He adds that by 1774 the insight into the actual historical evidence was

so advanced that it was suggested by a commission of Benedict XIV on breviary reform to put both "Cathedra Petri" festivals together. Out of deference to the Bull of Paul IV (1558), however, this was not done.

In I Peter 5:13, written at the end of the first century, we find early and fairly reliable testimony to the tradition that Peter visited Rome. This simple unelaborated assumption is also probably supported by Ignatius' *Epistle to the Romans* 4:3 (A.D. c. 110) and possibly, albeit very unlikely, by the fragment of Papias (A.D. c. 150) preserved by Eusebius. There is some further amplification in *I Clement* 5 (A.D. 96), discussed in Part II, and questionable elaboration by Dionysius of Corinth (A.D. 170) who makes the unlikely assumption that Peter and Paul founded both the Church at Corinth and the Church at Rome.

Further information is derived from the lists of the Roman bishops. However, there is no evidence that these made their appearance before the time of Hegesippus (A.D. c. 150). The monarchical episcopate certainly does not reach back to the period of the origins of the Roman Church, and, more important for this book, it is not possible to determine with any degree of definiteness the roles that Peter and Paul actually did play in the life of that community. It is certain that the proposal concerning the supposed twenty-five-year episcopate of Peter was born in the imagination or developed out of genuine confusion.

That Peter founded the Church of Rome without Paul or served as its bishop alone or did both, can be classified only as assumptions of the late second or early third century. In fact, the very idea that Peter was a bishop of Rome at all, in any sense of the word, or that he had any relation to its founding cannot be authenticated by any bishops' list or by any other literary document written before the middle of the second century. The liturgical celebration (January 18, February 22) which relates to the ascent of Peter to the Roman episcopacy makes its first appearance in the first half of the fourth century at the earliest. There is no tradition concerning the Roman episcopacy of Peter in the New Testament, *I Clement*, or Ignatius; it is only dimly discerned in Hegesippus and *may* be implied in the Letter of Dionysius of Corinth to the Romans. By the beginning of the third century, however, the early assumptions of tradition have been transformed into "facts" of history.

Information gathered from Clement of Alexandria, Tertullian, Hippolytus, and the apocryphal and liturgical material is to be considered as containing little or no independent testimony, but rather as interesting evidence of the direction in which the early development of the tradition moved. What, then, remains of the tradition concerning a Roman residence of Peter? It may be accepted that he did visit Rome. This tradition is too old, too varied, too unchallenged in antiquity to be challenged with any force in the present. But it is not known when he came to Rome, how long he stayed, nor what function of leadership he exercised in the Roman Church.

PART II

The Literary Evidence
for the Tradition
of the Martyrdom of Peter
in Rome

CHAPTER 4

The Traditions
of the Martyrdom

IT IS NOT possible to state precisely what the tradition is concerning the martyrdom of Peter in Rome. There is no single tradition but a number of traditions. The substance of each is basically similar; the details vary considerably. Before dealing with the various documents related to this question, it is necessary to enumerate and to discuss briefly the several categories in which the information gathered from these documents must be classified: 1) the fact of Peter's martyrdom, 2) the probable cause of his death, 3) the manner in which he died, 4) the date when the martyrdom occurred, and 5) the place of his death.

That Peter was martyred is assumed by all who take seriously the tradition pertaining to Peter in Rome. Others, who will not grant that he ever visited Rome, concede that he was martyred, but suggest that this incident took place in Jerusalem.[1] The view of a great majority is expressed adequately in the assured statement of Lietzmann, found in the two editions of *Petrus und Paulus in Rom* as well as in "Petrus römischer Märtyrer," that there is "Ergebnis einer Wahrscheinlichkeit, freilich einer hohen dafür, dass Petrus wirklich in Rom den Märtyrertod gestorben ist."[2]

Why was Peter martyred? Was it merely because he was a Christian and the profession of Christianity was in this early period a capital offense? Was it because the Christians were accused of immoral acts or some particular criminal act? Did he die as a result of a charge of atheism or of being sacrilegious? Or must it be admitted that the reason which lay behind the martyrdom is at the present beyond knowing?

A persistent tradition exists that Peter died either in that first Neronian persecution of the Christians, which followed shortly after the great fire of Rome, or in a later persecution under the same emperor, between A.D. 65 and 67. It is not probable that Peter died in the sixties of the first century in accordance with a law which made professing the "name" (being a Christian), a capital offense. In other words, it is unlikely that there existed in this period an *Institutum Neronianum*,[3] or

---

1. See the general view of Torrey, *Documents of the Primitive Church*, p. 10. Compare Heussi, in *Die Christliche Welt*, p. 168; Robinson, "Where and When Did Peter Die?" pp. 255–67; and Smaltz, "Did Peter Die in Jerusalem?" pp. 211–16. An early expression of this view is found in Erbes, "Petrus nicht in Rom, sondern in Jerusalem Gestorben," pp. 1–47 and 161–224. The basis of his thesis is found in the *Acts of Peter* where the sentence of death is handed down to Peter not by Nero but by a Roman prefect named Agrippa (see Acts 12). There was no prefect by that name in *Rome* at that time, and the Albinus also mentioned there could be the man by that name who succeeded Festus as Procurator of Judea. (See Josephus, *Antiquities* XX.9:1, in *The Works of Flavius Josephus*, trans. Shilleto, III, 404.) Only in Judea are the names Albinus and Agrippa found together. Therefore, Erbes claims that Peter was martyred by order of Herod Agrippa II at the end of A.D. 64, not in Rome but in Jerusalem. To this view Guignebert, *La primauté de Pierre*, p. 302, answers, "Pourtant il me semble impossible de considérer actuellement sa conclusion comme une résultat acquis. Si Pierre n'est pas mort à Rome, nous ne savons pas où il est mort, ni quand exactement."

2. "Petrus römischer Märtyrer," p. 410. Whether the written documents adequately support the tradition or not is immaterial to Barnes, *The Martyrdom of St. Peter and St. Paul*, p. 5: "Indirect evidence . . . is plentiful and continuing." In the words of Cardinal Newman, "Securus iudicat orbis terrarum [The whole world does not make a mistake].

3. Griffe, in *Bull. de Litt. ecclés.*, (1952), pp. 158–60, is doubtful that such a law existed at this time. He is joined in this opinion by Leclercq, *DACL*, IV, 1565 ff.; Duchesne, *Histoire ancienne de l'Église*, p. 107, and Goguel, *The Birth of Christianity*, pp. 537 ff.

special law of Nero against Christians such as existed later under Trajan (in whose reign the practice of Christianity was forbidden, even if the Christians were "not to be sought out" for persecution). This question has been hotly disputed, for there is no proof of the existence of such a law.[4] Although the view has a few proponents who find some support in the *Ad Nationes* of Tertullian,[5] there are strong objections,[6] not the least of which centers on the contents of Pliny's famous letter to Trajan written A.D. 112.[7] In this letter Pliny sought Trajan's advice concerning the treatment of Christians, but certain questions which he asked would have been unnecessary had there been an earlier general law prohibiting the practice of Christianity or the profession of the "name."[8] Furthermore, Tertullian, in the *Ad Nationes*, refers only to measures taken against the Christians after the burning of Rome and does not echo an early general law against this group.

Why were the Christians punished if not under the provisions of a general law? There is no indication that Christianity as an entity was condemned by the Romans prior to the fire in Rome, but it is possible that it was persecuted under existing laws concerning foreign and "unapproved" religions.[9] The Institutum of Nero, if such existed in *any* form, may refer merely to his "custom" or "practice" of persecuting the Christians. Christianity was subject to the same harsh restrictive measures as were meted out to other groups which were considered by the government to sponsor or permit "scelera" or "flagitia," that is, criminal or licentious conduct.[10] Because of an alleged antisocial tendency of such a group, confession of membership in that group, called "nomen," was forbidden. Those who persisted in their association with a proscribed group could be sentenced to death by direct order of a magistrate. The sentence was carried out by the police acting in accordance with their responsibility to keep order (coercitio). If a man were accused of "nomen," he was in fact charged with being a malefactor, "praesumatis de sceleribus nostris ex nominis confessione."

Tacitus accuses the Christians of "hatred of the human race."[11] Interestingly, as Hitchcock points out, Pliny uses the same term in referring to Nero,[12] in which passage the "human race" is equated with the Roman Empire.[13] The charge against the Christians, therefore, *may* be interpreted as a charge of hatred of or hostility toward the Roman Empire, or more explicitly toward the Roman government. Hitchcock is inclined to believe that Tacitus (A.D. c. 116) accused the Christians of "flagitia" because Pliny (A.D. 112) in his *Epistle* XCVI (the authenticity of which has been questioned) mentions such to Trajan. In comparing the letter of Pliny and the *Annals* XV.44 of Tacitus, there appears to be some evidence of a dependence of the latter upon the

4. See Grégoire, "Les Persécutions," p. 25.

5. *Ad Nationes* 1:7 (*MPL*, I, 637; *The Ante-Nicene Fathers*, III, 114): "Principe Augusto nomen hoc ortum est, Tiberio disciplina ejus illuxit, sub Nerone damnatio invaluit. . . . Et tamen permansit erasis omnibus solum institutum Neronianum, justum denique ut dissimile sui auctoris." [This name of ours took its rise in the reign of Augustus; under Tiberius it was taught with all clearness and publicity; under Nero it was ruthlessly condemned. . . . Now although every other institution which existed under Nero has been destroyed, yet this of ours has firmly remained—righteous, it would seem, as being unlike the author (of its persecution).]

6. "Institutum" in the passage of Tertullian may have had no legal significance whatsoever and may have referred only to a "custom" or "habit." Furthermore, if such "institutum" had existed, then, in such passages as *Ad Nationes* V.3, reference to it would be expected. The earliest concrete mention of the alleged "Institutum" is by Sulpicius Severus, *Chronica* II.29 (*MPL*, XX, 145): "post etiam datis legibus religio vetabatur, palamque, edictis propositis Christianum esse non licebat." See the discussion of this question in Goguel, *The Birth of Christianity*, pp. 506–10.

7. The English text of the letter (*Epistle* XCVI) and Trajan's answer (*Epistle* XCVII) are to be found in Mattingly, *Christianity in the Roman Empire*, pp. 36–38.

8. For example: "Should the name, if free from serious crimes, be punished or only the crimes that attach to the name?" *Ibid.*, p. 37.

9. See Tertullian, *Apologeticum*, IV and V (*MPL*, I, 333–47; *The Ante-Nicene Fathers*, III, 20–22) where presumably these laws are set forth and in which Tertullian seeks to have such laws modified.

10. Sherwin-White, "Early Persecutions and Roman Law Again," pp. 207, 208.

11. "Odio humani generis convicti sunt." *Annals* XV.44, trans. Jackson, IV, 284, 285.

12. "Hostis generis humani" [enemy of the human race] and "fax humani generis" [torch of the human race], *Naturalis Historia* VII:45–46, XVII:92.

13. Hitchcock, "Charges Against the Christians in Tacitus," p. 301.

former.[14] Suetonius characterizes the Christians in the same censorious manner stating that they are persecuted for being disturbers of the public order and given to a "new and nefarious superstition."[15]

Why were the Christians accused, in the words of Tacitus, of "odium generis humani"? This is a much-disputed question that is never answered to the complete satisfaction of all. Most probably, as may be gathered from Tertullian's argument in the *Apologeticum*, the magistrates did not take seriously the various reports concerning such crimes as incest and infanticide. What the magistrates did take seriously were the charges that 1) the Christians did not participate in public ceremonies and thereby exposed all men to the wrath of the gods and 2) they did not make ritual offerings to the emperor in demonstration of their loyalty and obedience. These were two essential points in the case of paganism against Christianity.[16] A man who bore "nomen" (professed Christianity) was one who would not sacrifice, ergo this man was a "public enemy."

Were the Christians also persecuted because of a belief that they had set fire to Rome? Tacitus in his *Annals* 38-43 describes the great fire of Rome which took place during the reign of Nero on July 17 and 18, A.D. 64.[17] Of the fourteen regions of Rome, four were not affected; three were totally destroyed and the remaining seven were in ashen ruins. No matter what the actual cause of the fire was, Nero could not dissuade the populace from their belief that somehow he was culpable and that the fire was a means to the fulfillment of his desire to build Rome anew.[18] In fear and cowardice Nero sought out victims, and with refinements of cruelty he found a multiple solution to his difficult situation by fixing the blame upon the Christians and using the means of their punishment to satisfy the desire of the populace for public spectacles. His acts were so savage and so ferocious that even pagans such as Tacitus were moved to pity for this unfortunate group.[19]

There is no doubt that the persecution, justly or unjustly, is related to the fire. The ferocity of the persecution as described in the *Annals*, however, may in part be a result of the impassioned imagination of Tacitus. There may be some exaggeration in Tacitus' account, not in the very fact of the persecution but in relation to its character and extent. As Mattingly indicates, Suetonius reports this persecution not as "an atrocity but as one of a series of salutary reforms."[20]

Tacitus accepted the charges of "flagitia," but not the allegation that Christians had set fire to Rome. Pliny disavowed the charges of "flagitia" and also took the position that mere "nomen" alone was not punishable.

The accounts of Tacitus and Suetonius and others are brief and tangled, but, from what can be gathered, it would seem that the Christians were informally accused in this period of "flagitia," "scelera," atheism, and sacrilege. Few Romans took seriously the charges of immorality and perhaps fewer still, that Christians were guilty of the burning of Rome. If there was any general proscription of the sect, it was most probably instituted after the time of the charge of incendiarism.

Further discussion of the causes of persecution is not necessary to this study. It remains to say that for whatever cause—whether, as is unlikely, there was a general law during the reign of Nero against the Christian sect or, as is more probable, that there were specific charges—it is presumed by most, on the basis of the tradition, that Peter died in the persecution of Nero

---

14. *Ibid.*

15. *Nero* XVI.2: "afflicti suppliciis Christiani, genus hominum superstitionis novae ac maleficae." See *Suetonius*, trans. Rolfe, II, 111; Suetonius, *Domitian* XV.1 in Rolfe, II, 371.

16. "Summa haec causa, immo tota est" [this is the greatest cause, or rather is all], *Apologeticum* X.1 (*MPL*, I, 380).

17. The great fire is also described by Suetonius, *Nero* XXXVIII, trans. Rolfe, II, 155; Pliny, *Historiae Naturalis* XVII.1:5, trans. Rackham, V, 5; Dio Cassius, *Roman History* LXII.16–18, trans. Cary, VIII, 110–17. See the excellent discussion in Goguel, *The Birth of Christianity*, pp. 510–23.

18. "Sed non ope humana, non largitionibus principis aut deum placamentis decedebat infamia, quin iussum incendum crederetur." [But neither human help nor imperial munificence

---

nor all the modes of placating heaven could stifle the scandal or dispel the belief that the fire had taken place by order.] Tacitus, *Annals* XV.44, trans. Jackson, IV, 282, 283.

19. *Ibid.*, p. 283–84. To those who question that *Annals* XV.44 is by Tacitus, Mattingly, *Christianity in the Roman Empire*, p. 31, argues that "the passage is unquestionably by Tacitus—if any part of the *Annals* is; the attempts of the old 'Higher Criticism' to discredit the passage have failed completely."

20. *Ibid.*, p. 32.

between A.D. 64 and 67. The strength or weakness of this position is discussed in the examination of the primary sources.[21]

There has never been any dispute concerning the manner of Peter's death. The unanimous verdict is that he died by crucifixion. A somewhat vague *vaticinium post eventum* appears in the New Testament, whereas more explicit indications are found in Tertullian,[22] Lactantius,[23] and Eusebius[24] who also distinguish between the types of death suffered by Peter and Paul. Once the tradition had been set, it was echoed again and again. Peter, Bishop of Alexandria (A.D. 300–11), testified to his belief in the crucifixion of Peter in Rome; the same is found in the works of John Chrysostom.[25] Jerome elaborated further by adding that Peter requested to be crucified head down, for he felt himself unworthy to die in the precise manner of his Lord.[26] This information concerning the position of Peter on the cross (but not the further elaboration) may have been derived from Origen who remarked that Peter simply made the request of his jailer without giving a reason.[27] That this was a well-known tradition by the fourth century is confirmed by the representation of Peter being crucified in this position on six sarcophagi dating from that period.[28] In 1299 Giotto was commissioned by Cardinal Stephanaschi to portray the figure of Peter in this position on a panel of the high altar of St. Peter's. It is possible that Origen and the later tradition ultimately derived this detail of the crucifixion of Peter head downward from the *Acts of Peter*,[29] which, it is interesting to note, makes no allusion to this martyrdom having taken place during the persecutions of Nero. An added apocryphal detail that Peter's wife was executed at about the same time and that he saw her being led away to execution, appears to have been known by Clement of Alexandria.[30]

There is much greater difference of opinion concerning the date and place of the martyrdom of Peter. The earliest date is suggested by Donald Robinson whose conclusion, reached by a careful comparison of the gospels (principally Luke 22–24) with Acts 12, is that Peter died in Jerusalem A.D. 44.[31] This theory is impressive and immediately attractive, but lacks confirmation elsewhere in the New Testament and contradicts the entire Roman tradition of Peter. Despite the support given by Davis,[32] Robinson's thesis cannot be accepted, any more than Heussi's theory, based on an improbable understanding of Galatians 2 (that Peter died A.D. 56 between the writing of 1 Corinthians and Galatians).[33] If Peter had died as early as A.D. 44, presuming that he did not reach Rome[34] for some time after the crucifixion of Christ, there would hardly have been time before his death for him to have become closely related to that

---

21. Serious persecutions of the Christians were not common in Rome between A.D. 64 and c. 250, and not a great many lost their lives as a result of them. This is confirmed by Origen, *Contra Celsum* III.8 (*MPG*, XI, 930), who states that, except for the persecution under Nero and that in Lyon and Vienna A.D. 177, the number of victims was comparatively small until the third century.

22. *De praescriptione* XXVI.2 (*MPL*, II, 50; Giles, *Documents Illustrating Papal Authority*, p. 22: "What a happy Church is that [Rome] on which the Apostles poured out their whole doctrine with their blood; where Peter had like passion with the Lord." *Scorpiace* XV (*MPL*, II, 151): "tunc Petrus ab altero cingitur cum cruci adstringitur."

23. *De mortibus persecutorum* II.6 (*MPL*, VII, 196–97).

24. *E. H.* II.25:5 (Lake, I, 181).

25. *On Genesis* XLVIII, *Homily* LXVI (*MPG*, LIV, p. 567); *On II Timothy* 5:2 (*MPG*, LXII, 626).

26. *De viris illustribus* I (*MPL*, XXIII, 639). In *Consolatio ad Marciam* XX, Seneca testifies to having seen "crosses on which men hung downwards." (Seneca, *Moral Essays*, trans. Basore, III, 68, 69). He also mentions in recounting the various tortures that "alia brachia patibulo explicuerunt" [others stretch out their arms on a fork-shaped gibbet].

27. In a passage quoted by Eusebius in *E. H.* III.1:2 (Lake, I, 190), Origen writes, "οὕτως αὐτὸς ἀξιώσας παθεῖν."

28. Wilpert, *Sarcophagi*, pp. 168–69, figs. 99, 100, cited by Josi, "Pietro, Apostolo, Santo," p. 1403.

29. Chapter XXXVII (James, *The Apocryphal New Testament*, p. 334), immediately after the so-called Quo Vadis legend. See also in this connection the work of the fifth century Spanish historian and theologian, Paulus Orosius, *Historiarum* VII.7 (*MPL*, XXI, 1077, 1078).

30. *Stromata* VII.11: ". . . τὸν μακάριον πέτρον θεασάμενον τὴν αὐτοῦ γυναῖκα ἀγομένην τὴν ἐπὶ θάνατον. . ." (*MPG*, IX, 488; *The Ante-Nicene Fathers*, II, 541).

31. In *Journal of Biblical Literature*, LXIV (1945), 255–67.

32. "Was Peter Buried in Rome?" pp. 167–71.

33. See above, pp. 12, 13. Compare Aland, "Petrus in Rom," p. 497.

34. A date early in the reign of Claudius is found in some segments of the tradition.

Church and to have assumed some leadership in it, as is implied in Ignatius, *Romans* 4:3.

Another complicated and untenable thesis, that Peter died A.D. 58, is advanced by Léon Hermann. His argument is based upon an ingenious and possible, but by no means certain, rearrangement of portions of the *Annals* of Tacitus.[35]

The *Liberian Catalogue*, mentioned in Part I and discussed further in Part III, contains a notice which would place the death of Peter and Paul A.D. 55.[36] This view is held by Mommsen, but has been correctly rejected by modern critics, such as Lietzmann, as historically useless. Aside from the early date for the martyrdom, we find in the notice of the *Liberian Catalogue* some evidence of manipulation which makes the document conform to the third-century tradition of the twenty-five-year episcopate of Peter: the notice involves the very improbable assumption that Peter entered upon his episcopal office at Rome in the year of, or in the year after, the death of Christ.

The *Fasti Vindobonenses priores* and the *Consularia Ravennatia* mention A.D. 57 as the year of martyrdom, while the *Consularia Constantinopolitana* places the date of death A.D. 58. But these documents are late and of little historic value.[37]

The great majority of early works places the martyrdom of Peter between A.D. 64 and 67. The former date has been argued forcefully by a number of prominent scholars, including Renan, Harnack, Duchesne, Lagrange, Styger, and Klauser.[38]

Those who prefer late A.D. 64 or early 65 depend upon Tacitus' *Annals*, or another like source, for they place the death between the fire of Rome and the later persecution.[39] This appears to be the reasoning of Tertullian and also of Epiphanius who mentions that the death of Peter came in the twelfth year of Nero (A.D. 65).[40]

Eusebius, in the Armenian version of the *Chronicle* together with the *Agapio*,[41] states that the death of Paul occurred in the thirteenth year of Nero (between October 3, A.D. 66, and October 12, A.D. 67) and that of Peter in the fourteenth year of Nero (A.D. 67–68). The Armenian version of the *Chronicle* also places the beginning of the episcopate of Linus A.D. 66. One of these dates presumably must have been a scribal error, for it could hardly be thought that Linus took office before Peter was martyred. This late reckoning by Eusebius results from the assumption (against Tacitus) that the persecution of Nero began A.D. 68 (which, as in the case of the *Liberian Catalogue*, may be an attempt to save the unsavable twenty-five-year episcopate of Peter).[42] Clement of Rome places the martyrdom of Paul ἐπὶ τῶν ἡγουμένων [before the rulers] (A.D. 67),[43] during

---

35. Hermann, "La mort de St. Paul et de St. Pierre," pp. 189–99.

36. "Petrus ann. XXV, mense uno, diebus VIIII. Fuit temporibus Tiberii Caesaris et Gai et Tiberi Claudi et Neronis, a consulatu Minuci [Venici] et Longini [A.D. 30] usque Nerone et Vero [Vetere] [A.D. 55]. Passus autem cum Paulo die III Kal. Iulias, consulibus suprascriptis imperante Nerone."

The *Liber Pontificalis*, which one would expect to follow the *Liberian Catalogue*, does not give a date for the martyrdom in the first edition (Duchesne, *Le Liber Pontificalis*, I, 51) and the Felician and Cononian Abridgments (*ibid.*, I, 50). The second edition states that the death of Peter took place "post passione Domini anno XXXVIII" (some MSS: XXXVI or XXXIIII), that is, between A.D. 65 and 67 if Christ died A.D. 29 or between A.D. 66 and 68 if Christ died A.D. 30 (*ibid.*, I, 118).

37. See Josi, "Pietro, Apostolo, Santo," p. 1401.

38. Renan, *The Antichrist*, p. 162. Harnack, *Die Chronologie*, I, 240. See also Zahn, *Introduction*, III, 480; Georgius Syncellus, *Historia ecclesiastica* (*MPG*, CVIII, 1196) for the year 5563 or 5564 (A.D. 63 or 64), "Petrus et Paulus divini apostoli pro Christi martyrii sunt agone coronati." Duchesne, *Histoire ancienne de l'Église*, I, 64. Lagrange, *Évangile selon St. Luc*, p. xxvi. Styger, *Die römischen Katakomben*, p. 347. Klauser, *Die römische Petrustradition*, p. 16.

39. Several things may have intervened between the fire in late July and the persecution of the Christians: caring for the immediate needs of those whose homes were destroyed, the rites of expiation, and the beginning of the great task of rebuilding.

40. *Homily* XXVII.6:6 (*MPG*, XLI, 373). See Marucchi, "La Crocifissione di S. Pietro in Vaticano," pp. 137–53.

41. Menbidj, *Kitab al-'Unvan* (Universal History) in *Patrologia Orientalis*, translated and edited by R. Graffin and F. Nau, VII.478, "Simon Cephas . . . died at Rome where he had been bishop for twenty-five years, in the thirteenth year of Caesar Nero. Nero killed him and Paul with him. Peter was crucified head downward."

42. Harnack, *Die Chronologie*, I, 242: "somit ist das Jahr 68 (67) nicht vertrauenswürdig."

43. *Epistle to the Corinthians* V.7 (*MPG*, I, 219, 220; *The Ante-Nicene Fathers*, I, 6).

which year Nero was in Greece and had left the government of Rome in the hands of Helius and the Praetorian Guards, headed by Tigellinus.[44] Of course, this reference does not necessarily give information concerning the death of Peter unless one is convinced that the death of Peter and Paul took place at the same time or at least within the same year.

Some help in reaching a decision as to the date is offered by Balleine.[45] If it is true that Peter died in the garden of Nero,[46] only the emperor himself could have given permission for such an event to take place. Nero, however, was in Greece from September, A.D. 66 to March, A.D. 68. Unless it is assumed that he gave permission *in absentia*, the choice of date is either before the first part of A.D. 66 or after the middle of A.D. 68. The latter date is unlikely. When Nero returned A.D. 68, he was far too busy seeking ways to save his crown to bother himself with such affairs as the death of Peter. On the other hand, he had a great deal more leisure A.D. 66. "Christians were still under suspicion of having caused the fire. The wholesale slaughter was over, but whenever a Christian was caught, he would be executed; and the crucifixion of a leader like Peter might well be made one grisly item in a public spectacle."[47] Balleine then explains that this reckoning would still make allowance for the traditional twenty-five-year episcopate of Peter; for if he arrived in Rome in the same year that he escaped from Herod, A.D. 42, his episcopate, ending A.D. 66, would have been roughly twenty-five years. As mentioned above, however, it is useless to attempt to preserve this item in the tradition which did not appear until the third century.

The view of Balleine notwithstanding, Jerome (who may, as Guignebert emphasizes, be too dependent upon Eusebius or, according to Harnack, upon Julius Africanus through Eusebius) sets the date of the martyrdom A.D. 67, at the latest possible moment.[48] In addition to the stipulation that the martyrdom of Peter took place in the "last year of Nero," Jerome makes doubly sure that his reader understands by stating that this was two years after the death of Seneca, who died A.D. 65.[49]

Eusebius, in *The Ecclesiastical History*, in a passage in which he quotes from Dionysius of Corinth, mentions that Peter and Paul ἐμαρτύρησαν κατὰ τόν αὐτὸν καιρόν.[50] This may not necessarily mean the same day, the same month, or even the same calendar year.[51] Considered *alone*, however, it cannot be construed to extend over a period of more than twelve months. From this note, together with information found in the *Chronicle*, it is gathered from Eusebius that Peter and Paul died at the same time of the year but in different years. This is also indicated by Tertullian.[52]

Although it is conceded by the majority of scholars that Peter died in Rome in the sixties of the first century and most probably A.D. 64,[53] there is still the problem of the place of execution. The testimony of tradition is widely divided on this question as on that of the date. In Part III, which deals with burial, the problem of place will be of vital importance; however, let us examine it briefly at this time.

If it is true that the topography of the ancients is much more reliable than their hagiography, it is defensible to conclude that the execution of Peter took place in the

---

44. See Dio Cassius, *Roman History* LXII.12:1, 19:1; LXIII.12:3, trans. Cary, VIII, 157, 165, 167. Compare Zahn, *Introduction*, II, 70.

45. Balleine, *Simon*, p. 82 (seen only in proof copy).

46. See below, p. 59.

47. Balleine, *Simon*, p. 82.

48. *De viris illustribus* I (*MPL*, XXIII, 638): "Romae . . . cathedram sacerdotalem tenuit ad ultimum annum Neronis, id est decimum quartum." He also places the death of Paul at the same time, *ibid.*, V (*MPL*, XXIII, 647).

49. *Ibid.*, XII (*MPL*, XXIII, 661).

50. *E. H.* II.25:8 (Lake I, 183). In *Demonstrationis evangelicae* III.5 (*MPG*, XXII, 209–10), Eusebius implies that the martyrdom of Peter and Paul took place on the same day but in different years. So Prudentius, *Peristephanon* XII.3 (*MPL*, LX, 557–60). See *Prudentius*, trans. Thomson, II, 322–27.

51. Compare Harnack's view, above p. 24; Lightfoot, *Apostolic Fathers*, Part I, Vol. II, p. 494.

52. *Scorpiace* XV (*MPL*, II, 181): "Tunc Petrus ab altero cingitur . . . tunc Paulus." See also *Against Marcion* IV.5 (*MPL*, III, 366): "Romani . . . quibus Evangelium et Petrus et Paulus sanguine quoque suo signatum reliquerunt." See also *De praescriptione* XXXVI (*MPL*, II, 50). Lactantius, *De mortibus persecutorum* II (*MPL*, VII, 196, 197), is vague at this point. See Lipsius, *Die apokryphen Apostelgeschichten*, II, 336 ff.

53. See above, p. 57.

Vatican area.[54] For more explicit information one must look to the apocryphal material which ever sought increased detail. In one tradition we find that Peter was alleged to have been martyred near a huge "Terebinth." In the Middle Ages this tradition merged with another to the effect that the martyrdom had taken place near a building called the "Tiburtinum Neronis."[55] In the interim the tree had been "changed" into a monument.

In *Pseudo Linus* we find the first mention that Peter was crucified at a place called the Naumachy "near the obelisk of Nero on the mountain."[56] This, of course, indicates the Vatican area near the Circus of Nero. The *Liber Pontificalis*, also interested in the preservation of all possible detail, agrees with this tradition.[57] In these notices the "palace" of Nero most probably refers to the circus, and the "mountain of gold" to the appearance of the sand on the Vatican. *Pseudo Marcellus* following *Pseudo Linus* also mentions that Peter met his death in the Naumachy. These general traditions reflect a belief that the martyrdom took place in the general area of the Vatican Hill.

Another legend of late vintage places the death between two pyramid-like monuments called the Metae.[58] This opinion was widely held between the twelfth and fourteenth centuries and then virtually abandoned. Peter Mellius in the twelfth century, indicating the "Meta Romuli" which was then known as the "Terebinth" in some quarters, stated that "juxta hoc aedificium crucifixus fuit beatus Petrus."[59]

The above sketch of the tradition is sufficient to suggest that although the general area indicated by the various documents is quite clear, the exact spot is not at all definite. The references in various texts mention the Naumachy or one of the following: the palace, garden, or Circus of Nero.

One further persistent tradition, which ought not to be taken seriously, maintains that Peter was crucified on the Janiculum. The genesis of the tradition may lie in an early misunderstanding of the words "montem aureum" which appear in the *Liber Pontificalis*, undoubtedly referring to the yellow sands of the Vatican Hill. This description later was confused with "Mons aureus," a term commonly applied to the Janiculum.[60] The tradition would have disappeared had it not been for: 1) the erection of a church on the Janiculum, known as the Church of San Pietro in Montorio, during the episcopate of Gregory X (1272-76), 2) the help the tradition received in 1472 from John II of Aragon, King of Spain, and 3) the erection of a small chapel in front of the thirteenth-century church by Bramante (1444-1514) in memory of the crucifixion of Peter.[61]

Maffeo Vegio (1406-57), while maintaining that Peter was crucified at the Vatican, also indicated the possibility that the references to the "Mons aureus" and "inter duas metae" reflected old and reputable traditions. This later tradition, that Peter was martyred "inter duas metae," is interesting in light of the fact that the Janiculum—the "Mons aureus"—lies in a direct line between the two Metae, that is, between the Meta of Romulus in the "Città leonina" and the Meta of Remus at the "Porta Ostiensis." Even as late as the beginning of the twentieth century, certain scholars such as Lugari were writing concerning the possibility that this tradition represented the truth.[62]

In this discussion the attempt has been made to introduce the tradition concerning the fact, cause, manner,

54. Even Guignebert, "La Sépulture de Pierre," p. 252, after some hesitation admits that Peter was most probably martyred under Nero on the Vatican Hill, but he does so only by analogy, since he is convinced that many Christians suffered in that area in that period.

55. The order of St. Benedict in the twelfth century added to the confusion by calling this mausoleum the "obelisk of Nero" (*MPL*, LXXVIII, 1032*n*16, 1045*n*50).

56. "Ad locum qui vocatur naumachiae juxta obeliscum Neronis in Montem." See Lipsius, *Die apokryphen Apostelgeschichten*, Vol. II, Part I, p. 400, and *Acta Apostolorum apocrypha*, pp. 11-22.

57. See the edition of Duchesne, *Liber Pontificalis*, Vol. I, Part I, pp. 52 and 118, in the biography of Peter, and p. 150 in the biography of Cornelius.

58. "Inter duas metas." See Grisar, "Le antiche Testimonianze," p. 722.

59. *Ibid.*, p. 722*n*2.

60. *Ibid.*, pp. 719-25. Lipsius, *Die apokryphen Apostelgeschichten*, Vol. II, Part I, p. 400, calls this "eine jungere tradition."

61. Grisar, "Le antiche Testimonianze," p. 723.

62. *Ibid.*, p. 725. See also Bosio, *Roma sotterranea* (1650), p. 74. The possibility is considered and discarded even by Barnes, *The Martyrdom of St. Peter and St. Paul*, p. 96, who (see above, p. 40) gives some credence to the legend of Peter and the Mamertine prison.

date, and place of Peter's martyrdom. The general picture is clear, but there is considerable confusion, especially in the details concerning the date and place. What is the truth that lies behind the traditions and legends? Before it is possible even to presume to answer this question, it is necessary to examine carefully the early documents which are thought to contain relevant information. It seems, therefore, most logical to begin by examining the evidence found in the New Testament itself.

CHAPTER 5

The Literary Evidence
for the Martyrdom of Peter in Rome

THERE is not one *explicit* statement in the New Testament to support the assumption that Peter was martyred, nor is there mention of where or when he died. The Scriptures do contain, however, two vague statements which give one reason to believe that traditions of his martyrdom were known.

THE GOSPEL OF JOHN

In discussing the evidence of the Gospel of John, first it is necessary to ascertain what may be inferred concerning the manner, date, and place of the death of Peter. Second, this information must be evaluated according to the period in which the passages in question first appeared.

John 13:36[1] has usually been viewed as an argument in favor of the assumption that Peter died in Palestine.[2] Christ addresses Peter and informs him that "where I go, there you cannot follow me now; you will, however, follow me later." It is a weak argument indeed to say that, since Christ died in Palestine, this statement concerning the death of Peter extends to the question of geography. It is weaker still to suppose that the manner of death is also prescribed in this vague prediction.[3] All that can be said safely is that it is prophesied that Peter, when he dies, will follow his Lord in death as in life. Furthermore, it is probable that, if chapter 21 is a part of the work of the author of chapters 1–20 (written at the same time or later), the awareness of the tradition which is surely represented in the last chapter may be dimly reflected here.

John 21:18, 19 clearly alludes to the death of Peter. The words are framed in the literary form of prophecy, but do they reflect the *ex post facto* knowledge that Peter was crucified? "When you are old, then you will stretch forth your hands and another will gird you and take you where you do not wish [to go]. (This he said to show by what death he was to glorify God.) And after this he said to him, 'Follow me.' "[4]

The author of the last chapter knows of the martyrdom of Peter and that this martyrdom was accomplished when Peter was an old man. But that he knew (or rather alluded to) the manner of the apostle's death in crucifixion, is open to question.

There is no mention of date or place. Does this mean that these facts are unknown to the author, or is it probable that behind 21:18, 19 stands a more detailed tradition of the martyrdom of Peter? Is it true, as Lietzmann maintains, that a martyrdom of Peter "ohne irgendwelche Ortsangabe undenkbar ist"?[5] If so, the place was known but not expressed, perhaps because the fact was so well known to John's intended readers.

---

1. Barrett, *The Gospel According to St. John*, p. 487.
2. Lietzmann, "Petrus römischer Märtyrer," p. 398.
3. Bernard, *The Gospel According to St. John*, II, 529, sees no reference here to the martyrdom of Peter. Compare Strachan, *The Fourth Gospel*, p. 279, who claims that the author presupposes the martyrdom of Peter in 13:36, 37.

4. "ὅταν δὲ γηράσῃς, ἐκτενεῖς τὰς χεῖράς σου, καὶ ἄλλος ζώσει σε καὶ οἴσει ὅπου οὐ θέλεις. τοῦτο δὲ εἶπεν σημαίνων ποίῳ θανάτῳ δοξάσει τὸν θεόν. καὶ τοῦτο εἰπὼν λέγει αὐτῷ· ἀκολούθει μοι.."

5. *Petrus und Paulus in Rom*, 2d ed., p. 235. Compare Heussi, in *Die Christliche Welt*, p. 164; Goguel, *L'Église primitive*, p. 209.

Both passages in John appear to Heussi to reflect legends; but if by chance they are not legend, then Heussi claims that they speak of a martyrdom of Peter, not in Rome but in Jerusalem. If it should somehow be proved, he continues, that the references are to Rome, this still would not be conclusive proof since the Gospel of John was written after 1 Clement, and an allusion to the martyrdom of Peter could be explained as an incorrect interpretation of this Epistle.[6]

Lightfoot is guilty of a paralogism in his discussion of this passage which is as serious an error as the skepticism of Heussi. He maintains that since there is no other place name given in John 21 for the crucifixion of Peter, it *must* be Rome because the tradition is so definite in placing the martyrdom in that city.[7] This reasoning would be defensible after the time of Gaius (A.D. c. 200), but not in this period with only the evidence of Clement and Ignatius to support it.[8]

It is equally precarious to see in this passage a transference to Peter of a report concerning the martyrdom of Paul. Heussi made this blunder (reminiscent of the position held by the Tübingen School) in his first article on the subject of Peter.[9]

The text of John 21:18 may reflect an ancient proverb: In youth man goes free where he wishes, in old age he must allow himself to be led even when he does not wish.[10] Nonetheless, the phrase, ἐκτενεῖς τὰς χεῖράς almost universally has been received as a reference to crucifixion.[11] But there are problems in the way

of the acceptance of such an assumption. The most prominent difficulty is the order of the words in John 21:18, 19. If there were a reference here to crucifixion, would one not expect that the "girding" would be mentioned first, followed by the "carrying," and lastly by the extension of the arms? And would it not also be more likely that "ἐκτενεῖς" would be found in the passive, that is, "your hands will *be* extended forward"?

It has been pointed out by Bultmann that ἐκτενεῖς τῶν χειρῶν does not indicate crucifixion, but rather ἐκτάσις τῶν χειρῶν.[12] The former phrase represents a forward extension of the arms and the latter, an extension to the side. If this interpretation is correct, John 21:18, 19 might reflect a belief on the part of the author of the Fourth Gospel that Peter in his old age was afflicted with blindness and that he had to be helped on with his clothing and led about as was the aged Oedipus. If this is to be the interpretation, however, how is one to account for the reference to the death by which Peter was "to glorify God?" Furthermore, this explanation does not take into account the fact that Epictetus appeared to understand ἐκτενεῖν as a reference to crucifixion.[13]

In view of the possibility that the author of the Fourth Gospel understood ἐκτενεῖν τῶν χειρῶν also to mean crucifixion and that the order of John 21:18, 19 represents not a considered opinion but a jumbled account of the order of events, an interpretation of these two verses as a prediction of Peter's crucifixion is defensible, but it must be recognized that it is by no means a certain conclusion, as was assumed by the later Church.[14]

To what period does this bit of evidence belong? If it could be shown to be sufficiently early to preclude

---

6. In *Die Christliche Welt*, p. 168.

7. Lightfoot, *Apostolic Fathers*, Part I, Vol. 2, p. 492.

8. See Goguel, *L'Église primitive*, p. 211n3.

9. "War Petrus in Rom?" p. 18; *Neues zur Petrusfrage* (1939), p. 24; *Deutschen Pfarrerblatt* (1949), p. 503; not mentioned in *Die römische Petrustradition* (1955). Compare Cullmann, *Peter*, p. 89n89.

10. Bultmann, *Das Evangelium des Johannes*, p. 552; Barrett, *The Gospel According to St. John*, p. 487; Cullmann, *Peter*, p. 88.

11. Barnabas 12:3 (*MPG*, II, 761–62) interprets the words in Is. 65:2 "ἐξεπέτασα τὰς χεῖράς μου" as referring to the crucifixion that will come. Also Irenaeus, *Against Heresies* V.17:4, "ὡς ἔφη τις τῶν προβεβηκότων διὰ τῆς (θείας) ἐκτασέως τῶν χειρῶν." (*MPG*, VII, 1171, *The Ante-Nicene Fathers*, I, 545). See also Justin Martyr, *First Apology* XXXV (*MPL*, VI, 384; *ibid*., I, 174) and Irenaeus, *Demonstration of the Apostolic Preaching* LXXIX, trans. J. H. Robinson, p. 136. In Ex. 17:12 there is mention of the outstretched hands of

Moses. Aaron and Hur ἐστήριζον τὰς χεῖρας αὐτοῦ" which is taken by Barnabas 12:2 (*MPG*, II, 761, 762; *The Ante-Nicene Fathers*, I, 145) and Justin, *Trypho* XC (*MPL*, VI, 692; *ibid*., I, 244) in the sense of crucifixion: "Μωυσῆς . . . τὰς χεῖρας ἐκατέρως ἐκπετάσας." See also Tertullian, *Scorpiace* XV, "tunc ab altero cingitur, cum cruci adstringitur" (*MPL*, II, 151).

12. Bultmann, *Das Evangelium des Johannes*, p. 552.

13. Epictetus III.26:22, trans. by Thomas Higginson, p. 259: "ἐκτενεῖς σεαυτὸν ὡς οἱ ἐσταυρομένοι" ("and extended yourself like a man crucified").

14. The pregnant meaning of the phrase "ἀκολούθει μοι" also tends toward the belief that the author intended to imply crucifixion here since this was the manner of death suffered by Christ.

any dependence upon 1 Clement, a dependence which Heussi assumes, its value would be great. A first century date, however, for the composition of the Gospel of John is very difficult to prove. Dibelius, Bauer, and Heussi date the Gospel between A.D. 115 and 150.[15] John knew Mark;[16] therefore, the Gospel is later than A.D. 70. Furthermore, since John was a product of Asia Minor (of Ephesus or Alexandria or Antioch, and most probably the first), it would have taken some time before the Gospel of Mark could possibly have reached that part of the world, been mastered, and accepted. Thus the *terminus a quo* for John cannot be earlier than A.D. 80 to 90.[17] The *terminus ad quem* is approximately fixed by the Rylands Papyrus 457 (P[52]) containing John 18:31–33, 37, 38, which Kurt Aland estimates to be from the period A.D. 90 to 100. If this dating were certain and if it were sure that the Papyrus MS at one time had contained the entire Gospel, the value of the passage under discussion would be raised immeasurably.[18] The usual dating of P[52], however, is between A.D. 125 and 150,[19] although it may be some years earlier.[20] If the "Papyrus Gospel,"known as the Papyrus Edgerton 2 (A.D. c. 150?) is not an actual copy of the Gospel of John but rather a fragment from a Gospel based upon John, then John could be dated well before the mid-second century.[21] Aside from these fragments there is no concrete evidence for the existence of the Fourth Gospel before A.D. c. 150. The *terminus ad quem* could be placed somewhat earlier if it were more certain that the Gospel of John had been used by

Basilides (A.D. 117–38) and the Valentinian Gnostics,[22] and earlier still if one were convinced that the author was John the Elder (died A.D. c. 100–10). After the time of Melito of Sardis (A.D. 160–70), there is no difficulty in finding allusions to the Fourth Gospel.[23]

Around A.D. 120 is the earliest date which safely can be adopted within the possible limits of A.D. c. 90–130 or 140. If 1 Clement was written in Rome A.D. 96, it may well have reached the East and become sufficiently well known and accepted by A.D. 110 to 115 to be considered authoritative. Therefore, the Gospel of John could well have been influenced by 1 Clement, and the two may not be as obviously independent as Aland would like to believe.[24]

In his article which appeared in 1939, Heussi did not seem to be aware of the Rylands Papyrus 457, for he still spoke assuredly of the Gospel of John as of "vermutlich sehr späten Ursprungs."[25] Heussi suggested in 1952 that the Gospel of John belonged to the period of the forming of the Four-Gospel Canon in the late second century. He was of the opinion that a trade had been made: Asia Minor had to accept Peter as a Roman martyr as the price for the acceptance of the Gospel of John by the Roman Church.[26] Perhaps this theory was suggested by Zahn who mentions that the ἑκατὸν πεντήκοντα τριῶν in John 21:11 stands for the year A.D. 153 "in which year Anicetus and Polycarp in Rome came to an agreement concerning the tradition of Peter's presence in that city."[27]

15. Dibelius, *Die Religion in Geschichte und Gegenwart*, edited by Hermann Gunkel and Leopold Zsckarnack, III, 363, suggests a date between A.D. 115 and 145. Bauer, *Theologische Literaturzeitung* (1936), p. 358, sees chapter 21 as a supplement and not later than A.D. 125–50, but in *Das Johannes Evangelium*, p. 244, he suggests A.D. 100–25. Heussi, *Die römische Petrustradition*, p. 43 mentions A.D. 150.

16. Barrett, *The Gospel According to St. John*, p. 34.

17. *Ibid.*, p. 108.

18. *Historische Zeitschrift*, CLXXXIII (April, 1957), 503.

19. An interesting discussion of the early-known fragments of the Gospel of John is found in an article by Filson, "A New Papyrus Manuscript," pp. 54–63, especially the discussion on p. 56.

20. Barrett, *The Gospel According to St. John*, pp. 92–94.

21. The facts concerning these fragments appear in Colin H. Roberts' *An Unpublished Fragment of the Fourth Gospel*.

22. Barrett, *The Gospel According to St. John*, p. 55.

23. *Homily* LXXVIII. Compare, John 11:39–44.

24. *Historische Zeitschrift*, CLXXXIII (April, 1957), 503.

25. *Neues zur Petrusfrage*, p. 24. This may not have been the case, however, for in *Die römische Petrustradition* (1955), he paid little attention to the Papyrus, placing it as late as A.D. 150.

26. *Theologische Literaturzeitung* (1952), p. 73.

27. Zahn, *Introduction*, II, 172, 173. The number has significance or it would not have been recorded. That it represents the accurate count of an eyewitness is not convincing, nor is the suggestion that it stands for A.D. 153. A writer of this period would more likely have noted the year in terms of the reign of the emperor or the consuls. Barrett's suggestion in *The Gospel According to St. John*, p. 484, is more plausible: 153 = "1 + 2 + 3 . . . + 17. Seventeen is the sum of 7 and 10 both numbers which even separately are indicative of completeness and perfection." The number 153 then represents the "full total of the Catholic and Apostolic Church."

In chapter 21 we are presented with a tradition of the death of Peter perhaps by crucifixion, a martyrdom in an unknown place on an unspecified date. While one may agree with Lietzmann that the author must have had a specific place in mind,[28] one may not jump to the conclusion as does Lightfoot, that this place *must* be Rome. In addition, since it is *possible* that the tradition in John 21 is dependent upon 1 Clement 5 or a similar source, such as the source used by Ignatius, Romans 4:3,[29] and since there is no mention of date or place, the passage is of very limited importance as evidence for the martyrdom of Peter in *Rome*.

THE FIRST AND SECOND EPISTLES OF PETER

The Petrine authorship of the two Epistles and their dates are discussed in Part I.[30] These questions are considered to be of importance in the evaluation of the testimony contained concerning the Roman residence of Peter. It is concluded that the word "Βαβυλών," which appears in 1 Peter 5:13, is a cryptic reference to Rome and, in addition, that 1 Peter, the earliest of the two Epistles, cannot be considered as valid evidence for a tradition earlier than A.D. 80–92 of the Roman sojourn of Peter.

The statement contained in 1 Peter 5:1 must be examined in considering the question of the martyrdom of Peter in Rome. Peter designates himself as a "witness of the sufferings of Christ."[31] These words when taken in conjunction with those which follow, "as well as a partaker in the glory that is to be revealed,"[32] tend to confirm the position that the author already knew of the martyrdom of Peter. This interpretation, however, is vigorously contested.[33]

Similarly, in 2 Peter 1:14 there is an awareness of a tradition that Peter had died a martyr's death: "since I know that the putting off of my body will be soon, as our Lord Jesus Christ showed me."[34] Here may be found a dim reflection of John 21:18, 19—a memory of the death of Peter, spoken as if a prediction of what was to come, and again without mention of place or time. In this instance there is not even a hint as to the manner by which Peter would "put off" his body. Even if this were an explicit statement, it could not be considered as of primary importance since 2 Peter cannot be dated definitely prior to the middle of the second century.[35]

---

28. "Es ist schlechterdings ausgeschlossen, dass je eine authentische Kunde von seinem Martyrium ohne Ortsangabe umlief: sie musste also zu finden sein." *Petrus und Paulus in Rom*, 1st ed., p. 170 (a martyr death "ohne irgendwelche Ortsangabe undenkbar ist," 2d ed., p. 235). This view is rejected by Bauer, in *Wiener Studien*, XXXVIII, 292: "Zurück projezieren der Denkweise und Interessen des II Jahrhunderts in die Frühzeit der römischen Gemeinde." Goguel, *L'Église primitive*, p. 209, also challenges this view by saying that the interest in the *place* of martyrdom only came with the later founding of the cult of martyrs (between A.D. 150 and 200). This is also the view of Heussi, in *Die Christliche Welt*, p. 164, who describes Lietzmann's position as an "anachronism."

29. Barrett, *The Gospel According to St. John*, p. 93, mentions that the supposition often made to the effect that Ignatius, *Magnesians* VII:1, VIII:2 (*MPG*, V, 763, 766, *Early Christian Fathers*, I, 96) and *Philadelphians* VII.1 (*MPG*, V, 701, 702), is dependent upon the Gospel of John is quite weak.

30. See above, pp. 14, 15.

31. "μάρτυς τῶν τοῦ χριστοῦ παθημάτων."

32. "ὁ καὶ τῆς μελλούσης ἀπὸ καλύπτεσθαι δόξης κοινωνός.."

33. See Cullmann, *Peter*, p. 87n83; Heussi, "War Petrus in Rome?" p. 31n21; Lietzmann, "Petrus römischer Märtyrer," p. 399; Bigg, *The Epistles of St. Peter and St. Jude*, p. 186; Strathmann, *Theologisches Wörterbuch*, IV, 499; Munck, *Petrus und Paulus in der Offenbarung Johannis*, p. 17.

34. "εἰδὼς ὅτι ταχινή ἐστιν ἡ ἀπόθεσις τοῦ σκηνώματός μου, καθὼς καὶ ὁ κύριος ἡμῶν Ἰησοῦς χριστὸς ἐδήλωσέν μοι."

35. Eusebius, *E. H.* II.25 (Lake, I, 256, 257), rejects 2 Peter in his ὁμολογούμενα. See above, p. 14. The Epistle was written (as the internal evidence in 1:14, 15; 3:15, 16 would suggest) in Rome A.D. c. 150. The author most likely knew the tradition of Papias (*E. H.* III.39:15) that Mark's Gospel was written embodying the ideas of Peter. There are some, however, including Barnes, *The Martyrdom of St. Peter and St. Paul*, p. 95, who maintain that 2 Peter is an authentic Epistle. Guarducci, *The Tomb of St. Peter*, p. 29, sees this verse as "another clear indication of the Apostle's martyrdom."

THE BOOK OF REVELATION

The last selection from the New Testament for discussion here is Revelation 11:3–13 because of the thought-provoking suggestions made by Johannes Munck. Munck suggests that contained in these few verses there is a cryptic reference to the martyrdom of Peter and Paul in Rome.[36]

The passage refers to "two witnesses" who will prophesy for a specified time, during which period they cannot be silenced. When their period of witnessing is completed, however, a "beast from the abyss" will ascend and will "conquer them and kill them." For three and one-half days their bodies will remain unburied. So great will have been the reaction against the witnesses that after their death there will be a great rejoicing on earth and even an exchange of presents.

At the end of the brief period in which their bodies were exposed (note the change of tense in 11:11) to the public view in the streets, "the breath of life from God entered them and they stood up" to hear a summons from God to which they responded by rising "up to heaven in a cloud." When this happened, there was on earth an earthquake in which a great part of the city fell and seven thousand people were killed. The rest of the multitude in fear "gave glory to the God of heaven."

Since the appearance of a work by R. H. Charles the passage is generally considered to have been borrowed from an unknown source written before the Fall of Jerusalem A.D. 70.[37] In his recent work, Johannes Munck is equally as positive that the fragment is not "zu jüdischen Vorstellungen, älter als die Apocalypse, zurückkommen können."[38] Indications are that Charles is correct, even if the possibility exists, which is discussed below, that an older Jewish fragment did receive a new interpretation in the hands of the author of Revelation.

The date of Revelation has been a subject of much discussion, and views range from the time of Nero to the end of the first century.[39] The earliest authorities almost unanimously assign the work to the last years of Domitian,[40] but since 11:1, 2 suggests that the temple in Jerusalem is still standing, the passage with which we are concerned gives some support to the argument for a date within the reign of Nero. If the position is accepted, however, that 11:1–13 is an earlier fragment, borrowed and adapted by the author of Revelation,[41] one must admit that these verses are of little importance in fixing the date of the work into which they most probably were introduced. The internal evidence favors a date during the reign of either Vespasian (A.D. 69–79) or Domitian A.D. 81–96), but the external evidence clearly supports a date in the reign of the latter.

Who are the "two witnesses" mentioned in verse 3? Cullmann is in error when he says that they "previously were *always* interpreted to be Moses and Elijah."[42] While it is true that by the use of the article the phrase τοῖς δυσὶν μάρτυσιν indicates that the passage deals with well-known personages, the obvious meaning of verses 5 and 6 on the one hand, and the apocalyptic tradition on the other, offer different possibilities for the identification. Tertullian is the earliest of those who identify the witnesses in the apocalyptic sense, that is,

---

36. *Petrus und Paulus in der Offenbarung Johannis*, p. 56.

37. Charles, *The Revelation of St. John*, I, lxii.

38. Munck, *Petrus und Paulus in der Offenbarung Johannis*, p. 84. See also p. 113, and the views to the contrary expressed by Joachim Jeremias, pp. 113, 114.

---

39. See Charles, *The Revelation of St. John*, pp. xci–xcvii, and Rist, "Revelation," p. 355.

40. See the evidence of Melito of Sardis in *E. H.* IV.26:9 (Lake, I, 391); Irenaeus as quoted in *E. H.* III.18:3, V.8:6 (Lake, I, 237, 457). The same material is found in Irenaeus, *Against Heresies*, V.30:3 (*MPG*, VII, 1207; *The Ante-Nicene Fathers*, I, 559–60).

41. Jeremias, "'Ἠλ(ε)ίας," *Theologisches Wörterbuch*, II, 942–43 (Munck, *Petrus und Paulus in der Offenbarung Johannis*, p. 113), convincingly identifies the tradition contained in Revelation 11:3–13 with that found also in the *Elias Apocalypse* fragment edited by Steindorf in 1899. Both contain mention of 1) the martyrdom of two witnesses, 2) bodies left unburied for three and one-half days, 3) resurrection, and 4) ascension.

42. *Peter*, p. 89.

as Elijah and Enoch.[43] The text of verses 5 and 6 strongly suggests Moses and Elijah, although it is difficult to match each promise here precisely with an occurrence in the Old Testament. The Elijah and Moses of the Old Testament are said to have produced mighty works such as those described in Revelation 11:3–13, and there are traditions which speak of their being taken up into heaven as well as traditions which mention the expectation of their return.[44] The most obvious reference to their return is found in Mark 9:2 ff., in which passage Moses and Elijah are present with Christ, when a confused Peter suggests that they "make three booths, one for you [Christ], one for Moses and one for Elijah."

Munck protests the identification of the "two witnesses" in Revelation 11:3 with Moses and Elijah on the grounds that the figure of a suffering Moses is not encountered in the New Testament or in late Judaism with the exception of the *Elias Apocalypse*.[45] Even in Hebrews 11:24–26 Moses is introduced only as an Old Testament example of faith, and his suffering is mentioned only insofar as he is one of the people of God.[46]

In spite of the objections of Munck it is most probable that the "two witnesses" referred to in Revelation 11:3–13 were intended to be Moses and Elijah in the *original* fragment appropriated by the author of Revelation.[47] Could it have been, however, that this author identified the "two witnesses" as Peter and Paul because some element of the original story reminded him of an aspect of the historical martyrdom of the two apostles? This is at least barely possible, especially if one considers other identifications made by the Primitive Church as a result of suggestions in the Old Testament. For example, the figures of the Suffering Servant (Isaiah 42:1–4, 49:1–6, 50:4–9 and 52:13–53:12) and the Son of Man (Daniel 7:13) suggested to the Church an interpretation of the life and work of Christ. The identification of the witnesses with Peter and Paul is not mentioned by R. H. Charles or Ernst Lohmeyer; the former sees any allegorical interpretation as "of very small moment,"[48] and the latter simply states that "hier ist die Beziehung auf Moses und Elias unverkennbar."[49]

The earliest identification of Peter and Paul with the "two witnesses" was made by Juan de Marianas in 1619.[50] It remained, however, for Johannes Munck to expand upon the possibility. He urges that the passage intends to suggest that Peter and Paul are endowed with the power of Moses and Elijah and that the removal of these two from Earth "introduces the perfect manifestation of the Antichrist and prepares therewith the

---

43. *De anima* L (*MPL*, II, 735), "Translatus est Henoch [Gen. 5] et Elias [2 Kings 2:11], nec mors eorum reperta est, dilata scilicet. Caeterum morituri [Rev. 11] reservantur, ut Antichristum sanguine suo exstinguant."

44. Charles, *The Revelation of St. John*, I, 281. Rev. 11:6 is to be compared with Exodus 7:14 ff.; 9:23 in relation to Moses, and 2 Kings 1:10 ff.; 1 Kings 17:1 ff., Eccles. 48:1, as well as Luke 4:25 and James 5:17 in relation to Elijah. That Elijah was taken up into heaven is mentioned in 2 Kings 2:11. That Moses was taken up into heaven may be derived from the *Assumption of Moses* X.12, written in the early first century. (See Charles, *Assumption of Moses*, pp. 44, 106, 107). The return of Moses (Deut. 18:15) and Elijah (Mal. 4:5, 6) were also awaited. See Mark 6:15.

45. Munck, *Petrus und Paulus in der Offenbarung Johannis*, pp. 118, 119.

46. *Ibid.*, p. 120n173.

47. Swete, *The Apocalypse of St. John*, p. 134: "Neither Moses and Elijah, nor Elijah and Elisha nor Enoch and Elijah . . . can exhaust the meaning of the two witnesses who

prophesy. . . . Though as the sequel (vv. 5, 6) shows, the first pair [Moses and Elijah] are in the mind of the writer, suggested undoubtedly by the visions of the Transfiguration [Mark 9:4]."

48. Charles, *The Revelation of St. John*, p. 282.

49. Lohmeyer, *Die Offenbarung Johannis*, p. 89.

50. *Scholia in Vetus et Novum Testamentum*, p. 1101. Chapter 11 refers to Nero's execution, and Marianas says of the two witnesses in vs. 3: "Hos plerique Enoch et Eliam putant"; however, concerning vs. 7 he adds that the beast who ascends from the abyss "haec est Nero vel Roma ipsa, ubi Apostoli occisi sunt." (The beast in 17:1 ff. is not *Nero*, however, but Rome). Concerning vs. 11 he says "et post tres dies surrecturos Enoch et Eliam ab Antichristo occisos credi potest. Petrum et Paulum revixisse non invenias. . . . Sed mystice revixerunt in suis: nam eorum morte fortiores ad evangelizandum sunt facti. Sic loci difficultatem emollire possumus. [S]ic ascensum eorum in coelum mystice interpretabar post mortem illustriores evasisse." In his comment on vs. 13 he mentions that the earthquake in Rome happened after the death of the Apostle. This work is cited by Munck, *Petrus und Paulus in der Offenbarung Johannis*, pp. 15–16n14, and Cullmann, *Peter*, p. 88n85.

return of Christ." That the martyrdom of Peter and Paul is meant here is "ein historisches Ereignis."[51]

This interpretation also must assume, beside the identification of Peter and Paul with the "two witnesses," that "the great city" mentioned in vs. 8 is Rome. Spitta and Wellhausen also identify "the great city" with Rome, but Charles rejects it, stating that "as the text stands 'the great city' can only mean Jerusalem."[52] As the text stands, this is the correct interpretation, but the reason given is weak. The *text* requires that Jerusalem be read for the "great city," not because there is no possible connection between Elijah or Moses and the City of Rome but because the phrase "where the Lord was crucified"[53] can only mean Jerusalem. If permitted to stand as part of the original work of the author of Revelation, this phrase would eliminate effectively the possibility suggested by Munck. Therefore, Munck accepts the convenient expedient that it is the work of a later hand—an argument equally as weak as that of Spitta and Wellhausen.[54] If an expedient were required, it would have been better, especially in light of the emphasis which Munck places upon the apocryphal material in the development of his view,[55] to have emphasized more prominently the possible relationship between the crucifixion of Christ and the City of Rome, as noted in the Quo Vadis legend in the *Acts of Peter*.[56] When Peter asks the Lord where he is going ("Quo vadis?"), Christ replies that he goes again to be crucified. This time the place is Rome.

In defense of Munck's thesis it must be said that "Sodom and Egypt" (11:8) could be a reference either to Jerusalem *or* to "Pagan ideas."[57] And "men of all people" (11:9) more plausibly suggests Rome rather than Jerusalem. (The suggestion of Bousset, to the effect that "men of all people" is a reference to the conquering army of Titus, is not convincing.)[58]

References to a possible resurrection and ascension of both Peter and Paul are not found elsewhere in the New Testament; the resurrection of Paul alone is mentioned, but not described, in the Martyrdom of Paul IV[59] and VI.[60] The idea of death, resurrection, and ascension are behind this apocryphal story, and the reference to burial could be explained as an addition made when the location of the tombs of the martyrs became increasingly important in the development of cultic interest.[61]

This same tradition of death–resurrection–ascension, Munck believes, also stands behind 1 Clement 5, in which both Peter and Paul are taken up to heaven after they have "witnessed." But whereas the interval in Revelation 11:9 is three and one-half days, in the passage from 1 Clement resurrection and ascension take place *immediately* after martyrdom.[62] Another similarity between these two documents is found in the implicit suggestion concerning jealousy contained in Revelation 11:9, 10 and the major motif of jealousy mentioned in 1 Clement 4–6.

In the *Acts of Peter*, Munck notes, the burial motif plays an increasingly important role, while in the earlier *Acts of Paul*, it is hardly mentioned and originally may not have been included at all.[63] The latter appears to

---

51. Munck, *Petrus und Paulus in der Offenbarung Johannis*, p. 56. See also pp. 17 ff. Compare meaning of Luke 24:48; Acts 22:15, 26:16.

52. Charles, *The Revelation of St. John*, p. 287. On p. 288, however, he admits, with Loisy, that Jerusalem no longer existed when the author of Revelation wrote, and thus the reference to Jerusalem could not have been taken seriously.

53. "ὅπου καὶ ὁ κύριος αὐτῶν ἐσταυρώθη."

54. Charles, *The Revelation of St. John*, p. 35.

55. *Ibid.*, pp. 78 ff.

56. Chapter XXV, James, *The Apocryphal New Testament*, p. 333, and in *Acts of Peter and Paul* LXXXII; also see Munck, *Petrus und Paulus in der Offenbarung Johannis*, p. 48n35. Compare texts of *Pseudo-Hegesippus* and *Pseudo-Linus* in Lipsius, *Die apokryphen Apostelgeschichten*, II, 103, and Ambrose, *Sermo de basilicis* (*MPL*, XVI, 1053).

57. Lohmeyer, *Die Offenbarung Johannis*, p. 90.

58. Munck, *Die Offenbarung Johannis*, p. 322.

59. Lipsius, *Die apokryphen Apostelgeschichten*, I, 112:13–114:1.

60. *Ibid.*, I, 116:3 f.

61. Lietzmann, *Petrus und Paulus in Rom*, 2d ed., pp. 123 f. and 226, points out that the location of graves only becomes important A.D. c. 200. He also admits the difficulty of getting behind the sources which show a date of about A.D. 200–20 and that although there is some "liturgische Überlieferung" there is no "historische Überlieferung." When the former fails "stehen wir vor dem Nichts," p. 123.

62. See Lightfoot, *Apostolic Fathers*, Part I, Vol. II, pp. 27–28.

63. See Munck, *Petrus und Paulus in der Offenbarung Johannis*, pp. 79 f. See the later *Acts of Peter and Paul* LXXXIV, *Acta Apostolorum apocrypha*, ed. Tischendorf, p. 37.

reflect an older tradition, cryptically described: "es liegt näher, es als historisches Faktum zu betrachten, dass Petrus und Paulus ungefähr zu gleicher Zeit Märtyrer in Rom geworden sind. Und es ist dies historische Faktum, dass sich in I. Klem. 5, Ignatius Röm. 4, 3 und Apok. 11, 3–13 widerspiegelt."[64]

There is much to be said for the theory of Munck in spite of his insistence that Revelation 11:3–13 is not borrowed from an older document. As has been emphasized, there is the possibility that the "two witnesses" could have stood for Peter and Paul in the mind of the author of Revelation; and it is possible that the "great city" meant Rome. The early records concerning the martyrdom of Peter and Paul (John 21, 1 Clement 5, and possibly Ignatius' *Epistle to the Romans*

4:3), do not mention burial; and therefore, a narrative such as this which speaks only of death, resurrection, and ascension does not contradict an early and trustworthy tradition. Since, however, as Cullmann indicates, "the cryptic manner of speech in the Apocalypse inevitably makes uncertain every interpretation in terms of contemporary history,"[65] we may neither unreservedly accept nor categorically reject Munck's suggestions. If, on the other hand, we should find that the roughly contemporary letter of Clement to the Corinthians alludes to the Roman martyrdom of Peter and Paul, then the contention of Munck that such a tradition lies behind Revelation 11:3–13 will be considerably more convincing and of greater value as evidence.

ASCENSION OF ISAIAH

It is possible that there is another early witness to the martyrdom of Peter in the *Ascension of Isaiah*. In 4:2 f. we read as follows:

then will arise Beliar, the great prince, the king of this world, who has ruled it since its origin; and he will descend from his firmament in human form, king of wickedness, murderer of his mother, who himself is king of the world; and he will persecute the plant which the Twelve Apostles of the Beloved shall have planted; one of the Twelve will be delivered into his hands.[66]

As the text stands, it is certain that Nero is meant by the term "Beliar." The question is whether the living Nero is indicated, or a Nero redivivus.[67] If the living Nero were intended, it is curious that the author added that this emperor had reigned "III annos et VII menses et dies XVIII...." (4:12)[68] Clemen calls this a slip, an "error which crept in for the author did not write in

Rome."[69] Rather than a slip, however, it is more probable that there is evidence here of a flowing together of two ideas and a compromise. On the one hand, Nero is seen as the Antichrist, and on the other, the Devil appears to be the Antichrist.[70] Gradually the second concept gained supremacy.

The mention of the "plant" may certainly refer to the Church, and it is permissible to see Peter *or* Paul in the reference to the "one of the Twelve" who will be "delivered into his [Beliar's] hands." If in 3:17 and 11:22 the author intends "the Twelve" in the technical sense as in 1 Corinthians 15:5, then Peter is the likely choice, and Paul is eliminated.

If Beliar is understood as a cryptic name for the historical Nero, then Rome is the logical geographical location of the scene. But the problem still remains that there is no explicit reference to place. If Rome was meant, then of "the Twelve" Peter is the most likely candidate for the "one who will be delivered into his

---

64. *Ibid.*, p. 70, see also p. 66.

65. *Peter*, p. 90.

66. Charles, *The Ascension of Isaiah*, p. 95.

67. *Ibid.*, p. 25. Charles, sees 4:2, 3 as a reference to the historical Nero, while the remainder of the passage has to do *only* with the Antichrist.

68. For the repeated reference to "three and one-half years" in New Testament apocalyptic literature see Luke

4:25, 21:24; Js. 5:17; and Rev. 11:2, 12:6, 14, 13:15, 11:9 ("three and one-half *days*").

69. C. Clemen, "Die Himmelfahrt des Jesaja, ein ältestes Zeugnis für das römische Martyrium des Petrus," *Zeitschrift für wissenschaftliche Theologie*, IV (1896), 399 f., as cited by Harnack, *Die Chronologie*, I, 715.

70. *Ibid.*

hands." The passage as it stands could, however, be a reference to any one of the Twelve. The martyrdom, if this is implied by "delivered into his hands," could have taken place anywhere. If "delivered" does not refer to martyrdom at all, then the verse may contain simply an allusion to the banishment of John to Patmos —in which event Beliar stands not for Nero but for Domitian.[71]

If the passage is read without prejudice, the most convincing interpretation is that "Beliar" is a cryptic name for Nero; "the plant" stands for the Church;[72] and Peter is the one of "the Twelve" who is "delivered into his hands" (in manum eius tradetur—ταῖς χερσὶν αὐτοῦ παραδοθήσεται).[73] The reason why Peter is not named may be explained from the standpoint of style. As in many passages pertaining to predictions of the future, this detail is omitted, that is, Acts 15:25, 26 and more clearly in Mark 14:18 (Matt. 26:21): "Truly, I say to you, *one of you* will betray me, *one who* is eating with me."

Given the possibility that the passage refers in a roundabout way to the martyrdom of Peter in Rome, it is necessary to consider the question of date in order to evaluate the evidence. The section 3:13–4:22 (Cullmann cites 3:13–4:19) has been described by Clemen and others as a Christian Apocalypse which was written in the time of Nero. He feels certain that the passage was borrowed by the author of the *Ascension of Isaiah* from an ᾽Αποκάλυψις ᾽Ησαΐου, which was written before Nero died and after the persecution of A.D. 64. He supports his claim by indicating that the material before 3:21 and after 5:1 is written in the third person in indirect discourse while intervening material, the Christian Apocalypse, appears in the first person and in direct discourse. The point is not well taken, however, for the difference in mode of expression may be explained as effectively by saying that the material in 3:21–5:1 originally may have been introduced by a formula such as "And Isaiah said." This type of formula is found often in the New Testament and also, for example, in the logia from the Gnostic library at Chenoboskion, that is, "λέγει ᾽Ιησοῦς" or "καὶ λέγει αὐτοῖς."[74] In addition, there is a close relationship between this passage and the remainder of the work.[75] It is sensibly argued against Clemen by Zeller that even if the passage does refer to the living Nero this is not a strong argument in favor of the assumption that the passage therefore *had* to be written in the lifetime of Nero. If the Neronic date is to be accepted, three important questions must be answered in the affirmative. First, is it necessary to suppose that the Church A.D. 64–68 would have been described as "the plant which the Twelve Apostles of the Beloved shall have planted"? Second, is it perfectly conceivable that a document written during or immediately after the persecution of Nero[76] would omit to elaborate upon the cruelties perpetrated against the Christians? This latter question occurred to Harnack who is convinced

71. See E. Zeller, "Der Märtyrertod des Petrus," p. 560.

72. In the Old Testament there are references to Israel as the "vineyard of the Lord" (Is. 5:17). See Enoch XCIII:2, 5 and Matt. 15:13 where "plant" stands for "ideas" or "doctrines."

73. This view is shared by Eugene Tisserant, *Ascension d'Isaie*, pp. 116–17; Charles, *The Ascension of Isaiah*, p. 26. (Consult his excellent bibliography concerning this question up to 1900, pp. xxxiv–xxxvi). Cullmann, *Peter*, p. 113, thinks that this is a possible witness to the martyrdom of Peter in Rome and "should not be simply ignored as has often happened in recent discussions." See also Goguel, *The Birth of Christianity*, p. 522.

The following Roman Catholic scholars have placed this text in evidence: Besson, *Saint Pierre, et les Origines de la Primauté*, p. 92; Peterson, "Das Martyrium des Hl. Petrus nach der Petrus Apokalypse," p. 181; Campiche, "Saint Pierre et son Martyre," pp. 262–66. Leclercq, *DACL*, Vol. XIV, Part I, p. 842, is more hesitant; the "one handed over" is *perhaps* Peter, and this *may be* a confirmation of the tradition.

In his criticism of the positive stand taken by Clemen, Harnack, *Die Chronologie*, I, 714–16, urges the inadvisability of placing this passage in evidence as a witness to the tradition of the martyrdom of Peter in Rome. Zeller, "Der Märtyrertod des Petrus," p. 560, is also very doubtful.

74. Notice the abrupt change from indirect to direct discourse in the beginning of the Sermon on the Mount. In Matt. 4:23–25 a narrator speaks about the teaching activity of Jesus; then a formula "καὶ ἀνοίξας τὸ στόμα αὐτοῦ ἐδίδασκεν αὐτοῖς λέγων." introduces the direct discourse of Jesus. If this formula were lost, an abrupt break similar to that in *Ascension of Isaiah* 3:20–21 would be noticed.

75. Zeller, "Der Märtyrertod des Petrus," p. 562, mentions a study by Dillmann, *Ascension of Isaiah*, pp. xi f., which supports this view.

76. *Tacitus: Annals XV.44*, trans. Jackson, IV, 282, 283.

that the description seems much too "conventionell und ohne concrete Färbung . . . (eine allgemeine Christenverfolgung ist ins Auge gefasst)."[77] Third, is it impossible that Beliar stands for Nero redivivus; must it be understood that the name can only stand for the living Nero? R. H. Charles, who is challenged by Guignebert, eliminates the questions put forth above by suggesting a date approximately a generation after the time of Nero.[78]

What is encountered in the *Ascension of Isaiah* 4:2 f. is not a passage from the time of Nero but a *vaticinium post eventum* written from the viewpoint of Isaiah, who sees in the future the coming of a Nero, whom he calls Beliar. Since it is possible to date this passage with some degree of certainty within the first quarter of the second century, if not earlier,[79] its value as an independent and valuable source for the tradition of the Roman martyrdom of Peter would be great if the information were more explicit. As it stands the information is too vague to serve as a strong argument for the martyrdom of Peter in Rome, but, on the other hand, the possibility that the passage does contain a cryptic reference to his martyrdom is so convincing that the evidence certainly ought to be proposed and considered.[80]

THE EPISTLE OF CLEMENT OF ROME TO THE CORINTHIANS

The Epistle to the Corinthians does not mention explicitly that the author was Clement, but there is no valid reason for refusing to grant that it was written by Clemens Romanus who flourished around A.D. 96 and is one of the so-called "Apostolic Fathers."[81] In the lists of bishops he is named either third or fourth, depending upon whether Cletus is considered as an alternate spelling for Anencletus or as a separate bishop. Origen without giving evidence identifies the author with the Clement who is mentioned in Philippians 4:3. Clement has also been associated in legends with a T. Flavius Clemens who was consul A.D. 95 with his cousin Domitian.[82]

The Epistle itself does not claim to be written by Clement. The tradition that this bishop is the author may be derived, however, from the fragments of

favour of his [Clemen's] main thesis, that we have in this work the oldest testimony to the martyrdom of St. Peter in Rome."

81. Harnack, *Einführung*, p. 50. The authorship of Clement is confirmed by the *Shepherd of Hermas* II.4:3 ". . . Clement then shall send to the cities which are without, for that is his commission. . . ." Compare *The First Epistle of Clement*, edited by W. K. Lowther Clarke, pp. 9–14.

82. See *Acts of Clement* (MPG, II, 617 ff.). The confusion (see Harnack, *Einführung*, p. 51) is logical since internal and external evidence places the writing of 1 Clement in the same period—A.D. 93–97. Zahn, *Introduction*, I, 60, suggests not later than A.D. 96. Harnack, *Die Chronologie*, I, 255, and *Einführung*, p. 52; and Lightfoot, *Apostolic Fathers*, Part I, Vol. I, p. 352, are inclined to accept A.D. c. 96 as the probable date. See also Guarducci, *The Tomb of St. Peter*, p. 30. A much later date A.D. c. 150 is proposed by Delafosse, "La Lettre de Clément romain" p. 82. He is convinced that the internal struggles in the Corinthian Church reflected in 1 Clement are those resulting from Marcionite propaganda in that city. This might be possible, were it not for the mention in 5:2 of "our generation" ($\tau\hat{\eta}s$ $\gamma\epsilon\nu\epsilon\hat{a}s$ $\dot{\eta}\mu\hat{\omega}\nu$), the only aid to chronology in this letter. Delafosse buttresses his position by stating that the *Epistle of Polycarp*, usually assigned to the second century, actually comes from the period A.D. 150–66, and therefore the utilization of 1 Clement by Polycarp may not be presented as evidence for the early date of 1 Clement. Loisy, *La Naissance du Christianisme*, p. 33, also offers a late date, A.D. 130–35.

---

77. Harnack, *Die Chronologie*, I, 715.

78. In *Ascension of Isaiah*, p. xliv, Charles sets the *Testament of Hezekiah* (3:13b–4:18) between A.D. 88 and 100. For a discussion of the *terminus ad quem* see pp. 30–31; for the *terminus a quo*, see pp. lxxi–lxxii.

79. Cullmann, *Peter*, p. 112, suggests, in agreement with Charles, that a date before A.D. 100 is probable. Harnack, *Die Chronologie*, I, 724, places the date of the *Ascension of Isaiah* in the second century, but the passage under discussion which he calls the *Visio apocalyptica* cannot be placed (see p. 579) before the middle of the third century. This position is reemphasized by Harnack in the *Sitzungsberichte der Berliner Akademie der Wissenschaften* (1900), p. 985.

80. Charles, *The Ascension of Isaiah*, p. xxxvi, is far too optimistic and positive when he says, in commenting upon the thesis of Clemen, "The balance of evidence seems to be in

Hegesippus[83] and Dionysius of Corinth[84] preserved in the *Ecclesiastical History* of Eusebius. Even Irenaeus who mentions the letter does not ascribe it to Clement, but merely states that "in this Clement's time no small discord arose among the brethren in Corinth, and the Church of Rome sent a powerful letter to the Corinthians."[85] The first explicit statement as to Clement's authorship of the letter is found in the *Stromata* of Clement of Alexandria: "the Apostle Clement, in the Epistle to the Corinthians. . . ."[86]

Whether the letter was written by Clement is only of incidental importance. Its value lies in the fact that it is a letter from Rome written at the end of the first century, *not* in the fact (if it is a fact) that Clement was its author.

A place of honor was early accorded 1 Clement among the writings of the Church, especially in Syria and Egypt. Although it was mentioned with great respect and was even appended to the fifth century Codex Alexandrinus, which was rediscovered in 1628 and presented by Cyril Lucar to Charles I, it was not Scripture.

The letter deals with the dissensions within the Church of Corinth,[87] called to Clement's attention about the time of the persecution of Domitian. It represents the one authentic act of the administration of Clement[88] and was probably written in a brief respite during the persecution. (This assumption is worth keeping in mind, especially as one interprets chapters 3 to 5.) Since there are no sources mentioned in the letter, Cecchelli suggests that the information reached Clement "di uomini vecchi e sagge"—two of the formal or informal envoys who must have traveled frequently from Corinth to Rome.[89]

The first question to be settled pertains to the character of the document. One can easily be led into error if he believes that this letter was intended to serve as a history, that is, the author intended to impart facts or to give a detailed account of the crisis at Corinth, such as would have served the purpose later of Eusebius in his writing of the *Ecclesiastical History*. Clement did not seek to write history nor to incite rebellion with vivid pictures of pain and martyrdom inflicted by the Roman government upon the Church. His purpose was in part to promote better relations between the Church and the government and thus to avoid future persecution, to preserve order in the world (20:11), in the state (60:4; 61:1), and in the Christian community (34:7; 50:5; 63:2; 65:1).[90]

Aland points out that in the passage which is of concern to us and its immediate context, Clement inveighs against the uproar in the Church of Corinth where ζῆλος ἄδικος is at work and where its effect has been to raise the ἄτιμοι against the ἔντιμοι, the ἄδοξοι against the ἔνδοξοι, the ἄφρονοι against the φρόνιμοι, the νέοι against the πρεσβύτεροι (3:3). In Corinth there is a state of ζῆλος καὶ φθόνος, ἔρις καὶ διωγμὸς καὶ ἀκαταστασία... (3:2).[91] In chapter 4 Clement presents a number of examples from the Old Testament to demonstrate the end to which such intracommunity difficulties can lead. He then follows in chapter 5 with examples from his own generation.

---

83. *E. H.* IV.22:2 (Lake, I, 235, 375). Eusebius mentions certain remarks by Hegesippus "about the Epistle of Clement to the Corinthians," but Hegesippus hesitates to testify that Clement wrote the letter. Compare *E. H.* III.16:1 which appears to make the testimony of Hegesippus more explicit than is the case in *E. H.* IV.22:2.

84. *E. H.* IV. 23:11 (Lake, I, 383). Dionysius of Corinth does not mention that the letter was written by Clement, but he does quote from it. Eusebius continues that Dionysius says that it is a letter which was formerly sent "*through Clement.*" (ὡς καὶ τὴν προτέραν ἡμῖν διὰ Κλήμεντος γραφεῖσαν).

85. *Against Heresies* III.3:3 (Lightfoot, *Apostolic Fathers*, Part I, Vol. I, p. 156 and *Early Christian Fathers*, trans. Richardson, p. 373).

86. *Stromata* I.7:38 (αὐτίκα ὁ κλήμης ἐν τῇ πρὸς κορινθίους ἐπιστολῇ). (*Apostolic Fathers*, Part I, Vol. I, p. 158; *MPG*, VIII, 735, 736). Also *Stromata* IV.17:11 (*MPG*, VIII, 1311, 1312).

87. Harnack, *Einführung*, pp. 88–97; *Early Christian Fathers*, trans. Richardson, pp. 34–36.

88. In addition there are the questionable details found in the *Liber Pontificalis* (see the edition of Duchesne, Vol. I, Part I, pp. 53, 123).

89. Cecchelli, "Un vecchio Errore," p. 3, col. 1. Katzenmeyer, "Zur Frage," p. 133, suggests that the author did know Hebrews 11:1–31. Clement is surely familiar with certain letters of Paul—2 Corinthians in particular (compare chapters 24, 49, 50). See below, p. 80.

90. See Dibelius, "Rom und die Christen," p. 25, and Harnack, *Einführung*, pp. 86–87.

91. Aland, "Petrus in Rom," p. 511.

Dibelius stresses that chapters 3, 4, and 5 are not historical and that their vocabulary is drawn from rhetoric and Hellenistic philosophy. Peter and Paul are described in language appropriate to the athlete, similar to that found in the description of Heracles by Dio Cassius.[92] A prominent error in the interpretation of the passage up to the present time, according to Dibelius, is that certain questions are asked of these chapters which, owing to the purpose for which they were written, they are not equipped to answer. Questions of a historical nature cannot be put to a document which deals with moral philosophy.

Whether the over-all analysis of Dibelius is correct must be considered after the passage is carefully studied, but the warning which he sounds, not to expect more from the material than it was designed to offer, cannot be ignored. Lietzmann in order to prove the Roman martyrdom of Peter, and Heussi in order to disprove such martyrdom may each have done violence to the text in their exegesis, since both clearly treat the material as an historical source. What might *appear* to be history may be little more than instructive examples from which historical conclusions must be drawn carefully and thoughtfully.[93]

In addition to the character of the material in 1 Clement 4–6, it is important, in evaluating what is said, to conjecture as to what both Clement and his intended hearers already know. If the Roman martyrdom of Peter and Paul were knowledge common to Clement and the Corinthians, there would have been no need to mention the *fact* of the martyrdom itself or any of the details other than those which were being presented for a specific purpose. All that was necessary was to show the relationship between the well-known "fact" of the martyrdom of Peter and Paul and its cause and the situation now existing at Corinth. Clement's interest then was not in the "when," "what," and "where" of the martyrdom of Peter and Paul but merely in the "why." This one-sided interest may explain the seemingly rhetorical style of the passage and serve to put one on guard against interpreting it out of context. Chapter 5 must be seen in relation to the whole letter and more particularly in relation to chapters 3, 4, and 6. Correct understanding, however, depends ultimately upon a careful exegesis of the passage itself. Therefore, since almost every word of chapters 5 and 6 is important, the Greek and English texts appear below in parallel columns.[94]

5:1 'Αλλ' ἵνα τῶν ἀρχαίων ὑποδειγμάτων παυσώμεθα ἔλθωμεν ἐπὶ τοὺς ἔγγιστα γενομένους ἀθλητάς. λάβωμεν τῆς γενεᾶς ἡμῶν τὰ γενναῖα ὑποδείγματα.

5:2 Διὰ ζῆλον καὶ φθόνον οἱ μέγιστοι καὶ δικαιότατοι στῦλοι ἐδιώχθησαν καὶ ἕως θανάτου ἤθλησαν.

5:3 Λάβωμεν πρὸ ὀφθαλμῶν ἡμῶν τοὺς ἀγαθοὺς ἀποστόλους.

5:4 Πέτρον, ὃς διὰ ζῆλον ἄδικον οὐχ ἕνα, οὐδὲ δύο, ἀλλὰ πλείονας ὑπήνεγκεν πόνους, καὶ οὕτω μαρτυρήσας ἐπορεύθη εἰς τὸν ὀφειλόμενον τόπον τῆς δόξης.

5:5 Διὰ ζῆλον καὶ ἔριν Παῦλος ὑπομονῆς βραβεῖον ὑπέδειξεν.

5:1 But, passing from examples in antiquity let us come to the heroes nearest our own times. Let us take the noble examples of our own generation.

5:2 By reason of rivalry and envy the greatest and most righteous pillars of the Church were persecuted, and battled to the death.

5:3 Let us set before our eyes the noble apostles:

5:4 Peter, who by reason of wicked jealousy, not only once or twice but frequently endured suffering and thus, bearing his witness, went to the glorious place which he merited.

5:5 By reason of rivalry and contention Paul showed how to win the prize for patient endurance.

---

92. Dibelius, "Rom und die christen," pp. 23, 24. This theme was, according to Heussi, discussed previously by Katzenmeyer in "Bemerkung zur Martyrien Literatur," pp. 437 f., who found philosophical associations in terms such as "the good," "toil," "to bear witness," "the herald of God," and "glory," and the like. See also Harnack, *Einführung*, pp. 80–86, esp. p. 84. Compare Heb. 12:1.

93. Harnack, *Einführung*, p. 106: "Dieses Kapitel und das folgende sind stark rhetorisch; diese Rhetorik ist unpräzis und steht auf keiner hohen Stufe: Die Apostel sind als Gladiatoren vorgestellt."

94. The Greek text is found in Lightfoot, *Apostolic Fathers*, Part I, Vol. II, pp. 25–34, and Heussi, *Die römische Petrustradition*, pp. 12–13. The English translation is that of Cyril Richardson, in *Early Christian Fathers*, pp. 45, 46.

5:6 ἑπτάκις δεσμὰ φορέσας, φυγαδευθείς, λιθασθείς, κῆρυξ
γενόμενος ἔν τε τῇ ἀνατολῇ καὶ ἐν τῇ δύσει, τὸ γενναῖον
τῆς πίστεως αὐτοῦ κλέος ἔλαβεν,

5:7 δικαιοσύνην διδάξας ὅλον τὸν κόσμον, καὶ ἐπὶ τὸ τέρμα
τῆς δύσεως ἐλθών· καὶ μαρτυρήσας ἐπὶ τῶν ἡγουμένων,
οὕτως ἀπηλλάγη τοῦ κόσμου, καὶ εἰς τὸν ἅγιον τόπον
ἐπορεύθη [ἀνελήμφθη] ὑπομονῆς γενόμενος μέγιστος
ὑπογραμμός.

6:1 Τούτοις τοῖς ἀνδράσιν ὁσίως πολιτευσαμένοις συνηθροίσθη πολὺ πλῆθος ἐκλεκτῶν, οἵτινες πολλαῖς αἰκίαις
καὶ βασάνοις διὰ ζῆλος παθόντες, ὑπόδειγμα
κάλλιστον ἐγένοντο ἐν ἡμῖν.

6:2 Διὰ ζῆλος διωχθ[ε]ῖσαι γυναῖκες, Δαναΐδες καὶ
Δίρκαι, αἰκίσματα δεινὰ καὶ ἀνόσια παθοῦσαι, ἐπὶ τὸν
τῆς πίστεως βέβαιον δρόμον κατήντησαν καὶ ἔλαβον
γέρας γενναῖον αἱ ἀσθενεῖς τῷ σώματι.

6:3 ζῆλος ἀπηλλοτρίωσεν γαμετὰς ἀνδρῶν καὶ ἠλλοίωσεν
τὸ ῥηθὲν ὑπὸ τοῦ πατρὸς ἡμῶν Ἀδάμ, ΤΟΥ͂ΤΟ
ΝΥ͂Ν ’ΟCΤΟΥ͂Ν ’ΕΚ ΤΩ͂Ν ’ΟCΤΕΩΝ ΜΟΥ ΚΑΙ͂
ΓΑ͂ΡΞ ’ΕΚ ΤΗ͂C ΓΑΡΚΟ͂C ΜΟΥ.

6:4 ζῆλος καὶ ἔρις πόλεις μεγάλης κατέστρεψεν καὶ ἔθνη
μεγάλα ἐξερίζωσεν.

5:6 Seven times he was in chains; he was exiled, stoned, became a herald of the Gospel in East and West, and won
the noble renown which his faith merited.

5:7 To the whole world he taught righteousness, and reaching
the limits of the West he bore his witness before rulers.
And so, released from this world, he was taken up into
the holy place and became the greatest example of
patient endurance.

6:1 To these men who lived such holy lives there was joined
a great multitude of the elect who by reason of rivalry
were victims of many outrages and tortures and who
became outstanding examples among us.

6:2 By reason of rivalry women were persecuted in the roles
of Danaïds and Dircae. Victims of dreadful and blas-
phemous outrages, they ran with sureness the course of
faith to the finish, and despite their physical weakness won
a notable prize.

6:3 It was rivalry that estranged wives from their husbands
and annulled the saying of our father Adam, "This is now
bone of my bone and flesh of my flesh."·

6:4 Rivalry and contention have overthrown great cities and
uprooted mighty nations.

In chapter 4 Clement enumerates seven examples
from the Old Testament in which "rivalry and envy"
are responsible for: fratricide, the fleeing of one brother
from another, persecution of a man by his brothers, the
fleeing of a man from his king, exclusion of a family
from their clan, the casting of two alive into Hades,
and the persecution of a young man by an old king.

To parallel those seven examples from the Old
Testament Clement draws seven examples from
"τῆς γενεᾶς ἡμῶν." This phrase is an aid in the dating
of the letter; if the author were writing immediately
after the persecution under Nero a specific number of
years or "last year" would have been used rather than a
vague term which connotes at least twenty-five and not
more than forty years (A.D. c. 90–105). If the examples
in chapters 5 and 6 are drawn from the time of Nero,
the phrase "our own generation" would still be applicable during the reign of Domitian, about A.D. 96.
While he does not argue against this date for 1 Clement,
Goguel draws attention to the inaccurate use by
Irenaeus (A.D. c. 190) of the term "day" or "generation"
in relation to John whom, Irenaeus claims, had his
revelation "almost in our own day [generation]."[95]

Zahn goes further than is reasonably possible when
he claims that Peter and Paul are οἱ ἔγγιστα γενόμενοι
ἀθληταί in time (τῆς γενεᾶς ἡμῶν) and place, namely
Rome.[96] Rome is not mentioned in the text, and there is
no possible way that this phrase can be interpreted as
definitely indicating Rome. If, after the entire passage
has been examined, it is determined that there is a strong
probability that the author is aware of a tradition that
Peter and Paul were martyred in Rome, then it may be
claimed fairly that this is the understanding behind 5:1.
As far as the text of 5:1 itself is concerned, however,
this conclusion is reached through reading into the
text rather than out of it.

In chapters 42–44 Clement speaks of the apostles as
a group in the past and hardly as members of "our own
generation." How is this to be explained in comparison
with 5:1? It is possible that the feeling of being of one

---

95. *Against Heresies*, V.30:3, *The Ante-Nicene Christian
Library*, IX, 138: "For that was seen no very long time since,
but almost in our own day, towards the end of Domitian's
reign." ἀλλὰ σχεδὸν ἐπὶ τῆς ἡμετέρας γενεᾶς πρὸς τῷ
τέλει τῆς Δομετιανοῦ ἀρχῆς (*MPG*, VII, 1207).

96. Zahn, *Introduction*, II, 69.

generation with the apostles may have become less vivid by A.D. 96. A writer of this period may have felt both a oneness with and a distinct distance from the apostolic generation and would express himself differently at different times. The generation of those who in their youth had known or worked with the apostles in their old age would have flourished between A.D. 60 and 95—a generation which had witnessed the death of James, Peter, and Paul and the persecutions under Nero and Domitian.[97]

The word "ἀθλητής" is used by Clement and later by Ignatius in Polycarp I:3.[98] The earlier use of the word as interpreted by the author of 2 Timothy *may* give us a clue to its meaning in Clement: "An athlete is not crowned unless he competes according to the rules."[99] We cannot be sure whether the meaning of "ἀθλητής" as a metaphor for martyrdom was known to Clement, but it is found in this sense in the *Martyrdom of Polycarp* 18:3.[100] Eusebius also, when speaking of those who have written concerning certain martyrs who waged war for "the peace of the soul, and men who therein have been valiant for truth rather than for country," speaks of "the struggles of the athletes of piety and their valor which braved so much."[101] The reference in the *Acts of Thomas* to Christ as "our true and undefeated 'athlete'" is vague, but martyrdom is suggested in the words that follow: "good shepherd that givest thyself for thine own sheep."[102]

It is obvious, then, that "ἀθλητής" did in time come to mean "martyr," but whether A.D. 96 this word was a conventional rhetorical term as Dibelius presumes[103] or a technical term for "martyr" is not completely clear. Surely the latter is not the meaning in 2 Timothy 2:5, quoted above. When the task of defining "ἀθλητής" in 1 Clement 5:1 is approached from the standpoint of its context, it appears likely that the author refers to those who have suffered martyrdom and not simply to those who have borne great hardships and burdens. A stumbling block is placed in the way of this interpretation, however, if 5:1 is considered as a general introduction to both chapters 5 and 6, for there is no reason to suppose that those mentioned in 6:3 met their *death* by reason of rivalry and envy—and of course the question is irrelevant to the example concerning "great cities and . . . mighty nations" in 6:4.

In the second verse of chapter 5 Clement speaks of the στύλοι, a familiar term from Galatians 2:9, referring to James, Cephas (Peter), and John. As pointed out by Ernest Burton, the term is a common designation in Classical, Jewish and Christian, writers for those who are in places of responsibility.[104] It may be admitted that στύλοι as used in 1 Clement 5:2 is not limited to Peter and Paul but includes a wider circle of apostles, and if not used in the precise manner of Galatians 2:9, it *may* also include others who suffered martyrdom in the Early Church—Stephen, the sons of Zebedee, James the Brother of the Lord, and others. The definite limitation of the term by Heussi to Paul and the Twelve is unjustified.[105]

The statement follows that these "Pillars" were persecuted because of "rivalry and envy unto death (ἕως θανάτου)." This clearly signifies that the persecution ended in death and does not mean that the "Pillars" were persecuted as long as they lived.[106] If 5:2 is

---

97. For further mention of this phrase see Harnack, *Die Chronologie*, I, 252, and Katzenmeyer, "Zur Frage," p. 133.

98. Lightfoot, *Apostolic Fathers*, Part II, Vol. II, p. 335; *Early Christian Fathers*, trans. Richardson, p. 118.

99. In 2 Timothy 2:5: "ἐὰν δὲ καὶ ἀθλῇτις, οὐ στεφανοῦται ἐὰν μὴ νομίμως ἀθλήσῃ." (*Novum Testamentum Graece*, 23d ed., eds. Nestle and Aland, p. 537.)

100. "In memory of those athletes who have gone before," Massey H. Shepherd, in *Early Christian Fathers*, p. 156.

101. *E. H.* V.1:1 (Lake, I, 407).

102. *Acts of Thomas* XXXIX; James, *The Apocryphal New Testament*, p. 384. See also Stauffer, "ἀθληταί," *Theologisches Wörterbuch zum N.T.* (1933), I, 167; Harnack, *Einführung*, p. 106; Altaner, "War Petrus in Rom?" p. 180; Calder, "Studies in Early Christian Epigraphy," p. 52. This meaning is also emphasized in Toynbee and Perkins, *The Shrine of St. Peter*, p. 131.

103. Dibelius, "Rom und die Christen," p. 22. Compare Heb. 12:1.

104. Burton, *The Epistle of Paul to the Galatians*, p. 96, mentions Euripides, *Iphigenia in Tauris* LVII, στύλοι γάρ οἴκων παῖδές εἰσιν ἄρσενες in ed. Flagg, p. 61; and in trans. Brynner *et al.*, II, 125, "The pillar of the family is the son."

105. *Die römische Petrustradition*, p. 14. Harnack, *Einführung*, p. 106, limits στύλοι even further to Peter and Paul, as does Giet, "Le Témoignage de Clément," p. 130.

106. Lightfoot, *Apostolic Fathers*, Part I, Vol. II, p. 493; Zahn, *Introduction*, II, 71; Katzenmeyer, "Zur Frage," p. 134; "dass der Tod der zeitliche Endpunkt ihres Kampfes war."

compared with 4:9 ("It was rivalry that caused Joseph to be persecuted as far as [up to] death [μέχρι θανάτου]"), it is Heussi's claim that there remains no grounds to insist that the persecution of the "Pillars" ended in death.[107] But it cannot be argued that there is sufficient distinction between μέχρι and ἕως to account for a radical difference in exegesis.

While Heussi's argument cannot be supported on the basis of a comparison of the meanings of "μέχρι" and "ἕως," there is some defense in the fact that in 4:9 μέχρι θανάτου is followed by μέχρι δουλείας εἰσελθεῖν, which definitely indicates that "μέχρι" here implies a point short of death itself. In the instance of 5:2, however, there is no such qualifying phrase, and the persecution is best understood in *this* case as ending in the death of Peter. Furthermore, there is a sense of finality in ἕως; the word often indicates a temporal end[108] and in one case also a definite geographical end point.[109]

Cullmann is correct in warning that "we must take into consideration the deliberately artificial arrangement of this section,"[110] but he is unjustified in countering Heussi's proposal (that the "Pillars" did not actually die under their persecution) by stating that the words "ἕως θανάτου" in 5:2 "are probably not merely rhetorical emotion as they are in the example of Joseph."[111] This may be true, but the assumption cannot be supported by the text.

The following verse has a degree of importance which is dependent upon a particular understanding of the structure. The question is whether ἡμῶν goes with ὀφθαλμῶν or ἀποστόλους. If it is related to the former, then the meaning of the phrase gives no support to the assumption that Peter and Paul had any unique relationship to Rome. If it is related to the latter, then the close relationship of Peter and Paul to Rome is suggested. Heussi in his earlier works held that ἡμῶν modified ὀφθαλμῶν, but recently has changed his position.[112] Zahn believes that ἡμῶν in this instance stands in an emphatic place before τοὺς ἀγαθοὺς ἀποστόλους.[113] The ἡμῶν is related to the τῆς γενεᾶς ἡμῶν which went before (5:1) and the ἐν ἡμῖν which follows (6:1). His position is weakened, however, by the use of ἡμῶν with ἀπόστολοι in the beginning of chapter 44, where ἀπόστολοι refers to all the apostles.[114] If this were a later period, it might

---

107. In *Die Christliche Welt*, p. 164; *Die römische Petrustradition*, p. 14. Lietzmann, "Petrus römischer Märtyrer," p. 398, considers this to be a weak argument. Compare Giet, "Le Témoignage de Clément," p. 133, "Clément ayant abordé chaque cas, poursuit la notice des apôtres jusqu'à leur mort, avant de passer à la notice suivante."

108. In 1 Clement 11:2, 50:3, 63:3.

109. *Ibid.* 25:3: "When it is full-fledged, it takes the burial nest containing the bones of its predecessor and manages to carry them all the way from Arabia to the Egyptian (ἀπὸ τῆς Ἀραβικῆς ἕως τῆς Αἰγύπτου εἰς τὴν λεγομένην ἡλιούπολιν) city called Heliopolis."

110. *Peter*, p. 93.

111. *Ibid.*, p. 93n99. Cullmann's opinion that the words in 4:9 are "rhetorical emotion" is based upon the assumption that the theme announced in 3:4 and 9:1 is a controlling one. If this were so, then either the example of Joseph would not have been used at all or the qualifying phrase "reduced to slavery" would have been omitted. It is not that 4:9 is "rhetorical emotion" while 5:2 is not, but that the two are not parallel and were not intended to be parallel.

Parallel cases for suffering *short of death* could have been derived from the recent past with ease, since the author would have found an ample number of examples among those who were touched by persecution. But as Cullmann says [*Peter*, p. 92]: "We must note the difficulty which Clement inevitably encountered finding for the relatively short period of the recent (that is, the Christian) past the number of examples that would correspond with the group taken from the Old Testament."

112. *Die römische Petrustradition*, p. 14. While admitting that "ἡμῶν" is related to "ἀποστόλους," he emphasizes that the "our" before "apostle" does not mean that Peter thereby *must* be considered as a member of the same group as that to which Clement belongs. Heussi calls attention to instances where the personal pronoun stands before the possessive but is *un*emphasized: 1 Clement 7:1: "καὶ ὁ αὐτὸς ἡμῖν ἀγὼν ἐπίκειται"; 36:2 "διὰ τούτου ἠνεῴχθησαν ἡμῶν οἱ ὀφθαλμοὶ τῆς καρδίς"; and 38:1 "Σωζέσθω οὖν ἡμῶν ὅλον τὸ σῶμα ἐν χριστῷ Ἰησοῦ." From the point of view of grammar his position is well taken. The examples cited, however, do not afford the same possibility of confusion as does 5:4. Compare Aland, "Petrus in Rom," p. 514.

113. *Introduction*, II, 69. See also Monceaux, "L'Apostolat de Saint Pierre," p. 225, who emphasizes that the construction intimates that Peter and Paul have a relationship both with Rome and with Corinth. Another understanding would result in a platitude, "Let us set before our eyes," and Monceaux believes that Clement is incapable of platitudes. See Goguel, *L'Église primitive*, p. 205n3.

114. Richardson, *Early Christian Fathers*, p. 46, and Lightfoot, *Apostolic Fathers*, Part I, Vol. II, p. 274, have preferred to take ἡμῶν with ὀφθαλμῶν.

be presumed on extratextual grounds that Clement is referring to local martyrs—those whose graves were "known" to lie within the vicinity of Rome, that is, Clement is invoking "the memory of the Roman Apostles, Peter and Paul; a memory which remained alive in the local community."[115] The adjective ἀγαθοὺς in the phrase τοὺς ἀγαθοὺς ἀποστόλους is a term of "affectionate remembrance and not an impersonal substitute for πρότους or ἀγίους."[116]

The theory of Zahn, Monceaux, Heussi, and others that ἡμῶν is to be taken with τοὺς ἀγαθοὺς ἀποστόλους rather than with ὀφθαλμῶν has been very forcefully challenged by Giet.[117] He notes that in sixty of the sixty-three times that Clement uses ἡμῶν it follows the word it modifies. The remaining three cases (15:2, 36:2, 38:1) present unique problems, which is *not* true of 5:3. The verse, therefore, should be translated "Let us set before our eyes the good apostles." The "our" is not to be understood, he believes, in the broad sense of "we Christians" nor necessarily in the strictly limited sense of "we Romans." More likely the "our" refers to both the Romans *and* the Corinthians: The author "désire vraisemblablement remettre sous les yeux de ses correspondants une image familière, celle *d'apôtres dont ils connaissent la bonté* et qui ont donné aussi peu de prise que possible à la jalousie."[118]

The meaning of the word "μαρτυρήσας" is of central importance in 5:4. Related to the problem of its meaning is the question of cause as indicated by διὰ ζῆλον and the question of result indicated by τόπον τῆς δόξης.

There is some difference of opinion concerning the meaning of μάρτυς (μαρτυρεῖν) in the period in which 1 Clement was written. The great majority, however, see the later meaning of "martyr" as appropriate here, especially in view of the context.[119] Others are more

doubtful,[120] and some, such as Heussi, completely reject the possibility. The phrase "after he had borne witness," Heussi claims, does not mean that Peter died a martyr's death; such a conclusion is only read into the text from the meaning given to the word in a later period. At the end of the first century the verb "μαρτυρεῖν" in no instance referred to martyrdom, and the noun "μάρτυς," as in the case of Stephen (Acts 22:20), merely indicated a "witness" to Christ: "Stephen was not a witness *because* his blood was poured out, rather he was

---

115. Monceaux, "L'Apostolat de Saint Pierre," p. 226.

116. Lightfoot, *Apostolic Fathers*, Part I, Vol. II, p. 25. Compare Harnack, *Einführung*, p. 107, who takes ἀγαθούς here to mean "tapfer" (valiant). Clarke, *The First Epistle of Clement*, p. 89, agrees with Harnack.

117. Giet, "Le Témoignage de Clément," pp. 124–30.

118. *Ibid.*, p. 130.

119. The noun "μάρτυς" is used in the New Testament frequently for a testimony in blood; Acts 22:20; Rev. 1:5,

---

2:13, 3:14, 17:6. The word can be traced, at least after the middle of the second century, in both noun and verb forms, to mean martyrdom: Melito of Sardis in *E. H.* IV.26:3 (Lake, I, 387) and Dionysius of Corinth, *E. H.* II.25:8 (Lake, I, 183); Hegesippus, *E. H.* II.23:18, IV.22:3 (Lake, I, 175, 375).

The meaning "martyrdom" is accepted by Lightfoot, *Apostolic Fathers*, Part I, Vol. II, pp. 27, 493; Zahn, *Introduction*, II, 70, 71; Lietzmann, "Petrus römischer Märtyrer," p. 394; Delehaye, in *Analecta Bollandiana* (1921), p. 44; Harnack, *Einführung*, p. 107; Campenhausen, *Die Idee des Martyriums in der alten Kirche*, p. 54; Altaner, "War Petrus in Rom?" pp. 179, 184, and "Neues zum Verständnis vom I Clem. V:1–6, 2," pp. 25–30 where Altaner devoted a short article to this problem; Molland, "Petrus in Rom," p. 441; Dibelius, "Rom und die Christen," p. 27; Cullmann, *Peter*, p. 96; Toynbee and Perkins, *The Shrine of St. Peter*, p. 131.

R. Reitzenstein, *Bemerkungen zur Martyrien literatur* (1929), p. 438 (cited by Heussi, *Die römische Petrustradition*, p. 17), claims that "μαρτυρήσας" is to be understood in relation to the sufferings "of which the end is death." The *sufferings* are the witness. Heussi would agree except that he does not believe that Clement intended to say that the sufferings did end in death.

120. Katzenmeyer, "Zur Frage," p. 136, points out that although the meaning only later came to be associated with martyrdom, the definition *seems* to be required by the context, especially in light of the words which immediately follow. Goguel, *L'Église primitive*, p. 206, is more doubtful: "the idea of a martyrdom is not excluded"; compare Munck, *Petrus und Paulus in der Offenbarung Johannis*, p. 61. Strathmann, in *Theologisches Wörterbuch*, IV, 511, sees the opinion (that the word refers here to martyrdom) as disputed. The martyr-death of Paul is certain, but in the case of Peter it is a question of his sufferings and not of his death. Strathmann bases his decision in part on the fact that the words "μαρτυρεῖν" and "μάρτυς" for martyrdom are unknown in Ignatius and Justin and seen first only in the relatively late *Martyrdom of Polycarp* 19:1. Bauer, in *Wiener Studien*, pp. 282 ff., also held that Peter and Paul in 1 Clement 5 are not shown as martyrs, but "die ersten Autoritäten der Kirche."

a witness and *therefore* his blood was poured out."[121] Even in the beginning of the third century, says Heussi the noun did not necessarily mean martyrdom but could also indicate the witness one gave to Christ while living.[122]

Interestingly, Heussi marshals in support of his position the very passages in Revelation which most commentators cite to support their view that "μαρτυ-ρήσας" in the first century indicated martyrdom. He contends that even if it is conceded that the noun "μάρτυς" may possibly mean "martyr" in this period, the verb does not. Another verb "ἀποκτενεῖν" which is found in Revelation 2:13 is used to indicate that one has died for the faith. In this same verse the noun "μάρτυς" also appears and refers to a "witness." Antipas is not a "witness" *because* he was killed, but he was killed *because* he was a witness. Nevertheless, Heussi will not allow that the verb "μαρτυρεῖν" was used to indicate the suffering of the death of a martyr until around A.D. 160 and claims that it is indefensible to recognize in 1 Clement 5:4, 7 a meaning for the word which it did not possess until a half century after the document was written. His thesis is strengthened somewhat by the fact that Clement did not mention Stephen, the sons of Zebedee, and James in this passage along with Peter and Paul. These last two apostles were mentioned alone, he maintains, because they were the greatest of all the apostles and they both had suffered many troubles. The emphasis throughout is upon their troubles and not upon their death.[123]

In an earlier articles in *Die Christliche Welt*, Heussi had maintained that the death of Paul is only indicated by the words "ἀπηλλάγη τοῦ κόσμου" which follow μαρτυ-ρήσας. No such phrase expands upon the witnessing of Peter. He has not "witnessed" before a court (the sentence of which carried the death penalty for Paul), but only through his sufferings, which need not be interpreted as ending in his death.

It must be pointed out against Heussi's conclusions that if στύλοι in 5:2 refers to *both* Peter and Paul, then it means that both apostles were at least in danger of death. Furthermore, since the passage clearly states that Paul was martyred, a different understanding of ἕως θανάτου in relation to Peter is hardly admissible.[124] It appears also that μαρτυρεῖν is more than "on the way to becoming the technical term for martyrdom."[125] It has arrived, even if very recently, and its assured use in the sense of "martyr" in the noun form, at least in Acts and Revelation, is difficult to dispute.

Undoubtedly, the Neronian persecution had a great deal to do with the development of the meaning of the word "μαρτυρεῖν" in the direction of "martyrdom" although the earlier meaning of "witness" was not discarded. It has been pointed out concerning Peter that the details found in 1 Clement 5 may be little more than what could have been derived from Acts 12.[126] This is an attractive hypothesis; however, faced with the parallel wording in the notice concerning Paul, which must be

---

121. *Die römische Petrustradition*, p. 24. He claims support for his position from Seneca, *Epistles* XX:9, to the cynic Demetrius; see also Epictetus I.29:47–49, III.22:86, IV.8:32. The evidence from the *Epistle* of Seneca is not valid since the word "Testis" (witness) is used, which tells us nothing concerning the word "μάρτυς" (see Seneca, *Epistles* XX trans. Gumere, pp. 138, 139). He is justified, however, in calling attention to the references in *Epictetus* I.29:46 ff., trans. Oldfather, I, 198, 199; see also *Epictetus* III.22:86 (*ibid.*, II, 160, 161) and IV.8:32 (*ibid.*, II, 386, 387).

122. E. H. III. 20:6 (Lake, I, 239); Tertullian, *Against Valentinus* IV, "Sed alium ex martyrii praerogativa locis potitum indignatus, de Ecclesia authenticae regulae abrupti" (*MPL*, II, 516); "Being indignant, however, that another obtained the dignity by reason of a claim which confessorship [martyrii] had given him, he broke with the Church of the true faith." (*The Ante-Nicene Fathers*, III, 505). E. H. V.18:5–7 (Lake, I, 489).

123. Compare Lightfoot, *Apostolic Fathers*, Part I, Vol. II, p. 493. Peter and Paul alone are mentioned by name and not such martyrs as Stephen and James, "because Clement was appealing to examples which they themselves [the Romans] had witnessed."

124. This untenable view of Heussi was attacked in the same year that it was advanced by Molland, "Petrus in Rom," p. 441 and Altaner, "War Petrus in Rom?" pp. 187–88.

125. Zahn, *Introduction*, p. 71; Cullmann, *Peter*, p. 96; Guarducci, *The Tomb of St. Peter*, p. 31.

126. This is the thesis of a brief article of Morton Smith (*New Testament Studies*, VII [1960], 86–88) who holds that all of Clement's remarks concerning Peter in Chapter 5 are derived from Acts, which nullifies the value of this testimony as evidence for Peter's Roman martyrdom. Compare the following verses: 1 Clement 5:1, 2 with Acts 12:1, 2; and 1 Clement 5:4 with Acts 12:4–12, 17. Note the possible relationship between "Then he departed

accepted as a reference to martyrdom, it does not add to our understanding of 1 Clement 5.

Granted that Clement testifies to the martyrdom of Peter and Paul, what lay behind this martyrdom? This is the question that for the most part has been neglected. The key to the explanation lies in the meaning of ζῆλος. Cullmann in 1930 suggested that "la jalousie engendre le malheur."[127] In his *Epistle to the Corinthians*, Clement uses ζῆλος sixteen times, φθόνος four times, and ἔρις three times. These terms indicate interparty friction and jealousy, the presence of which in the Roman Church led to the martyrdom of Peter and Paul.[128] The Christians themselves were indirectly responsible for the death of the two apostles since their internal strife had moved the Roman government to intervene in order to maintain order. This explanation prompts the question: Why was Clement not more explicit? A satisfactory answer lies in the fact that such information was not at all edifying, and the details would have added little to the argument of Clement. The particulars (how, when, and where) concerning the death of Peter and Paul were not important. What was important was the end result, precipitated by the disorder and friction within a Christian Church. Clement exhorted the Corinthians to learn from what had happened in the distant and recent past as a result of interparty rivalry so that they might not meet with similar disaster.[129] Chapter 47 appears to support this interpretation; Clement clearly reminds the Corinthians of the letter

written to them years before by Paul himself in which the apostle warned them concerning factiousness. How disgraceful it is, Clement continues, that "because of one or two individuals the Corinthian Church is now in revolt against the presbyters." He further warns that by such activity the Corinthians are "exposing themselves to danger."[130] Notice too the similarity between the vocabulary used by Clement in chapter 5 and that used by Paul in Philippians 1:15 when he speaks of interparty rivalry: φθόνος, ἔρις, ἐριθεία.

What could have precipitated this interparty rivalry at Corinth? A convincing answer is given by Cullmann. After Antioch (Gal. 2:11–14) Peter had come more and more under the influence of Paul and by A.D. 64 both apostles had been repudiated by the Jewish Christians, whose opposition was behind the decision of the Roman authorities to intervene.[131]

Tacitus adds his support to the theory that some interparty strife was involved when he writes concerning the persecution under Nero: "Igitur primum correpti, qui fatebantur, deinde, *indicio eorum*, multitudo ingens, haud perinde in crimine incendii quam odio humani generis, convicti sunt."[132]

The theory of Cullmann is challenged by Munck on the ground that, while the Old Testament examples undoubtedly illustrate the evil workings of jealousy, the case is not so obvious in the more recent examples.[133] It is not clear to Munck that "ζῆλος" can mean jealousy among members of the same group:[134] "Here [1 Clement 5] it is a question concerning a direct opposition between the Church and the heathen world, and ζῆλος must mean there evil zeal, not however, jealousy."[135]

---

and went to another place" (Acts 12:17) and "went to the glorious place which he merited" (1 Clement 5:4).

Note also that the "witnessing" mentioned in 1 Clement 5:4 *could* be interpreted to mean the words spoken by Peter to those in the house of Mary in Acts 12:17 rather than a suggestion of martyrdom.

127. "Les Causes de la Mort de Pierre et de Paul," pp. 294–300. See also Cullmann, *Peter*, pp. 102 f.

128. This view may find support in *The Shepherd of Hermas* (A.D. c. 148) 3.2:2 (*The Apostolic Fathers*, trans. Lake, II, 19): "your seed Hermas, have set God at naught and have blasphemed the Lord, and have betrayed their parents in great wickedness and they are called the betrayers of parents, and their betrayal has not profited them." Compare the views of Munck and Giet, below, p. 79.

129. This same reason that such a discussion would be unedifying may lie behind the absence of any mention of the final days or the death of Peter and Paul in the Book of Acts.

---

130. Does he not perhaps mean danger of intervention by the Roman authorities as was the case a generation ago when through such interparty jealousy "Peter suffered . . ."?

131. "Les Causes de la Mort de Pierre et de Paul," p. 300. *Early Christian Fathers*, trans. Richardson, p. 46n27, also mentions this possibility.

132. *Annals* XV.44, trans. Jackson, pp. 282, 283. Giet, "Le Témoignage de Clément," p. 344, questions that Tacitus refers here to interparty jealousy.

133. Munck, *Petrus und Paulus in der Offenbarung Johannis*, pp. 60, 61.

134. See Stumpf, "ζῆλος," pp. 879 f. Compare 1 Clement 45:4, where "ζῆλος" has a good meaning.

135. Munck, *Petrus und Paulus in der Offenbarung Johannis*, pp. 60, 61.

Stanislas Giet also challenges the conclusions of Cullmann at this point.[136] He admits that certain of the Old Testament examples can be construed to fit the pattern of internal jealousies, but not all. And in the New Testament examples none is most convincingly explained in this way. It is more probable, he maintains, that the meaning is to be found in the jealousy of the Jews. Both Peter and Paul had suffered at the hands of this group, and it is most natural to think that "comparant ces examples de l'Ancien Testament à ceux du passé chrétien, il mît en regard la jalousie entre Israélites et celle qui oppose les frères de la religion nouvelle."[137] He admits, however, that "il y ait eu à Rome, vers la fin du règne de Néron, des dissensions dans l'Église, c'est fort possible: le texte de Clément n'exclut pas cette hypothèse, mais il ne la fonde pas."[138]

Despite the objection levelled by Munck, Cullmann iterates his position in *Peter, Disciple, Apostle, Martyr*[139] and explains further that διὰ ζῆλον in 5:4 is related grammatically both to the bearing of the sufferings by Peter and to the result, "he went to the place of glory." In the verse following 5:5, which is concerned with Paul, the grammatical connection between διὰ ζῆλον καὶ ἔριν and martyrdom is not a necessary one, but this is clearly the intention of the author. Finally, Cullmann calls attention to the similar motif in 2 Corinthians 2:26 and 1 Clement 3:4, 9.

If jealousy, in a form which existed within the Christian community itself had precipitated the martyrdom of Peter, what, according to Clement, was the direct result of the martyrdom? The answer to this question involves a discussion of the grammatical relationship of καὶ οὕτω. If the words are understood in one way, the interpretation of 5:4 as evidence for a Roman martyrdom of Peter is jeopardized, and if in another way, then the words introduce an explanation of what happened as a result of the martyrdom of Peter.

Heussi consistently maintains that καὶ οὕτω is related to μαρτυρήσας and means simply "thus having witnessed [by his suffering] Peter went."[140] This connotes that the sufferings did not lead to death and that there was an indefinite time between the witnessing and the going. According to the more widely accepted interpretation καὶ οὕτω is related to ἐπορεύθη which expresses result: "thus [Peter], having witnessed, went." (If the "going to the promised land" is a result of witnessing, this is further evidence that "witnessing" means martyrdom.)[141]

From the grammatical point of view the most convincing explanation indicates an intimate cause-and-effect relationship between καὶ οὕτω and ἐπορεύθη (aorist).[142] There is a relationship between a happening in the past and a direct result which, from the point of view in Clement, is also in the past: "Thus having witnessed, he went."[143]

The term "ὀφειλόμενον" clearly reflects the primitive Christian belief that the suffering of martyrdom insured the right to, or made a claim upon, heaven.[144] This is

---

136. "Le Témoignage de Clément," pp. 130–32, 333–45.

137. *Ibid.*, p. 337.

138. *Ibid.*, p. 345.

139. *Peter*, pp. 102 f. The reasons which he gives for the fact that more details do not appear and for the abruptness of the ending of Acts are the same given in his article written in 1930. He also refers (*Peter*, p. 108) to the motif of jealousy which appears in Mark 15:10—jealousy is behind the handing over of Jesus to Pilate.

140. For example, *Die römische Petrustradition*, p. 23. The possibility has been suggested that καὶ οὕτω μαρτυρήσας refers to Acts 12:17. Peter *witnessed* to his miraculous escape from prison and then "ἐπορεύθη εἰς ἔτερον τόπον.." This general view presupposes that all that Clement writes concerning Peter is derived from the New Testament. But see Oscar de Gebhardt and Adolf Harnack, "Clementis Romani ad Corinthos quae dicuntur Epistulae," *Patrum Apostolorum*, Fasc. I, Part II, Ed. 2, pp. liii–liv, "attamen ea quae p. 145 collegi, certe non sufficiunt ad usum Actorum in ep. nostra probandum." See Lightfoot, *Apostolic Fathers*, Part I, Vol. II, p. 516.

141. *Early Christian Fathers*, trans. Richardson, p. 46; Cullmann, *Peter*, p. 95n96. Compare E. H. II.23:18 in which Eusebius (or Hegesippus) explains the martyrdom of James in the same way: "καὶ οὕτως ἐμαρτύρησεν" (Lake, I, 175).

142. Harnack, *Einführung*, p. 107, sees ἐπορεύθη [A,C] (vss. 4 and [?] 7) as equivalent to ἀνελήμφθη [Latin, Syriac, and Coptic versions for 5:7] which refes to "ascension" or "assumption" in apostolic symbolism.

143. See Altaner, "War Petrus in Rom?" pp. 180, 181. Campenhausen, *Die Idee des Martyriums in der alten Kirche*, pp. 54–55, explains that the οὕτω in the expressions "καὶ οὕτω μαρτυρήσας" and "καὶ μαρτυρήσας . . . οὕτως ἀπηλλάγη τοῦ κόσμου" belongs to the technical expressions used in the reports of martyrdoms. See also Molland, "Petrus in Rom," p. 441.

144. Lietzmann, "Petrus römischer Märtyrer," p. 395.

interpreted otherwise by Heussi who sees here a reference to Peter's being worthy of earthly happiness due to his confession and witnessing concerning Christ. Once the basic assumption is made, in accordance with which the whole passage is interpreted, both views can be defended.

A more detailed notice concerning the life of Paul begins in 5:5. The length implies that Clement had either *more* information concerning Paul or more of the type of information which was useful for his present purpose. Actually there is little contained in the notice which could not have been derived from 1 and 2 Corinthians, Romans and perhaps Acts or the traditions behind Acts. The "rivalry and contention" (1 Clement 5:5) may be assumed behind all of the difficulties which Paul details in various places. Parallel to 1 Clement 5:5, 2 Corinthians 11:23–28 mentions "far more imprisonments," "once I was stoned," and "on frequent journeys." The "prize for patient endurance" mentioned by Clement could easily have been written after a reading of Romans 5:3,[145] 1 Corinthians 9:24,[146] and 2 Corinthians 1:6.[147] The reference to the "limits of the West" could be a deduction from Romans 15:24, 28.[148] The claim that "he [Paul] bore witness before rulers" is mentioned explicitly in Acts 16:19 f. and 18:12 f.[149] The indication of these parallels is not meant to imply that Clement is necessarily dependent upon these sources although acquaintance with 1 Corinthians is fairly obvious (chapters 24, 49, and 50).[150] The facts which lay behind these passages in the letters of Paul and Acts may have been common knowledge, may even have been told over and over in the meetings of the

Roman Church by "the trustworthy and discreet persons who from youth to old age have lived irreproachable lives among us."[151] The surprising factor is, however, if 1 Clement 5 were not mainly dependent upon the letters of Paul and Acts, why is the notice of Peter so much shorter? In consideration of the amount of material written in the second century concerning Peter in Rome, it would seem plausible that, if the tradition were trustworthy, the basic elements would have been mentioned by Clement. The explanation for his silence must lie therefore either in the tradition not being trustworthy or in the *purpose* for which the letter was written.

In keeping with his theory that Clement is presenting Peter and Paul as examples of the "philosophical athlete," Dibelius points out that Paul alone is a good example for Clement's purpose.[152] Peter was not a κήρυξ of the "Gospel of Christ to the East and West." Perhaps, Dibelius ventures, he never carried the Gospel in the West at all. The wandering career of Paul, on the other hand, can be pictured as similar to that of the "athlete" Heracles who, according to Dio Cassius, wandered over Europe and Asia.

The comparative brevity of the notice of Peter has given some concern to many writers on the subject. Harnack imagines that the facts of the life of Peter were so well known in the Roman and Corinthian churches that further mention of them was unnecessary.[153] This assumption is contested by Heussi who is sure that if Clement had known more about the career of Peter he would have said so.[154] Goguel also refuses to see the notice of Peter as a condensation of what is known, and while conceding that the passage cannot be treated as an

---

145. "More than that, we rejoice in our sufferings, knowing that suffering produces endurance." Compare Acts 9:22 ff. and 13:44 ff.

146. "Do you not know that in a race all runners compete, but only one receives the prize? So run that you may obtain it."

147. "It is for your comfort, which you experience when you patiently endure the same sufferings that we suffer."

148. Rom. 15:24, "I hope to see you in passing as I go to Spain, and to be sped on my journey there, by you." Rom. 15:28, "I shall go on by way of you to Spain."

149. Acts 16:19 f., "they seized Paul and Silas and dragged them into the market place before the rulers." Acts 18:12 f., "But when Gallio was proconsul of Achaia, the Jews made a united attack upon Paul, and brought him before the tribunal."

150. See *The First Epistle of Clement*, ed. Clarke, pp. 30–36.

151. 1 Clement 63:3, *Early Christian Fathers*, trans. Richardson, p. 73. See Zahn, *Introduction*, II, 60.

152. "Rom und die Christen," pp. 27 f. Paul is the one who suffers with perseverance, and in the notices of Paul we find such "philosophical" terms as "ὑπομονή," "πόνοι," and "ἔργα." In addition (p. 29) Peter's notice is purposely short for political reasons. Clement did not wish to foment political unrest. See also Goguel, *The Birth of Christianity*, p. 553. See 1 Clement 20:11, 34:7, 40:4–41:2, 57:2, 60:4, 61:1, 63:4, 65:1. In these passages Clement preaches obedience, mutual trust, and peace.

153. Harnack, *Einführung*, p. 107.

154. *War Petrus in Rom?* p. 27.

historical source he maintains that it does not suggest further knowledge but ignorance.[155] If we concede that Clement knew at least some of the letters of Paul, the criticisms of Heussi and Goguel are not completely valid, for the comparative brevity of the notice of Paul is then *also* astonishing. From Paul's letters there is a great deal more that Clement might have added about the apostle to the Gentiles but did not. Therefore, he may also have had more material or more specific material concerning the life and martyrdom of Peter, but he chose *not* to use it.[156] The explanation of why he did not use it may be found in a combination of the views of Harnack and Dibelius. On the one hand, the facts concerning the life of Peter were so well known in A.D. 96 that mention of them was unnecessary. On the other hand, only certain general elements of the Petrine tradition were included since these alone contributed to the argument that Clement was presenting to the Corinthians. Prudence also may have been a factor in the brevity of the notice; Clement may have refrained from mentioning details that would have endangered relations between the Church and the State.

Whatever the conclusion is concerning the comparative lengths of the notices of Peter and Paul, it cannot be disputed that the notices are intended to be parallel. Both Peter and Paul suffer and witness (are martyred) and go to the "holy place" (or the "place of glory"). The sufferings and martyrdom of Peter were caused διὰ ζῆλον ἄδικον and those of Paul διὰ ζῆλον καὶ ἔριν. These terms are most often interpreted as allusions to the hate and jealousy of the evil world for the children of God,[157] but they are explained more convincingly as indicating friction between various groups within the Christian Church itself. As Cullmann indicated in

an article,[158] in the seven Old Testament examples and those from τῆς γενεᾶς ἡμῶν the suffering was caused by ζῆλος, φθόνος, and ἔρις. The disputes were between those who were closely related, between brothers, and between friends. The last two in both series of examples dealt with some form of ζῆλος and ἔρις, namely that which existed between married couples and citizens of the same country and the same city.

The "seven times he [Paul] was in chains" appears to provide further grist for the mill of those who seek to prove that there is no historical value in 1 Clement 5.[159] There is no record in the New Testament of the tradition of seven imprisonments of Paul. In addition to the "far more imprisonments" mentioned in 2 Corinthians 11:23, there are only the two other known imprisonments, at Philippi and at Rome. Some have suggested that Clement added the captivities at Philippi and Rome to the "five" mentioned in 2 Corinthians 11:24, which would be a convenient solution were it not for the fact that the "five" refers to beatings and has nothing whatsoever to do with imprisonments. The reference to "seven imprisonments" leads Lightfoot to guess that Clement "must have derived his more precise information from some other source."[160] This is countered from an unexpected quarter. Heussi is probably right in stating that "seven times" indicates nothing more precise than "very often."

While opposing the interpretation that 1 Clement 5 alludes to the martyrdom of Peter, Heussi supports the view that we do find a reference to the martyrdom of Paul in this passage. He claims that κήρυξ is parallel to the μαρτυρήσας in the notice of Peter (5:4) and refers to Paul as a witness, that is, herald, of Christ.[161]

An interesting problem in 5:7 surrounds the meaning of ἐπὶ τὸ τέρμα τῆς δύσεως. Does "the limits of the

---

155. *L'Église primitive*, p. 208. Lietzmann's explanation, "Petrus römischer Märtyrer," p. 396, is unconvincing: "Seine [Peter's] Reise nach Rom steht hinter der weltumspannenden Wirksamkeit des Paulus so stark zurück. . .."

156. Compare Heussi, *Die römische Petrustradition*, p. 29.

157. Lietzmann, "Petrus römischer Märtyrer," p. 394; Munck, *Petrus und Paulus in der Offenbarung Johannis*, p. 63. Leclercq, *DACL*, VII, 491, and *The First Epistle of Clement*, ed. Clarke, p. 89, imagine that this is a reference to Jewish denunciations. This is hardly the case as Goguel, *The Birth of Christianity*, p. 503, and Cullmann, *Peter*, p. 102n22, point out.

158. "Les Causes de la Mort de Pierre et de Paul," pp. 295 ff.

159. Conversely, it might be argued that it favors the opinion that 1 Clement 5 has some historical reliability since it depends upon sources *other than* the Pauline Epistles.

160. *Apostolic Fathers*, Part I, Vol. I, p. 29. Also Dibelius, "Rom und die Christen," p. 25.

161. Heussi, *Die römische Petrustradition*, p. 17, indicates that support for this interpretation of the word "κήρυξ" can be found in 1 Timothy 2:7, 2 Timothy 1:11, and 2 Peter 2:5.

West" refer to Spain or Rome?[162] The importance of the question for this part of my study is paramount: if the two notices of Peter and Paul are parallel and related temporally and geographically, then it is necessary to locate where Paul witnessed "before the rulers" and was executed in order to locate where Peter was martyred. In Romans 15:24, 28 Paul mentioned a projected trip to Spain, and it would seem that 1 Clement 5:7 proves that what had been planned did take place. This confirmation appears more explicitly in the *Muratorian Canon* XXXVII.[163] That Spain is a plausible translation for τὸ τέρμα τῆς δύσεως is plain from a passage in Strabo.[164] If one agrees that Spain is meant by "the limit of the West" and that ἐλθών and μαρτυρήσας are related temporally and geographically, then it must be concluded that Paul reached Spain, appeared before the rulers (or magistrates) in that area and died there. However, if Spain is still accepted as the meaning, but the close temporal relationship between ἐλθών and μαρτυρήσας is not deemed necessary, then Paul may have reached Spain, been tried there, and then returned

to Rome for execution. The problem, however, is that there is no hint of any appreciable interval between the time he reached the "limits of the West" and the time "he bore his witness." In the absence of such an indication, it is most natural (but not imperative) to take the two together as following one upon the other.[165] If this is so, then Paul died in Spain or in Rome.

If Clement was writing from Rome, which is not disputed, and had meant to indicate Spain,[166] would he not have been more explicit? Furthermore, if Peter and Paul had died in Spain, how is one to explain the absence of any mention to this effect in the early tradition and the apparent close temporal and geographical relationship between the Roman martyrdom of the "great multitude of the elect"[167] (mentioned in 6:1) and that of Peter and Paul?

If it is claimed that Paul visited Spain at all, but did not die there, then it must be accepted that there were two imprisonments in Rome and that Paul visited Spain in between these two visits. Such tradition is only found in a disputed portion of the *Acts of Peter* and later writings dependent upon it.[168]

While it is difficult to explain that a man living in Rome would refer to Rome as the "limits of the West," any more than a man living in Arizona would claim that Tucson was the limit of the West, the absence of a

---

162. Zahn, *Introduction*, II, 72–75, discusses the whole problem and concludes that Clement intended that Rome should be understood here. Lightfoot, *Apostolic Fathers*, Part I, Vol. II, pp. 30–31, agrees, as does Heussi, *Die römische Petrustradition*, pp. 62–68. Compare Schmiedel, *Encyclopaedia Biblica*, IV, 4599–600.

Guignebert, *La Primauté de Pierre*, p. 27, is doubtful, and mentions that Harnack, *Patres Apostolorum Opera*, II, 16, believes that Clement referred here to Spain. (See also Harnack, *Einführung*, p. 107.) See Molland, "Petrus in Rom," p. 441, and Katzenmeyer, "Zur Frage," *Internationale kirchliche Zeitschrift*, p. 137, and *The First Epistle of Clement*, ed. Clarke, pp. 89–90.

Dibelius, "Rom und die Christen," p. 27, professes that if *Paul* is the main interest in 5:7 then the meaning of "τὸ τέρμα τῆς δύσεως" is Spain, but if the "philosophical athlete" is the main interest the phrase may not mean Spain at all. On the matter of Spain, see Zahn, *Introduction*, II, 72–75.

163. "Sicuti et semote passionem Petri evidenter declarat, sed et profectionem Pauli ab urbe ad Spaniam proficiscentis." *Ibid.* Zahn, dates this fragment A.D. 160–70, and Lightfoot, *Apostolic Fathers*, Part I, Vol. II, p. 30, says A.D. c. 180.

164. Strabo II.1, "πέρατα δὲ αὐτῆς [τῆς οἰκουμένης] τίθησι, πρὸς δύσει μὲν τὰς Ἡρακλείους στήλας [Gibraltar]." *The Geography of Strabo*, trans. Jones, I, 253. See the discussion in Lightfoot, *Apostolic Fathers*, Part I, Vol. II, pp. 30, 31; Harnack, *Einführung*, p. 107.

165. In opposition to Lightfoot, *Apostolic Fathers*, Part I, Vol. II, p. 31, and Zahn, *Introduction*, II, 73.

166. That Paul *visited* Spain is affirmed by Epiphanius, *Panarium* XXVII.6; Isidorus (A.D. c. 636), *De Ortu et Obitu Patrum* LXIX (*MPL*, LXXXIII, 150): "usque ad Iliricum, et Italiam Hispaniasque processit"; and Gregory of Rome (A.D. c. 595), *Moralium* XXXI.103 (*MPL*, LXXVI, 630, 1454). These sources, however, do not mention that he *died* there. Belief in the Spanish sojourn of Paul was forbidden by Gelasius A.D. 495, *Epistle* XXX.11. He also condemned the view that Peter and Paul died at separate times. (This reference is cited by Zahn, *Introduction*, II, 74, 75.)

167. See below, pp. 83–85.

168. *Acts of Peter* (*The Vercelli Acts*) III. James, *The Apocryphal New Testament*, p. 306, says that this tradition that Paul was imprisoned twice in Rome with a trip to Spain in between may be an excerpt from the *Acts of Paul*: "The question is a difficult one. All allow that the writer of the *Acts of Peter* used the *Acts of Paul*; but there is strong opposition to the idea that the *Acts of Paul* related two visits to Rome." See also, Zahn, *Introduction*, II, 74 and Goguel, *L'Église primitive*, p. 207.

tradition to support a martyrdom in Spain and above all the context of 1 Clement 5–6 argue for the interpretation that Clement did refer to Rome in 5:7.[169]

The term "μαρτυρήσας" means the same in 5:7 as it did in 5:4; it refers to a "witnessing" which in the mind of Clement most probably meant martyrdom. In this instance the witnessing can be thought of as including both a last confession which took place ἐπὶ τῶν ἡγουμένων and an actual execution.[170] Among those who have been suggested as the οἱ ἡγούμενοι (5:7) are Helius and the Praetorian Prefect Tigellinus who were left in charge of Rome when Nero visited Greece during A.D. 67.[171] If Paul had appeared before the emperor himself, the fact would surely have been noted. The ἡγουμένοι could mean almost any one in authority, even local authorities or magistrates in Rome,[172] but according to Zahn, the absence of any local designation and the inclusion of the οἱ seems to indicate the supreme rulers.[173] Who they are, we can only guess.[174]

After having come to the "limits of the West," and having borne "his witness before the rulers," thus (οὕτως) Paul "was released from the world and went to the holy place." The οὕτως shows that his release was contingent upon his witnessing (compare καὶ οὕτω . . . μαρτυρήσας in 5:4), and the ἀπηλλάγη τοῦ κόσμου reinforces μαρτυρήσας to emphasize that Paul was martyred. Heussi is of the opinion that ἀπηλλάγη τοῦ κόσμου definitely refers to martyrdom and insists that it

is *this* element which distinguishes the notice of Paul from that of Peter. This view permits one to maintain that while 1 Clement clearly refers to the martyrdom of Paul, it says nothing about a martyrdom of Peter. It has been mentioned above that this is not a necessary or even the most plausible conclusion.[175] The parallelism which exists between the two notices indicates strongly that if martyrdom is implied in the one notice, it is implied in the other.

Chapter 6 which is very important for the correct understanding of chapter 5 begins with the words: "To these men [Peter and Paul] who lived such holy lives there was joined a great multitude of the elect who by reason of rivalry were the victims of many outrages and tortures and who became outstanding examples among us."[176]

The "great crowd of witnesses," especially in this context, can only mean those who suffered in the Neronian persecution. (Tacitus also mentions a "multitudo ingens"—a huge multitude[177] who died at this time.) There were surely some who died after the time of Nero and before the time of Clement (between A.D. 68 and 96), but those who are mentioned here (6:1) are represented as being roughly contemporary with Peter and Paul as well as τῆς γενεᾶς ἡμῶν (5:1).[178]

It is mentioned by Clement that those who died in the Neronian persecution were "joined to" or "gathered

---

169. See Fridrichsen, "Propter Invidiam. Note sur Clém. V.," pp. 161–74. This also seems to have been the interpretation put upon the verse as reflected in later liturgical usage. For example, see *The Office for the Commemoration of the Holy . . . Apostles . . . Peter and Paul . . . According to the Byzantine Rite in the Byzantine Office*, ed. Wainewright, pp. 51, 129, 140.

170. Compare Zahn, *Introduction*, p. 70. Dibelius, "Rom und die Christen," p. 27, sees μαρτυρήσας ἐπὶ τῶν ἡγουμένων as possibly referring to a "Vernehmung" [trial] and not necessarily to death as in the notice of Peter.

171. See above, p. 57.

172. Acts 7:10 mentions that Joseph is appointed ἡγούμενον, governor, over Egypt by Pharaoh. In Hebrews 13:7 the word refers to church leaders. Most, as for example Katzenmeyer, "Zur Frage," p. 136, admit candidly that they do not know who is meant here.

173. Zahn, *Introduction*, p. 71.

174. Harnack, *Einführung*, p. 107, "Die weltliche Obrigkeit ist hier gemeint ohne nähere Bestimmung."

175. See above, p. 77.

176. *Early Christian Fathers*, trans. Richardson, p. 46.

177. Tacitus, *Annals* XV.44, trans. Jackson, IV, 282, 283. See Guarducci, *The Tomb of St. Peter*, p. 30: "without a doubt, St. Clement was referring to the victims of the persecution of Nero. This is clearly demonstrated by consulting a famous passage in the *Annals* of Tacitus."

178. Lightfoot, *Apostolic Fathers*, Part I, Vol. II, p. 32; Schmiedel, "Peter," *Encyclopaedia Biblica*, IV, 4599; Lietzmann, *Petrus und Paulus in Rom*, 2d ed., pp. 231–32, holds that this is a reference to those who died in the Neronian persecution and that it is "keine rhetorische Gruppierung"; Delafosse, "La Lettre de Clément romain," p. 77; Harnack, *Einführung*, p. 107; Molland, "Petrus in Rom," p. 440; Cullmann, *Peter*, p. 98; Toynbee and Perkins, *The Shrine of St. Peter*, p. 131; Aland, "Petrus in Rom," p. 514.

Heussi, *Die römische Petrustradition*, p. 20, and Goguel *The Birth of Christianity*, p. 511, both ask if the phrase, "great crowd of witnesses" is not dependent upon Tacitus, *Annals* XV.44 which is a definite possibility.

with" (συνηθροίσθη) Peter and Paul. Cullmann wisely suggests the possibility that this could mean simply that the *example* in 6:1 is joined to those which precede it.[179] But it can also be interpreted as indicating a reunion in heaven[180] or a reference to the martyrdom of Peter and Paul and the "huge multitude" in Rome.

179. *Peter*, p. 97. Otherwise we would be obliged to agree that Peter and Paul died first in the persecution, an assumption which is unlikely in view of the notice of Tacitus which does not permit one to suppose that Nero's attention was drawn to the apostles individually at this critical time. See Giet, *Le Témoignage de Clement,"* p. 134.

180. Harnack, *Die Chronologie*, p. 243n1, mentions that this is a possibility, but he is inclined to accept the view that Peter was martyred "zwar in Rom unter Nero"; Guignebert, *La Primauté de Pierre*, p. 273; Lipsius, *Die apokryphen Apostelgeschichten*, II, 12. Katzenmeyer, "Zur Frage," p. 137, in agreement with his view that Peter and Paul died before the Neronian persecution, believes that the meeting was in heaven. For Dibelius, "Rom und die Christen," p. 23, the meeting place is "die imaginäre Arena in der die Kämpfe der christlichen 'Athleten' stattfinden." Heussi, *Die römische Petrustradition*, p. 20, definitely believes that the place of meeting is "der unmittelbar vorher zweimal genannte 'Ort der Herrlichkeit,'" see also pp. 68–70.

Others are not sure whether the meaning is Rome or heaven. Molland, "Petrus in Rom," p. 440, sees the possibility of the view of Lipsius, Guignebert, and Heussi, but does not agree with it nor considers it a necessary conclusion; in fact, he believes that it is unlikely. Heussi's view also presupposes that Peter and Paul died before the Neronian persecution and were already in "the place of glory." Altaner, "War Petrus in Rom?" p. 182, points out that it is possible to understand it "both ways," but that the most probable meaning is not a meeting in heaven but in the "earthly event." This interpretation, he warns, is dependent upon seeing a close connection between 5:1 and 6:1. See Lietzmann, *Petrus und Paulus in Rom*, 1st ed., pp. 169 f.; 2d ed., pp. 234 f., and "Petrus römischer Märtyrer," p. 394.

Cullmann, *Peter*, p. 97, claims that "were gathered with" [or "were joined to"] need not be a geographical designation but may be theological; it need not answer "where" at all. He suggests that examples 2–5 are probably related to the Neronian persecution.

181. Lightfoot, *Apostolic Fathers*, Part I, Vol. II, p. 32; Lebreton and Zeiller, *The History of the Primitive Church*, I, 235; Katzenmeyer, "Zur Frage," p. 137; Cullmann, *Peter*, p. 97, believes that if Clement wrote 5:1 at Rome, then ἐν ἡμῖν for the πολὺ πλῆθος ἐκλεκτῶν would mean "among us Romans." Heussi in *War Petrus in Rom?*, p. 21, agreed with

This last interpretation seems the most likely, especially if ἐν ἡμῖν (6:1) is understood to mean "among us Romans."[181] This argument would be considerably weakened, however, if it could be proved that ἐν ἡμῖν means "among us Christians."[182]

Cullmann correctly warns that we must not be hasty in saying that ἐν ἡμῖν links Peter and Paul as well as the πολὺ πλῆθος ἐκλεκτῶν to Rome. This is clear if we include Stephen and James among the "Pillars" (5:2) who have died, for these surely did not die in Rome,[183] and therefore ἐν ἡμῖν cannot refer to them. Furthermore, in 5:3 the ἡμῶν does include the Corinthians, and if 5:2 and 3 are not included in the ἐν ἡμῖν, why is 5:4 to be included? We are justified in extending the ἐν ἡμῖν to the notice of Peter *only* if it "can be proved that other really important features connect examples two to four (and perhaps also five) so closely together that we must assume that all three or four occurred at the same time and at the same place."[184] That such a close relationship existed has been suggested above in the discussion of the internal strife within the Roman Christian community which resulted in such a degree of internal disorder that, as Cullmann says,

the magistrates were encouraged by the attitudes of some members of the Christian Church, and perhaps by the fact that they turned informers, to take action against others. In just the same way Moses, in one example of the first group, had

this position (but in note 9 of the same page he acknowledged that it could mean "among us Christians," a position which he definitely held at a later date); Harnack, *Einführung*, p. 107; *The First Epistle of Clement*, ed. Clarke, p. 90; Toynbee and Perkins, *The Shrine of St. Peter*, p. 131. Cecchelli, in *Osservatore Romano*, November, 18, 1951, p. 3, col. 1, believes that "fra noi" is meaningless unless there is behind it the idea of a precise locality. See 1 Clement 63:3.

Bauer, in *Wiener Studien*, XXXVIII, 287 (refuted by Lietzmann, *Petrus und Paulus in Rom*, 2d ed., p. 232), proposes that ἐν ἡμῖν only applies to those martyrs mentioned in 6:1 and indeed helps to indicate a temporal division: Peter died *far* from Rome and *before* the time of Nero.

182. Guignebert, *La Primauté de Pierre*, p. 272; and Heussi, *Die römische Petrustradition*, p. 20. See 1 Clement 21:9, 27:3, and 55:2.

183. Cullmann, *Peter*, p. 97.

184. *Ibid.*, pp. 97–98. Compare Duchesne, *Histoire ancienne de l'Église*, pp. 62–63; Aland, "Petrus in Rom," p. 512.

to flee from the Egyptian King because of the jealousy of a fellow-countryman.[185]

Thus internal "jealousy," "rivalry," and "contention" may have resulted in the persecution and death of Peter and Paul.

Cullmann concedes that what happened in the Roman Church could also have happened elsewhere, and similar internal strife could have caused the death of Peter and Paul at different places and at different times. He offers the rather weak argument that

this is improbable, and in any case the fact remains that the existence of such jealousy is attested only for Rome, where it is attested by I Clement 6:1, almost certainly by Paul's letter to Philippi [1:15-17], and indirectly also by the letter to the Romans. Therefore the indication of place in ch. 6:1, "among us," that is, in the church of Bishop Clement of Rome, quite probably refers to all the Christian martyrdoms mentioned by the author and caused by jealousy.[186]

The remainder of chapter 6 is not important for this discussion since verse 2 is simply an elaboration of verse 1,[187] and the final two illustrations (6:3, 4) more than likely were included simply to complete the seven examples from τῆς γενεᾶς ἡμῶν to parallel the seven drawn from the Old Testament.

What does I Clement communicate concerning the martyrdom of Peter in Rome? Before this question is answered, it must be emphasized again that I Clement 4–6 is a rhetorical passage, not an historical one, and that the information which it contains must be judged in light of its intent. The notices of Peter and Paul are parallel but unequal in length; this does not necessarily imply that Clement knew more about Paul or less about Peter. It does, however, suggest that the details of the career of Paul better served the purpose of Clement at this point in his argument.

After listing seven examples from the Old Testament in which jealousy between those closely associated had

resulted in great suffering or death, Clement turns to indicate these examples collectively in 5:2 and then proceeds to describe them individually. Peter and Paul are set before the eyes of the Corinthians and Romans since these apostles are known to both groups. It is explained that because of jealousy and envy within the Christian community (or possibly, as Giet indicates, jealousy harbored by members of the Jewish community against the Christians) the two apostles were betrayed to the Roman authorities and executed. The why, when, and where of their execution may be explained only cautiously and provisionally, for the thread which connects the elements of the argument is exceedingly fragile.

If by the "great crowd of witnesses" is meant the "multitudo ingens" of which Tacitus speaks and if it appears likely that ἐν ἡμῖν means "among us Romans" *and* may be extended to include Peter and Paul, then it may be accepted that Clement means to imply that Peter and Paul died in the Neronian persecution either immediately or sometime after the great fire in A.D. 64.

Most would agree that the "great multitude of the elect" refers to victims of the Neronian persecution, and it is likely that ἐν ἡμῖν *does* mean "among us Romans," *but* are Peter and Paul included in this term? Although the possibility cannot be stated as a certainty, which has been done in the past by a number of those who have supported the tradition of a Roman martyrdom of Peter, neither can the possibility be rejected as impossible or highly improbable, as others have done.

The question of where the interest and emphasis of Clement lies is very important to the correct understanding of the passage. If one places the emphasis upon the individuals involved in the examples, it becomes puzzling that certain "facts," if they were known at all, were not expressed or that one notice is longer than another. In this case silence appears to imply ignorance. If one thinks mainly of the individuals, whether they are conceived to be historical personalities or "christlichen Athleten," it is natural to interpret what is said from the personal standpoint in terms of human endurance or patience. The emphasis in Clement, on the contrary, is not upon the personalities of his examples (as the interest of Jesus did not lie in the personalities involved in his parables), but upon certain disruptive

185. Cullmann, *Peter*, p. 102. One must not forget, however, the factiousness of the Corinthians reflected in Paul's retort in I Cor. 12 f. or the disagreements at Antioch which lie behind Gal. 2:11-14.

186. *Ibid.*, p. 108. See the entire argument supporting this conclusion, pp. 104-8.

187. See Heussi, *Die römische Petrustradition*, excursus 3, pp. 69-71; Barnes, *The Martyrdom of St. Peter and St. Paul*, p. 92.

attitudes (ζῆλος, φθόνος, ἔρις) and actions of individuals and groups which lead to destruction. The Pillars, Peter and Paul, the Great Multitude of the Elect, and the Danaïds and Dircae were chosen by Clement not just to give information about them but to offer to the Corinthians the opportunity to contemplate the fate of Peter and Paul and the others, so that they might mend their ways. And for just this reason these examples do not *have* to be considered as connected temporally or geographically because their presence together is adequately explained by the element of cause. On the other hand, they *may* be connected in time and place as well as cause, for there is nothing associated with the latter which would preclude the former.

Errors in interpretation of 1 Clement 5 arise because some have judged the passage either as history which must include all known details or as moral philosophy which need not be limited to historical "facts" at all. These interpreters have been too preoccupied with the examples themselves to see them correctly in relation to their purpose in the argument of Clement; they have confused his interests with their own.

We cannot interpret 1 Clement 4–6 in light of other texts, since those which give information concerning the martyrdom of Peter in Rome are later than the end of the first century. And we cannot be sure in the case of even later texts that they are not dependent upon 1 Clement which was widely read in the second century.[188]

Despite the objections of those who deny that Clement had any knowledge of Peter's martyrdom in Rome[189] (for which assumption Heussi mistakenly believes he has "unwiderlegbare Beweise") and those who see in 1 Clement 5 and 6 the beginning of the Roman legend of Peter and Paul,[190] it is most probable that Clement believed, on the basis of written or oral tradition or both, that Peter and Paul (in that order) died at about the same time in Rome during the persecution under Nero.[191] Clement neither states nor implies any more than this. There is not even a hint of: 1) when Peter came to Rome and how long he stayed, 2) what relationship he had to the Roman Church, 3) the manner of his death or where he was buried.

THE EPISTLE OF IGNATIUS TO THE ROMANS

Despite the observations of Cullmann, there is no indication in the *Epistle to the Romans* of a tradition concerning the martyrdom of Peter and Paul in Rome.

Ignatius does emphasize the difference between himself and the two apostles, but it is precarious to further deduce that the writer is "nevertheless conscious that

188. See Lightfoot, *Apostolic Fathers*, Part I, Vol. I, pp. 148–60; Goguel, *L'Église primitive*, p. 210.

189. Zeller, *La légende de Saint Pierre premier évêque de Rome*, p. 90, cited by Guignebert, *La Primauté de Pierre*, p. 273; Schmiedel, "Peter," in *Encyclopaedia Biblica*, IV, 4599, 4601; Erbes, "Petrus nicht in Rom, sondern in Jerusalem gestorben," p. 24; Dannenbauer, "Nochmals die römische Petruslegende," p. 83 (refuted by Lietzmann, "Petrus römischer Märtyrer," p. 396).

Others are confident that Clement knew that Peter was martyred, but that he did not know where: Guignebert, *La Primauté de Pierre*, p. 273; Bauer, in *Wiener Studien*, XXXVIII, 287 f. (discussed by Lietzmann, *Petrus und Paulus in Rom*, 2d ed., pp. 231–33); Katzenmeyer, "Zur Frage," pp. 136–39. Heussi argues (an *argumentum e silentio*) that Clement did know of a tradition relating the martyrdom of Paul to Rome but was ignorant of any tradition that Peter died in Rome: *War Petrus in Rom?*; in *Die Christliche Welt*, pp. 163; 164; *Die römische Petrustradition*, pp. 28–30. This position is less tenable

than that which holds that Clement knew nothing of a Roman martyrdom of Peter *or* Paul.

190. Delafosse, "Le Lettre de Clément romain," p. 81. "At the moment when Clement writes the fable comes to be born. It still has its primitive character and does not press to enhance the glory of the Roman church"; Goguel, *L'Église primitive*, p. 231: "The small germ constituted by a very vague [creuse] phrase of Clement of Rome has given birth on the whole to a tradition of the martyrdom of the Apostle"; see also Goguel, *The Birth of Christianity*, pp. 510n4, 552n2.

191. Lightfoot, *Apostolic Fathers*, Part I, Vol. I, pp. 74–75; Zahn, *Introduction*, II, 61; Harnack, *Die Chronologie*, I, 710; Duchesne, *Origines du Culte chrétien*, p. 79; Monceaux, "L'Apostolat de Saint Pierre," p. 226; Lietzmann, *Petrus und Paulus in Rom*, 2d ed., p. 235, and *Petrus römischer Märtyrer*, pp. 394, 396, 405; Altaner, "War Petrus in Rom?" pp. 179–82; Molland, "Petrus in Rom," p. 442; *The First Epistle of Clement*, ed. Clarke, p. 18; Cullmann, *Peter*, p. 109; Leclercq, *DACL*, Vol. XIV, Part I, p. 852; Aland, "Petrus in Rom," p. 515.

he has something in common with them. This is not the apostolic office, but probably the martyrdom in Rome."[192] Of course, this is not to deny that Ignatius was acquainted with a tradition of martyrdom; he surely was if he knew 1 Clement, and it is at least possible that he did.[193] It is not possible, however, to find in Romans 4:3 a reference to Peter's death in Rome that is sufficiently explicit to be presented as evidence.

LATER EVIDENCE FOR THE MARTYRDOM OF PETER IN ROME

A number of the following sources are mentioned in the introduction to the subject of the martyrdom of Peter in Rome in chapter 4, but to give a picture of the trend in the development of the tradition, I evaluate them here in this section.

Cullmann rightly reminds us that evidence from a period after the middle of the second century does not add facts to the meager amount of knowledge concerning the martyrdom of Peter in Rome; it simply attests "the development of the tradition."[194]

Nothing is derived from the works of Justin Martyr,[195] and the martyrdom of Peter in Rome is only mentioned in passing in a fragment of the works of Dionysius of Corinth (A.D. c. 170) preserved by Eusebius. This Corinthian bishop, who was according to his own testimony acquainted with the letter of Clement to the Romans, may have derived all that he knew of Peter and Paul in Rome from this source. His only comment concerning the death of the two apostles is that "ἐμαρτύρησαν κατὰ τὸν αὐτὸν καιρόν."[196]

Irenaeus (A.D. c. 185), who also had read 1 Clement, does not refer to the martyrdom of Peter, although he alludes to the founding of the church of Rome by Peter and Paul and states that "they handed over the ministry of the episcopate to Linus."[197] Tertullian (A.D. c. 200) is the first orthodox writer to refer explicitly to the Roman martyrdom of Peter in the time of Nero.[198]

While one may find testimony concerning the death of Peter in the writings of Dionysius and Tertullian, their statements must be received with caution. The former, in the same passage in which he mentions that Peter and Paul were "martyred at the same time," makes the very improbable assumption that these apostles founded the church at Corinth. And in one passage in which Tertullian reports the martyrdom of the apostles he adds the fantastic story that John was dipped in boiling oil and emerged from the experience unharmed.[199]

There is no mention of the death of Peter in the works of Clement of Alexandria (A.D. c. 200), and although the author of the *Muratorian Canon* does mention in line 37 the "passio Petri," he does not give any exact indication of place. There can be little doubt, however, that he meant Rome.[200] In a fragment attributed to Hippolytus (A.D. c. 235), there is mention of the legend that Peter was crucified head downward.[201] The same apocryphal detail, which *may* ultimately be derived from the *Epistle of Clement to James* (fourth century)[202] or its source, is reported by Origen in Book

---

192. *Peter*, p. 111. See Guarducci, *The Tomb of St. Peter*, p. 33.

193. Evidence that Ignatius may have known 1 Clement is derived from *Ephesians* XV and *Polycarp* V. Lightfoot, *Apostolic Fathers*, Part I, Vol. I, p. 149; Part II, Vol. II, pp. 69–71, 347–50.

194. *Peter*, p. 115.

195. See above, p. 26.

196. *E. H.* II.25:8. See above, p. 24.

197. *Against Heresies* III.3:3 (*MPL*, VII, 849). See above, pp. 28–30.

198. *De praescriptione haereticorum* XXXVI.12 (*MPL.* II, 50; Giles, *Documents Illustrating Papal Authority*, p. 22). See also *Scorpiace* XV (*MPL*, II, 151); *Adv. Marcion* IV.5 (*MPL*, II, 366).

199. *De praescriptione haereticorum* XXXVI (*MPL*, II, 50).

200. See Heussi, *Die römische Petrustradition*, p. 46.

201. "Hippolytus on the Twelve Apostles," a fragment preserved in *The Ante-Nicene Fathers*, Vol. II, Part II, p. 130. See above p. 26.

202. See above, pp. 38–39, 56.

III of his *Commentary on Genesis*.[203] Lactantius (A.D. c. 313) refers briefly to the death of the two apostles in the time of Nero.[204] Eusebius a few years later follows Origen, the *Epistle of Clement to James*, or another oral or written source when he writes: "Moreover, Simon Peter was crucified in Rome head downwards [κατὰ κεφαλῆς] and Paul was put to death, and John was consigned to an island."[205] In the *Ecclesiastical History* and in the *Chronicle* under the notices for anno Abraham 2083 (A.D. 67), Eusebius (A.D. c. 326) merely states that Peter died under Nero.[206]

The last literary witness to be mentioned here for the martyrdom of Peter in Rome is a statement found in the works of Macarius Magnus which derives its importance from the fact that the information goes back to Porphyry (d. A.D. 304), a Neoplatonic opponent of Christianity who cannot possibly be accused of Christian bias.[207] Whether this testimony is "eine höchst kostbare Nachricht," as Harnack assumes, is questionable. First of all, the statement is late and second, it is vague, only mentioning Rome by implication.[208] The most interesting aspect of this testimony is the observation that Peter did little to carry out the wishes of his Master (John 21:15-17), for he came to Rome only a short while before his death. The statement of Porphyry thus implicitly discredits the traditions that Peter founded the Roman Church or was its first bishop, much less that he spent twenty-five years in Rome in the latter capacity.

The *Liberian Catalogue* (A.D. 336) assumes the tradition that Peter died in Rome and states that he "passus autem cum Paulo die iii Kl. Iulius, cons. s̅s̅, imperante Nerone."[209] The *Martyrologium Hieronymianum* for June 29 mentions no more than that Peter and Paul "passi sub Nerone." In the first edition and the Felician abridgment, the *Liber Pontificalis* mentions vaguely that after Peter had done these things, "hic martyrio cum Paulo coronatur."[210] The second edition is more explicit adding that the martyrdom took place "post passionem Domini anno XXXVIII."[211] Both editions leave no doubt that Rome is meant as the city in which the martyrdom occurred.

Several apocryphal works which are discussed in Part I and mentioned again earlier in this chapter allude to the martyrdom of Peter. These are the *Acts of Peter*, which contains the Quo Vadis legend and first mentions the legend that Peter was crucified head downward,[212] the *Acts of Andrew and Paul*,[213] and the *Epistle of Clement to James*, which serves as the introduction to the *Clementine Homilies*.[214]

---

203. *E. H.* III.1:2 (Lake, I, 191); Heussi, *Die römische Petrustradition*, p. 46, holds that the addition is "eine blosse Addition verschiedener Überlieferung." Lipsius, *Die apokryphen Apostelgeschichten*, II, 337, considers the possibility that the entire tradition of the head-downward position of Peter on the cross (a late addition, perhaps, to the *Acts of Peter and Paul*) rests upon a misunderstanding of the word "ἄνωθεν" in Origen, *Commentary on Genesis*, Book III. The word can mean either "again," "from above," or simply "above," "on high."

204. *De mortibus persecutorum* II (*MPL*, VII, 195-97), "cumque jam Nero imperaret, Petrus invenit . . . [Nero] Petrum cruci affixit et Paulum interfecit."

205. *De theophania* V.31, *De theophania*, trans. Lee, p. 315. The same statement is found in *Demonstrationis evangelicae* III.5:65, trans. Farrar, I, 134.

206. *E. H.* II.25:5 (Lake, I, 181).

207. Heussi, *Die römische Petrustradition*, p. 47; Cullmann, *Peter*, p. 122. Macarius Magnus III.22 "ὅμως ἱστορεῖται μὴ δ' ὀλίγους μῆνας βοσκήσας τὰ προβάτια ὁ πέτρος ἐσταυρῶσθαι." (*Macario Magnete*, ed. Duchesne, p. 102, mentions that Peter was "crucified after he had shepherded the flock only a few months.")

208. This point is emphasized by Dannenbauer, "Die Petruslegende," p. 253, and mentioned by Heussi, *Die römische Petrustradition*. Cullmann, *Peter*, p. 122, however, rightly states that no other place but Rome need be considered. "This results at once from the simple consideration that Porphyrius, in speaking of the brief 'feeding of the sheep,' can only have thought of the same place at which occurred the crucifixion mentioned in the same sentence."

209. Lightfoot, *Apostolic Fathers*, Part I, Vol. I, p. 253; see above, p. 41.

210. *Liber Pontificalis*, 1st ed., Vol. I, Part I, pp. 50-52.

211. *Ibid.*, 2d ed., p. 118.

212. XXV, XXXVII (James, *The Apocryphal New Testament*, pp. 333, 334), compare Lipsius, *Die apokryphen Apostelgeschichten*, II, 337 f.; see above, pp. 35-37.

213. James, *The Apocryphal New Testament*, p. 474; see above, p. 37.

214. *The Ante-Nicene Fathers*, VIII, 218; see above, pp. 38-39.

Liturgical Sources

A discussion of the meaning of the festival of Peter and Paul held on June 29 could be undertaken in this section. It seems more fruitful, however, to deal with it in Part III, in connection with the liturgical evidence for the burial of Peter in Rome and the difficult problem of the alleged "translation" of the relics.

BRIEF SUMMARY OF THE LITERARY EVIDENCE FOR THE MARTYRDOM OF PETER IN ROME

It is generally accepted that Peter was martyred and that he suffered death by crucifixion. The detail concerning his head-downward position on the cross is apocryphal, perhaps invented by the author of the *Acts of Peter*.

Why he was martyred still remains a problem. It may have been in connection with the great fire of Rome or a refusal to make ritual offerings to the emperor in demonstration of loyalty and obedience or as a result of a number of charges which an unfriendly community might bring against a group which it disliked and distrusted. On the one hand, the absence of strongly conflicting traditions as to time and place may cause some to be too hasty in accepting the tradition; while, on the other hand, the vagueness of the earliest sources may cause others to discard the tradition entirely. The answer does not appear to be at either extreme.

It must be admitted that the earliest sources such as 1 Clement and John 21 (and perhaps Ignatius, Romans 4:3, and Revelation 11:3–13), while they knew that Peter had been martyred, do not mention where or when it took place. But if the suggestions and implications of these and later sources *are taken together*, the tradition is most persistent in setting the time of Peter's martyrdom in Rome within the reign of Nero and between A.D. 64 and 67. Only the later and less trustworthy sources appear to be concerned with *where* the crucifixion took place. There seems to be virtual agreement among these, however, that Peter was martyred in the vicinity of the Vatican. This topographical detail may be trustworthy or it may simply be an inference drawn from the tradition that Peter died in the great persecution, described by Tacitus and others, which took place in the Vatican area.

PART III

The Literary, Liturgical, and Archeological Evidence for the Tradition of the Burial of Peter in Rome

CHAPTER 6

Traditions of Burial in Rome

IF IT BE accepted that Peter did reside in Rome (if even for only a short time at the end of his life) and that he was martyred in the Vatican area during the latter part of the reign of Nero, the question of where he was buried must still be answered.

There is the possibility that if Peter died as a condemned criminal his body was never buried at all.[1] The friends and relatives of the condemned had the right to claim the body of the deceased under Roman law.[2] But it seems doubtful that the law was honored in this period,[3] for A.D. 177 the faithful at Lyon, even though under one of the more temperate emperors, Marcus Aurelius (A.D. 161–80), could not recover their dead.[4] After the martyrdom of Polycarp the authorities ordered the body to be burned so that the faithful of Smyrna might not hide and treasure it.[5] Carcopino also stresses that A.D. 110 the body of Ignatius was ordered thrown to beasts so that it could not be reclaimed by the Christians. It can be argued, however, that the martyrdom

of Peter took place somewhat earlier and the gathering of relics by Christians had not previously taken place, an activity which at a later time called forth restrictive measures on the part of the authorities. Carcopino is convinced that, as later in the disposal of Ignatius' remains, only a few bones were left to the Christians for burial.[6]

Assuming for the moment that there were at least portions of the body of Peter remaining for burial after his crucifixion, and possible mutilation, and also that these remains were not thrown into the Tiber, what is the probability that they were buried by the faithful? "As far as one can learn from the sources in a number sufficient for the period in question," says Capocci, "it seems that the concession of sepulture for one punished in the manner of the cross was dispensed by discretionary powers, properly of the judging authority that had issued the condemnation."[7]

It is possible that Peter was buried furtively so that those who claimed the body might not be identified publicly with the Christian group. If this were so, the Vatican Hill would be a likely place geographically, assuming that Peter was martyred by Nero in that immediate area. But there are also arguments against this proposal: 1) legal permission *could* be obtained, 2) the Vatican Hill was part of the gardens of Nero or very near such property[8] (and there is the distinct possibility

---

1. Toynbee and Perkins, *The Shrine of St. Peter*, p. 156. The topography speaks against the probability that Peter's body was buried at the Vatican. The area would have had to become extremely derelict to permit private burials, and according to Tacitus the deaths did take place within the imperial gardens: "hortos suos ei spectaculo Nero obtulerat et circense ludicrum edebat" (*Annals* XV.44).

2. "Corpora animadversorum quibuslibet petentibus ad sepulturam danda sunt." Julius Paulus, *Sententiae Receptarum ad Filium* I.21:16 in *Jurisprudentia Vetus, Ante Justinianea*, ed. Schultingh, p. 266. This entry does appear, however, in modern editions of Julius Paulus such as "The Opinions of Paulus," *The Civil Law*, ed. Scott, Vol. I. p. 266. Book I ends with I.21:15.

3. Carcopino, *Études*, p. 180.

4. *E. H.* V.4 (Lake, I, 444, 445) and Gregory of Tours, *De gloria confessorum* XLIX (*MPL*, LXXI, 865).

5. See in *The Martyrdom of Polycarp* XVII.1–2 (compare XVIII. 1–2), trans. Massey H. Shepherd, in *Early Christian Fathers*, pp. 155–56. Grégoire, *Les Persécutions*, pp. 102–4.

6. *Études*, p. 181.

7. Capocci, "Notae," p. 202. Compare the treatment accorded the body of Jesus: Mark 15:42–46, Matt. 27:57–60, John 19:38–42 (Luke 22:50–56). Philo, *Against Flaccus* chap. XI, trans. Yonge, IV, 78.

8. See the inscription of Popilius Heracla, below, p. 163; Platner and Ashby, *A Topographical Dictionary of Ancient Rome*, pp. 113–14, 264–65, 547–48 (cited by Capocci, "Notae," p. 203). See also Leclercq, *DACL*, Vol. XIV, Part I, p. 854, "Saint Peter was buried along the route which bordered the gardens in a way that Nero knew nothing of it."

that the area was patrolled), and 3) if ever it were discovered that the burial had taken place without legal
authorization, the remains would be removed and cast
into the Tiber or into the sea, and the testimony of Suetonius shows that this was not simply a theoretical
danger.[9] If the Christians would risk so much to recover
the body of the apostle, would they risk an illegal burial
so near the imperial gardens? If the Primitive Church
had wished to "invent"[10] a burial place for the relics of
Peter and Paul would they have chosen such a location?

One who was careless or meant to deceive would be likely to
"find" the remains in the Catacombs near those of other
Christians, where Christian sentiment was dominant, where
Christian worship was easy. The relics might have been
"invented" [gefunden] lying side by side. The ancient unanimous tradition, however, finds the graves of Peter and Paul
widely separated, hard by well-travelled roads, each alone in
the midst of heathen graves. The natural explanation is that
the ancient sites are genuine: that beneath the hall of the three
Emperors there actually rest the remains of Paul and under
the mighty dome of Bramante those of Peter.[11]

This conclusion may seem obvious to Lietzmann, but
upon the basis of the same evidence other conclusions
have been formulated. Paul Styger is confident that
Peter and Paul were buried on the Via Appia immediately after their martyrdom[12] and that Gaius meant a
place of martyrdom by the word τρόπαιον. From this

they claim (but it is exceedingly unconvincing) that it
follows logically that Constantine built his basilicas not
over the graves of the apostles but over the places most
closely associated with their deaths. The same evidence
has led the Bollandist, Hippolyte Delehaye, to state
with equal conviction that Peter and Paul were buried
in the traditional locations in the Vatican and on the
Via Ostia, and that the Via Appia is related to the
veneration of the apostles in another way.[13] Josef
Wilpert suggests a solution similar to that of Delehaye:
while the basilicas for the apostles were still unfinished,
Peter was buried at San Sebastiano in an "ehemaliger
Wohnung" (in a place where Peter had once actually
lived—the "Domus Petri").[14]

The elements of the tradition of Peter's burial on
the Vatican are many and varied. The general impression
that one receives in viewing and comparing the sources
is a confused one. The picture of claim and counter-
claim among ancient writers as well as the modern
scholars leads Chadwick to conclude that the "Christians
of Rome during the second and early third centuries
had no reason to be much more certain about the true
sites of the apostolic graves than we are today, and in
fact . . . most of our modern confusions and doubts
are little more than a consequence of theirs."[15]

In reaching a decision concerning the burial of the
apostle, we must examine: 1) the various types of literary
evidence chronologically, but separately; 2) the liturgical evidence, especially the meaning of the festival of
Peter and Paul held on June 29 and the enigmatic
reference to "Basso et Tusco consulibus" (in this
connection it is also necessary to study carefully and
evaluate the intricate "Translation" theories); and 3) the
excavations at San Sebastiano and beneath St. Peter's
at the Vatican.

---

9. *Domitian* VIII:5, *Suetonius*, trans. Rolfe II, 356, 357.

10. Lipsius, *Die apokryphen Apostelgeschichten*, II, 21. Renan,
The Antichrist, p. 165. It is difficult to agree with Grisar,
Geschichte Rom und der Päpste im Mittelalter, I, 234, in the latter
part of the following sentence: "if there had been a tomb of
St. Peter it could not have been forgotten and if there had not
been one, it could not have been invented."

While Guignebert, "La Sépulture de Pierre," p. 229, does
not accuse the Roman Catholic Church of a "voluntary fraud,"
he does say that the Church "was perfectly able to discover
the opportune moment when it felt the need to possess the
tomb of Peter . . . by one of the means of which hagiography
offers us a copious choice: revelation, inspired dream, pro-
vidential luck, etc."

11. English translation of this passage by W. W. Rockwell,
Journal of Theology (1918), p. 121. Lietzmann, *Petrus und
Paulus in Rom*, 1st ed., p. 177.

12. Styger, *Römische Märtyrergrüfte*, Vol. XLVIII.

---

13. Delehaye, *Les Origines*, pp. 267, 268. See below, pp.
131-34.

14. Wilpert, "La Tomba di S. Pietro," pp. 28-30. The subject
of the "Domus Petri" is dealt with in chapter 9.

15. Chadwick, "St. Peter and St. Paul," p. 51. He adds on
the following page that "nothing is harder than the discovery
of the martyred apostles of history when almost all the extant
evidence concerns only the saints of faith."

CHAPTER 7

The Literary Evidence
for the Burial of Peter in Rome

OF ALL THE literary evidence for the burial of Peter in Rome, the fragment of Gaius (sometimes written Caius) is the most important. While it is the earliest evidence (A.D. c. 200) of which we have any knowledge and bears witness to a tradition which is at least a generation earlier (A.D. c. 165), it cannot be said "to support all alone all the weight of the Roman tradition touching upon the burial of Peter."[1] The statement of Gaius must be read with caution, for he includes, in addition to the designation of the location of the apostles' τρόπαια, the apocryphal detail that Peter and Paul "founded this Roman Church."[2]

THE FRAGMENT OF GAIUS PRESERVED BY EUSEBIUS[3]

Gaius is described by Eusebius as ἐκκλησιαστικὸς ἀνήρ, which is rendered by Valois (1659) in his Latin translation "vir catholicus."[4] This designation has been variously interpreted. Some take it to mean "a man of the Church" and not "an orthodox Christian." Eusebius, however, called such a man ὀρθοδόξων μὲν καὶ ἐκκλησιαστικῶν.[5] In the ninth century Photius identified Gaius as a priest and even a bishop living at Rome.[6] Harnack refers to him as "Caius the Roman," and Liddell and Scott suggest that Eusebius meant to imply that Gaius was not a layman but an "ecclesiastic"—of or belonging to the Church, "clerical."[7] Lightfoot in the middle of the last century advanced the theory that Gaius was "only the double of Hippolytus and that all the works ascribed to the former belong rightfully to the latter." In his later years, however, he retracted his earlier statements and admitted that he was now quite certain "that there was a certain Gaius against whom

---

1. Guignebert, "La Sépulture de Pierre," p. 229.

2. See above, pp. 24–25, 29. This warning is sounded by Guignebert, *ibid.*, p. 226, who mentions that Harnack, *Die Mission und Ausbreitung des Christentums*, II, 205, also is cautious, since Gaius is capable of making a statement without knowing the facts.

3. *E. H.* II.25:6, 7 (Lake, I, 180–83) "οὐδὲν δὲ ἧττον καὶ ἐκκλησιαστικὸς ἀνήρ, Γάϊος ὄνομα, κατὰ Ζεφυρῖνον Ῥωμαίων γεγονὼς ἐπίσκοπον· ὃς δὴ Πρόκλῳ τῆς κατὰ Φρύγας προϊσταμένῳ γνώμης ἐγγράφως διαλεχθείς, αὐτὰ δὴ ταῦτα περὶ τῶν τόπων, ἔνθα τῶν εἰρημένων ἀποστόλων τὰ ἱερὰ σκηνώματα κατατέθειται, φησίν· ἐγὼ δὲ τὰ τρόπαια τῶν ἀποστόλων ἔχω δεῖξαι· ἐὰν γὰρ θελήσῃς ἀπελθεῖν ἐπὶ τὸν βασικανὸν [preferred over βατικανόν] ἢ ἐπὶ τὴν ὁδὸν τὴν Ὠστίαν, εὑρήσεις τὰ τρόπαια τῶν ταύτην ἱδρυσαμένων τὴν ἐκκλησίαν." ("no less than does a writer of the Church named Caius, who lived when Zephyrinus was Bishop of Rome. Caius in a written discussion with Proclus, the leader of the Montanists, speaks as follows of the places where the sacred relics of the apostles in question are deposited: "But I can point out the trophies [τρόπαια] of the Apostles, for if you will go to the Vatican or to the Ostian way you will find the trophies of those who founded this Church.")

4. *MPG*, XX, 207–10.

5. *E. H.* V.27:1 (*MPG*, I, XX, 512; Lake, I, 514, 516). See *Commentarii in Eusebii Pamphili Historiam Eccl. . . .*, ed. F. Heinichen, pp. 63, 64.

6. The statement that Gaius lived at Rome is most probably an inference from Eusebius.

7. *A Greek–English Lexicon*, eds. Liddell and Scott, I, 509.

Hippolytus wrote."[8] Peterson, on the other hand, is convinced that the adjective indicates that Gaius was orthodox and not a heretic, which does *not* mean that he was a member of the clergy. Perhaps he was a presbyter whose ministry in Asia Minor was to transmit the oral tradition to the churches.[9] Peterson further contradicts the claim of Eusebius, that it was during the pontificate of Zephyrinus (A.D. 199–217), by suggesting instead the immediately preceding pontificate of Victor (A.D. 189–99).[10]

In any case, whether he was a clergyman or a layman and whether he served in the time of Zephyrinus or Victor, Gaius (or Caius) is described by Taillez (after an analysis of the references to Gaius in Eusebius[11]) as a well-intentioned conservative who wrote originally in Latin, not in Greek, and who, not having been "condemned by the Church, could be called the first 'father' of the Latin Patrology."[12]

Eusebius in the preparation of his text used early records of the history of the Church which included reflections on the time of Nero by Tertullian. And Rufinus, when translating the text of Eusebius into Latin (MS L, A.D. 402), also used the works of Tertullian, which fact is an aid in checking the text of Eusebius. The Latin text of Rufinus is more an interpretation than a translation;[13] Taillez suggests that it may contain archeological testimony which is independent and interesting.[14] Also, he is of the opinion that Eusebius has omitted four words in the Greek text and that Rufinus' "via regali quae ad Vaticanum ducit" correctly preserves the original. In copying the Greek uncial, which probably contained 19 to 22 letters to the line, Eusebius

or his source omitted a whole line.[15] Such errors resulting from the same or a similar word appearing at the end of a line (homoeoteleuton) are common, and in this case would easily explain the variant in Rufinus. There is, however, no way to prove whether the difference between the Greek and Latin texts is to be explained as resulting from an error by a scribe in copying a pre-Rufinian Greek manuscript or through an interpretation of the text by Rufinus himself. The Βασιλικὴ ὁδός in later Greek, according to Taillez, meant a "via publicus" (and could, of course, refer to the Via Cornelia). Notice also in the text of Rufinus that he has "vaticanum" for "βατισανόν." This error in the Greek might have been in the original text of Gaius, but more likely it was made by Eusebius or a later copyist.

Gaius is represented by Eusebius as taking part in a "written discussion" with a Phrygian named Proclus.[16] To understand the reply of Gaius, it is first necessary to understand the position of his opponent. In speaking about the death of Philip and his daughters, Proclus says, "after him the four daughters of Philip who were prophetesses were at Hierapolis in Asia. Their grave is there and so is their father's (ὁ τάφος αὐτῶν ἐστιν ἐκεί καὶ ὁ τοῦ πάτρος αὐτῶν)." [17] Proclus boasted that Hierapolis could claim the real grave, ὁ τάφος (not a cenotaph), of Philip and his daughters, and Gaius' answer, if it is to be considered as effective at all, must be understood as a response to this claim.

Gaius boasts, "but I can point out the trophies of the apostles," and the emphatic ἐγὼ δὲ appears to oppose the pretention of Proclus. They argue like two small boys, the first claiming that his father is strong and the second

---

8. Lightfoot, *Journal of Theology* (1868), I, 98 ff. and *Apostolic Fathers*, Part I, Vol. II, pp. 380–84.

9. Peterson, "A propos du Tombeau," p. 491n1 (a French translation by Paul Orgels of the original article which appeared in *Schweizer Rundschau*, LII (1952), 328.

10. This view is accepted by Guarducci, *Cristo e San Pietro in un Documento precostantiniano*, p. 105n208 and by Peterson, "A propos du Tombeau," p. 491.

11. *E. H.* II.25:6 (Lake, I, 181–83); III.28:1, 2 (Lake, I, 263); III.31:4 (Lake, I, 271). See also V.24:2 (Lake, I, 505).

12. Taillez, "Notes conjointes," p. 447.

13. "Si enim procedas via regali quae ad Vaticanum ducit, aut via Ostiensi, invenies tropaea defixa quibus ex utraque parte statutis Romana communitur Ecclesia."

14. Taillez, "Notes conjointes," p. 433.

15. *Ibid.*, pp. 434, 435: "ἀπελθεῖν ἐπὶ τ(η)ν βασι[λίκην ὁδὸν εἰς (τόν) βασι] κανόν, ἡ ἐπὶ ὁδὸν 'Ωστίαν."

16. Lake, I, 183, adds concerning Proclus that he is "the leader of the Montanists." Literally the Greek reads "the opinion among the Phrygians." The addition is justified as a point of information, since Proclus was a successor of Montanus.

17. *E. H.* III.31.5 (Lake, I, 270, 271). It must be mentioned that most probably Polycrates has made an error in confusing the apostle Philip with the deacon Philip (see Acts 21:9). The latter Philip had four daughters; Polycrates, however, mentions only three daughters (*E. H.* III, 31:3), which may be a copyist's error. This confusion of the two Philips was common, see Clement of Alexandria (A.D. c. 190), *Stromata* III.6:16 (*MPG*, VIII, 1156, 1158). Perhaps the identification had been made even as early as Papias (*E. H.* III.39:9).

replying that his father is stronger. Proclus asserts that Hierapolis boasts of the graves of Philip and his daughters, but Gaius counters that Rome can boast of the τρόπαια of the apostles Peter and Paul.

The central problem in dealing with the fragment of Gaius is to determine the meaning of "τρόπαια." If it is understood to indicate something other than "graves," "tombs," or "relics," then there is *no* evidence here that in the last half of the second century the grave of the apostle Peter was located by tradition on the Vatican Hill or that of Paul on the Via Ostia.

Although those who support the tradition that Peter resided, was martyred, and was buried in Rome are likely to define τρόπαια as "tombs" or "relics" and those who oppose the tradition mention more frequently the meanings "monuments" or "victories" or the like, this is not always the case.

The most complete analyses of the word "τρόπαιον" are to be found in the studies of Friedrich Lammert and Christine Mohrmann,[18] and upon these studies the following brief historical survey is based in part.

Since the text of Gaius is derived from a Roman milieu, it must be understood in light of Latin linguistic facts. Originally the word referred to the tree trunk or pole in the vicinity where a victory had been won and upon which was hung the plunder taken from the enemy in battle.[19] Later the τρόπαιον was associated with something more permanent than these comparatively temporary locations for the trophies of victory, and the word was used to describe a monument which bore some memory of victory.[20] Later still the notion of a physical monument was deemphasized as the word was increasingly associated with the *idea* of "victory" itself.[21] In fact, according to Mohrmann, the words "victory" and "tropaeum" became in time quasi-synonymous. In the period of the Empire the meaning of "tropaeum" as monument was revivified and was applied in this sense also to representations in art.

Christians used the word "τρόπαιον," or tropaeum, always metaphorically, Mohrmann claims, and never in the sense of monument. While this conclusion is disputed, it is true that the word is semipoetic and figurative in character, a fact especially apparent to Christians who used the word in connection with the cross[22] in particular and with martyrdom in general. The cross as a tropaeum is an understandable development in view of the classical meaning of the word, since the cross, by its very shape, suggests the form of the τρόπαιον on which the spoils of the victory were hung. In addition, the cross is a symbol of victory—a victory over death, a victory of God over the Devil. The word is often used to mean the Cross of Christ.[23] Tertullian mentions "per tropaeum crucis triumphavit,"[24] and Augustine: "ipsam enim crucem suam signam habiturus erat, ipsam crucem de diabolo superato tamquam tropaeum in frontibus fidelium positurus."[25] At times, though infrequently, the body of Christ is referred to as a tropaeum.[26]

---

18. Lammert, "τρόπαιον," pp. 663–73. Mohrmann, "A propos de deux Mots controversés," pp. 154–73.

19. Lammert, "τρόπαιον," Vol. VI, cols. 2165 f.; Zahn, *Introduction*, II, 82.

20. See *E. H.* VII.18:1 (Lake, II, 175), where the bronze monument, etc., in Caesarea Philippi are called τρόπαια: "καὶ τῆς ὑπὸ τοῦ σωτῆρος εἰς αὐτὴν εὐεργεσίας θαυμαστὰ τρόπαια παραμένειν." ("and those marvelous memorials of the good deed, which the Saviour wrought upon her, still remained").

21. Lammert, "τρόπαιον," p. 664, quotes the following from *Etymologicum Magnum*, an etymological compilation of the Middle Ages written A.D. c. 1100: τρόπαιον = Tropaeum. "πᾶν κτητικὸν οὐδέτερον ἀπὸ θηλυκοῦ γεγονὸς τρίτην ἀπὸ τέλους ἔχει τὴν ὀξεῖαν. οἷον κεφαλὴ κεφάλιον γυνὴ γύναιον. ὅθεν καὶ τροπὴ τρόπαιον. οἱ δὲ παλαιοὶ Ἀττικοὶ πρὸ περὶ πῦσιν. εἴρηται δὲ ἀπὸ τοῦ τρέψαι καὶ διῶξαι τοὺς πολεμίους τὰ ἱστάμενα σύμβολα τῆς νίκης." Lammert comments, "Bemerksamkeit ist die Sinndeutung als Siegehrung."

22. Justin Martyr, *Apology* I.55:3 (*MPL*, VI, 411, 412; *The Ante-Nicene Fathers*, I, 181–82); Tertullian *Ad Nationes*, I.12 (*MPL*, I, 650; *The Ante-Nicene Fathers*, III, 122); *Apology* 16:6 (*MPL*, I, 422, "Sed et victorias adoratis, cum in tropaeis cruces intestina sint tropaeorum;" *The Ante-Nicene Fathers*, III, 31).

23. Mohrmann, "A propos de deux Mots controversés," pp. 156 f. and Leo I, *Sermon* LXXXII.5 (*MPL*, LIV, 425).

24. "And through the trophy of the Cross he triumphed," *Adv. Marcion* IV.20 (*MPL*, II, 407; *The Ante-Nicene Fathers*, III, 379).

25. *In Evangelium Johannis* XXXVI.4 (*MPL*, XXXIV, 1665; *The Nicene and Post-Nicene Fathers*, VII, 209): "That very cross, a trophy, as it were."

26. Augustine, *Sermon* CCLXXIX:3 (*MPL*, XXXVIII, p. 1277): "Vide ergo mitem et humilem corde, ut ad istam gloriam tropaeum mortificatae carnis adduceret."

From the idea of the cross as a symbol of Christ's victory it is easy to see how the meaning of "tropaeum" was extended to include martyrdom itself; the very dying of the martyrs was the symbol of their victory. As Mohrmann points out, Ambrose[27] used the word in this way as did Damasus, often at the end of a verse of poetry.[28]

It is frequently mentioned that Prudentius in the *Peristephanon* employs the word "tropaeum" in the sense of sepulture,[29] but many have interpreted the word in this instance as indicating a place of martyrdom or the relics *in* the tomb.[30]

In determining the meaning of the word, some scholars have referred to an inscription found at Tabarka containing a reference to a number of martyred virgins.[31] The words "portantes tropaea" are interpreted as both "the victory of the martyr" and the "relics of the martyr." The former is the more probable since the "tropaea" in this instance are no doubt the "trophies" of their virginity consecrated to God by their faith.

Although there is a great diversity of opinion, there appears to be a development in the pagan and Christian history of the word: 1) the commemorative tree together with the spoils that hung upon it, 2) the monument which is reminiscent of the victory, 3) the Cross of Christ, 4) the Body of Christ, 5) the victory itself without a monument to commemorate it, 6) the martyrdom of Christians in the sense of this being a victory over Satan, 7) the body or the relics of the martyr, 8) the tomb of the martyr which contains the relics (the actual symbols of victory).

One encounters these various elements in most discussions of the meaning and development of the word "τρόπαιον." No one writer will agree that all these elements are accurate definitions of the word, and none will agree completely that this is the order of development. The problem for this study, however, is not the development of the word nor its many shades of meaning in various periods, but the meaning of the word *for Gaius* A.D. 200.

The views of the great majority of scholars may be divided into two main categories: those who claim that Gaius used the word "τρόπαια" in the exact way which Eusebius a century and a quarter later interpreted his meaning (in the sense of tombs or relics within the tombs or both),[32] and those who are equally positive

---

27. *De virginibus* I.2:7 (*MPL*, XVI, 201).

28. Damasus XII.4; XIV.4; XVII.8 (*Damasi Epigrammata*, ed. Ihm, pp. 18, 21, 24):
"Hic comites Xysti, portant qui ex hoste Tropaea;
hic numerus procerum, serut qui altaria Chr(ist)i;
hic positus longa vixit qui in pace sacerdos;" [xii.4]
"Iudicus populos Stephanum meliora monentem perculerat saxis, tulerat qui ex hoste Tropaeum, martyrium primus rapuit levita fidelis." [xiv.4]
". . . Tulerat qui ex hoste (T)ropaeum." [XVII.8 (a fragment)].

29. XII:7 f., *Prudentius*, trans. Thomson, II, 322, 323.
"Scit Tiberina palus, quae flumine lambitur propinquo,
Binis dicatum caespitem tropaeis,
Et crucis et gladii testis, quibus inrigans easdem
Bis fluxit imber sanguinis per herbas."
See Lietzmann, *Petrus und Paulus in Rom*, 2d ed., p. 210.

30. Carcopino, *Études*, pp. 252–53. The view of Carcopino was presupposed by Jacques Zeiller, *Histoire de l'Église*, I, 223.

31. ". . . privata cum Victoria gaude, triumpha, consecratae virginitatis et confessionis victricia portantes tropaea veste indutae angelica in pace." See Leclercq, *DACL*, Vol. XIV, Part I, p. 854, who cites the inscription from P. Monceaux, "Enquête sur l'Épigraphie chrétienne d'Afrique," *Mémoires présentés à l'Academie des Inscriptions et Belles Lettres*, LXXXVIII (1908), 260. See *Inscriptiones Latinae Cristianae Veteres*, ed. Diehl, Vol. I, No. 2032A, p. 401.

32. Zahn, *Introduction*, II, 83, is confident that in the last analysis we must define Gaius' meaning of the word in relation to the later interpretation by Eusebius. Bauer, in *Wiener Studien* (1916), p. 272n2, while maintaining that Gaius is mistaken, believes that he meant "tomb" by the word "τρόπαιον." Lietzmann, *Petrus und Paulus in Rom*, 2d ed., p. 210, reaches the same conclusion in view of the claim made by Proclus: "Was man zur Zeit des Gaius, also um 200, auf dem Vatikan zeigte, war das Petrusgrab." Delehaye, *Les Origines*, p. 264. The anonymous author of the article, "Sulle Memorie e i Monumenti dei SS. Apostoli Pietro e Paolo a Roma," *La Civiltà Cattolica*, LXXXVI (1935), 250, is positive that the word is never used in a completely figurative sense and that Eusebius' meaning (tombs) must also have been in the mind of Gaius. He criticizes Marucchi, whom he believes gives too much attention to the views of C. Erbes in *Memorie dei SS. Apostoli Pietro e Paolo a Roma*, p. 31 (that tropaeum is to be understood as a "place of martyrdom") even though he gives his own, more orthodox position on p. 29. Capocci, "Notae," p. 200, remarks that Gaius' statement "cannot refer except to two burial monuments each above a sepulcher . . . and relative to the Apostle Peter such a monument must be

that the word means not a tomb, but a monument that designates either the place of martyrdom or a victory symbol erected near the place of martyrdom[33]

---

the Aedicula." After tracing the history of the word, Leclercq, *DACL*, Vol. XIV, Part II, p. 854, concludes that "il n'est donc guère douteux que les trophées de Caius sont réellement les tombeaux des deux apôtres." Carcopino, in the following books and articles affirms his position that the word does not, strictly speaking, refer to the tombs but to the relics within the tombs: "Note sur deux Textes controversés de la Tradition apostolique romaine," p. 428; *Études*, p. 257 (σκηνώματα, i.e., "mortal remains" is probably a synonym for "τρόπαια" in the mind of Eusebius. See 2 Peter 1:14 and Prudentius, *Peristephanon* V:397–400); In *De Pythagore*, pp. 251–55, he cites further examples to support his contention in the works of Gregory of Nyssa (*MPG*, XLVI, 737, 753, 761), Basil (*MPG*, XXXI, 521), and Gregory of Nazianzus (*MPG*, XXXVI, 257). Further discussion by Carcopino in "Encore 'Tropaeum' et 'nomen'," *Studi in onore di A. Calderini e R. Paribeni*, pp. 385–90. See Bernardi, "Le Mot τρόπαιον appliqué aux Martyrs," pp. 174, 175. Josi, in *Comptes rendus de l'Académie des Inscriptions et Belles-Lettres* (1954), p. 350, mentions that since Eusebius uses "τόπος" and "κατάθεσις" (*E. H.* II.25:6; Lake, I, 183) in the immediate context and these words indicate a tomb, another literary link is found in the chain to prove that Gaius meant a tomb containing the relics of the martyred apostles when he spoke of trophies (Josi's position was supported at this session of the Académie by Jacques Zeiller). It is necessary to point out that the meaning in question is not that of Eusebius but that of Gaius. Mohrmann, "A propos de deux Mots controversés," pp. 166 f., concludes her careful analysis by saying that "tropaeum" as "place of martyrdom" lacks textual support and that, since Cyprian by the end of the fourth century and Eusebius at the beginning of the fourth century meant by "τρόπαια" the relics of the tombs, Gaius (A.D. c. 200) did not use the word to refer to a monument "but rather to their [Peter and Paul] bodies recumbent in their tombs." For this reason she suggests that the researchers no longer refer to the Aedicula beneath the Basilica of St. Peter as the "tropaeum." Cullmann, *Peter*, pp. 118 f. sees the meaning of tombs likely if the arguments of Proclus and Gaius are taken to be parallel, but he also points out certain criticisms of this conclusion. Klauser, *Die römische Petrustradition*, p. 81n161, mentions the possibility that the trophies are in fact cenotaphs, but is quick to add that the *ancients* could not have considered them to be cenotaphs, for such would not have been a guarantee of apostolic succession (the development which for Klauser explains the "sudden interest" concerning Peter's grave A.D. c. 165). Guarducci, *The Tomb of St. Peter*, p. 41.

33. Renan, *The Antichrist*, pp. 164–65 (see Eusebius, *Vita Constantina* II.40: *MPG*, XX, 1018); Lipsius, *Die apokryphen Apostelgeschichten*, Vol. II, Part I, p. 21, "τρόπαια sind nicht die Gräber, sondern die Todesstätten der beiden Apostel"; Zahn, *Introduction*, II, p. 83, is convinced that the meaning in *this* case is tombs, but sees the *possibility* that the tropaeum could also be a marker at the approximate place of execution. He bases this suggestion on Eusebius, *E. H.* II.23:18 (Lake, I, 175), who implies that there was such a marker over the tomb of James the Just, "καὶ ἔθαψαν αὐτὸν ἐπὶ τῷ τόπῳ παρὰ τῷ ναῷ, καὶ ἔτι αὐτοῦ ἡ στήλη μένει παρὰ τῷ ναῷ." (Eusebius claims that this is an account given by Hegesippus in agreement with Clement). Guignebert, *La Primauté de Pierre*, is sure that Gaius "en écrivant trophées n'a certainement pas entendu tombeaux"; Erbes, *Die Todestag*, pp. 68 f.; Guignebert, "La Sépulture de Pierre," pp. 226–28, maintains that if Gaius had meant a tomb he would have used another word in an attempt to be more definite. The word "τρόπαιον" probably means some landmark in the area of the martyrdom of the apostles, which for Peter may have been the Terebinth and for Paul, the Pine (which on the testimony of the *Acti Petri et Pauli* was near the Acquae Salviae). He also calls attention to the view of Shotwell and Loomis, *The See of Peter*, p. 180. Lemerle, "Les Fouilles de Saint Pierre de Rome," p. 403 (see p. 410n8): "Trophée signifie trophée de victoire . . . en parlant de martyrs . . . concrètement le lieu où ils sont morts." The same view, which claims that any other understanding is "unreasonable," is found in a second article by Lemerle, "La Publication des Fouilles," p. 224. See also his article the year before in *Revue Archéologique* entitled "Les Persécutions et le Tombeau de Saint Pierre." This opinion is shared by Burger, *La Tombe*, pp. 15 ff., who also will not admit that the Aedicula found in the recent excavations beneath St. Peter's Basilica is the "Trophy" of Gaius. See De Bruyne, "La Tomba apostolica," p. 220, who believes that the Tropaeum of Gaius and the Aedicula are clearly the same. Leo Kunibert Mohlberg, "Historisch-kritische," p. 55n22, concluded (*after* only "ein leeres Grab" was found under the Vatican) that the Tropaeum of Gaius was intended to indicate a "monument of victory" and not a grave. (Of course, this view, as well as a number of others, does not allow for the possibility that Gaius *believed* there was a tomb there, even if there was not.) Only after A.D. 225 did the idea arise that Peter's grave was there. Grégoire, "Le Tombeau de Valerius Herma," p. 399, is sure that the monument relative to Peter, to which Gaius refers by the word "τρόπαιον" is really the tomb of the Valerii; and see his "Le Problème de la Tombe de Saint Pierre," p. 49. Von Gerkan in "Kritische Studien," p. 45, objects that some incorrectly say that "τρόπαιον" *cannot* mean "grave"; it can mean a grave in the figurative sense—it does not mean a grave expressly. It could not have meant a place of execution, for Gaius seems to represent the trophies of both apostles as similar, which is not applicable to

or a cenotaph.[34] In other words the designation of τὰ τρόπαια ἀποστόλων is meant to imply that: 1) this is the spot where one may seek the relics of the apostles or 2) it is not necessarily the spot or 3) there is no relationship between the τρόπαια of the apostles and their tombs or relics or both.

---

the places of martyrdom. See his "Die Forschung nach dem Grab Petri," pp. 201, 204. The tropaeum was not a place of burial but *near* a place of burial which, in the case of Peter in A.D. 200, no one could locate exactly. See also his article in *Evangelische Lutherische Kirchenzeitung*, VI (1952), 379 ff. Schäfer, "Das Apostelgrab," p. 313, assumes that Gaius meant the general areas of the executions of the apostles Peter and Paul—the Vatican and the Via Ostia. See also Alfons Schneider, "Die Memoria Apostolorum," pp. 2 f., and "Das Petrusgrab im Vatikan," pp. 322 ff. Torp, "The Vatican Excavations," p. 60, is confident that Gaius meant "a place of martyrdom," for the idea of a martyr's relics in A.D. 200 had not yet been used as an argument in political and ecclesiastical discussions. By Cyprian's time this had changed (see p. 62n171). Marrou, *DACL*, Vol. XV, Part II, pp. 3343, 3344, is not dogmatic on the question of whether tropaeum means tomb or monument: "c'est en tout cas ainsi qu'Eusèbe l'a compris [as a tomb]; it n'est en tout assuré que c'est ainsi que l'entendait Caius." The word "τρόπαιον" could mean a grave or a monument and he admits that "il parait difficile de faire un choix entre ces diverses hypothèses." See Klauser, *Die römische Petrustradition*, pp. 38 ff., 85, 86. Heussi, *Die römische Petrustradition*, p. 47, "Einerlei, ob die Gräber der Apostel oder ihre Hinrichtungsstätten gemeint sind, in jedem Falle lässt sich der Stelle entnehmen, dass damals in Rom die Tradition über Petrus und Paulus mit bestimmten Örtlichkeiten verbunden war." Guarducci, *I. Graffiti*, II, 404–5, is confident that Gaius in his argument "allude certamente ad oggetti bene visibili, e non a reliquie celate nella Terra o dentro un ripostiglio." The "τρόπαια" here are "monumenti di vittoria."

34. While this possibility is mentioned by some, there are only a few who appear to take it seriously. Peterson, "A propos du Tombeau," p. 492, says: "One can well designate the place of martyrdom as a place of victory. One can also qualify by 'trophy' the relics of the martyrs. One can even speak of a 'trophy' *a propos* of a monument of bronze. . . . It is possible that the term had been suggested to Gaius by his Montanist disputant, for . . . it is presented twice in a short passage. . . . But one can ask if this imprecise word was not chosen by Gaius precisely because the tombs were not in Rome, but some monuments to oppose to the pretentions of the Asiatics"; perhaps τρόπαιον means a cenotaph (see also p. 494). Chadwick, "St. Peter and St. Paul," p. 44, mentions that the language of Gaius is not decisive for or against the view that τρόπαια means tombs or graves. Chadwick asks

Before one decides hastily as to the intention of Gaius in his use of the word "τρόπαιον," one should heed the warning of Toynbee and Perkins that "in the present state of knowledge it would certainly be unwise to press the claims of either interpretation on purely philological grounds."[35] The decision must be reached only after having considered carefully which meaning is the more likely in the context of the dispute between Gaius and Proclus.

The introduction to the statement of Gaius by Eusebius shows that Gaius meant by τρόπαια the graves of Peter and Paul, for he says that Gaius "speaks as follows of the places where the sacred relics of the apostles in question are deposited." If Proclus in the *Ecclesiastical History* III.31:4 boasts of the *graves* ("their grave [ὁ τάφος] is there and so is their father's"), it is most reasonable to think that Gaius countered by mentioning the *graves* (τρόπαια) of the apostles.[36] Proclus refers to the burial place of the apostle Philip and his four daughters in order that what he claims in his argument may appear to have "apostolic" authority. The location of the grave of Philip is "proof" that this apostle had had contact with the people of Hierapolis and therefore Proclus intended it to be assumed that his teaching was obtained from Philip through an authorized succession.[37] If this interpretation

---

whether, it would not be probable however, that at a later time the memorial monument which is now under the Vatican (which was a cenotaph marking the place of Peter's martyrdom) was taken for the actual grave. This is very possible, he claims, but proves nothing in relation to the meaning of Gaius A.D. 200.

35. *The Shrine of St. Peter*, p. 154.

36. This argument from the parallel relationship between the two statements may be advanced even though the reference to Proclus' claim is made in a different section of the *E. H.* (II.25:7 and III.31:4; Lake, I, 183 and 271). Eusebius is surely referring to the same debate in both places and included the material concerning Proclus in III.31:4 because it served his purpose at that point and not earlier.

37. Notice how Polycrates argues (*E. H.* V.24:2 ff., Lake, I, 505 ff.) from the standpoint of apostolic authority in his Easter controversy, see above, p. 25, with Victor. He mentions that Philip and his three daughters (III.31:5) were among "those who kept the fourteenth day of the Passover according to the gospel." Possession of graves appears to be growing in importance. See Cullmann, *Peter*, p. 120.

of the reasoning of Proclus is sound, would it have been probable that Gaius would claim simply that Rome possessed cenotaphs dedicated to the apostles? It doesn't seem likely, since this would imply no personal contact between the apostles and the Church at Rome.

From the standpoint that both disputants wished to demonstrate the apostolic authority of their respective churches, Gaius could have spoken *either* of two monuments which marked the places of martyrdom, that is, the places of victory of the two apostles *or* of their graves. Possession of proof that Peter and Paul had *died* in Rome would guarantee as much personal contact between the Church and the apostles as would possession of their graves. On the other hand, the possession of the place of martyrdom is not as "tangible" evidence as is the possession of the tomb (which presumably contains the relics). There is more certainty in a statement about tombs, which presupposes the ability to back up the claim if greatly pressed; the relics presumably could be produced while a vague "place of martyrdom" could only be verified by fallible human testimony. Furthermore, Gaius appears to be making a claim parallel to that of Proclus, for if it were not intended to be parallel, one would naturally expect him to explain the difference in his argument and *why* the difference is important.

Even if it were conceded that it is at least most probable that Gaius alluded to the graves of Peter and Paul and testified to his belief that these were situated at the Vatican and the Via Ostia, this does not guarantee that what he says corresponds to the facts.[38] It is important to note that there is not one allusion in the New Testament to the burial of Peter, although there is a possible mention of his martyrdom in John 21[39] and Revelation 11:3–13.[40] And while Clement of Rome clearly alludes to the death of Peter and Paul, he too says nothing of their burial. In fact, it might be argued that ἐπορεύθη (5:4) and ἀνελήμφθη or ἐπορεύθη (5:7) might instead suggest ascension. The apocryphal *Acts of Peter* and *Acts of Paul* do not emphasize the idea of burial, and what reference to it they do contain may be caused by the influence of later cultic interests.[41] In addition, it may be doubted whether the faithful would have been permitted to recover the remains of the apostles,[42] and in the case of Peter whether they would have recognized the remains had they been permitted to recover them. Also it must be mentioned that there is not the slightest evidence that a cult of martyrs' relics existed in the West at this time (A.D. c. 165), although it is conceivable that such a cult *may* have existed in this period.

On the other side, it may be argued that if graves had been "invented" [found], because of the growing interest in the relics of the martyrs, for cultic or apologetic purposes, the choice of the Vatican and the Via Ostia was not fortuitous.[43] The tombs would more naturally have been "discovered" in the Catacombs where cultic activities could have been carried on in comparative safety.[44] Furthermore, it would have been natural, but not necessary, in light of the evidence available in the apocryphal material, to have "invented" the graves of Peter and Paul in the same place or at least in the same vicinity.

Finally, as mentioned above, it does not make a substantial difference to the argument of Gaius whether he indicated the "place of martyrdom" or the "tombs" for, as Cullmann points out, it is most natural to believe that the place of burial (if there was a burial at all) would be close by the place of execution.[45] But it *does* make a great deal of difference to this study which seeks to ascertain where Peter was buried and whether the Aedicula recently discovered beneath the Vatican (an hypothesis which I discuss in detail in Chapter 9 below) really marks the exact location.

---

38. Lipsius, *Die apokryphen Apostelgeschichten*, II, 21, claims that Gaius was duped and that the tomb of Peter was not intentionally, but nevertheless actually, invented around A.D. 170.

39. See above, pp. 61–64.

40. See above, pp. 65–68.

41. See above, pp. 67–68; Cullmann, *Peter*, pp. 109n55, 119.

42. See above, p. 93.

43. See below, pp. 131–32.

44. See below, pp. 127–28. Goguel, *Les premiers Temps de l'Église* (cited by Grégoire, "Les Persécutions," p. 102), suggests that "vers 200 on a pu nommer le Vatican comme lieu de supplice de Pierre, ce peut être tout simplement parce qu'on pensait qu'il avait peri au cours des massacres qui avaient suivi l'incendie de Rome. Il pourrait bien n'y avoir là qu'une conjecture et presque un aveu d'ignorance."

45. *Peter*, p. 120.

LATE AND SECONDARY EVIDENCE

The Evidence from the Apocryphal Acts of Peter and the Acts of Peter and Paul

If the burial places of Peter and Paul were known at all, it is curious that they were not mentioned at least by Clement of Rome and Dionysius of Corinth. Gaius indicates the Vatican as the burial place of Peter, but this is not the only tradition of the location. The *Acts of Peter* in the late second century says nothing of a burial of Peter on the Vatican, and near the conclusion of the document it is stated simply that "Marcellus not asking the leave of any, for it was not possible, when he saw that Peter had given up the ghost, took him down from the cross with his own hands and washed him in milk and wine . . . and perfumed the body . . . and laid it in his own tomb."[46] The location of the tomb is not mentioned. In a Syriac *Preaching of Simon Cephas in Rome*, Linus buries the body of Peter, but again no definite place is mentioned.[47] The *Acts of Peter and Paul* (sixth century) and other apocryphal documents mention that Peter was buried "under the Terebinth near the Naumachy in a place called the Vatican,"[48] on June 29,[49] but that the body remained Ad Catacumbas for one year, seven months (the Greek πράξεις τῶν

ἁγίων ἀποστόλων Πέτρου καὶ Παύλου reads one year, six months)[50] prior to his burial on the Vatican. In a version of the πράξεις τῶν ἁγίων ἀποστόλων preserved by Johannes Malalas (sixth century), it is stated that Nero prohibited the burial of the bodies of Peter and Paul.[51]

The Linus text (L) of the *Passion of Peter and Paul* written probably at Rome in the fifth or early sixth century contains the information that Peter was buried in a place "qui vocatur Naumachia iuxta obeliscum in montem."[52]

Lipsius is confident that these texts in their statements concerning the burial place of Peter have made a deduction from the assumed place of martyrdom. He bases his position upon the belief that in the second century it was commonly held that Peter and Paul had died in the Neronian persecution.[53] In accordance with this tradition, Lipsius claims, Gaius pointed to the τρόπαια, the place of martyrdom, of Peter and Paul. The early editions of certain apocryphal documents also referred to the Vatican as the place of the *martyrdom* of Peter, but later recensions extended the reference to the Vatican to include the place of *burial*.

I suggested earlier[54] that Gaius most probably meant to indicate tombs or graves by the word "τρόπαια." If this was his meaning, then the authors of certain apocryphal *Acts* may have been aware of a second-century tradition which held that Peter was buried on the Vatican. The various details, "Naumachy," "Obelisk," "Terebinth," and the like, reflect attempts to locate the particular place of burial within the large Vatican area. While the details in themselves cannot be

---

46. *Acts of Peter* XL (in James, *The Apocryphal New Testament*, p. 336). Lipsius, *Die apokryphen Apostelgeschichten*, Vol. II, Part I, pp. 93, 118.

47. Cureton, *Ancient Syriac Documents*, pp. 35–41; Lipsius, *Die apokryphen Apostelgeschichten*, Vol. II, Part I, p. 306: "Isus (Linus) hebt die Leichname des Nachts auf und bestattet sie."

48. *Acta Petri et Pauli* LXXXIV, "καὶ αὐτοὶ ἅμα Μαρκέλλῳ ἀνδρὶ ἰλλουστρίῳ, ὅστις καὶ πεπίστευκε πέτρῳ καταλιπὼν τὸν Σίμονα ἧραν τὸ σῶμα αὐτοῦ λάθρα καὶ ἔθηκαν αὐτὸ ὑπὸ τὴν τερέβινθον πλησίον τοῦ ναυμαχίου εἰς τόπον καλούμενον βατικανόν." in *Acta Apostolorum apocrypha*, ed. Tischendorf, p. 37. Notice the variant tradition, Lipsius, *Die apokryphen Apostelgeschichten*, Vol. II, Part I, p. 102, in which an angel loosens the body from the cross and the Christians (unspecified number) take the body down and bury it "in a place called the Vatican." See Vol. II, Part I, pp. 336, 391.

49. *Acta Petri et Pauli* LXXXVIII, in *Acta Apostolorum apocrypha*, ed. Tischendorf, pp. 39, 304.

50. Lipsius, *Acta Apostolorum apocrypha*, I, 174, 220. See also the Syriac *Acta of Scharbil* (Cureton, *Ancient Syriac Documents*, p. 61).

51. Lipsius, *Die apokryphen Apostelgeschichten*, Vol. II, Part I, p. 212: "Nero befiehlt, die Leiber der beiden heiligen Apostel sollten unbestattet bleiben."

52. *Ibid.*, pp. 273–74.

53. 1 Clement 5, 6. (Lightfoot, *Apostolic Fathers*, Part I, Vol. II, pp. 25–34; *Early Christian Fathers*, trans. Richardson, pp. 45–46).

54. See above, p. 101.

considered as representing authentic traditions, they do demonstrate a growing cultic interest in the relics and tombs of the apostles and martyrs.[55]

A Statement of Julian the Apostate

Julian the Apostate (emperor, A.D. 361–63) in *Contra Christianos*,[56] at a point in which it was mentioned that John the Evangelist first spoke of Christ as God, added that in this period the "tombs of Peter and Paul although hidden were adored." If this statement were accurate, it would mean that in the period when "John" wrote (A.D. c. 125), the tombs of the apostles Peter and Paul were already venerated. Corte warns that this claim of Julian *may* be an unfounded tradition. He could have stated it more strongly; a tradition such as this, appearing for the first time in the fourth century, is *surely* unfounded.[57]

The Evidence of Eusebius

It has been shown that Eusebius interpreted the word "τρόπαια," as used by Gaius, to mean the tombs of Peter and Paul. Furthermore, since he did not question the indication of the Via Ostia and the Vatican by Gaius, it must be accepted that he considered these locations to be accurate.[58] In *De theophania* (A.D. 330–39) Eusebius writes that "the memory of him [Peter] now is greater among the Romans than it was earlier so that he is deemed worthy of a glorious sepulture by the State to which hastens, as to a great Sanctuary and Temple of God, a myriad amount of Roman riches [sic]."[59] If this work was written before A.D. 339 and the statement refers to a basilica built over what was considered to be the tomb of Peter, it witnesses to a general belief in the early fourth century that the apostle was buried in the Vatican area.[60]

THE DAMASUS INSCRIPTION

Documents such as the *Liber Pontificalis* are greatly dependent upon the apocryphal *Acts*, which definitely refer to the Vatican as the burial place of Peter. Some scholars maintain that there was another relatively early tradition which claimed that Peter was buried originally not on the Vatican but Ad Catacumbas on the Via Appia.[61] They find support for this view in an inscription by Pope Damasus (A.D. 366–84),[62] which must be analyzed before deciding whether their position is at all justified.

That Pope Damasus was popular with the people of Rome may be due in part to his zeal in recovering the graves of the martyrs. He composed numerous inscriptions in indifferent verse which were incised in marble and set up in the tombs. One of these inscriptions, known only in a copy made by a pilgrim in the seventh century,[63] originally was set up either inside the Church of San Sebastiano or in the adjoining building called the "Platonia":[64]

55. These various topographical details are considered at length in the discussion of the archeological evidence.

56. See Cyril of Alexandria, *Contra Julianum* X.

57. Cecchelli, *Il Tempo*, December 11, 1952; Cristiani, "Les Fouilles de Saint-Pierre," p. 62; Corte, *Saint Pierre est-il au Vatican?* p. 142.

58. *E. H.* II.25:7 (Lake, I, 183). See above, pp. 95–101.

59. *De theophania* IV.7, *Theophania*, trans. Lee, p. 221.

60. This fragment is preserved only in the Syriac. A German translation was made in 1904 by H. Gressman. The word translated here as "sepulture" is rendered from the Syriac by Gressman as "Grabstätte." He cites R. Payne Smith as his authority for this translation, *Thesaurus Syriacus*, col. 3481.

61. For example, Tollotti, *Memorie degli Apostoli in Catacumbas*.

62. See *MPL*, XIII, 1215, 1216; and *Le Liber Pontificalis*, ed. Duchesne, Vol. I, Part I, pp. 212–15.

63. Barnes, *The Martyrdom of St. Peter and St. Paul*, pp. 47–59, believes that he has recovered some of the fragments of the lost inscription. See especially the plates after pp. 50 and 52. He is of the opinion that the fragments he has found are from the first three lines and that the original may have been smashed in the Saracen invasion in the ninth century. The inscription was recognized as Damasian because of the distinctive Philocalian lettering.

64. This building is described below, pp. 137–38.

Hic habitasse prius sanctos cognoscere debes
Nomina quisque Petri pariter Paulique requiris.
Discipulos Oriens misit, quod sponte fatemur;
Sanguinis ob meritum Christumque per astra secuti,
Aetherios petiere sinus regnaque piorum.
Roma suos potius meruit defendere cives,
Haec Damasus vestras referat, nova sidera, laudes.[65]

The main interest and the main problem of the inscription lie in whether it implies that Peter and Paul once lived in this vicinity or that their relics were buried here, immediately after their martyrdom or at a later time. The interpretation of the inscription is difficult,

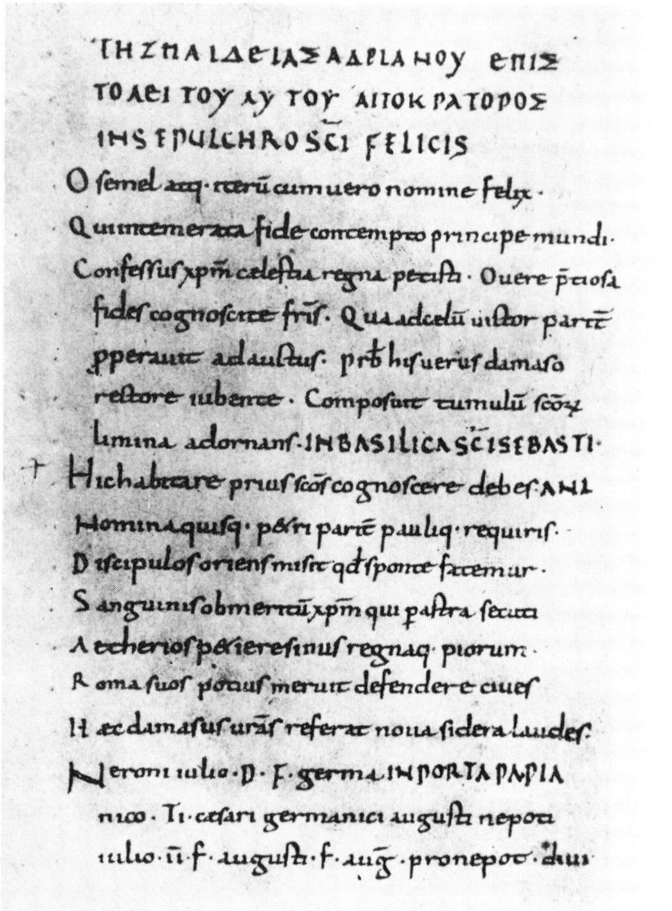

PLATE 2   Damasus' "habitasse" inscription in honor of Peter and Paul copied by a pilgrim at the beginning of the Middle Ages and preserved in the Syllogium Einsiedelnensis. This MS is preserved at the Abbey of Einsiedeln and is from the eighth century—cod. 326, fol. 78 verso. Notice the "habitare" in place of the "habitasse" in the MS on line 11 (Besson, Saint Pierre et les Origines de la Primauté romaine, Fig. 44, p. 65).

as an understatement of Delehaye suggests: "cette poésie ne pèche point par excès de clarté."[66]

The inscription begins with the word "hic." If this demonstrative pronoun was used in an extremely limited sense, it could be interpreted as indicating the precise location of the apostolic tomb.[67] But it could also mean the general location of the church or "hic, in catacumbis" or even "hic Romae."[68] The wider meaning, "hic Romae," is defended by Boulet: "here [in this place], in Rome" either Peter and Paul actually resided or at one time their relics were located. This less local meaning is most appropriate if the inscription were designed not for those living in Rome, for whom information concerning a Roman burial of Peter and Paul would be superfluous, but for those pilgrims who would naturally enter Rome from the eastern countries on the Via Appia. This meaning also has the advantage of binding together the two parts of the inscription, aiding in the presentation of a single idea instead of two unrelated ideas. If the "hic" refers to the City of Rome, then this also explains the confusion of those who read the inscription having come out *from* the City of Rome, a confusion which led to the apocryphal legend of the stealing of the relics of Peter and Paul by the Orientals.[69] Even if either interpretation is *possible*, it must be said, for a number of reasons which will become more clear after the excavations at San Sebastiano have been examined, that the less local interpretation is the more probable.

65. *Damasi Epigrammata*, trans. Ihm, Number 26: "Here you should know that the saints dwelt at one time, you who seek the names of both Peter and Paul. We freely acknowledge that the East sent them as disciples [of the Lord]. For Christ's sake and the merit of his blood, they followed him across the stars, and sought the heavenly regions, Kingdom of pious souls. Rome has merited to claim them as citizens. Damasus has wished to proclaim these things, O new stars, to your praise." (Trans. A. S. Barnes.)

66. *Histoire ecclésiastique*, II, 5, cited by Griffe, in *Bull. de Litt. ecclés.* (1953), p. 135. Guignebert, "La Sépulture de Pierre," p. 238, says simply, "the form is miserable and the sense obscure."

67. Hertling and Kirschbaum, *Die römischen Katakomben*, p. 105.

68. Testini, "Noterelle sulla 'Memoria Apostolorum,'" p. 228; Tolotti, *Memorie*, pp. 282, 283.

69. Boulet, "À propos des Fouilles," pp. 405–6.

Does the "prius" in this instance mean "at first" or "formerly" and what does it modify? The second question has been asked, but the answer is fairly obvious: "prius" goes with "habitasse" and not with "cognoscere." The first question is more complicated. It is argued by Duchesne, and others who follow his reasoning, that "prius" implies that the relics of Peter and Paul were here, but they are not here *now*. If the word were used to inform the pilgrim that Peter and Paul had once *lived* here, the "prius" no longer opposes a situation past to a condition or situation present, and "prius" adds nothing to the sense. It would have been superfluous for Damasus (d. A.D. 384) to explain that Peter and Paul (d. A.D. c. 64) had lived in this vicinity prior to his writing.[70] Whether the statement is true or false, the priority is obvious. What is meant here by "prius," according to Guignebert, is "formerly," that is, the relics of Peter and Paul were here in some period before the time when Damasus wrote.[71] Any other interpretation, he explains, would conflict with the tradition preserved by the *Depositio Martyrum* and the *Martyrologium Hieronymianum*.[72] The opposite point of view is taken by Boulet who interprets "prius" not in the sense of "previously" or "at one time" but as meaning "first" or "first of all." To support his view he cites an inscription of Sixtus III, from a period approximately fifty years after Damasus, found at St. Pierre-aux-Liens: "Cede prius nomen novitati, cede vetustas."[73] No matter how the word is interpreted, either implication is at variance with what is most probably the truth. All evidence taken together makes it very doubtful that Peter and Paul ever lived Ad Catacumbas or were buried there "eo tempore quo passi sunt."

The central word in the problem of the inscription is "habitasse."[74] Duchesne and others take the word in its funerary sense. Their argument is that one could examine the history of the Early Church and not find one example of veneration attached to a private dwelling —the place where once the saint in question had lived, "be it of an apostle, of other great ecclesiastics, martyrs, bishops, etc. Christian piety is always oriented around the burial place, not around the common dwelling; sometimes one sees, if it is a question of a martyr, to be also attached to the place of martyrdom, but that is all."[75] Against this assured assertion Delehaye cites a

70. Duchesne, "La 'Memoria Apostolorum,'" p. 7; Leclercq, *DACL*, Vol. XIV, Part I, p. 873. Testini, "Noterelle sulla 'Memoria Apostolorum,'" p. 229; Prius means "prima della pace prima che si reportassero le reliquie ai loro siti originali."

71. Guignebert, "La Sépulture de Pierre," p. 238.

72. These liturgical documents, however, must not be looked upon as necessarily trustworthy. See below, pp. 116–26.

73. Boulet, "À propos des Fouilles," p. 404.

74. Ferrua and others favor this "hard" reading found in MSS Turonensem (VII) and Laureshamensi (IX). "Habitare" is found in MSS Einsiedlensem (VIIII) and Petropolitanus (IX). See *Damasi Epigrammata*, trans. Ihm, and *CIL*, Vol. VI, Part I, pp. ix f. Giulio Belvederi's preference for "habitare" would place the bodies of Peter and Paul Ad Catacumbas at the time when Damasus wrote (A.D. 366–84) and have them transferred to the Vatican and Via Ostia in the sixth century. *Le Tombe apostoliche nell'età paleocristiana*.

75. Duchesne, "La 'Memoria Apostolorum,'" p. 7; F. Grossi-Gondi, "Il 'Refrigerium,'" p. 246n3. Lietzmann, *Petrus und Paulus in Rom*, 1st ed., pp. 107 f.; 2d ed., p. 149. Leclercq, *DACL*, Vol. XIV, Part I, pp. 872, 873, admits that the more common meaning is "to live," but he favors the less common meaning found in inscription No. 31 of Damasus (*DACL*, Vol. IV, p. 182n31). An argument in favor of the latter view is that Peter and Paul are mentioned together; it is very improbable that they lived together in the same place. We do know, however, from 1 Clement, Ignatius, and Romans 4:3 that the Church did not hesitate to join them *after* their deaths. See *DACL*, Vol. XIV, Part I, p. 876. See Lemerle, in *La Nouvelle Clio*, IV (1952), p. 401n4. Guignebert, "La Sépulture de Pierre," p. 238, agrees with this position since the meaning must be the same as that found indisputably in inscription No. 31 (Ihm): "inveniet vicina in sede habitare beatos;" Goguel, *L'Église primitive*, p. 211; Hertling and Kirschbaum, *Die römischen Katakomben*, p. 111. In Carcopino, "Note sur deux textes controversés," p 430, *Études*, p. 260, and *De Pythagore*, pp. 246, 247, Peter is never mentioned in any hagiographic source Ad Catacumbas and Paul is mentioned in Acts 28:16 as dwelling by himself and guarded by a soldier, an assumption which is elaborated in the later *Acts of Peter and Paul*. Testini, "Noterelle sulla 'Memoria Apostolorum,'" p. 229, rejects Delehaye's view on archeological grounds; the existence of the nearby "Villa," which some scholars hold supports the view that Peter *lived* Ad Catacumbas, was not built before the second century. Toynbee, "The Shrine of St. Peter and Its Setting," p. 14; Toynbee and Perkins, *The Shrine of St. Peter*, p. 168; Chadwick, "St. Peter and St. Paul," p. 34; Schäfer, *Die Bedeutung der Epigramme des Papstes Damasus I*, p. 26, "Pilger oder Mönchsführer des frühen Mittelalters bezeichneten ein Gemach in unmittelbarer Nähe der 'Platonia'

conciliar statement from Africa.[76] Guignebert agrees with Duchesne and Lietzmann that "habitasse" must be taken in the funerary sense by analogy with Damasus Inscription, Number 31.[77] There are others, including the famous hagiographer Delehaye, however, who take seriously the view that Peter and Paul actually lived Ad Catacumbas at some time during the period when they were in Rome.[78] This latter meaning cannot be easily accepted on the grounds that there surely would have been some surviving tradition to that effect. The words "Domus Petri" on the wall of the small building adjoining the Church of San Sebastiano cannot serve as evidence since they are much too late, as is shown

below.[79] Furthermore, the words "Domus Petri" were most likely suggested to a pilgrim by the very inscription which is now under discussion. There are, however, legendary traditions concerning a Roman residence of Peter such as that found in the *Acta Marcelli*, where the Ostian cemetery is identified with a place "ubi Petrus baptizabat ad nymphas sancti Petri."

If "habitasse" refers to an original burial of Peter and Paul Ad Catacumbas, this contradicts the early literary and liturgical evidence; and if taken to mean a later burial, this involves the question of a translation of the relics which will be discussed in the following chapter.

"Nomina" is another important word found in the inscription. Christine Mohrmann traces its meaning historically as she did with the word "τρόπαια" used by Gaius. She discovered that there were two streams actively flowing into the meaning of the word in the period when Damasus wrote. In the Old Testament the familiar שֵׁם יהוה refers to the "presence of Jahweh"; in Greek this is rendered ὄνομα Θεοῦ. There is a mysterious, power-filled quality in the idea of a name which is derived from very primitive belief. In Latin the word was used commonly as the designation of a people; for example, the "nomen Latinum," meaning "all those who call themselves Latins." The New Testament reflects the Hebrew influence in its use of the word in Acts 4:12: "And there is salvation in no one else, for there is no other name under heaven given among men by which we must be saved."[80] The same understanding of the word is also found in Ignatius[81] and 2 Clement.[82]

Cyprian also used the word in the term "confessio nominus" or "confessio nominis Christi" which parallels in part the biblical idea of שֵׁם or ὄνομα.[83] The Church Fathers, such as Tertullian, used the term "confessio nominis" partially in the biblical sense and partly in the old Roman sense of identifying the person

durch ein Graffito das im Jahre 1909 zum Vorschein kam als 'Domus Petri.' Dass wir am 3 Meilenstein der Via Appia nicht das wirkliche Haus des Apostels Petrus suchen dürfen, in dem gar auch Paulus zeitweise gewohnt haben soll, sondern dass derjenige, der das Graffito einritzte, das 'habitasse' im ersten Vers unseres Gedichtes allzu wörtlich nahm, ist evident."

76. Delehaye, *Les Origines*, p. 305, cites *Codex Eccl. Africanae* LXXXIII, Bruns, I, 176, "Omnino nulla memoria martyrum probabiliter acceptur, nisi ubi corpus aut aliquae reliquiae sunt aut origo alicuius habitationis vel possessionis vel passionis fidelissima origine traditur." He also mentions the three separate basilicas of Cyprian which are described by Monceaux, in *Histoire littéraire de L'Afrique chrétienne*, II, 71–86.

77. "Martyris hic tumulus magno sub vertice montis
　　Gorgonium retinet, servat qui altaria Christi.
　Hic, quicumque venit, sanctorum limina [Martyr's
　　　graves] quaerat,
　　inveniet vicina in sede habitare beatos,
　　ad caelum pariter pietas quos vexit euntes."
(*Damasi Epigrammata*, trans. Ihm, Number 31).

78. Delehaye, "Le Sanctuaire des Apôtres," pp. 294–304; Erbes, "Die geschichtlichen Verhältnisse der Apostelgräber in Rom," pp. 38 ff.; Lanciani, "La Memoria Apostolorum e gli Scavi," pp. 57–109; La Piana, "The Tombs of Peter and Paul ad Catacumbas," 67 ff.; Wilpert, "Domus Petri," pp. 117–22, and "La Tomba di S. Pietro," pp. 27–41; Schuster, "Domvs Petri," pp. 160 f. The most prominent scholar of recent times to hold this opinion is E. Griffe. He claims in *Bull. de Litt. ecclés.* (1951), p. 199, that the verb in the past tense makes it necessary to eliminate the funerary meaning; if the verb were in the present tense, the funerary meaning would be obvious. On page 200 he continues that Damasus wished to explain that Peter and Paul were honored Ad Catacumbas because they had *lived* there at one time, "l'inscription n'est pas sans doute des plus claires, mais elle se comprend suffisamment," in *Bull. de Litt. ecclés.* (1953), pp. 131, 132, 137, 138.

79. See below, p. 138.

80. Acts 5:41: "Then they left the presence of the council, rejoicing that they were counted worthy to suffer dishonor for the name."

81. *Ephesians* 3:1 (*Early Christian Fathers*, trans. Richardson, p. 88); *Ephesians* 7:1 (*ibid.*, p. 89); *Philadelphians* 10:1 (*ibid.*, p. 111).

82. In 2 Clement 13:1 (*ibid.*, p. 198).

83. See Cyprian, *De habitu virginis* VI (*MPL*, IV, 446); *De unitate ecclesiae* XIV (*MPL*, IV, 510).

or persons with the group ("nomen Latinum"). As Mohrmann emphasizes, there was in this period and later a wedding of the two streams of thought. The term came to denote the presence of something in a specific group of people, as well as a differentiation.

The meaning of ὄνομα as a "person" is found in Acts 1:15: "In those days Peter stood up among the brethren (the company of persons [ὀνομάτων] was in all about one hundred and twenty)." This same meaning of the word, Mohrmann shows, is found in classical Latin writers such as Cicero and Seneca and others, and in popular usage, as reflected in the *defixionum tabellae*. The popular idiom in turn influenced the Vulgate translation, for example, in Revelation 11:13, where ὀνόματα is rendered "nomina."[84] From the popular understanding of the word, "nomen" as "person," it is not difficult to imagine the development of "nomina" meaning "relics," as found in a number of Latin inscriptions. For example, there is the inscription, discovered in Algeria in 1890 near Tixter, written in Vulgate Latin: "et dabula [for *tabula*] it [for *id*] de lignu [for *ligno*] crucis de ter(r)a promisionis [for *promissionis*], ube [for *ubi*] natus est Christus, apostoli Petri et Pauli, nomina marturu[m] Datani, Donatiani, Cipriani, Nemesani, (C)itini, et Victo(r)ia(nu)s."[85] Here "nomen marturu" does not mean the relics of the cross nor the relics of Peter and Paul, Mohrmann claims, but "persons"—African martyrs—that is, their remains.

The funerary meaning is most probably not a Christian innovation but a derivation from the common language of the day. And even though the definition "relics" for "nomina" is possible, Mohrmann is convinced that it is by no means assured that this is the meaning in the Damasus Inscription. She warns that the inscriptions where "nomina" is defined in this way derive only from Africa, not from Italy. In addition, Damasus uses the word elsewhere, but never in the sense of "relics."

Lietzmann is convinced that the word "nomen" in this inscription means "person,"[86] and he is followed by Last, Griffe, Chadwick, and Toynbee.[87] Carcopino alone takes the stand that the word "nomina" definitely means "relics."[88]

---

86. Lietzmann, "The Tomb of the Apostles ad Catacumbas," p. 150; *Petrus und Paulus in Rom*, 2d ed., p. 148. For the names of these African saints, see Delehaye, *Les Origines*, pp. 376, 383, 386.

87. Last, in *The Journal of Roman Studies*, XLIV (1954), 115, suggests that at a place where the veneration of the apostles Peter and Paul was active, as in the Basilica Apostolorum, the word "nomina" could well be interpreted as meaning simply "names"—the "names of the blessed dead which in the Roman rite were recited in one of the prayers of the Synaxis before the Mass, much as such names were read from one leaf of the diptychs in the Eastern and Gallican rites." This interpretation is followed by Griffe, in *Bull. de Litt. ecclés.* (1953), pp. 133, 134, who challenges the idea that "relics" is *really* meant by "nomina" in the Algerian inscriptions, and even so, doubts that this is the meaning in the Damasus Inscription. He questions Carcopino who accepts the definition of Gsell that "nomen" can mean "memoria" or "reliquiae." The former does not necessarily mean "relics" in any sense. It can mean anything which calls to mind the memory of the martyr—the tomb, casket, or reliquary, or even the part of the church where one assumes the tomb of the saint to be—or the whole church; in other words, it need not indicate the precise place where the relics are assumed to be. Griffe also cites African inscriptions where "nomina" does not mean either "relics" or "memoria." See also in this regard, Delehaye, in *Analecta Bollandiana*, XXII (1903), 478, and XXV (1906), 350. Delehaye, *Les Origines* (1912), p. 308, mentions that if Damasus, not being a slave to meter, wanted to say "relics," he could have used the word "corpora" instead of "nomina." (See *Damasi Epigrammata*, trans. Ihm, Numbers 4, 12, 27, and for "nomen," Number 10:2, "hic soror Damasi, nomen si quaeris, Irene," and Number 42.) The meaning of "names" is also supported by Toynbee, in *Gnomon*, XXIX (1957), 265, who sees the phrase "nomina Petri Paulique" as meaning nothing more than "Petrum Paulumque" in a poetic way. And even if Damasus did mean relics these need not be "corporeal relics"; it could be simply a place where the "names" of the apostles were commemorated. See also Chadwick, "St. Peter and St. Paul," p. 35.

88. He relies heavily on the findings of Gsell, *Inscriptions Latines de l'Algérie*, pp. 430 f. See Carcopino, "Note sur deux textes controversés," pp. 431–33; *Études*, pp. 261–63. He cites, among others, the following inscriptions from the fourth century: 1) "Nome(n) marturis Calendionis A(d)iutes(eos) qui botum (pour Votum) cum compleberunt (pour compleverunt)," 2) "Stiddin Miggin nomina m(ar)tiru(m) perf(ectorum)."

---

84. "Et in illa hora factus est terraemotus magnus, et decima pars civitatis cecidit: et occisa sunt in terraemotu nomina hominum septem millia: et reliqui in timorem sunt missi, et dederunt gloriam Deo caeli." *Novum Testamentum Graece et Latine*, ed. Vogels, p. 768.

85. See Carcopino, *Études*, p. 263, and "Encore 'Tropaeum' et 'nomen,'" pp. 385–90.

PLATE 3 The original deposition of the bodies of Peter and Paul Ad Catacumbas after the "robbery" (Bosio, *Roma sotterranea*).

PLATE 4 The taking of the bodies of Peter and Paul from their resting place in the Catacombs (Bosio, *Roma sotterranea*).

It could be that there was a custom, as Griffe has suggested, that the pilgrim in passing by a funerary inscription was supposed to pronounce the name of the martyr. This is possible, as a passage in a poem by Prudentius will illustrate: "Incisos tumulis titulos et singula quaeris Nomina?"[89] Whether pronounced by

the pilgrim or not, one of the most probable explanations of the word "nomen" in the Damasus inscription is "name." At the Vatican the pilgrim remembered and called upon (or "sought") the name of Peter; in the Via Ostia he called upon the name of Paul and in the Basilica Apostolorum, Ad Catacumbas, he called upon the names (nomina) of both apostles.

An inscription composed in such ambiguous terms was certain to foster misinterpretations. Orazio Marucchi, Arthur Barnes, and others see in a careless reading of the words "discipulos oriens misit" ("discipulos" read as "messenger" instead of "disciple") the genesis of the fantastic story of the theft of the bodies of Peter and Paul by Orientals, which is found in a number of late apocryphal documents, including the *Passio Sanctorum Apostolorum Petri et Pauli* (sixth century), *Passio Sebastiani* LXXVIII,[90] and the *Acts of Scharbil* (sixth century).[91] Misinterpretations of the terms found their way into art as well as the literary works. Three frescoes (Plates 3, 4, and 5), originally found in the Atrium of St. Peter's Basilica, depicted the interpretation of the reburial of Peter and Paul by the "Orientals" after the "crime." The frescoes were destroyed in 1606, but reproduced in the mid-seventeenth century by Antonio Bosio in *Roma sotterranea*.[92]

---

89. "Do you seek the engraved inscriptions in the tombs and names of each?" See Prudentius, *Peristephanon* XI.2, *Prudentius*, trans. Thomson, II, 304, 305.

90. Marucchi, *Manual of Christian Archeology*, 4th ed., p. 164. See also Lipsius, *Die apokryphen Apostelgeschichten*, Vol. II, Part I, pp. 312, 335, 393, and *Acta Apostolorum apocrypha*, I, 175. Griffe, in *Bull. de Litt. ecclés.* (1951), p. 200. See also *Bull. de Litt. ecclés.* (1953), p. 138. Leclercq, *DACL*, Vol. XIV, Part I, p. 874. La Piana, "The Tombs of Peter and Paul ad Catacumbas," pp. 63–65. Testini, "Noterelle sulla 'Memoria Apostolorum' in Catacumbas," p. 229. Klauser, *Die römische Petrustradition*, p. 27, also saw this inscription as the beginning of this "reines Phantasiegespinst." Chadwick, "St. Peter and St. Paul," p. 35n2. *Atti Sebastiani* (fifth or sixth century): "Hoc tu dum levaveris perduces ad Catacumbas et sepelies in initio cryptae, iuxta vestigia apostolorum." Tolotti, *Memorie*, p. 7; *MPL*, XVII, 1150.

91. *The Acts of Scharbil* (sixth century) in Cureton, *Ancient Syriac Documents*, p. 61, records approximately the same incident, except that the unpleasant role of the thieves is no longer assigned to men from the East and that the event took place during the pontificate of Fabian (A.D. 235–50) and not Cornelius (A.D. 251–53) as in the *Liber Pontificalis*.

92. Bosio (whose opinion can hardly be judged authoritative) considered these frescoes to be at least a thousand years old.

PLATE 5   The final deposition of Peter at the Vatican (Bosio, *Roma sotterranea*).

In view of the foregoing analysis, what is the probable meaning of the inscription? Does it provide evidence for the theory of some, such as Tolotti, that Peter was buried Ad Catacumbas immediately after his martyrdom? Does it testify to a translation of the relics at some later time, or is it simply a testimony to the fact that this was *a* place in which the names of Peter and Paul early were venerated? In addition, it must be asked whether it is not very probable that there is a claim made by Damasus in this inscription which reflects a tradition and not necessarily the facts.

The Letter of Gregory the Great to Empress Constantina and the notice of Cornelius in the *Liber Pontificalis*, both of which are considered briefly below, support the theory that Peter and Paul were buried Ad Catacumbas immediately after their martyrdom. But these documents are late and contradict all known earlier evidence.[93] In addition, their statements may well be based upon a misinterpretation of this very inscription, a possibility which will be considered further in the examination of the evidence compiled from the reports of the excavations at San Sebastiano.

Although a number of writers, including Griffe,[94] disagree it seems very possible that Damasus believed that the relics of Peter and Paul had once rested Ad Catacumbas.[95] This judgment is based not upon the

93. See Guignebert, "La Sépulture de Pierre," p. 238.

94. In *Bull. de Litt. ecclés.* (1951), p. 200.

95. Chadwick, "St. Peter and St. Paul," p. 34; Grégoire, "Le problème de la Tombe de Saint Pierre," p. 56, suggests that the Damasus inscription is an attempt to reconcile the ancient localization of the relics of Peter with that which was presupposed by the Constantine basilica. A misunderstanding of Damasus' efforts resulted in the 'tale' of translation in a time of persecution, attributed to Cornelius in the *Liber Pontificalis*.

interpretation of Carcopino concerning the word "nomen" (which is far too uncertain) but upon the character of the celebrations carried on in the vicinity of Ad Catacumbas in the third century, discussed in Chapter 9. This does not mean, however, that what Damasus *believed* to be true *was* true, but only that there is sufficient evidence to warrant the assumption that in A.D. 366 to 384 the leader of the Roman Church could have postulated an original burial of Peter and Paul Ad Catacumbas. It is also possible that the element of ambiguity which is inherent in the inscription may not be accidental, but may reflect a lack of certainty on the part of Damasus himself. Perhaps he too was not positive concerning the meaning or implications of the ceremonies held in the Triclia (an area set aside for the partaking of cultic meals) Ad Catacumbas a century before his time.[96]

In agreement with Lietzmann, against La Piana and Griffe, it seems farfetched to assume that the inscription reflects a claim to Peter and Paul by the Roman Church, in opposition to a now unknown claim by a church or churches of the East.[97]

SUPPORTING EVIDENCE FROM THE FIFTH THROUGH THE SEVENTH CENTURIES

The Letter of Gregory the Great to the Empress Constantina

In A.D. 594 Gregory the Great (A.D. 590–604) wrote a letter to Empress Constantina, who had asked him for relics of Peter and Paul ("Caput eiusdem sancti Pauli, aut aliud quid de corpore ipsius"). Contained in his letter of refusal in which he told her she must be content with "brandea," Gregory recounted the legend of the theft of the relics of Peter and Paul (which he may have derived from the apocryphal *Acts of Peter and Paul*[98] or another written or oral source seemingly based ultimately on a misunderstanding of the Damasus Inscription). He mentions that the theft had taken place "eo tempore quo passi sunt," that is, under Nero. The bones were later taken to the Vatican and the Via Ostia.[99] This letter appears to contradict the tradition as found in the fragment of Gaius and the evidence of Eusebius, as well as the common belief reflecting in the building of the Basilica of St. Peter at the Vatican in the fourth century. The theory is not without support, however, as is apparent from the notice of Cornelius in the *Liber Pontificalis*.

The Peristephanon of Prudentius

Aurelius Clemens Prudentius (A.D. c. 348–410) was one of the most accomplished of the early Western Christian poets. The *Peristephanon* (A.D. 405), with which we are alone concerned, consists of fourteen hymns to martyrs, inspired either by images in the various churches or by the inscriptions of Damasus.[100]

Hymn XII suggests, as Carcopino expresses it, that by A.D. 405 "le culte des Apôtres à Catacumbas avait été abrogé."[101] Lines 4 through 6 mention the festival of Peter and Paul held on June 29:

---

96. See Lipsius, *Die apokryphen Apostelgeschichten*, Vol. II, Part I, pp. 312, 313; Mohrmann, "A propos de deux Mots," p. 173. Klauser, *Die römische Petrustradition*, p. 26, suggests the inscription may reflect confusion; "for Damasus the Apostolic tradition, which was related to the Via Appia, was as enigmatic as for us, and his statement that the [relics of the] Apostle had once lain on the Via Appia was likewise only an hypothesis with which he sought to remove the contradictions in the Roman tradition." See Bauer, in *Wiener Studien*, pp. 272, 273.

97. Lietzmann, "The Tombs of the Apostles ad Catacumbas," p. 150. See La Piana, "The Tombs of Peter and Paul ad Catacumbas," pp. 57–94; Griffe, in *Bull. de Litt. ecclés.* (1953), p. 138.

98. *Acts of Peter and Paul*, LXXXVII, Tischendorf, *Passio Sanctorum Apostolorum Petri et Pauli*, pp. 38–39.

99. *Epistle* IV (*MPL*, LXXVII, 703).

100. See Delehaye, *Les Origines*, p. 367.

101. *De Pythagore*, p. 241.

Festus Apostolici redit hic dies triumphi cruore
. . . . Unus utrumque dies pleno tamen innovatus anno
vidit superba morte laureatum.[102]

The dependence of Prudentius upon the tradition which represented that the graves of Peter and Paul were to be found in the Vatican and on the Via Ostia is implied in lines 29 to 32 and 45 to 46:

Dividit ossa duum Ti[y]bris, sacer ex utraque ripa,
  Inter sacrata dum fluit sepulcra.
Dextra Petrum regio tectis tenet aureis receptum,
  Canens oliva, murmurans fluento. . . .
Parte alia titulum Pauli via servat Ostiensis,
  Quia stringit amnis c[a]espitem sinistrum.[103]

This interpretation is also supported by lines 57 through 58 and 61 through 62:

Aspice, per bifidas plebs Romula funditur plateas,
  Lux in duobus fervet una festis. . . .
Ibimus ulterius qua fert via pontis Hadriani
  Laevam deinde fluminis petemus.
Transtiberina prius solvit pervigil sacerdos
  Mox huc recurrit duplicatque vota.[104]

Is it most plausible to suppose that the reason Prudentius did not mention the Basilica Apostolorum Ad Catacumbas as the resting place of the relics of the apostles was 1) ignorance or 2) a rejection of the assumption that the relics of Peter had ever been there or 3) an acceptance of the theory that the relics, which were allegedly there in the time of Damasus, were no longer there A.D. 405 but had been removed to the Vatican and the Via Ostia? This question can be answered only after the Translation Theory is discussed and the results of the excavations at San Sebastiano are examined.

THE LIBER PONTIFICALIS[105]

The *Liber Pontificalis*, mentioned in Part I,[106] is usually dated in the sixth century. If we accept the opinion of Lipsius, Duchesne, and Lightfoot, the Felician Epitome

(F) (A.D. c. 530)[107] represents a summary of the original text of the *Liber Pontificalis*, written according to Duchesne A.D. c. 514 and according to Lipsius A.D. c. 496. The Cononian Epitome (K) (A.D. c. 687) is a summary of the first edition of the text supplemented by an abridgment of a seventh-century recension. On the other hand, Mommsen believes that the original document is no older than the seventh century and that the

---

102. *Peristephanon* XII.4–6 in *Prudentius*, trans. Thomson II, 322, 323:
> Today we have the festival of the Apostles'
> triumph coming round again, a day
> made famous by the blood of Peter
> and Paul. The same day, but recurring
> after a full year, saw each of them
> win the laurel of a splendid death.

See also lines 7–10, above, pp. 96–97 where tropaeum [τρόπαιον] is to be understood in the same way as in the fragment of Gaius. Compare Carcopino, *Études*, pp. 253–58.

103. *Peristephanon* XII.29–32 in *Prudentius*, trans. Thomson, II, 324–25:
> Tiber separates the bones of the two and both its
> banks consecrated as it flows between the hallowed
> tombs. The quarter on the right bank took Peter
> into its charge and keeps him in a golden
> dwelling [legend of the bronze coffin] where there is the
> grey of olive trees and the sound of a stream. . . .

Lines 45, 46, pp. 326, 327:
> Elsewhere the Ostian Road keeps the
> memorial church of Paul, where the river
> grazes the land on its left bank.

104. *Peristephanon* XII.57–58, 61–62, *ibid.*, II, 326–27:
> See, the people of Romulus goes pouring
> through the streets two separate ways for
> the same day is busy with two festivals. . . .
> We shall go further on, where the way leads
> over Hadrian's bridge and afterwards seek
> the left bank of the river. The sleepless bishop
> performs the sacred ceremonies first across the Tiber
> [Vatican],
> then hastens back to this side and repeats his offerings.

105. The *Liber Pontificalis* was listed, even as late as Migne, among the works of "Anastasius" (*MPL*, Vols. CXXVII, CXXVIII).

106. See above, pp. 32–35.

107. See above, p. 33, and Duchesne, *Le Liber Pontificalis*, Vol. I, Part I, p. xxxiii ff. See also Barker, *Rome of the Pilgrims*, p. 60.

recensions (*F*, *K*) are roughly contemporary with it, that is, around the time of Gregory the Great (A.D. 590–604).[108]

The *Liber Pontificalis* is dependent indirectly upon the earlier papal lists of Hegesippus, Irenaeus, Hippolytus, Julius Africanus, and Eusebius and more directly upon the *Liberian Catalogue*. For the life of Peter, the author of the *Liber Pontificalis* was especially dependent upon *De viris illustribus* of Jerome, and, especially for the life of Clement, he drew upon the so-called *Clementine Recognitions* and the *Epistle of Clement to James*.[109] The prefatory letters to the *Liber Pontificalis*, allegedly written by Damasus and Jerome, are forgeries of the sixth or seventh centuries. Even if we may account confidently for the papal list and certain material found in the lives of the early popes by citing sources, the decrees of the early popes down to the middle of the fifth century are spurious, almost without exception. The author undoubtedly wished to assign to each pope some enactment of significance. In addition, popular martyrologies gave him information concerning early persecutions and miraculous happenings in the history of the Early Church such as the finding of the cross and the healing of Constantine. The great detail and the character of the information concerning the construction of the various churches and the size and value of the imperial donations suggest that the author also possessed some written source for this information. Perhaps, at least for the later popes, there was also a written record of all ordinations upon which the author might draw. For the earlier popes, such details were no doubt completely lacking, and the information was supplied in order to give an appearance of accuracy.[110]

As Loomis points out, "because of its unmistakable antiquity and because of the profound importance of its early subject matter it was reckoned as a source of unimpeachable veracity and as one of the indisputable proofs of the primitive power and activity of the popes."[111] In actuality the second part, from the seventh to the eighteenth centuries, is fairly reliable, but the earlier part is a combination of fact and fable, containing a number of errors honestly made and a number of fabrications included for specific purposes:

One can observe in this single document a blending of most of the processes by which a history may be constructed, the use of sober, reliable, sometimes first-hand reports of events and again marvelous legends, the creations of generations of enthusiasm and piety, intentional manufacture of data for a specific purpose, the distortion of other data through prejudice and ignorance.[112]

As this introduction implies, it is dangerous to take seriously any information which the *Liber Pontificalis* supplies concerning the lives of the earliest popes.

While the Cononian (*K*) abridgment is concerned with the "monumental notices," it is the Felician (*F*) abridgment which is interested in the notices of depositions. For this information, *F* is "précis, exact, fidèle: il ne néglige aucun détail."[113] Therefore, for these details we have a document which is probably very close to the original text of the *Liber Pontificalis*.

The notice of Peter in the first edition of the *Liber Pontificalis* contains the following information concerning his burial: "Qui et sepultus est via Aurelia, in templum Apollonis, iuxta locum ubi crucifixus est, iuxta palatium Neronianum, in Vaticanum, in territurium Triumphale, via Aurelia, III k. iul."[114] The second edition contains the following changes: the "et" in the first sentence is omitted, as is "via Aurelia" at the end. In addition, "iuxta" replaces "in" before "territurium Triumphale."[115]

The geographical details of the notice depend upon various sources; for example, the "via Aurelia" is

108. See Duchesne, *Le Liber Pontificalis*, Vol. I, Part I, p. xxxvii. Lightfoot, *Apostolic Fathers*, Part I, Vol. I, p. 307, conjectures that the *Liber Pontificalis* may have grown out of a "looking at the past" occasioned by the rivalry over the papacy between Symmachus (d. 514) and Laurentius.

109. Duchesne, *Le Liber Pontificalis*, Vol. I, Part I, p. lxviii.

110. See *The Book of the Popes*, trans. Loomis, pp. xvi–xvii; Heussi, *Die römische Petrustradition* (1955), excursus 4, pp. 71–77. Heussi also quotes O. Bardenhewer, *Patrologie*, 3d ed., III (1910), 565, as saying "der erste und ältere Teil ist . . . ebenso unzuverlässig wie inhaltsarm."

111. *The Book of the Popes*, trans. Loomis, p. x.

112. *Ibid.*; see also Duchesne, *Le Liber Pontificalis*, Vol. I, Part I, p. lxviii.

113. Vielliard, "Les Titres romains et les deux Éditions du *Liber Pontificalis*," p. 90, including note 2.

114. Duchesne, *Le Liber Pontificalis*, Vol. I, Part I, p. 53.

115. *Ibid.*, notes 10–12 and p. 118.

mentioned in the Berne MS of the *Martyrologium Hiero-nymianum*.[116] The Vatican and Via Ostia were associated with the burial of Peter at least since the time of Gaius (A.D. 200). The remaining details, such as the "templum Apollonis" and "territurium Triumphale" could easily have been inferred from the location of the Basilica of St. Peter, which was a familiar site on the Vatican at the time when the *Liber Pontificalis* was written. The reference to the "templum Apollonis" is incorrect; actually it is an allusion to a sanctuary of Cybele (Magna Mater) which is known to have stood in the area in the period when the Basilica of St. Peter was under construction.[117] Duchesne also mentions that the second edition is correct in changing "in templum Apollonis" to "iuxta templum Apollonis"; the sanctuary of Magna Mater was not precisely on the spot where the Basilica is situated, but in the vicinity.

It is claimed that eleven of the early popes are buried "iuxta corpus beati Petri."[118] These are Linus (A.D. 67–76), Cletus (Anencletus) (A.D. 76–88), Evaristus (A.D. 97–105), Xystus (A.D. 115–25), Telesphorus (A.D. 125–36), Hyginus (A.D. 136–40), Pius (A.D. 140–55), Anicetus (A.D. 155–66), Soter (A.D. 166–75), Eleutherus (A.D. 175–89), and Victor (A.D. 189–99).[119]

Since the recent excavations there has been a great deal of discussion about the possibility that the eleven graves which were originally found in the vicinity of the alleged grave of Peter are in actuality the graves of a number of early popes. The coincidence in number between these eleven graves and the fact that exactly eleven early popes were reported by the *Liber Pontificalis* to have been buried "near the body of the blessed Peter" has been often pointed out. It is much more likely that these early popes would have been buried in the graves of their families or near the place of their martyrdom.[120] Whether the statement is accurate or not, however, the belief that Peter was definitely buried in the Vatican area is reflected in the claim.

Although it cannot be considered in depth here, it must be noted that there was a great deal of uncertainty concerning the names of Cletus and Anencletus. It is most probable that the two names were confused and what ought to have been considered as a variant spelling of the name of a single pope was early seen as the names of two separate popes.[121]

In the notice of Cornelius is found the following:

Hic temporibus suis rogatus a quodam matrona [some MSS enter Lucina here] corpora apostolorum *beati* Petri et Pauli de Catacumbas levavit noctu. Primum *quidem* corpus beati Pauli accepto beata Lucina posuit in praedio suo, via Ostiense, iuxta locum ubi decollatus est; beati Petri accepit corpus *beatus* Cornelius episcopus et posuit iuxta locum ubi crucifixus est, inter corpora sanctorum *episcoporum*, in templo Apollonis, in monte Aureo, in Vaticanum palatii Neroniani, III Kal. iul.[122]

---

116. See below, pp. 121 ff.

117. *CIL*, Vol. VI, Part I, Nos. 497–504, pp. 93–95. See Duchesne, *Le Liber Pontificalis*, Vol. I, Part I, p. 210. A list of the Taurobolia held in this period, their dates, and position in the *CIL* appear in Carcopino, *Études*, p. 275.

118. The formulae differ, but the meaning is the same: "Sepultus est in basilica beati Petri in Vaticanum"; "Ex precepto beati Petri in Vaticano sepultus est"; "Sepultusque est iuxta corpus beati Petri"; and the like.

119. See Duchesne, *Le Liber Pontificalis*, Vol. I, Part I: Linus, pp. 52, 53, 121; Cletus, pp. 52, 53, 122; Anencletus, pp. 54, 55; Evaristus, pp. 54, 55, 126; Xystus, pp. 54, 55, 56, 57, 128; Telesphorus, pp. 56, 57, 129; Hyginus, pp. 56, 57, 131; Pius, pp. 58, 59, 132–33; Anicetus, pp. 58, 59, 134; Soter, pp. 58, 59, 135; Eleutherus, pp. 58, 59, 60, 61, 136; Victor, pp. 60, 61, 137–38. Compare p. lxi for the burial of Anicetus and Soter. See also *The Book of the Popes*, trans. Loomis, pp. 3–19.

120. Toynbee and Perkins, *The Shrine of St. Peter*, p. 264; Guarducci, *Cristo e San Pietro in un Documento precostantiniano*, p. 85n45. Compare Ruysschaert, *Réflexions sur les Fouilles vaticanes*, p. 26, who concludes that this idea of a papal cemetery around the grave of Peter was not a creation of the *Liber Pontificalis* but dependent upon a tradition going back to the time of the building of the Basilica by Constantine.

121. See above, pp. 28, 30, 32. See also Heussi, *Die römische Petrustradition*, pp. 71–77; Kirschbaum, "Das Petrusgrab," p. 331; Toynbee and Perkins, *The Shrine of St. Peter*, p. 265.

122. Duchesne, *Le Liber Pontificalis*, Vol. I, Part I, p. 67. The *italicized* words appear in one or the other of the abridgments. See *The Book of the Popes*, trans. Loomis, p. 26, "He during his pontificate at the request of a certain matron [Lucina], took up the bodies of the apostles, blessed Peter and Paul from the catacombs by night; first the body of the blessed Paul was received by the blessed Lucina and laid in her own garden on the Via Ostia near [beside] the place where he was beheaded; the body of the blessed Peter was received by the blessed Cornelius, the bishop, and laid near the place where he was crucified, among the bodies of the holy bishops, in the shrine of Apollo, on the Mons Aureus, in the Batican [*sic*], by the palace of Nero, June 29." Notice "*de* Catacumbas." No other document prior to this notice in the *Liber Pontificalis*

This notice would seem to corroborate one interpretation of the Damasus Inscription and place the burial of Peter and Paul at the cemetery Ad Catacumbas immediately after their martyrdom. The document clearly states that the Via Ostia and the Vatican are the places of martyrdom of the two apostles, but it does not mention that they had been *first* buried in these places and then at a later time had been *translated* Ad Catacumbas (from which place they were *returned* to the Vatican and to the Via Ostia), although this is the interpretation of the notice by Duchesne.[123]

The last notice of the *Liber Pontificalis* to be mentioned is that of Damasus, the author of the enigmatic inscription considered in the last section. In the Cononian abridgment we find mention that Damasus "dedicavit platomum in Catacumbas, ubi corpora Petri et Pauli apostolorum iacuerunt quam et versibus ornavit."[124] In the second edition is a slightly different form of the same thought, "et in Catacumbas, ubi iacuerunt corpora sanctorum apostolorum Petri et Pauli, in quo loco platomam ipsam, ubi iacuerunt corpora sancta, versibus exornavit." While it is taken for granted by Loomis and Duchesne that the notice implies that the bodies of Peter and Paul lay Ad Catacumbas during the persecution begun by Valerian,[125] this interpretation is not required by the text of the notice itself.

THE SALZBURG ITINERARY

This Itinerary was published first in 1777 as an appendix to the works of Alcuin, but it has no more relationship to Alcuin than the *Liber Pontificalis* has to Anastasius, among whose works this latter document appeared even as late as Migne.[126] The Itinerary is found in two documents, the *Notitia ecclesiarum urbis Romae* and the *De Locis Sanctis Martyrum*.[127]

Doufourcq claims that the *Notitia* (A.D. c. 640) is based upon an original Itinerary written under Sixtus III (A.D. 432–40) and that this in turn depends upon the Roman *Calendar of 312* which is contemporary with the reorganization of the Church under Sylvester, and is also, claims Doufourcq, the source for the *Depositio Episcoporum* and *Depositio Martyrum*.[128] If this is true which is debatable, we should know the names, places of burial, and anniversaries of the early martyrs from a date about ten years after the end of the last persecution.

According to the *Notitia* the pilgrim is to go clockwise in his visit to the various churches and ends at St. Peter's in the Vatican; the pilgrim using the *De Locis* (seventh century) should begin at St. Peter's and go counterclockwise. Interestingly, the errors made in each document are identical, which suggests that the authors of both used a common source.

The *Salzburg Itinerary* contains these notices:

Postea pervenies via Appia ad S. Sebastianum martyrem cuius corpus iacet in inferiore loco, et ubi sunt sepulcra apostolorum Petri et Pauli in quibus XL annorum requiescebant, et in occidentali parte ecclesiae per gradus descendis ubi S. Cyrinus papa [he never was a pope, but Bishop of Siscia in Pannonia] et martyr requiescit [pausat]. . . . Et sic intrabis via Vaticana donec pervenies ad basilicam beati Petri, quam Constantinus imperator totius orbis condidit, eminentem super omnes

---

mentions a translation *from* Catacumbas. This notice can be interpreted to confirm the assumption that Peter and Paul were buried originally Ad Catacumbas, as found also in the *Epistle* of Gregory the Great, *Pseudo-Marcellus*, The *Salzburg Itinerary*, *Acts of Sharbil* and the Damasus Inscription, Number 26. See Chadwick, "St. Peter and St. Paul," p. 38.

123. *Le Liber Pontificalis*, Vol. I, Part I, pp. civ–cvii. Compare Toynbee and Perkins, *The Shrine of St. Peter*, pp. 169, 188n48. The appearance of the name Lucina in this notice is interpreted by Lietzmann, *Petrus und Paulus in Rom*, 2d ed., p. 188, to mean that in the fifth or sixth century the Church of Rome possessed some benefices which carried the name of a donor, Lucina; See Goguel, *L'Église primitive*, p. 224n2.

124. Duchesne, *Le Liber Pontificalis*, Vol. I, Part I, p. 84. For an English translation of this portion of the notice of Damasus, see *The Book of the Popes*, trans. Loomis, p. 81.

---

125. See Duchesne, *Le Liber Pontificalis*, Vol. I, Part I, p. civ; *The Book of the Popes*, trans. Loomis, p. 81n2.

126. See de Rossi, *La Roma sotterranea*, I, 139.

127. Barker, *Rome of the Pilgrims*, p. 114, and Marucchi, *Manual of Christian Archeology*.

128. Barker, *Rome of the Pilgrims*, p. 114, cites Doufourcq, *Études sur les Gesta Martyrum romains*, p. 21.

ecclesias et formosam, in cuius occidentali plaga beatum corpus eius quiescit.[129]

The statement that Peter and Paul lay in the crypt of San Sebastiano for forty years[130] is clear, but from the standpoint of the main interest of this study it leaves one very important question unanswered: *When* were the bodies of Peter and Paul assumed to have rested there? Was it immediately after their martyrdom or between the alleged translations to and from the original burial places on the Vatican and the Via Ostia? It may

be concluded that by the fifth or sixth century there were various traditions which claimed that the bodies of Peter and Paul resided Ad Catacumbas, but they cannot agree upon the epoch or the length of the stay.

Other Itineraries, such as the *Notitia Portarum Ecclesiarum circa Urbem Romam*, the *Itinerary of Ein-siedeln*, and the *Index Oleorum* could be cited, but these are late and of no value for determining the belief of the Early Church concerning the place where the bodies of Peter and Paul were originally buried.[131]

129. De Rossi, *La Roma sotterranea*, I, 139; Leclercq, *DACL*, Vol. XIV, Part I, p. 874, and Marucchi, *Manual of Christian Archeology*; Tolotti, *Memorie*, p. 7. The English translation is found in Toynbee and Perkins, *The Shrine of St. Peter*, p. 188n49: "Next you will proceed along the Via Appia to San Sebastian the martyr, whose body lies in the crypt. There, too, are the tombs of the Apostles Peter and Paul, where they lay for forty years, and at the west end of the

Church you go down by steps to where Saint Quirinius, pope and martyr, rests."

130. Notice the conflict with the testimony of the *Acts of Peter and Paul*, where it mentions that the bodies rested in the crypt for one month and seven days; see above, p. 102.

131. See de Rossi, *La Roma sotterranea*, Vol. I, p. 181, cols. 4, 5.

CHAPTER 8

The Liturgical Evidence
for the Burial of Peter in Rome

Now THAT the literary evidence for the martyrdom of Peter and Paul has been considered and before examining the reports of the excavations at San Sebastiano and the Vatican, let us study the liturgical evidence. As Cullmann has correctly observed, both literary and liturgical sources of information are closely related and mutually dependent. The liturgical texts give information of Peter and Paul "and so can serve as a clue for the archeological investigation; the excavations . . . can confirm these statements or even show their lack of historical value."[1]

The liturgical texts which are of help in this study are the *Depositio Martyrum* (which appears in the *Philocalian Calendar*) and the *Martyrologium Hieronymianum*. The principal problem in both centers on the meaning of the date "III Kal. iul. Basso et Tusco consulibus" (A.D. 258).

The *Depositio Martyrum*, written around A.D. 310, contains a list of festivals celebrated in Rome in the fourth century.[2] Each date is followed by the name of a particular saint and the cemetery where the liturgical meeting was held. The notice pertaining to Peter and Paul appears as follows: "III Kal. iul. Petri in Catacumbas et Pauli Ostense, Tusco et Basso consulibus" (or A.D. 258).

If the notice could be taken literally and the consuls mentioned had served A.D. 64, there would be no problem at all. The notice could *only* be taken to mean that on this date, when Tusco and Bassus were consuls, it was *believed* by the author of the *Depositio Martyrum* that Peter was buried Ad Catacumbas and Paul on the

Via Ostia. However, the consuls are those not for A.D. 64, but for 258. In view of this the notice must be explained in another way, and one is faced with a number of mutually exclusive possibilities. Is the consular notation in this notice 1) an error or does the notice refer *not* to a date of martyrdom or original burial but to 2) an "invention" of the relics of Peter and Paul in these places, 3) the inauguration of a liturgical feast, or 4) the translation of the relics of the apostles? Each of these possibilities has been vigorously challenged and defended. Before reconsidering them, however, it is necessary to introduce the text of the *Martyrologium Hieronymianum* for A.D. 258 and decide whether the notice of the *Depositio Martyrum* ought to be corrected in terms of this later document or whether each represents belief in two different stages of the tradition.

The *Martyrologium Hieronymianum* according to the eighth-century Berne Manuscript contains the following notice for June 29:

III kal. iul. Romae via Aurelia natal. s̄corum apostolor̄ Petri et Pauli,[3] Petri in Vaticano, Pauli vero in via Ostensi, utrūque in Catacumbas, passi sub Nerone, Basso et Tusco consulib. In eadem urbe Aurelia sanctorum Novatiani et aliorum nongentorum septuaginta et septem martyrum et dedicatio baptisterii antiqui Rome. In Persida natale sancti Simonis Judae apostolorum.[4]

---

1. Cullmann, *Peter*, p. 123.
2. See above p. 41.

---

3. The words "apostolorum Petri et Pauli" are over an erasure; it was first written "Petri et Pauli apostolorum." See Plate 7.
4. The Codex Epternacensis for the same date contains the following: "III Kal. iul. Rome n̄t. apostolor̄ Petri et Pauli et aliorum DCCCCLXXVIIII martyrum item Romae Novatiani

In the fourth century we know that the day of June 29 was celebrated with great magnificence. On that day the great door of the Vatican was opened and a large tub made of boxwood leaves was displayed—a piscatorial symbol. Among the many pilgrims who journeyed to the Vatican for the occasion was Paulinus, a wealthy patrician, a Senator and a Consul of Rome. He gave up his political career A.D. 394 and entered monastic poverty with his wife at Nola in South Italy. He became a bishop A.D. 409 and mentions in his works that he went on an annual pilgrimage to Rome on June 29, "beatorum Apostolorum natalis."

We learn that at a much later period the festival was still kept with great enthusiasm. In Stow's *Survey of London*, 1598, it is noted that "on Peter's Vigil every man's door was garnished with garlands of flowers and had lamps burning all night."[5]

The basic questions in this study are not how or for what reason the day was celebrated in the fourth or the sixteenth century but what was the original meaning of the festival and why was this particular date chosen?

Barnes, despite arguments to the contrary, maintains that this is the actual date of Peter's martyrdom A.D. 67.[6] It is much more probable, however, that the date was chosen for the same reason that February 22 or January 18 were chosen.[7] On June 29 the pagan Romans at one time had celebrated *Quirinus in colle*; it was a time which marked the foundation of the *Aedes Quirini*, accompanied by the rejoicings in honor of the founders of Rome. This interpretation finds support in a sermon given on this date by Leo the Great in which he said, "the Apostles have better protected the city than those who built its walls and soiled it by fratricide."[8]

It is taken for granted that June 29 is an arbitrary date, which may well have been chosen by the Church because it had been previously associated with the pagan celebration of the founding of Rome and thus would be a logical date for the commemoration of the alleged founders of the Roman Church. The primary problem, however, is not the choice of the *day* but the meaning of the *date*. What precisely was celebrated on this day in the year 258?

---

in Persida Simonis et Judae apostolorum." The last part of the notice including the number of martyrs and "Novatiani" does not appear in most MSS, e.g., Corbiense, Senonense. See Codex Wissemburgensis: "III kl. iul. Rom. nat. s̄corum Petri Pauli Apostolorum. Petri in Vaticano. Pauli vero Via Ostensi et aliorum DCCCCLXXVII martyrum et dedicatio baptistirii anteque Roma."

Berne Manuscript, as expected, contains the topographical details as does Codex Wissemburgensis. The Codex Epternacensis has only the names of the saints. (See Plate 6.)

See Duchesne, *Le Liber Pontificalis*, Vol. I, Part I, pp. cv ff., and p. 11; Lietzmann, *Petrus und Paulus in Rom*, 1st ed., pp. 81 ff.; Johann Peter Kirsch, "Das 'Martyrologium Hieronymianum,'" pp. 259 ff., and "Le Feste degli Apostoli," pp. 54, 55; Quentin, "Per la Critica," pp. 103–8; Carcopino, *Études*, pp. 266–69.

5. See Balleine, *Simon*, p. 94.

6. Barnes, *Christianity at Rome in the Apostolic Age*, p. 2. See Guignebert, "La Sépulture de Pierre," p. 247. Several Eastern documents refer to June 29 as the date of martyrdom: the *Consularia Constantinopolitana* and *Consularia Ravennatia*. See also Pseudo-Chrysostom on "SS. Petrum et Paulum" (*MPG*, LIX, 496). The Syriac Martyrology (A.D. 411–12) sets the date of the martyrdom of Peter and Paul on December 28 (see Lietzmann, *Die drei älteste Martyrologien*, p. 9). This last date, however, is arrived at automatically; the first martyr,

Stephen, was commemorated on December 26; James and John, on December 27; and Peter and Paul, therefore, on December 28. There was surely no tradition of the actual day of death of Peter before the third century at the earliest. The idea that June 29 marks the actual date of martyrdom is dismissed by most scholars, for example, Duchesne, *Origines du Culte chrétien*, p. 227, and La Piana, "The Tombs of Peter and Paul ad Catacumbas." p. 58. But at the time of the copying of the *Depositio Martyrum* by Philocalus, June 29 was *considered* to be the "dies natalis," showing that the original significance of the date had been forgotten by the mid-fourth century.

7. See above pp. 42–45, 48–49.

8. *Epistle* LXXXII, "In Natali Apostolorum" (*MPL*, LIV, 422 f.). This relationship of June 29 in the pagan and Christian calendars is urged by Erbes, *Die Todestage*, pp. 39 f., but Klauser, *Die römische Petrustradition*, p. 77, citing G. Wissowa, *Religion und Kultus der Römer* (1912), pp. 155, 574 f., 578, holds that the view is untenable since June 29 had not played a role in the Temples of Quirinus as the feast day of Romulus-Quirinus since 49 B.C. In the period of the Empire the festival of the founding of the state was held on April 3, and the foundation date of the new Quirinus Temples was February 17. Erbes' explanation cannot be completely discarded, however, since even if June 29 no longer was celebrated in connection with the founding of Rome, the memory of its former significance no doubt was still well known.

THE DEPOSITIO MARTYRUM

If the notice of June 29 in the *Depositio Martyrum* is taken literally, we are told that A.D. 258 Peter was commemorated in the Catacombs and Paul on the Via Ostia; there is no mention of the Vatican. The notice in the *Martyrologium Hieronymianum*, on the other hand, if taken literally, is unintelligible. It says that on June 29 in Rome on the Via Aurelia is celebrated the "natale" of Peter and Paul;[9] Peter in the Vatican and Paul on the Via Ostia and the latter also Ad Catacumbas. The document continues with the statement that this date is related to the martyrdom "passi sub Nerone" which is followed by the names not of the consuls who held office A.D. 64, but those who served A.D. 258.

The Berne MS of the *Martyrologium* is thought by some to represent the original more faithfully than the others.[10] The Epternacensis MS, according to Leclercq, Kirsch, and others, shows abridgment of the notices and deletion of the topographical details. These details were not invented by the author but drawn from a source, perhaps the Roman Calendar of 312 and thus indirectly the *Chronograph of 354* or the *Depositio Martyrum*. There is another possibility, that both the *Depositio* and the *Martyrologium* had a common source in the *Calendar of 312*, known also as the *Calendar of Miltiades*.[11] Quentin, however, disagrees with those who would maintain that the Roman notices in the *Martyrologium* predate the edition of A.D. 592 and suggests that these appeared first as marginal notes, drawn from hagiographic literature, itineraries, and earlier liturgical documents. In the later editions these marginal notes were entered directly into the text.[12]

The text of the *Depositio* can be viewed in one of three ways: 1) the present form represents the errors of scribes, 2) it must be understood in relation to the fuller notice in the Berne MS of the *Martyrologium*, or 3) it faithfully reflects the belief at the time of writing. The first two views involve a reconstruction, which has been suggested by many and in various ways and must now be considered.

Paul Monceaux finds a possible origin of the problem by suggesting that either the author of the *Depositio* or the author of his source copied incorrectly the names of the consuls because of the presence of a homonym; "Bassus and Crassus" who held office A.D. 64 were intended and not "Bassus and Tuscus," consuls A.D. 258.[13] He offers the following reconstruction: "Passi sub Nerone, Basso [et Crasso consulibus (A.D. 64), translati in Catacumbas, Basso] et Tusco consul [ibus] (A.D. 258)."[14]

Another reconstruction made by Dom Quentin[15] involves the thesis that the date A.D. 258 or the more original equivalent, "Tusco et Basso consulibus," was originally attached as a marginal note beside the notice of Cyprian, September 14. The theory requires that the original text of the *Depositio* was written on one page divided into two columns of exactly the same length. As it happens the editions of Duchesne, Mommsen (in the *Monumenta Germaniae*), and that of Lietzmann (in *Die drei älteste Martyrologien*) contain the complete text of the document on one page of two equal columns of twenty-five lines each. This arrangement reveals that the notice of Cyprian and the notice of Peter and Paul are exactly opposite to each other, and that the date under these *precise* conditions, could have been easily

---

9. See above, p. 42, for a discussion of "natale."

10. Johann Peter Kirsch, "Das 'Martyrologium Hieronymianum,'" p. 259; Leclercq, *DACL*, Vol. XIV, Part I, p. 862. This is challenged by Quentin, "Per la Critica," p. 108, and Chadwick, "St. Peter and St. Paul," p. 37n2. Grégoire, "Le Problème da la Tombe de Saint Pierre," p. 53, notes that the Berne Manuscript is "unhappily interpolated," depends upon the Damasus Inscription, and contains a number of errors made by the later copyists.

11. Barker, *Rome of the Pilgrims*, p. 225. Duchesne, "La 'Memoria Apostolorum,'" p. 2, also mentions that the two are derived from a common source, but does not identify it.

12. Quentin, "Per la Critica," p. 108.

13. Monceaux, "L'Apostolat de Saint Pierre à Rome," p. 235. See also Guingnebert, *La Primauté de Pierre*, p. 236 and Leclercq, *DACL*, Vol. XIV, Part I, p. 860.

14. The brackets are those of Paul Monceaux.

15. Quentin, "Per la Critica," pp. 103–8.

transferred from the right- to the left-hand column, especially if the consular dates appeared in a small center column or to the left of the right-hand column. While it is certainly possible that such an "accident" might have happened,[16] this solution may only be accepted as an interesting hypothesis, for there are no MSS which reveal this arrangement, and there is no extant information whatsoever as to the ancient form of the text. If the original was longer or shorter than the modern text, by even a line, the value of the suggestion would be lost, for in the original, the two notices would not have been in juxtaposition.

Griffe's solution involves the assumption that there were two successive modifications in the text to accommodate it to changed conditions. The original notice indicated the initiation of a celebration of Peter *and* Paul on the Via Appia: "Petri et Pauli in Catacumbas, Tusco et Basso consulibus." In other words, the cult of the apostles was located Ad Catacumbas A.D. 258. Later, between the period when the circumstances which were described in the *first* edition of the *Depositio* existed and the more permanent conditions which came into being, and are known to us through the

poem attributed to Ambrose,[17] there was an interim set of conditions which correspond to the present form of the *Depositio*. The relics of Paul had been moved to the Basilica on the Via Ostia, but the relics of Peter still remained on the Via Appia ("III kal. iul. Petri in Catacumbas et Pauli Ostense, Tusco et Bassus consulibus") (= A.D. 258). When the Basilica at the Vatican was finished and the relics of Peter were moved there, a set of conditions was produced which corresponds exactly to those described in the *Martyrologium*. If the "Basso et Tusco" element of the notice is to be retained at all, this appears to Griffe to be the only solution.[18] In addition, it must be remembered that this view does not necessarily involve a transfer of relics but only the transfer of cultic celebration.

The present text of the *Depositio*, according to Duchesne, does not represent tradition older than that reflected in the *Martyrologium*. In fact, "D'après ce que nous savons sur la composition du martyrologe hiéronymien en particulier pour ce qui regarde les fêtes romaines, on a tout droit de considérer de texte comme [of the *Martyrologium*] un témoignage des usages publics et officiels de l'église romaine pendant le IVe siécle."[19] The *Depositio* which appears in the *Chronograph of 354* represents a later redaction. He denies that the conditions it describes represent accurately a temporary condition between A.D. 336 and 354 (that is, between the two editions of the *Depositio*). On the contrary, if the body of *one* of the apostles had been removed from the Catacombs first, it would have been that of Peter, because the Basilica of Paul was not completed; for it was only A.D. 386 that the Emperors Valentinian II, Theodosius, and Arcadius gave the orders to build it. Therefore, this document as it stands is opposed to the *Martyrologium*, the "Hic habitasse" inscription of Damasus ("nomina Petri pariter Paulique"), the *Liber Pontificalis* in its notices for both Cornelius and Damasus, and among other apocryphal documents,

16. Griffe, in *Bull. de Litt. ecclés.* (1951), p. 204, too quickly dismisses the possibility by saying that the redactor of the *Chronograph of 354* could not have made such an error for the tradition A.D. 354 was that Peter died *not* A.D. 64 but A.D. 55. While it is true that this is the calculation of the *Chronograph*, it may have been less founded upon actual conviction and strong tradition than upon a desperate attempt to preserve the "twenty-five years" episcopate of Peter. (Quentin's thesis is criticized and dismissed by most scholars including Leclercq, *DACL*, Vol. XIV, Part I, p. 860.) See Griffe, in *Bull. de Litt. ecclés.* (1951), p. 205. Delehaye, "TVSCO ET BASSO CONS.," p. 204, says that the theory is "extrêmement problématique," especially since Philocalus no doubt had not copied the names of cemeteries and the names of "vias," and the like, which were most probably in the earlier text. And unless we say that the *Martyrologium* is dependent upon the *Depositio*, we have to reckon that the "Basso et Tusco cons." was also in the source document. See also the objections of A. M. Schneider, "Die Memoria Apostolorum," p. 4.

17. "Tantae per urbis ambitum/Stipata tendunt agmina/Trinis celebratur viis/Festum sacrorum martyrum." (*MPL*, XVII, 1215.) See Styger, *Die römischen Katakomben*, p. 346. Chadwick, "St. Peter and St. Paul," p. 37, suggests that the poem is "attributed probably rightly to Ambrose." Griffe, in *Bull. de Litt. ecclés.* (1951), 207n33, disagrees.

18. *Ibid.* (1951), pp. 206, 207, and *ibid.* (1958), pp. 119–22. See also Duchesne, *Le Liber Pontificalis*, Vol. I, Part I, p. cv.; Kirschbaum, "Petri in Catacumbas," pp. 221–29; Vallin, "Le culte des Apôtres Pierre et Paul," p. 261; and Kirschbaum, *Die Gräber*, p. 155. See Klauser, *Die römische Petrustradition*, p. 22.

19. Duchesne, *Le Liber Pontificalis*, Vol. I, Part I, p. cv.

the Syriac *Acts of Scharbil*, as well as the later Letter of Gregory to the Empress Constantina. All these and other documents allege that at one time or another the relics of Peter and Paul rested Ad Catacumbas—"ils y ont séjourné ensemble, ils en sont partis ensemble."[20] The proper understanding of the June 29 notice of the *Depositio* depends, both Duchesne and Lietzmann believe, upon the *Martyrologium* (Berne MS), and the interpretation "Petri et Pauli in Catacumbas."[21] Barnes, who admits that the document is not in its original form, agrees in the reconstruction, "Petri et Pauli in Catacumbas," but for reasons other than those which Duchesne advances. The form of the notice in the *Depositio* was the work not of Philocalus[22] but of a convert of Valentinus. The original notice of Peter *and* Paul Ad Catacumbas, he claims further, did not describe a situation peculiar to the third century but preserved the original date of the apostles' burial on the Via Appia immediately after their martyrdom. The "Pauli Ostense" element in the notice of the *Depositio* was brought in later as a result of the tradition which grew up around the date of January 25.[23]

Both Carl Erbes and Adolf Bauer reject the claim by Lietzmann and Duchesne that the reconstruction is to be based upon the text of the *Martyrologium*. But they agree that A.D. 258 Paul was not at the Catacombs on the Via Ostia, nor was Peter at the Vatican. The original notice read simply "III kal. iul. Petri et Pauli in Catacumbas, Tusco et Basso cons." As later changes came about in the tradition, changes were made in the texts, first in the recording of the *Depositio* in the *Chronograph of 354* and later in the appropriation by the *Martyrologium*.[24]

Delehaye explains the date A.D. 258 in relation to the beginning of the cultic celebration Ad Catacumbas. In a similar manner, both Bettini and Lemerle[25] agree in their interpretation that the reasons behind the emergence of this particular date are to be found in the struggle of the Church with the Montanists. The cult of martyrs begins first in the East, probably in Smyrna with the martyrdom of Polycarp.[26] By the time of Tertullian, the cult is established at least in Africa and later introduced into Rome. In the year 258 the battle between East and West is raging over the claim to primacy of the bishop of Rome in the name of "Tu es Petrus," and the Eastern Church, supporting Cyprian, argues against this interpretation. But Rome reasons that 1) Peter was the Prince of the apostles, 2) the bishops of Rome are heirs of the prerogatives of Peter, therefore, 3) the Roman bishops are supreme over all other bishops. And in the entire controversy, of course, possession of the tomb of Peter is of great importance. "Now it is just at this moment exactly, in A.D. 258 that we report the mention there [in the *Depositio*]. 'III kal. iul. Petri in Catacumbas et Pauli Ostense Tusco et Basso consulibus.' If this were a coincidence it would be remarkable."[27]

The present form of the *Depositio* may represent the belief of the Church or a group within the Church in the early fourth century. On the other hand, the present form may represent a corruption of the original. If so, the foregoing reconstructions are all within the realm of possibility. Which of them is the more probable can only be determined after further evidence is examined.

20. *Ibid.*, p. cv; "La 'Memoria Apostolorum,'" p. 19.

21. Duchesne, *Le Liber Pontificalis*, p. cv. See also Burger, *La Tombe*, p. 17. The original text, according to Lietzmann, *Petrus und Paulus in Rom*, 2d ed., p. 114; "III kal. iul. Natale sanctorum apostolorum Petri et Pauli; Petri in Vaticano, Pauli vero in Via Ostensi utriusque in Catacumbas. Basso et Tusco cons." (= A.D. 258.)

22. Delehaye, "TVSCO ET BASSO CONS.," p. 204.

23. See Barnes, *St. Peter in Rome*, pp. 122–29.

24. Bauer, in *Wiener Studien*, p. 272. He also cites Erbes, *Texte und Untersuchung*, N. F., IV, 81, in support of his thesis.

25. Bettini, "Tusco et Basso consulibus," pp. 67–87, and Lemerle, "Les Persécutions," pp. 147–55.

26. *Ibid.*, p. 151. Delehaye, "TVSCO ET BASSO CONS.," p. 205, remarks that "it is interesting to remember that the first institution of a feast of martyrdom which they [the Church] kept the memory of, dates from the moment when the books of St. Polycarp were still burning."

27. Lemerle, "Les Persécutions," p. 152.

THE MARTYROLOGIUM HIERONYMIANUM[28]

The Berne MS of the *Martyrologium* is not considered to be the original form of the notice, but it is curious that Wissemburgensis and other MSS do not mention Ad Catacumbas when this location is clearly set forth in the literary tradition and is confirmed by the archeological excavations at San Sebastiano. Duchesne offered the explanation that this topographical detail was dropped since the *Martyrologium* was originally intended for use outside of Rome and the celebration Ad Catacumbas was peculiarly Roman.[29] In addition, by the time that the *Martyrologium* was written,[30] the celebration Ad Catacumbas was no longer held, having been suppressed by the Church, and the site was in the possession of the cult of St. Sebastian. The mention of Catacumbas in the Berne MS is an anachronism from the standpoint of the religious activity of the day and, as such, most probably was contained in the archetype.

Duchesne also suggests that the following phrases in the notice as found in the Berne MS are additions: "Via Aurelia," "passi sub Nerone," "utrumque," and "Basso et Tusco consulibus." The first two can be explained as dependent upon literary (The *Liber Pontificalis*: Peter, "Qui sepultus est via Aurelia") and oral traditions. The last two are more difficult to explain and were probably contained in the source which lies behind both the *Depositio* and the *Martyrologium*. Since it is obvious that both Peter and Paul were commemorated Ad Catacumbas, Lietzmann and Leclercq favor the suggestion made by Duchesne that "utriusque" should be read in place of "utrumque."[31]

The original notice of the *Martyrologium*, according to Guignebert, involved only Peter: "Romae Via Aurelia, natale [sancti?] Petri [apostoli?] in Vaticano sub Nerone, in Catacumbas Basso et Tusco consulibus." Paul, he says, was only introduced into the notice at a later date, and when this happened it made the notice almost unintelligible.[32] The argument immediately arises against this proposal that the graffiti found on the wall of the Triclia, Ad Catacumbas unmistakably contain the name of Paul.[33]

In the conclusion to his discussion of the Vatican excavations, Hjalmar Torp states that "the development in the beginning of the fourth century in an ever-increasing rhythm goes from Ad Catacumbas to the Vatican, from a common celebration of Peter and Paul to a particular feast of Peter, from a funeral celebration of the relics of the Apostles to a hierarchical feast of funeral origin, but predominantly associated with Peter the Bishop."[34] He is convinced that the veneration of relics began Ad Catacumbas and ended when the relics were brought to the Vatican (although nothing is

---

28. Plate 6 shows the notice for June 29 in the Codex Epternacensis and Plate 7, the notice in the Berne Manuscript.

29. *Le Liber Pontificalis*, Vol. I, Part I, p. cv; and his "La 'Memoria Apostolorum,'" p. 2.

30. The text was written, at the earliest, in the mid-fifth century, and the first Gallic redaction appeared a century or more later. Johann Peter Kirsch, "Das 'Martyrologium Hieronymianum,'" p. 253, cites the following as the best introductions to this document: Duchesne, "Les Sources du Martyrologe hiéronymien," pp. 120–60; *Acta Sanctorum*, eds. de Rossi and Duchesne, Vol. II, Part I (1894), esp. pp. 84 and 342, 343; Duchesne, *Analecta Bollandiana*, XVII (1898), 421–47; Delehaye, "Le Témoignage des Martyrologes," pp. 78–99.

31. *Acta Sanctorum*, eds. de Rossi and Duchesne, Vol. II, Part I, p. 84; Lietzmann, *Petrus und Paulus in Rom*, 1st ed., pp. 81 ff.; 2d ed., pp. 109 ff.

Duchesne's reconstruction: "Romae natale sanctorum Petri et Pauli apostolorum: Petri in Vaticano, Pauli vero in via Ostensi, utriusque in catacumbas. Basso et Tusco consulibus."

Leclercq's reconstruction, *DACL*, Vol. XIV, Part I, p. 975, is based in part upon the reasoning of Duchesne: "Romae apostolorum Petri et Pauli [or Romae Petri et Pauli apostolorum]. Petri in Vaticano, Pauli vero via Ostiensi, utriusque in Catacumbas." In addition to these phrases which Duchesne discards as secondary, he also eliminates the enigmatic "Basso et Tusco consulibus."

32. Guignebert, "La Sépulture de Pierre," p. 237.

33. See below, pp. 150–51.

34. Torp, "The Vatican Excavations," pp. 64–65.

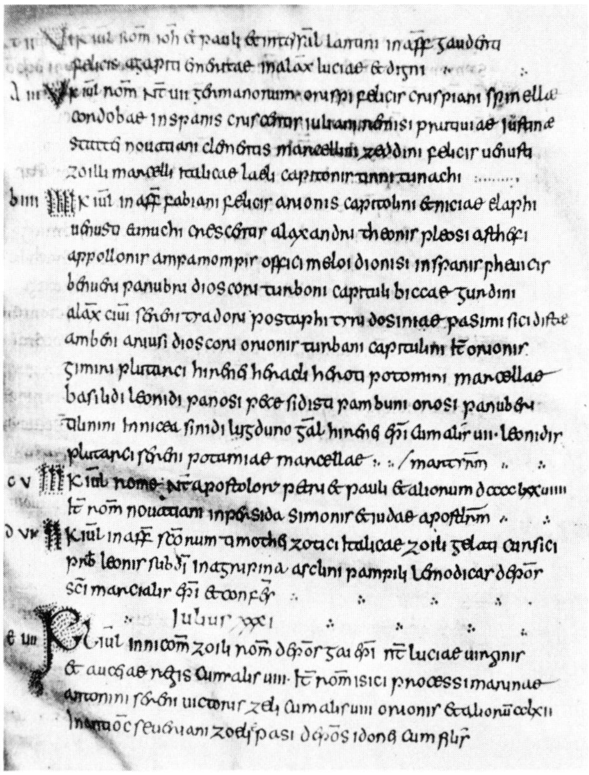

PLATE 6 This page of the *Martyrologium Hieronymianum*, Codex Epternacensis, mentions the feast of Peter and Paul held on June 29. The MS is preserved in the Bibliothèque Nationale de Paris, Lat. 10.837, fol. 20—from the eighth century (Besson, *Saint Pierre et les Origines de la Primauté romaine*, fig. 45, p. 67).

really known of a translation) in the sixth century. This late translation, he claims, may explain the notice in the *Martyrologium* which gives June 29 as the day of commemoration to Peter on the Vatican. The "Petri in Vaticano," then, was not left out of the *Depositio* (as Duchesne and Lietzmann believed) but was added by the *Martyrologium*.

The original wording of the *Martyrologium* can be recovered, Kirsch observes, by a combination of the Berne, Ottoboniano, and the Wissemburgensis MSS.[35] "III Kal. Iul. Romae [via Aurelia] natale sanctorum apostolorum Petri et Pauli.[36] Petri in Vaticano. Pauli vero (in) via Ostiensi (utrumque in Catacumbas, passi sub Nerone). [Basso et Tusco consulibus]." The material common to all MSS is original; in addition, Kirsch is convinced that "utriusque in Catacumbas" belongs to the archetype for it is beyond doubt that a commemoration of Peter and Paul was held Ad Catacumbas in the Basilica Apostolorum. His "proof," in part, for this conclusion depends upon the poem attributed to Ambrose, a poem which he considers genuine. "Via Aurelia" is no doubt a marginal note that crept into the text, perhaps inspired by the *Liber Pontificalis* or a common tradition. The reference to "Basso et Tusco consulibus," which appears in the Berne MS only, may be derived from the original or may have appeared only in the source used by the Berne MS author. The same may also be said for "passi sub Nerone," which is one of the more than sixty-eight hagiographic details found in the *Martyrologium*.[37] The original text, Kirsch suggests, was as follows: "Romae apostolorum Petri et Pauli [or Roma Petri et Pauli apostolorum]. Petri in Vaticano, Pauli vero via Ostiense, utriusque in Catacumbas."

An important and thought-provoking analysis of the text is made by Leo Kunibert Mohlberg. In disagreement with Duchesne and others, he maintains that the only part of the *Depositio* or the common source used in this notice is the "III kal. iul." He claims that the last part of the notice of June 29 in the *Martyrologium* does

35. Johann Peter Kirsch, "Le Festi degli Apostoli," p. 59. The brackets indicate words found only in the Berne Manuscript. The parentheses indicate words found in the Berne and Ottoboniano manuscripts (the latter is found in the Vatican Library, Lat. 38—and is considered by Kirsch to be valuable) and not in the Codex Wissemburgensis.

36. Codex Wissemburgensis has "sanctorum Petri et Pauli apostolorum."

37. As his source for this information, Kirsch cites H. Achelis, "Die Martyrologien, ihre Geschichte und ihre Wirt," *Abhandlungen der Gesellschaften der Wissenschaften zu Göttingen*, III, 155–88.

The DCCCCLXXVII which follows the first part of the notice is probably later than the original, but earlier than the archetype of our recensions. The word "Romae" was certainly added by the Gallic editor of the *Martyrologium*. In a Roman document, such as the *Depositio*, this detail would be superfluous.

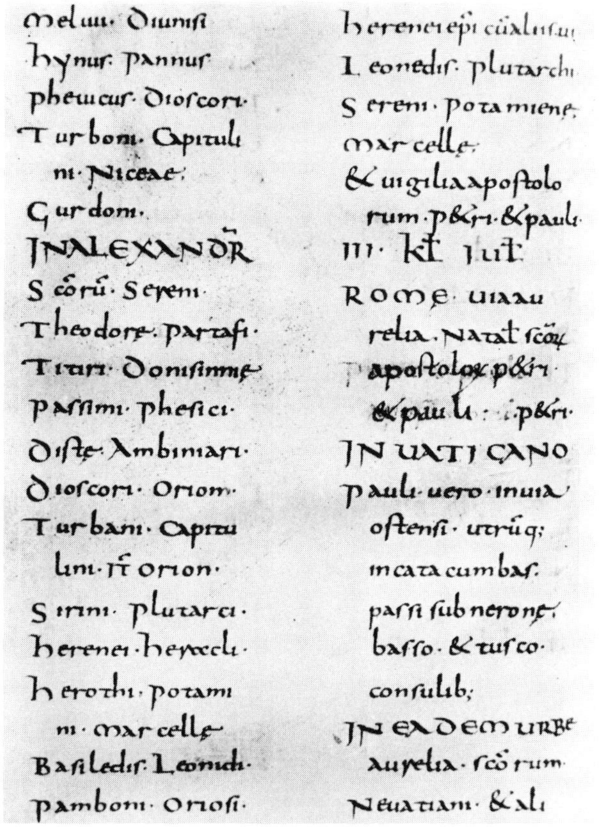

PLATE 7 This page, from the *Martyrologium Hieronymianum*, Codex Bernensis, mentions the feast of Peter and Paul held on June 29. The MS is preserved in the Bibliothèque de la Ville de Berne, Codex 289, fol. 101.v—eighth century (Besson, *Saint Pierre et les Origines de la Primauté romaine*, fig. 46, p. 68). Notice the erasure at lines 10 and 11 in column 2.

not belong to the date following but is an integral part of the reference to the celebration of Peter and Paul; in fact, it holds the key to the entire mystery.[38] The ending of the June 29 notice appears in two recensions: "et aliorum martyrum DCCCCLXXVIIII item Romae Novatiani et dedicatio baptisteri antiqui Romae,"[39] or "in eadem urbe Aurelia sanctorum Novatiani et

aliorum DCCCCLXXVII et dedicatio baptisteri antiqui Romae."[40]

Mohlberg claims that the discovery of the grave of Novatian on April 1, 1932, has made this interpretation possible. The last five digits in the number DCCCCLXX*VIIII* and the last three digits in the number DCCCCLXX*VII* represent the nine milestones of the Via Tiburtina and the seven sons of Symphorosa. This statement is explained by reference to the notice of "V Kal. Iul."

I	II
Romae natale *VII germanorum* Crispi, Felicis, Crispiani, Spinellae	Romae via Tiburtina *milario VIIII* Crispi, Crispiani, Felicis, Spinellae et *septem germanorum*

Cordubae in Spania Criscentis, Juliani Remisi, Prutiviae, Justinae, Stattei, Eugeni, Novatiani, Clementis, Marcellini Zeddini, Felicis, Venusti
Zoilli, Marcelli Italicae Laeli, Capitonis Tinni Tunachi

et in insula Oia
translatio corporis
sanctis Florenti.

The numbers 977 and 979 originated in connection with Nero's persecution "through a late folk legend."[41] The connection with Novatian explains why the *Depositio* does not mention the celebration of the date at the Vatican, an orthodox shrine.[42]

It is a source of wonder to Mohlberg that no one ever asked why the Church built three sanctuaries almost at the same time to the two apostles—one on the Vatican to Peter, another on the Via Ostia to Paul, and one to both apostles on the Via Appia. The close connection of the Basilica Apostolorum with the

38. Mohlberg, "Historisch-kritische," pp. 52–74. See Grégoire, "Le Problème de la Tombe de Saint Pierre," pp 53–57, looks favorably upon the position of Mohlberg.

39. Mohlberg, "Historisch-kritische," p. 63n61. The text is from the Codex Epternacensis, Paris, Bibliothèque Nationale, Lat. 10837 (from the beginning of the seventh century).

40. Mohlberg, "Historisch-kritische," p. 63n61. The text is the Laureshamensis MS, Rome, Bibl. Vatican pal., Lat. 238; Metz MS, Berne, Stadt Bibl. 289; Sens MS, Paris, Bibliothèque Nationale, Lat. 1064; and Rome, Bibl. Vatican, Reg. Lat. 507.

41. Mohlberg cites *Ephemerides Liturgicae*, LI (1937), 244.

42. Mohlberg, "Historisch-kritische," p. 64, "Es besteht zwischen der Petrusnotiz in dem Depositio Martyrum und dem Novatianstag in der ältesten und besten Überlieferung des Martyrologien Hieronymianum ein innerer historischer Zusammenhang."

Depositio (through the notice of "Petri in Catacumbas") and the very significant Novatianist character, which he sees in the entire list, compel Mohlberg to conclude that the Basilica Apostolorum was a sanctuary of Novatian. This connection also explains easily the reason why the cult of Peter and Paul was suddenly dropped Ad Catacumbas and why the Basilica Apostolorum became known later as the Church of San Sebastiano. The early Itineraries refer to the sanctuary as San Sebastiano; therefore, the mention in the *Liber Pontificalis* and the *Acta Quirini* of the "Basilica Apostolorum" can be explained only as an anachronism.[43]

Sebastian probably died under Diocletian A.D. 303 or 304, and his relics were buried Ad Catacumbas before the mid-fourth century, when the *Chronograph of 354* was written. If one follows the various notices gathered by Mohlberg to indicate the changing fortunes of the Novatianists, it appears evident that the Basilica Apostolorum could well have "changed hands" during the pontificate of Innocent I (A.D. 401–17).[44]

If Mohlberg is correct, the *Depositio Martyrum* and *Depositio Episcoporum*, which previously were looked upon solely as sources of topographical information, would now have some importance in shedding light on one short period in the history of the Early Church. And, according to Mohlberg, they join the grave catalogues which are made known to us in the controversies between Proclus and Gaius and between Polycrates and Victor. Our documents contribute to the understanding of the tradition since "they stem from the time of similar spiritual interest and controversies."[45]

The Novatianist character of the *Depositio Martyrum* and *Depositio Episcoporum* can be seen, Mohlberg adds, by the fact that both documents lack any reference to Bishop Cornelius (foe of Novatian), and there is no mention of the festival of Peter "in Vaticano."[46] The date, June 29, A.D. 258, can only be satisfactorily explained as contemporary with the cult on the Via

---

43. Lietzmann, *Petrus und Paulus in Rom*, 2d ed., p. 151.

44. The outline of the changing fortunes is organized by Mohlberg, "Historisch-kritische," pp. 69–71: 1) The name of Novatian stands in a calendar of feasts written by Miltiades between A.D. 311 and 314. 2) The attitude in Canon 8 of the Council of Nicea is friendly toward Novatianists; surely they were not treated as heretics in this period. 3) *Cod. Theod.*, XVI.5:2 allows the Novatianists to have cemeteries. 4) Later, A.D. 326, Constantine changed his position and treated the Novatianists as Marcionites and Valentinians. Their public services were forbidden and their books prohibited and rejected, but according to Mohlberg, "das gesetz hatte wenig Erfolg" (Eusebius, *Vita Constantini* III.64; *MPG*, XX, 1040–41). The authenticity of this tradition, however, has been disputed; see Mohlberg, "Historisch-kritische," p. 69n110. 5) Under Constantius (A.D. c. 337) the Novatianists were grouped with the orthodox and the emperor stood with the Arians against them. The orthodox in this period used the Novatianist churches in Constantinople (Socrates, *Historia Ecclesiastica* II.38; *MPG*, LXVII, 323–27). 6) Julian's politics (A.D. 361–63) were favorable to the Novatianists (Socrates, *Hist. Eccl.*, pp. 327–32). 7) Under Valens (A.D. 364–78) we learn from Socrates (*Hist. Eccl.*, IV.9; *MPG*, LXVII, 477–80) that the fortunes again changed and the sect of Novatianists were persecuted under the influence of Dominica, the wife of the emperor, and the bishop of Constantinople. The churches were closed and their bishop, Agelius, was banished. At the same time Athanasius was sent into exile for the fifth time. 8) Under Theodosius (A.D. 379–95), when he was at odds with the

Arians, the Novatianists prospered. In *Cod. Theod.* XVI.5:6 it is learned that on January 10, A.D. 381, legislation was passed against the heretics, but the Novatianists were not named. After A.D. 381 the Novatianists were allowed "frei Religionsübung" and Bishop Leo A.D. 391 was an important figure in the court of Theodosius. 9) In Socrates, *Hist. Eccl.*, VII.9; *MPG*, LXVII, 755, is found the following notice relative to Innocent I: "ὃς πρῶτος τοὺς ἐν Ῥώμῃ Ναυατιάνους ἐλαύνειν ἤρξατο, πολλάς τε αὐτῶν ἐκκλησίας ἀφείλατο." This is the period, between A.D. 401 and 417, when Mohlberg, "Historisch-kritische," p. 71, is convinced that the Novatianists moved from the Basilica Apostolorum, "als in Rom der Vernichtungskampf gegen die Novatianer begann." The persecution reached its height under Celestine I (A.D. 422–32) according to Socrates, *Hist. Eccl.* (VII.11; *MPG*, LXVII, 757).

45. Mohlberg, "Historisch-kritische," p. 73. See Vallin, "Le Culte des Apôtres Pierre et Paul," p. 267.

46. The later notice concerning Silanus, Mohlberg claims ("Historisch-kritische," p. 74), is a later addition by an anti-Novatianist hand. Furthermore (*ibid.*, p. 60), he notes that the *Depositio* begins with the period of antipope Hippolytus, A.D. 217–35 (who opposed Callistus, A.D. 217–22; Urbanus, A.D. 222–30; and Pontianus, A.D. 230–35) and the *Depositio Episcoporum* begins with the period of the antipope Novatian, A.D. 251–58 (who opposed Cornelius, A.D. 251–53; Lucius, A.D. 253–54; Stephanus, A.D. 254–57; and Xystus II, A.D. 257–58). He asks if it is but chance that the last pope buried near Peter at the Vatican is Victor (A.D. 189–98). Even Zephyrinus, Callistus' predecessor, is buried "iuxta Callistum."

Appia, and the only satisfactory explanation of the date in the *Martyrologium* lies in its relationship to the following notice of the commemoration of Novatian celebrated on the Via Tiburtina (this date A.D. 258 marks the death and deposition of Novatian). The Basilica Apostolorum was built after A.D. 336 in a period when the Novatianists had official recognition. At this spot the cult of Peter and Paul was conducted until the pontificate of Innocent I. Interestingly, at almost the same time that the cult of Peter and Paul was suppressed at the Catacombs, the cult of Cornelius on the Via Appia was begun, "which is the counterevidence for the above mentioned facts."[47] In other words, recognition was given to an orthodox bishop when a cult sponsored by his rival, a Novatianist bishop, ceased to be recognized.

The theory is interesting and convincing if one makes the initial admission that the liturgical documents discussed above were written or edited by the Novatians, but there is no direct evidence to warrant this conclusion. In addition, there is the entry, "hunc Silanum martyrum Novati furati sunt," which must be conveniently dismissed as a late entry by an orthodox writer who imputed the theft of relics to the Novatianists. The main problem of the theory is that it is in opposition to that which follows from the Damasus inscription. If the area Ad Catacumbas were simply a Novatianist cult center and *never did* contain the relics or the tombs of the apostles *and* if this sect did not give up the site until the beginning of the fifth century, what meaning must be attached to the words of Damasus: "Hic habitasse prius sanctos cognoscere debes, nomina quisque Petri pariter Paulique requiris"? We must either say that Damasus was ignorant of the Novatianist character of the cult center *or* that he meant literally "to live" by the verb "habitare"—both suggestions are extremely unlikely.

Chadwick finds another explanation for the decline of the importance of the cult center Ad Catacumbas, not in the actual *fact* of a translation of the apostles' relics to the Vatican and the Via Ostia but in the *belief* that such a translation had taken place. This most simply explains the decline of the site on the Via Appia and its rededication to the cult of Sebastian. After the relics

had been moved, or the belief was abroad that they had been moved, all except the occasional curious pilgrim would have forsaken the area of the Via Appia for the Vatican and Via Ostia.[48]

Which, if any, of the explanations and reconstructions of the *Depositio* and *Martyrologium* is correct? What are the implications of the reconstructions? Since there is no textual evidence to support any one of them, they are based upon individual reasoning arrived at from consideration of relevant evidence drawn from other literary and liturgical documents and from the reports of the excavations at San Sebastiano and the Vatican. In brief, the various theories are determined in a large part by individual decisions concerning the meaning of the date A.D. 258 which—aside from the convenient but arbitrary avoidance of the problem altogether by Paul Monceaux and Dom Quentin—cannot be eliminated.

As the text of the *Depositio* stands, there is no mention of veneration of Peter at the Vatican nor Paul Ad Catacumbas. If this notice is believed to be accurate for the time in which it was written (A.D. 336–54), and unless one is willing to defend the theory that Peter and Paul originally were buried Ad Catacumbas, one must admit that it was believed by the Church or by some within the Church in the fourth century that at some time (logically when Basso and Tusco were consuls) the cult or the relics *and* cult of Peter were transferred to the Catacombs. One must further admit that at this time it was also believed either that the cult or the relics *and* cult of Paul had been transferred back to the Via Ostia from the Catacombs or that they had never left the Via Ostia.[49] If the text is to be reconstructed on the basis suggested by Duchesne and Lietzmann, this involves a belief in a prior translation of the relics of Peter and Paul to the Catacombs and presupposes a later translation back to the original burial places (unless an original

47. Mohlberg, "Historisch-kritische," p. 74.

48. Chadwick, "St. Peter and St. Paul," p. 47. See Toynbee, "The Shrine of St. Peter and Its Setting," p. 15; Lowe, *St. Peter*, p. 40. Klauser, *Die römische Petrustradition*, p. 77. A. M. Schneider also believed that the shrine on the Via Appia was in the hands of schismatics or heretics, but he did not identify them. "Die Memoria Apostolorum," p. 14. See review by Toynbee, in *Gnomon*, pp. 269, 270.

49. A conclusion which, however, is challenged by the evidence found in the Triclia Ad Catacumbas.

burial of Peter in the Catacombs and Paul on the Via Ostia can be defended, which is unlikely).

The text of the Berne MS of the *Martyrologium* as it stands is unintelligible and *must* be interpreted. Without the words "Via Aurelia" and "passi sub Nerone," which are obviously later additions based on other traditions and understandable confusion, the notice makes it logical to assume, as does the original or reconstructed text of the *Depositio*, either that a translation of the relics took place *or* that a cult of Peter and Paul existed. One

obvious conclusion may be drawn from the ambiguity and vagueness of the liturgical sources: the Church possessed no historical record whatsoever concerning the date of the martyrdom or burial of Peter in Rome.

The next problem to examine is which, if any, of these explanations is correct or, in the absence of conclusive proof, which is the more plausible. Was the transfer limited to the cult or did it involve also the moving of relics? What actually took place on June 29, A.D. 258?[50]

THE TRANSLATION THEORY

In the *Depositio* and *Martyrologium* does "III kal. iul. Basso et Tusco consulibus" (= A.D. 258) indicate a translation of some kind, an "invention" of relics, or an inauguration of a cult? Or might the inclusion of the date be explained as a conscious fabrication, intended to serve some forgotten purpose during the persecution which raged at the time of Valerian?

Almost all of the modern writers refer to the Translation Theory as if it were an original solution to the problem conceived by Louis Duchesne. As Barnes pointed out at the beginning of the century and Chadwick commented within the past few years, it would be better to say that the theory was revived and modified by Duchesne.[51] The idea had been suggested previously by John Pearson in *Annales Cyprianici* (printed in John Fell's edition of Cyprian in 1682, p. 62, and criticized by Tillemont, *Mémoires pour servir à l'Histoire ecclésiastique des six premiers Siècles*, Vol. I, Part 2, 1701).

The Translation Theory does not represent a single point of view but appears in a number of quite different versions. There are a number who explain that the bodies of the apostles were buried Ad Catacumbas immediately after their martyrdom and that around A.D. 251, *prior* to the persecution of Valerian, the relics were moved to the Vatican and the Via Ostia. Others

take the position that Peter was originally buried at the Vatican, and Paul, on the Via Ostia. At the time of the Valerian persecution, the relics were brought to the Catacombs, and at a later time they were returned to their original resting places. A third group of scholars claims that if there were a translation at all, it was only partial and that some of the relics of the apostle Peter had always remained at the Vatican. Still another version proposes that Peter was buried originally at the Catacombs and that his relics were brought to the Vatican as late as the seventh century.

The earliest of those who supported the first version of the theory was Cardinal Baronius (1538–1607) in the *Annales Ecclesiastici*. He based his theory on information gathered from the *Acta Petri*, the Damasus Inscription, and the Letter of Gregory to the Empress Constantina.

In order not to conflict with the evidence of Gaius, E. Paperbroche, who wrote on the translation in the Bollandist *Acta Sanctorum*, claimed that the translation ("de Catacumbus" in the notice of Cornelius in the *Liber Pontificalis*) to the Vatican and Via Ostia did not take place until the reign of Cornelius in A.D. 251 or 252. Paperbroche also argued that since eleven of the earliest bishops were said to have been buried near the body of Peter at the Vatican, the relics of Peter could not have been removed to the Catacombs until about A.D. 200.[52] If this hypothesis is correct, an explanation

---

50. Goguel, *L'Église primitive*, pp. 217–31, persists in writing June 28.

51. Barnes, *St. Peter in Rome*, pp. 112–16; Chadwick, "St. Peter and St. Paul," pp. 41–42.

52. See Barnes, *St. Peter in Rome*, p. 112.

is provided for the degree of cultic interest in the site of the Catacombs in the third century. But what reason was there for a translation to the Vatican and Via Ostia in the mid-second century, for there seems to be no record of any custom in this period that would make it necessary for the body of a martyr to be brought back to the place of martyrdom, and why were the relics transferred to the Catacombs in the beginning of the century? The only reason given is unconvincing: Perhaps at the time of Heliogabulus (A.D. 218–22) the Circus of Nero beside the Vatican Hill was widened to accommodate races with elephants, which endangered the apostolic tomb.[53] In addition, this theory does not offer any explanation of the enigmatic date of A.D. 258 which appears in the *Depositio* and the *Martyrologium*. More recent scholars who have championed the view of a post martyrdom burial of Peter Ad Catacumbas are Alfons Schneider, Pasquale Testini, and Francesco Tolotti.[54]

The most popular form of the Translation Theory is that which admits that Peter was buried originally at the Vatican and Paul on the Via Ostia, and which maintains that the relics of both apostles were transported Ad Catacumbas not "eo tempore quo passi sunt" (Tolotti and others) or around A.D. 200 (Paperbroche) but during the persecution of Valerian. At some later time the bodies were returned to their original and final resting places on the Vatican and Via Ostia. This view satisfies the requirements of the liturgical documents as reconstructed by the proponents of this form of the Translation Theory, but it disregards the "evidence" of the Letter of Gregory to the Empress Constantina, the apocryphal *Acta*, and the notice of Cornelius in the *Liber Pontificalis*. Since this is the most widely held interpretation and since there are many "proofs" and objections, it is instructive to view separately the positions of the most important writers.

Duchesne pointed out that A.D. 258 was a year of persecution. Gathering in the cemeteries, including those on the Vatican and Via Ostia, was forbidden,[55] and since these areas were certain to be guarded it was exceedingly dangerous to hold such meetings. He claims therefore that

la prudence commandait d'en extraire les reliques des apôtres et de les cacher en quelque endroit où la police ne fût pas tentée d'aller les chercher, où même les fidèles n'eussent pas autant de facilité de se réunir pour les vénérer. Le monument des Catacombes satisfait admirablement à cette condition.[56]

That the Catacombs was a safer place than the Vatican and Via Ostia is challenged by A. M. Schneider. Only a few hundred yards away there was an imperial police station near the tomb of Caecilia Metella,[57] near one of the busiest of the Roman highways. The danger of gatherings in the Catacombs became especially imminent when, on August 6, Bishop Sixtus II, while officiating at a ceremony held near the tombs of his predecessors who had been buried there since A.D. 217, was martyred in a surprise attack. Perhaps the attackers involved were from that very police station.[58]

Duchesne concludes, nevertheless, that the relics were transported to the Catacombs for safety, probably on the date recorded in both the *Depositio* and the *Martyrologium*, and remained there for about sixty years

---

53. *Ibid.*, p. 112. This refers, most probably, *not* to the area of the Vatican Hill but to the Gaianum to the northeast of the Vatican area.

54. A. M. Schneider, "Die Memoria Apostolorum," pp. 1 ff.; Testini, "Noterelle sulla 'Memoria Apostolorum' in Catacumbas," pp. 209–31; Tolotti, *Memorie,* pp. 111–14, 220.

55. *E. H.* VII.11:10 (Lake, II, 159): "οὐδαμῶς δὲ ἐξέσται οὔτε ὑμῖν οὔτε ἄλλοις τισὶν ἢ συνόδους ποιεῖσθαι ἢ εἰς τὰ καλούμενα κοιμητήρια εἰσιέναι." ("And it shall in no wise be permitted either to you or to any others either to hold assemblies or to enter the cemeteries, as they are called." Trans. by J. E. L. Oulton. This was an order given by Aemilianus, Prefect of Egypt, to the bishop of Alexandria.

See *Acta Cypriani* VII (*MPL*, III, 1500): "ne in aliquando [aliquibus] locis conciliabula fiant, nec coemeteria ingrediantur."

56. Duchesne, *Le Liber Pontificalis*, Vol. I, Part I, pp. cvi–cvii, compare p. 151n7 and p. 81. See also his *Origines du Culte chrétien* (1889), p. 268. Harnack, *Die Chronologie*, I, 709, agreed with this conclusion in saying that on June 29 "erfolgte i.J. 258 unter den Consuln Tuscus und Bassus die Beisetzung der Apostel in den Katakomben." Tuker and Malleson, *Handbook to Christian and Ecclesiastical Rome*, p. 239; Zahn, *Introduction*, II, 79.

57. A. M. Schneider, "Die Memoria Apostolorum," p. 5.

58. Cyprian, *Epistle* LXXXII (*MPL*, IV, 430). See A. M. Schneider, "Die Memoria Apostolorum," p. 5. For evidence of the police station in this area, see *CIL*, Vol. VI, Nos. 230, 3329. Schneider calls attention to O. Hirschfeld, *Die Sicherheitspolizei im röm Kaiserreich* (Berlin, 1891), Nos. 39, 860. See Marucchi, *Manual of Christian Archeology*, 4th ed., p. 52, for

or more until the erection of the basilicas for Peter and Paul on the Vatican and the Via Ostia. When the relics had been replaced, the memory of the temporary burial Ad Catacumbas was forgotten, but the topographical detail remained for a long while and continued to be associated with the solemn commemoration on June 29. Duchesne's theory was supported by Marucchi, Grossi-Gondi, and Styger, who, despairing of the inconsistencies and contradictions in the literary and liturgical traditions, arrived at this position through a study of the excavations Ad Catacumbas.[59] Scholars have frequently criticized the Translation Theory of Duchesne by saying that the Romans would not have harmed the grave.[60] It was, however, a question not of the safety of the relics alone and whether or not the Romans would molest the grave but of the safety of the faithful, the Christians who felt the need to congregate near the relics. Such congregations, Duchesne maintained, were safer in the vicinity of the Via Appia than at either the Vatican or the Via Ostia.[61]

Certain writers have argued against the Translation Theory that it was illegal for the Christians to move the body once it had been buried. Against this objection might be stated that "in Roman law . . . where the relics are deposed in a temporary place with the intention to transfer them elsewhere, neither the permission of the emperor nor of the pontiffs is needed."[62] And as Trajan's Letter to Pliny shows, permission could be obtained to move a body.[63] Permission was given according to the conditions involved. Against the theory, in addition to the arguments mentioned above, La Piana stresses that the Christians in a time of persecution would hardly have dared to enter a guarded cemetery and commit a crime of this type, which carried the extreme penalty.[64] Moreover, there are no recorded instances of translations of martyrs in the West (in the East there are occurrences after the Peace of the Church) during the first five centuries of the Christian era, except the "bringing home" of bodies of martyrs such as Pontianus and Hippolytus.[65] La Piana in this theory

---

the view that the Valerian persecution was not greatly severe and a translation of relics would have been unnecessary. See Delehaye, *Les Origines*, pp. 302–8, and in *Analecta Bollandiana*, XLV (1927), 297; La Piana, "The Tombs of Peter and Paul," pp. 67 ff. See Duchesne, *Le Liber Pontificalis*, Vol. I, Part 2, p. 155.

59. Marucchi, "Osservazioni intorno al cimitero delle Catacombe sulla Via Appia," *Römische Quartalschrift*, VI (1892), p. 281 f.; Styger, in *Römische Quartalschrift*, p. 189; Grossi-Gondi, "Il 'Refrigerium'," pp. 243, 244.

60. This belief is considered by Capocci, "Notae," pp. 199–212. However, Tertullian in a letter to Scapula A.D. 203 tells of pagan profanation of Christian graves to the cry of "area non sint" [down with Christian cemeteries], see Carcopino, *Études*, p. 185. See Julius Paulus, *Sententiarum receptarum ad Filium* I.21:8, ed. Schultingh, p. 264 and note 6; Cumont, "Un rescrit impérial sur la violation de sépulture," pp. 241–66, esp. 257–66.

61. This article by Styger was written before that of Schneider which pointed out the close proximity of the police station.

62. Attention is called by Grossi-Gondi, "Il 'Refrigerium,'" p. 243n1, to this law found in V. Quenstedius, I. Andreas, "De sepultura veterum" CXII in Gronovio (*Thes. Graec. Antiq.*, Venetiis, 1737, Vol. XI, col. 1296).

63. *Epistle* X.69, Pliny, *Letters*, trans. Melmoth II, 368, 369: "It will be a hardship upon the provincials to oblige them to address themselves to the College of Pontiffs whenever they have just reasons for removing the ashes of their ancestors. In this case therefore it will be better that you should follow the example of the governors, your predecessors, and grant or deny them this liberty as you shall see reasonable."

("Durum est iniungere necessitatem provincialibus pontificum adeundorum si reliquias suorum, propter aliquas iustas causas, transferre ex loco in alium locum velint. Sequenda ergo potius tibi exempla sunt eorum, qui isti provinciae praefuerunt, et ex causa cuique ita aut permittendum, aut negandum.")

See also Julius Paulus, *Sententiae Receptarum ad Filium* I.21:1, ed. Schultingh, p. 261, "ob incursam fluminis, vel metum ruinae, corpus jam perpetuae sepulturae traditum, solemnibus redditis sacrificiis, per noctem transferri locum potest." ("The Opinions of Paulus," ed. Scott, I, 266, "A body after it has been permanently buried . . . can be transferred by night to another place on account of the overflow of a river, or the fear of ruin.")

64. "The Tombs of Peter and Paul," p. 68. To this objection advanced by both La Piana and Delehaye (*Les Origines*, pp. 305 ff.), Duchesne made the classic reply, "La 'Memoria Apostolorum,'" p. 20; "Sans doute si l'on avait procédé régulièrement il aurait fallu une autorisation; on ne se fût pas risqué, bien entendu, à la demander. Mais en tous les temps on a fait sans autorisation des choses pour lesquelles une autorisation n'était ni riquise, ni possible." [The Church often did what was not permitted to them!] "Les translations, évidemment non autorisées, de martyrs chrétiens, sont souvent mentionées dans les textes."

65. See Carcopino, *Études*, p. 185.

discounts Lietzmann's position that the other consular dates found in the *Depositio* (May 19, A.D. 304, commemorating Parthenius and Calocerus, and September 22, A.D. 304, commemorating Basilla) are records of translations,[66] which view he sees as based upon an unfounded hypothesis of de Rossi.[67] The year 304 in the above cases are records of translations not of relics but of martyrdoms. In Rome (A.D. c. 600) relics were not even moved in accordance with the wish of a Roman empress,[68] or even of an emperor himself.[69] If the translation of the relics of the apostles took place A.D. 258, says La Piana, it would have been a unique situation.

The thesis is supported by Leclercq, who cautions, however, that it is a theory only and not a proved fact, but that it is a theory which has corroboration from the *Martyrologium*, and the archeological discoveries Ad Catacumbas.[70] While some still support the Translation Theory as formulated or revivified by Duchesne,[71] there has been in the past twenty years a growing tendency to discard it.[72]

66. *Petrus und Paulus in Rom*, 1st ed., pp. 84–87; 2d ed., pp. 114–18. Compare Delehaye, in *Analecta Bollandiana*, XLV (1927), 307–9; "Not any proof has been brought forth in the case of SS. Parthenius and Calocerus and the problem of the double festival ought not to be resolved by an hypothesis which has no reasonableness."

67. *La Roma sotterranea*, II, 214.

68. See above, p. 110.

69. In A.D. 519 Justinian asked Hormisdas for relics of St. Laurentius, but the papal legates told him of the "consuetudo Romana" which was to send "brandea" and not relics.

70. Leclercq, *DACL*, Vol XIV, Part I, pp. 894 f.

71. It is still supported by a few specialists and a number of texts, such as Jacquin, *Histoire de L'Église*, I, 231, 232; Piganiol, *Histoire de L'Église*, I, p. 63; Finegan, *Light from the Ancient Past*, pp. 376–78; Daniel-Rops, *The Church of the Apostles and the Martyrs*, p. 101. It is also defended by De Bruyne, "La Tomba apostolica," p. 221; Ferrua, "A la Recherche," p. 43; and Corte, *Saint-Pierre est-il au Vatican?*, pp. 82, 98. Toynbee and Perkins, *The Shrine of St. Peter*, p. 181, admit that translation was possible, but it is not provable, and the burden of proof is upon those who propose the theory. To date such proof has not been forthcoming. Hertling and Kirschbaum, *Die römischen Katakomben*, pp. 111, 202, accepted the theory (compare the position of Kirschbaum in 1957), but saw a number of objections to it; in addition to the ones already pointed out, they mention that translation is pointless if there was a recognized Christian cemetery Ad Catacumbas A.D. 258. Also, no definite place was ever found in that area where Peter and Paul were buried, and it is very doubtful that no trace would have remained. Jean Bernardi, in *Vigiliae Christianae*, p. 160; Carcopino, *Études*, pp. 112, 113, 184–88, 193 ff., and *De Pythagore*, pp. 280–322. In both works Carcopino emphasizes that the excavations at San Sebastiano and the Vatican support the theory that after the time of Gaius (A.D. c. 199–217) A.D. 258, the relics of Peter and Paul were transported Ad Catacumbas. At a later date, January 18, A.D. 336 (*Études*, p. 202), the relics of Peter were probably returned to the

Vatican. See Testini, "Le 'presunte' reliquie dell' Apostolo Pietro e la traslazione 'ad Catacumbas'," pp. 529–38; Klauser, "Die Deutung," p. 36, and Belvederi, "La cripta di Lucina," pp. 121–64

72. The most important alternatives to the Translation Theory of Duchesne will be considered separately. The following are a few of those who have discarded the view in favor of a modification or a totally different explanation of the date A.D. 258. Franchi De Cavalieri, "Note agiografiche," pp. 124–25; Johann Peter Kirsch, "Die beiden Apostelfeste Petri Stuhlfeier und Pauli Bekehrung im Januar," pp. 48–67. Delehaye, *Les Origines*, p. 64, sees the theory as a "result of a series of ingenious combinations rather than a fact supported by testimonies. . . . Certainly once one has accepted the idea of translation, one is better able to harmonize the texts which appear discordant." Cardinal Schuster, "DOMVS PETRI," pp. 147, 148, sums up his views, "Ma io non vedo come tale duplice traslazione sarebbe stata allora possibile," due to all the difficulties involved—"né i documenti, né i monumenti conservano alcuna traccia di una situazione simile" (see p. 167); Goguel, *L'Église primitive*, p. 228. Boulet, "À propos des Fouilles," pp. 401 f., emphasizes that a translation of the relics presupposes an interest in the relics of the martyrs in this period and this he believes is an anachronism. Veneration of relics did not begin until later. Boulet does not agree with any of the interpretations of the Translation Theory; but if *forced* to choose, he would take the position of Delehaye that the translation was not of relics but of cult; Griffe, in *Bull. de Litt. ecclés.*, LII (1951), 202–4, 208 says, "c'est que la légende forgée par l'érudition moderne"; see also the same author, *ibid.*, LIV (1953), 142; and LIX (1958), 119–22. See Bettini, "Tusco et Basso consulibus," pp. 67–87. Mohlberg, "Historisch-kritische," p. 74, agrees with Capocci that the Translation Theory is untenable; Berra, "Lo Sviluppo architettonico della Tomba di S. Pietro," p. 97n14; Kollwitz, "Die Grabungen," p. 15; Capocci, "Notae," p. 204; Toynbee, "The Shrine of St. Peter and Its Setting," p. 13, 14; Tolotti, *Memorie*, pp. 182, 183; Cristiani, "Les Fouilles de Saint Pierre," p. 54; Guarducci, *Cristo e San Pietro in un Documento precostiniano*, p. 74, also, in *Osservatore Romano*, November 22, 1953; von Gerkan, "Kritische Studien," p. 53, "Die Forschung nach dem Grab Petri," p. 204, "Zu den Problemen des Petrusgrabes," pp. 79–93, and "Petrus in Vaticano et in Catacumbas," p. 25. In

Another form of the Translation Theory is that adopted by F. Marchi and Charles Lugari, who combined the views of those who maintain that Peter was buried Ad Catacumbas immediately after his martyrdom (his body was later brought to the Vatican) and those who state that Peter was buried at the Vatican (his body later brought Ad Catacumbas and, at some later period, around the time of the building of the Basilica, returned again to the Vatican). Both writers maintain that two translations of the relics took place. In the first translation the bodies of the apostles were brought Ad Catacumbas shortly after their matryrdom and later returned to the Vatican and the Via Ostia. In the second translation the relics of Peter were again brought Ad Catacumbas (A.D. c. 200) at the time when Heliogabalus widened the circus to accommodate elephant races (but this took place most probably not in the Campus Vaticanus but in the Gaianum to the northeast, Plate 20) and the relics of Paul were also later brought to this place as a result of the presumed danger to his tomb during the Valerianic persecution. The bodies were returned to the Vatican and the Via Ostia at the time of the Peace of the Church (A.D. c. 312).[73]

recent articles such as "Basso et Tusco consulibus," (1958), pp. 89–105, von Gerkan appears to reverse himself explaining the damage to the Red Wall (MR) as a result of later Christians who were searching for the relics of Peter which they transported Ad Catacumbas. Burger, *La Tombe*, p. 26: "Cette hypothèse ne repose sur aucun texte, elle est tout gratuité"; O'Callaghan, "The Vatican Excavations and the Tomb of St. Peter," p. 83, Chadwick, "St. Peter and St. Paul," pp. 41, 42, states the theory "can claim only the dubious merit of being irrefutable only because it is unverifiable. . . . Seldom has so much history been constructed out of so little actual testimony." The translation is an etiological myth and we ought to look not for an event which took place but for the *belief* that an event had taken place. (See Lietzmann, *Petrus und Paulus in Rom*, 2d ed. p. 297.) See J. Ruysschaert, in *Revue d'histoire ecclésiastique*, pp. 791–837; Vallin, "Le Culte des Apôtres Pierre et Paul," pp. 258–62, and Winter, *St. Peter and the Popes*, pp. 99–112.

73. The following studies by F. Marchi and Charles Lugari are cited by Styger, in *Römische Quartalschrift*, p. 189, and Barnes, *St. Peter in Rome*, pp. 112, 114; Marchi, *Monumenti delle Arti cristiane primitive*, pp. 200 ff.; Lugari, *Le Catacombe; ossia, il Sepolcro apostolico, dell' Appia* (1888) and "I varii seppellimenti degli apostoli Pietro e Paulo sull'Appia, contirmati e chiariti dagl'ultima scavi," *Bessarione Roma*, II (1897), p. 317n17. See also de Rossi, "La Cathedra de S. Pietro," p. 31.

Against this hypothesis (beside its discordance with the *Depositio* or the *Martyrologium*), as well as that of Duchesne, it might be argued that neither explains why this emperor took such infinite pains to see that the Basilica was placed immediately over the alleged burial place of Peter. If the relics had been transported Ad Catacumbas A.D. 200 and not returned until after or in the period of the building of the Basilica, would it not be more reasonable to believe that the Basilica would have been built at the foot of the Vatican Hill? This move would still have placed the Basilica in the vicinity of the alleged place of martyrdom and burial. But the exact spot, no longer hallowed by the relics of the apostle (which were Ad Catacumbas A.D. 258 to c. 336) would no longer have been sacrosanct, and there would have been no further necessity to bury the large pagan necropolis and to move a million cubic feet of earth.

In an attempt to eliminate the more prominent objections to the Translation Theory and to accommodate the hypothesis to the findings of the excavations both at San Sebastiano and the Vatican, Enrico Josi evolved what may be called the "partial translation theory."[74] The hypothesis maintains, on the authority of the Roman jurist Julius Paulus in the third century, that the relics of a saint are considered to be where the head is to be found.[75] This solution by Josi that the head and some other bones were moved Ad Catacumbas in A.D. 258 and that the rest remained at the Vatican: 1) eliminates the objections concerning the danger of detection during the translation, 2) explains the fact that there was no evidence of a sarcophagus or large receptacle for relics either at San Sebastiano or beneath the Vatican, and 3) provides an interpretation for the

74. "Ipotesi sulla traslazione delle sole teste degli apostoli in Catacumbas," pp. 94–95.

75. The following is cited in Kirschbaum, *Die Gräber*, p. 246n20, which calls attention to *Corpus iuris civilis*, eds. P. Krüger and T. Mommsen, 1877, D. XI.7:44, "Cum in diversis locis sepultum est, uterque quidem locus religiosus non fit, quia una sepultura plura sepulchra efficere non potest: mihi autem videtur illum religiosum esse, ubi quod est principale conditum est, *id est caput*, cuius imago fit, inde cognoscimur, cum autem impetratur, ut reliquiae transferantur, desinit locus religiosus esse." (Italics are mine.)

THE LITURGICAL EVIDENCE 131

loculus in wall *g* of the Aedicula beneath the Vatican.[76] In addition, the hypothesis eliminates the objection made on the basis of the seemingly unshakable desire of Constantine to build his Basilica on a precise spot, despite the great difficulties—for the remainder of the relics were beneath the Red Wall (behind the Aedicula) and had never been moved. Because of these advantages, some who were skeptical of the old Translation Theory were won to the new interpretation, even though the documents relating to an original burial Ad Catacumbas remained unexplained.[77]

For one who accepts the possibility of a translation at all, a partial translation is rationalized on the basis of a wish of the Christian community, or hierarchy, A.D. 258 not to desecrate entirely the area of the Vatican. It follows then that, in the event that the cult of Peter had been transferred to the Catacombs with the major relic (the skull), there naturally would have been no graffiti calling upon the name of Peter on wall *g* (constructed in the interval A.D. 258–325) adjacent to the Aedicula beneath the Vatican.

A theory, concerning "III kal. iul." A.D. 258, more radical than any version of the Translation Theory is the one which claims that on this date the relics of the apostles were "invented." A plausible objection to this hypothesis is offered by Lietzmann. If the relics were "invented" at all, they would have been found together.[78] This is challenged by Goguel who claims that "if the tradition had always associated the two martyrs, as much as they were products of the same period, then they had also differentiated them as far as place."[79] A second objection by Lietzmann is more damaging: if there had been an invention it would have taken place

somewhere else. The relics would have been "found" in a Christian cemetery and not, as in the case of the Vatican and the Via Ostia, in the middle of a pagan burial ground. In addition, Gaius' statement in the *Ecclesiastical History* of Eusebius shows that the tradition of the relics of Peter was known A.D. 258, and therefore this date is much too late for an "invention."[80] Despite Lietzmann's arguments, Goguel still maintains that "l'invention reste tout aussi possible que la 'translatio.'"[81]

Another view, championed by Delehaye, maintains that the relics of Peter and Paul were never Ad Catacumbas. But the cult was established there A.D. 258 because the rites could not be observed in safety at the Vatican or the Via Ostia as a result of the Edict of Valerian, which had been published the year before.[82] Later, when the basilicas were built on the Vatican and the Via Ostia the cult returned to these places, but remained also for a time at the Catacombs, as the poem attributed to Ambrose indicates.

Against this view may be urged the conclusion of the most popular interpretation of the Damasus Inscription, that the relics of Peter and Paul were *believed*—at least in the time of Damasus (A.D. 366–84)—to have rested at one time Ad Catacumbas. This objection also may be countered, because a cult could be located in places

---

76. See below, pp. 200–2.

77. Cristiani, "Les Fouilles de Saint Pierre," p. 54; Testini, "Noterelle sulla 'Memoria Apostolorum' in Catacumbas," pp. 213–18, 230, 231, a.ıd "Le 'presunte' reliquie dell'Apostolo Pietro e la Traslazione 'ad Catacumbas," pp. 529–38 (see Kirschbaum, *Die Gräber*, p. 203). Ruysschaert, *Réflexions sur les Fouilles vaticanes*, pp. 48–52. Kirschbaum, *Die Gräber*, p. 142; "Demnach können wir um diese Zeit, d. h. im Jahre 258, die Enthebung der Gebeine des heiligen Petrus aus seinem Grabe annehmen, und zwar glauben wir, dass man nur das Haupt entnahm." See also pp. 208–11.

78. *Petrus und Paulus in Rom*, 2d ed., pp. 246 f.

79. *L'Église primitive*, p. 228.

80. Against this objection must be urged that it is most probable but not *certain* that Gaius meant the relics or the tombs of the apostles by the word "tropaeum." He may have intended only to indicate the place of martyrdom, that is, the place of "victory." See above, pp. 95–101.

81. Goguel, *L'Église primitive*, p. 229. (See the development of his theory of the relation of the idea of a "translatio" to an "inventio" on the following pages.) See also Grégoire, "Les Persécutions," p. 102. The year 258 "pourrait n'avoir été qu'une 'inventio,' et non une 'translatio'." See also his article, "Le Problème de la Tombe de Saint Pierre," pp. 48–58. After considering all this evidence, Chadwick, "St. Peter and St. Paul," pp. 47 ff., concludes: "I venture to submit that the most reasonable interpretation of the available evidence is that the year 258 marked an 'invention' on June 29 in consequence of a Revelation [the location was surely in private hands]. . . . We have plenty of evidence for the frequency of 'invention' by private revelation" (for example, *Passio Sebastiani* and the dream of Lucina). See below, p. 158.

82. *Les Origines*, pp. 267, 302–8 and his article in *Analecta Bollandiana*, p. 305.

where the relics were not to be found. This fact is illustrated by the existence of the three basilicas of Cyprian and in our own day by the veneration of the saint at Lourdes: "Here would the immaculate girl be honored *as* in her permanent dwelling place."[83] Another argument against this view is one which may be presented also against the hypothesis of Duchesne. If the date refers to an establishment of cult practices Ad Catacumbas and it is only the cult that is transferred later to the Vatican (in other words, that actual relics were not in either site), then the precise placement of the Basilica on the Vatican by Constantine cannot be adequately explained. With some minor elaborations Delehaye's hypothesis has found favor with a number of modern writers.[84]

In an article written around the turn of the century, Carl Erbes suggested that the answer to the problem of the date A.D. 258 in the liturgical documents lay in both a commemoration *and* a translation. He is cautious, however, to distinguish between fact and belief. The Church in the third and fourth century *believed* that the relics of Peter and Paul resided in Catacumbas as the Damasus Inscription intimates. The notice "III kal. iul." in the *Chronograph of 354* indicates that on this day the Roman Church commemorated her founder-apostles. On this date A.D. 258 the Church commemorated Peter at the Catacombs and the transfer of the relics of Paul to the Via Ostia. And since the *Chronograph of 354*

does not mention a transfer of the relics of Peter, Erbes is confident that it was still believed (A.D. c. 354) that the relics of this apostle remained Ad Catacumbas.[85] Constantine built the Basilica at the alleged place of execution and not at the place of burial. Besides the familiar argument of the exact placement of the Basilica at the Vatican, it may also be asked of this theory why the relics of Paul were moved to the Via Ostia long before the Basilica was built? If there were some danger Ad Catacumbas, would not the relics of Peter also have been moved?

Guignebert considers the possibilities that the date in June, A.D. 258, could mark a translation, a presumed date of the original burial, the beginning of a cultic festival, or even an invention. "There remains," he says, "only this . . . that something of importance had taken place A.D. 258, since that date is brought out by the famous notices of the *Depositio* and the *Martyrologium* and certainly in the course of the third century the Roman community believed it possessed the relics of the two apostles Ad Catacumbas. That and nothing more!"[86]

As a result of the excavations beneath St. Peter's, Klauser rejects the Translation Theory.[87] He suggests instead that the veneration of Peter on the Vatican began with the finding of a vague inscription (perhaps like that which Damasus set up Ad Catacumbas) and then imagination, aided by the tradition of the martyrdom of Peter in that area did the rest. He cannot find any other more satisfying explanation for the remaining two locations, the Via Ostia (Paul) and Ad Catacumbas (both apostles). It could be also, he suggests, that the search for the grave site of Peter was inspired by the developing idea of apostolic succession. In any event, the various sites must have been known and pointed out by at least A.D. 165. This occurs, however, a generation before Gaius, who only mentions the Vatican because either he takes this one site seriously or he does not wish to weaken his argument with Proclus. It may

---

83. "In hac sua veluti sede Immaculata Virgo iugiter colitur." See Hertling and Kirschbaum, *Die römischen Katakomben*, p. 111.

84. Boulet, "À propos des Fouilles," p. 401; Bettini, "Tusco et Basso consulibus," pp. 67–87. Lemerle, "Les Persécutions," p. 152, argues against Bettini's thesis that the "memoria" Ad Catacumbas was built a long time before A.D. 258, but was only "inaugurated" at that time—sometime between the martyrdom of Stephen (August 2, A.D. 257) and the martyrdom of his successor Sixtus II (August 6, A.D. 258). Lemerle asks why an "inauguration" is more plausible during a persecution than a construction? In addition, he does not know of any other such "inauguration" in Christian history. He also attacks Bettini's thesis (similar to Tolotti's) of a continuous veneration Ad Catacumbas (p. 153). Compare Lemerle, "La Publication des Fouilles," pp. 224, 225. Others who follow Delehaye and Bettini are Berra, "Lo Sviluppo architettonico della Tomba di S. Pietro," p. 97; Celi, "La Memoria apostolica sull'Appia," *La Civiltà Cattolica*, No. 2, pp. 483–90 and No. 3, pp. 387–98; Batiffol, *Cathedra Petri*, p. 174.

85. Erbes, *Die Todestage*, pp. 39 f. See also his conclusions in "Die geschichtlichen Verhältnisse des Apostelgräber in Rom," p. 91. Compare Klauser, *Die römische Petrustradition*, p. 77.

86. Guignebert, "La Sépulture de Pierre," p. 246.

87. Klauser, *Die römische Petrustradition*, pp. 73 f., and "Die Deutung," p. 36.

also be, surmises Klauser, that Gaius did not mention Ad Catacumbas because this site was not considered authentic by the orthodox Christians of this period or that the celebration on the Via Appia was only held in a private manner in the early third century. In the year 258 this state of affairs may have changed; what had been previously a private celebration came to be recognized officially by the Church, and the date deemed worthy to be entered into the official Calendar. The date was remembered by the Church because it coincided with a year of persecution under Valerian, when visits to martyr's graves were prohibited.[88]

One is faced, as this survey of solutions indicates, with three choices (each with its variations) to explain the year 258 which appears in the liturgical documents: invention, translation, and liturgical commemoration. Each has its difficulties; no one theory can satisfy all literary, liturgical, and archeological evidence. The situation is not helped by adding one more conjecture, nor by categorically eliminating any one of those proposed in favor of one which supposedly represents the truth. 1) There *could* have been a translation from the Vatican and Via Ostia to Ad Catacumbas, but the evidence is slight and the objections many, including one that this writer considers to be quite important: in neither the *Ecclesiastical History* nor the *Theophania* does the Church historian Eusebius seem to know of any other tradition concerning the burial of Peter and Paul than that received on the authority of Gaius and others of the faithful. Surely, if he had known of a tradition, that at one time the relics of Peter and Paul had been buried at or removed to Ad Catacumbas he would have alluded to this fact in some way. 2) There *might* have been an "invention" stimulated by the growing concern with apostolic succession or perhaps emanating from an alleged revelation to a member of a cult associated with a private cemetery. Such a revelation may have been officially recognized as authentic A.D. 258. 3) It is *possible* that the cult Ad Catacumbas was schismatic or Novatianist and that the documents which mention this date are Novatianist in origin, but evidence of this is far from conclusive. 4) That the whole problem of the date proceeds from an error in copying the

Depositio and that the date belongs not to the notice concerning the commemoration of Peter but to the notice of Cyprian is also *possible*, but depends upon a remarkable and improbable coincidence between the length of the text in the modern copies and the original document. After careful consideration of the various alternatives, I believe it most probable that the date had some relationship to *cultic commemoration*, the official recognition of some event related to Peter which had taken place or which was *believed* to have taken place.

The inauguration of a cultic celebration must have a reason. And there are a number which are possible. As Chadwick suggests, the date *could* be the cultic recognition of what at base is no more than an etiological myth "and that it is accordingly to be explained as an attempt to comprehend two originally rival and antithetical traditions."[89] Or, since the cult of martyrs began in Rome approximately in this period, the date *could* mark the inauguration of the martyr cult at the place *or* places where the relics of Peter and Paul were believed to reside.

The problems raised by the liturgical documents remain, but the most probable solution as to the original form of the notices of the *Depositio* and the *Martyrologium* is to be found in the reconstruction of both documents by Duchesne[90] followed by Lietzmann.[91] The most probable original meaning of the June 29 notice in the *Depositio* is discovered when it is understood in the light of the corrected form of the notice in the *Martyrologium*. Together they represent a development: "Romae natale sanctorum Petri et Pauli apostolorum: Petri in Vaticano, Pauli vero in via Ostensi, utriusque in Catacumbas. Basso et Tusco consulibus." While Duchesne and Lietzmann then continue to interpret the reconstructed notice in terms of a translation, it is equally defensible to take it to mean that on this date, when Bassus and Tuscus were consuls, celebration to Peter and Paul was inaugurated at the Catacombs. This inauguration took place around A.D. 258 because it was at this time that Valerian had forbidden the Christians to meet in their own cemeteries.

---

88. *Die römische Petrustradition*, pp. 73–75.

89. Chadwick, *St. Peter and St. Paul*, p. 42.
90. Duchesne, *Le Liber Pontificalis*, Vol. I, Part I, pp. cv ff.
91. Lietzmann, *Petrus und Paulus in Rom*, 2d ed., pp. 110 f.

The cemetery of Callistus, where pontiffs had been buried since 217, was nearby; Ad Catacumbas, a *pagan* burial area, was a logical choice. The cult was also celebrated on the Vatican and on the Via Ostia. And even in the period when the earliest form of the *Martyrologium* appeared, mention of the celebration at the Catacombs, which was so popular at the time of the writing of the *Depositio*, was an anachronism.

The emergence of a cult of martyrs in the mid-third century also adequately explains the period of inauguration. The appropriation by the Church of the pagan festival of Romulus-Quirinus, founder of Rome, may have suggested the day. The various places in Rome where the relics of Peter were thought to be or to have been, at one time, supply a reason for the fact that there are three places mentioned. But what lay *behind* these facts of the cultic celebration appears to be hidden in impenetrable mystery. The "where" must be accepted, but the "why" behind the "where" appears to be unknowable at the present time.

It remains now to examine carefully the excavations at San Sebastiano and the Vatican in order to see how far the findings challenge or corroborate the literary and liturgical evidence.

CHAPTER 9

The Archeological Evidence
for the Burial of Peter in Rome

UP TO THIS point we have considered that literary and liturgical evidence which provides information concerning the burial of Peter in Rome. It has been discovered that certain documents are vague in their geographical references, while others appear confident, providing certain particulars such as surrounding landmarks near which the original burial place is supposedly to be found. The literary and liturgical documents serve in the capacity of "maps" which must be accepted or rejected in view of the results of the archeological investigations undertaken upon the authority of such "maps." The documents consistently mention either the Church of San Sebastiano or the Church of St. Peter or both. And no discussion of the question of burial would be complete unless it took into account these two monuments, both of which have had an interesting as well as an extremely complicated history.

THE EXCAVATIONS AT THE CHURCH OF SAN SEBASTIANO
ON THE VIA APPIA

The first monument to be considered is that of San Sebastiano, located three miles from Rome on the Via Appia. After a brief survey of the history of the excavations and an account of the development of the monument itself, it will be necessary to consider in detail the several locations within the monument indicated by various archeologists as the temporary resting place of the remains of the apostles. In this section the history and general development in the discussion will follow that of Francesco Tolotti in his most comprehensive work, *Memorie degli Apostoli in Catacumbas.*

Socrates in his *Ecclesiastical History IV* affirms that the Basilica Apostolorum Ad Catacumbas (or Ad Catacumbas as the area is often called) was the first martyrium of the relics of Peter and Paul.[1] Ammonius, an Egyptian monk who visited Rome with Athanasius, about A.D. 340, said that he only paid attention to *the* martyrium of the apostles Peter and Paul: "μόνον δὲ ἰδεῖν τὸ Πέτρου καὶ Παύλου μαρτύριον."[2] Thus, at a time *after* the Basilica on the Vatican was built and after the death of Constantine (A.D. 337), there was in Rome, according to this fourth century writer, only one martyrium common to Peter and Paul, only one Basilica Apostolorum:

By confirming that the Basilica Apostolorum was the martyrium of Saint Peter, the fifth century historian [Socrates] also corroborates the view that the Monument in the apse of the Vatican Church did not contain the relics of the Apostle, and that this was generally known to be so. The holy relics were, indeed, commemorated Ad Catacumbas at the time when the veneration of our monument [the Memoria at San Sebastiano] starts (240–260) and even later, when the erection of the magnificent Vatican Basilica began.[3]

Three excellent histories of the excavations at San Sebastiano, written by Paul Styger, Adriano Prandi,

---

1. *MPL*, LXVII, 520 f.

2. See Torp, "The Vatican Excavations," p. 61, and his reference to B. J. Kidd, *A History of the Church to A.D. 461* (Oxford: Clarendon Press, 1922), II, 72 ff.

3. Torp, "The Vatican Excavations," p. 61.

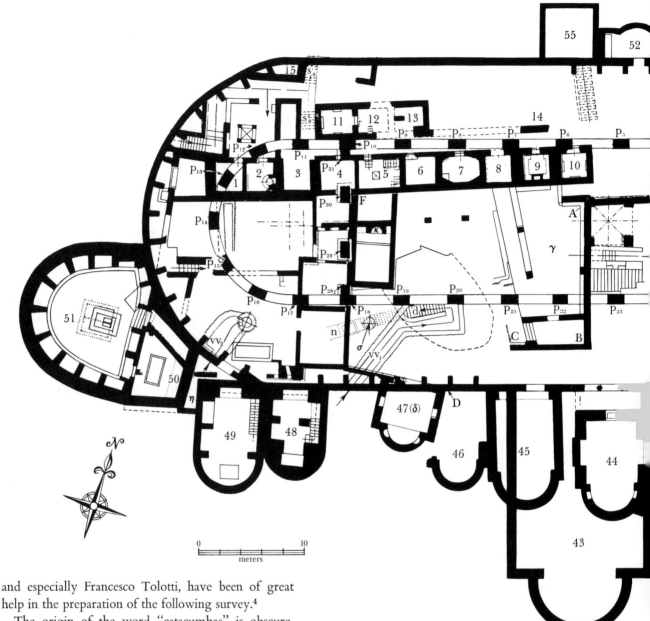

and especially Francesco Tolotti, have been of great
help in the preparation of the following survey.[4]

The origin of the word "catacumbas" is obscure.
Antonio Bosio in 1650 testifies that it was thought by
some in his day to be derived from the Greek "κατά"
and the Latin "tumba," that is, "iuxta tumba," since
the area was near a tomb of the martyrs. Others later
saw the word as ultimately derived from κατακύμβη

---

4. Styger, "Il Monumento apostolico"; Prandi, "La
Memoria Apostolorum in Catacumbas"; Tolotti, *Memorie*,
pp. 10–46.

PLATE 8 A general plan of the Church of San Sebastiano and
the area beneath, showing the Memoria, columbaria, villa,
Basilica, and mausolea (Tolotti, *Memoria*, Plate 1).

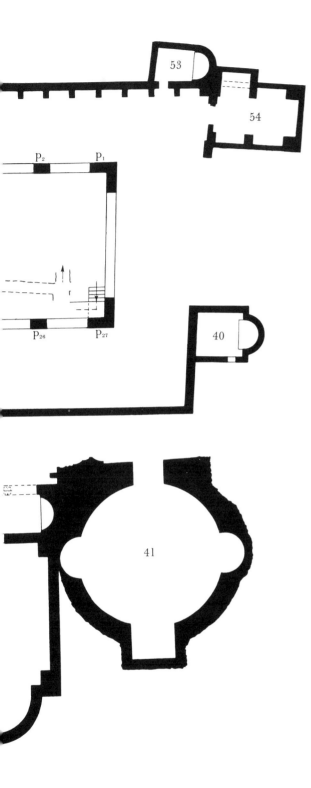

"un luogo cava, e profundo," which definition is favored by Bosio himself.[5] A novel theory is held by R. Egger: the term may refer to a nearby public house which had on its shield a picture of a tankard or ship (either could have been represented by the word "cumba"); therefore, a landmark had given the name to the region. The word "κύμβη," meaning a goblet, cup or bowl, and "κύμβη," meaning a ship, are both possible in Greek, but according to Latin philologists such as Kahn, the term could not have lived on in the Latin "cumba," (or "cymba," a small boat or skiff). In spite of such doubts Schneider concludes, "I would therefore take it that at San Sebastiano stood a truly striking ship monument and the region was called after it."[6] Tolotti, on the contrary, is of the opinion that the idea behind "bacino" ("basin" in English) best interprets Catacumbas—a basin continually filled with water rather than a dry area shaped like a basin. Therefore the well beneath the monument of San Sebastiano may have given the Catacombs their name: "il luogo presso il bacino, il cemeterio del bacino."[7]

In the middle of the last century Giovanni Battista de Rossi spoke briefly of the Platonia (Plate 8, No. 51), which is located to the west of the church, as the place in which the bodies of the apostles Peter and Paul were hidden for a while after their death.[8] A few years later Louis Duchesne indicated that this was the place to which the bodies of the apostles had been brought for temporary burial during the persecution under Valerian.[9] Neither of these scholars had studied the Platonia, but their remarks did much to call forth the archeological investigations. Giovanni Battista Lugari first studied the Platonia in 1888, but added little to our

5. *Roma sotterranea*, p. 257. A. M. Schneider (in quoting from *Monumenta Germaniae Historica Auctorum Antiquissimorum* [Berlin: Weidmann, 1892], IX, 148) also sees the definition in terms of a depression or valley, "Die Memoria Apostolorum," p. 3.

6. See *ibid.*, p. 4, for the view of R. Egger, *Anzeiger der Öesterr. Akad. D. Wiss.* (1950), No. 10, pp. 162 f.

7. Tolotti, *Memorie*, pp. 85, 86. Compare his "Ricerche intorno alla Memoria Apostolorum," pp. 19–20, 61, where he defines the word as "next to the baptistery." See also Carcopino, *De Pythagore*, pp. 227n4, 340n28.

8. *La Roma sotterranea*, I, 188.

9. *Le Liber Pontificalis*, Vol. I, Part I, p. cvii.

knowledge of the monument.[10] His contribution was simply an involved interpretation of the Translation Theory which attempted to reconcile all of the many conflicting statements contained in the prominent literary and liturgical sources. During the last decade of the nineteenth century a more scientific investigation of the Platonia was undertaken by Anton de Waal, a student of de Rossi. His investigations, which resulted in the discovery of the vestibule and stairway within the Platonia, convinced him that this structure was built not in the first century but in the third century, and that the bodies of the apostles had never rested there. The Platonia was, he said, a mausoleum built for Quirinius whose body had been brought from Pannonia to Rome in the fourth or fifth century.[11] Although opposed by de Rossi, Lugari, and Marucchi, he was confident that the real Memoria would be found when excavations were undertaken beneath the center of the present church.

The mausoleum (Plate 8, No. 50) by the side of the Platonia was further investigated by P. Mariano Colagrossi in 1908 where the now famous ancient graffito DOMVS PETRI was found.[12] Building upon these discoveries, Josef Wilpert in 1912 advanced the theory that this graffito confirmed that interpretation of the Damasus Inscription which maintained that Peter and Paul had *lived* in this area at some time during their Roman sojourn.[13]

Up to this point no part of the monument other than the Platonia had been investigated. It remained for Fra Damiano Pinna, custodian of the church, to find evidence in 1910 and 1913 of: 1) what later came to be known as the large villa, located beneath the northeast part of the church, 2) the stairway (Plate 8, s_8), and 3) one of the columbaria (Plate 8, No. 15). These discoveries began the second series of investigations, the excavations having been suspended since the work done by de Waal in 1894–95.

In February, 1915, the excavations under the leadership of Paul Styger commenced in the area of what was later called the Triclia (an area reserved for the celebration of cultic meals, Plate 8, γ). At the same time de Waal, who had abandoned his investigations in the Platonia, began excavating beneath the center of the church. The uncovering of the Triclia and surrounding structures was the most important advance that had been made thus far, and, when fully analyzed, yielded a great deal of information concerning the Christian funerary customs in the late third century.[14] When the aging de Waal first witnessed the discovery of the Triclia and the graffiti which appeared to confirm the one time presence of the apostolic relics, it is reported that on

quel giorno stesso, e, inginocchiatosi accanto allo scavo, levando le braccia, ringraziò Dio que gli aveva permesso di vedere, prima di chiudergli gli occhi per sempre, la memoria degli Apostoli, lì, in quel luogo, nel mezzo della chiesa.[15]

As it proved later, however, the optimistic confidence of Styger and de Waal was unfounded. This was obviously a place where the apostles had been commemorated, as we shall see, but this did not establish as fact that the bodies of the apostles had ever been in the

---

10. *Le Catacombe: ossia, il Sepolcro apostolico dell' Appia.*

11. A. de Waal, "La Platonia ossia Sepolcro apostolico della Via Appia," p. 141, and "Die Platonia ad Catacumbas," p. 111.

12. "Di un Monumento recentemente scoperto presso il Sepolcro apostolico dell'Appia," p. 51. Guarducci, *I Graffiti,* I, 381–83, has studied the graffito very carefully and concludes that there is more meaning in these words than is immediately evident. The graffito, which she dates in the late fourth or early fifth century, can be read also as DOMVS PATRIS and DOMVS DOMINI. The second letter of the first word can be read easily as either an A or an E (see fig. 195a, p. 382) and the plainly visible mark over the R links the M of the first word with the ending of the second word making possible the reading DOMVS DOMINI. While these readings are possible, the further conclusion is farfetched that the author of the graffito in writing these two simple words meant to imply an identification of Peter with Christ and with the Church (p. 382).

13. Wilpert, "Domus Petri," pp. 117–22, and "La Tomba di S. Pietro," pp. 28 ff.; Lanciani, "La Memoria Apostolorum e gli Scavi," pp. 96–109; Duchesne, "La 'Memoria Apostolorum,'" p. 7; Armin von Gerkan in Lietzmann's *Petrus und Paulus in Rom,* 2d ed., p. 293. See also Besson, *Saint Pierre et les Origines de la Primauté romaine,* p. 77; Carcopino, *De Pythagore,* p. 293.

14. These discoveries were described by Paul Styger in *Römische Quartalschrift* (1915), pp. 73–110, 149–221. See in addition Tolotti, *Memorie,* p. 22n18.

15. *Ibid.,* p. 18.

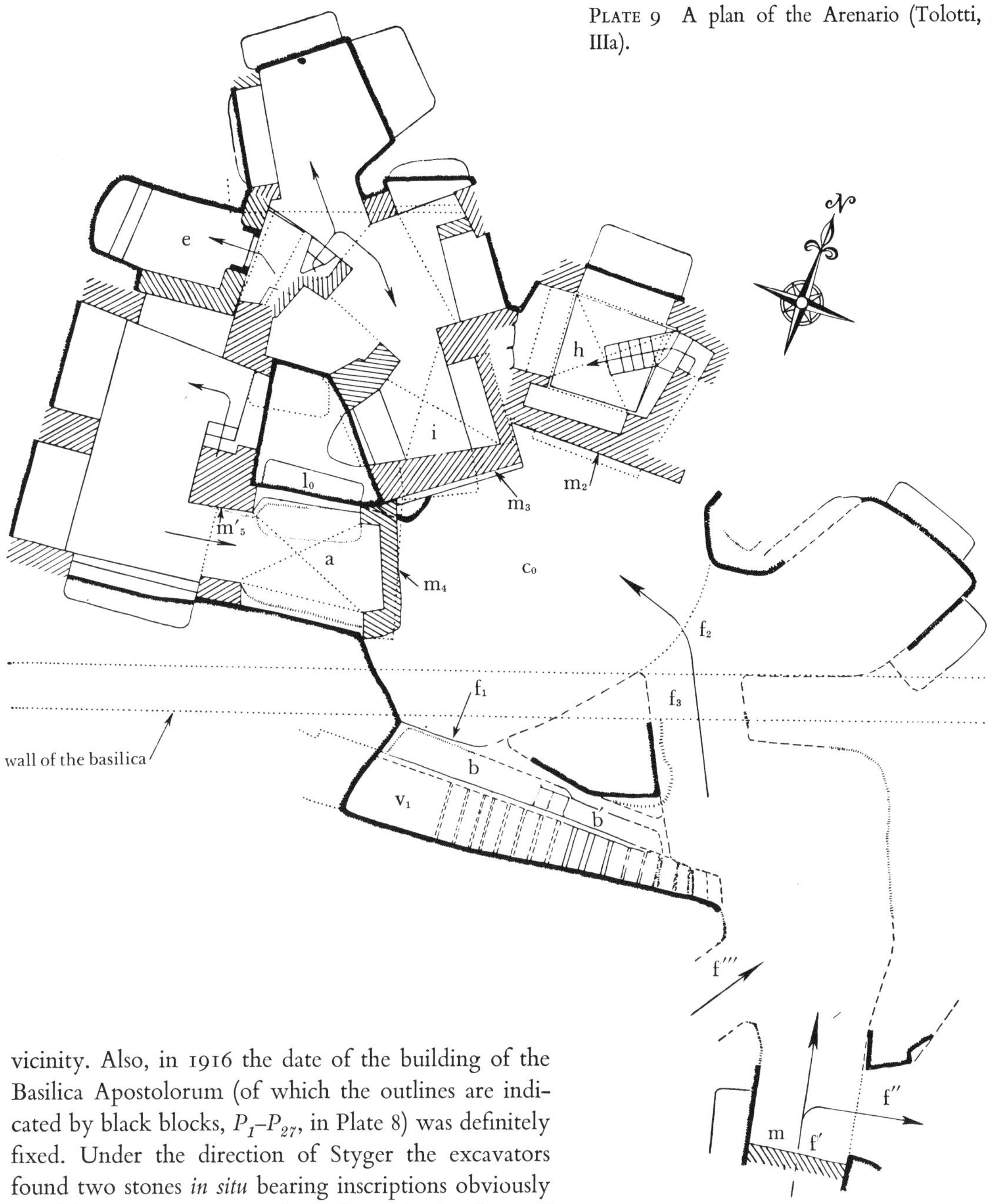

PLATE 9 A plan of the Arenario (Tolotti, *Memorie*, Plate IIIa).

vicinity. Also, in 1916 the date of the building of the Basilica Apostolorum (of which the outlines are indicated by black blocks, P_1–P_{27}, in Plate 8) was definitely fixed. Under the direction of Styger the excavators found two stones *in situ* bearing inscriptions obviously dated between A.D. 356 and 400 beneath the floor of the Basilica. These inscriptions are testimony that the building was erected prior to the earlier date, and thus prior to the pontificate of Damasus, who up to this time had been credited with the construction of the Basilica. The Cortile, or enclosed paved courtyard, to the south of columbaria 6 and 7 (Plate 8) was also

discovered, together with a stairway beside wall *B-C* (Plate 8). The stairway, at the time, could not be explained.

By 1917 the excavations still had not uncovered an apostolic tomb. In this year Styger had to abandon his research, de Waal died, and for a short time the progress of the work became the responsibility of F. Fornari, who extended the explorations into the area of the pagan columbaria (Plate 8, *1–10*).[16] In 1919 Gioachino Mancini of the R. Sovraintendenza divided the responsibility for the excavations with Orazio Marucchi of the Pontifical Commission of Sacred Archeology. Mancini worked underneath the church and Marucchi assumed Styger's work at the long stairway (Plate 8, *d–n*) which, Marucchi believed, went down to a very deep tomb under the nave of the Basilica. During 1919 three pagan tombs were located beneath the area later occupied by the Cortile, which later became known as the hypogea (from "ὑπόγαιος" or "ὑπόγειος," meaning an underground area) of the Hermete, Innocenti, and Ascia (Plate 9, *h, i, a*).[17] It was also discovered that the long stairway (Plate 8, *d–n*) extended to a gallery excavated in the tufa (a form of porous limestone deposited by springs or the like). The walls of the gallery were stuccoed for about a meter, and on this surface was found a number of graffiti containing the names of Peter and Paul. The Constantinian monogram, also found on the stuccoed wall, demonstrated that while the stairway had been built before the construction of the Básilica, access to the well remained even after the Basilica was in use. Later it was found that this stairway extended even further.[18]

In 1924 Fra Damiano and F. Fornari located structures adjacent to the apse of the Basilica which predated it, since the walls of these structures were destroyed when the Basilica was built (Plate 8, *η*). These researches confirmed the view that the Memoria Apostolorum was much more extensive than had been believed previously.

---

16. Since these structures are obviously pagan and have no relationship to the Memoria or the cult of the apostles, they are not discussed in this book. See *ibid.*, pp. 55–58.

17. The tomb *h* (the tomb of the Hermete) is so called because it is identified by an inscription "M. CLODIVS HERMES" over the doorway. (See Lietzmann, *Petrus und Paulus in Rom*, 2d ed., fig. 8). Tomb of the Innocenti, *i*, is so identified by the late burials in this tomb bearing this inscription, A.D. 238–344. The tomb of the Axe is so named because of the presence of the axe symbol found on the front of the building.

18. Tolotti, *Memorie*, p. 25, fig. 1.

In 1928–29 further work, carried on under the Cortile, took approximately two years because of the time-consuming precautions taken to shore up the structures above. Since that time only minor discoveries have been made, none of which is directly relevant to this study.

There has been little dispute concerning what has been found, but *wide* differences of opinion as to the interpretation of the discoveries. Let us examine carefully the development of the area from its earliest period up to the building of the Basilica and note the principal theories concerning the relation of each part to that which preceded it and to the burial or cult of the apostles Peter and Paul.

The present Church of San Sebastiano is situated upon what in the first century A.D. was the site of a quarry for pozzuolana, a black volcanic deposit, used by the Romans in the making of concrete. When the quarry was in operation, the land on which the church is now built constituted a small valley surrounded by steep slopes. Into these slopes were dug the galleries and passages necessary to the mining operation. At an undetermined time, when the mine was either exhausted or for some other reason abandoned, the galleries and passageways, which were remarkably suited for the purpose, were converted into burial areas. The name given to this first- or early second-century phase in the development of the area is the Arenario, literally "sand pit." (Plate 9). The burial galleries lead off from the central cavity C_0 (Plate 9), beneath which Tolotti is convinced there is a vault—the area, however, has never been excavated. Typical galleries are noted at the bottom of Plate 9 at *f, f^{11}* and *f^{111}*, the second of which contains the grave of Marcus Ulpius Calocerus, a freedman (or possibly the son of a freedman) of Trajan (A.D. 98–117). This burial serves as the *terminus post quem* for the Arenario. It is argued by Tolotti, however, that this grave belongs not to the first but to the second phase of the development which slightly overlapped the first[19] and was not entirely independent of it, as Prandi is inclined to believe. This latter archeologist maintains further that when the sepultures immediately above this level were used, the areas below had been abandoned, an assumption, he claims, which can be proved by the formation of the various walls. Tolotti and Prandi also

---

19. *Ibid.*, pp. 73–74.

disagree as to the underlying reason for the building of the level above, the Piazzuola. Tolotti is of the opinion that the Arenario was buried in definite deliberate stages and not, as Prandi believes probable, by a gradual unplanned raising of the level by a constant enlarging and leveling process.

The stairway to the area south of C_0 (Plate 9) was most likely in use when the Arenario served as a mine. Tolotti, however, in keeping with his improbable theory that the area was associated with a Christian cult from almost the very beginning, is convinced that the stairway served as a primitive baptistery.[20] He argues that the grade of the stairway is 75 percent rather than the usual 50 percent and it becomes wider as one descends to the floor, approximately 9 feet below the level of the Arenario. At the foot of the stairway, there is a landing which is under water part of the time (and thus could never have been used as a sepulcher as Marucchi claims). Near the bottom of the stairs and over the gallery b (Plate 9), there is an opening f which served as a source of light for the dark recess below. Tolotti admits that the depth of the stairway and certain aspects of its excavation compel one to admit that it had been planned "dare accesso a una conserva d'acqua."[21] But the unique feature is that the stairway goes deeper than the water level (which could not have varied to any appreciable degree over the years) and therefore does not appear to have been used *only* to secure water for cultic needs. The well appears to be eminently suited to serve also as a location for conducting the rite of immersion. A person could descend the stairs standing and continue down until the water covered a large part of his body. The several stairs permitted its use as a place of baptism by people of varying heights and also allowed for any changes in the water level.[22] Certain arguments against this view are admitted by Tolotti, but he is convinced that such an interpretation

best explains the various aspects of the stairway which remain a mystery if the function of the well is conceived to be limited to the supplying of water for the cultic celebrations in the Triclia.

If it can be maintained, after consideration of the entire monument, that there was Christian influence in the area as early as the time of the construction of the stairway and well, Tolotti's theory is entirely plausible. But, as it will be seen, Christian occupation at such an early date is extremely unlikely.

For whatever reason the Arenario was filled in after the caving in of parts of the old quarry, whether the gradual filling was haphazard or by design, the next stage in the development of the area known as the Piazzuola soon appears. A number of the lower vaults were destroyed; the abandoned caverns were filled in to about 3 m. above the old level. The Piazzuola extended over area C_0 (Plate 9), where the older caverns, the reservoir v_1 (Plate 9), and the connecting passageways had been. When the Piazzuola was finished it looked a bit like a crater, on the north side of which over the three caverns a, i, h (Plate 9), were built three hypogea a^1, i^1, h^1 (Plates 10 and 11).[23] Entrance into the Piazzuola, according to Tolotti, was still gained by means of the same passageway f^5 (Plate 10; see also the arrows in the lower part of Plate 9) and not from above as might be expected. Access to the well was still possible by way of an extended stairway, and the whole area was delimited (see Plate 8) by the row of columbaria to the north and the basalt walls A–B, B–C, D–E, E–F to the west, south, and east.

Before discussing the possibility of Christian occupation of the hypogea[24] and when, if at all, such occupation took place, let us consider the construction of the hypogea. They stand side by side, consist of more than one floor, and face out upon a courtyard. Each has a brick façade similar to the tombs recently discovered beneath the Vatican.[25] The lower floor of each utilized those passageways of the old quarry that still remained open; for the most part the hypogea were limited within

---

20. *Ibid.*, pp. 74–82.

21. *Ibid.*, p. 78.

22. *Ibid.*, p. 82. This conclusion is challenged by A. M. Schneider, "Die Memoria Apostolorum," p. 9, who claims that an area for baptism requires flowing water or well water. See Didache 7:2, "ἐὰν δὲ μὴ ἔχῃς ὕδωρ ζῶν, εἰς ἄλλο ὕδωρ βάπτισον" (*Apostolic Fathers*, trans. Lake, I, 318, 319). The well was built to serve the needs of the workers in the pozzuolana mine (at the level of the pagan Arenario).

---

23. The various burials d^1–d^7 around the walls of the Piazzuola (Plate 10) are later than the building of the hypogea.

24. Dated by A. M. Schneider, "Die Memoria Apostolorum," p. 11, A.D. c. 150–200.

25. See Lietzmann, *Petrus und Paulus in Rom*, 2d ed., fig. 8.

the natural excavations and were not bound by artificial walls. There were, however, a number of *inside* walls which were built at various times. Each of the hypogea was a unit and its present aspect, according to Tolotti, is very much like that which was seen by the first owners; all later changes were minor. The new burials were placed on side platforms, between the pilasters, and into niches in the walls. From an examination of the front walls m^2, m^3, m^4 (Plate 9) of the hypogea, one is able to determine that the hypogea were built from east to west, h^1 first and a^1 last.

It is not possible, nor is it important for the purpose of this study, to describe the interior of the three hypogea,[26] but a discussion of cella a is important because it contains the loculus l_0 (Plate 9). This immediate vicinity assumes great importance in the theory of Tolotti concerning the meaning of the entire area.[27] Cella a^1, he proposes, at some time became filled and burials were then made in the newly dug and richly stuccoed cella a, which was accessible only through a^1.

26. Tolotti, *Memorie*, pp. 105–8.
27. *Ibid.*, pp. 108–14.

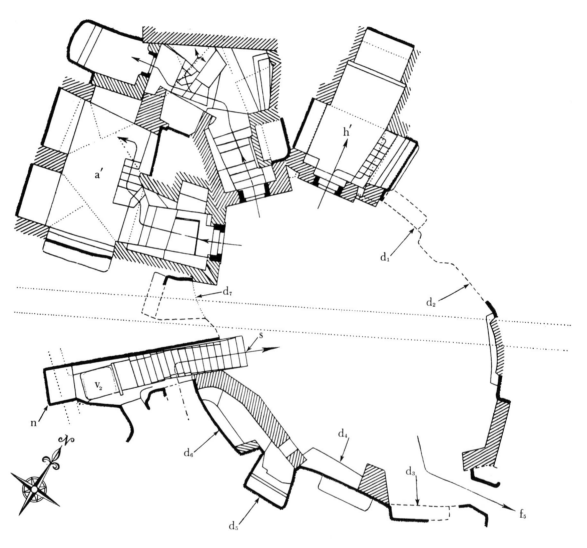

PLATE 10   A plan of the Piazzuola (Tolotti, *Memorie*, Plate IIIb).

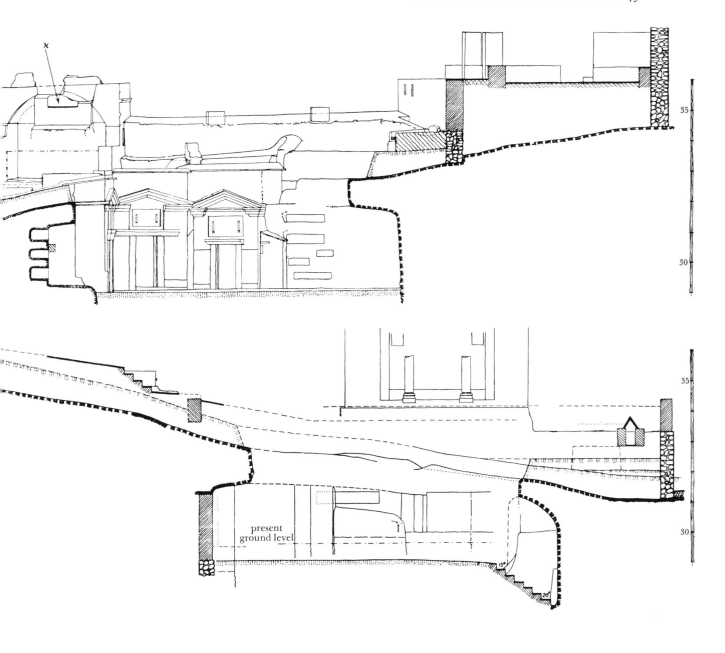

PLATE II   Sections of the Piazzuola (above) and Memoria (Tolotti, *Memorie*, Plate V).

Since it was hidden and protected, cella *a* was a "unico luogo possibile per il deposito dal quale sepolcreto sarebbe stato santificato."[28] Cecchelli, who sees this

28. *Ibid.*, p. 109.

immediate area as the temporary resting place of the relics of the apostles and not, as Tolotti defends, the original burial place, is convinced that "dei tre sepolcri a camera quello di fondo secondo noi è il più indiziato

come luogo in cui dovettero custodite le salme apostoliche."[29] Tolotti admits that cella *a* was built at a late
date and dug out of the tufa from above, but mentions
the presence in the area of a much older hidden loculus
l^0 between walls m^4 and m^5 which were excavated in
the tufa. This space when sealed off with plaster made
cella *a* appear completely empty. He sees l_0 as much
earlier than cella *a* and the hypogea; for if l_0 had been
of one build with these structures, it would have been
placed in a more favorable position, and it would have
been provided at least with an entrance in the wall.
This loculus, he maintains, is a tomb of eminence which
determined the transformation of the entire zone
surrounding it. Loculus l_0 belongs to the level of the
Arenario and goes back to the most primitive period—
perhaps the hypogeum of which it was originally a
part was destroyed at some earlier time. It is conceivable,
Tolotti surmises, that this loculus locates the burial
place of the apostles Peter and Paul over which one of
the most important structures of the later Memoria
was to be built.

The theory that there is evidence of a continuous
history of Christian occupation from the earliest times
is strongly and correctly challenged by Paul Styger. He
maintains that the era of the columbaria and the hypogea is definitely pagan. Even if it is admitted that the
latter structures were utilized by Christians at a later
time, they were not *built* by Christians.[30]

One point in favor of Tolotti's view of continuous
Christian occupation of the site is the common Christian
refusal to use the grave places of the pagans. Cyprian
informs us, however, that during the persecution of
Decius (A.D. 249–51), there were a number of apostates.
He adds that Basilides, Bishop of Lyon, sacrificed to
idols and that Martialis, Bishop of Merida, was on
friendly terms with pagans and even permitted his son
to be buried in a grave belonging to one of the pagan
funerary guilds.[31] It is suggested by Marucchi that the

Church early may have used "legal" funerary societies
as "fronts" to provide for needed burial space, especially
in times of persecution, and that perhaps the hypogea
represent such "front" societies.

It is true, as von Gerkan points out, that there are
some signs of a period of Christian occupation in the
later history of the hypogea.[32] In hypogea h^1 a grave was
found decorated with the anchor and the fish—both
are usually identified as Christian symbols. One
inscription found in this structure bore the Christian
epithet φιλόχηρος, a word which appears in the
Apostolic Constitutions II.4:1 and 50:1.[33] Around A.D.
200 the owners of h^1 plastered the brick façade, and
inside, dating from this period, are found Christian
paintings such as the Good Shepherd—paintings which
could have been either Roman Catholic or sectarian in
character.

The hypogeum of the Innocenti also contains certain
elements which must be considered as Christian. For
example, on the site of a grave added later than the
actual construction of the hypogeum we find the word
"*ΙΧΤΘΥΣ*." It has been argued by some that the symbol
was also used by the pagans, but this cannot adequately
explain the *T* (tau cross) between the chi and the theta,[34]
unless it is simply a matter of misspelling.[35]

At one time there must have been a "changeover"
from the pagan to Christian ownership, and it must
have been carried out in such a way that the Christians
did not feel an overwhelming repugnance at using
these particular pagan hypogea for their own burials.
Paul Styger convincingly describes the changeover in
terms of an important event—a change in the faith of
those who owned the tombs. If such a conversion had
taken place, the pagans who were already buried in the

---

29. Cecchelli, *Monumenti cristiani—eretici di Roma*, p. 185.

30. "Il Monumento apostolico," pp. 12–15.

31. *De Basilide et Martiale Hispaniae Episcopos Libellaticis*, V
(*MPL*, III, 1029–31): "Martialis quoque praeter gentilium
turpia et lutulenta conviva in collegio diu frequentata et filios
in eodem collegio exterarum gentium more apud profana
sepulchra depositos et alienigenis consepultos."

32. In Lietzmann, *Petrus und Paulus in Rom*, 2d ed., p. 159.

33. *MPG*, X, 1553b. Compare Toynbee and Perkins, *The
Shrine of St. Peter*, p. 191n61.

34. Styger, *Die römischen Katakomben*, p. 339: "Die akro-
stiche Formel sowie Anker und Fisch gibt es bekanntlich auch
auf heidnischen Texten." He does not, however, offer any
examples. See Lietzmann, *Petrus und Paulus in Rom*, 2d ed.,
Table 10.

35. The insertion of the tau cross in a word is common, as is
illustrated by Guarducci, *I Graffiti*, I, 302–32. See especially
her discussion of this graffito on pp. 309–10.

hypogea would have been relatives of the new Christians, in which case the feeling of repugnance would no doubt have been slight or nonexistent.[36] The key to the relationship between the two phases of the hypogea is found by Carlo Cecchelli in the possibility of the presence of syncretistic cults.[37] This general position is also adopted by Alfons Schneider, who estimates that the hypogea were built between A.D. 150 and 200 and that the Innocenti were among the last burials in the hypogeum i^1, about A.D. 238–44. Soon after this date the hypogea were closed and the Memoria was built above. The cult of the apostles entered into the site at this time and built the Triclia and the other sections, which were "unabhängig von den darunter liegenden völlig verschütteten und unbekannten Gräbern."[38]

While the evidence of Christian interest in the site of Ad Catacumbas prior to the building of the Memoria is not conclusive, it cannot be disregarded. The possibility, however, that this interest goes back to the first century, as Tolotti would suggest, is extremely unlikely and from lack of evidence can be virtually eliminated. From the early third century there appears to be a good deal of evidence, when taken together, that indicates a definite Christian interest. But whether the group was orthodox or schismatic, whether public or private, cannot be established.[39] Jérôme Carcopino devotes a long section in his *De Pythagore aux Apôtres* to the development of the theory that the hypogea a^1, h^1, and i^1 illustrate in various features the presence of heretical Christian sects.[40] Some of these sects came to Christianity from the various pagan philosophies, Gnosticism, Neo-Pythagoreanism, and "ensuite il est non moins certain que plusieurs des morts de Catacumbas étaient venus à l'hérésie chrétienne par leur divorce d'avec Israël."

For example, Carcopino includes a number of Nazareans among the members of the college of the Innocenti (tomb i^1).[41]

Around A.D. 200, when the limitations of the area of the Piazzuola had been definitely set and, no doubt, the area below in the tombs was slowly being filled with burials, there is evidence to support the assumption that the cultic activities were transferred to the roofs or attics of the hypogea. The "sigma" (curved chamber with a bench) on the top of h^1 may be explained in this way, and perhaps there were similar chambers over a^1 and i^1. But because of the destruction caused by the later construction of the Memoria, this is not certain. At a still later time the sigma over h^1, with its waterproof concrete floor, was replaced by a barrel-shaped structure which covered a^1 and extended also partly over i^1. In front of the sigma there was an opening connecting with the well below, which had served the area during the period of the Arenario and the early phase of the Piazzuola.

In the last period of the Piazzuola more and more excavations were made within the hypogea and the level of the ground outside rose steadily, to such a degree that it was necessary to reach the doorways of the structures by means of stairways from above.

According to Tolotti there is an early stage in the history of the Christian Memoria which precedes the filling of the Piazzuola.[42] The new area (Plate 12), the reconstruction of which Tolotti agrees is largely hypothetical, is approximately 9 by 12 m. and is limited by wall A–B on the west, E–F on the east, the columbaria on the north, and E–D together with the remains of an early wall B–C on the south. This stage in the development is prior to the building of the important elements γ, β, and α (Plate 12), all of which are discussed below. This is the period when the attics over the hypogea are of great importance, such as the irregular quadrilaterial α over h^1, the terrace of which sloped toward f^8 to drain away the water. While the level of the Piazzuola is filled with tombs in this period, area α had none until after its destruction, when it was covered with burials even up to the level of the pavement of the Basilica. The Piazzuola beneath and α above are related but

36. Styger, *Die römischen Katakomben*, p. 339.

37. This view of Cecchelli is explained and challenged by Antonio Ferrua, "Questioni di Epigrafia eretica, romana," pp. 193–206. Ferrua in this article analyzes a number of graffiti found in the tombs.

38. A. M. Schneider, "Die Memoria Apostolorum," p. 12; See Leclercq, *DACL*, Vol. XIV, Part I, p. 886; Carcopino, *De Pythagore*, pp. 342–49.

39. Compare A. M. Schneider, "Die Memoria Apostolorum," p. 11; Mohlberg, "Historisch-kritische," pp. 52–74. Torp, "The Vatican Excavations," p. 47.

40. *De Pythagore*, pp. 342–49.

41. *Ibid.*, p. 359.

42. Tolotti, *Memorie*, pp. 115–53.

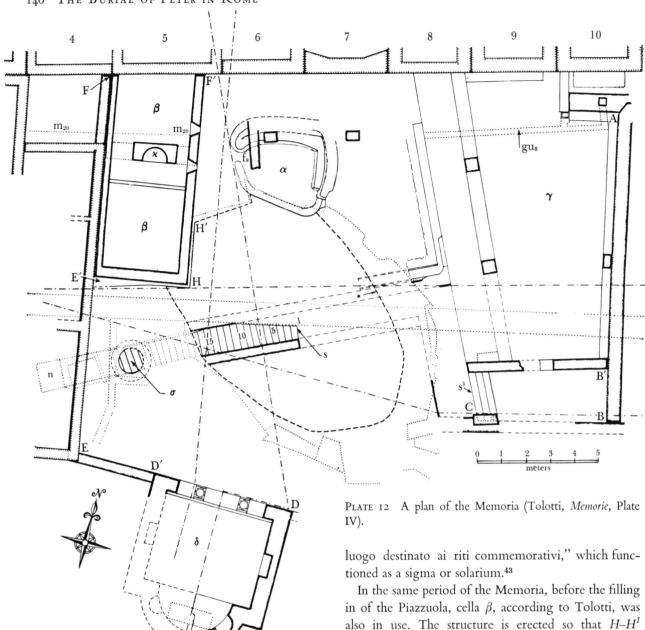

PLATE 12 A plan of the Memoria (Tolotti, *Memorie*, Plate IV).

distinct, and there is no connection between the two. But, Tolotti claims, it must not be forgotten that α was so placed simply *because* the Piazzuola was beneath; the Piazzuola was "il luogo destinato alle sepolture e il

luogo destinato ai riti commemorativi," which functioned as a sigma or solarium.[43]

In the same period of the Memoria, before the filling in of the Piazzuola, cella β, according to Tolotti, was also in use. The structure is erected so that $H-H^1$ (Plate 12) is directly over the façade of a^1 (see Plate 10) and the rear of the cella is attached to columbarium 5 (Plate 12). Tolotti, in disagreement with Prandi, imagines that the north and south sections of β are a unity and not originally divided by a partition or wall,[44] although there may have been a parapet about a meter in height between them. The pavement most assuredly sloped toward E^1 and there may have been a doorway

43. *Ibid.*, p. 127.

44. *Ibid.*, pp. 142–53.

in $H–E^1$, but this is only a suggestion. While the outside walls of the cella suggest to Tolotti the type of constructions popular in the period of the Flavii and the inside walls contain pictures which are characteristic of the period prior to the age of Augustus, he does admit that both are imitations of an earlier style. When he takes into account the walls, the art work, and the like, he is inclined to date the cella at the end of the second century at the latest and prefers to say the mid-second century. In any case, he is convinced that the cella is later than the columbaria, the hypogea, and the basalt walls ($A–F$). On the other hand, Mancini dates the cella A.D. c. 250;[45] von Gerkan, A.D. c. 180;[46] and Prandi, in the epoch of Alexander Severus (A.D. 222–35).[47] Despite the opinions to the contrary Tolotti remains convinced that this area "ad sepulcra" was built between A.D. 150 and 180 and destroyed around 250.

Cella β was probably a structure built to house the cult related to the burials below in the crypt. Tolotti suggests that it may have been Christian from the beginning,[48] but this, it may be repeated, is very doubtful.

In the mid-third century the Piazzuola was filled in— it may have happened, as Prandi suggests, as a result of landslides in the area or, according to Tolotti, followed upon further systematization and the gradual accumulation of earth from the digging of tombs in the relatively small area. Perhaps the truth lies in a combination of both views: Landslides filled in a large part of the area and the remainder was accomplished by design. In any case it seems worthy of mention that the project of filling in, which when completed obliterated nearly all of the previous structures, took place in the mid-third century, approximately at the same time indicated in the mysterious notice in the *Depositio Martyrum* ("Tusco et Basso consulibus").[49] Between

A.D. 200 and 258 the site may have been in the hands of a private or an heretical Christian sect group, which would adequately account for the Christian decorations in the attic structure over h^1 during the *first* phase of the Memoria.[50] The construction of the *later* Memoria must have occurred after A.D. 238–44 since the last burials in the hypogea i^1 (inaccessible after the building of the Memoria) date from this period. And the pre-Constantinian type pictures and inscriptions on the wall of the Triclia provide a *terminus ad quem* of A.D. c. 340 at the latest.[51]

Against Styger who sees this area as "neutraler Bau auf neutralem Boden," Tolotti claims "che una continuità di disposizioni e una continuità giuridica risalgono *in Catacumbas* dal II al IV secolo." There was surely a continuity; the placing of the Memoria is definitely related to the structures which precede it, but a theory which claims a continuity of *Christian* interest in the site since the second century is not defensible.[52]

The history of the monument up to this point has been sketched briefly based upon the assumption that there is no evidence of a cult of the apostles Ad Catacumbas prior to the building of the complex now to be discussed. The word "triclia" was first given to one part of this important area (Plate 12 and the rectangle at the right of Plate 13) by Paul Styger. The word appears elsewhere in relation to chambers annexed to burial places where refrigeria took place and varies considerably in spelling: triclia, trichlia, tricla, trichilium. For example, one pagan inscription mentions that a freedman of Claudius dedicated "triclum cum columnis

---

45. Mancini, in *Notizie degli Scavi* (1923), p. 3.
46. In Lietzmann, *Petrus und Paulus in Rom*, 2d ed., p. 263.
47. Prandi, "La Memoria Apostolorum in Catacumbas," p. 41.
48. Tolotti, *Memorie*, pp. 173, 174.
49. See above, pp. 116–120. Of course, the work may have been undertaken during the pontificate of Cornelius (A.D. 251–53); his notice in the *Liber Pontificalis* mentions a transfer of the relics Ad Catacumbas. Or the work may have taken place in the pontificate of Dionysius (A.D. 259–69), whose notice in

the *Liber Pontificalis* mentions that "presbyteris ecclesias divisit coemeteria constituit."

50. Toynbee and Perkins, *The Shrine of St. Peter*, p. 174.
51. Compare *ibid.*, p. 178, where the authors suggest A.D. 349 for the *terminus ad quem* with Guarducci, *The Tomb of Peter*, p. 171, who stipulates A.D. 315–25.
52. Tolotti, *Memorie*, pp. 170, 176–78. Compare Styger, *Die römischen Katakomben*, p. 339; A. M. Schneider, "Die Memoria Apostolorum," p. 9. Testini, "Noterelle sulla 'Memoria Apostolorum' in Catacumbas," p. 216, claims that the closing in, or filling in, of the Piazzuola was not gradual, but was an act of violence and was incompatible with what came later. A continuous tradition does not cut off its ties with the past.

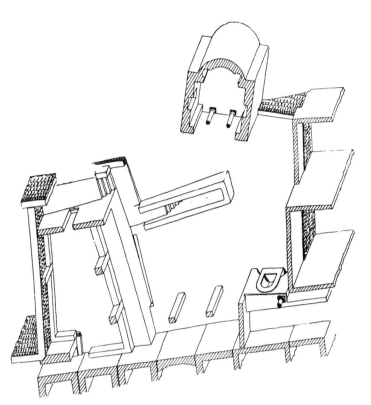

PLATE 13   A drawing of the four areas of the Memoria. In addition to the top of the stairway, the reconstruction of the niche and the parts above it are largely hypothetical (Tolotti, *Memorie*, Fig. 43).

et mensis et maceria"[53] to the memory of the Empress Livia in the columbarium of her slaves and freedmen.

Wall *A–B* of the Triclia, called the "wall of the graffiti," was covered with frescoes containing representations of sheep, doves, and the like, and scribbled statements and prayers. Along this wall was found the remains of a bench 50 cm. high and 37 cm. wide. At right angles to this bench there was another at point *A* which led to a small fountain[54] (noted in Plate 12 as a small indented square). On the other side of the fountain the bench continued to the wall of columbarium *10*. The height of the bench was 15 cm. and may have been

intended for resting vases of wine or water.[55] Beneath the floor a conduit gu_5, in which were found bits of vases and a small piece of gold thread, ran from the fountain and under the bench near point *A*. And since there is no evidence of any "pipe" feeding into the fountain, it may be that such was affixed to the north wall and later destroyed. That the water did flow in the conduit gu_5 is proved by the fact that the sand still found within it was clean and free from earthy material. A third bench most probably ran along the wall of columbarium *9*. The outer wall of the Triclia (now completely destroyed) had no bench attached to it and probably was not over a meter in height, permitting one to look out over the Cortile. Later, however, it was established that there was a stairway at point s^1 which was related directly to *s* (Plates 12 and 13; see also Plate 14).

As Styger pointed out fifty-three years ago, a triclia is not new to those who are familiar with pagan monuments.[56] It is analogous to the "cubiculum memoriae," the "alogia," and the "locus scholae"; all these terms denote places where the pagan family and friends gathered to commemorate the dead ("ad confrequentandam memorian"). Often these structures in which funerary banquets were held contained paintings on the walls and were covered by a tile roof, as verified by numerous frescoes and inscriptions. Styger has marshaled considerable evidence to prove that such banquets were also held by early Christians to commemorate their dead.[57]

The relationship of the Triclia to the cult of the apostles can be best illustrated by a consideration of the graffiti which were found on wall *A–B*. Before that, however, let us examine briefly the type of activity which was conducted in the Triclia. The "refrigerium," mentioned briefly in Part I,[58] is a term meaning basically

---

53. See Spence-Jones, *The Early Christians in Rome*, p. 37.

54. In the fountain were found bones of poultry, fish, and hares, testifying to the fact that the rite of refrigeria was celebrated here.

55. Styger, in *Römische Quartalschrift* (1915), p. 151. See also Tolotti, *Memorie*, pp. 18–23, Klauser, *Die römische Petrustradition*, fig. 1, pp. 102, 103, and Goodenough, *Jewish Symbols in the Graeco-Roman Period*, p. 106.

56. Styger, in *Römische Quartalschrift* (1915), p. 157.

57. *Ibid.*, pp. 159–67. See also A. M. Schneider, "Die Memoria Apostolorum," p. 13.

58. See above, pp. 42–44. See also "Refrigerium," in Leclercq, *DACL*, Vol. XIV, Part II, pp. 2179 ff. and Toynbee and Perkins, *The Shrine of St. Peter*, pp. 189–90n56.

"refreshment," "restoring," a "banquet," or "a rest in a place of pain, or joy eternal of the heavens."[59] In this last, figurative sense it appears in the Old and New Testament (Psalms 65:11, Jeremiah 6:16, and Acts 3:20) and in Tertullian.[60] The word is used literally, however, in the graffiti on the wall of the Triclia, where it definitely suggests a banquet held in commemoration of Peter and Paul. In this sense also the word is not unknown in Christian literature; perhaps this meaning is found in 2 Timothy 1:16, "May the Lord grant mercy to the household of Onesiphorus, for he often refreshed me." In Tertullian the word is equated with "agape," which, it is mentioned, indicates the common banquet of the faithful.[61]

The pagans celebrated the refrigeria not on the date of death but on the date of birth (indicative perhaps of their estimate of the afterlife). The Christians, on the other hand, commemorated the date of death which for them was also a date of birth—birth into the life eternal. Thus the anniversary is often called the "natale" in Christian liturgical documents.[62] Both Tertullian and Augustine assure us that from the second to the fifth centuries Christians took part in these refrigeria.[63] The chief participants, who were the poor, considered the meal as an act of piety proffered to the dead. The more

PLATE 14   A reconstruction of the Triclia (Styger, *Römische Märtyrergrüfte*). A slightly different reconstruction appeared in *Römische Quartalschrift* (1915), p. 155.

affluent conceived of it also as an act of sharing extended to the living. In this spirit Pammachius, we are told, gave a copious banquet (A.D. 397) to the poor in the Church of St. Peter in the Vatican for the soul of his wife.[64] The refrigeria were held often for immediate practical reasons: The martyrs might be moved to intercede with God on behalf of those celebrating the cultic meal.

Owing to obvious abuses in the conduct of the refrigeria the Church looked with increasing disfavor upon them, and they were only suffered at all because it was felt to be expedient not to turn the new converts too abruptly from their pagan ways. But, as I mentioned earlier, Augustine urged the people to end these feasts and withheld the permission given freely by his predecessors in Carthage.[65]

Many had thought, until the recent discovery by Marichal of an early graffito on the wall of the Triclia, that the celebrations had not been practiced in Rome until after the Peace of the Church.[66] It is now known,

59. Grossi-Gondi, "Il 'Refrigerium,'" pp. 222 f.; La Piana "The Tombs of Peter and Paul ad Catacumbas," pp. 78, 79. See de Rossi, in *Bullettino di Archeologia cristiana* (1884–85), pp. 43–61; (1894), p. 60. See also the extensive article on the history of "refrigeria" by André Parrot, "Le 'refrigerium' dans l'au-dèla," in *Revue de l'Histoire des Religions*, CXIV (1936), 69–92, 158–96 and CXV (1937), 53–89 (especially the last excellent analysis relative to the celebrations held in Rome).

60. *De Monagamia* X (*MPL*, II, 942).

61. *Apology* XXXIX: "De solo Triclinio Christianorum refractatur. Coena nostra de nomine rationem sui ostendit; id vocatur, quod dilectio penes Graecos est [some MSS have "vocatur, ἀγάπη" or "vocatus enim id ἀγάπη quod dilectio penes Graecos est"] . . . siquidem inopes quosque refrigerio isto juvamus" (*MPL*, I, 538). "Our feast [Triclinio] explains itself by its name. The Greeks call it *agape* [alternate reading] i.e. affection . . . since with the good tidings of the feast [refrigerio] we benefit the needy (*The Ante-Nicene Fathers*, III, 47).

62. As in the Notice of the *Depositio Martyrum* for February 22 "viii kal. martias *Natale* de Cathedra." (Italics are mine.)

63. See Duchesne, *Origines du Culte chrétien*, p. 272; Delehaye, *Les Origines*, p. 41.

64. Paul of Nola, *Epistle* XIII.11 (*MPL*, LXI, 213).

65. *Epistle* XXIX.11 (*MPL*, XXXIII, 118). Compare *Epistle* XXII.3 (*MPL*, XXIII, 91).

66. Grossi-Gondi, "Il 'Refrigerium,'" p. 228; von Gerkan, in Lietzmann, *Petrus und Paulus in Rom*, 2d ed., p. 282.

PLATE 15 Graffiti on the wall of the Triclia (Styger, "Scavi a San Sebastiano," *Römische Quartalschrift* [1915], Plates II, IIIa).

however, that they were held as early as A.D. 260 and perhaps before. It is also known that the celebrations were prohibited by Ambrose,[67] but there appear to have been instances of them as late as about A.D. 400.

The date and description of the area of the Triclia and the dates on which these feasts were held in Rome all point toward a funerary celebration—which most

naturally presupposes the presence or, what is more probable, a *belief* in the presence of the relics of the apostles.[68]

The following are a few of the graffiti found on the wall (see Plate 15), written in capitals and cursive, Latin and Greek, and Latin written in Greek script:[69]

1. *ΠΕΤΡΕ ΕΤ ΠΑΥΛΑΙ IN METE*
2. PAVLE ET PETRE PETITE PRO VICTORE
3. AT PAVLV (m) ET PETR (um) REFRI(geravi)
4. PETRE ET PAVLE PETE PRO PRIMITIVO BENE BENE
5. DALMATIVS BOTVM IS PROMISIT REFRI-GERIVM
6. PETRVS ET PAVLVS IN MENTE ABEATIS ANTONIVS BASSVM ////// NIVS E . . . IN GELASIVS MENTE ABETE
7. PAVLE PETRE PETITE PRO ERATE ROGATE.

The following graffito was found on the left side of the wall of the cubicle on the stairway descending to the well:

PETRE ET PAVLE IMMENTEM HABETE PRIMVM ET PRIMAM IVgaLE EIVS ET SATVRNIMAM CONIVGEM FILI PRIMI ☧ ET VICTORINVM PATREM ejus IN ☧ SEMPER IN AETERNO ET . . .

Until very recently most scholars dated the graffiti on the wall *A–B* of the Triclia in the early fourth century[70] and not before (a later date for the graffiti on the wall leading to the well is made obvious by the presence of the Constantinian monogram). But an interesting and convincing study undertaken by Robert Marichal of one particular graffito has produced evidence which makes it fairly certain that these scribblings appeared on wall *A–B* of the Triclia

67. See above, p. 44.

68. See Leclercq, *DACL*, Vol. XIV, Part I, p. 889.

69. Of the 191 graffiti discovered, 33 were in Greek and the majority in low Latin.

70. Belvederi, *Le Tombe apostoliche*; Lemerle, "La Publication des Fouilles," pp. 223, 224. Oscar Cullmann, *Peter*, 1st ed., p. 133, was inclined to agree. However in *Peter*, 2d ed., p. 132, he dates the Triclia "probably in the year 258" and thus the graffiti at any time after this date.

as early as A.D. 260.[71] Paul Styger in his study in 1918[72] offered the following reading of the graffito in question:

> . . . CELGRA . . . (?)
> VVIVS AVG
> FARSVL . . . (?)
> ET DONAT . . . (?) . . .

The same graffito was rendered by Marichal in 1953 as:

> . . . CELERI . . .
> V IDVS AVG
> SACCVL
> ET DONAT . . .

He then proceeds to reconstruct the graffito as:

> . . . CELER(INVS)
> V IDVS AVG(VSTAS)
> SAECVL(ARI II)
> ET DONAT(O II COS.).

This graffito as reconstructed testifies to a refrigerium held on August 9, A.D. 260, when Cornelius Saecularis and C. Iunius Donatus were consuls for the second time. And since this graffito is written over another, "PAVLE ET P . . ." some of these scribblings at the Triclia may be even older. Marichal observes that the graffiti Ad Catacumbas are a mingling of capitals, minuscules, and cursives and that the minuscules are extremely early[73]—the earliest known examples of this type of writing in the Occident (possibly because many pilgrims visiting Ad Catacumbas were from the East). The minuscule writing provides the *terminus a quo*, and another graffito[74] in ancient cursive provides the *terminus ad quem*. This particular cursive used only up to

about A.D. 300, according to Marichal,[75] is particularly reminiscent of that found in the Oxyrhynchus papyri 103 (third century) and 114 (more precisely dated A.D. 237). Marichal is inclined to date all the graffiti (and therefore the building of the Triclia) between A.D. c. 258 and 300.[76] "Their [the graffiti] homogeneity is opposed to their being spread out much more than a generation."[77]

The importance of the Triclia and the graffiti is great, since these scribblings are always found near where the relics are buried (or are *believed* to be buried).[78] Toynbee and Perkins point out, however, that at least from the fourth century on, a phrase such as "ad Paulum et Petrum refrigeravi" *could* indicate the proximity of "brandea" and not necessarily relics. They cite, as an example from Castellum Tingitanum (Orléansville) in Algeria, an epitaph on a memoria erected for a child by its parents "aput/[sancto]s apostolos Petru(m) et/ [Paulu(m)]." They also conclude that if this cult center Ad Catacumbas was schismatic (Schneider) or Nova-tianist (Mohlberg), we would have to conclude the presence not of the relics but of cult objects—a fore-shadowing in the third century of a fourth-century practice.[79]

The Cortile (Plates 12, 13, 14) is located in front of the Triclia, extending from the columbaria on the north and H–F' (Plate 12) on the west to cella δ on the south. At the west side of the Cortile is found niche κ, which assumes great importance in several studies of the area and is dealt with in detail below. The Cortile, lower than the Triclia but connected with it by means of stairway

---

71. Robert Marichal (Directeur d'Études à l'École pratique des Hautes Études), "La Date des graffiti," in *La Nouvelle Clio*, V (1953), 119–20. Concerning the view that these graffiti are from the third century see Hertling and Kirschbaum, *Die römischen Katakomben*, p. 104.

72. "Il Monumento apostolico."

73. See *CIL*, Vol. VIII, Number 2391. The earliest from Egypt, Africa, and the Orient date between A.D. 225 and 250.

74. *Ibid.*, Plate XXIV.

75. Marichal, "La Date des graffiti," p. 120. See also Styger, *Die römischen Katakomben*.

76. A further account of Marichal's investigations is found in "Les Dates des Graffiti de Saint-Sébastien," in *Comptes Rendus de l'Académie des Inscriptions et Belles-Lettres* (1953), pp. 60–68. Cullmann, *Peter*, p. 132; Carcopino, *Études*, Appendix VI, pp. 279 ff., and *De Pythagore*, pp. 314–16.

77. Marichal, "Les Dates des Graffiti de Saint-Sébastien," p. 63; acceptance of the dating of Marichal is urged by von Gerkan, "Petrus in Vaticano et in Catacumbis," p. 25.

78. Grossi-Gondi, "Il rito funebre del 'Refrigerium,'" pp. 263–77. Klauser, *Die römische Petrustradition*, p. 24, states that these graffiti force one to conclude that it was at least believed that the relics of Peter and Paul rested in the area during this time. Tolotti, *Memorie*, p. 179, is sure that this is a fact, not simply a belief.

79. Toynbee and Perkins, *The Shrine of St. Peter*, p. 193n74.

s^1, was built after the Triclia. The flooring of this area evened out the complex which preceded it, establishing some order out of the earlier disorder (see Plate 12). In part it lies over e of the Arenario (Plate 9) which long since had been filled in when β was constructed.

Cella δ (Plates 8, No. 47, [δ]; 12; 13) was attached to the basalt wall D–E (Plate 12) which served as one of the southern limits of the Cortile.[80] The cella faced out on the Cortile through a wide opening divided into three spaces by columns. Tolotti is convinced that the cella was closely related to the Memoria and up to this time was unfortunately neglected by students of the monument. The construction of the cella, of one build with the Cortile (which in turn was a bit later than the Triclia), began around A.D. 250—"forse dal 258"—and ended with the destruction of the entire complex to permit the building of the Basilica. The cella contained two floors, the lower one for burials and the upper one for commemorative activities, a plan not without parallels in other Christian cemeteries. A great number of similar cellas are found in Milan, Africa, and Greece.[81] Cella δ most probably served not as a martyrium but as the tomb of a Christian noble family, as was the early opinion of Colagrossi and Marucchi. Further, it belonged to the last phase of the Memoria and served to "systematize with dignity a venerated place."[82]

This examination of the Christian Memoria (including the Triclia and its connection with the well and the Cortile, and finally cella δ) prepares us for the following discussion concerning the various areas of the monument which have been suggested as the resting places for the relics of the apostles.

The earliest of the designated places was the Platonia.[83] Antonio Bosio in his *Roma sotterranea* mentions this structure as that which served as the sepulture of the apostles.[84] Anton de Waal agreed with this conclusion until the findings of the excavations of 1894 convinced him that the Platonia was originally the tomb of Quirinius, whose bones had been brought from Pannonia about A.D. 380.[85] In 1900 Arthur S. Barnes still accepted the view uncritically that the apostles' bodies were brought to this building immediately after their crucifixion and placed in the "bisoma" (two sepulchers side by side—Plate 8, No. 51), remaining there for one year and seven months, after which time they were moved to their final resting places. In keeping with general opinion since the beginning of the twentieth century,[86] Barnes gradually accepted the fact that there was no basis to this legend.[87]

The Platonia itself (Plate 8, No. 51) is closely related to the "Domus Petri" (Plate 8, No. 50) beside it. The two are separated only by three arches, each of which in turn is separated by two columns. The entrance to the Platonia was originally from the ground; later this was changed and entrance was effected from within the Basilica itself (to the left of vv_2, Plate 8). A number of arcosolia found in the structure belong to a late phase of the building (fourth or fifth century). The floor was paved with mosaic, which causes Tolotti to suggest a relationship in this early stage of the Platonia to the Cortile and Triclia. The Platonia is later than the Basilica; there are a number of spurs contained in its walls which served as buttresses. The Platonia is little more than a large cella "built to contain burials and extend hospitality to a commemorative cult . . . we know there

---

the marble slab which bore the Damasus Inscription and not to the building as a whole, as has been commonly the belief. In the notice of Liberius which appears in the *Liber Pontificalis* (ed. Duchesne, Vol. I, Part I, p. 208), it is mentioned that he decorated the tomb of Agnes with a "Platomis marmoreis." Compare Barnes, *The Martyrdom of St. Peter and St. Paul*, pp. 50–59.

84. Bosio, p. 260. See the same view in Spence-Jones, *The Early Christians in Rome*, p. 243.

85. A. de Waal, "Gli Scavi nel Pavimento della Basilica di San Sebastiano," p. 145.

86. For example, see Lietzmann, *Petrus und Paulus in Rom*, 2d ed., pp. 151–55; Mancini, "La Depositio dei SS. Pietro e Paolo Ad Catacumbas," p. 200.

87. *St. Peter in Rome*, p. 140 (see pp. 135–58). But see his *The Martyrdom of St. Peter and St. Paul*, p. 85. Compare H. Stuart Jones, "The Memoria Apostolorum on the Via Appia," pp. 30–39.

---

80. See Tolotti, *Memorie*, pp. 193–212.

81. *Ibid.*, p. 197, fig. 44.

82. *Ibid.*, p. 212.

83. The word "platonia" is a corruption of "platoma" (Alexander Souter, *Glossary of Later Latin to 600 A.D.* [Oxford: Clarendon Press, 1949]), which means a marble slab. The confusion has resulted in a number of alternate spellings. Leclercq, *DACL*, Vol. XIV, Part I, accepts Platonae as the preferred form, but also cites the alternate spellings, Platoniae and Platuniae ($\pi\lambda\alpha\tau\acute{\upsilon}\nu\iota\omicron\nu$). The word originally referred to

existed an episcopal chair at the center of the curve of the bench now at Pisa—a gift of Innocent XII to Grand Duke Cosimo III."[88] On the upper floor, in front of the bishop's chair, was a bisoma and an altar. The latter is late Renaissance, dating from the time of Cardinal Borghese; the former is no earlier than the building of the Platonia (fourth century) and, therefore, could not have been the receptacle for the relics of Peter and Paul. The only relationship between this structure and the cult of Peter and Paul is that after the Basilica was built it served as a place in which the rite of refrigerium might be conducted.

In addition to the Platonia the "hic" of the Damasus Inscriptions has been identified with other areas of the Memoria. The inscription, written about forty years after the building of the Basilica, perhaps indicates that Damasus himself did not know where the relics of the apostles had lain:

With the passing of years this "hic" had caused the fantasies of the faithful to form, hastened by the desire moved in every period to provide a material object for their piety. And one had been led to believe from time to time according to the words of the *Liber Pontificalis* that the adverb of Damasus referred directly to the slab of the inscription "platoniam ipsam ubi iacuerunt corpora sancta versibus exornavit," and at another time to localize, perhaps first under the altar and then on the two sides of it, the sepulchers of Peter and Paul: in "initio cryptae, iuxta vestigia Apostolorum" [fifth century]; "et ibi sunt sepulcra Apostolorum" [seventh century]; "dipoi furono trovati li corpi, furono messi a mezza la chiesa: dove e quella feriata S. Pietro: e dove e dalla scala S. Paulo" [sixteenth century]. Down the many centuries the same double tradition is found, indicating in the same period two places for the deposition of the bodies, in the middle of the Church and in the Platonia, which is a clear sign of a product of the imagination [un prodotto fantastico].[89]

A space beneath the Memoria off the stairway leading down to the well was indicated by Marucchi and Grossi-Gondi as the place which once contained the relics of the apostles. This space, 12 m. below the floor of the Basilica, and only a little over a meter square, was finished in plaster, on which were found numerous graffiti containing the names of Peter and Paul. In addition to the absence of *any* sign that there ever had

been a sepulcher (caskets of lead, according to Marucchi) here, it appears to be an extremely unlikely place for a burial. The area is humid (at times under water) and public, with no adequate place to hide the relics. The presence of the graffiti in this area is plausibly explained if it is remembered that those who were taking part in the refrigeria in the Triclia (or later in the Basilica) required water for their celebrations. The conclusions of Marucchi and Grossi-Gondi are rejected by Duchesne, Mancini, and Tolotti,[90] even though they admit that graffiti are found usually in the immediate vicinity of the relics of a matryr.[91] But why, it may be asked, do Marucchi and Grossi-Gondi believe that the graffiti found on the stairway more adequately locate the hiding place of the relics than the graffiti on the wall of the Triclia? Perhaps, Marucchi explains weakly, the graffiti were placed at the space on the stairway after all of the available space up above was taken. It might be asked, in addition, if one wanted to *hide* the bodies of the apostles, why were there more than two hundred graffiti permitted to remain in clear sight on the wall of the Triclia above? Carcopino attempts to clarify the situation by suggesting that the niche indicated by Marucchi housed the relics and served the cult in part during periods of persecution, such as those under Valerian and Diocletian, while the Triclia was used in periods of calm.[92]

For many years Lietzmann believed that the relics of the apostles once lay in sarcophagi behind the Triclia.[93] This tradition which is not found prior to the Middle Ages is indicated by the Salzburg Itinerary (seventh century).[94] The center of the church as the burial place of the apostles is also mentioned in: the

88. Tolotti, *Memorie*, p. 249.
89. *Ibid.*, pp. 283–84.

90. "La 'Memoria Apostolorum,'" p. 16. See also Leclercq, *DACL*, Vol. XIV, Part I, p. 893. Marucchi's position is also rejected by Mancini in "La Depositio dei SS. Pietro e Paolo Ad Catacumbas," p. 200.
91. Marucchi, in *Nuovo Bullettino di Archeologia cristiana*, XXVII, p. 6, and in *Notizie degli Scavi* (1923), pp. 88–89.
92. *De Pythagore*, pp. 318–22. Even this suggestion is unlikely, as fig. 9, p. 321, of Carcopino's book will illustrate. The niche would have been under water a large part of the time.
93. *Petrus und Paulus in Rom*, 2d ed., pp. 155 and 167. See also fig. 1 A.
94. See above, pp. 114–115; see also Tolotti, *Memorie*, p. 7.

Acta Sebastiani, "in initio cryptae iuxta vestigia aposto-lorum"[95] and the notice of Leo III (A.D. 795–816) in the *Liber Pontificalis,* "et inibi super tumbas apostolorum Petri ac Pauli fecit vestes II de stauraci et fundato seu blati."[96] In addition, there is the testimony of Onofrius Panvinius (d. 1569) who says simply that the relics lay "propre altare in medio ecclesiae a dextra introeuntibus est craticula ferrea sub qua iacuisse dicitur S. Petrus Apostolus multis annis."[97]

In view of these traditions and because excavations proved that the relics had never been in the Platonia, Lietzmann continued to indicate the center of the church as the most probable area until von Gerkan's excavations seemed to indicate that this tradition also was false. Von Gerkan maintained that the Triclia could not have been built until after the Peace of the Church and, therefore, the room behind the Triclia, probably built in the same period, could not have existed in A.D. 258. Lietzmann's abandonment of his original thesis was wise, considering the fact that "there was not found the slightest trace of an apostolic grave."[98]

Duchesne and Mancini clung to the belief that the apostolic tomb lay beneath the place known in the Middle Ages as the "altar of the relics," very near the center of the nave of the Basilica and a bit to the east of the place indicated by Lietzmann.[99] Duchesne's argument centered on the idea that the area of the greatest concentration of the early graves indicated the location that was early believed to be the burial place of the apostles. Such a clustering was noticed markedly in the space beneath the "altar of the relics" in the vicinity of the Triclia.[100] Of course, he admits, there is no evidence *now* of an apostolic grave.

Leclercq attempts to explain the existence of the two traditions concerning the placement of the relics of the apostles as follows.[101] Prior to the ninth century the body of St. Sebastian was venerated in the center of the church, but was transferred (at least partially) by Gregory IV (A.D. 827–44) to the Basilica of St. Peter's and placed under the altar of St. Gregory.[102] The monks of the Church of San Sebastian sought another focus for their devotion, and they chose St. Fabian, supposedly buried near the apostles. In the thirteenth century the relics of St. Sebastian were restored by Honorius which resulted in the existence of two cults within the same church. In this period also the tomb of Quirinius was again venerated, and the Platonia once more fired the imagination. It was remembered that this tomb had long been associated with the name "Catacomb" and with a tradition of the apostles. This was enough for imagination to prompt the assured statement that the bisoma, or double sepulcher, in the center of the Platonia was at one time the burial place of Peter and Paul. Now there were two definite traditions of apostolic sepulture within the same church, two traditions which were constantly in conflict. The Platonia had the bisoma, but the Basilica had the objects of long veneration such as the slab of Damasus (which was taken down by Cardinal Borghese in 1563). The conflict continued into the present century and was brought to an end only when the excavations forced the recognition that both traditions were unfounded.[103]

The loculus l_0 (north of *a*, Plate 9), which is mentioned above in connection with the Arenario, was, according to Tolotti, the original resting place of the relics of the apostles.[104] The view was not originated by Tolotti, but had been mentioned *en passant* by Mancini and developed further by Cecchelli, neither of whom took the possibility seriously.[105] Testini has carefully reviewed Tolotti's theory and arrives at the defensible conclusion that this loculus is not exceptional in any way.[106] For a time it did perhaps influence the placement

---

95. *MPL*, XVII, 1150.

96. Duchesne, *Le Liber Pontificalis,* II, 13.

97. Codex Vaticanus Lat. 6780, f. 43. See Lietzmann, *Petrus und Paulus in Rom,* 2d ed., p. 155n1; Tolotti, *Memorie,* p. 6; Carcopino, *De Pythagore,* p. 325n193.

98. *Petrus und Paulus in Rom,* 2d ed., p. 167. Compare Carcopino, *De Pythagore,* pp. 325 f.

99. Mancini, in *Notizie degli Scavi* (1923), p. 78; Duchesne, "La 'Memoria Apostolorum,'" pp. 12, 17–18. See Tolotti, *Memorie,* p. 281.

100. See Styger, "Il Monumento apostolico," Plate I.

101. *DACL*, Vol. XIV, Part I, pp. 879 f.

102. Duchesne, *Le Liber Pontificalis,* II, 74.

103. See for the above, Styger, in *Römische Quartalschrift* (1915), pp. 197 ff.

104. See above, Plate 9, p. 139.

105. See especially Cecchelli, *Monumenti cristiani—eretici di Roma,* p. 185.

106. "Noterelle sulla 'Memoria Apostolorum' in Catacumbas," p. 213. Compare Tolotti, *Memorie,* p. 113.

of the various burial spaces in the area, but later it was unceremoniously sealed off and ignored to such a degree that the plaster did not even contain so much as a simple graffito to explain who was buried within. Testini continues, "The deposition [of the apostles] in that place 'eo tempore quo passi sunt' is urged against insuperable difficulties."[107] Klauser adds that perhaps the loculus l_0 was only spared at all by the later owners of the hypogea because of: 1) the Roman laws against disturbing a permanent grave and 2) their own pagan

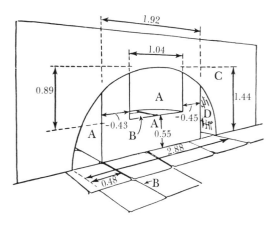

PLATE 17 A reconstruction of niche κ (Prandi, "Sulla Ricostruzione della 'mensa martyrum'").

superstition. Furthermore, that the loculus lay under niche κ is pure chance—it was out of sight, and most likely out of mind, after the Arenario was abandoned.[108]

Another place that has been named as the resting place of the relics of the apostles is found in the area of cella β (Plate 12), mentioned briefly above.[109] To find any likely tomb of the apostles one must look, according to Testini, in the complex which comprises the Triclia, Cortile, and cellas δ and β; it is "illogico e antistorico cercare altrove."[110] He continues that *the* place, if it exists at all, must be κ (Plate 12, also Plate 16 which shows the niche in detail), an aedicula, or a niche.[111] The niche, however, could not have been an *original* apostolic tomb since it is a part of cella β which belonged to the last stage of the building of the Memoria. The

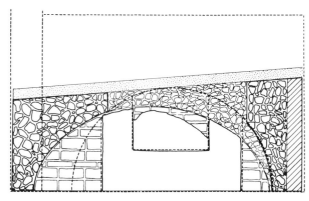

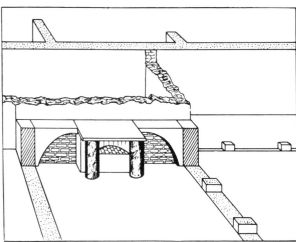

PLATE 16 A reconstruction—and cross section (above)—of niche κ. Note that the rampart on the right is smaller than the one on the left. This asymmetry is found also in the reconstructions of von Gerkan and Prandi (Testini, "Noterelle sulla 'Memoria Apostolorum' in Catacumbas," fig. 5).

107. "Noterelle sulla 'Memoria Apostolorum' in Catacumbas," p. 213.

108. Klauser, *Die römische Petrustradition*, p. 80. See also the same arguments in J. B. Ward Perkins' review of Tolotti's *Memorie degli Apostoli in Catacumbas* in *The Journal of Roman Studies*, XLV (1955), 206, in which he concludes that Tolotti's view is built only upon flimsy circumstantial evidence.

109. See above, pp. 146–47.

110. "Noterelle sulla 'Memoria Apostolorum' in Catacumbas," p. 217.

111. For descriptions of the niche see: A. M. Schneider, "Die Memoria Apostolorum," pp. 12 ff.; Prandi, "La Memoria Apostolorum in Catacumbas," figs. 16–17, and "Sulla Ricostruzione della 'mensa martyrum,'" pp. 345–53; Belvederi, "Le Tombe apostoliche," figs. 15, 17, 20, 21; Tolotti, *Memorie*, pp. 213, 218 f. The structure is also mentioned by Toynbee and Perkins, *The Shrine of St. Peter*, p. 177.

PLATE 18 The arcosolium of "the small apostles," depicting Peter (left), Paul (right), the Constantinian monogram, and an orant. The arcosolium is found in the Cemetery of Domitilla (Wilpert, *Roma sotterranea*, fig. 4, p. 350).

niche entered into wall m^{20} (Plate 12) is approximately 1.5 m. high, and is approximately 6.5 m. above *e* (Plate 9) of the Arenario. Paul Styger originally saw in *κ* "a niche destined to contain a statue,"[112] but later came to think of it as a cathedra of the type frequently found near the tombs of the dead.[113] And while von Gerkan imagined it to be on the style of a lararium of Hercules,[114] the structure suggested a mensa martyrum to Enrico Josi and Adriano Prandi.[115] As may be seen in the traces that remain, *κ* was once faced with marble, and there are no signs that it was ever decorated on the outside (Plate 17). In front of the niche originally were two columns. On one of these, found in pieces and identified as belonging to a type of Roman column construction of the third century, was found the graffito "Petre et Pavle in mente." Together with Josi

and Ferrua, Prandi ventured that in *A* and *D* (Plate 17), which were covered on the inside surfaces with marble and on the outside concave surfaces with a polychrome mosaic,[116] were at one time the reliquaries containing the bones of Peter and Paul.[117] The niche suggests an arcosolium to Prandi, many of which are compartmental, as is this one. In the Cemetery of Domitilla there appears to be, Prandi mentions, a representation of the niche (Plate 18).[118] The two pictures follow the usual fourth-century representations of Peter on the left and Paul on the right. The way in which the figures are placed does not suggest that the pictures appeared in the original niches, but it does hint at what the niches were *believed* to contain. The presence of the orant (praying figure) and the Constantinian monogram are further indications that the representations (Plate 18) were not intended to duplicate the decorations of the original niche but to serve as symbols of the *meaning* of the niche in the cult of Peter and Paul. The pictures, originally published in the work of Josef Wilpert, go back to the middle of the fourth century. Perhaps, as Prandi observes, the mensa *κ* was still accessible at this

---

112. "Il Monumento apostolico," p. 93; also Mancini, in *Notizie degli Scavi* (1923), p. 40.

113. *Römische Märtyrergrüfte*, p. 34. See also above, pp. 42–44 and Plate 1; and Klauser, *Die Cathedra im Totenkult*, p. 99.

114. See *Petrus und Paulus in Rom*, 2d ed., pp. 163, 271 and fig. IX.

115. Such a view was mentioned by Josi to the members of the Pontifical Institute of Archeology on January 16, 1936. This interpretation was also followed by Ferrua, "Scavi a San Sebastiano," *La Civiltà Cattolica*, II (1937), 361–65, and Prandi, "Sulla Ricostruzione della 'mensa martyrum,'" pp. 349 ff.

116. The mosaic was made from a material for decoration —a tin alloy which glistens, producing a silver-leaf effect.

117. See also Carcopino, *De Pythagore*, p. 303.

118. Plate 18 is found in Josef Wilpert, *Roma sotterranea, le Pitture delle Catacombe romane*, p. 370, and reproduced in Prandi, "Sulla Ricostruzione della 'mensa martyrum,'" p. 350.

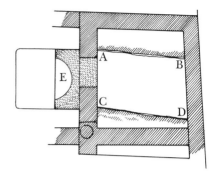

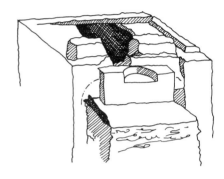

PLATE 19 A reconstruction of niche κ showing a top (above) and front view (Belvederi, *Le Tombe apostoliche*, figs. 20, 21).

time, or perhaps an artist of the period wished to preserve the *meaning* of the niche just prior to its destruction in the preparations for the building of the Basilica. A while later Damasus (A.D. 366–84) also wished to preserve the memory of the apostolic associations of the place in his "Hic habitasse" inscription.

Belvederi, like Prandi and others, interprets the niche itself as a cathedra, but one which stood in front of a vaulted tomb (Plate 19).[119] This combination is not new, as Torp points out, and is found in a number of Christian and pagan cemeteries, especially in Egypt.[120] But whereas Belvederi thinks in terms of an actual tomb containing the relics of the apostles, it must be remembered that Torp considers this niche as one element in a complex which served the martyr cult—a cult organized around an "invention" of the apostolic relics.[121]

Testini follows Prandi's theory in part and, unlike Tolotti, who believes the elements of κ are too destroyed to make any reconstruction possible,[122] he does propose a plan of the original (Plate 16). He considers that there is little similarity between this niche and the newly discovered Aedicula in the Vatican cemetery; while the latter and most pagan lararia are built into walls, niche κ is free standing. Each part of his reconstruction has parallels in monuments of this type and of this period, and he is careful to point out these similarities as he defends his interpretation.[123] It would not have been strange, he adds, if the niche were used to support a statue or holy object, but Testini holds that it served mainly to protect the coffin containing the relics. The bones were not in reliquaries at each side of the niche, however, as is suggested by Prandi and others. If such a niche had existed, it would have been entirely unique, for there is no similar arcosolium known where the sides remained securely open to leave the container with the relics open to view.

If one could go beyond and conclude that if the excavations in the Vatican have furnished one of the most ancient martyriums, the "manufatto" [κ] Ad Catacumbas would represent the prototype—at least for now—of an altar "ad corpus."[124]

Testini, furthermore, believes that it is to this small niche that Damasus referred when he wrote the "hic" in the first line of his famous inscription.

It must be remembered that these are only theories concerning the meaning of κ and that Tolotti's estimate is probably correct—the area is too completely destroyed to render possible any defensible reconstruction of the original niche. Furthermore, as there is no way of knowing the appearance of the original structure, there is no chance to determine its function.

In what appears to be an artificial attempt to combine and harmonize the various traditions and modern views concerning the several suggested burial places of Peter and Paul Ad Catacumbas, Carcopino suggests that originally (upon translation of the relics of the apostles

---

119. "Le Tombe apostoliche," pp. 146, 150, 153.
120. "The Vatican Excavations," p. 54*n*119–22, is especially helpful for examples and bibliography concerning this proposition.
121. *Ibid.*, pp. 55, 56.

122. Tolotti, *Memorie*, p. 214.
123. "Noterelle, sulla 'Memoria Apostolorum' in Catacumbas," p. 223*n*18, 19.
124. *Ibid.*, p. 227. See also Klauser, *Die römische Petrustradition*, p. 78.

from the Vatican and the Via Ostia) the relics were placed in the niche designated by Marucchi at the bottom of the stairs, and at this time the services in memory of the apostles were held at the mensa martyrum above. Later, after the time lapse in the episcopate between August 9, A.D. 258 and August 22, A.D. 259, a new bishop was elected, and a more proper setting was found for the relics in the space behind the Triclia.[125]

It may be definitely established that a cult of the apostles existed at the Catacombs by A.D. 258 or 260, while Christian influence in the monument *may* have been felt as early as A.D. 200. It cannot be convincingly supported, however, that Christians buried their dead in this cemetery prior to the turn of the third century, nor that the bodies of Peter and Paul rested here "eo tempore quo passi sunt." None of the excavations in the areas indicated as temporary hiding places of the apos-

tolic relics has produced any evidence whatsoever, and it is very doubtful that any of them would have been suggested as the burial place of the two apostles had it not been for the traditions found in the literary and liturgical documents. If these documents may be likened to maps, it can be said that they have not led to the discovery of the promised treasure, nor to any signs that the treasure had ever been there. This leads us then to conclude that the *early* literary documents were misunderstood or were the products of misunderstanding. Either they did not intend to indicate that the relics of the apostles would be found Ad Catacumbas or they harbored a mistaken belief. Furthermore, the liturgical documents testify *not* to a translation of the relics but to an inauguration of the cult of the apostles at the Catacombs A.D. 258—perhaps marking the completion of and first celebration at the Triclia.[126]

THE EXCAVATIONS AT THE CHURCH OF
SAINT PETER ON THE VATICAN

On August 22, 1949, the New York *Times* carried a front-page news story which bore the headline, "Bones of Saint Peter, Found under Altar, Vatican Believes." Follow-up articles appeared in *Time*,[127] *Life*,[128] and a number of other popular and scholarly magazines and journals. Behind the headlines there was a story that had taken ten years to write. For this amount of time the archeologists and *sampietrini* had worked in comparative secrecy in the crypt below the Sacred Grotto. During the 1940s the few articles that appeared in Italian journals such as *La Civiltà Cattolica*, did little more than hint at the magnitude of the project that was being undertaken.

Monsignor Ludwig Kaas, at that time administrator of St. Peter's, was actually the instigator behind the modern excavations. He was appointed by Pius XI to be in charge of the area of St. Peter's beneath the surface. In the process of clearing up the confusion of centuries which existed in the sacred grottoes he decided to ask

for permission to investigate the area in its entirety. Pope Pius XI was not in favor of the idea, but, indirectly, his wish to be buried near the remains of Pius X and as close as possible to the area of the Confessione precipitated the excavations. Thirty-six hours before the funeral of Pius XI, in the spring of 1939, Ludwig Kaas was searching in the crypt for a suitable place for the burial, and in the process he ordered a marble plaque to be removed from a wall. As this was being done, the wall caved in and exposed an ancient vault. When the new pontiff, Pius XII, heard of this, he ordered at the vigil of the feasts of the apostles Peter and Paul on June 28, 1939, a full-scale investigation of the area down to the virgin soil; but he cautioned that the excavations were to be undertaken in secret. The work was to be done under the supervision of the College of Architects of St. Peter's and a committee of archeologists: B. M.

---

125. Carcopino, *De Pythagore*, p. 319.

126. Perhaps, too, up to this time the site was in the hands of a schismatic group and this celebration served as an official recognition of the site and of the cult.

127. September 5, 1949, p. 61; March 27, 1950, p. 70.

128. March 27, 1950, pp. 65–85. Then in *Osservatore Romano*, December 20, 1951, appeared the following: "La parola definitiva è stata pronunciata. La scienza, che non crede se non vede, ha veduto. Crede con la chiesa, con la tradizione, con la storia, con l'arte."

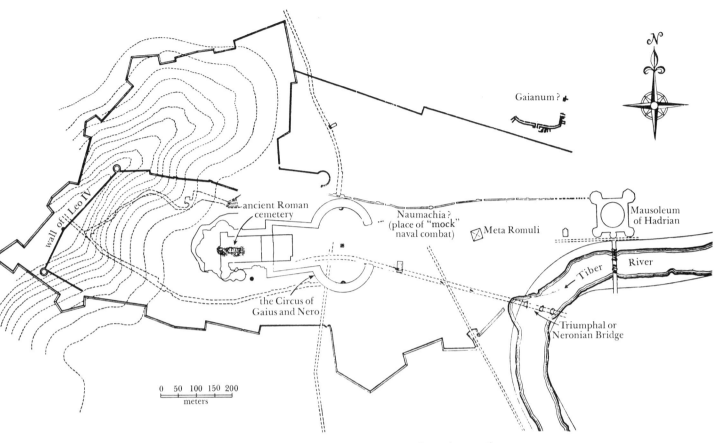

PLATE 20 The Vatican area (*Esplorazioni*, Vol. II, Plate CIV).

Apollonj-Ghetti, Antonio Ferrua, Enrico Josi, and Englebert Kirschbaum. There have been two phases to this investigation: the first carried on from 1939 to 1949 and a second from 1953 to the present.

Since the time of Gaius (A.D. 200)[129] at least, the general Vatican area (Plate 20) has been associated with the burial of Peter.[130] Furthermore, a number of the later literary and liturgical documents mentioned more specific landmarks which supposedly were to be found

near the place of his burial—the Via Aurelia, Via Triumphale, and Via Cornelia, the Naumachy, the obelisk, the Circus of Nero, the Metae, and the monte aureo. The exact spot, which has been venerated since before the time of Constantine, has now been thoroughly and carefully investigated; the findings have been published and criticized. Here, concerning the traditions of the burial of Peter in Rome, this study is based upon the findings as published in the Official Report[131] and the separate individual statements of its four authors who have had the opportunity to see and to study the necropolis at length. However, an examination and

129. See above, pp. 95–101.

130. The word "Vatican" is derived from the Latin adjective "vaticanus" and thus in turn from the noun "Vatica" or "Vaticum"—a word which comes from the Etruscan. The area originally belonged to the most southerly of the Etruscan cities. The Vatican area became part of the City of Rome in 396 B.C. and was included in the 14th region of Rome under the Emperor Augustus. See Guarducci, *The Tomb of St. Peter*, pp. 44–45.

131. *Esplorazioni sotto la Confessione di San Pietro in Vaticano*, eds. Apollonj-Ghetti, Ferrua, Josi, and Kirschbaum, Vols. I, II, 1951 (hereafter referred to as *Esplorazioni*). The first volume contains the text and numerous illustrations; the second volume presents a wealth of valuable and instructive photographs.

evaluation of the disagreements in interpretation which have arisen among the experts are essential to arrive at a decision concerning the probability that this was or was not the tomb of Peter.

The purpose of this section of the book is similar to the over-all intent of the *Esplorazioni*, in that only the immediate area of the alleged tomb is considered in detail. The Vatican area, however, and the various "landmarks" mentioned in the literary documents are also discussed briefly. But, I have made no attempt to provide "English readers with a comprehensive, connected, critical . . . account of the whole area" which is the main purpose of the excellent study of the excavations made by Jocelyn Toynbee and John Ward Perkins.[132] My concern is not with the entire cemetery, but with one small part of it, area *P* and its immediate surroundings (Plate 23). And my interest is in one question alone: Is it reasonable to suppose that this is the place where Peter was buried shortly after his alleged martyrdom in the Circus of Nero?

An excellent short introduction to the Vatican area is provided by Toynbee and Perkins; a few of the more relevant facts are mentioned here.[133] The area was approached from the Tiber River over the Pons Neronianus or the Pons Aelius, after A.D. 134 (Plate 20). In the days when the cemetery was active, there had to be avenues of approach from the city. The exact location of these avenues, however, is a matter of great disagreement. The Gaianum (an open space used by the Emperor Gaius for chariot races) has been variously located: off to the right as one approaches the present site of St. Peter's, or near Hadrian's tomb on the site of the Church of Santa Maria in Transpadina where appropriate inscriptions have been recovered (Plate 20). Closer to the recently excavated area of the cemetery was seen the Mons Vaticanus rising sharply to the north and falling off more gradually to the west down to the Vallis Vaticana. The entire region was included, as mentioned above, in the trans-Tiberine district of the fourteenth administrative region into which the

Emperor Augustus had divided the City of Rome. As Toynbee and Perkins point out, the district was rural and poor.[134] The chief occupations were the making of a rather poor grade of wine and the manufacture of bricks and pottery. Furthermore, we are told by Tacitus that the Vatican area was not healthy; but in spite of this, imperial gardens were found there. In the first century the gardens belonged to Agrippina, later to Gaius, and then to Nero. Since in no document yet discovered are the limits of the gardens described, it is not possible to know for certain whether or not the cemetery with which we are concerned lay within these gardens or just beyond them.

Of those topographical details provided by the literary documents in connection with the burial of Peter, it is perhaps best to start with the highways. The grave site is traditionally located in the vicinity of three thoroughfares: Jerome places it in the vicinity of the Via Triumphalis;[135] the *Liber Pontificalis* mentions the Via Aurelia;[136] while the *Notitia portarum et viarum* names the Via Cornelia.[137]

The position of these highways is not known positively. The authors of the *Esplorazioni* and *The Shrine of St. Peter* are more cautious than von Gerkan who surmises that: 1) the Via Triumphalis ran to the north and east of the cemetery and may have intersected with the Via Cornelia at the Meta Romuli, 2) the Via Cornelia continued north from this point of intersection to the north of the cemetery,[138] 3) the Via Aurelia Nova

---

132. *The Shrine of St. Peter*, p. xx.

133. *Ibid.*, pp. 3–17. The map used in Plate 20 is that found in *Esplorazioni*, Vol. II, fig. CIV, which is similar to fig. I in Toynbee and Perkins, *The Shrine of St. Peter*, p. 4, and von Gerkan, "Kritische Studien," fig. I.

134. *The Shrine of St. Peter*, by Toynbee and Perkins, pp. 17–20, contains an excellent bibliography related to the various aspects of the Vatican area.

135. *De viris illustribus* I (*MPL*, XXIII, 639, 640). Peter is "sepultus Romae in Vaticano iuxta viam triumphalem."

136. Duchesne, *Le Liber Pontificalis*, Vol. I, Part I, p. 118. Peter "sepultus est via Aurelia, in templum Apollonis, iuxta locum ubi crucifixus est, iuxta palatium Neronianum, in Vaticanum, iuxta territurium triumphalem, iii Kal. Iul."

137. See also the *Catalogue loci martyrum* compiled in the seventh century, which mentions that "Saint Peter reposes in the region west of the city, beside the Via Cornelia, near its first mile marker."

138. Ferrua, "Nuove Scoperte sotto S. Pietro," p. 241; *Esplorazioni*, I, 26 ("senza dubbio essa doveva correre note volemente più a sud"); Toynbee and Perkins, *The Shrine of St. Peter*, fig. I, shows this road to the south of the cemetery. Klauser, *Die römische Petrustradition*, p. 40, does not believe

was south of the gardens, but the location of the Via Aurelia Vetus is not known.[139]

These three highways are all related and certainly were well-known landmarks of the Vatican area, for which reason they were chosen by the literary documents to locate *approximately* the burial place of Peter. In the mid-second century it seems that Antonius Pius (A.D. 138–61) appointed an official, Caius Popidius Pedo, as administrator of the three highways.[140]

The old Itineraries as well as writers such as Grimaldi, Duchesne, and Lanciani, are in error in their claim that the Via Cornelia ran beneath St. Peter's.[141] No remains of this or any other highway were uncovered during the excavations.[142] Could it be, since there are stairs leading over the roofs of the northerly row of mausolea and down (for example, at tomb O—Plate 23), that the Via Cornelia was situated slightly to the north of the cemetery?[143] The problem of the exact location of the highways in the vicinity of the Vatican in the first century still remains a problem. But Carcopino, while doubting the old proverb that "all roads lead to Rome," is sure in the case of the three highways under discussion that all led to the Vatican.[144]

The two Metae and the Terebinth mentioned in the apocryphal literary documents can also be located. The Meta of Romuli (destroyed in April, 1499) stood on the road (traced by von Gerkan and suggested by Toynbee and Perkins) from the Pons Aelius to the cemetery (Plate 20). The Meta of Remus was located near the Porta S. Paolo, and the τερεβίνθος (Terebinth) was later identified with the "Tiburtinus [or Terebinthus] Neronia," *possibly* the Obelisk of Nero.[145]

The Naumachy indicated in the fourth century Regionary Catalogue as being in the fourteenth district is mentioned in the *Passio Petri et Pauli*, as being located "iuxta obeliscum Neronis in montem." According to Charles Hülsen this was located northwest of the Mausoleum of Hadrian,[146] but Lietzmann states definitely that the author "meint augenscheinlich nichts anderes als den Circus mit dem worte 'Naumachie.'"[147] The term comes from the Greek "ναῦς" (ship) and "μάχη" (battle) and was employed by the Romans to describe a mock naval battle which took place in a flooded amphitheater called a naumachia. The first of these "battles" on record was that staged by Julius Caesar in 46 B.C. on a lake constructed in the Campus Martius. The crews of these vessels included gladiators, prisoners, and, in later times, volunteers. The Naumachy in the Vatican area is thought today to have been located either due west of the Mausoleum of Hadrian or three hundred yards north of that point (Plate 20).[148]

In the notice of Peter in the *Liber Pontificalis*, we find mention of a "templum Apollonis" in the vicinity of the

---

that this road to the south is to be connected with the Via Cornelia of medieval handbooks. Besides, he thinks that if there had been a road to the south the name would have appeared on the inscription of Popilius Heracla. (See discussion of this inscription below.) This seems doubtful, for there must have been *some* road from the Tiber to the gardens which lay to the south of the cemetery.

139. See Carcopino, *Études*, pp. 144, 145 and Platner and Ashby, *A Topographical Dictionary of Ancient Rome*, p. 561.

140. *CIL*, Vol. XIV, Number 3610, "curatori viarum Aureliae Veteris et Novae Corneliae et Triumphalis."

141. The assumption was doubted by André Piganiol, *L'Empereur Constantin*, p. 210, "Il est peu vraisemblable que l'Église St. Pierre ait barré une rue."

142. See in Kirschbaum, *Die Gräber*, p. 41, Lanciani, *Forma Urbis Romae*, fig. 1A. Kirschbaum sees the Via Cornelia as proceeding from the Pons Aelius in a westerly direction a bit north of the cemetery, along the slope of the hill. See fig. A in the front inside cover of his book. See also his article, "Gli Scavi sotto Basilica di S. Pietro," pp. 554–56; and Carcopino, *Études*, pp. 141 ff.; Klauser, *Die römische Petrustradition*, pp. 84, 85.

143. This possibility also occurred to Kirschbaum, *Die Gräber*, p. 41, and Cullmann, *Peter*, p. 143.

144. Carcopino, *Études*, p. 149.

145. See above, p. 59. The Terebinth is mentioned in the *Passio Petri et Pauli* (Marcellus Text), "Sub terebinthum iuxta Naumachiam in locum qui appellatur Vaticanis" (*Acta Apostolorum apocrypha*, eds. Lipsius and Bonnet, I, 172, 216). The "Terbentinum Neronis" appears in the twelfth-century *Mirabilia*. See Lietzmann, *Petrus und Paulus in Rom*, 2d ed., pp. 177–78, and Carcopino, *Études*, pp. 139–40.

146. "Il Gaianum e la Naumachia Vaticana," fig. IX, cited by *Esplorazioni*, p. 13n7.

147. Lietzmann, *Petrus und Paulus in Rom*, 2d ed., p. 167.

148. *Esplorazioni*, Vol. II, fig. CIV. See also *Liber Pontificalis*, II, 28, 57. The first reference mentions the construction of a hospital in the Naumachy in the pontificate of Leo III. The word also appears in the biography of Pascal I. See Guignebert, *La Primauté de Pierre*, p. 297.

place where Peter was buried.[149] Lugli believes that this is a reference to a statue that once stood on the spina of the circus.[150] But this is improbable, if only because the notice mentions a temple and not a statue. Duchesne's suggestion, that this is a reference to the Phrygianum believed to have been located in the vicinity of the Vatican in the third and fourth centuries, is more plausible. Since "rays" of some sort are at times found in representations of Attis (consort of the Magna Mater), this god could have been mistaken for Apollo.[151] The *Notitia regionum* mentions that a Phrygianum stood in the fourteenth district. One of the many inscriptions (the first dating from A.D. 160) refers to a taurobolium celebrated in the area "ex imperio Matris deum" by L. Aemilius Carpus who "vires excepit et a Vaticano transtulit."[152] Although other inscriptions witness to the fact that the taurobolia were celebrated until about A.D. 390 (but not in the period of continuous Christian activity in the area during the building of the Basilica in the early fourth century), the placement of the Phrygianum cannot be determined since none of the inscriptions were found *in situ*. It may have been located immediately to the south of St. Peter's, for a number of reliefs and inscriptions referring to the Phrygian divinities have been located on foundations in this area.[153] The last inscription (dated July 19, A.D. 324) to be found was located in 1949 in the Piazza S. Pietro, 1 m. north of the statue of Peter and 2.5 m. beneath the pavement.[154] Even if the Phrygianum, or Temple of Apollo (*if* this is how the Phrygianum is referred to in the *Liber Pontificalis*) cannot be located exactly, surely it stood somewhere within the Vatican area.

Carlo Cecchelli is of the opinion that the Temple of Apollo was the present rotunda of St. Andrea, immediately to the south of the present church (Plate 20). He mentions that in an attempt to deal with the water problem beneath the Vatican, excavations were made which came upon a structure in the vicinity of what was considered to be the original site of the obelisk. The structure, which was identified as a tomb at the time of the excavations, was dated in the second century. Cecchelli contends that it was not built in the second century, that it was not a tomb, and that it may have been the "templum Apollonis."[155] He further suggests that Caligula or Claudius placed the obelisk beside it because in Egypt the obelisk may have been associated in some way with a solar symbol. It is defensible to believe, he adds, that Constantine left the structure standing, instead of destroying it along with a great number of other buildings with pagan associations, because this emperor had come out of a solar faith and this structure, standing beside the Basilica, might have served to symbolize his conversion from faith in Apollo Sol to his new faith in Sol Novus (Christ).[156] This view is doubtful, for there is a funerary inscription on the base of the structure which shows it was not a temple but a tomb.

Even less tenable is the suggestion made by Jérôme Carcopino[157] that the "templum Apollonis" was located in mausoleum *M* (Plate 23). He estimates that this structure, approximately 2 m. long, 1.5 m. wide, and 2 m. high, dates from about A.D. 210 to 230. Sometime between the building of the mausoleum and its partial destruction around A.D. 320, the owners became Christian—a number of the paintings have Christian motifs: a fisherman, a shepherd with a sheep on his shoulder, and a figure of Christ as a sun god figure. It would be natural, continues Carcopino, for a

149. Duchesne, *Le Liber Pontificalis*, Vol. I, Part I, p. 64.

150. In *Il Vaticano nel 1944*, pp. 16, 17.

151. Duchesne, *Le Liber Pontificalis*, Vol. I, Part I, pp. 119, 120, 150, 176. Compare von Gerkan, "Kritische Studien," p. 30. Even if Attis was popularly worshiped as a moon god rather than a sun god, the error might still have been made.

152. *CIL*, Vol. XIII, Number 1751. The text is reproduced in *Esplorazioni*, p. 14 (see also figs. 2, 3); and Toynbee and Perkins, *The Shrine of St. Peter*, pp. 6, and 18n12.

153. See Guarducci, *The Tomb of St. Peter*, p. 51.

154. *Esplorazioni*, p. 15.

155. *Il Tempo* (January 31, 1950), p. 2.

156. Cecchelli, "L'Obelisco Vaticano," pp. 66, 67. He also maintained that the present obelisk in the Piazza S. Pietro is not the one originally in Nero's circus; this monument is still to be found. A more recent study by Castagnoli, "Il circo di Nerone in Vaticano," pp. 97–121, demonstrates that the foundations of the obelisk in the Piazza S. Pietro have been found in the area traditionally noted to the south of the Basilica. Thus this area is now surely to be identified as the "Gai et Neroni principium."

157. Carcopino, *Études*, pp. 150–57.

later age to have labeled this tomb a "templum Apollonis" as a result of mistaking this figure of Christ (drawn from the context of the artist's pagan background) for that of Apollo.

The traditional scene for the martyrdom of Peter was the Circus of Nero. It was believed until recently that the southern foundation wall of the Basilica built by Constantine rested upon the northern wall of this circus.[158] The recent excavations, however, failed to uncover any sign of this latter wall.[159] The error is easily traced to Giacomo Grimaldi.[160] In addition to the fact that his assumption was based upon a preconceived idea that the obelisk was located on the spina of the circus (which may well have been the case) what this early

seventeenth-century writer thought were the walls of the circus were really the substructures of the foundation walls of the Constantinian Basilica itself. Although it is true that the walls of the circus were not found, this does not mean *ipso facto* that the Basilica was not built over the area that had been previously occupied by the circus. The stands bordering the circus could have been made of wood, or perhaps there were no walls at all and the people simply viewed the spectacles from the Vatican hillside.[161] However, some evidence that the Circus was in the *vicinity* of the Basilica was found in the process of the excavations. Tomb *A* (Plate 23), the property of C(aius) Popilius Heracla, bore a long inscription over the door which contained in part: "Vti monvmentvm mihi faciatis in Vatic ad Circvm ivxta monvmentvm Vlpi Narcissi."[162] Heracla ordered his heirs to build his mausoleum near that of Ulpius Narcissus "in Vaticano ad Circam." It may be that this tomb, the farthest from the area *P*, was the closest to the circus. The *exact* location is not known and may never be known. While the circus was omitted in the *Notitia* of A.D. 334 and the *Curiosum* of A.D. 357, it is probable that it was near a necropolis, for it is recorded in Aelius Lampridius XXII that when Elagabalus converted the circus into a track for racing elephants, his widening of the circus destroyed part of a cemetery.[163] Another

158. Lietzmann, *Petrus und Paulus in Rom*, 2d ed., pp. 207–8; *La Civiltà Cattolica*, LXXXVI (1935), 254 f. Marucchi, *Éléments d'Archéologie chrétienne*, 2d ed., III, 110, defends this view (which is repeated in the *Manuale di Archeologia cristiana* [Rome, 1923], p. 148), in which he says of the circus, "il existe encore quelques restes des murs." An excellent bibliography of the works of those who perpetuated this fiction is prepared by Giuseppe Nicholosi, "Questioni nuove intorno alla Basilica costantiniana in Vaticano," in *Il Vaticano nel 44*, pp. 201–3. It is difficult to understand how the following assured statement could appear as late as 1957: Werner Kellner, "The Search for Peter's Tomb," pp. 106–7, says that the stones for St. Peter's "came from the old circus of Caligula, the north arena wall was included in the foundations of the Church, and the south end of the Church extended into the race course."

159. Ferrua, "Nuove Scoperte sotto S. Pietro," p. 433; Kirschbaum, *Die Gräber*, p. 14; *Esplorazioni*, I, 16, 17; De Visscher, in *L'Antiquité classique*, pp. 117–20; Boulet, "À propos des Fouilles," p. 386n1; Carcopino, *Études*, p. 159.

160. *Codex Ambros*. A. 178, as quoted in Hülsen, "Il circo di Nerone al Vaticano," p. 272: "Perche il muro perimetrale e il doppio colonnato verso mezzodi erano fondati su tre grandi muri del circo di Gaio e di Nerone, i quali non valevano a reggere il peso del tetto e delle colonne. Le pareti del circo essendo di mattoni e spesse palmi 13 [or about 2.9 m.] avrebbero certo sostenuto il peso del tetto e delle colonne se fossero state fondate sulla solida argilla; al contrario erano fondate su terra mossa." Grimaldi was followed by Maffeo Vegio and others (see Kirschbaum, *Die Gräber*, p. 224n7). See Pliny, *Historiae Naturalis* XXXVI.14, ed. Brotier, VIII, 4207–13: "tertius [obelisk] est Romae in Vaticano Gai et Neronis principum circo"; Suetonius, *Caligula* LIV, *Claudius* XXI, *Nero* XXII in *Suetonius*, trans. Rolfe, I, 486, 487; II, 40, 41, 120, 121; and Tacitus, *Annals*, XIV.14, trans. Jackson, IV, 128, 129.

161. Von Gerkan, "Kritische Studien," p. 29, points out that the Circus of Maxentius on the Via Appia had no walls. This same view is expressed by Michelangelo Cagiano de Azevédo, "L'Origine della Necropoli Vaticana secondo Tacito," pp. 575–77; Toynbee and Perkins, *The Shrine of St. Peter*, p. 10. Gavin Townsend, "The Circus of Nero," pp. 216–18, mentions that if the structures were of wood, they would have disappeared without a trace. To support this, he cites the wooden theater of Augustus by the Tiber, or Nero's wooden amphitheater mentioned in Suetonius, *Nero* XII.1, trans. Rolfe, II, 102, 103. See also Tacitus, *Annals* XIV.13, trans. Jackson, IV, 128, 129, and Dio Cassius LIX.10:5 in *Dio's Roman History*, trans. Cary, VIII, 290, 291.

162. The text is found in: Marrou, *DACL*, Vol. XV, Part 2, p. 3299; Toynbee and Perkins, *The Shrine of St. Peter*, p. 19n28; de Visscher, in *L'Antiquité classique*, pp. 121–26.

163. It is probable, however, that the race course mentioned in connection with Elagabalus is an extension of the Gaianum and not the Circus of Nero. The cemetery in question, then, is not that beneath the Vatican but that newly discovered (1957) cemetery of the first century approximately 300 m.

PLATE 21   The obelisk, in its original location, as it appeared in an early work by D. Fontana (*Della Trasportazione dell'-Obelisco Vaticano et delle Fabbriche di N. S. P. Sisto V*). To the rear of the obelisk is the mausoleum which served in that period as the sacristy of St. Peter (Cecchelli, "L'Obelisco Vaticano," p. 62).

explanation for the inclusion of the term "circus" in the inscription of Heracla (in view of the failure to locate the walls) might be made on the grounds that even in

his day the circus no longer existed in fact, but the name lingered on to identify the general area. This phenomenon is met with frequently in the names of streets in New York City: Canal Street marks the site of a canal that no longer exists; Wall Street recalls the former position of a wall which served as the northern border of the town located on the tip of Manhattan; Maiden Lane refers to a long forgotten footpath used by the women of the colonial town as they went down to the river to wash clothes. The names have lingered on, used every day by thousands who have no knowledge of the original topographical meaning. The proposal by Toynbee and Perkins is overly imaginative when they say that perhaps "Heracla was a circus-fan"[164] or that the circus was "certainly still in use as a place of public entertainment when the tombs were going up."[165] Townsend's conclusions are convincing: 1) Caligula put the Egyptian obelisk (discussed below) in his gardens, which became the center of his race course; 2) Claudius may then have built some further structures in the area to house his animals and the like; 3) Nero further delimited the area for his races, but it is *possible* that he did not build any permanent structures, such as stands. In this case no permanent road may have been needed, or perhaps *allowed*.[166]

The question of the Obelisk of Nero is related both to the problem of the location of the Circus of Nero and to the burial of Peter. In the first instance, it has been commonly believed that the obelisk was situated on the spina of the Circus as was the case of the Circus Maximus, the largest arena in Rome. If this is true the circus must have been in part under the area now covered

---

northeast of the Basilica. See Kirschbaum, *Die Gräber*, pp. 44, 45. Toynbee and Perkins, *The Shrine of St. Peter*, p. 10, cites *Scriptores Historiae Augustae, Vita Elagabalus* XXIII. See also Dio Cassius, LIX. 14, in *Dio's Roman History*, trans. Cary, VIII, 290, 291.

164. *The Shrine of St. Peter*, p. 10.

165. *Ibid.*, p. 20n33.

166. In this same note (*ibid.*), Toynbee and Perkins maintain that there *had* to be "a road immediately to the south of the excavations." Heussi, *Die römische Petrustradition*, p. 51, is much too positive in his statement that the Vatican cemetery was in the circus, and the circus was in the gardens of Nero. See Ruysschaert, *Réflexions sur les Fouilles vaticanes*, p. 42.

PLATE 22   The raising of the obelisk in its new location in the square in front of St. Peter's.
This drawing also appeared in the early work by Fontana (Cecchelli, "L'Obelisco Vaticano,"
p. 65).

by the Church of St. Peter and its axis parallel to it.
Second, one version of the *Acts of Peter* (A.D. c. 170)
explains that Peter is buried "ad locum qui vocatur
Naumachiae, iuxta obeliscum Neronis in montem" or,
in another version, "apud palatium neronianum iuxta
obeliscum inter duas metas."

It is known that the obelisk was moved by Domenico
Fontana in 1586 (Plates 21, 22), under a commission
given by Sixtus V, from a place immediately to the south
of the present church and to the east of the rotunda of
St. Andrea (Plate 20 indicates the spot by a small black
dot) to the Piazza S. Pietro. According to the opinion
of most, the structure had been placed in the position
where it stood prior to 1586 when it was first imported
from Egypt; it had not been moved in antiquity from
some other location.[167] This appears to pose a problem:

167. *The Shrine of St. Peter*, p. 12; Kirschbaum, *Die Gräber*,
p. 14.

If the obelisk moved in 1586 is the one mentioned by Pliny as standing within the circus and if it stood on the spina, which is the natural place for it, "there would have been no room between the outer wall of the Circus and the recently excavated tombs for the road of which the remains were found when the south-east corner of the present church was built."[168]

It is argued further by Toynbee and Perkins that if the obelisk was on the spina, then the outer *walls* of the circus would have been found under the Basilica. But this does not allow for the very possible and even probable conclusion reached by many authorities, mentioned above, that the outer walls were not of the permanent stone type.

Boulet's suggestion, that the obelisk may have been moved in the time of Elagabalus from a point further south,[169] is not credible, for the foundations of the obelisk have recently been located to the east of the rotunda of St. Andrea (Plate 20).[170] If he had been correct, the spina would have been an undetermined distance further south than has usually been thought, and the stands also, if they ever existed at all, would have been further south than the area which has been excavated.

Two studies concerning the Vatican obelisk are available, in addition to the latest one by Ferdinando

Castagnoli, one by Carlo Cecchelli and another by Giuseppe Zucchetti.[171] In brief, the main questions center on the interpretation of a notice in the *Historiae Naturalis* (A.D. 77) of Pliny, which states that in addition to the Egyptian obelisks brought to Rome by Augustus and set up in the Campus Martius and the Campus Maximus, "tertius est Romae in Vaticano Gai et Neronis principum circo—ex omnibus unus omnino fractus est in molitione [one edition of Pliny published in the seventeenth century reads "imitatione"]—quem fecerat Sesosidis filius Nencoreus. Eiusdem remanet et alius centum cubitorum quem post caecitatem visu reddito ex oraculo soli sacravit."[172] The question remains: Which of the obelisks mentioned by Pliny was moved in 1586 from the south side of the church and now stands in St. Peter's Square? For this study, the comparison of the meaning of the word "circus" as used by Pliny ("in Vaticano Gai et Neronis principum circo") and as used by C(aius) Popilius Heracla ("in Vatic[ano] ad circum") is important. If the obelisk which now stands in the Vatican is the one mentioned by Pliny as being in the circus in the first century and *if* this obelisk was not moved in antiquity from another location to the place from which it was moved in the sixteenth century[173] (which is not now seen as a matter for serious consideration), then we may be fairly sure that the circus was in the immediate vicinity of the present Church of St. Peter. One further complication

---

168. Toynbee and Perkins, *The Shrine of St. Peter*; p. 12. There is the possibility, however, that the sixteenth-century excavators were as much in error in their identification of what had been found as they were in their identification of the walls of the Constantinian Basilica as the walls of the circus. Although Toynbee and Perkins disparage the view of von Gerkan (p. 20*n*33), it is possible that there was no road to the south of the grounds. If this road did run parallel to the cemetery on its north side, this would solve the problem of the placement of the obelisk on the spina of the circus.

In this connection it may again be emphasized that some tombs, e.g., tomb O, did have stairs leading down from the hillside above, which at least makes plausible the suggestion that the road was above to the north of the cemetery and not below to the south. On the other hand, it must be mentioned that the tombs are oriented north to south and open to the south.

169. "À propos des Fouilles," p. 386*n*1.

170. Castagnoli, "Il circo di Nerone in Vaticano," pp. 97–121.

171. Cecchelli, "L'Obelisco vaticano," pp. 53–71; notice the excellent bibliography covering the main studies on this problem on pp. 57, 58. Zucchetti, in *Ecclesia*, pp. 523–26. In addition, the three principal views concerning the identification of the obelisk are briefly but carefully reviewed in Toynbee and Perkins, *The Shrine of St. Peter*, pp. 20–22*n*34.

172. *Ibid.*, p. 20*n*34, offers the following translation: "there is a third [obelisk] in Rome in the Circus of the Emperors Gaius and Nero—it is the only one of all of them to have been broken during transport—which was made by Nencoreus, son of Sesosis. There remains another obelisk of the same Nencoreus, a hundred cubits high, which he dedicated to the Sun on the instructions of an oracle after regaining his sight from blindness."

173. Kirschbaum, *Die Gräber*, p. 14: "Immerhin ist die Errichtung eines Obelisken keine Kleinigkeit, und man ist gern geneigt, anzunehmen, dass der vatikanische Obelisk vor dem Eingriff Sixtus V. noch an seiner ursprünglichen Stelle stand."

is suggested by the fact that it is not known exactly how the word "circus" was used by Pliny. For, as Toynbee and Perkins point out,

when Livy speaks of the Temples of Juno and Diana "in circo Flaminio" (xl. 52, 2–3), he does not mean that they stood within the Circus, but in its immediate neighbourhood (in fact, they stood within the Porticus Octaviae, a hundred yards to the south of the Circus). Similarly, Pliny could well have described a funerary obelisk set up by the roadside near the Circus of Gaius and Nero . . . as being "in circo."[174]

In any event the literary evidence that the grave of Peter lies "iuxta obeliscum Neronis" is too uncertain to be used to support a reasonable claim that Peter is buried in the cemetery located on the Vatican hill.

It must appear obvious from the discussion above that not one of those "landmarks" mentioned in the literary sources as indicating the approximate place of the burial of Peter in the Vatican is of great value. The Via Cornelia cannot be located; it may have been either north or south of the tombs. Undoubtedly, the Terebinth[175] was originally a reference to a tree that stood in the Vatican area. When the particular tree disappeared the name was transferred to the Obelisk of Nero. The position of the Naumachy is only approximate and, as the above discussion indicates, the exact location of the circus, is still uncertain. Since the literary documents fail to limit the burial place of Peter more precisely than the general "Vatican area," it is now necessary to focus attention upon the cemetery located beneath the present Church of St. Peter.

In a study which is specifically concerned with the burial place of Peter, it is not necessary to discuss the pagan mausolea in detail.[176] Some mention of them must be made, however, in order to show the geographical and temporal relationship of the remainder of the cemetery to the area which contains the alleged tomb of Peter. The discovery of a pagan cemetery (except for mausoleum M of the Julians adorned with Christian mosaics[177]) beneath the church was not a complete surprise, for its existence had been known since the sixteenth century.[178] It is now surmised that the cemetery existed beyond the limits of the present extensive excavations, west to the Church of St. Stephen and east as far, perhaps, as the Tiber. As may be seen in Plate 23 the mausolea are grouped in two files A to Q and ψ to R. The existence of tombs A to L was rediscovered during the building of the pillars of the "Grotte vecchie"; H and I had been known since the early seventeenth century as a result of the building of the eastern foundations of the cupola. In this same period, when the western columns of Bernini's baldacchino were built, R and S came to light, but in this case, as in those above, no formal explorations were undertaken.[179] Tomb T was known to Maffeo Vegio; and Δ was discovered in the court of St. Peter's in 1574 by Tiberio Alfarano. Another tomb,

---

174. *The Shrine of St. Peter*, p. 21n34.3. See also Toynbee, "The Shrine of St. Peter and Its Setting," pp. 1–26.

175. The *Pistacia terebinthus* is a small tree which is found in southern Europe and around most of the Mediterranean. When the stem is cut, there is a liquid exudation called Scio or Cyprus turpentine.

176. Discussions of the mausolea are to be found in *Esplorazioni*, I, 29–91, Vol. II, figs. I–XLI; Toynbee and Perkins, *The Shrine of St. Peter*, pp. 24–124; Klauser, *Die römische Petrustradition*, pp. 38–40; Kirschbaum, *Die Gräber*, pp. 18–45.

Earlier discussions of the tombs include: Ferrua, "Nelle Grotto di S. Pietro," pp. 358–65, 424–33; and "Nuove Scoperte sotto S. Pietro," pp. 73–86, 228–41; Josi, "Gli Scavi nelle sacre Grotte Vaticane," pp. 188–99; Kirschbaum, "Gli Scavi sotto la Basilica di S. Pietro," pp. 544–57; O'Callaghan, "The Vatican Excavations and the Tomb of St. Peter," pp. 70–87; Speier, "Die neuen Ausgrabungen unter der Peterskirche in Rom," pp. 199–218; *Time*, March 27, 1950, p. 70; *Life*, March 27, 1950, pp. 65–85; Carcopino, *Études*, pp. 134–68. The tombs in the immediate vicinity of the most important area are described by Prandi, *La zona*, chap. I.

Hans Ulrich Instinsky, "Christen und Heiden im Umkreis des Petrusgrabes," p. 588, makes the thought-provoking but unlikely suggestion that many of the seemingly pagan tombs and sarcophagi *could* be Christian. First of all, what criteria were chosen to make the decision in each case? Do we have enough examples of early Christian graves *to be able* to decide? Could it not be that some of the pre-Constantinian sarcophagi, deemed pagan, were "disguised" by Christians for the sake of safety? He cites an example of this in the pagan decoration of the sarcophagus of L. Aurelius Prosenes buried on the Via Labicana.

177. See Guarducci, *The Tomb of St. Peter*, pp. 74–76 and Cullmann, *Peter*, p. 143.

178. Lietzmann, *Petrus und Paulus in Rom*, 2d ed., pp. 191–208, 304–10; *Esplorazioni*, I, 23–27.

179. Lietzmann, *Petrus und Paulus in Rom*, 2d ed., p. 194.

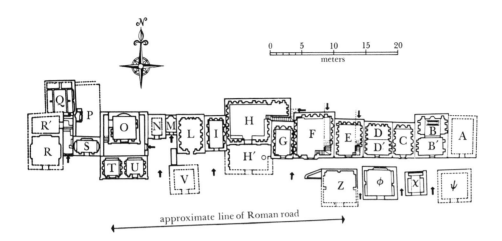

PLATE 23 The Vatican cemetery. The dotted lines indicate suggested reconstructions and the arrows indicate the entrances to the tombs or the tomb areas (Toynbee and Perkins, *The Shrine of St. Peter*, fig. 3).

ε, was found in the Piazza S. Pietro in 1616 by Grimaldi. Finally, *N* and *O* were also known in the building of the new Basilica in the sixteenth century.

The mausolea are all similar,[180] all (except for *M*, the mausoleum of the Julians) of pagan origin and composed of one large room. These are the mausolea not of noblemen, but of freedmen. Socially, they did not rank, but economically they were able to build beautiful tombs for themselves and their families. Each of the mausolea is covered, and many are served by a terrace or cult area, such as *B'*, *D'*, *H'* and *R'* (Plate 23). Many of the tombs are richly decorated, indicating the status of those who originally built them. But in many cases the mosaics and paintings were later covered over and replaced by decoration of greatly inferior quality, denoting that the last occupants did not have the means of the earlier owners.[181] Most of the mausolea have a number of niches, designed to receive urns containing the ashes of the dead. The older tombs show signs that at some time *after* they were built, provision was made for arcosolia to accommodate inhumations. The newer tombs indicate that they had been built to provide facilities for both types of burial. A number of the tombs were found with the titulus still *in situ*, as for example, over the door of the Tomb of the Caetennii

(*L* in Plate 23). Both files of tombs, oriented north to south and opening to the south, lie approximately along the line of the apse of the Basilica. The development was certainly from the east to the west. The *Esplorazioni* concludes its discussion of these mausolea by saying that "è facile concludere che i cristiani de sec. II e III veneravano il sepolcro del Principe degli Apostoli in mezzo ad una necropoli essenzialmente pagana."[182]

Two points should certainly be of interest to us here:

1) It is freely admitted that the mausolea are, with one exception, pagan, not Christian, in origin.

2) Christians of the second and third centuries venerated the alleged tomb of Peter in the midst of this pagan metropolis.

The *Esplorazioni* dates the mausolea "secondo secolo più o meno avanzato,"[183] but there has been some discussion concerning a more exact dating. Ferrua dates tomb *C* between A.D. 174 and 225; *A* and *B* (A.D. c. 150) are earlier than *C* but after *D* to *T*. The *Esplorazioni* dates the tombs in the area of the alleged sepulture of Peter as follows: tomb *L* from the end of the second century (p. 30); *M* and *N* a bit later; and *O* somewhat earlier (A.D. c. 120–30); *S* from the middle of the second

---

180. See the discussion of the cemetery in general in *Esplorazioni*, I, 25–27.

181. Kirschbaum, *Die Gräber*, p. 45.

182. *Esplorazioni*, I, 27.

183. *Ibid.*, I, 25; Ferrua, "Nuove Scoperte sotto S. Pietro," pp. 236–41.

half of the second century (p. 74) about the same time as *R* and *R'* (p. 88) and *Q*[184] (pp. 103, 104). This same work finds no Christian traces in the mausolea before the third century.[185] Von Gerkan,[186] followed by Klauser,[187] comes to approximately the same conclusions, depending for his dating upon:

1) the relationship of the facilities for incineration and those for inhumation,

2) wall construction,

3) inscriptions,

4) the constructions of the façades of the mausolea,

5) paintings and decorations, and

6) the various seals which must be considered but which may *not* be taken alone.

Hjalmar Torp is criticized by Klauser for his late dating of the mausolea (A.D. 180–230), because he ignores the evidence of the seals completely[188] and because he is too dependent upon the Van Deman method of determining the date of a monument by brick measure and the like.[189]

In conclusion, it may be said that the Vatican necropolis was used for a period of about two hundred years, from about A.D. 120 to the period of the building of the Basilica of Constantine or about 333. By that time when the tombs were fast becoming inaccessible and all of the available places for sepultures were filled, including the spaces beneath the mosaic and marble

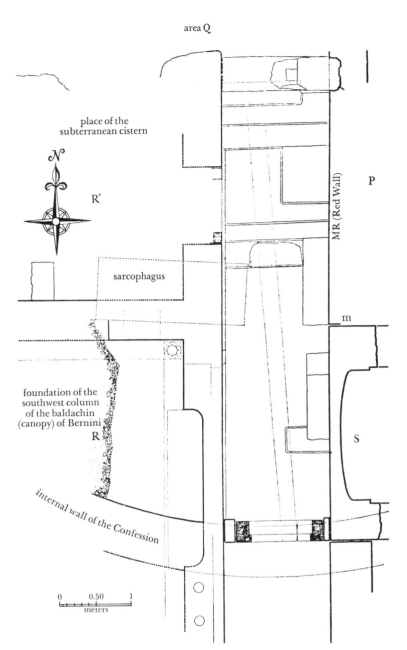

PLATE 24   A plan of mausoleum *R*, area *R'*, and the adjacent Clivus, or sloping passageway (*Esplorazioni*, Vol. I, fig. 54).

floors, burials were placed side by side above the floors and covered over, necessitating the raising of the floors and the doorsills.

184. Prandi, *La zona*, pp. 8–15, determines, *O* was built in the period of Hadrian, A.D. c. 135. (See Toynbee and Perkins, *The Shrine of St. Peter*, pp. 32–33; *S* is later.)

185. Kirschbaum, *Die Gräber*, pp. 26–36. For example, tomb *Z* (the "Tomb of the Egyptians") contains a grave which is possibly Christian. The inscription no longer contains the name and date, but does include the word "deposita," which is almost exclusively Christian in use. In mausolea *F* (Tomb of the Caetennii) is found the probable Christian burial of Aemili(a)e Gorgoniae. The word "deposita" appears again in the burial of Valerinus Vasatulus in tomb *H*. Christian influences are also found in *M*, which is termed by Kirschbaum "the only purely Christian one of all the so far known mausolea of the Vatican necropolis." Compare von Gerkan, "Kritische Studien," p. 35.

186. *Ibid.*, pp. 32–35.

187. *Die römische Petrustradition*, p. 39.

188. Torp, "The Vatican Excavations," pp. 30–44.

189. See Van Deman, "Methods," pp. 230–51.

More important for this study than the placement of the obelisk or the circus, the Terebinth, the Naumachy, or the Via Cornelia, and more important than the predominantly pagan mausolea (which, it is agreed, arose in the second century) is the question of whether there is any evidence that there was a first-century Christian grave in this area, a grave which plausibly might be identified as that of Peter.

Before examining the important area *P*, containing the Aedicula which for approximately eighteen hundred years has been venerated as marking the grave of Peter, let us examine the immediate vicinity somewhat more carefully.

Tomb *S* (Plates 23 and 24) is described in the *Esplorazioni* as partially destroyed.[190] Originally, it was about 3.40 m. by 1.86 m., and, while the majority of the spaces in the mausoleum were intended for inhumations, there was some space set aside to accommodate incinerations. In 1626 a few post-Constantinian burials which had been lowered beneath the floor of the Basilica were discovered in *S*. A sarcophagus was also found which contained the bodies of an adult and a child.[191] From what was discovered in the recent excavations together with what was reported by Ubaldini concerning his excavations in 1626, the mausoleum has been dated about A.D. 150.[192] It is surely later than *O* and somewhat earlier than *R* and *R'* which are discussed next.

Area *R* (Plate 24) was damaged a number of times by: 1) Constantine in the building of the foundations for the apse of the Basilica, 2) the lowering of a number of sarcophagi into the area from above, during the post-Constantinian period,[193] and 3) the construction of the southwest column of the baldacchino of Gianlorenzo Bernini[194] around 1626. Tomb *R* contains a few niches

for incinerations, but principally it was built to accommodate arcosolia for inhumations. At one point the tomb was found to be too small, and a number of burials were lowered beneath the floor. One of the sarcophagi which had been lowered from above through the floor of the Basilica contains an inscription dating from A.D. 382. In origin, *R* is a bit later than *S*, somewhere between A.D. 150 and 200.[195]

The theory as outlined by Margherita Guarducci to the effect that a graffito incised on three layers of brick to the right of the entrance of area *R* is the oldest witness to the proximity of the apostolic sepulcher is unconvincing.[196] The editors of the *Esplorazioni* did not emphasize its importance,[197] and indeed it is far from proved that the graffito was done by a Christian. The drawing of the fish which appears above the inscription may have been drawn at any time in the second or early third centuries and may have been pagan in origin.[198] In any event, the statement is unjustified that there is "la presenza sul sepolcro *R* di altri graffiti certamente cristiani."[199]

Area *R'*, of which only fragments of the walls remain, is later than and physically and functionally related to *R*, and its pavement level is a little higher than that of *R*. The area, built before the Red Wall, or Muro Rosso (MR), was probably a solarium or a space in which cultic meals were celebrated[200] and most probably was not used for burials—although there may have been a few niches around the walls to accommodate urns. In the northeast corner was found a cistern constructed, undoubtedly, for the use of this and perhaps other mausolea.

Area *Q* (Plate 25), immediately to the north of *R'*

190. *Esplorazioni*, I, 69–77.

191. Lietzmann, *Petrus und Paulus in Rom*, 2d ed., pp. 305–6; *Esplorazioni*, I, 74.

192. Kirschbaum, *Die Gräber*, p. 222, suggests A.D. 125–35.

193. One of these sarcophagi is decorated with roughhewn figures of Peter and Paul.

194. *Esplorazioni*, I, 79–91. Prandi, *La zona*, p. 16, admits that his investigation of *R* has led to results very similar to those of the *Esplorazioni*.

195. Kirschbaum, *Die Gräber*, p. 222, suggests A.D. c. 135.

196. *I Graffiti*, II, 415–40. See especially pp. 435–40; See also *The Tomb of St. Peter*, pp. 136–44.

197. *Esplorazioni*, I, 103. Compare Carcopino, *Études*, p. 178n2.

198. *I Graffiti*, II, 433. See also Guarducci, *The Tomb of St. Peter*, p. 142.

199. *I Graffiti*, II, 440.

200. See Klauser, *Die römische Petrustradition*, p. 43. Prandi, *La zona*, pp. 17–18 and figs. 19, 22, and 23, is unquestionably correct that *R* and *R'* are not of one build and that *R'* was constructed after *R*.

(Plate 24), has been called "l'area per inumazione."[201] The south wall of area Q (the wall on the right in Plate 25) does not belong to Q but is the north wall of R', and thus Q is somewhat later than R'. The west wall (at the bottom of Plate 25) was almost completely destroyed when the baldacchino of Bernini was constructed. The north wall is 28 cm. thick as is the south wall (the north wall of R').[202] The east wall, which is the best preserved, lies between areas P and Q and bears slightly to the west from the point where it intersects with the Red Wall (MR).[203] The area, thus delimited, is 3.97 m. (east to west) by 4.63 m. (north to south). The floor was of mosaic, some of which still remains at various points. At the sides beneath the flooring were found two files of burials, oriented north to south and east to west, six in all, two to a side; all were used for inhumations. Above these empty spaces and related to them were corresponding arcosolia. The most important of these arcosolia—which is, incidentally, the best preserved—is the one situated immediately to the right of the doorway to area Q (upper right in Plate 25) and immediately behind the Aedicula.[204] At the time of Constantine, this arcosolium was cut off and left filled with a wall structure. This theory is maintained because the "fill" differs from the material used in the construction of the arch and because the arcosolium rests on the large yellow tiles covering the empty space below (Plate 25). The center of the area (1.8 m. by 3.5 m.) was not utilized at the time when Q was in use. It was, however, almost completely destroyed later during the construction of the "half ring" Confessio and especially when the sarcophagi were lowered from the Basilica above. It is stated by the authors of the *Esplorazioni* that no trace was found there of niches or urns (as was the case in the other areas of the cemetery);[205] this has led a few to conclude that Q was built and used by Christians. This theory

PLATE 25 A view of area Q from above and toward area P (*Esplorazioni*, Vol. I, Plate F).

was at one time elaborated upon by José Ruysschaert, who, noticing that the arcosolia were empty when the area was excavated, proposed that when the Basilica of Constantine was under construction, area Q was emptied systematically, and the remains reburied in area P.[206] Four such graves (α, δ, ε, μ) were thus moved

---

201. *Esplorazioni*, I, 93–104.

202. This *may* indicate that both walls were constructed by the same builder at approximately the same time.

203. See below, pp. 177–78.

204. For further particulars concerning the construction and the peculiarities of that which remains, see *Esplorazioni*, I, 100–4.

205. This conclusion is challenged by Ferrua, "La Storia," p. 22.

206. *Réflexions*, pp. 32–35, shows that at one time Ruysschaert held that the area was built by Christians "pour servir de nouveau champ commun de sépulture réservé aux évêques de Rome." See also Kirschbaum, "Das Petrusgrab," p. 408, and *Die Gräber*, p. 134.

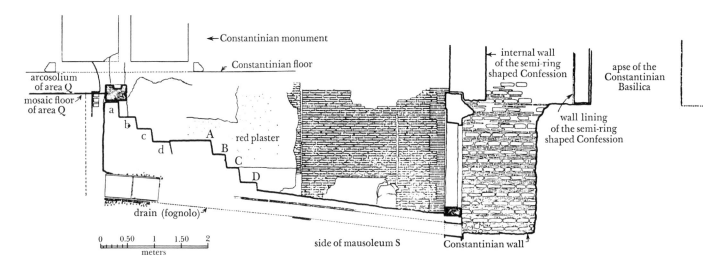

PLATE 26 A north-to-south section of the Clivus, looking east toward tomb *S* and area *P* (*Esplorazioni*, Vol. I, fig. 65).

and are to be found now, he believed, above grave *β* on the south and above grave *λ* on the north. This theory does explain the close relationship between areas *Q* and *P*: the same level of mosaic pavement, the same character of the burial field, and other similarities. Nevertheless, one must be mindful always that simply because the theory is convenient does not mean that it is correct. And in addition to the lack of evidence to warrant such a conclusion, there are good reasons to believe that it is not true.[207] He was further attracted to the theory because, at the time that he wrote, exactly eleven graves had been excavated in area *P* and there are exactly eleven early bishops who are, notes the *Liber Pontificalis*, buried "near the body of Peter." Therefore, he concluded that the eleven graves were indeed those of early bishops.[208] However, this theory is destroyed in the recent discovery by Adriano Prandi of further graves in the area, the type of grave found in area *P* hardly would have been provided by the fourth-century Church for their early bishops.[209] Furthermore,

that this area was constructed by Christians is not at all certain, and the assumption has been denied emphatically by von Gerkan.[210]

After this brief "look" at the cult and burial areas in the immediate vicinity of area *P*, it still remains for us, before going on to the area of *P* itself, to mention the Clivus or sloping passageway which is found between *R* and *R'*, beginning at a point even with the façade of *S* on the south and proceeding to area *Q* on the north (Plates 24 and 26).[211]

According to the *Esplorazioni* the area must be described as follows: for the most part the Clivus, which is paved with cement, is 1.47 m. wide and rises first gently and then more rapidly to the north (Plate 26). The eastern wall of the Clivus is known as

207. See below, pp. 174–77.

208. Ruysschaert, *Réflexions*, p. 33.

209. Others have been attracted by the theory that papal tombs are found in area *P*. Among them is Carcopino, *Études*,

pp. 181, 182. Karl Busch, "Das Petrusgrab," p. 316, identifies grave *θ* with that of Linus. Luigi Berra, "Lo Sviluppo architettonico della Tomba di S. Pietro," p. 93n5, is more hesitant.

210. "Kritische Studien," p. 196: "Q hat nur Bestattungsgräber, ohne deshalb unbedingt christlich sein zu müssen, denn nach Hadrian wurde die Inhumation wieder üblich." Lemerle, "La Publication des Fouilles," p. 212, joins von Gerkan in this opinion.

211. *Esplorazioni*, I, 94–97, 102–4, 107.

the Red Wall, or Muro Rosso (MR),[212] the first part of which extends from the southern tip of *S* to the entrance of *Q*. On the west side of the Clivus was attached a stairway (each step topped with travertine) which enabled one to proceed between *R* and *S* and into area *Q*. In the opinion of the *Esplorazioni* wall *R'* is later than the Clivus, since it was built to receive the stairway. As may be seen in Plate 26, there is a landing in the middle of the staircase in front of the door to *R'*. Originally the stairway began at the level of the present landing after a rather steep incline, and the first three steps were simply a later addition, making entrance to *R'* easier. The archeologists who prepared the *Esplorazioni* conclude, however, that the Clivus, areas *Q*, and *R*, *R'* were built at the same time.[213]

In the construction of *Q* it was noticed that a drain would be necessary to carry off the water from this uncovered area. To accomplish this a well was constructed at the point where *Q* and the Clivus met (Plate 26).[214] Beneath the Clivus, at the base of this well, was constructed a drain leading southeast, which carried the water away to the northern wall of *S* where it then proceeded to the east.[215] The drain at the northern end was constructed by placing three building tiles in the shape of a triangle, but toward the southern end the construction was in the form of a square.[216]

After the Clivus, the drain and *R* and *R'* were constructed, MR was built but "certamente il muro rosso appartiene a un atto costruttivo diverso da quella delle strutture adiacenti; e anzi fu l'ultimo, in ordine di tempo."[217] MR formed the western wall of area *P*. It

---

212. From this point the Red Wall will be referred to as MR. The wall derives its name from the decided red color of the stucco used in its decoration.

213. Compare von Gerkan, "Kritische Studien," p. 36–38, and Toynbee and Perkins, *The Shrine of St. Peter*, p. 59n7. This conclusion has been challenged by Prandi, *La zona*, pp. 41–56, who agrees that the stairway between *A* and *D* is a bit later than *R'*, but built before *Q*. The older set of stairs (*a, b, c, d*) at the point where *Q* meets the Clivus, unrelated in time or function to *A* and *D* were also later than *R'* and earlier than *Q*.

214. Compare the later interpretation of Prandi, *La zona*, pp. 54–57.

215. Von Gerkan, "Kritische Studien," p. 37, doubts that the drain turned to the east at the northern wall of *S*.

216. *CIL*, Vol. XV, No. 401; a sixth tile was discovered by Prandi, *CIL*, Vol. XV, Nos. 1527, 1528. See *Esplorazioni*, I, 103; Ferrua, "A la Recherche," p. 41; Torp, "The Vatican Excavations," p. 41n62. See also O'Callaghan, "The Vatican Excavations and the Tomb of St. Peter."

217. Prandi, *La zona*, p. 57.

appears superficially to have been a single wall also serving as the eastern wall of area Q with a break at a point near the rear of the Aedicula—a break which the *Esplorazioni* explains as the result of the insertion of the shoulder of the door opening into Q.[218] Prandi without question has correctly interpreted that there is not one but two walls (the wall from the intersection and north, he calls *mq*). The wall *mq* is different from MR in direction and thickness. The function of MR was to separate the Clivus and the area to the east.[219]

If the various elements (Clivus, drain, Q, R, R', and MR) belonged to roughly one complex and were built at about the same time, then in the event that one element can be dated definitely, all can be dated at least approximately. Such a possible aid to dating the complex is found in the presence of five tiles (Plate 27) dated from the seals of Marcus Aurelius Caesar (A.D. 140–61) and Faustina Augusta (A.D. 147–75); thus between A.D. 147 and 161.[220]

One criticism of the *Esplorazioni* arises over the dating of the complex by means of these tiles; even though there seems to be little chance that five reused tiles would be found together, it is a possibility.[221] Torp has pointed out that the Memoria Apostolorum Ad Catacumbas was paved with tiles from the periods of Hadrian (A.D. 117–38) and of Severus (A.D. 222–35).[222] In addition, six tiles (which dated from a period between A.D. 60 and 93) were used above mausoleum *h'* (A.D. c. 200).[223] Lemerle attempts to explain away the possibility of using the tiles for purposes of dating by saying that they might have been sold to the builders

of MR years after they were made because of an over-supply of the dealer.[224] If we take this observation seriously, it must be said that if there were any delay at all, it would not have been more than a few years at the most.

The unity of the complex as stated by the authors of the *Esplorazioni* has been challenged by some to differing degrees. Torp takes the position that R and R' were built at about the same time,[225] but not with Q, and that the two sections of MR were not built at the same time.[226] The southern part of the wall was built with R, R' and was built to establish boundaries and to protect R' from the rising level of the earth to the east during the building of O and S (which he dates considerably later than do the *Esplorazioni* and Prandi). The northern part of MR is only the eastern wall of Q and was built later. The important implication of this is that if the two parts of the wall are of different *periods*, the Aedicula in area P (discussed at length below), which was built at the juncture of the two walls, must be posterior to both sections.[227] Torp further argues incorrectly on the basis of wall construction, and the like,[228] that S is to be dated around A.D. c. 200, R, R between A.D. 200 and 220, Q around A.D. 230, and the Aedicula in area P, which is the center of interest in the search for the grave of Peter, between A.D. 230 and 250. (Plate 28). He supports his late dating of Q by citing the fact that all burials in this area are inhumations, and thus the area must be dated within the third century.[229] From the standpoint of the assumption, made unavoidable by the results of the investigations of Prandi, that

218. *Ibid.*, p. 65.

219. Prandi, *La zona*, p. 65.

220. *Esplorazioni*, I, 38.

221. As is pointed out by Toynbee and Perkins, *The Shrine of St. Peter*, p. 32.

222. Torp, "The Vatican Excavations," pp. 41–42. See *CIL*, Vol. XV, Numbers 693, 625 and 762b. See also Mancini, "Scavi sotto la Basilica di S. Sebastiano sull'Appia antica," p. 41.

223. (See Plate 10.) *CIL*, Vol. XV, Number 998. Von Gerkan mentions in Lietzmann's *Petrus und Paulus in Rom*, 2d ed., p. 254, that "die Ziegel mit stempeln der domitianischen Zeit datieren das Grab nicht, da sie nicht dem Fassadenmauerwerk angehören." Toynbee, "The Shrine of St. Peter and Its Setting," p. 15, agrees. See Styger, "Il Monumento apostolico," pp. 12 ff. and figs. 7, 8.

224. Lemerle, "La Publication des Fouilles," p. 211.

225. Torp, "The Vatican Excavations," p. 36. Prandi, *La zona*, p. 17, has convinced most, including Kirschbaum, *Die Gräber*, pp. 217–21, that R and R' are not contemporary and that the cistern definitely related to R is to be dated A.D. c. 135. R was already standing when R' was built (A.D. 147–61).

226. Torp, "The Vatican Excavations," pp. 36–40. For example, he points out that the southern portion is 40 cm. wide while the northern portion is 54 cm. wide. In addition the northern portion is 1 m. deeper than the part to the south.

227. *Ibid.*, p. 38*n*50.

228. Van Deman, "Methods," pp. 423 ff.

229. As has been mentioned previously, this blanket evaluation of the type of burials in the area has been challenged by Ferrua, "La Storia," p. 22.

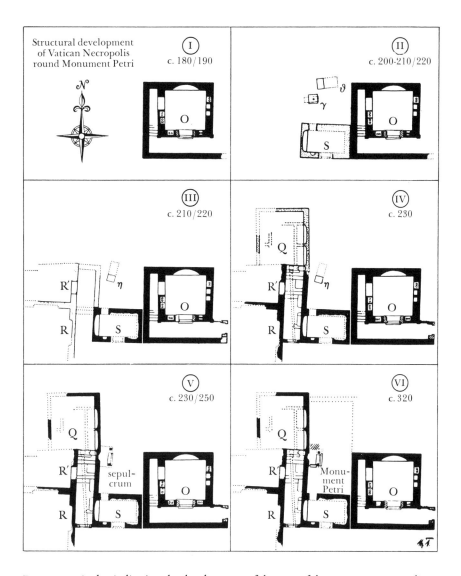

PLATE 28   A plan indicating the development of the area of the cemetery surrounding
area *P* and the Aedicula (Torp, "The Vatican Excavations," fig. 15).

MR was built in two sections, the dating of the whole complex in the mid-second century is not affected. The northern part of MR might have been built a year, or even less, later than the southern part.[230] More damaging, however, is Torp's contention that R, R', and Q were built in the third century which necessitates the assumption that the Aedicula could not have been built until at least the middle of the third century. His dating is, however, based upon a rigid application

of the Van Deman method, which according to Toynbee and Perkins, "cannot be used indiscriminately

230. *Esplorazioni*, I, 108, argues that the northern part may have been constructed first. In this event the southern point of the northern section would have been fixed, and when the southern portion of the wall was built from the northern corner of tomb *S*, it had to deflect a bit to meet the fixed point. Whether correct or not, this would explain adequately the slight difference in direction of the two portions of the wall.

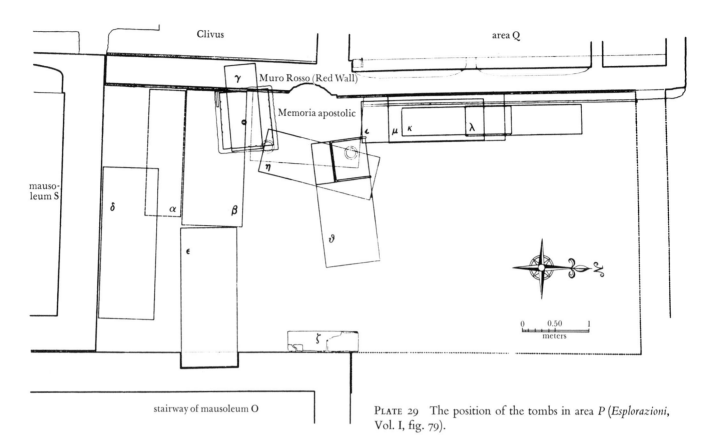

Clivus

area Q

γ Muro Rosso (Red Wall)

Memoria apostolic

μ κ λ

ι

σ

η

mauso-
leum S

δ α β

ϑ

ε

ζ

0   0.50   1
meters

stairway of mausoleum O

PLATE 29 The position of the tombs in area P (*Esplorazioni*, Vol. I, fig. 79).

to date private monuments like the mausolea of the Vatican cemetery."[231] Furthermore, if, as he claims, Christian interest in the area is first evidenced in the graffiti of wall *g* (third century) of the Aedicula, then the definite reference of Gaius to the Vatican (A.D. c. 200) cannot be associated with this monument.

The break in MR at point *m* (Plate 24) was caused, according to the *Esplorazioni*, by a flaw introduced at the time of the insertion of the shoulder of the door to Q.[232] The latest theory, advanced by Prandi and challenged by Kirschbaum, is that the break is not the result of a flaw, but, admitting that the two sections were built separately, is in reality a seam.[233]

In a short article, J. Gwyn Griffiths argues with the conclusion reached in the *Esplorazioni*, and by Ruys-schaert, Toynbee and Perkins, and others: *if* the drain is of one build with the Clivus and the Clivus is of one build with MR and the Aedicula (which is inserted in that wall), then the Aedicula dates from about A.D. 150.[234] While he admits that the large number of tiles with dated seals is evidence against the assumption that they were reused, this possibility is not precluded. In addition, the Clivus *could* have been built in stages at different periods and thus the drain *could* be older than MR (which he dates in the third century). Again, as in

231. *The Shrine of St. Peter*, pp. 268–69.

232. *Esplorazioni*, I, 97. See also von Gerkan, "Kritische Studien," p. 201.

233. *Esplorazioni*, I, 88; Prandi, *La zona*, p. 65. See Kirschbaum, *Die Gräber*, p. 218, who argues that this is *not* a seam, and its presence was *not* intentional.

234. Griffiths, in *The Hibbert Journal*, pp. 285–86. See also Kollwitz, "Die Grabungen," p. 20; von Gerkan, "Die Forschung nach dem Grab Petri," p. 380; Fink, "Archäologie des Petrusgrabes," p. 83, Marrou, *DACL*, Vol. XV, Part II, p. 3344; Cullmann, *Peter*, p. 146; Schäfer, "Das Apostelgrab," p. 312; Lemerle, "La Publication des Fouilles," p. 221.

the case of Torp, his argument is only effective because of his late dating of parts of the complex.[235]

Area *P* (Plates 23 and 29), which originally was about 7 m. long and 4 m. wide, lies immediately to the east of the Clivus and area *Q*. It is bounded on the south by the northern wall of *S* and on the east for about half its probable original length by the western wall of *O*. The northern boundary is hypothetical, but it is likely that it abutted upon MR at a point near its northern end. The location of the entrance to *P* is not known, but it most probably was on the north or northeast side of the area.[236] This is challenged by Lemerle, who mentions in passing that at that time when *P* was bounded by *O*, *S*, *R*, and *Q*, it was either abandoned or no longer used and, therefore, it may very well be that there was no entrance (as the term is usually used) to it at all. A more serious alternative is proposed by Margherita Guarducci, who mentions that a stairway to the south of a small off-room of *H* (Plate 23) leads east, from which one might reach "una strada corrente lungo il lato settrionale della necropoli."[237] This could have been a lane that led to *O* over the top of which was a stairway that *may* have led down into *P*. The surface of *P* was at one time covered with a mosaic which slopes 7 cm. toward the south. In the later stages this flooring consisted of a green and white mosaic and marble. The

pavement was destroyed, however, in construction work in 1615.[238]

Before entering upon the discussion of the level of area *P* and the various graves contained within it around the so-called "central grave," it is necessary to consider the role of MR, this time from the vantage point of its role as the western wall of area *P*. MR, as mentioned above, was constructed in two parts. It is built on an incline toward the north, but its foundations toward the northern end instead of rising in proportion to the rate of the rise of the land go deeper into the hillside. On the east side of the wall there is a coating of opus signinum,[239] and the earth is banked up against it.

MR is important in this discussion only because of its relationship to the "central grave." For the *basic* question of this section is, *if* there was a central venerated grave, did MR cut through it or pass over it? The legal aspects of the question have been examined by Valentino Capocci who agrees with the *Esplorazioni* that there was a grave (of Peter) which he believes must have been originally "un sarcophago in terra cotta," and that MR did pass over it.[240] MR was an "operis refectio salva religione," and thus "non costituto alcuna offesa per le tombe e per il riposo dei morti," for nothing in the progress of MR in relation to a central grave would have violated the then existing Roman laws. Furthermore, since no grave was moved, the Christian would not have been legally required to make a sacrifice.[241] Ferrua is undecided whether the wall went through or beside the grave which, he maintains, was already short and contained the incinerated remains of Peter in an "arcula" (casket). In this case all that would

---

235. Griffiths' arguments were answered by J. Toynbee, "The Vatican Excavations and the Tomb of St. Peter," pp. 284–86. Griffiths again answered Toynbee by admitting that the drain and MR are related, but that the wall may have been built later simply because the drain did not work. See also Ruysschaert, *Réflexions*, pp. 17–18.

236. *Esplorazioni*, I, 109; von Gerkan, "Kritische Studien," p. 41, agrees but does not explain. In "Die Forschung nach dem Grab Petri," p. 197, he states that entrance from the north is necessary since *P* is not related to *Q* and is later than *Q*. See also Klauser, *Die römische Petrustradition*, p. 44; Kirschbaum, *Die Gräber*, p. 80; Torp, "The Vatican Excavations," p. 48.

237. Guarducci, *Cristo e San Pietro in un Documento pre-costantiniano*, p. 4; *Esplorazioni*, Vol. I, fig. 32. Toynbee and Perkins, *The Shrine of St. Peter*, pp. 182–83n2, mention that "it is not improbable that the staircase within the precinct of *O*, originally designed to give access to *O* from the north, was later made available to the owners of *P* as a means of access from the south after the blocking of the alleyway between tombs *L* and *N* by the construction of Tomb *M*."

238. Lemerle, "La Publication des Fouilles," p. 210, mentions his amazement that there was no entrance from the south. See Ruysschaert, *Réflexions*, p. 34.

239. A type of plaster for walls and pavements.

240. Capocci, "Notae," pp. 206, 207. Compare the cautious position of de Bruyne, "La Tomba apostolica," p. 224. See also Cumont's ("Un rescrit impérial sur la violation de sépulture," pp. 257–66), discussion of Roman laws concerning the moving and robbing of graves. Sentences of deportation, forced labor and even "death" (p. 257) were, at times, meted out to offenders, by the end of the second century.

241. Capocci, "Notae," p. 207.

have been needed was a "cognitio" of the pontiffs that the grave had not been opened.[242]

If, on the other hand, Capocci points out, the grave was of normal adult size and had been disturbed, then new legal aspects emerge. The bones would have been carefully laid aside and placed in an arcula, an act which could have been justified under Roman law for any one of the following reasons: 1) "metus ruinae" (fear of ruin), 2) "incursus fluminis" (danger of flood), or 3) "iusta et necessaria causa" (just and necessary causes). In this case the first would have been the most probable reason, if any had been offered at all.[243] *If* the relocation were to be effected legally, permission would need to have been granted (which is extremely unlikely). Such a request was sent to the collegium, who examined the case, and if they so desired, they gave a favorable answer. If the pontiffs agreed, then a piaculum was required—a sacrifice of an "ovis atra" (black sheep)—which would have been odious to Christians. Since it is assumed that Peter had been executed, Capocci examines also the possibility that imperial permission would have been required. Unless, he concludes, the Christians had access to some important personage close to the emperor, this would have been impossible. Therefore, either the grave was not cut or the relocation of the central grave (if there were such a grave), if undertaken by Christians, was done without permission.[244] Capocci suggests also that the archeologists look more closely beneath the stairs of the Clivus for a grave.

A graffito, not recorded in the *Esplorazioni* and first mentioned by Ferrua,[245] was found on MR at the right

side of the Aedicula about 1.10 m. above the soil, at the point where wall *g* meets MR. The only certain letters are *ΠΕΤΡ/ΕΝΙ*. Kirschbaum does not find it difficult to believe that if this is the grave of Peter there are not other graffiti mentioning his name,[246] but the lack of graffiti is a problem to others.[247] The graffito, with letters averaging about 0.7 cm. high, was originally read by Carcopino as follows:

ΠΕΤΡ/ΕΝΙ[ΡΗΝΗ] for *ΠΕΤΡ/ΕΝ[Ε]Ι[ΡΗΝΗ]*.

This, he suggests, might have been a second-century epitaph for Peter—"Petrus in pace."[248] After seeing a projection of the graffito by Antonio Ferrua at the Vᵉ Congrès d'Archéologie chrétienne d'Aix-en-Provence, Carcopino became convinced that he had been wrong in his reconstruction. Line one, *ΠΕΤΡ*, is very plain, but the roughness of the remainder precludes its being an epitaph of Peter. He then offered the reading[249] *ΠΕΤΡ[ΟΣ]ΕΝΔ[ΕΙ]* or *ΠΕΤΡ[ΟΥ]ΕΝΔ[ΕΙ]*, which he interprets to mean "Peter is wanting" or "Peter is not here." This understanding of the graffito supports his theory that the bones, at the time when the graffito was scrawled, were not at the Vatican but Ad Catacumbas. The reading *ΠΕΤΡ[ΟΣ]ΕΝΔ[ΟΝ]* "Peter is here," is discarded by Carcopino for this would challenge the Translation Theory. One further fanciful note is added

---

242. Ferrua, "La Storia," pp. 22–24. Compare "A la Recherche," pp. 42–43, and von Gerkan, "Kritische Studien," p. 42. Griffe is confident, in *Bull. de Litt. ecclés.* (1964), p. 16, that "Si le corps de l'apôtre, après avoir été crucifié, a servi de Torche, les chrétiens désireux d'ensevelir ses restes n'ont recueilli que des cendres ou au mieux des ossements plu ou moins carbonisés ou même calcinés qui pouvaient mal resister à l'effritement."

243. Capocci, "Notae," p. 208.

244. *Ibid.*, p. 210.

245. "La Storia," p. 26. He says in this article that there were "tre o quattro almeno." See also his article, in *Il Messagero* (January 16, 1952), in which he repeats the story of the discovery. Kirschbaum, *Die Gräber*, p. 222, suggests a date for the graffiti between A.D. 180 and 200.

246. "Das Petrusgrab," p. 330.

247. For example, Seston, "Hypothèse sur la date de la basilique constantinienne de Saint-Pierre de Rome," p. 155, emphasizes that one would imagine that *if* this were a grave of Peter, many inscriptions in the area would be witness to the fact. See also Cullmann, *Peter*, p. 146. Kirschbaum, *Die Gräber*, p. 138, suggests that there were more than this one graffito *originally*, but that we have only a small portion of the original plaster—perhaps the complete plaster facing of the wall would have revealed many more.

248. *Études*, p. 281. See also *Inscriptiones Latinae Cristianae Veteres*, ed. Diehl, Vol. II (1927), Nos. 2715, 2716A, 2731, and 3406. Ruysschaert, *Réflexions*, p. 63, while admitting that the graffito is mutilated and difficult to read, is inclined to agree with Carcopino that this is some prayer to Peter which dates between A.D. 160 (when the wall was built) and the mid-third century. See Josi, "Pietro, Apostolo, Santo," p. 1407, Kirschbaum, "Das Petrusgrab," p. 330, and *Die Gräber*, p. 137.

249. *De Pythagore*, pp. 283 and 284n10. See Corte, *Saint Pierre est-il au Vatican?*, pp. 135–37. Compare J. Toynbee, a review of *De Pythagore aux Apôtres* in *Gnomon*, XXIX (1957), 261–70, and Klauser, *Die römische Petrustradition*, p. 72.

by O'Callaghan. Since the graffito is only 1.10 m. above ground, it may be that one of the worshipers, prostrating himself before the shrine of the apostle, scrawled a pious prayer or just the name of Peter on the wall.[250] Some such graffiti, suggests Chadwick, may be at the base of the entire erroneous association of the name of Peter with this location.[251]

Guarducci made a careful examination of the graffito and after considering the theories advanced to date came to the following very plausible conclusions.[252] The first row of letters definitely contains part of the name of Peter ΠΕΤΡ|, the last vertical line being the bottom of a rho. The graffito was written on a slope downward, perhaps caused by the difficulty in writing at that particular point. The form of the epsilon (ϵ) in both the first and second rows indicates that the writing took place in the second or early third century, which accords well with what is known concerning the date of the building of MR.[253] She is confident that the second row contained only three letters since if it had extended further it would have run into the OC at the end of the sloping first row. The last letter of the second row was not a θ or a δ but an ι. *ENI* is the complete word which in prose and poetry stands often for ἔν ἐστι.[254] Thus the graffito ΠΕΤΡΟΟ ΕΝΙ exclaims the belief that "Peter is here within." Guarducci is also confident that the verb ἔνι signified not only that Peter was venerated in that spot but that he was buried there.[255] It is reasonable to agree with her that the graffito was incised either at the time of the recognition

of the tomb or when some change had taken place in the area which altered its appearance to some extent. Perhaps it was written, as she suggests, after wall *g* had been erected and the area of the loculus was opened. This is a possibility, for such a graffito would have been required to authenticate the contents of the loculus.[256]

At this point a Christian graffito found in the Tomb of the Valerii warrants attention. The graffito was first mentioned by Ferrua, but he did not comment upon it at length because he believed that it was too indistinct to be read with confidence.[257] Margherita Guarducci, however, during an intensive study between June, 1952, and June, 1953, addressed a meeting of the Pontificia Accademia romana di Archeologia in November, 1952, at which she argued that the graffito could be interpreted and that the interpretation was relative to the question of the grave of Peter beneath the Vatican.[258]

The graffito, she explained, was found in the tomb of C. Valerius Hermes, the largest and most richly appointed of the tombs discovered in the Vatican necropolis. It is believed either that the family who owned the sepulcher was devoted to more than one religion or, which seems more likely, that different generations of the family had embraced different religions. There are signs of the worship of both Isis and Dionysus, whose cults emphasize a belief in life beyond the grave. The center niche of the mausoleum was occupied by Apollo, who among the Egyptians was worshiped as a symbol of light.[259] An important figure for the study by Guarducci is the one (to the right of this representation

250. "The Vatican Excavations and the Tomb of St. Peter," p. 87; see Ferrua, "La Storia," p. 27. Compare Guarducci, *I Graffiti*, II, 411.

251. Henry Chadwick, a review of Klauser, *Die römische Petrustradition* in *Gnomon*, XXX (1958), 409, and Klauser, *Die römische Petrustradition*, p. 72.

252. Guarducci, *I Graffiti*, II, 389–96, and *The Tomb of St. Peter*, pp. 133–35.

253. Guarducci, *I Graffiti*, II, 399.

254. See I Cor. 6:5, "οὕτως οὐχ ἔνι ἐν ὑμῖν οὐδεὶς σοφός...."

255. Guarducci, *I Graffiti*, Vol. II, fig. 22d, p. 401. "A me pare che la frase . . . debba piuttosto essere intesa come un'annotazione avente lo scopo di precisare il luogo del sepolcro venerato . . ." (p. 402). See *The Tomb of St. Peter*, figs. 38, 39, and *Le Relique di Pietro*, pp. 35–42.

256. See below pp. 200–4.

257. Ferrua, in *Il Messaggero* (January 16, 1952). See Carcopino, in *Giornale d'Italia* (November 22, 1952), and *Études*, p. 282.

258. *Osservatore romano* (November 22, 1952), p. 3, cols. 1–6.

259. Guarducci's study led Grégoire, "Le Tombeau de Valerius Herma," p. 399 (also "Le Problème de la Tombe de Saint Pierre," p. 50), to suggest that the mention in the *Liber Pontificalis* of a "templum Apollonis" in relation to the burial of Peter refers to the Tomb of the Valerii (*H*). Furthermore, this tomb *not* the Aedicula was the area sacred to the memory of Peter.

The figure of Apollo in this instance is Apollo-Arpocrates, a combination (which was common in the early Empire) of the son of Isis and Apollo. "'Απόλλωνα Ὥρον Ἁρποκράτην."

of Apollo) which she identifies with Marcus Aurelius.[260] If she is correct in this, the graffito, mentioned below, must date after March 17, A.D. 180.

There are undoubtedly some Christian burials in tomb *H*—probably those arcosolia in the lower part of the walls which disfigured the harmony of the original architecture. Those which have been opened, however, do not reveal any recognizable Christian signs. One third-century sepulture of Christian origin belonged to Valerinus Vasatulus and bears the following inscription: "D(is) M(anibus)/Valerinus/Vasatulus/vixit annis/XXI m(ensibus) IIII d(iebus) X h(oris) III Flo/rentia coius/ fecit marito/suo anime/benemerenti d(e)p(ositio) eius

PLATE 30 The head and inscription allegedly of St. Peter in the Tomb of the Valerii (*H*). The lines are darkened with charcoal to aid in the reading of the inscription (Guarducci, *Cristo e San Pietro in un Documento precostantiniano*, Plate 17).

VII idus sep(te)m(bres)." The "anime benemerenti" and the "depositio" both suggest that the occupant was of the Christian faith, and the pagan scenes which appear on the sarcophagus are common in the early Christian period. Guarducci dates the case itself around A.D. 260 and the cover between A.D. 270 and 290.[261]

The graffito is found in the central niche of the solar god immediately opposite the entrance, between the left edge of the niche and the right shoulder of the deity. A wall, built by the workmen of Constantine from the doorway to the central niche, covers most of the graffito, which indicates that the drawings and text must have been scribbled before the wall was built in the early fourth century. The graffito is composed of a sketching of two heads, one above the other, "e ambedue accompagnato dai epigrafi."[262] The heads were identi- fied tentatively by Ferrua as those of Peter and Paul, but Guarducci insists that the head which Ferrua believed to be that of Paul is in reality that of Christ. She main- tains this in spite of the findings of the paleographer Giovanni Muzzioli, who, with some reserve, read "PAVL" near the upper head and, "non senza esita- zione," read "PETRV" near the lower one. Muzzioli presented his conclusions to the Reverend Fabbrica di S. Pietro in July, 1951, and Guarducci began her work in an attempt to confirm his findings.

The upper figure which she identified with Christ is, she believes, the work of one who, though unskilled, had some ability. The figure appears to her to have a wrinkled face, large eyes and nose, and a pointed beard; all in all "non mancaro alcune caratteristiche semitiche."[263] The lower head depicts an old man with furrowed forehead, large eyes, and a beard to the neck

260. Grégoire, "Le Tombeau de Valerius Herma," p. 399, suggests that the figure is a statue of Peter and that this "est devenue une certitude depuis la travaille de Mme. Guarducci." This mausoleum, he believes, is also the Tropaeum of Gaius.

261. Guarducci, *Cristo e San Pietro in un Documento preco- stantiniano*, pp. 22-24. See *The Tomb of St. Peter*, pp. 144-47.

262. Guarducci, *Cristo e San Pietro in un Documento preco- stantiniano*, p. 14 and figs. 15, 16.

263. *Ibid.*, p. 25. From pages 28 to 60, Guarducci deals with the graffito associated with this figure which is not related to this study. See *The Tomb of St. Peter*, pp. 146–47.

opening of his clothing.[264] (Plates 30 and 31). The first word of the inscription, which is generally recognized as PETRU, begins at the left of the head; the S of PETRUS and the remainder of the graffito is found on the right side of the head (compare Plates 30 and 31). She maintains that the graffito was written in small letters and that some were traced over later. As a result of the building of the Constantinian wall, the filling in of earth, and the great humidity, the graffito is very difficult to read, and it continues to deteriorate.[265] The text, which she describes as the earliest known prayer to Peter is as follows: "Petrus roga ☥ xs ⁺hs/ pro sanc(ti)s hom(ini) bus/ Chrestianis/ (ad) co(r)pus tuum sep(ultis)."[266] The name of Christ, xs hs (Chrestus Hiesus for χρίστος Ἰήσους), is preceded by the crux ansata, or ankh used by the ancient Egyptians and adapted by the Christians to symbolize the concept of life. On the "h" of "hs" is found the ✗ which symbolizes the cross.[267] The object or "roga" is most probably Christ, and "corpus" refers to the relics of a martyr—a rare meaning for the word in the early Christian centuries, but very common later as is shown, for instance, in the notices of the *Liber Pontificalis*. Grégoire suggests that the crux ansata *may* be a sign for the imperative of "roga."[268] Thus, it would seem to Guarducci that whoever scratched this prayer on the wall of the niche was asking that Peter intercede for those who were buried near him—an early proof of the desire of the faithful to be

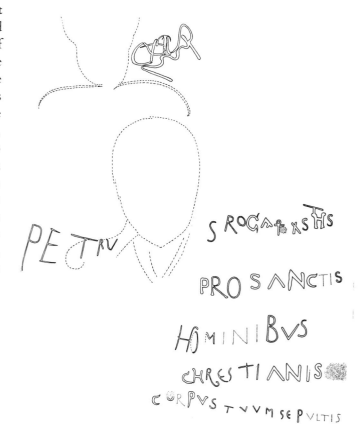

PLATE 31 A reproduction of the drawing and inscription of St. Peter by Guglielmo Gatti. The dotted lines show the letters supplied by Margherita Guarducci (Guarducci, *Cristo e San Pietro in un Documento precostantiniano*, Plate 44).

buried near the bodies of the martyrs and an early witness to the belief that the relics of Peter were buried nearby.[269]

It is generally agreed that the graffito would not have been scrawled on the wall of the Tomb of the Valeri, when it was first built. And since, if Guarducci is correct, the mausoleum contains a statue of Marcus Aurelius,

---

264. Schäfer, "Das Apostelgrab," p. 311, also agrees that the lower head is that of Peter.

265. Guarducci, in *Osservatore romano* (November 22, 1952), p. 3, col. 2, "Gli elementi essenziali pero erano, grazio a Dio, salvi al momento della decifrazione, ed è stato anche illustreranno la publicazione, alla quale già si attende." *Cristo e San Pietro in un Documento precostantiniano*, p. 16.

266. *Ibid.*, p. 18. The graffito is interpreted somewhat differently by Carcopino, *Études*, p. 283.

267. Guarducci, *Cristo e San Pietro in un Documento precostantiniano*, pp. 18–21. See the Epistle of Barnabas IX.8 which contains what is perhaps the oldest allusion to the tau cross (*Apostolic Fathers*, trans. Lake, I, 372, 373): "τὸ δεκαοκτὼ ἰ δέκα, ἡ ὀκτώ· ἔχεις Ἰησούν. ὅτι δὲ ὁ σταυρὸς ἐν τῷ ταῦ ἤμελλεν ἔχειν τὴν χάριν, λέγει καὶ τοὺς τριακοσίους." The eighteen is ι [= 10] and H [= 8]—you have Jesus—and because the Cross was destined to have grace in the ✝ he says 'and three hundred.'"

268. "Le Problème de la Tombe de Saint Pierre."

269. In *Osservatore Romano* (November 22, 1952), p. 3, col. 2. Guarducci, *Cristo e San Pietro in un Documento precostantiniano*, p. 76, lists eight other experts whom she consulted in the reading of this graffito (including Gisela Richter, former director of the Classical Collection of the Metropolitan Museum of New York), all of whom supported her, "esprimendo poi ciascuno anche per iscritto il proprio consenso." Her reading of the graffito is sharply criticized by others, however, including Carcopino, *Études*, pp. 283–84.

the graffito must have been written after A.D. 180. In fact, it is safe to say that it would not have been written until the family of the Valerii became Christian, perhaps generations after the time of Marcus Aurelius. It must have been written, however, before the Constantinian wall was built, but not necessarily, as Guarducci maintains, "almeno di qualche anno anteriore all'interramento del sepolcreto."[270] It could have been done a *day* before. She dates the graffito at the end of the third century, but does add that "non potendo escludere che si debba scendere fino ai primi anni del IV."[271] Grégoire prefers to say that the graffito is from the fourth century due to the presence of the "croix ansée" (crux ansata) which, he maintains, "absolutely is not found before the end of the fourth century."[272]

If it is granted that the graffito dates from the end of the third century at the earliest (but more likely it is from the beginning of the fourth) and if it is granted further that it contains a prayer to Peter that he might intercede for those who are buried near him, what is the importance of the graffito for this study? According to Guarducci the graffito proves that the relics of Peter are buried in the vicinity.[273] This conclusion is unjustified, for all that the graffito implies is that it was *believed* in

the late third or early fourth century that the relics of Peter were buried in the vicinity. This "discovery," however, is not overly important in view of the statement of Gaius almost a century *earlier* and the witness to the belief in the act of Constantine a decade or less later, who overcame immense obstacles to build his Basilica over the *exact* spot of the alleged grave. We may readily agree, however, with the second conclusion of Guarducci that "il esisteva anche prima un culto di Pietro strettamente collegato alla presenza della sua tomba."[274] That this graffito, dating from the same period as those found on wall *g*, is a strong argument against the Translation Theory, as Guarducci claims, is not convincing. The graffiti on wall *g could* have been written on the day before the alleged translation and this graffito on the day after. It may be admitted that graffiti are *usually* found in or near the place where the relics of the saint or martyr are believed to be, but this is not always the case. Graffiti abound at San Sebastiano: on the wall of the Triclia, on the wall of the niche on the stairway to the well and on the wall of the building beside the Platonia (the so-called Domus Petri). But no definite sign of an apostolic grave had been found during the more than sixty years of excavations. Furthermore, as is pointed out by Toynbee and Perkins, by the fourth century graffiti can be explained as implying the nearness of *brandea* rather than corporeal relics.[275]

The foregoing comments assume that the lower of the two heads was that of Peter and that a graffito containing a prayer to Peter actually did exist, as interpreted by Guarducci. These concessions, however, are considerable. "Le fotografie," warns Josi, "sia a luce normale che raggi ultraviolati e infrarossi, sia a luce monocromotiche, non permettono di leggere con sicurezza l'intergrazione proposta."[276] Perhaps the stronger doubt expressed by Voelkl is more in accord

---

270. In *Osservatore Romano* (November 22, 1952), p. 3, col. 3.

271. *Ibid.*, see also *Cristo e San Pietro in un Documento precostantiniano*, pp. 14, 64. On p. 69 she further delimits the date between A.D. 270 and 320. The scribbling must be from this period, she maintains, because of the manner in which the eyelids and the pupils of the eyes are drawn. In addition the cult of St. Peter is strong in this period and the Feast of the Cathedra begins. (It is more probable that it began earlier, perhaps A.D. 258.) She is followed in her dating by Prandi, "Lettre de Rome," p. 396. Prandi also states that Guarducci read the graffito "con eccezionale perizia." See also Cristiani, "Les Fouilles de Saint Pierre," p. 59.

272. Grégoire, "Le Tombeau de Valerius Herma," p. 398. Ruysschaert, *Réflexions*, pp. 64, 70–72, also suggests a late date—around the time of the filling in of tombs by the workmen of Constantine (or at least in the period after the area had been "condemned" by the emperor). Toynbee and Perkins, *The Shrine of St. Peter*, p. 198: "and it was assuredly during the earliest stages of the dismantlement of the same tomb that Christian workmen scribbled on its walls portraits and inscriptions" (see also p. 15).

273. In *Osservatore Romano* (November 22, 1952), p. 3, col. 4. Compare col. 5. See *Cristo e San Pietro in un Documento precostantiniano*, p. 74.

274. *Ibid.*, p. 74.

275. Toynbee and Perkins, *The Shrine of St. Peter*, p. 193n74. Brandea are usually bits of cloth, e.g., handkerchiefs, which are thought by some to become sanctified by contact with the tomb of a saint (p. 209).

276. "Zona archeologica e Basilica," *Enciclopedia Cattolica*, XII, 1066. See Cristiani, "Les Fouilles de Saint Pierre," p. 59; Ruysschaert, *Réflexions*, pp. 67, 73–74.

with the facts: the letters in five rows are "today practically no longer readable."[277] Toynbee and Perkins ask searchingly, in view of the claim that various conditions hastened the deterioration of the graffito, why "Petru" is still completely legible while the contested remainder of the text has faded beyond recognition.[278] The importance of the graffito is not in the fact that it is convincing evidence that the relics of Peter *are* nearby tomb *H* but that it is confirmatory evidence that it was *believed* by those who were filling in the pagan mausolea in preparation for the building of the Basilica that the grave of Peter was in the vicinity. Perhaps, it is best to follow Toynbee and Perkins, who "are happy to leave to others more competent than themselves" the matter of the reading and the technical criticisms of the reading of the graffito.[279]

The *Esplorazioni* argues concerning the dating of the various graves in area *P* from the standpoint of their depth in the soil[280] in relation to the supposed natural level of the earth, at the time of burial such level being the result of a *natural* filling in of the area between MR, *S*, and *O*. Perhaps the most significant difference between the *Esplorazioni* and Toynbee and Perkins is at this point. The latter do not believe that any precise judgment can be made concerning the age of the graves in area *P* by means of their depth since the filling in was *not* natural (or at least cannot be *proved* to have been such), but may very well have been the result of the further systematization of the area.[281] Kirschbaum's extended discussion, "Das Gelände," concerning the slope of the land within area *P* and its importance, causes one to pause

before making any judgments on the dating of the graves using this criterion alone.[282]

The foundation level of *O* is 3.90 m. beneath the floor of the Constantinian pavement; the level of the foundation of *S* is only 2.85 m. Von Gerkan, also disagreeing with the *Esplorazioni*, contends that this difference of about 1 m. cannot be natural. It is to be accounted for by the gradual collecting of the material left over from the building of *O*, and the like. *R* is 2.3 m. beneath the floor of the Basilica and *R'*, only 1.50 m. below. Thus between *R'* and *O* there is a difference in the level of the depth of the foundations of about 2.5 m., which, von Gerkan observes, cannot be explained in terms of natural filling in over a thirty-year period. Furthermore, MR at *S* is 2.40 m. below the level of the Constantinian Basilica (the dirt had not yet been taken away for the building of the steps of the Clivus). The level of the foundations on the east side of MR are only 1.50 m. deep, showing clearly that there were piles of earth in area *P* which may or may not have been leveled and which permitted the builders of MR to save that much on the waterproofing of the brick on that side of the wall.[283] Until the work of Prandi had been completed, it was believed, by the authors of the *Esplorazioni* and others, that there were only twelve graves located in area *P* (α–μ).[284]

A quantity of earth was disturbed during this work, which included fragments of tiles, bricks, and human bones. Since this material was not *in situ*, an accurate description of the total number or placement of burials was impossible. Prandi conducted his careful explorations in area *P* in two principal sections: along the back of *O* toward the east, and from the northwest corner of *O* northward. A brief tunneling also followed along the east side of MR (the section which Prandi indicates as *mq*) in the northwest corner of *P*.[285] In the course of these investigations, nine pre-Constantinian graves were

---

277. Voelkl, "Vaticano," p. 245.

278. Toynbee and Perkins, *The Shrine of St. Peter*, p. 22n39. Cullmann in a review of *The Shrine of St. Peter* by Toynbee and Perkins in *The Journal of Ecclesiastical History*, XII (1956), 17, agrees in their criticisms of Guarducci's reading and evaluation of the graffito.

279. Toynbee and Perkins, *The Shrine of St. Peter*, pp. 15, 22,23n39.

280. *Esplorazioni*, I, 133–34. See Vogt, "Sepulcrum S. Petri," fig. facing p. 172, and A. M. Schneider, "Das Petrusgrab im Vatikan," p. 323. Both came to the same conclusion independently. (See fig. b, p. 324.)

281. Toynbee and Perkins, *The Shrine of St. Peter*, pp. 147, 148.

---

282. *Die Gräber*, pp. 93–100. The discussion in Prandi's *La zona*, pp. 75–89, is also valuable.

283. Von Gerkan, "Kritische Studien," p. 39. See Torp, "The Vatican Excavations," pp. 34, 35 and figs. 6, 7, also Von Gerkan, "Die Forschung nach dem Grab Petri," p. 200.

284. For a discussion of these graves, see *Esplorazioni*, I, 111–17.

285. See Prandi, *La zona*, pp. 75–76.

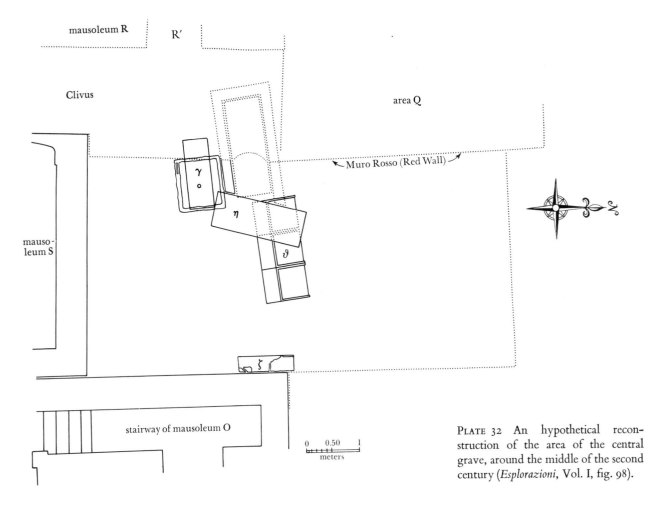

mausoleum R

R'

Clivus

area Q

γ
○

⟵ Muro Rosso (Red Wall) ⟶

mauso-
leum S

η

ϑ

ζ

stairway of mausoleum O

0   0.50   1
meters

PLATE 32 An hypothetical reconstruction of the area of the central grave, around the middle of the second century (*Esplorazioni*, Vol. I, fig. 98).

examined (two of these could not be dated with precision). An additional twenty-one burials were determined to be anterior to the building of the Basilica and at least four were later. Others were noted, but the remains were too fragmentary to yield any information.

In general, the twenty-one newly discovered graves are "cappuccine" or "mezza cappuccine" (the body is placed in the ground and covered by two tiles or one tile in an inclined position).[286] Some, however, had no protecting tiles at all. A very few marble sarcophagi and burials protected by stones were found, all of which were post-Constantinian.[287]

---

286. The graves that come to a point, made by two tiles leaning against each other gable-wise, remind one of the hood of the Capuchin monks and are called "Kapuzinergräben" by the Germans or "a cuppucina" by the Italians. See Villiger, "Die Ausgrabungen," p. 324.

287. The depth at which each of the twenty-one burials was found is noted in Prandi, *La zona*, p. 91.

Burials, numbered by Prandi, 3, 4, 5, 8, 17 to 22, 24, 26, and 34 were oriented along MR (*mq*); 9, 10, 11, and 15 were in contact with MR (*mq*), and 16 was in the area of MR (*mq*). It is interesting to note here that Prandi found "infine, che le direzioni delle tombe di ambedue i gruppi sembrano convergere nella nicchia N_1."[288] The direction, furthermore, cannot be construed as accidental. As a result of their presence near the Aedicula and their obvious orientation, the question of chronology is of great interest and importance. None of these burials contained a seal; therefore their relation to MR is most important. For if a burial is related to the direction of a wall, it is reasonable to suppose that it is later than that wall—in this case later than A.D. 160, since MR (*mq*) is related definitely to the stairway which has been dated by the seals[289] around

---

288. *Ibid.*, p. 78.
289. *CIL*, XV, 401.

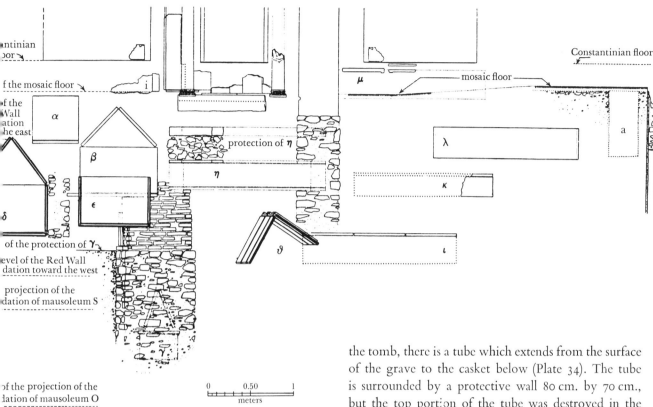

ntinian
oor

f the mosaic floor

f the
Wall
ation
he east

α

β

i

protection of η

η

ε

δ

ϑ

μ

λ

κ

ι

Constantinian floor

mosaic floor

a

b

of the protection of γ

evel of the Red Wall
dation toward the west

projection of the
dation of mausoleum S

γ

of the projection of the
lation of mausoleum O

0   0.50   1
meters

PLATE 33   A north-to-south section of area *P* across the front
of the central grave (*Esplorazioni*, Vol. I, fig. 81).

A.D. 160. Thus a *terminus a quo* is provided. Burials 9,
15, and 16 were made prior to the external "rivesti-
mento" of MR (*mq*), which Prandi had previously
indicated was related to the institution of Q, thus mid-
second century. Others in this group and burial 33 are
from the general period of A.D. 160.[290]

It is not necessary to this study to discuss the later
graves, but two of the earliest burials (γ, or 3, and θ, or
8) do warrant careful description, if only because so
much has been written about them.

Grave γ, indicated as 3 by Prandi (Plates 29, 32–34),[291]
is a little north of β. The casket itself is 1.26 m. long,
44 cm. wide, and 31 cm. high, and thus must have
contained the body of a child. Between the tiles covering

the tomb, there is a tube which extends from the surface
of the grave to the casket below (Plate 34). The tube
is surrounded by a protective wall 80 cm. by 70 cm.,
but the top portion of the tube was destroyed in the
construction of grave β, which lies partly over γ
(Plate 33). The foundations of grave γ are the deepest
in the area, 3.65 m. beneath the level of the Constantine
Basilica; 1.50 m. from S, but 75 cm. more shallow than
S; 2.8 m. from O, but 1.80 m. more shallow than O.
The grave is also partly beneath MR, which means that
it is anterior to it (that is, before A.D. 141–61). The tube
is undoubtedly for the purpose of pouring libations, a
common pagan practice. Even if the authors of the
Esplorazioni, caution "non è altrettanto sicuro indizio
del carattere pagano della tomba," it would seem to
establish the fact fairly well.[292] The superstructure of γ

290. Prandi indicates the three earliest second-century
graves as 3, 8, and 33.

291. See *Esplorazioni*, I, 111–13.

292. *Ibid.* The *Esplorazioni* supports its contention by citing
A. Profumo, "La Memoria monumentale 'in Catacumbas'
degli Apostoli Pietro e Paolo," *Studi Romani*, II (1914), 457,
who located near San Sebastiano a Christian sarcophagus, containing a metal tube for libation. What is not emphasized,
however, is that this grave is from the fourth, *not* the first,
century; Ferrua, "La Storia," pp. 18, 20; Carcopino, *Études*,
p. 176. See Goodenough, *Jewish Symbols in the Graeco-Roman
Period*, p. 71.

has been defined as a pagan grave altar,[293] but this is denied by Kirschbaum, who is confident that when the grave was built the slope and the level of the land in that immediate area would have left the "altar" much too low to have been used for this purpose. He too cautions that we cannot be *sure* whether γ is Christian, for we have no other Christian graves of that period with which to compare it.[294] The crucial question in connection with grave γ, in addition to whether or not it is Christian, is its date. The authors of the *Esplorazioni* hazard that it is from the first century,[295] but a number of other scholars challenge the conclusions for a variety of reasons.[296] Since the discovery of a seal by Prandi,

however, which establishes the *terminus a quo* of the grave to have been between A.D. 116 and 123,[297] any discussion of the various arguments (including the long and seemingly convincing one by Kirschbaum)[298] is academic. Grave γ is *not* of the first century but was built about the same time as tomb *O*—the earliest of the mausolea.

Before turning attention to the "central grave" and the Aedicula, grave θ (indicated as 8 by Prandi) merits discussion. As in the case of γ, there has been a great deal of argument as to whether it is from the first or the second century. The decision of each writer is largely based upon whether or not he accepts as decisive the date of the Vespasian tile (Plate 35) found over the grave. The opinion of the majority is that a single tile bearing a seal cannot be used as independent evidence in determining the *terminus ad quem*, because of the common custom, especially in the poorer grave areas, to reuse tiles.[299] It is unconvincingly argued by Kirschbaum that even though the grave is poor it is arbitrary

That this grave with the libation tube is Christian is doubted by von Gerkan, "Kritische Studien," p. 42, "Die Forschund nach dem Grab Petri," pp. 200-1 and "Zu den Problemen des Petrusgrabes," p. 85; A. M. Schneider, "Das Petrusgrab im Vatikan," pp. 323, 324; see Ruysschaert, *Réflexions*, p. 38, esp. note 1; Toynbee and Perkins, *The Shrine of St. Peter*, p. 148; Klauser, *Die römische Petrustradition*; Lemerle, "La Publication des Fouilles," p. 212; Cullmann, *Peter*, p. 148.

293. Von Gerkan, "Kritische Studien," p. 41; Toynbee and Perkins, *The Shrine of St. Peter*, p. 184; Klauser, *Die römische Petrustradition*, p. 46. See also Ferrua, "La Storia," pp. 18, 20.

294. Kirschbaum, *Die Gräber*, pp. 103, 104.

295. *Esplorazioni*, I, 116, 134-35. This view is supported by Villiger, "Die Ausgrabungen," p. 325; De Bruyne, "La Tomba apostolica," pp. 218-24; Speier, "'Memoria' Sancti Petri," p. 264. Marrou, *DACL*, Vol. XV, Part II, p. 3319, is more skeptical but concludes by saying, "il est difficile de proposer des dates précises pour les différentes tombes de ce dernier groupe [including γ]: il n'est pas exclus qu'il faille les placer toutes à l'antérieur du IIe siècle." See also Kirschbaum, *Die Gräber*, pp. 100-3 and Guarducci, *The Tomb of St. Peter*, p. 85.

296. A. M. Schneider, "Das Petrusgrab im Vatikan," p. 324, using the Van Deman method (mentioned above) came to the conclusion that bricks used in the superstructure are not from the period of Nero. The use of the Van Deman method for small private monuments is criticized by Kirschbaum, *Die Gräber*, p. 233n31, and by Toynbee and Perkins, *The Shrine of St. Peter*, pp. 268-69. Lemerle, "La Publication des Fouilles," p. 212, also challenges the first-century date. Von Gerkan, "Kritische Studien," pp. 41, 42, argues for a second-century date, since the level of the grave cannot be used to prove it is from the first century. He also believes that the superstructure and the slab decoration bespeak a later period. See also his "Die Forschung nach dem Grab Petri," p. 200. In this regard, see A. M. Schneider, "Das Petrusgrab im Vatikan," p. 324. Torp, "The Vatican Excavations," dates the grave at the time of the building of *S* A.D. c. 200. This, however, is much later

than it is reasonable to accept. Klauser, *Die römische Petrustradition*, mentions that the *Esplorazioni* dates grave γ in "the decade immediately after the death of Peter," when actually all that is claimed is that the grave was from the first century (I, 134); Klauser estimates γ was built not before A.D. 150. Cullmann, in the second edition of *Peter* (p. 137), modifying his earlier position, after the publication of Prandi, *La zona* (1957), dates these pagan graves "from the years 150 to 300."

297. *CIL*, Vol. XV, No. 1220a (dated by Dressel A.D. 123 and by Block between A.D. 115 and 123). See Prandi, *La zona*, p. 40 (or Kirschbaum, *Die Gräber*, pp. 217-21, 222), who argues on other grounds that "appare insostenibile . . . assegnare al primo secolo una costruzione, cui è pertinente la stessa quota che segna il livello 'tipico' degli edifici della metà del secondo."

298. See *Die Gräber*, pp. 83-85, 93-100.

299. *CIL*, Vol. XV, Number 1273. Among those that accept the authority of the tile are: *Esplorazioni*, I, 115; Josi, *Enciclopedia Cattolica*, IX (1952), 1405; Castagnoli, "La Tomba di S. Pietro," p. 31; A. M. Colini, "Il Sepolcro di S. Pietro," p. 8; Kirschbaum, "Das Petrusgrab," p. 403; De Bruyne, "La Tomba apostolica," pp. 218-24; Marrou, *DACL*, Vol. XV, Part II, p. 3319; Cristiani, "Les Fouilles de Saint Pierre," p. 54; Kirschbaum, *Die Gräber*, pp. 85, 104, 105. See also Fink, "Archäologie des Petrusgrabes," p. 95; Carcopino, *Études*, p. 176. Ruysschaert, *Réflexions*, p. 31. Prandi, *La zona*, p. 86, in rejecting a first-century date completely, emphasizes that *if* it were first century "questa tomba l'unico (si repete l'unico) monumento del primo secolo dell'intera zona archeologica finora posta in luce sotto la basilica vaticana."

to state, as does Klauser,[300] that the one who built or repaired θ "procured an old tile,"[301] for the grave is composed of only six tiles which could have been afforded by even the poorest person.[302]

A discussion of the dating of the grave from the standpoint of the slope of the land is meaningless, since this manner of dating proved incorrect in the case of

PLATE 35   The seal—STAT-MARCIUS DEMETRIUS—from the time of Vespasian (A.D. 69–79) found on the covering tile of grave ϑ (*Esplorazioni*, Vol. I, fig. 84).

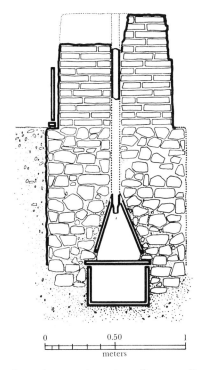

0   0.50   1

meters

PLATE 34   A north-to-south section of grave γ (*Esplorazioni*, Vol. I, fig. 80).

grave γ. Grave θ does, however, lie below η, and is older, and parallel to γ (Plates 29 and 30). The body was placed in the bare earth and was protected merely by tiles (Plate 33). The grave is 1.69 m. under the level of the Basilica, somewhat higher than γ (Plate 33), but because of the *probable* slope of the land, it may be argued that when both were built it lay 40 cm. to 50 cm. below the corresponding level of γ. This, however, is very uncertain.[303]

The suggestion of Fink that grave θ is the grave of Peter [304] is completely untenable; it is justly discounted

---

300. Klauser, *Die römische Petrustradition*, p. 46, is joined in his opinion by Lemerle, "La Publication des Fouilles," pp. 213, 221; von Gerkan, "Kritische Studien," p. 200, and "Zu den Problemen des Petrugrabes," p. 85; A. M. Schneider, "Das Petrusgrab im Vatikan," p. 324; Kollwitz, "Die Grabungen," pp. 18–19. Schäfer, "Das Apostelgrab," p. 313, argues that there is not one piece of evidence that θ is from the first century. No Christian graves of simple tiles are known from this time, nor until c. 313. He thinks that those buried in P may have been domestics of the family of the Matucci (tomb O). See also Torp, "The Vatican Excavations," p. 43*n*67. Grave θ, he says, dates from about A.D. 210. See also Toynbee and Perkins, *The Shrine of St. Peter*, p. 183*n*7.

301. Kirschbaum, *Die Gräber*, p. 104.

302. Guarducci, *The Tomb of Peter*, pp. 57–59, argues that this tile is not reused and that the additional evidence of a terra cotta lamp, the presence of burned bones, and other fragmentary objects related to funeral rites prove this to be a first-century burial area. The terra cotta lamp was made by L. Munatius Threptus, who made at least two other known lamps which can be dated "with certitude in the first century." Based upon this discovery and others, she is positive that this area was a burial ground in the first century, long before the construction of the mausolea of the second and third.

303. For similar type graves in the Isola Sacra, see Kirschbaum, *Die Gräber*, and fig. 22, after p. 120.

304. Fink, "Archäologie des Petrusgrabes," pp. 81–102.

by Kirschbaum on the grounds of the position of the Aedicula and the careful placement by Constantine of the Basilica, not over grave θ, but over the "central grave."[305] Equally weak, however, is Kirschbaum's argument against Prandi (who would, as has been pointed out, date grave θ with γ in the mid-second century before the building of MR but after the construction of S). Kirschbaum still employs arguments involving the slope of the land in area P, which evidence, however, may no longer be admitted; he arbitrarily dismisses the possibility that area P was leveled artificially. Also, he is unconvincing when he criticizes Prandi for the latter's dismissal of the evidence provided by the Vespasian tile.[306]

At this point, because of the work described by Filippo Magi, director of the Vatican Museum, in the uncovering in 1956 of a first-century pagan cemetery less than 400 m. to the north,[307] it is not possible to say definitely either that no burials would have been permitted in this Imperial area until the death of Nero, or that there was no burial ground in the Vatican area until the second century. The group of tombs was discovered while preparing ground for a new garage inside the Vatican City. One of the tombs was found to belong to a slave of Nero, Nunnius, and his wife (probably an Asiatic), who had the unusual name of Ma. This grave and another which can be assigned by the type of masonry used to the very early first century means that it would have been perfectly *possible* for there to have been burials in area P, on the same slope of the Vatican Hill, as early as the Neronian persecution. It is still valid to object, however, that if the obelisk stood on the spina in the Circus of Nero, then the cemetery on the lower part of the hill which includes area P would have been closer to the circus—perhaps too close to have have been permitted.[308] As in the case of the cemetery beneath St. Peter's, the ancient burial place less than 400 m. to the north was in use until the fourth century.

Are the graves clustered about the Aedicula Christian? Surely there is *no* valid ground for the assumption that the graves belong to the early Roman pontiffs.[309] But whether there are any Christian graves among the pagan graves (aside from the obviously pagan grave γ) is a moot question.[310] The certainty that they are Christian is definitely and unwarrantedly claimed by Carcopino and Cristiani as well as Ferrua, who argues from the standpoint that all the graves in this vicinity were constructed for inhumations.[311] On the other hand, Torp, though uncertain, is more inclined to see all the graves as pagan.[312] If the graves are Christian, then it follows that they are grouped around a "central grave," and *if* they belong to the second century instead of the first,[313] the supposition is more logical in light of the notice of Gaius written around A.D. 200 and reflecting a tradition which is at least a generation older (A.D. c. 165). That they are Christian, however, cannot be stated with any confidence whatsoever, and to be any more positive than this is to mix "find" and "fancy," against which Schneider, for one, has

305. Kirschbaum, *Die Gräber*, p. 234*n*43.

306. *Ibid.*, pp. 219–20.

307. See Magi, "Realazione preliminare sui ritrovamenti archeologici nell' area dell'autoparco vaticano," p. 99, and Perkins, "A Roman Cemetery Newly Discovered in the Vatican," pp. 849–50.

308. See Smothers, "The Bones of St. Peter," pp. 81–82.

309. Luigi Berra, "Lo Sviluppo architettonico della Tomba di S. Pietro," p. 93*n*5, "There are ten [tombs in area P] from the II to the V centuries. No one can affirm or deny that any of these tombs does not conceal the body of one of the first pontiffs that, according to the *Liber Pontificalis* [ed. Duchesne, I, 122–26], had their sepulture there." Compare Ferrua, "A la Recherche," p. 421. Fink, "Archäologie des Petrusgrabes," suggests that κ "perhaps is the grave of Linus." Compare the view of Derouou, "Les récentes Fouilles à Saint-Pierre de Rome," p. 155, who believes that area P was established by the Christian community as "un terrain pour inhumation des plus pauvres parmi des frères."

310. The possibility is neither admitted nor completely denied by the following: von Gerkan, "Kritische Studien," p. 42; Toynbee, "The Shrine of St. Peter and Its Setting," p. 16; Klauser, *Die römische Petrustradition*, p. 46. The possibility is put more positively in Toynbee and Perkins, *The Shrine of St. Peter*, p. 148. See also Schäfer, "Das Apostelgrab," p. 314; Cullmann, *Peter*, p. 150.

311. Ferrua, "A la Recherche," p. 421; Carcopino, *Études*, p. 187; Cristiani, "Les Fouilles de Saint Pierre," pp. 147, 149.

312. "The Vatican Excavations," p. 44.

313. Prandi, *La zona*, p. 40, as early as 1953 at a conference at Brussels, stated what today is the common opinion based upon his investigations that ". . . on doit considerer toutes les tombes commes posterieures d'au moins 70 ans à la époque du martyre de St. Pierre."

PLATE 36 A reconstruction of the Aedicula (*Esplorazioni*, Vol. I, Plate G).

The Aedicula, as interpreted in the *Esplorazioni*, situated on the eastern side of MR and facing area *P*, is composed of three superimposed niches, which are recessed into MR at the point where, on the west side of the wall, the Clivus and Q meet. Various parts of the monument were so completely destroyed during its eighteen-hundred-year history that their restoration is only conjectural, but two interpretations as to the original appearance of the Aedicula are shown in Plates 36 and 37.[316] In the *Esplorazioni*, it is maintained

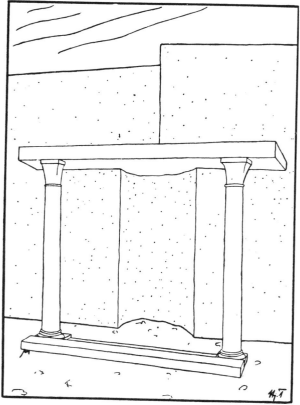

PLATE 37 A reconstruction of the Aedicula (Torp, "The Vatican Excavations," fig. 52).

warned.[314] Is there sufficient evidence to suppose that the "empty space" around which the graves near the Aedicula in *P* are grouped contains, or did at one time contain, the grave of Peter?[315] It is hoped that this question may be answered after a careful consideration of the Aedicula itself.

It will be most fruitful first to examine the Aedicula briefly and in a general way, then to discuss each part of the monument in detail, and to reserve the important matters of interpretation until after the details have been presented.

314. A. M. Schneider, "Das Petrusgrab im Vatikan," p. 326.

315. See Kirschbaum, *Die Gräber*, p. 221.

316. See also the reconstruction of Marrou, *DACL*, Vol. XV, Part II, p. 3342, criticized by Toynbee and Perkins, *The Shrine of St. Peter*, p. 183n4. The reconstruction of the *Esplorazioni* is criticized by the following who, however, offer no alternative: Lemerle, "La Publication des Fouilles," p. 216, and A. M. Schneider, "Das Petrusgrab im Vatikan," p. 324. The reconstruction of *Esplorazioni* is defended by Ferrua, "La Storia," p. 25; Perkins, "The Shrine of St. Peter," p. 511; Villiger, "Die Ausgrabungen," p. 222. Guarducci, *The Tomb*

that, except for the lowest underground niche, the Aedicula was built at the same time as MR[317]; while others argue, on the basis of various aspects of the relationship between the niches and MR, that the monument was built at a slightly later time.[318] In any case it is reasonable to assume that the Aedicula was built in the mid-second century.

Concerning the question as to who built the Aedicula, there are three principal theories. In the case of those who imagine that the monument was expropriated from the pagans the question of the builder is irrelevant.[319] A number of those who recognize its Christian origin cite the notice of Anencletus (also called Anacletus and often confused with Cletus) in the *Liber Pontificalis*: "Hic memoriam beati Petri construxit et composuit (dum presbiter factus fuisset a beato Petro), [seu alia loca] ubi episcopoi reconderentur [sepulturae]; (ubi tamen) et ipse sepultus est (in pace) [iuxta corpus beati Petri].[320] The probable original form of the notice read as follows: "Hic memoriam beati Petri construxit et composuit, dum presbiter factus fuisset a beato Petri, ubi episcopi reconderentur. . . ."[321] The notice would seem to account for the building of the Memoria and the construction of an episcopal cemetery in area *P*

around A.D. 76–88. The excavations, however, cast serious doubt on the existence of the latter, because there is no evidence that the graves in question are Christian and because the graves are extremely poor.[322] The more probable interpretation is that: 1) there was some confusion between the names Anencletus (A.D. 76–88) and Anicetus (A.D. 157–68),[323] 2) the statement concerning the establishment of an episcopal cemetery was an "invention" of the author of the *Liber Pontificalis* or his source, 3) it was Anicetus, not Anencletus, who constructed the "Memoria." The dates of the pontificate of Anicetus agree well with what we know of the date of the building of MR and the Aedicula and also with the tradition known to Gaius (A.D. 200), which appears to have been at least a generation older than his time. Carcopino's view that the remains of the body of Peter were not collected and buried until the time of Anencletus is without any foundation.[324] He is confident that at this time the remains of the apostle were gathered and buried in a casket at the spot over which the Aedicula was later built.[325]

Various other interpretations have been offered. Torp, as mentioned above, disassociates the Aedicula from the cult of Peter altogether, saying that the monument was related to grave η.[326] Klauser is convinced that the "Memoria" in the notice of Anencletus refers to another monument, and that the small size of the

---

of St. Peter, p. 86, avers that "we may almost class this reconstruction as certitude."

317. *Esplorazioni*, I, 137: "In questa fase fu disposto nel muro rosso, nell'atto stesso della costruzione—come ci garantisce la sua conservazione per un'altezza di m. 2,45 nella parte settentrionale—, e precisamente là dove incontrammo il misterioso quadrato circondato da tombe antiche, il sistema delle tre nicchie sovrapposte." See also Toynbee and Perkins, *The Shrine of St. Peter*, pp. 140–41.

318. On this point, see Kollwitz, "Die Grabungen," p. 22; Lemerle, "La Publication des Fouilles," pp. 205–7; von Gerkan, "Kritische Studien," p. 43. Compare Torp, "The Vatican Excavations," pp. 46 f. (see Plate 28); Klauser, *Die römische Petrustradition*, p. 48.

319. Torp, "The Vatican Excavations," pp. 47–48.

320. *Le Liber Pontificalis*, Vol. I, Part I, pp. 54, 55, 125. The parentheses indicate words found in the Felician and not the Cononian abridgment. Square brackets indicate words found only in the second edition.

321. This is translated by Toynbee and Perkins, *The Shrine of St. Peter*, p. 262: "He built and put in order a *memoria* of the blessed Peter, since he had himself been ordained priest by Peter, in order that the bishops might be buried there. . . ."

322. Ruysschaert's view, *Réflexions*, pp. 77–93, that this is an episcopal cemetery was correctly challenged by Klauser, *Die römische Petrustradition*, p. 49n81. See also Toynbee and Perkins, *The Shrine of St. Peter*, pp. 155, 262–65, and Kirschbaum, *Die Gräber*, p. 90.

323. Kirschbaum, "Das Petrusgrab," p. 331, and *Die Gräber*, pp. 131–32; Toynbee and Perkins, *The Shrine of St. Peter*, p. 262. See also Vielliard, "Les Titres romains et les deux Éditions du *Liber Pontificalis*," pp. 90–92, and Busch, "Das Petrusgrab," p. 315.

324. Hertling and Kirschbaum, *Die römischen Katakomben* (1950): "When we speak today of the tombs of the Apostles, we must not imagine that there is a tomb at a great depth which contains a body miraculously undecomposed for nineteen centuries, but, as in the case of most of the tombs of the saints or other famous historical personages, we must say: here is the place where the bones became dust."

325. Carcopino, *Études*, pp. 181–83.

326. "The Vatican Excavations," p. 43.

Aedicula proves it to have been a private undertaking, *not* a community project.[327]

Although complete certainty on this point is not possible, it seems most likely that the Aedicula is the τρόπαιον to which Gaius referred, a monument which *he* associates with the tomb of Peter.[328] Whether the opinion of Gaius accords well with what has been found cannot be answered until the Aedicula is carefully examined.

The main interest in N^1 (the lowest of the three niches, Plate 38) is centered on the questions: Did the niche at one time contain a grave? and, if so, Is there sufficient evidence to warrant the conclusion that the grave belonged to Peter? The authors of the *Esplorazioni* believe that there *was* a central grave and that this grave extended to the west beyond MR,[329] but they are uncertain as to whether MR passed over the grave or cut through it (Plate 32).[330] Ferrua avoids this difficulty in affirming that the original grave was not full length, but consisted of an urn that need not have been disturbed in the construction of MR.[331] He is quick to add, however, that it is impossible to ascertain any more concerning the grave, since the structure of the tomb has been completely destroyed in the intervening centuries, and there remains only a nondescript "empty space." A few scholars, such as von Gerkan and Klauser, take a totally different point of view. The former proposes that the Memoria was built *after* MR and that originally it was not erected over some grave below, but rather in relation to the window in MR (Plate 36) that gave light to the Clivus (which he believes was in part covered).[332] Klauser denies that the grave, *if* there was a grave in the "misterioso quadrato," belonged to

Peter on the grounds that a first-century grave would have to be at a level well *below* that of γ (which he estimates is from the mid-second century). On the contrary, the level of the grave indicated in the *Esplorazioni* as that which once belonged to Peter is *above* γ.[333] Furthermore, Klauser does not agree with the *Esplorazioni* that MR seems to "lift up" over N^1, indicating that the builders of MR had respect for a grave at this point.[334] In the matter of the oblique direction indicated for the central grave,[335] Klauser observes that if there had been a grave there in the beginning, its orientation may have been determined in the same way as graves γ and θ, by the slope of the land. Thus γ and θ were oriented in relation to the central grave not out of respect for it but for a reason or reasons completely irrelevant to it. The builders of MR, on the other hand, may well have deduced that because of the direction of γ and θ, the bones of Peter (perhaps identified by these same builders with the bones found under MR) had lain not perpendicular to MR but at an oblique angle parallel to γ and θ. Thus the travertine plate over N^1 was placed obliquely to the wall.[336] Kirschbaum states positively, however, that this grave, oblique to MR, was considered by the builders of the wall to be the grave of Peter:

Die Erbauer der Memoria legten soviel Wert auf diesen Grabrest, dass die darüber in der Memoria eingebaute Verschlussplatte der Richtung des Grabes folgen musste und

---

327. *Die römische Petrustradition*, p. 49*n*81.

328. See above, pp. 95–101.

329. See fig. 98, p. 136 and Kirschbaum, *Die Gräber*, pp. 90–91.

330. The various legal problems related to this question are mentioned above, pp. 177–78, and discussed in detail by Capocci, "Notae," pp. 206–8.

331. Ferrua, "La Storia," p. 22. Kollwitz, "Die Grabungen," p. 22, is sure that the builders of MR would not have cut through the grave of Peter. See Carcopino, *Études*, p. 179 and De Bruyne, "La Tomba apostolica," p. 220.

332. "Kritische Studien," p. 43, "Die Forschung nach dem Grab Petri," p. 202.

---

333. *Die römische Petrustradition*, p. 53. Capocci, "Notae," p. 210, also comes to this same conclusion. If this is a grave of Peter it must be at a decidedly lower level than that indicated in the *Esplorazioni*.

334. Klauser, *Die römische Petrustradition*, p. 52. Von Gerkan, "Kritische Studien," p. 43, agrees with him. See Toynbee and Perkins, *The Shrine of St. Peter*, p. 140. Kirschbaum, *Die Gräber*, p. 88, definitely believes that MR was raised at point N^1.

335. Plate 32 and the oblique direction of the travertine plate at the base of the reconstructed Aedicula in Plate 36.

336. Klauser, *Die römische Petrustradition*, p. 55. Lemerle, "La Publication des Fouilles," p. 217, holds that the builders of MR would not have built in that place with all its difficulties (any more than Constantine would have built there later with such great difficulty) if they had not *believed* that this was the precise spot of the grave of the apostle. Bernardi, in *Vigiliae Christianae* (1957), p. 157, agrees.

PLATE 38   A view into N^1 from the northeast side (*Esplorazioni*, Vol. I, fig. 89).

nicht der des Grabmonumentes selbst. Damit dürfte endgültig klar sein, dass die Apostelmemorie nicht nur über dem Grabe, sondern auch wegen des Grabes erbaut worden ist, das seine leicht abweichende Lage so klar in das Monument selber einzeichnen konnte.[337]

To me the correct interpretation of the so-called N_1 (the symbol used in the discussion below) was given by Prandi.[338] He noted that MR (that is, MR and *mq*) were never a single continuous wall, but two walls which differ in function, direction, and thickness. The place where the two walls meet is not where "la fondazione del muro rosso rientra, dando luogo a quell'incamerazione che nel volume *Esplorazioni* è indicata comme 'nicchia N_1.' "[339] Nor, he argues further, was N_1 caused by a later destruction; it was not an accidental incameration. It is the result of an impression made by something solid when the wall was made.

In other words, at this point existed, firmly set in the ground, a "quid" against which the semiliquid colature of the conglomerate concrete would have adhered when the foundations of the Red Wall [MR] were poured. This "quid" removed in later times would have left obviously its own imprint in the mortar.[340]

This concavity, so formed, would have the appearance of a "niche." Prandi adds that in this case a look at the niche itself would be much more convincing than even the most careful examination of a number of photographs. Whatever this "something" was, which when removed later left the incameration under discussion, it was in full view of the builders when they poured the foundations of MR, and it was not removed by them.[341] He suggests various possibilities: that the imprint was made by a cippus (a half column used for marking something), a column of stone, or perhaps a gravestone

337. Kirschbaum, "Das Petrusgrab," p. 405.
338. See Prandi, *La zona*, pp. 63–73.
339. *Ibid.*, p. 69.

340. *Ibid.* This view is supported by Guarducci, *Le Relique di Pietro*, p. 10.
341. *Ibid.*, p. 71.

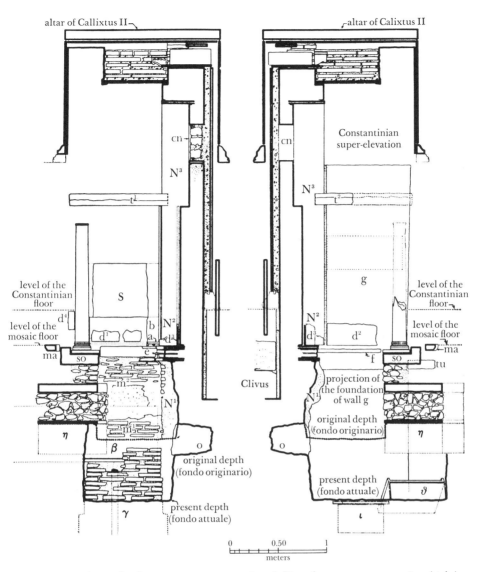

PLATE 39 The Aedicula: an east-to-west section (left) and a west-to-east section (right)
from the *Esplorazioni* (Vol. I, figs. 90a and 90b).

covering. "Osiamo appena, invece, e sanza porvi l'accento, in omaggio alla stretta osservanza della più rigorosa obbiettivtà far notare che questo 'quid' sorgeva nello stesso preciso luogo indicato come sacro alla memoria del Principio degli Apostoli."[342] While he does not state that the area or vault under MR at this point is from the first century, he does not deny

the possibility. There are too many uncertainties involved.

This "empty space," then, beneath the Aedicula was not a total surprise to the archeologists. Hartmann Grisar in 1892 first partially and with difficulty investigated the floor of the niche beneath the Niche of the Pallia.[343] He called the space the "Katarakt," but could

---

342. *Ibid.*, p. 73.

343. Grisar, "Le Tombe apostoliche," pp. 321 ff. and in *Analecta romana* (1899), pp. 274–97, and Fig. VIII.

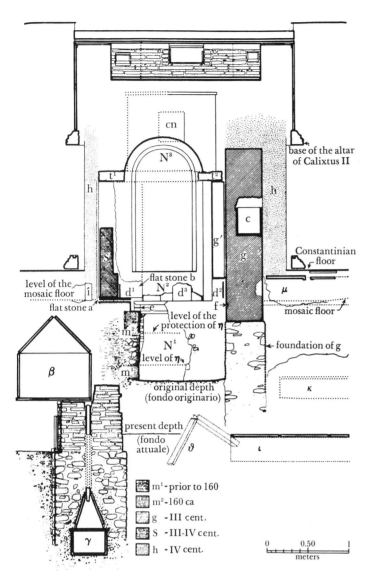

with a layer of very thin bricks and mortar, 50 mm. thick. Both parts of m^2 were constructed together. In the *Esplorazioni*, it is estimated that m^2 was later than MR since it rests against it. The wall m^1, however, precedes MR for one of its bricks penetrates into the structure of the MR foundation. Both walls were built against the earth; and when they were built, the level of the earth was above grave γ.

Various questions arise in connection with m^1, principally those which have to do with its age and function. Several writers claim that it is from the first century or at least prior to grave η.[345] Others will only say definitely that it is older than MR (A.D. c. 160).[346] More serious disagreement, however, surrounds the theory that it served as a protective wall for the central grave.[347] The authors of the *Esplorazioni* imagine that m^1 is one section of a small wall that originally went entirely around the central grave (Plate 32) and served to protect the grave against the rise in the level within area P.[348] Ruysschaert is in agreement, except that he believes that the wall delimited an area approximately

PLATE 40   A south-to-north section of the Aedicula (*Esplorazioni*, Vol. I, fig. 91).

not carefully observe it. N^1 is very irregular, but may be said to be approximately 72 cm. wide and 1.40 m. high (Plates 38 and 39). On the south it is bounded by wall m^1 (north of grave γ, Plate 40).[344] This small wall, covered with traces of red stucco, is 56 cm. long, 16 cm. wide, and 11 cm. to 13 cm. high and in two parts; the lower part is 37 cm. high, made of tufa and covered

344. *Esplorazioni*, I, 119–20.

345. De Bruyne, "La Tomba apostolica," p. 220, and Carcopino, *Études*, suggest the age of Vespasian. Ruysschaert, *Réflexions*, p. 46, sees the wall as prior to η and not contemporary with it, as the *Esplorazioni*, I, 135, estimates. He is supported in this by von Gerkan, "Kritische Studien," p. 47, and "Die Forschung nach dem Grab Petri," p. 202; Fink, "Archäologie des Petrusgrabes," p. 96; Kirschbaum, *Die Gräber*, pp. 107, 234*n*50. The date each assigns to m^1, however, is relative to the date given to η.

346. For example, A. M. Schneider, "Das Petrusgrab im Vatikan," p. 325, and Toynbee, "The Shrine of St. Peter and Its Setting," p. 20.

347. The view that it served as a protective wall is taken by Romanelli, "La Documentazione scientifica," p. 1, col. 5; Josi, *Enciclopedia Cattolica*, IX, 1406; Fink, "Archäologie des Petrusgrabes," pp. 94–95; A. M. Schneider, "Das Petrusgrab im Vatikan," p. 325, admits the *possibility* that m^1 was a protective wall for the central grave, but does not admit that the grave belonged to Peter (p. 326). On the other hand, Carcopino, *Études*, pp. 177, 178, thinks that walls m^1 and m^2 guarded the apostolic grave and were built later than γ and before θ. See Ruysschaert, *Réflexions*, p. 46; Kirschbaum, *Die Gräber*, p. 90. Toynbee and Perkins, *The Shrine of St. Peter*, p. 153, admit only the *possibility* of this interpretation. See Edgar R. Smothers, "The Excavations under Saint Peter's," p. 314.

348. *Esplorazioni*, I, 139.

square in shape on the eastern side of MR. The eastern side of this protective wall m^1 was destroyed, he adds, in the construction of grave η; the north side disappeared in the construction of wall g, and the west side was replaced by the foundations of MR.[349]

The idea of m^1 as a protective wall for the central grave is criticized by von Gerkan. Because one cannot establish that m^1 had counterparts on the west and north without some evidence, he also maintains that the role attributed to grave η as a protection on the eastern side is false; the grave did not contain a coffin which could have served as a protection, and its thin walls were of insufficient strength for this purpose.[350] Toynbee, Klauser, and von Gerkan[351] (challenged by Kirschbaum)[352] point out that it is equally possible that m^1 served as a protective wall for γ to which it is parallel. If m^1 had been intended originally as a protection for γ no other walls need be postulated since adequate protection for γ would have been given by this one wall on the north. (This is not the case if we speak of m^1 as a *southern* protective wall for the central grave.) But Kirschbaum believes that if the view of von Gerkan and others is to be accepted, we *must* say that originally there were walls on the four sides of γ, of which, however, there is no trace.[353] Nor, he continues, does there seem to be any sign of destruction which would permit the possibility that such walls had once existed. He is sure that a northern wall would have been insufficient; a southern wall would have been needed to protect γ against the rise in level resulting from the construction of S. Furthermore, it is reasonable to assume that a protective wall would have been built on the existing superstructure of γ and *not*

upon loose earth. The second objection is stronger than the first, for when the wall was built there was the ever-present danger from the hillside to the north; but S may not have been under construction. Perhaps the best judgment concerning m^1 is given by Lemerle and von Gerkan (in a later article): In its present condition the wall is impossible to interpret.[354]

Wall m^2, which lies above m^1 and is posterior to MR, would somehow be related to the Aedicula *if* the monument was built in approximately the same period as MR, but its exact function is a mystery.[355]

On the west side of N^1 is MR (Plates 38 and 39), into which the lower part of N^1 extends, about 90 cm. in depth and 30 cm. in width. Some bricks at the top of N^1 are broken, which suggests that the space had later been opened with an instrument such as a chisel.[356] Perhaps this was the time when the "quid" which Prandi is convinced was the original cause of N^1 was removed.[357]

The north side of the niche was destroyed in the various invasions and modifications of the Aedicula, and the east side was formed by the west side of both η and θ. The bottom of N^1, the "fondo originario" (level before the excavations of 1940–49), is of earth, about 1.5 m. above the "fondo attuale" (level after the excavations of 1940–49) (Plate 39). The "fondo originario" in N^1 is 1.20 m. deep and at one point even a bit deeper where the coins, to be discussed later, were found.[358] The present top of the niche is composed of a slab of marble taken from mausoleum E and referred to

349. Ruysschaert, *Réflexions*, p. 46. Kirschbaum, *Die Gräber*, p. 139, agrees in the matter of the destruction of the northern side of wall m^1 in the construction of wall g.

350. Von Gerkan, "Kritische Studien," p. 47, and "Die Forschung nach dem Grab Petri," p. 202. Kollwitz, "Die Grabungen," p. 22, is doubtful.

351. Toynbee, "The Shrine of St. Peter and Its Setting," p. 20, and Toynbee and Perkins, *The Shrine of St. Peter*, p. 153; Klauser, *Die römische Petrustradition*, p. 54. Von Gerkan, "Kritische Studien," p. 47, points to the decoration on the north side of m^1.

352. *Die Gräber*, pp. 107–8. This is also doubted by Kollwitz, "Die Grabungen," p. 22.

353. *Esplorazioni*, I, 121–22.

354. Lemerle, "La Publication des Fouilles," p. 219; von Gerkan, "Die Forschung nach dem Grab Petri," p. 202, maintains that m^1 is an isolated remains "of a wall of unknown meaning."

355. Von Gerkan, "Kritische Studien," p. 48, maintains that m^2 is earlier than MR, that it was *cut off* when MR was built, thus that it had nothing to do with the Aedicula, for it is oblique to it. Kirschbaum, *Die Gräber*, p. 108, holds that m^2, like m^1, is related to the central grave.

356. *Esplorazioni*, I, 120.

357. See Prandi, *La zona*, pp. 69 f.

358. Von Gerkan, "Kritische Studien," p. 46, is sure that the "terra vergine" has not been reached in this precise area (as, he claims, the level of γ, which is only .25 m. away and .30 m. deeper, shows). What has been called the bottom of the niche is still filled-in ground.

as the Slab of Isidorus.[359] This marble closure, first seen by Grisar in 1899, is 1.12 m. long, 0.65 m. wide and 0.35 m. thick and bears the inscription, "D(is) M(anibus) S(acrum) /P(ublio) Aelio Isidoro seniori/parenti bene-merenti filie/ ius fecerun[t]/ liberti(s) liber[tabus] posteris/que eo[rum]." There is a hole in the slab 0.25 m. by 0.19 m. (roughly the same size as the hole in the slab *a*, which was cut to give access to the cavity below through the shaft in the Niche of the Pallia). It is evident from the remains of N^1 that at one time coins were permitted to fall through the shaft to the niche

PLATE 41 Bones discovered in the bottom and to the rear of N^1 (*Esplorazioni*, Vol. I, fig. 87).

below. It is interesting to note that the *Esplorazioni* does not mention this point.[360] Whatever lid originally covered the niche, however, was oriented in the direction m^1, m^2, γ, and θ, that is at an angle at 11° to the axis of the Aedicula.

Within the "empty space" in N^1 were found coins (all catalogued in the *Esplorazioni*[361]) from various places and from various periods, which suggested to the archeologists preparing this report that "questo fatto, già da solo, sta a significare che quest'umile vano sotterranea è un vero centro di culto che era reso unicamente a S. Pietro."[362]

In addition to a number of coins, bones were found in N^1 (Plate 41). Immediately it was conjectured that the grave and partial remains of Peter had at last been discovered.[363] The excavators were cautious and while intimating that there was a probability that these were the bones of the apostle, stated definitely only that they had been removed, presumably for study. Others were not so prudent. Ruysschaert claimed that the authors of the *Esplorazioni* (I, 120) had been too cautious in not making definite claims concerning the bones; he was fairly certain that these were the bones of the apostle: 1) this is the area "qu'elle n'a jamais cessé d'être entourée d'un grand soin," and 2) there is no real reason to believe that these bones were taken away in A.D. 258 nor that they were reached in the later profanations of the tomb.[364] Others, however, were doubtful.[365]

361. *Esplorazioni*, I, 229–44.

362. *Ibid.*, I, 122.

363. Bernardi, in *Vigiliae Christianae* (1957), pp. 159–60, develops an interesting and imaginative theory concerning the reason that these bones were left behind in the supposed translation of A.D. 258. He admits, however, that this is only conjecture; see Kollwitz, "Die Grabungen," p. 22. Toynbee, "The Shrine of St. Peter and Its Setting," p. 20, asks the question but does not answer it, for actually it cannot be answered definitely. But she does mention that it is unlikely that the bones were from one of the known surrounding graves, for these were sealed. See Corte, *Saint Pierre est-il au Vatican?* p. 134; Kirschbaum, *Die Gräber*, pp. 198, 199: "We can only say that they have taken away the bones which we today recognize as those of the blessed Peter, and that it is really the bones of an old man. And Peter was by [the time of] his death an old man. There is certainly a great justification in dealing with the bones as those of the blessed Peter." (See also p. 88.)

364. Ruysschaert, *Réflexions*, p. 53. See also the interesting theory of Bernardi, in *Vigiliae Christianae* (1957), pp. 159–60; and Carcopino, *Études*, 2d ed.

365. Eltester, "Epimetron," p. 280: If they are the bones of Peter, they are at too high a level to be *in situ*; A. M. Schneider, "Das Petrusgrab im Vatikan," p. 325n4. Fink, "Archäologie des Petrusgrabes," suggests they are perhaps

359. This is not unique. An epitaph from the Tomb of the Valerii (*H*) was used in ε.

360. Notice that Plate 36 does not indicate a hole in the slab which covered N^1. It is the opinion of Toynbee and Perkins, *The Shrine of St. Peter*, p. 184n14, that "in view of the heavy rainfall in Rome in the winter months, it seems probable that the means of access was some sort of a removable lid."

The bones were turned over originally to Dr. Galiazzi-Lisi, a general physician to the Pope, who believed they belonged to one individual. Later the bones were entrusted to a specialist, Venerando Correnti, who occupies the Chair of Anthropology in the University of Palermo.[366] He ascertained that the bones in N^1 belonged not to one person but to three: an elderly woman, probably seventy to seventy-five years of age; a mature man of robust stature between fifty and sixty years of age; and another man of less robust build between fifty and sixty years of age. In addition, bones of animals were found. Although such scientific study does not completely eliminate the possibility that any of the bones found belonged to the apostle, it in no way confirms this statement.[367] By far the most probable explanation is that earlier graves had been disturbed by the workmen in the construction of MR and the bones hastily reburied.

The lowest niche, if we may continue to call it a niche, is crude in contrast to the more artistic arrangement of N^2 and N^3. It seems very reasonable to me, in agreement with Prandi, that MR did not cut through N^1 but passed over the solid object which originally occupied that space and was later presumably removed.

---

from a grave destroyed in the laying of m^1. Torp, "The Vatican Excavations," p. 47n80, considers the possibility that we have bones that had been placed in the niche at a late date when the Clivus had been remodeled. See Carcopino, *Études*, pp. 229, 230, and Cullmann, *Peter*, p. 147. See also Lietzmann, "Petrus römischer Märtyrer," p. 408. Fink, "Archäologie des Petrusgrabes," p. 85, reminds us that in the investigations of Martinetti in the eighteenth century no bones were discovered, but in 1835 J. Settele identified two bones when he was making an investigation of the area through the shaft of the Niche of the Pallia. (See Cugnoni, "Settele e il suo Diario," p. 272— entry for April 8, 1835.) Settele does *not* identify these bones with Peter and asks where they could possibly have come from. (Of course, in that day it was believed that the body of Peter was encased in an "unmovable bronze coffin," which had been provided at the time of Sylvester.)

It is interesting to note that Lemerle has nothing to say concerning the bones in "La Publication des Fouilles."

366. See Guarducci, *Le Relique di Pietro*, pp. 14–16, and the careful analysis of the bones by V. Correnti, pp. 83–85, 93, 94, 96–103, 107–24.

367. See the results of Correnti's study of this group of bones in Guarducci, *Le Relique di Pietro*, pp. 157–58.

Any of the later damage which is noted may be variously explained. Is the damage to be interpreted as a result of an attempt to steal some alleged valuables or coins thrown into the cavity by the pious visitors; or, was the damage done in connection with an attempt to *remove* the presumed relics of Peter during the persecution of Valerian or perhaps with a *return* of the relics about A.D. 336?[368] These are questions that cannot be settled. If we ignore Klauser's reference to N^1 as being "cut out," a satisfying answer to the mystery is offered by him (with some modifications based on later studies). He points out that there is nothing to indicate that the Roman Church venerated the relics of Peter at this spot before the building of MR. The niche N^1 may have been "cut out" while seeking the *grave* of Peter beneath the spot which for some time had been venerated as marking the place of his *martyrdom*. Perhaps this damage came about immediately prior to the building of N^2 and N^3 or in the time of Constantine. During this search the bones under discussion were found, and it may be that imagination helped to convince the Church that these were the bones of Peter.[369] But that it was *believed* around A.D. 160 that a grave of Peter was to be found in N^1 does explain, according to Toynbee and Perkins: 1) the rise and fall of MR, 2) the orientation of N^1 at an oblique angle to MR and N^2, N^3, and 3) the location of the Aedicula at this particular point.[370]

The middle part of the Aedicula, N^2, is situated above N^1 and cuts into MR, with which it is roughly contemporary.[371] Beginning at the southeast corner of

---

368. See Ferrua, "A la Recherche," p. 45 and Carcopino, *Études*, pp. 230–32; and Ruysschaert, *Réflexions*, p. 56.

369. Klauser, *Die römische Petrustradition*, pp. 54–55.

370. Toynbee and Perkins, *The Shrine of St. Peter*, p. 160. On page 161, they admit that "although it is not certain that the Aedicula marks the site of an earlier grave, the hypothesis that it does so explains much that is otherwise obscure; and although there is nothing to prove that this was the grave of St. Peter, nothing in the archeological evidence is inconsistent with such an identification." To this, of course, must be added that the burden of proof is definitely upon those who claim that this *is* the grave of Peter.

371. For a description of N^2, see *Esplorazioni*, I, 123–31. Compare the different opinions of Ferrua, "La Storia," p. 24; von Gerkan, "Kritische Studien," p. 43; Klauser, *Die römische Petrustradition*, p. 78; and Ruysschaert, *Réflexions*, p. 11.

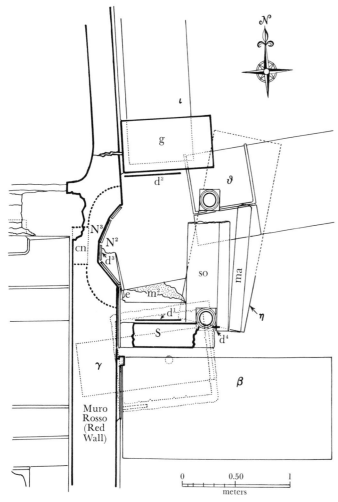

PLATE 42 A view from above area *P*, after the building of walls *S* and *g*, which shows the facing slabs *d¹*, *d²*, and *d³* (*Esplorazioni*, Vol. I, Fig. 88).

the base of N^2, a small wall is noticed over m^2 which goes a bit further to the south and touches the older ε, which is found between two horizontal slabs. Above e is slab a (Plates 38–40), upon which rests a later thin wall S which in turn leans upon the vertical marble slab b. On the north side of S are the remains of a marble covering d^1. The original height of S may have been at t^1, a travertine slab 1.34 m. above slab a.[372]

This travertine slab, originally 1.78 m. wide and

11 cm. thick (surviving only in its two broken ends), is inserted into MR above the vertical marble slab b–b^1 (Plate 39). On the east t^1–t^2 rests upon its one vertical southern column (the other was removed in antiquity) which is still *in situ* and 74 cm. in front of the niche (see *Esplorazioni*, Vol. II, fig. 55 *a, b*). The column was originally 72 cm. from b and rests not upon a but upon the horizontal travertine slab SO (Plate 42), which is 12 cm. below a.[373] This interpretation of t^1–t^2 is challenged by von Gerkan. He envisages not a slab extending from between the two pillars but two separate slabs from MR to the columns, leaving a space between.[374] This view, however, does not take into consideration the broken inside edges of t^1–t^2, which seem to indicate that each extended further toward the center (Plate 40). The pillars were originally 1.18 m. high with base of 9.7 cm. including the plinth. The missing capital of the only remaining pillar measured between 17 cm. and 20 cm. in height.

On the west side of N^2 stands MR. On the south side of this west wall are found traces of gray plaster over which was placed vertical slab b (Plate 38), 1.5 cm. thick and 1.33 m. high, and a little over 53 cm. wide, beneath the horizontal travertine slab. N^2, which opens on the north side of b into a space 1.10 m. wide and 1.40 m. high, is now filled with later walling but appears to have been faced at one time with gray marble, d^3, similar to d^1 over wall S. To the north of the niche is a wall, b^1, of the same height and thickness as b but 29 cm. wide (originally 53 cm. wide), corresponding in function to b to the south (Plate 43).

The authors of the *Esplorazioni* note interesting peculiarities in the orientation of N^2, which cause one to wonder if the niche originally did not face in the direction parallel to m^1 and the graves γ and θ.[375]

---

372. The *Esplorazioni* states that the vertical slab a goes across and beneath N^2. This is only an hypothesis, not a fact, as Marrou points out, *DACL*, Vol. XV, Part II, p. 3339.

373. Compare the measurements of t^1–t^2 and the columns in *Esplorazioni*, Vol. I, p. 126, with Ferrua, "A la Recherche," p. 38. See also Toynbee and Perkins, *The Shrine of St. Peter*, p. 163; Kirschbaum, *Die Gräber*, pp. 75, 230n30. *Esplorazioni* maintains that t^1–t^2 is perpendicular to MR; Ferrua, "La Storia," p. 25, sees it as oblique to MR.

374. "Die Forschung nach dem Grab Petri," p. 203; "Kritische Studien," p. 45. See Marrou, *DACL*, Vol. XV, Part II, p. 3342; and Klauser, *Die römische Petrustradition*, p. 51.

375. See *Esplorazioni*, I, 127–28, and fig. 92.

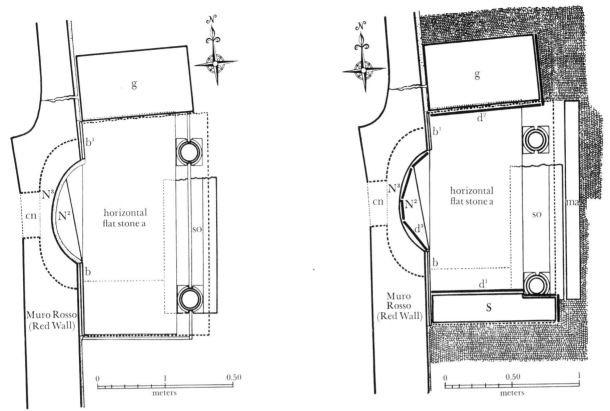

PLATE 43   Two views from above the Aedicula, after the construction of wall *g* and the
relocation of the northern pillar (*Esplorazioni*, Vol. I, figs. 100 and 101).

Further, they mention the third-century construction
of wall *g*, 85 cm. long and 47 cm. thick (Plates 39–40)
and describe the various destructions which took place
while clearing the way for the building of wall *g* and
the modifications which resulted because of it.[376] The
horizontal slabs t^1–t^2 and SO (under which some coins
were found) had to be cut by 20 cm. on the north side.
The northern column had to be moved further to the
south, and the northern part of *η* had to be sacrificed.
But what was the need for wall *g* in the first place?
Ferrua gives no reason except that it was needed because
of the partial destruction of N^1.[377] Kirschbaum, in

error, but in agreement with the *Esplorazioni* (fig. 88),
accepts the interpretation that wall *g* was built to
sustain MR as a result of a fault in the latter.[378] Prandi,
in his later investigations, demonstrated that no "fault"
exists. Behind wall *g* was the "seam" at the point where
the two separate and distinct parts of MR (or MR and
mq) meet.[379] Wall *g* does not in any way strengthen MR;
it merely touches it. It may well be that wall *g* served as
a retaining wall, necessary because of the constant
danger of earth washing down from the slope above.
(We do not know anything about the height or length
of a north wall of *P*, if such a wall existed at all.) In
any case, according to the *Esplorazioni*, before the
construction of *g*, care was taken concerning the exact
place and direction of the supposed tomb; but after

376. *Ibid.*, I, 140. Compare Ruysschaert, *Réflexions*, pp.
48–52. See the very different interpretation of the later
changes in the Aedicula in Torp, "The Vatican Excavations,"
pp. 47–51. Von Gerkan, "Kritische Studien," p. 49, says that
the wall was not built prior to A.D. c. 313.

377. Ferrua, "A la Recherche," p. 43.

378. Kirschbaum, "Das Petrusgrab," pp. 328, 409.

379. Prandi, *La zona*, p. 66.

the construction of this wall the whole monument had to be remodeled to repair the damage to its symmetry. To accomplish this, wall S was built (late third century), 20 cm. thick. Later both S and g, together with N^2, were faced on the inside with gray marble. The new slab a at the base of the niche, which was once oblique to MR, was placed in a position that "conformed to the axis of the Red Wall" and the superstructure of the Aedicula.[380] Next, b and b^1 were placed over the north and south portions of N^2 over a and beneath t^1–t^2. Later, wall S was added over a beneath t^1–t^2 abutting the gray marble slab b. Thus S is later than these elements, but still is considered to be pre-Constantinian. This wall was then faced on the north side with marble slab d^1. Later still, area P was covered with a mosaic of green and white tiles which is 6 cm. higher than the floor of the Memoria. Marble strip ma also may have been laid at this time.

The importance of wall g for this study does not lie in the fact that it did or did not brace MR or that it served as a retaining wall to protect the Aedicula from the washing down of earth from the north but that it contained a loculus and its northern surface was covered with graffiti.

The loculus of wall g (Plates 40 and 44) was about .77 m. long, .315 m. deep, and .29 m. wide, at a distance of about .80 m. above the mosaic pavement of P. Whether it was built with wall g or inserted at a later time is questionable. According to Ferrua, the loculus, made of thin slabs of marble, was constructed by Constantine to contain what was left "of the mortal remains of Peter," supposedly after their return from Ad Catacumbas.[381] It can be urged against this hypothesis that, if this were true, the shrine of Constantine would have been oriented over the loculus instead, as it was, over the center of the Aedicula; and a Constantinian wall (Plate 40, h) would not have sealed the loculus in place. Furthermore, it is argued by von Gerkan that if

PLATE 44 The empty space surrounded by marble inside of wall g (Guarducci, *Le Reliquie di Pietro sotto la Confessione della Basilica Vaticana*, fig. 4).

the space for the loculus had been opened in wall g after it had been built, as is claimed in the *Esplorazioni*,[382] the overhang above the loculus would not have sustained the shock. On the other hand, if the wall and the space had been built together, then the slim overhang would have remained intact. In any case, he explains, the loculus was opened from above (or from the east side where some traces remain of a possible entrance), and at a later time coins from the Middle Ages were inserted.[383] Thus the loculus was most probably not the work of Constantine, but belongs to the pre-Constantinian history of the Aedicula.

---

380. Toynbee and Perkins, *The Shrine of St. Peter*, p. 164.

381. "A la Recherche," p. 45. This theory is rejected by Toynbee and Perkins, *The Shrine of St. Peter*, p. 166, and Klauser, *Die römische Petrustradition*, p. 58. Guarducci, *I Graffiti*, I, 15, 26, agrees with Ferrua that the loculus was built into the wall at the time of Constantine, but she rejects the Translation Theory.

---

382. *Esplorazioni*, I, 162; Josi, *Enciclopedia Cattolica*, IX, 1407; Kirschbaum, *Die Gräber*, p. 67.

383. "Kritische Studien," p. 48; "Die Forschung nach dem Grab Petri," p. 203; Klauser, *Die römische Petrustradition*, p. 57. Kirschbaum, *Die Gräber*, p. 230n23, deems this interpretation

In an exhaustive study of the loculus by Guarducci, it is determined that it contained remains of bone, coins, and cloth.[384] The contents of the loculus had been removed by the first group of excavators about 1943 and were transferred by the foreman, Giovanni Segoni, to a box which was deposited in the confessio of the crypt to the rear of the Niche of the Pallia. This material was examined, returned to its box, stored by Monsignor Kaas, and not examined further. In 1956, Guarducci recovered the loculus and handed over its contents to Venerando Correnti for analysis. His conclusions were that the bones, apart from the few fragments identified by Luigi Cardini as being sheep, goat, ox, cock, and a half of a skeleton of a mouse (which probably entered the loculus, open at the top, at a later time), were 19 fragments from a single human skeleton.[385] It was determined that the bones had belonged to one individual: a male between sixty and seventy years of age, of average height, and robust. In addition, the earth found in the loculus, analyzed by Carlo Lauro and G. C. Negretti, was found to contain fragments of plaster from MR and was the same earth as that found in the vicinity of N^1 in area P.[386] Furthermore, fragments of purple (imperial color) cloth which had been decorated with gold thread and some threads of gold-plated copper were found. It is reasoned by Guarducci that the cloth was used to wrap the bones, which demonstrates that *in the age of Constantine* the contents of the loculus of wall *g* "degna non soltanto di rispetto ma addirittura (ce lo dimostra la porpora) di onori regali."[387] She is certain that in that period the bones considered to be those of Peter were taken from the ground of area P, near the Aedicula, and placed in the loculus and thence into wall *g*. In order to explain the animal bones in the loculus it is conjectured that they were already in the earth

around N_1 and had been disinterred unknowingly along with the human bones. The presence of the human and animal bones together leads Guarducci to believe that the original tomb is from the first century, when the Vatican area was known as the *horti Neronis* and was in an area "di carattere agricolo. Si risale, dunque, all'età do san Pietro."[388] She concludes, based on the investigations of Correnti and others, that "Si puo dunque concludere che le ossa rinvenute nel vano del muro *g* e considerate ai tempi di costantino ossa di Pietro provengono dalla tomba esistente sotto l'edicola del muro Rosso e sono veramente le reliquie dell'-Apostolo."[389]

On the northern surface of wall *g*, about 1 m. above the ground, there is a space covered with whitewash which has preserved fragments of various graffiti: "vite in ☧," "Nicasi vibas in ☧," "Victor cum svi[s] Gavdentia vibatis in ☧," "Prima vivas," "Paulina vivas," "in ☧ Venerosa vea." There are numerous instances of the use of the XP, chrismon (☧) or Constantinian monogram, which the emperor began to use on his coins between A.D. 317 and 320. The chrismon, however, was used, according to Carcopino, before this date,[390] and thus he would date the graffiti of wall *g* between A.D. 298 and 313. The name of Peter on the wall of what has been identified as his shrine, and surely recognized as such by the end of the third century, is conspicuous by its absence.[391] For those who accept the Translation Theory, this does not present a problem, for during the period when the graffiti were supposedly written, the body of Peter was not at the Vatican but at the Catacombs on the Via Appia.[392] The absence of the apostle's

impossible considering the Roman type of wall construction. The overhang would have needed some support during construction. This support, granting that it may have been necessary, *could* have been temporary and removed when the loculus was inserted.

384. See Guarducci, *Le Relique di Pietro*, pp. 26–35, 86–92, 96–105, 134–60.

385. *Ibid.*, fig. 8 (p. 90), pp. 134–55.

386. *Ibid.*, pp. 73, 179.

387. *Ibid.*, p. 71.

388. *Ibid.*, p. 74.

389. *Ibid.*, p. 75. Pope Paul VI agrees with this conclusion. In a Statement given three days before the feast of Sts. Peter and Paul, at a weekly general audience, on June 26, 1968, he averred that "the relics of St. Peter have . . . been identified in a way we believe convincing and we praise those who have dedicated careful study and long and great efforts to this . . . we must be all the more eager and exultant when we are right in believing that the few but sacred mortal remains have been traced of the Prince of Apostles." But see below, pp. 205–9.

390. See Carcopino, *Études*, pp. 191–93.

391. M. Guarducci, *I Graffiti*, I, 19–23.

392. See Carcopino, *Études*, pp. 188–93, 281–82. Compare Ruysschaert, *Réflexions*, pp. 63–64.

name is attributed by Toynbee to the facts that 1) it was so well known that this was the tomb of Peter and Peter alone and 2) the writing of the names of the apostles Ad Catacumbas was perhaps necessary *if* this sanctuary was new and schismatic, and set up in competition with the cult at the Vatican and the Via Ostia. Toynbee concludes that the absence of the name *can* be explained and therefore cannot be used as evidence for or against the supposition that this is the tomb of Peter.[393]

But is the name of Peter really absent? Before concluding the discussion concerning the graffiti on the wall *g* it is necessary to give some attention to the observations and theory of Margherita Guarducci in regard to these graffiti. Since her explanation that the form in which the *name* Peter was scribbled on wall *g* does not appear as such, it is understandable that more than three quarters of Volume I of *I Graffiti sotto la Confessione di San Pietro in Vaticano* is devoted to the examination of the theory that the early Christians assigned a mystical value to the majority of the letters of the alphabet. By this means and by the further expedients of transforming certain letters into other letters, ciphers, or figures of symbolic character, these early Christians expressed affirmations of faith, Christian thoughts of hope, and prophecies of happy future life. These cryptographs used "anche da gente umilissima" experienced their greatest period of development in the second and third centuries, but were used commonly as late as the sixth century. The resort to cryptographs, a result of the persecutions under Nero, Diocletian, and others, enabled the early Christians to express ideas and hopes which, if understood by the authorities, might have led to their detection and punishment. This type of writing which helped "celare lo spirituale dietro il sensibile" was not new, but borrowed. It originated in the Orient, and became popular among the ancient Hebrews and Greeks of the Hellenistic-Roman Age

and, in fact, in all of the Mediterranean area in the period of the early Empire. Early Christians who had contact with Hebrew, Greek-Hellenistic, and Gnostic elements of the population adopted and created, Guarducci explains, a number of cryptographs: for example, A-Ω(ω) (Latin O) as a sign of the beginning and the end and thus of deity in general and Christ in particular; IX as a symbol for Christ; D for *Deus*; P for *Pax*; and γ for ὑγίεια. Less well known are a number of other symbols, such as the Orans (praying figure), which represented the spirit of the dead; the dove, standing for the spirit of the dead in flight or preparing for the flight to Paradise; and the vase, representing the restoration of life eternal. In addition, the letters L or LV were the symbols for light; R or RE for resurrection; RS for a combination of the two ideas of resurrection and salvation; and tau for the cross. Less well known also is the symbolic meaning of A as life or the living Christ; B for Bita (vita) meaning life; CO or COR for corona or crown of life; E for Eden or Paradise; NI (νίκα) for victory. And there are a great many others.

In a given graffito containing the name of the deceased a palm leaf or the branch held in the mouth of a dove might touch a certain letter. That letter, then, not only functioned as a symbol in the spelling of the name but had a further meaning depending upon its religious significance. For example, if in a graffito containing the word "AURELIVS," a chrismon appears over the "L," the "L" then not only serves to complete the spelling of the name but expresses the sentiment that Christ is light, or the hope that Aurelius might live in the future life in the light of Christ. So also the chrismon above the "R" in APRILIS suggests the hope of resurrection in Christ. Letters found over or near others render combinations of a mystical nature: the chrismon in the midst of three A's shows the centrality of Christ in the divine Trinity. In the graffito

MARCIAHILAR

O

IN PACE[394]

O over A indicates the hope of the passage of the dead from life (Alpha as the beinning) to death (Omega—in Latin expressed as O) and thence to life eternal (Alpha

---

393. Toynbee, "The Shrine of St. Peter and Its Setting," p. 26*n*13a; Toynbee and Perkins, *The Shrine of St. Peter*, p. 166; Kirschbaum, *Die Gräber*, p. 66. See also Guarducci, *I. Graffiti*, I, 105; Castagnoli, "La Tomba di S. Pietro," p. 7*n*5. The opposite point of view is taken by Hugh Last in his review of *Études* by Jérôme Carcopino, *The Journal of Roman Studies*, LIV (1954), 114; and Klauser, *Die römische Petrustradition*, p. 58.

394. Guarducci, *I Graffiti*, I, 359, fig. 183.

as the absolute for life). At other times a mystical symbol was entered into the text of a word itself to inject its meaning. At San Sebastiano is found the graffito IXTΘYC,[395] which contains the tau and more closely links the idea of the fish, the cross, and Christ. In a few cases actual letters are transformed so that they have a symbolic meaning within the words: CRIS✳INA CO₽ONI. In some instances letters are changed within a word so that while the letter which is displaced is clearly understood, the one which is added has a definite symbolic value: "CONSTANTIAOAE VIXIT XXX. . . ." The graffito was meant to read "Constantia quae vixit . . .," but the "O" was entered for the "QU" in order to show the order A-O-A with its symbolic meaning.[396]

The explanation concerning Christian cryptographs is meant to serve as an introduction to the main premise of Guarducci's *I Graffiti*, that the name of Peter appears frequently in a number of forms on wall *g* in a symbolic manner:

P, PE, PET, ⴱ, ⴱ, ⴱ, Ⴒ, Ⴒ.

Any symbol for the name of the apostle may also be linked with A standing for "life" or for the preposition *ad:* AP, APE, APET.[397] She also argues that in time, and perhaps as early as the period which is of interest here (A.D. 290–315), the rho in the chrismon standing for Christ was also understood by the Romans as a Latin P standing for Peter.[398] These symbolic representations for the name of Peter, according to Guarducci, "sembra trovare spiegazione facile e ragionevole in tutti i documenti in cui ricorre."[399] For example, one of the graffiti on wall *g* appears

NIBEAPE VIVE [400]

Nibe is the vocative for Nibus and APE is the symbol for "ad Petrum." The hope is expressed that Nibus may live in Paradise with Peter. To Guarducci such sentiments are most convincing proof that those who

recorded their religious sentiments on wall *g* believed that the tomb of Peter was to be found in the immediate vicinity. It is impossible, especially for one who is not a trained epigraphist, to argue from photographs with the author concerning what she has found on wall *g*. To the untrained eye the general appearance of the graffiti on this wall is one of utter confusion, increased by the numerous cracks in the stucco which crisscross the many scribblings which themselves crisscross over one another.[401] The careful groundwork that she has laid for her main premise is convincing. *If* the various suggested symbolic representations of the name of Peter were as widely known as she has intimated and *if* they are as clearly discernible on the wall itself as they are in the diagrams prepared for her text, it is possible that those who wrote on wall *g* were aware of the proximity of a precinct venerated as being the place of the burial of Peter.[402]

However, even if one concedes that the graffiti contain symbolic references to Peter, it is not *necessary* to believe that those who scribbled these pious phrases believed that Peter's relics were buried nearby, for such symbolic representations of the name of Peter were found in numerous places which were not dedicated to the veneration of Peter.[403]

Furthermore, since these graffiti were probably written between A.D. 290 and 315, or shortly thereafter,

---

395. See above, p. 144.

396. Guarducci, *I Graffiti*, I, 377.

397. *Ibid.*, II, 45, 89, 119, 158, 163, 228, 231, 281, 327.

398. *Ibid.*, I, 406, fig. 206.

399. *Ibid.*, I, 440.

400. *Ibid.*, I, 465. See also *ibid.*, II, 335–36.

401. For example, examine *ibid.*, III, 15, fig. 6; III, 47, fig. 22; III, 69, fig. 33; III, 107, fig. 52.

402. A number of writers to differing degrees criticize her basic premise or her method altogether. Her sternest critic is Ferrua. See "La criptografia mistica ed i Graffiti Vatican," pp. 246–47: "we believe that it is of little use to accumulate observations, on these or other letters, this or that result, when we have shown clearly that the method itself, that is the theory of mystical epigraphy . . . is not proved." He praises Guarducci for her industrious work, but believes that it is time wasted. Toynbee, "Graffiti beneath St. Peter's," p. 234, sees her work as a "labor of love." Toynbee would at least partially agree with Guarducci in mystical values for certain letters, and the like, but she insists Guarducci has gone much too far (see p. 237–40); at times her methods are questionable and at times her results are absurd. But see the more favorable reactions of Coppo, "De inscriptionibus cryptographicis basilicae vaticanae," p. 115.

403. See Guarducci, *I Graffiti*, I, 381–83; I, 395, fig. 201; I, 431, fig. 221; I 467, fig. 243.

the sentiments of the writers have no relation to the *basic* question of whether the relics of Peter actually did rest beneath the Memoria, or whether by then it was simply *believed* that the relics of Peter were buried there. The name of Peter appearing at this time (A.D. 290–315) on wall *g* is important, however, as an argument to weaken to some extent the Translation Theory. For if the appearance of the name of Peter on wall *g* does indicate a belief that the relics of the apostle rested beneath the Memoria and if the graffiti were written at a period when it was held by those presently maintaining the Translation Theory that the relics were at San Sebastiano, then either their presence there was not well known or the Translation Theory is even more doubtful than has been heretofore generally believed.

If it is *not* conceded that the name of Peter is to be found on wall *g* in any form, it is certain that the Aedicula and the cult of Peter cannot be disassociated, especially at the time when the graffiti on wall *g* were written. And the explanations offered for the absence of the name of Peter are not convincing in light of the appearance of the martyr's name in places such as San Sebastiano. It is not enough to be reminded that San ·Sebastiano *may have been* a schismatic cult center or that, since there were two apostles honored there, the names had to be written out to distinguish which one was being called upon for intercession (most often *both* names appear in the graffiti.)

The uppermost niche, N^3, is larger than N^2 (Plate 36). At a point (Plates 39 and 40) .40 m. above t^1–t^2 in the center of the curve (Plate 36 but cf. Plate 37), there is a square (*cn*, Plate 40) that at one time *may* have been a small window which later was walled up. The meaning of this window is not clear unless it was cut to give light to the Clivus to the west. On the north side of N^3 is the top part of wall *g* (Plate 40). Von Gerkan's theory that N^3 is the oldest part of the monument and the only part of the Aedicula that was built with MR is not convincing. It may be, however, as he also mentions, that the purpose of the alleged window within N^3 was to permit light within the Clivus and the entrance to Q, which may have been covered. To say that N^2 is independent of N^3 above is, it seems, somewhat arbitrary.[404]

If it is acknowledged that the Aedicula was related in some way to the cult of Peter, whether or not it was the actual site of his tomb, what then is the meaning of N^2 and N^3, which rise to a height of approximately 2.30 m. above the ground?[405] Thus, several possible uses of N^3 suggest themselves. For instance, it was made to contain a vase for flowers, a votive lamp, or a statue. The last is the most likely suggestion.[406] The shallowness of N^2 is a problem, but N^3, which was wider and deeper, is more likely to have contained an object of this kind. The height of t^1–t^2 is too great for it to have served as a mensa martyrum and too low for a man to stand beneath. If it was designed for those who would be before it, it was intended that they be in a kneeling position. The question, however, is much easier to ask than to answer, and von Gerkan reminds us that empty niches provide a familiar theme for conjecture.[407]

Torp explains the monument as a "poor or rather insignificant variant of a common pagan type of Aedicula grave, one that is often connected with cremation burials.[408] The monument as reconstructed, Kirschbaum admits, is not common, but similar monuments are to be found, such as that of Sabinus Taurus at the Isola Sacra.

This is a small grave monument built up against an adjoining mausoleum, and consists of a pedimented, column-flanked niche, containing a representation of the dead boy standing at the open doors of his tomb, and below this a smaller recess, which held the ash urn was sealed by the commemorative inscription.[409]

---

404. Von Gerkan, "Kritische Studien," p. 52. He is followed by Schäfer, "Das Apostelgrab," p. 312.

405. Guarducci, *I Graffiti*, II, 411, emphasizes that more recent excavations than those conduced by the editors of the *Esplorazioni* "do not exclude the possibility of a greater height than that indicated."

406. Ferrua, "La Storia," p. 27.

407. Von Gerkan, "Kritische Studien," pp. 45–46. See above, pp. 155–58. Compare Marrou, *DACL*, Vol XV, Part II, pp. 3340–41.

408. "The Vatican Excavations," pp. 47, 51. Compare *Esplorazioni*, I, 138, and Vol. II, fig. XVIII. See Lemerle, "La Publication des Fouilles," pp. 218–19.

409. Toynbee and Perkins, *The Shrine of St. Peter*, p. 163 (see also fig. 18). See Kirschbaum, *Die Gräber*, pp. 78, 136; Ferrua, "A la Recherche," p. 39; Klauser, *Die römische Petrustradition*, p. 109, fig. 10. Compare the suggestion in the *Esplorazioni*, p. 138*n*1. See Lugli, "Scavo di un Sepolcreto

When all aspects of this unique monument have been taken into consideration, there is no proof that there ever existed a central grave beneath the Aedicula; on the other hand, there is no proof that one did not exist. The bones that have been found in N^1 cannot be identified as those of Peter. The loculus of wall g did contain fragments of bone, but there is not sufficient evidence to permit us even to suggest that they belonged to Peter, except that they were no doubt at one time wrapped in purple cloth containing gold thread and were found within a monument which, at least since the time of Constantine, and most likely back to the time of the construction of MR, had been associated with the apostle. The absence of the name of Peter, apart from the possibility that it is present in certain letters with mystical values, on wall g is startling, but is not conclusive evidence that this was *not* Peter's tomb. Therefore, faced with the possibility of two *completely* different answers, neither one contradicted by the archeological evidence, it is not defensible to say with the authors of the *Esplorazioni* and Kirschbaum and others, that the Aedicula, without doubt, stands above the tomb of Peter.[410] Nor is it defensible to state definitely

that it is merely a monument or a cenotaph.[411] It is extremely likely, however, that the Aedicula is to be identified with the Tropaeum of Gaius,[412] and it is beyond doubt that by the time of Constantine the Aedicula was *believed* to have been erected above the actual grave of Peter. Furthermore, the excavations give no real support to the Translation Theory. Some who come to an interpretation of the excavations, already convinced of the truth of this theory, maintain that a breakthrough into N^1 from MR took place A.D. 258. But this is not demonstrable. If it were true, one would expect to find some remains of the ossuary or at least of its having been there. It is argued by Ferrua that the loculus in wall g contained the remains of Peter when they were returned from the Catacombs in the early fourth century. Wall g, however, is much older than this (third century), and the space for the loculus was

---

romano presso la Basilica di San Paulo," pp. 300-1, figs. 7, 12, 15 and 29; Calza, *La Necropoli del Porto di Roma nell'Isola Sacra*, pp. 79, 80, 317; fig. 30; p. 79 and Plates I, IV. These last two works are cited in Marrou, *DACL*, Vol. XV, Part II, p. 3340. See Fink, "Archäologie des Petrusgrabes," pp. 87-93. Compare Ruysschaert, *Réflexions*, pp. 9-10, 16-17.

410. *Esplorazioni*, I, 144, "Gli scavi hanno dunque rivelato quello che nessuno sospettava, cioè che la tomba del Principe degli Apostoli aveva avuto già prima di Costantino una propria sistemazione monumentale, la quale, nel corso di un secolo e mezzo, subì numerose modifiche e rinnovazioni che documentano chiaramente la continua venerazione concentrata in questo luogo." See also Kirschbaum, *Die Gräber*, p. 112; Carcopino, *Études*, pp. 121-28, 133-34, 174; Capocci, "Notae," p. 200; Ruysschaert, *Réflexions*, p. 36; Griffiths, in *The Hibbert Journal*, p. 286; Corte, *Saint Pierre est-il au Vatican?* p. 144; Romanelli, "La Documentazione scientifica," p. 1, col. 4; Jung, "Where is St. Peter Buried?", p. 113; von Gerkan, "Petrus in Vaticano et in Catacumbas," p. 32; Sullivan, "Excavations under St. Peter's," p. 42; Ruysschaert, *The Tomb of St. Peter*, pp. 13-14; Rimoldi, "L'Apostolo San Pietro," p. 344. At the end of a summary article by Smothers, "The Bones of St. Peter," p. 88, he states that "there is a positive, serious probability, however, that thsee are the bones of St. Peter." See the belief that the tomb of Peter has been

located in the words spoken to a group from Philadelphia (Pa.), by Pope Paul VI, *Osservatore Romano*, June 26, 1963, p. 1. M. Guarducci, *The Tomb of St. Peter*, p. 91, states that it is absurd to imagine the Aedicula as a marker for a martyrdom, "The only alternative is to admit that it refers to the tomb."

411. The following are uncertain: Cullmann, *Peter*, pp. 148-57; Marrou, *DACL*, Vol. XV, Part I, pp. 3344-45; Toynbee, "The Shrine of St. Peter and Its Setting," p. 26. The following are certain that the Aedicula is either a monument or a cenotaph: Peterson, "A propos du Tombeau de Saint Pierre," *Le Flambeau*, XXXV (1952), 493 ("Über das Petrusgrab," pp. 328-29); A. M. Schneider, "Das Petrusgrab im Vatikan," pp. 322, 325, 326; von Gerkan, "Kritische Studien," p. 55; H. Grégoire, "Le Problème de la Tombe de Saint Pierre," p. 48. Lemerle, "La Publication des Fouilles," p. 222; "Avoir montré . . . que tout sans execption peut être contesté ou doit être rejeté"; further, he denies that the Aedicula can be identified with the Tropaion of Gaius, nor can *any* certain Christian remains be located in the area investigated. See also his "Les Fouilles de Saint Pierre de Rome," p. 409. See the excellent bibliographical note in Heussi, *Die römische Petrustradition*, pp. 49-50n5, and p. 51. See Klauser, *Die römische Petrustradition*, pp. 69-70; Schulze-Kadelbach, "Die Stellung des Petrus in der Urchristenheit," p. 13; Schäfer, "Das Apostelgrab," pp. 315 ff; Vogelsanger, "Petrusgrab und Papsttum," 311; Burger, *La Tombe*, pp. 29, 31.

412. Chadwick, "St. Peter and St. Paul," p. 31 (compare p. 43), despite the caution of those, including Fink, "Archäologie des Petrusgrabes," p. 83, and the rejection of some, including A. M. Schneider, "III Abteilung: Bibliographie, 7B, Kunstgeschichte," pp. 494-95.

built *with* the wall (not later as maintained in the *Esplorazioni*). In addition, the loculus is not the central point of the Aedicula and, therefore, would hardly have contained what would have been considered the precious relics of the apostle Peter.

Archeology has solved neither the question of the tomb of Peter nor the riddle which some have sought in vain to solve by means of the Translation Theory. The final conclusion of von Gerkan is sober and fair: *If* the body of Peter was recovered at all, a grave must have existed, and it *may* have been in the area of the Aedicula. But if the "central grave" is that of Peter no remains exist today.[413]

Since it is not seriously disputed that Constantine believed the grave of Peter to be beneath the Aedicula, it is unnecessary to describe the development of the monument further. It remains to note briefly, however, the herculean task which was begun by Constantine, and accomplished in about the year A.D. 333 by his son Constantius,[414] in order that this second-century Aedicula might be situated directly below his Basilica— a task which would have been unnecessary if he had been content to build on the Vallis Vaticana only slightly to the south. He was faced with the physical problem of moving a million cubic feet of earth by digging into the side of the hill and carefully depositing this amount on the lower, gradual slope to the east and the sharper slope to the south to create an artificial platform.[415] In addition to this physical problem, there were the legal and moral problems. According to Roman law it was a crime to violate sepulchers, and this had to be done over and over again in the process of the dismantlement and filling in of the large, predominantly pagan necropolis which lay approximately on the north-to-south axis of his intended Basilica.[416] But Constantine, as Pontifex Maximus as well as emperor, could absolve himself and avoid all penalties. His determination to build upon this precise spot in the face of all obstacles is proof that he believed the body of him to whom he was to dedicate his Basilica was buried in a grave beneath.[417]

---

413. Von Gerkan, "Die Forschung nach dem Grab Petri," p. 205.

414. See Cullmann, *Peter*, p. 141*n*72, for an excellent bibliography concerning the exact date when the Basilica was begun. The dates vary from A.D. 324–33.

415. See *Esplorazioni*, I, 152, fig. 107, and Kirschbaum, *Die Gräber*, p. 146, fig. 37.

416. Cod. Theod. IX.17:2 (*The Theodosian Code*, trans. Pharr, p. 239): "those persons also shall be held liable to the same penalty who demolish a monument or diminish its ornamentation."

417. For information concerning the Constantinian Basilica see Barnes, *St. Peter in Rome*, pp. 158–78; Wilpert, "La Tomba di S. Pietro," pp. 27–41; Seston, "Hypothèse sur la date de la basilique constantinienne de Saint-Pierre de Rome," pp. 153–59, and "Les récentes Fouilles de Saint Pierre," pp. 389–92; Wand, "The Location of Constantine's Gold Cross," pp. 84–88; Lemerle, "Les Fouilles de Saint Pierre de Rome," pp. 393–411; Toynbee and Perkins, *The Shrine of St. Peter*, pp. 195–239; *Esplorazioni*, I, 161–72; Marrou, *DACL*, Vol. XV, Part II, pp. 3328, 3329; Carcopino, *Études*, pp. 203–10; Klauser, *Die römische Petrustradition*, pp. 59–66; Guarducci, *Cristo e San Pietro in un Documento precostantiniano*, p. 97*n*161. Kirschbaum, *Die Gräber*, pp. 143–56. See also Lemerle, "Les Fouilles de Saint Pierre de Rome," p. 409.

Conclusions

Two RELATED, but not necessarily interdependent, questions must be answered if the problem of Peter in Rome is to be solved with any degree of satisfaction. If it is found that there is insufficient evidence that Peter was buried beneath the Aedicula on the Vatican, it is not proved thereby that he is not buried somewhere else on the Vatican Hill. If, in addition, it could be proved, which it cannot, that Peter was never buried on the Vatican Hill or at San Sebastiano, that his body had not been thrown into the Tiber and further that he had not been martyred in the Circus of Nero, this evidence still would be insufficient to prove that Peter had never been in Rome. The question of his residence in Rome and that of his possible martyrdom and death there are completely distinct. If, on the other hand, it could be proved, which it cannot, that Peter had never been in Rome, then of course, a discussion of his martyrdom and burial in that city would be superfluous.

In view of the meager information which is available at the present time, no certain statement can be made concerning Peter's Roman residence, martyrdom, and burial. One must continually speak in terms of possibilities and probabilities. The positive aspects of each scrap of evidence must be weighed against the negative. The philological and dating problems must receive careful attention because it is necessary to ascertain exactly what is claimed in a given statement; and late evidence must be discounted, no matter how conveniently it fits into any theory, unless it can be shown that it is directly dependent upon a primitive source. The implications of each bit of evidence must be evaluated not only in their isolated relationship to a single issue but in their relationship to the entire question.

The almost complete silence of the New Testament, and in particular the silence of Paul's Epistle to the Romans and the Book of Acts, is not decisive evidence for or against the theory of a Roman residence of Peter.

On the other hand, 1 Peter 5:13 is plausibly interpreted as testifying to a Roman residence of the apostle. Further positive evidence is found in Ignatius, *Epistle to the Romans* 4:3, and possibly in the fragment of Gaius preserved in the works of Eusebius. The evidence of Dionysius of Corinth, who elaborates upon the simple assumption that Peter at some time in his life did reside in Rome, is suspect. That Peter founded the Church at Rome is extremely doubtful and that he served as its first bishop (as we understand the term today) for even one year, much less the twenty-five-year period that is claimed for him, is an unfounded tradition that can be traced back to a point no earlier than the third century. The liturgical celebrations which relate to the ascent of Peter to the Roman episcopacy do not begin to make their appearance until the fourth century at the earliest. Furthermore, there is no mention of the Roman episcopacy of Peter in the New Testament, 1 Clement, or the epistles of Ignatius. The tradition is only dimly discerned in Hegesippus and may be implied in the suspect letter of Dionysius of Corinth to the Romans. By the third century, however, the early assumptions based upon invention or vague, unfounded tradition have been transformed into "facts" of history.

The evidence which supports the assumption of a Roman residence of Peter cannot be said to be conclusive. It is scarce, vague, and relatively late (nothing antedates the last decade of the first century—at least a generation after he most probably died). But it does seem highly probable that Peter did visit Rome. As has been stated previously, the tradition is too old and too unchallenged in antiquity to be challenged *with any force* in the present. Nothing can be determined, however, about when he came to Rome, how long he stayed, or what function of leadership, if any, he exercised within the Roman Church.

It is somewhat precarious to build upon the insecure foundation of Peter's residence in Rome in order to reach a decision concerning his martyrdom there, "but without hypotheses we can reach no conclusions in this question."[1] It is generally accepted on the basis of 1 Clement and the Gospel of John that Peter was martyred and that, on the basis of the latter document alone, the manner of his death was crucifixion. Both documents can be and have been interpreted in ways that would preclude such a conclusion, but it seems most probable that they do testify to the death of Peter and to the manner in which he died. Details such as his hanging head downward on the cross are obviously apocryphal.

Nothing positive is known concerning the reason for his martyrdom. It may have been in connection with the great fire of Rome or with a refusal to make ritual sacrifice to the emperor in demonstration of loyalty. It may have been caused by some trumped-up charge which an unfriendly community would find possible to bring up against one who was a prominent member of a group which it disliked and distrusted.

None of those early documents which are interpreted as referring to a Roman martyrdom of Peter mentions the time or the place that such a martyrdom supposedly took place. But if the suggestions and implications which are drawn from certain of these early notices are studied with those of the later sources, there results a most persistent tradition which sets the martyrdom of Peter in Rome within the reign of Nero (most probably between A.D. 64 and 67). Only later, less trustworthy sources seem concerned with the place where Peter died, and there appears to be virtual agreement among them that he died in the vicinity of the Vatican.

It does not necessarily follow that if Peter died in the Circus of Nero immediately to the south of the Vatican Hill that he must be buried in the vicinity. It is more than a mere possibility that his body was not recovered for burial at all.[2] The right to claim the body of a condemned criminal could be exercised under Roman law; but in this case, under the conditions which prevailed at that time, the submitting of the request, whether legal or not, would have been tantamount to suicide. Furthermore, if the body had been recovered, it does not necessarily follow that the burial took place in the vicinity of the Vatican Hill, only a bit north of where the imperial gardens were located.

It is entirely probable—more than possible—and not refuted by any known literary, liturgical, or archeological evidence, that the Aedicula on the Vatican is the tropaeum to which Gaius refers. The evidence is not contradicted either if it is further conjectured that the early community knew that the martyrdom of Peter took place in the Circus of Nero to the south of the Vatican Hill and erected some small monument or marker there to commemorate his victory. Later, perhaps in the building of the Red Wall, bones were discovered in the vicinity of the monument or marker at the base of the present Aedicula. Following this discovery a rumor may have arisen which later developed into an accepted tradition, that this was in fact the grave of Peter. It is not a serious problem that the tropaeum is found in what today is a cemetery (an unlikely place for a monument of victory), and there is *some* evidence that the beginning of the recently excavated cemetery was located there as early as the first century A.D. It is true that all of the mausolea date after the first quarter of the second century, and even the oldest grave, γ, in area P was not constructed until after A.D. 116. But it could well be that when the first humble marker or extremely simple monument was erected (perhaps constructed of some perishable material), the area was a plain hillside as yet unmarked by even the gable-like covering of a single grave. The nearest cemetery at that time may have been the one recently discovered over 300 m. to the north of St. Peter's containing 15 mausolea and 70 individual tombs or perhaps a few stately mausolea along the road leading west from the bridge over the Tiber known as the Pons Neronianus.

Whether or not the tradition is based upon fact, Gaius accepted it as true and considered the tropaeum to be the grave of Peter when he referred to it in his disputation with Proclus. The same tradition was accepted by the pilgrim who scribbled the name of Peter on the Red Wall (before or during the erection of wall g).

---

1. Cullmann, *Peter*, p. 153. This statement which Cullmann made in relation to a more limited question is applicable to the larger one as well.

2. The objections of Guarducci, *The Tomb of St. Peter*, p. 92, notwithstanding.

perhaps also by the later pilgrims who scratched their pious phrases on the north side of wall *g*, as well as by the Constantinian workmen who testified to their faith in the nearness of the grave of the apostle Peter by scribbling "Petrus" and the like on the wall at the rear of the center niche in the Tomb of the Valerii. By the time of Constantine the tradition was firmly established and not seriously contested except perhaps by those who *may* have represented some schismatic interest located Ad Catacumbas on the Via Appia.

The relationship between the cult site at the Catacombs and the one on the Vatican is no doubt important, but defies solution. It is possible that the shrine at the Catacombs began as a private or schismatic cult center which looked to Peter and Paul as their patrons. Their choice may have been dictated by a chance finding of a graffito or picture decoration (possibly left from the time—prior to A.D. c. 200—when pagan families or funerary societies celebrated their refrigeria in the cellas above the hypogea), which was interpreted as the names or representations of Peter and Paul (see Plate 18). It would then have been a simple thing for pious imagination to weave a plausible and convincing theory that it was *here* in the Catacombs and not on the Vatican and the Via Ostia that the apostles were buried. In their enthusiasm for their discovery, refrigeria were held, and the names of Peter and Paul, together with pious prayers, were scribbled on the walls of the newly built Triclia. And it may have been still later, A.D. 258, that the now fully organized cult of Peter and Paul was officially recognized by the Church.

The Translation Theory is an ingenious attempt to explain why the site was recognized and to reconcile the obvious conflict of interest between Ad Catacumbas and the Vatican, but it is fraught with as many problems as it solves. It may have been that the Church itself in this period was uncertain concerning whatever claims were made by the cult at the Catacombs, and for a period of a half century or more the fate of the cult was undecided. The destruction of the Memoria Apostolorum, however, and the later dedication of the Basilica to the cult of Sebastian testify to the fact that a decision was finally made in favor of the claims made by the cult at the Vatican: this was the place of the martyrdom of Peter; this was the place of his burial!

In answer to the question of burial we must speak in terms of *belief* and not in terms of true and false. We must ask where was it *believed* that Peter was buried and how early is the evidence which we find for the *belief*? Behind the belief there was probably a *discovery*, and before the discovery there was most probably only a vague association of Peter with the Vatican area as a result of the tradition connected with his martyrdom in the Circus of Nero.

In summary, it appears *more plausible than not* that: 1) Peter did reside in Rome at some time during his lifetime, most probably near the end of his life. 2) He was martyred there as a member of the Christian religion. 3) He was remembered in the traditions of the Church and in the erection of a simple monument near the place where he died. 4) His body was never recovered for burial by the Christian group which later, when relics became of great importance for apologetic reasons, came to believe that what originally had marked the general area of his death also indicated the precise placement of his grave.

Appendix

Chronological Chart, A.D. 90 to 405[1]

	Residence	Martyrdom	Burial
90–100	[1]1 Peter 5:13	[2]Revelation 11:3–13; [1]1 Clement 4–6	
100–110	[1]Ignatius, *Romans* 4:3	[3]Ignatius, *Romans* 4:3	
110–120		[3]John 13:36; [2]John 21:18–19	
115–130	[4]Papias (*E.H.* III. 39:15)		
150?		[2]*Ascension of Isaiah* 4:2–3	
c. 165	[2]Papal list of Hegesippus		[4]The Red Wall (MR) and the Aedicula at the Vatican
160–175	[4]*Acts of Paul*	[4]*Acts of Paul*	
c. 170	[2]Dionysius of Corinth (*E.H.* II. 25:8)	[2]Dionysius of Corinth (*E.H.* II. 25:8)	
175?		[3]*Muratorian Canon* 37	
190	[2]Irenaeus, *Adversus haereses* III. 1:1		
190–200	[3]Silence of Victor in the Easter Controversy with Polycrates		
200	[3]Tertullian, *De praescriptione haereticorum* XXXII		[1]Gaius of Rome (*E.H.* II. 25:6)
200–225	[3]*Acts of Peter* XXXV	[3]*Acts of Peter* XXXV	

1. Each item of the evidence is evaluated from 1 to 4. 1 stands for evidence which strongly supports the tradition; 2 stands for evidence that is fairly strong; 3 indicates weak evidence; and 4 indicates evidence which is often cited but cannot be used in support of the tradition.

	Residence	Martyrdom	Burial
c. 210–220	[3]Clement of Alexandria, *Hypotyposes* VI		
c. 211	[3]*Against the Heresy of Artemon* (*E.H.* V. 28:3)		
220–235	[4]Papal list of Julius Africanus	[4]Origen, *Commentary on Genesis* (*E.H.* III. 1:2)	
256	[4]Cyprian, *Epistle* LXXIV. 2		
260–c. 300			[4]Graffiti at San Sebastiano
c. 300			[4]Graffiti at the Vatican
300–330	[4]*Didascalia*		[3]Eusebius, *Ecclesiastical History*, II. 25:5–7
300–350	[4]*Clementine Homilies*	[4]*Clementine Homilies*	
313		[4]Lactantius, *De mortibus persecutorum* II	
326		[4]Eusebius, *Chronicle*	
330–339			[4]Eusebius, *De theophania* IV.7
336–354	[4]*Depositio Martyrum* viii Kal. Mart.		[4]*Depositio Martyrum* III Kal. iul.
350–400	[4]*Death and Assumption of the Virgin*		
366–384			[4]Damasus 'habitasse' Inscription
c. 380	[4]Papal list of Epiphanius		
405			[4]Prudentius *Peristephanon* XII:4–6

Selected Bibliography

Acta Apostolorum apocrypha. Edited by Constantinus Tischendorf. Leipzig: Avenarius and Mendelssohn, 1851.

Acta Apostolorum apocrypha. Edited by R. A. Lipsius and M. Bonnet. Leipzig: H. Mendelssohn, 1891.

Acta Sanctorum. Edited by J. B. de Rossi and L. Duchesne. Brussels: Socios Bollandianos, 1894.

Aland, Kurt. "Wann starb Petrus? Eine Bemerkung zu Gal. 2:6," *New Testament Studies,* II (1956), 267–75.

—— "Petrus in Rom," *Historische Zeitschrift,* CLXXXIII (April, 1957), 497–517.

—— "Petrus in Rom. Eine notwendige Bemerkung," *Deutsches Pfarrerblatt,* LVIII (1958), 79–81.

—— "Der Tod des Petrus in Rom," *Kirchengeschichtliche Entwürfe.* Berlin: Gerd Mohn, 1960.

—— "Eine abschliessende Bemerkung zur Frage Petrus in Rom," *Historische Zeitschrift,* CXCI (1960), 585–87.

Allen, E. L. "On This Rock," *Journal of Theological Studies,* New Series, V (1954), 59–62.

Altaner, Berthold. "War Petrus in Rom?" *Theologische Revue,* XXXVI (1937), 177–88.

—— "Omnis ecclesia Petri propinqua," *Theologische Rundschau,* XXXVIII (1939), 130–38.

—— "Neues zum Verständnis vom I. Clem. 5, 1–6, 2," *Historisches Jahrbuch der Görresgesellschaft,* LXII–LXIX (1949), 25–30.

Ancient Christian Writers. Translated by James Kleist, Vols. I, VI. Westminster, Md.: The Newman Press, 1946.

The Ante-Nicene Christian Library. Edited by Alexander Roberts and James Donaldson. Vol. II. Edinburgh: T. & T. Clark, 1869.

The Ante-Nicene Fathers. Revised edition by Cleveland Coxe. Vols. I–VIII. Grand Rapids, Mich.: Wm. B. Eerdman's, 1950.

Apostolic Fathers. Translated and edited by Kirsopp Lake. 2 vols. London: William Heinemann, 1924.

Audin, A. "Le memoria de Saint Pierre au cimetière du Vatican," *Byzantion,* XXIV (1954), 265–94.

Augustine: Confessions and Enchiridion. Translated and edited by Albert Cook Outler. (Vol. VII of the *Library of Christian Classics,* edited by John Baillie *et al.*). London: S. C. M. Press, Ltd., 1955.

Bacchus, Francis. "The Twenty-five Years of Peter," *Dublin Review,* Fourth Series, CXX (1897), 386–96.

Balboni, D. "Natale Petri de Cathedra," *Ephemerides Liturgicae,* LXVIII (1954), 97–126.

Balleine, G. R. *Simon Whom He Surnamed Peter.* London: Skeffington and Son, 1958.

Barker, Ethel Ross. *Rome of the Pilgrims and Martyrs.* London: Methuen and Co., 1913.

Barnes, Arthur Stapylton. *St. Peter in Rome and His Tomb on the Vatican Hill.* London: Swan Sonnenschein and Co., 1900.

—— *The Martyrdom of St. Peter and St. Paul.* London: Oxford University Press, 1933.

—— *Christianity at Rome in the Apostolic Age.* London: Methuen and Co., 1938.

—— "The Apostles at Rome," *The Early Church in the Light of the Monuments.* London, New York, Bombay, Calcutta: Longmans, Green and Co., 1913.

—— "A Lost Apostolic Sanctuary," *The Dublin Review,* CLXXV (July, 1924), 1–20.

Barrett, C. K. "Paul and 'Pillar' Apostles," *Studia Paulina in honorem J. de Zwaan,* Haarlem (1953), pp. 1–19.

—— *The Gospel According to St. John.* New York: The Macmillan Co., 1955.

Batiffol, Pierre. *Cathedra-Petri: Études d'histoire ancienne de l'Église.* Paris: Les Éditions du Cerf, 1938.

—— "Natale Petri de Cathedra," *Journal of Theological Studies,* XXVI (1925), 399–404.

Bauer, Adolf. *Das Johannes Evangelium.* Tübingen: J. C. B. Mohr, 1933.

—— "Die Legende von dem Martyrium des Petrus und Paulus in Rom," *Wiener Studien: Zeitschrift für klassische Philologie,* XXXVIII (1916), 270 ff.

—— A Review of An *Unpublished Fragment of the Fourth Gospel,* edited by C. H. Roberts, *Theologische Literaturzeitung,* LXI (1936), 358–59.

Baur, F. Christian. "Die Christuspartei in der korinthischen Gemeinde, der Gegensatz des petrinischen und paulinischen Christentums in der ältesten Kirche, der Apostel Petrus in Rom," *Tübinger Zeitschrift für Theologie* (1831), pp. 137 ff.

Beaupère, René. "Dialogue oecuménique autour du 'Saint Pierre' de M. Oscar Cullmann," *Istina,* II (1955), 347–72.

Belvederi, Giulio. *Le Tombe apostoliche nell'età paleocristiana* (Collezione "Amici delle Catacombe," Vol. XII). Vatican City: Società "Amici delle Catacombe," 1948.

—— "La Tomba di S. Pietro e i recenti lavori nelle Grotte Vaticane," *Bollettino degli Amici delle Catacombe*, XIII (1943), 1–16.

—— "Depositio Petri in Vaticano, Pauli in Via Ostiensi, Utriusque in Catacumbas," *Bollettino degli Amici delle Catacombe*, XIII (1943), 47–64.

—— "All'Osservatore Romano," *Bollettino degli Amici delle Catacombe*, XIII (1943), 43–46.

—— "La cripta di Lucina," *Rivista di Archeologia Cristiana*, XXI (1945), 121–64.

Benoit, Pierre. "La Primauté de Saint Pierre dans le Nouveau Testament," *Istina*, II (1955), 304–34.

Berger, Adolf. "Encyclopedic Dictionary of Roman Law," *Transactions of the American Philosophical Society*, New Series, XLIII (1953), 473, 573, 688.

Bernard, J. H. *The Gospel According to St. John*, Vol. II. New York: Charles Scribner's Sons, 1929.

Bernardi, Jean. "Le Mot τρόπαιον appliqué aux Martyrs," *Vigiliae Christianae*, VIII (1954), 174–75.

—— "A propos des Ossements de la Niche I," *Vigiliae Christianae*, Vol. II, No. 3 (1957), pp. 152–60.

Berra, Luigi. "Lo Sviluppo architettonico della Tomba di S. Pietro," *Arte Cristiana*, XXXIX (May, 1952), 91–104.

—— "Vaticano: II, La tomba di S. Pietro alla luce degli ultimi scavi," *Dizionario Ecclesiastico.*, Vol. III, Turin, 1958.

Bésobrasoff, Cassien. "Saint Pierre et l'Église dans le N.T.," *Istina*, II (1955), 267–304.

Besson, Marius. *Saint Pierre et les Origines de la Primauté romaine*. Geneva: Société d'Éditions artistiques, 1929.

Bettini, S. "Tusco et Basso consulibus. A proposito della tomba di San Pietro," *Jahrbuch der Österreichisches byzantinische Gesellschaft*, I (1951), 67–87.

Bickersteth, E. "A Note on the Festival Commemorating the Primacy of Peter," *Eastern Churches Quarterly*, XIII (1959), 154–55.

Bigg, Charles. "The Clementine Homilies," *Studia Biblica et Ecclesiastica*. Vol. II. Oxford: Clarendon Press, 1890.

—— *The Epistles of St. Peter and St. Jude*. New York: Charles Scribner's Sons, 1901.

Birchler, L. "Das Petrusgrab," *Schweizer Rundschau*, LX (1960), 308–15.

The Book of the Popes (Liber Pontificalis). Translated by Louise Ropes Loomis. New York: Columbia University Press, 1916.

Bosio, Antonio. *Roma sotterranea*. Rome: Ludovico Grignani, 1650.

Boulet, Nöele Maurice-Denis. "À propos des Fouilles de Saint Pierre: Questions historiques et liturgiques," *Recherches de Science religieuses*, XXXIV (1947), 385–406.

Bousset, Wilhelm. *Die Offenbarung Johannis*. Göttingen: H. A. W. Meyer, 1906.

Bultmann, Rudolf. *Das Evangelium des Johannes*. Second edition. Göttingen: Vandenhoeck and Ruprecht, 1952.

Burger, Jean-Daniel. *La Tombe de Saint Pierre, est-elle identifiée?* Geneva: Les Cahiers de 'Foi et Verité,' 1954.

Burton, Ernest de Witt. *The Epistle of Paul to the Galatians*. Edinburgh: T. & T. Clark, 1921.

Busch, Karl. "Das Petrusgrab," *Das Münster*, V (1952), 313–21.

The Byzantine Office. Edited by John Bannerman Wainewright. London: Cope and Fenwick, 1909.

Cajetan, Thomas de Vio. *De Comparatione Auctoritatis Papae et Concilii* (written at Rome, 1511). Edited by Vincentius M. Jacobus Pollet. No. 39. Rome: Institutam 'Angelicum,' 1936.

Calder, W. M. "Studies in Early Christian Epigraphy," *Journal of Roman Studies*, X (1920), 42–59.

Calza, G. *La Necropoli del Porto di Roma nell'Isola Sacra*. Rome: La Libreria dello Stato, 1940.

Campenhausen, Hans von. *Die Idee des Martyriums in der alten Kirche*. Göttingen: Vandenhoeck und Ruprecht, 1936.

Campiche, Michel. "Saint Pierre et son Martyre," *Revue de l'Université d'Ottawa*, XXII (1952), 249–73.

Capocci, Valentino. "Notae: gli Scavi del Vaticano alla Ricerca del Sepolcro di S. Pietro e alcune Note Diritto funerario romano," *Studia et Documenta Historiae et Iuris*, XVIII (1952), 199–212.

Carcopino, Jérôme. *Études d'Histoire chrétienne: le Christianisme secret du Carré magique: les Fouilles de Saint-Pierre et la Tradition*. Paris: Albin Michel, 1953. (Second edition, 1963.)

—— *De Pythagore aux Apôtres*. Paris: Flammarion, 1956.

—— "Note sur deux Textes controversés de la Tradition apostolique romaine," *Comptes Rendus de l'Académie des Inscriptions et Belles-Lettres* (1952), pp. 424–34.

—— "Qu'ont prouvé les Fouilles de Saint-Pierre?" *Historia*, CXVI (1956), 73–79.

—— "Encore 'Tropaeum' et 'nomen,'" *Studi in onore di A. Calderini e R. Paribeni*. Vol. I. Milan, 1956.

Caspar, E. *Die älteste römische Bischofliste*. Berlin: Verlagsgesellschaft für Politik und Geschichte, 1926.

Castagnoli, Ferdinando. "La Tomba di S. Pietro," *Studium*, XLVIII (January, 1952), 30–36.

—— "Il circo di Nerone in Vaticano," *Rendiconti della Pontificia Accademia Romana di Archeologia*, Third Series, XXXII (1959–60), 97–121.

Cecchelli Carlo. *Monumenti cristiani—eretici di Roma*. Rome: Fratelli Palombi, 1944.

—— "L'Obelisco Vaticano," *Capitolium*, XXV (1950), 53–71.

—— "Un vecchio Errore," *Osservatore Romano* (November 18, 1951), p. 3, cols. 1, 2.

—— *Il Tempo*, January 31, 1950, and December 11, 1952.

—— "La tombe di N. S. Gesu Cristo e le 'Memorie' Apostoliche," *Universita degli studi di Roma*, Rome: Editrice F. Ferrari (1952–53).

Celi, C. "Sulle memorie e monumenti dei SS. Apostoli Pietro e Paolo a Roma," *La Civiltà Cattolica*. LXXXVI, No. 2 (1935), 247-57; 587-94; LXXXVI, No. 3 (1935), 157-73; 582-89.

—— "La Memoria apostolica sull'Appia," *La Civiltà Cattolica*. LXXXVII, No. 2 (1936), 483-90; LXXXVII, No. 3 (1936), 387-98.

Chadwick, Henry. "Pope Damasus and the Peculiar Claim of Rome to St. Peter and St. Paul," *Neotestamentica et Patristica*. Leiden: E. J. Brill, 1962, pp. 313-18.

—— "St. Peter and St. Paul in Rome: the Problem of the Memoria Apostolorum ad Catacumbas," *Journal of Theological Studies*, New Sereies, VIII (1957), 31-52.

—— A Review of Theodor Klauser's *Die römische Petrustradition im Lichte der neuen Ausgrabungen unter der Peterskirche*, *Gnomon*, Vol. XXX, Part 5 (1958), pp. 409-10.

Charles, R. H. *The Ascension of Isaiah*. London: Adam and Charles Black, 1900.

—— *The Revelation of St. John*. Vol. I. New York: Charles Scribner's Sons, 1920.

—— *The Apocalypse of Baruch*. London: Macmillan & Co., 1929.

Clementis Romani, Homiliae. Edited by Adelbertus Schwegler. Stuttgart: Sumtibus A. Becheri, 1847.

Colagrossi, P. Mariano. "Di un Monumento recentemente Scoperto presso il Sepolcro apostolico dell'Appia," *Nuovo Bullettino di Archeologia cristiana*, XV (1909), 51-61.

Colini, A. M. "Il Sepolcro di S. Pietro," *Capitolium*, XXVII (1952), 1-16.

Congar, Y. "Cephas-Céphalè-Caput," *Revue du Moyen Age Latin*, VIII (1952), 5-42.

Confessions and Enchiridion of Augustine. Translated by Albert Cook Outler. (Vol. VII of the *Library of Christian Classics*, edited by John Baillie, *et al.*, 13 vols.) London: S. C. M. Press, 1955.

Connolly, R. H. "Eusebius H. E. V.28," *Journal of Theological Studies*, XLIX (1948), 73-79.

Coppo, A. "Gli scavi della necropoli vaticana in una recentissima pubblicazione," *Ephemerides Liturgicae*, LXXIV (1960), 128-32.

—— "De inscriptionibus cryptographicis basilicae vaticanae," *Ephemerides Liturgicae*, LXXVII (1963), 115.

Corpus Inscriptionum Latinarum. Edited by Theodore Mommsen, Johannes Battista de Rossi, *et al.* Vol. I, Part I. Berlin: Akademie der Wissenschaften, 1876.

Corpus Scriptorum Ecclesiasticorum Latinorum. Editum consilio et impensis Academiae Litterarum Vindobonensis, 1866.

Corte, Nicholas. *Saint Pierre est-il au Vatican?* Paris: Librarie Arthème Fayard, 1956.

Craig, Clarence T. "I Corinthians," *Interpreter's Bible*, Vol. X. New York: Abingdon Cokesbury Press, 1953.

Cristiani, L. "Les Fouilles de Saint Pierre du Vatican," *L'Ami du Clergé*, LXIII (January, 1953), 49-62; LXIII (April, 1953), 229-31.

Cross, F. L. *I Peter, A Paschal Liturgy*. London: A. R. Mowbray & Co., 1954.

Cugnoni, Giuseppe. "Settele e il suo Diario," *Scuola romana*, IV (1886), 272.

Cullmann, Oscar. *Le Problème littéraire et historique du Roman pseudo-clémentin*. Paris: Librairie Félix Alcan, 1930.

—— *Peter, Disciple, Apostle, Martyr*. Second edition. Translated by Floyd V. Filson. Philadelphia: The Westminster Press, 1962.

—— "Les Causes de la Mort de Pierre et de Paul d' après le Témoignage de Clément romain," *Revue d'histoire et de Philosophie religieuses* (1930), pp. 294-300.

—— A Review of Jocelyn Toynbee's and John Ward Perkins' *The Shrine of St. Peter and the Vatican Excavations*, The *Journal of Ecclesiastical History*, XII (1956), 238-40.

Cumont, F. "Un rescrit impérial sur la violation de sépulture," *Revue historique*, CLXIII (1930), 241-66.

Cureton, William. *Ancient Syriac Documents*. London and Edinburgh: Williams and Norgate, 1906.

D. Martin Luthers Werke. Weimar edition. Vol. LIV. Weimar: Herman Böhlaus, 1928.

Damasi Epigrammata. Maximillianus Ihm. Leipzig: B. C. Teubner, 1885.

Danes, G. "La tomba di S. Pietro. Un ventennio di ricerche archeologiche," *Rivista Biblica*, VIII (1960), 144-65.

Daniel-Rops, H., *The Church of the Apostles and the Martyrs*. Translated by Audrey Butler. London: J. M. Dent, 1960.

Dannenbauer, Heinrich. "Die Petruslegende," *Historische Zeitschrift*, CXLVI (1932), 239 ff.

—— "Nochmals die römische Petruslegende," *Historische Zeitschrift*, CLIX (1939), 81-88.

Davis, Guy M. "Was Peter Buried in Rome?", *Journal of Bible and Religion*, XX (1952), 167-71.

De Azevédo, Michelangelo Cagiano. "L'Origine della Necropoli Vaticana secondo Tacito," *Aevum*, XXIX (1955), 575-77.

De Bruyne, Luciano. "La Tomba apostolica in Vaticano," *Rivista di Archeologia cristiana*, XXVII (1951), 218-24.

De Labriolle, P., "Refrigerium," *Bulletin d'ancienne littérature et d'archéologie chrétienne* (1912), pp. 214-19.

Delafosse, Henri. "La Lettre de Clément romain aux Corinthiens," *Revue de l'histoire des Religions*, XCVII (1928), 53-89.

Delehaye, Hippolyte. *Legends of the Saints*. Translated by V. M. Crawford. London: Longmans, Green and Co., 1907.

—— *Les Origines du Culte des Martyrs*. Tenth edition. Brussels: Société des Bollandistes, 1933.

—— "Le Témoignage des Martyrologes," *Analecta Bollandiana*, XXVI (1907), 78-99.

—— "Refrigerare, Refrigerium," *Journal des savants* (November, 1926), pp. 385-90.

—— "Le Sanctuaire des Apôtres sur la Voie apienne," *Analecta Bollandiana*, XLV (1927), 294–304.

—— "Hagiographie et Archéologie romaines," *Analecta Bollandiana*, XLV (1927), 304–322.

—— "TUSCO ET BASSO CONS.," *Mélanges Paul Thomas*. Bruges: Sainte Catherine, 1930.

—— "The Martyrdom of St. Peter and St. Paul," *Analecta Bollandiana*, LII (1934), 69–72.

De Marco, Angelus A. *The Tomb of Saint Peter*. Leiden: E. J. Brill, 1964.

Demonstrationis Evangelicae. Translated by W. J. Farrar. London: Society for Promoting Christian Knowledge, 1920.

de Rossi, Giovanni Battista. *La Roma sotterranea cristiana*. Vol. I. Rome: Cromo-litografia pontificia, 1864.

—— "La Catedra di S. Pietro nel Vaticano e quella del Cemetero ostriano," *Bullettino di Archeologia cristiana*, V (June, 1867), 33–48.

Derouou, W. "Les récentes Fouilles à Saint-Pierre de Rome et la Découverte du Tombeau de Saint Pierre," *Les Études classiques*, XXI (1953), 145–55.

De Visscher, Fernand. "A propos d'une Inscription nouvellement découverte sous la basilique Saint-Pierre," *L'Antiquité classique*, XV (1946), 117–26.

—— "Locus religiosus," *Atti del Congresso internazionale di diritto romano e di storia del diritto*. Vol. III. Milan: Giuffrè, 1948.

—— "Un texte négligé dans les controversés autour de la tombe de l'apôtre Pierre," *Studia et documenta historiae et juris*, XXVI (1960), 362–65.

Dibelius, Martin. *Die Religion in Geschichte und Gegenwart; Handbuch für Theologie und Religionswissenschaft*. III, 1929. Edited by Hermann Gunkel and Leopold Zscharnack. 6 vols. Tübingen: J. C. B. Mohr, 1927–32.

—— "Rom und die Christen im ersten Jahrhundert," *Sitzungsberichte der Heidelberger Akademie der Wissenschaften: philosophisch-historische Klasse*, 2 Abhandlung (1941–42), pp. 18–29.

Didascalia Apostolorum. Translated by R. H. Connolly. Oxford: Clarendon Press, 1929.

Diekmann, H. "Das Zeugnis des Polykrates für die Apostelgräber in Rom," *Zeitschrift für katholische Theologie*, LXV (1921), 627–34.

Dinkler, E. "Die Petrus-Rom-Frage," *Theologische Rundschau*, XXV (1959), 189–230; 289–325; XXVII (1961), 33–64.

—— "Die 'Memoria Apostolorum' an der via Appia," *Die Petrus-Rom-Frage, Theologische Rundschau*, XXV (1959), 326–35.

—— "Petrus Apostel," *Religion in Geschichte und Gegenwart*, V (1961), 247–49.

Diodorus of Sicily. Translated and edited by C. H. Oldfather. Vol. II. London: William Heinemann, 1935.

Dio Cassius, Roman History. Translated by Earnest Cary. Vol. VIII. London: William Heinemann, 1917.

Downey, Glanville. A Review of Jocelyn Toynbee's and John Ward Perkins' "The Shrine of St. Peter and the Vatican Excavations," *American Journal of Archeology*, LXII (1958), 247–48.

Duchesne, Louis. *Le Liber Pontificalis, Texte, Introduction et Commentaire*. Vols. I¹, I², and II. Paris: Bibliothèque des Ecoles Français d'Athènes et de Rome, 1884–1892.

—— *Origines du Culte chrétien*. Tenth edition. Paris: Ancienne Librairie Thorin et Fils, 1898. (English translation by M. L. McClure, *Christian Worship*. London: Society for Promoting Christian Knowledge, 1903.)

—— *Histoire ancienne de l'Église*. Paris: Fontemoing, 1906.

—— "Les Sources du Martyrologe hieronymien," *Mélanges d'Archéologie et d'Histoire*, V (1885), 120–60.

—— "La 'Memoria Apostolorum' de la Via Appia," *Atti della Pontificia Accademia romana di Archeologia: Memorie*, Third Series, Vol. I, Part I (1923), pp. 1–22.

Early Christian Fathers. Translated and edited by Cyril C. Richardson *et al.* (Vol. I of the *Library of Christian Classics*. Edited by John Baillie *et al.* 13 vols.) London: S. C. M. Press, 1953.

Eltester, W. "Epimetron: die Gebeine des Petrus," *Zeitschrift für neutestamentliche Wissenschaft*, XLIII (1950–51), 280.

Elton, G. E., *Simon Peter*. London: Peter Davies, 1965.

Encyclopedia Biblica. Vol. IV, 1903. Edited by T. K. Cheyne. 4 vols. London: Charles Black, 1899–1907.

Epictetus. Translated by W. A. Oldfather. London: William Heinemann, 1928.

Epictetus. Translated by Thomas Higginson. New York: Walter Black, 1944.

Erbes, C. *Die Todestage der Apostel Paulus und Petrus und ihre römischen Denkmäler*. Leipzig: J. C. Hinrichs, 1899.

—— "Petrus nicht in Rom, sondern in Jerusalem Gestorben," *Zeitschrift für Kirchengeschichte*, XXII (1901), 1 ff., 161 ff.

—— "Die geschichtlichen Verhältnisse der Apostelgräber in Rom," *Zeitschrift für Kirchengeschichte*, XLIII (1924), 38–92.

Esplorazioni sotto la Confessione di San Pietro in Vaticano. Edited by B. M. Appollonj-Ghetti, Antonio Ferrua, Enrico Josi and Englebert Kirschbaum. Vols. I, II. Vatican City: Tipografia Poliglotta Vaticana, 1951.

Essays on the Early History of the Church and the Ministry. Edited by Cuthbert Hamilton Turner. Oxford: Clarendon Press, 1921.

The Ethiopic Didascalia. Translated by J. M. Harden. London: Macmillan & Co., 1920.

Euripides, Iphigenia in Tauris. Edited by Isaac Flagg. Boston: Ginn and Co., 1899. (English translation by Witter Brynner *et al.* Chicago: University Press, 1956.)

Eusebii Scripta Historica. Edited by Fredericus Adolphus Heinichen. Vol. I. Leipzig: Hermann Mendelssohn, 1868.

Eusebius. *The Ecclesiastical History.* Vol. I. Translated by Kirsopp Lake. Vol. II. Translated by J. E. L. Oulton. London: William Heinemann, 1926.

Ewig, E. "Petrus- und Apostelkult im spätromishen und Frankischen Gallien," *Zeitschrift für Kirchengeschichte,* LXXI (1960), 215–51.

Feltoe, Charles Lett. *Sacramentarium Leonianum.* Cambridge: University Press, 1896.

Ferrua, Antonio. "Nelle Grotto di S. Pietro," *La Civiltà Cattolica,* XCII (1941), 358–65, 424–33.

—— "Nuove Scoperte sotto S. Pietro," *La Civiltà Cattolica,* XCIII (1942), 73–86, 228–41.

—— "Sulle Orme di S. Pietro," *La Civiltà Cattolica,* XCIV (1943), 81–102.

—— "Questioni di Epigrafia eretica, romana," *Rivista di Archeologia cristiana,* XXI (1945), 193–206.

—— "Cataracta," *Enciclopedia Cattolica,* III (1949), 1086.

—— "A la Recherche du Tombeau de Saint Pierre," *Études,* CCLXXII (1952), 35–47.

—— "Il Sepolcro di S. Pietro è di certo nella Basilica Vaticana," *Il Messagero* (January 16, 1952).

—— "La Storia del Sepolcro di San Pietro," *La Civiltà Cattolica,* CIII (1952), 15–29.

—— "La criptografia mistica ed i graffiti Vaticani," *Rivista di Archeologia Cristiana,* XXXV (1959), 231–47, with 2 figs.

—— "Lavori a S. Sebastiano," *Rivista de Archeologia Cristiana,* XXXVII (1961), 203–36.

Filson, Floyd. "A New Papyrus Manuscript of the Gospel of John," *The Biblical Archaeologist,* XX (1957), 54–63.

Findlay, J. Alexander. *A Portrait of Peter.* New York: The Abingdon Press, 1935.

Finegan, Jack. *Light from the Ancient Past.* Princeton: Princeton University Press, 1946.

Fink, Josef. "Archäologie des Petrusgrabes," *Theologische Revue,* L (1954), 81–102.

The First Epistle of Clement. Edited by W. K. Lowther Clarke. London: Society for Promoting Christian Knowledge, 1937.

Foakes-Jackson, F. J. *Peter, Prince of the Apostles: A Study in the history and tradition of Christianity.* New York: George H. Doran, 1927.

—— "Evidence for the Martyrdom of Peter and Paul in Rome," *Journal of Biblical Literature,* XLVI (1927), 74–78.

Foakes-Jackson, F. J., and Kirsopp Lake. *The Beginnings of Christianity.* Vol. V. London: Macmillan & Co., 1933.

Fontana, D. *Della Trasportazione dell'Obelisco Vaticano et delle Fabbriche di N. S. P. Sisto V.* Vol. I. Rome: Domenico Basa, 1590. Vol. II. Naples: 1603.

Fornari, F. *San Sebastiano* (Collezione "Amici delle catacombe," IV), Società "Amici delle catacombe, 1934, Vatican City, 1934.

Fouard, C. *St. Peter and the First Years of Christianity.* Translated by G. F. X. Griffith. New York: Longmans, Green and Co., 1903.

Franchi De Cavalieri, P. "Note agiografiche," *Studi e Testi,* XXVII (1915), 124–25.

Fridrichsen, A. "Propter Invidiam. Note sur Clém. V.," *Eranos,* XLIV (1946), 161–74.

Gagov, G. M. "Il termine 'nomina' sinonimo di 'reliquiae' nell' antica epigrafia cristiana," *Miscellanea Francescana,* LV (1955), 3–13.

Gealy, Frank. "The Second Epistle to Timothy," *Interpreter's Bible,* XI, 475–76. New York: Abingdon-Cokesbury Press, 1955.

Gebhardt, Oscar de, and Adolf Harnack. "Clementis Romani ad Corinthos quae dicuntur Epistulae," *Patrum Apostolorum,* Fasc. I, Part II, Ed. II. Leipzig: J. C. Hinrichs, 1876.

Giet, Stanislas. "Le Témoignage de Clément de Rome," *Revue des Sciences religieuses,* XXIX (1955), 123–36, 333–45.

Giles, E. *Documents Illustrating Papal Authority.* London: S. P. C. K., 1952.

Gilg, Arnold. "Die Petrusfrage im Lichte der neuesten Forschung," *Theologische Zeitschrift,* XI (1955), 185–206.

Goguel, Maurice. *L'Église primitive.* Paris: Payot, 1947.

—— *The Birth of Christianity.* Translated by H. C. Snape. New York: The Macmillan Co., 1954.

—— "L'Apôtre Pierre a-t-il joué un Rôle personnel dans les Crises de Grèce et de Galatie?" *Revue d'Histoire et de Philosophie religieuses,* XIV (1934), 461–500.

Goodenough, Erwin R. *Jewish Symbols in the Graeco-Roman Period.* Vol. I. Kingsport, Tenn.: Kingsport Press, 1953.

Goodspeed, Edgar J. *An Introduction to the New Testament.* Chicago: University of Chicago Press, 1945.

Grant, Frederick C. *Hellenistic Religions.* New York: The Liberal Arts Press, 1953.

—— *Rome and Reunion.* New York: Oxford, 1965.

Greek-English Lexicon. Edited by Henry George Liddell and Robert Scott. Revised by H. S. Jones. Oxford: Clarendon Press, 1940.

Grégoire, Henri. "Les Persécutions dans l'Empire romain," *Mémoires de l'Académie des Sciences de Belgique.* Second Series, Classe des Lettres, XLVI (1950), 24–35, 47–54, 101–2.

—— "Le Tombeau de Valerius Herma (Hermas) et l'Inscription relative à S. Pierre," *La Nouvelle Clio,* IV (1952), 398–401.

—— "Le Problème de la Tombe de Saint Pierre," *La Nouvelle Clio,* V (1953), 48–58.

Gregoire, Henri, and Paul Orgels. "La véritable date du martyre de S. Polycarpe (23 février 177) et le 'Corpus Polycarpianum,'" *Analecta Bollandiana,* LXIX (1951), 1–38.

Gregorovius, Ferdinand. *The Ghetto and the Jews of Rome.* New York: Schocken Books, 1948.

Griffe, H. "A propos de la date du martyre de saint Polycarpe," *Bulletin de Littérature ecclésiastique*, LII (1951), 170–77.

—— "La Légende du Transfert des Corps de Saint Pierre et de Saint Paul *Ad Catacumbas*," *Bulletin de Littérature ecclésiastique*, LII (1951), 193–209.

—— "Institutum Neronianum," *Bulletin de Littérature ecclésiastique*, LIII (1952), 158–60.

—— "La Question du Transfert des Reliques de Saint Pierre 'ad Catacumbas'," *Bulletin de Littérature ecclésiastique*, LIV (1953), 129–42.

—— "Nouvelle visite 'ad catacumbas'," *Bulletin de Littérature ecclésiastique*. LIX (1958), 119–22.

—— "La Persécution contre les Chrétiens de l'an 64," *Bulletin de Littérature ecclésiastique*, LXV (1964), 3–16.

Griffiths, J. Gwyn. "The Vatican Excavations and the Tomb of St. Peter," *The Hibbert Journal*, LV (1957), 140–49, 285–86.

Grisar, Hartmann. *Analecta Romana*. Vol. I. Rome, 1899.

—— *Geschichte Rom und der Papste im Mittelalter*. Freiburg: Herder, 1901.

—— "Le Tombe apostoliche di Roma," *Studie Documenti di Storia e Diritto*, XIII (1892), 321–73.

—— "Le antiche Testimonianze sulla Luogo della Crocifissione di S. Pietro," *La Civiltà Cattolica*, LVI (1905), 719–25.

Grossi-Gondi, F. "Il 'Refrigerium' celebrato in Onore dei SS. Apostoli Pietro e Paolo nel sec. IV ad Catacumbas," *Römische Quartalschrift*, XXIX (1915), 221–49.

—— "Il rito funebre del 'Refrigerium,'" *Atti della Pontificia Accademia romana di Archeologia: Dissertazioni*, Second Series, XIV (1920), 263–77.

Guarducci, Margherita. *Cristo e San Pietro in un Documento precostantiniano della Necropoli Vaticana*. Rome: "l'Erma" di Bretschneider, 1953.

—— *I Graffiti sotto la Confessione di San Pietro in Vaticano*. Vols. I–III. Vatican City: Libreria Editrice Vaticana, 1958.

—— *The Tomb of St. Peter, the New Discoveries in the Sacred Grottoes of the Vatican*. Translated by J. McLellan. New York: Hawthorn Books, 1960.

—— *Le Reliquie di Pietro sotto La Confessione della Basilica Vaticana*. Vatican City: Libraria Editrice Vaticana, 1965.

—— "Un Documento precostantiniano su San Pietro nelle Grotte vaticane," *Osservatore Romano* (November 22, 1952), p. 3, cols. 1–6.

—— "Nuove iscrizioni nella zona del circo di Nerone in Vaticano," *Atti della Pontificia accademia romana di Archeologia, Rendiconti*, Third Series, XXXII (1959–60), 123–32.

Guignebert, C. *La Primauté de Pierre et la Venue de Pierre à Rome*. Paris: Librairie critique, Émile Nourry, 1909.

—— "La Sépulture de Pierre," *Revue historique*, CLXVIII (1931), 225–53.

Haenchen, E. "Petrus-Probleme," *New Testament Studies*, VII (1961), 187–98.

Haller, Johannes. *Das Papsttum, Idee und Wirklichkeit*. (Vol. I, 1934.) 3 vols. Stuttgart: Cotta, 1934–45.

Harnack, Adolf. *Die Chronologie der altchristlichen Literatur bis Eusebius*. 2 vols. Leipzig: J. C. Hinrichs, 1897.

—— *Die Mission und Ausbreitung des Christentums*. Vol. II. Second edition. Leipzig: J. C. Hinrichs, 1915.

—— *Einführung in die alte Kirchengeschichte*. Leipzig: J. C. Hinrichs 'sche Buchhandlung, 1929.

Harris, Rendel. "Hadrian's Decree of Expulsion of the Jews from Jerusalem," *Harvard Theological Review*, XIX (1926), 199–206.

Harrison, P. N. *Polycarp's Two Epistles to the Philippians*, Cambridge: University Press, 1936.

Headlam, A. C. "The Epistle of Polycarp to the Philippians," *The Church Quarterly Review*, CXLI, (1945), 1–25.

Hermann, Léon. "La mort de St. Paul et de St. Pierre, 811 U.C. = 58 ap. J.C.," *Revue de l'Université de Brussels*, XLI (December, 1935–January, 1936), 189–99.

Hertling, Ludwig, and Englebert Kirschbaum. *Die römischen Katakomben und ihre Martyrer*. Vienna: Herder, 1950.

Heussi, Karl. *War Petrus in Rom?*. Gotha: L. Klotz, 1936.

—— *Neues zur Petrusfrage*. Jena, 1939.

—— *Die römische Petrustradition in kritischer Sicht*. Tübingen: J. C. B. Mohr, 1955.

—— "War Petrus wirklich römischer Märtyrer? *Die Christliche Welt*, LI (February, 1937), 162–71.

—— "Die Entstehung der römischen Petrustradition," *Deutsches Pfarrerblatt* (1949), pp. 82 f., 301 f., 501–4.

—— "Papst Anekletus I und die Memoria Petri auf dem Vatikan," *Deutsches Pfarrerblatt*, XLIX (1949), 301 ff.

—— "Gal. 2 und der Lebensaugung der jerusalemischen Urapostel," *Theologische Literaturzeitung*, LXXVII (1952), 67–72.

Hirsch, Emmanuel. "Petrus und Paulus," *Zeitschrift für neutestamentliche Wissenschaft*, XXIX (1930), 63–76.

Hitchcock, F. R. Montgomery. "Charges Against the Christians in Tacitus," *The Church Quarterly Review*, CIX (January, 1930), 300–16.

Hudec, Ladislas E. "Recent Excavations under St. Peter's Basilica in Rome," *Journal of Bible and Religion*, XX (1952), 13–18.

Hülsen, Charles. "Il Gaianum e la naumachia Vaticana," *Dissertazioni della Pontificia accademia romana di archeologia*, Second Series, VIII (1903), 3–34.

—— "Il circo di Nerone al Vaticano," *Miscellanea Ceriani*. Milan, 1910.

Hunter, Archibald. "The First Epistle of Peter," *Interpreter's Bible*. Vol. XII. New York: Abingdon-Cokesbury Press, 1957.

Inscriptiones Latinae Cristianae Veteres. Edited by Ernestus Diehl. Vols. I–III. Berlin: Weidmannos, 1925–31.

Instinsky, Hans Ulrich. "Christen und Heiden im Umkreis des Petrusgrabes," *Hochland*, L (August, 1958), 586–88.

Irenaeus. *Demonstration of the Apostolic Preaching.* Translated by J. H. Robinson. New York: Society for Promoting Christian Knowledge, 1920.

Jacquin, A. M. *Histoire de l'Église.* Vol. I, 1928. 2 vols. Paris: Éditions de la Revue des Jeunes, 1928–36.

James, Montague Rhodes. *The Apocryphal New Testament.* Oxford: The Clarendon Press, 1924.

Jones, J. Stuart. "The Memoria Apostolorum on the Via Appia," *Journal of Theological Studies,* XXVIII (1927), 30–39.

Jongkees, J. H. "The Tomb of St. Peter," *Mnemosyne,* Fourth Series, XIII (1960), 143–55.

Josephus, Flavius: Works of. Translated by C. W. Wilson. Vol. III. London: George Bell and Sons, 1889.

Josephus, Flavius: Works of. Translated by A. R. Shilleto. Vol. III. London: G. Bell and Sons, 1912.

Josi, Enrico. "Paolo, Apostolo, Santo," *Enciclopedia Cattolica,* IX (1952), 717–20.

—— "Pietro, Apostolo, Santo," *Enciclopedia Cattolica,* IX (1952), 1400–27.

—— "Ipotesi sulla traslazione delle sole teste degli apostoli in Catacumbas in seguito all editto di Valeriano del 258," *Rivista di Archeologia Cristiana,* XXIX (1953), 94–95.

—— "Les 'KOIMHTHPIA' d'Eusèbe de Césarée et les Tombes apostoliques," *Comptes Rendus de l'Académie des Inscriptions et Belles-Lettres* (1954), p. 350.

—— "Zona archeologica e Basilica," *Enciclopedia Cattolica,* XII (1954), 1053–97.

—— "Gli Scavi nelle sacre Grotte Vaticane," *Il Vaticano nel 44* (1944), 188–99.

Journet, Charles. *The Primacy of Peter.* Translated by John Chapin. Westminster, Maryland: The Newman Press, 1954.

Jung, Eva-Maria. "Where Is Saint Peter Buried?," *Catholic World,* CCII (1965), 107–13.

Juster, Jean. *Les Juifs dans l'Empire romain.* Vols. I, II. Paris: Librairie Paul Geuthner, 1914.

Kaas, Ludwig. "The Search for the Bones of St. Peter," *Life,* March 27, 1950, pp. 65–85.

Karrer, Otto. *Peter and the Church: An Examination of Cullmann's Thesis.* Edinburgh and London: Nelson, 1963.

Katzenmeyer, H. "Bemerkung zur Martyrien Literatur," *Göttingen gelehrte Nachrichten* (1916), pp. 437 ff.

—— "Zur Frage, ob Petrus in Rom war," *Internationale kirchliche Zeitschrift* (1938), pp. 129–40.

Kellner, Werner. "The Search for Peter's Tomb," *Catholic Digest,* XXI (March, 1957), 106–10.

Kesich, V. "The Problem of Peter's Primacy," *St. Vladimir's Seminary Quarterly,* IV (1960), 26–48.

Kirsch, J. B. "Peter," *The Catholic Encyclopedia.* Edited by Charles G. Herbermann *et al.* Vol. II. New York: The Encyclopedia Press, 1913.

Kirsch, Johann Peter. "Das 'Martyrologium Hieronymianum' und die römische 'Depositio Martyrum' im Chronographen von 354," *Beiträge zur Geschichte des christlichen Altertums und der byzantinischen Literatur: Festgabe Albert Ehrhard.* Bonn: Kurt Schroeder, 1922.

—— "Die 'Memoria Apostolorum' an der Appischen Strasse zu Rom und die liturgische Festfeier des 29. Juni," *Jahrbuch für Liturgiewissenschaft,* III (1923), 33–50.

—— "Le Feste degli Apostoli S. Pietro e S. Paolo nel Martirologio Gerolimiano," *Rivista di Archeologia cristiana,* II (1925), 54–83.

—— "Die beiden Apostelfeste Petri Stuhlfeier und Pauli Bekehrung im Januar," *Jahrbuch für Liturgiewissenschaft,* V (1925), 48–67.

Kirschbaum, Englebert. *Die Gräber der Apostelfürsten.* Frankfurt on Main: Heinrich Scheffler, 1957.

—— *The Tombs of St. Peter and St. Paul.* Translated by J. Murray. New York: St. Martins Press, 1959.

—— "Gli Scavi sotto la Basilica di S. Pietro," *Gregorianum,* XXIX (1948), 544–57.

—— "Petri in Catacumbas," *Miscellanea liturgica in honorem L. C. Mohlberg,* I (1948), 221–29.

—— "Das Petrusgrab," *Stimmen der Zeit,* CL (August, 1952), 321–32; (September, 1952), 401–10.

—— "Besprechung von Klauser, 'die römische Petrustradition,'" *Römische Quartalschrift,* LI (1956), 247–54.

Klauser, Theodor. *Die Cathedra im Totenkult der heidnischen und christlichen Antike.* Münster: Aschendorffschen Verlagsbuchhandlung, 1927.

—— *Die römische Petrustradition im Lichte der neuen Ausgrabungen unter Peterskirche.* Cologne: Westdeutscher Verlag, 1956.

—— "Die Deutung der Ausgrabungsbefunde unter S. Sebastiano und am Vatikan," *Jahrbuch für Antike und Christentum,* V (1962), 33–38.

Klein, C. "Der Verleugnung des Petrus: eine Traditions geschichtliche Untersuchung," *Zeitschrift für Theologie und Kirche,* LVIII (1961), 285–328.

Knox, John. "Epistle to the Romans," *Interpreter's Bible.* Vol. IX. New York: Abingdon-Cokesbury Press, 1954.

Kollwitz, Johannes. "Die Grabungen unter Sankt Peter," *Hochland,* XLV (1952–53), 15–25.

Kretschmar, Georg. "St. Peter's Place in the Apostolic Church," *The Ecumenical Review,* IX (1957), 85–90.

Kuhn, Karl Georg. "βαβυλών," *Theologisches Wörterbuch zum neuen Testament.* Edited by Gerhard Kittel. Vol. I. Stuttgart: W. Kohlhammer, 1933.

Kunzle, P. "Sul carme damasiano 'Hic habitasse'," *Rivista di Archeologia Cristiana,* XXVII (1951), 192–93.

—— "Bemerkungen zum Lob auf Sankt Peter und Sankt Paul von Prudentius (Peristeph. XII)," *Revista di Storia della Chiesa in Italia,* II (1957), 309–70.

Lagrange, M. J. *Évangile selon St. Luc*. Paris: Librairie Lecoffre, 1927.

Lake, K. "Simon Cephas, Peter," *Harvard Theological Review*, XIV (1921), 95–97.

Lammert, Friedrich. "τρόπαιον," *Real Encyclopädie der classischen Altertumswissenschaft*, Second Series, Vol. VII (Neue Bearbeitung), Part I (1939), pp. 663–73.

Lanciani, R. "La Memoria Apostolorum e gli Scavi di San Sebastiano," *Atti della Pontificia Accademia romana di Archeologia: Dissertazioni*, Second Series, XIV (1920), 57–109.

—— "The Memoria Apostolorum on the Appian Way," *The Dublin Review*, CLVIII (1916), 220–29.

La Piana, George. "The Tombs of Peter and Paul ad Catacumbas," *Harvard Theological Review*, XIV (1921), 53–94.

Last, Hugh. A Review of Jérôme Carcopino's, *Étude d'histoire chrétienne*, *The Journal of Roman Studies*, XLIV (1954), 112–16.

Lebreton, Jules, and Jacques Zeiller. *The History of the Primitive Church*. Translated by Ernest C. Messenger. Vol. I. London: Burns, Oates and Washbourne, 1942.

Leclercq, Henri. "Saint Pierre," *Dictionnaire d'Archéologie chrétienne et de Liturgie*, Vol. XIV, Part I (1939), cols. 822–981. 15 vols. Paris: Libraire Letouzey et Ané, 1907–53.

Lemerle, Paul. "Les Fouilles de Saint Pierre de Rome," *La Nouvelle Clio*, II (1950), 393–411.

—— "Les Persécutions et le Tombeau de Saint Pierre," *Revue Archéologique*, XXXVIII (1951), 147–55.

—— "La Publication des Fouilles de la Basilique Vaticane et la Question du Tombeau de Saint Pierre," *Revue historique*, CCVIII (1952), 205–27.

Lewin, Thomas. *Fasti Sacri*. London: Longmans, Green and Co., 1865.

Lietzmann, Hans. *Die drei älteste Martyrologien*. Second edition. Bonn: Marcus und E. Weber, 1912.

—— *Petrus und Paulus in Rom*. First edition. Bonn: Marcus und E. Weber's Verlag, 1915.

—— *Petrus und Paulus in Rom*. Second edition. Berlin: Walter de Gruyter & Co., 1927.

—— "The Tomb of the Apostles ad Catacumbas," *Harvard Theological Review*, XVI (1923), 147–62.

—— "Zwei Notizen zu Paulus," *Sitzungsberichte der preussischen Akademie der Wissenschaften: philosophisch-historische Klasse* (February 20, 1930), pp. 151–56.

—— "Petrus römischer Märtyrer," *Sitzungsberichte der preussischen Akademie der Wissenschaften: philosophisch-historische Klasse* (December 3, 1936), pp. 391–410.

Lightfoot, J. B. *Apostolic Fathers*. Second edition. Part I, Vols. I, II; Part 2, Vols. I, II. London: Macmillan & Co., 1889–1890.

Lipsius, R. A. *Die apokryphen Apostelgeschichten und Apostellegenden*. Vol. II. Braunschweig: C. A. Schwetschke und Sohn, 1887.

Lohmeyer, Ernst. *Die Offenbarung Johannis*. Tübingen: J. C. B. Mohr, 1926.

Loisy, Alfred, *La Naissance du Christianisme*. Paris: E. Nourry, 1933.

Lowe, John. *Saint Peter*. New York: Oxford University Press, 1956.

Lucian. *Charon*. Translated by A. M. Harmont. Vol. II. London: William Heinemann, 1915.

Lugari, Giovanni Battista. *Le Catacombe: ossia, il Sepolcro apostolico, dell'Appia*. Rome, 1888.

—— "I varii seppellimenti degli apostoli Pietro e Paulo sull'Appia, confirmati e chiariti dagl'ultimi scavi," *Bessarione*, II (1897), 317n17.

Lugli, Giuseppe, *Il Vaticano nel 44*, pp. 16–17.

—— "Scavo di un Sepolcreto romano presso la Basilica di San Paolo," *Notizie degli Scavi di Antichità*, Fifth Sereies, XVI (1919), 285–354.

Macario Magnete. Edited by Louis Duchesne. Paris: Fr. Klincksieck, 1877.

Macgregor, G. H. C. "The Acts of the Apostles," *Interpreter's Bible*. Vol. IX. New York: Abingdon-Cokesbury Press, 1954.

MacKendrick, P. "Caesar and Christ," *The Mute Stones Speak*. New York: St. Martin's Press, 1960.

Magi, Filippo. "Realazione preliminare sui ritrovamenti archeologici nell'area dell'autoparco vaticano," *Triplici omaggio a Sua Santità Pio XII*. 2 vols. Vatican City, 1958.

Mancini, Gioacchino. "Scavi sotto la Basilica di S. Sebastiano sull'Appia antica," *Notizie degli Scavi di Antichità*, XX (1923), 3–79.

—— "La Depositio dei SS. Pietro e Paolo Ad Catacumbas," *Atti del I° Congresso nazionale di Studi romani*, I (1929), 195–201.

Manson, T. W. "St. Paul's Letter to the Romans—and Others," *Bulletin of the John Rylands Library* (1948), pp. 3 ff.

Marcora, C. "San Pietro," *Storia dei Papi*. Vol. I. Milan: Edizioni Librarie Italiane (1961).

Marianas, Juan de. *Scholia in Vetus et Novum Testamentum*. Madrid: Ludovicus Sanctius, 1619.

Marichal, Robert. "La Date des graffiti de la Basilique de Saint-Sébastien à Rome," (Académie des Inscriptions et Belles Lettres, 20 février, 1953), *La Nouvelle Clio*, V (1953), 119, 120.

—— "Les Dates des Graffiti de Saint-Sébastien," *Comptes Rendus de l'Académie des Inscriptions et Belles Lettres* (1953), pp. 60–68.

Marrou, Henri. "Les Fouilles du Vatican," *Dictionnaire d' Archéologie chrétienne et de Liturgie*. Vol. XV, Part 2, cols. 3291–346. Paris: Libraire Letouzy et Ané, 1953.

Martyrologium Hieronymianum ad Fidum Codicum. Edited by J. B. de Rossi and L. Duchesne in *Acta Sanctorum Bollandiana*. Vol. II. Brussels: Socios Bollandianos, 1894.

Marucchi, Orazio. *Éléments d'Archéologie chrétienne*. Second edition. Paris: Desclée, Lefebre & Co., 1909.

—— *Pietro e Paolo a Roma*. Fourth edition. Revised by Carlo Cecchelli. Turin: Casa Editrice Marietti, 1934.

—— *Manual of Christian Archeology*. Fourth edition. Revised by Guilio Belvederi and translated by Hubert Vecchierello. Patterson, N.J.: St. Anthony Guild Press, 1935.

—— "Osservazioni intorno al cimitero delle Catacombe," *Römische Quartalschrift*, VI (1892), 275–309.

—— "Ulteriori Osservazioni sulla Memoria della Sede primitiva di S. Pietro," *Nuovo Bullettino di Archeologia cristiana*, Vol. VII (1901).

—— "La Crocifissione di S. Pietro in Vaticano," *Nuovo Bullettino di Archeologia cristiana*, XI (1905), 137–53.

—— "La Memoria sepolcrale degli Apostoli sulla Via Appia secondo il Resultato delle ultime Ricerche," *Nuovo Bullettino di Archeologia cristiana*, XXVI (1920), 5–31.

—— "L'Ipogei con i graffiti degli Apostoli Pietro e Paolo," *Nuovo Bullettino di Archeologia cristiana*, XXVII (1921), 3 ff.

—— "Gli ultimi Scavi nella Basilica S. Sebastiano," *Nuovo Bullettino di Archeologia cristiana*, XXVIII (1922), 3 ff.

—— "Nota sulle Memorie cristiane," *Notizie degli Scavi di Antichità*, XX (1923), 80–103.

Mattingly, Harold. *Christianity in the Roman Empire*. Dunedin, New Zealand: University of Otago, 1955.

Maurice-Denis, N., and R. Boulet. "A propos des fouilles de Saint-Pierre. Questions liturgiques et historiques," *Recherches de Science Religieuse*, XXXIV (1947), 403–6.

McGiffert, Arthur Cushman. *A History of Christianity in the Apostolic Age*. Revised edition. New York: Charles Scribner's Sons, 1932.

—— "Peter's Sojourn in Rome," *American Journal of Theology*, I (1897), 145–49.

McGuire, Martin R. P. "Clementine Literature," *Encyclopaedia Britannica*. Vol. V. Chicago: Encyclopaedia Britannica, Inc., 1951.

Menbidj, Agapius (Mahbaub) de. *Kitab al-'Unvan* [Universal History] in *Patrologia Orientalis*. Edited and translated by R. Griffiths and F. Nau. Vol. V, Part 4, 1909, 27 vols. Paris: Firmin Didot, 1903–55.

Menzies, A. "Acts of Peter," *Expository Times*, XIV (1903), 399–401.

Meslin, Michel, "Fouilles archéologiques à Rome," *Larousse Mensuel illustré*, Vol. XIII, No. 461 (January, 1953), pp. 199–201.

Meyer, C. R., "Recent Excavations Under St. Peter's Basilica," *Chicago Studies*, I (1962), 89–103.

Moffatt, James. *Introduction to the Literature of the New Testament*. New York: Charles Scribner's Sons, 1915.

Mohlberg, Leo Kunibert. "Petri ad Catacumbas. Una parola per la soluzione del problema della considdetta 'Memoria Apostolorum' alla via Appia," *Atti della Pontificia Accademia romana di Archeologia*, Third Series, Rendiconti, XV (1939), 16.

—— "Historisch-kritische Bemerkungen zum Ursprung der sogenannten 'Memoria Apostolorum' an der Appischen Strasse," *Colligere Fragmenta: Festschrift Alban Dold*. Beuron in Hohenzollern: Beuroner Kunstverlag (1952), pp. 52–74.

Mohrmann, Christine. "A propos de deux Mots controversés de la Latinité chrétienne—tropaeum—nomen," *Vigiliae Christianae*, VIII (1954), 154–73.

Molland, Einar. "Petrus in Rom," *Theologische Literaturzeitung*, LXII, 24 (1937), 439–44.

Monceaux, Paul. "L'Apostolat de Saint Pierre à Rome à propos d'un Livre récent," *Revue d'histoire et de Littérature religieuses*, New Series, XV (1910), 216–40.

Munck, Johannes. *Die Offenbarung Johannis*. Göttingen: Vandenhoeck und Ruprecht, 1906.

—— *Petrus und Paulus in der Offenbarung Johannis*. Copenhagen: Rosenkilde og Bagger, 1950.

Murphy, Francis X. "Professor Cullmann's St. Peter," *The Irish Ecclesiastical Record*, LXXXI (1954), 436–43.

Nesbitt, C. F. "What Did Become of Peter?", *Journal of Bible and Religion*, XXVII (1959), 10–16.

New York *Times*, December 24, 1950, pp. 1, 27.

The Nicene and Post-Nicene Fathers. Edited by Philip Schaff. New Series. Grand Rapids, Michigan: Wm. B. Eerdman's Publishing Co., 1956.

Nicholosi, Giuseppe. "Questioni nuove intorno alla Basilica costantiniano in Vaticano," *Il Vaticano nel 44.*, pp. 201–7.

North, R. *Verbum Domini*, XXXII (1954), 244–47.

—— "Domus Petri, Domus Domini, Domus Patris," *Biblica*, XXXVI (1955), 156–57.

Novum Testamentum Graece. Edited by Erwin Nestle and Kurt Aland. 23. Auflage. Stuttgart: Privileg. Württ. Bibelanstalt Stuttgart, 1957.

Novum Testamentum Graece et Latine. Edited by Henry Joseph Vogels. Freiburg Breisgau: Herder, 1955.

Nunn, H. P. V. "St. Peter's Presence in Rome," *Evangelical Quarterly*, XXII (1950), 126–44.

O'Callaghan, Roger T. "Recent Excavations Underneath the Vatican Crypts," *The Biblical Archaeologist*, XII (1949), 1–23.

—— "The Vatican Excavations and the Tomb of St. Peter," *The Biblical Archaeologist*, XVI (1953), 70–87.

O'Dogherty, Eamonn. "The Tomb of Saint Peter," *The American Ecclesiastical Review*, CXXVIII (January–June, 1953), 438–44.

The Office for the Commemoration of the Holy . . . Apostles . . . Peter and Paul . . . according to the Byzantine Rite in the Byzantine Office. Edited by John Bannerman Wainewright. London: Cope and Fenwick, 1909.

O'Hare, Charles M. "St. Peter in Rome," *Irish Ecclesiastical Record*, XXXVII (1931), 337–54.

"The Opinions of Paulus," *The Civil Law*. Vol. I. Edited by S. P. Scott. 17 vols. Cincinnati: Central Trust Co., 1932.

Oracula Sibyllina. Edited by C. A. Leyandre. Paris: Firmin Didot, 1869.

Parrot, André. "Le 'refrigerium' dans l'au-dèla," *Revue de l'histoire des Religions,* CXIV (1936), 69–92, 158–96; CXV (1937), 53–89.

Patrologiae Cursus Completus. Greek Series (*MPG*). 165 vols. 1857–66. Latin Series (*MPL*). 221 vols. Second edition. Edited by Jacques Paul Migne. Paris: Garnier Frères, 1878 seq.

Paul VI (pope). *Osservatore Romano.* June 26, 1963, p. 1.

Paulus, Julius. *Sententiae Receptarum ad Filium in Jurisprudentia Vetus, Ante Justinianea.* Edited by Antonii Schultingh. Leipzig: Weidmanniana, 1737.

Pausanius. *Description of Greece.* Translated by J. S. Frazer. London: Macmillan and Co., 1898.

Perkins, J. B. Ward. "The Shrine of St. Peter," *The Listener,* XLVIII (Spetember 25, 1952), 509–11.

—— A Review of Francesco Tolotti's, *Memorie degli Apostoli in Catacumbas, The Journal of Roman Studies,* XLV (1955), 205–7.

—— "A Roman Cemetery Newly Discovered in the Vatican," *The Illustrated London News,* December 12, 1959, pp. 849–50.

Peterson, Erik. "A propos du Tombeau de Saint Pierre," *Le Flambeau,* XXV (1952), 486–95 (a translation by Paul Orgels of an article, "Über das Petrusgrab," which appeared in the *Schweizer Rundschau,* LII (September, 1952), 326–31.

—— "Das Martyrium des Hl. Petrus nach der Petrus-Apokalypse," *Miscellanea Giulio Belvederi, Collezione "Amici delle Catacombe,"* XXIII (1954–55), 181–85.

Philo. *Against Flaccus.* Translated by C. D. Yonge. Vol. IV. London: Henry G. Bohn, 1955.

Philonis Alexandrini. Edited by Leopold Cohn. Vol. V. Berlin: Georgii Reimeri, 1906.

The Philosophumena. Translated by F. Legge. Vols. I, II. London: Society for Promoting Christian Knowledge, 1921.

Photius. "Bibliotheca," 273, *Patrologiae cursus Completus.* Greek Series. Vol. CIV. Edited by Jacques Paul Migne. Paris: Garniér Frères, 1860.

Piganiol, André. *L'Empereur Constantin.* Paris: Les Éditions Rieder, 1932.

Platner, Samuel B., and Thomas Ashby. *A Topographical Dictionary of Ancient Rome.* London: Oxford University Press, 1929.

Pliny the Younger. *Historiae Naturalis.* Edited by Gabrielis Brotier. Vols. II, VIII. London: H. J. Vapy, 1836.

—— *Historiae Naturalis.* Translated by H. Rackham. London: William Heinemann, 1950.

—— *Letters.* Edited by William Melmoth. London: William Heinemann, 1915.

Prandi, Adriano. *La zona archeologica della Confessione Vaticana. I Monumenti del II secolo.* Vatican City: Tipografia Poliglotta Vaticana, 1957.

—— "La Memoria Apostolorum in Catacumbas," *Roma sotterranea cristiana per Cura del Pontificia Accademia di Archeologia cristiana.* Vol. II. Vatican City, 1936.

—— "Sulla Ricostruzione della 'mensa martyrum' nella Memoria Apostolorum in Catacumbas," *Atti della Pontificia Accademia romana di Archeologia: Rendiconti,* XIX (1943), 345–53.

—— "La Cripta di S. Sebastiano," *Atti della Pontificia Accademia romana di Archeologia: Rendiconti,* XXV–XXVI (1949–50), 139–52.

—— "Lettre de Rome," *La Nouvelle Clio,* IV (1952) 395–97.

Profumo, A. "La Memoria monumentale in Catacumbas degli Apostoli Pietro e Paolo," *Studi Romani,* II (1914), 415 ff.

Prudentius. Translated by H. J. Thomson. London: William Heinemann, 1953.

Quentin, Enrico. "Per la Critica del Martirologio Gerolimiano," *Atti della Pontificia Accademia romana di Archeologia: Memorie.* Third Series, Vol. I, Part II (1924), pp. 103–8.

—— "Tusco et Basso consulibus," *Rendiconti della Pontificia Accademia Romana di Archeologia,* V (1927), 145–47.

Rehm, Bernard. "Zur Enstehung der pseudoclementinischen Schriften," *Zeitschrift für neutestamentliche Wissenschaft,* XXXVII (1938), 73–184.

Renan, Ernest. *The Antichrist.* Translated by Joseph Henry Allen. Boston: Roberts Brothers, 1897.

Rimoldi, Antonio, "L'Apostolo S. Pietro nella letteratura apocrifa dei primi sei secoli," *La Scuola Cattolica,* LXXXIII (1955), 196–224.

—— "L'Apostolo San Pietro," *Analecta Gregoriana,* Vol. XCVI (1958).

Rist, Martin. "Revelation," *Interpreter's Bible.* Vol. XII. New York: Abingdon-Cokesbury Press, 1957.

Roberts, Colin Henderson. *An Unpublished Fragment of the Fourth Gospel in the John Rylands Library.* Manchester, England: Manchester University Press, 1935.

Robinson, Donald Foy. "Where and When Did Peter Die?" *Journal of Biblical Literature,* LXIV (1945), 225–67.

Romanelli, Pietro. "La Documentazione scientifica del Ritrovamento della Tomba di San Pietro al Vaticano," *Osservatore Romano,* December 20, 1951, p. 1, Cols. 1–6.

Roth, Cecil. "Simon Peter," *Harvard Theological Review,* LIV (1961), 91–97.

Ruysschaert, José. *Réflexions sur les fouilles vaticanes. Le rapport officiel et la critique: données archéologiques, données épigraphiques et littéraires.* Louvian: E. Nauwelaerts, 1954.

—— "Les documents littéraires de la double Tradition romaine des tombes apostoliques," *Revue d'histoire ecclésiastique,* LII (1957), 791–837.

—— *The Tomb of St. Peter* (translated by Sesto Prete), *Thought,* XXXIV (1959), 5–15.

Schäfer, Ernst. *Die Bedeutung der Epigramme des Papstes Damasus I. für die Geschichte der Heiligenverehrung.* Rome: Ephemerides Liturgicae, 1932.

—— "Das Petrusgrab und die neuen Grabungen unter St. Peter in Rom," *Evangelische Theologie,* X (1951), 459–79.

—— "Das Apostelgrab unter St. Peter in Rom," *Evangelische Theologie,* XII (1952–53), 304–20.

Schmidt, Carl. *Die alten Petrusakten.* Leipzig: J. C. Hinrichs, 1903.

—— *Studien zu den Psuedo-Clementinen.* Leipzig: J. C. Hinrichs, 1929.

Schmitz, J. "Fouilles et Découvertes sous la Basilique de Saint-Pierre de Rome," *Revue Diocésaine de Namur,* II (1947), 48–63.

Schneider, Alfons Maria. "Die Memoria Apostolorum an der Via Appia," *Nachrichten der Akademie der Wissenschaften in Göttingen, philosophisch-historische Klasse,* III (1951), 1–15.

—— "III Abteilung: Bibliographie, 7B Kunstgeschichte," *Byzantinische Zeitschrift,* XLV (1952), 494–95.

—— "Das Petrusgrab im Vatikan," *Theologische Literaturzeitung,* LXXVII (June, 1952), 321–26.

Schneider, Fedor. "Über Kalendae Januariae und Martiae in Mittelalter," *Archiv für Religionswissenschaft,* XX (1921), 386.

Schulze-Kadelbach, Gerard. "Die Stellung des Petrus in der Urchristenheit," *Theologische Literaturzeitung,* LXXXI, (January, 1956), 2–14.

Schuster, I. Cardinal. "DOMVS PETRI," *Ambrosius,* XIV (1938), 157–63.

Scivoletto, N., "Pietro e Paolo nel quartiere ebraico dell'-Appia," *Giornale italiano di filologia,* XIII (1960), 1–24.

Selwyn, Edward Gordon. *The First Epistle of St. Peter.* London: Macmillan & Co., 1952.

Seneca. *Epistles.* Translated by R. M. Gumere. London: William Heinemann, 1917.

—— *Moral Essays.* Translated by J. W. Basore. Vol. III. London: William Heinemann, 1935.

Seppelt, Franz Xavier. "Das Petrusgrab," *Hochland,* XLII (June, 1950), 456–66.

Seston, W. "Les récentes fouilles de Saint-Pierre de Rome et la date de la Construction de la Basilique constantinienne," *Revue de l'histoire des Religions,* CXXX (1945), 186–88.

—— "Hypothèse sur la date de la basilique constantinienne de Saint-Pierre de Rome," *Cahiers Archéologiques,* II (1947), 153–59.

Sherwin-White, A. N. "Early Persecutions and Roman Law Again," *Journal of Theological Studies,* III (1952), 199–213.

Shotwell, J. T., and L. R. Loomis. *The See of St. Peter.* New York: Columbia University Press, 1927.

Sigrist, F. A. *Petrus der erste Papst.* Switzerland: Verlag Weggis, 1930.

Simon, Thomas Collins. *The Mission and Martyrdom of St. Peter.* London: Seeleys, 1852.

Smaltz, Warren M. "Did Peter Die in Jerusalem?" *Journal of Biblical Literature,* LXXI (1952), 211–16.

Smith, Morton. "The Report about Peter in I Clement, 5, 4," *New Testament Studies,* VII (1960), 86–88.

Smothers, Edgar R. "The Excavations under Saint Peter's, *Theological Studies,* XVII (1956), 293–321.

—— "The Bones of St. Peter," *Theological Studies,* XXVII (1966), 79–88.

Speier, Hermine. "Die neuen Ausgrabungen unter der Peters-kirche in Rom," Reinhard Herbig ed., *Vermächtnis der antiken Kunst.* Heidelberg: F. H. Kerle, 1950.

—— "'Memoria' Sancti Petri, die Auffindung des Apostel-grabes," *Wort und Wahrheit,* VII (April, 1952), 262–72.

Spence-Jones, H. D. M. *The Early Christians in Rome.* London: Methuen and Co., 1910.

—— "The Foundation of the Church in Rome. The Influence of St. Peter," *The Early Christians in Rome.* New York: John Lane, 1911.

Stamm, Raymond T. "Epistle to the Galatians," *Interpreter's Bible.* Vol. X. New York: Abingdon-Cokesbury Press, 1953.

Stauffer, Ethelbert. "ἀθληταὶ," *Theologisches Wörterbuch zum neuen Testament.* Vol. I. Herausgegeben von Gerhard Kittel. Stuttgart: W. Kohlhammer, 1933.

Stern, H., "Le calendrier de 354. Étude sur son texte et ses illustrations," *Institut français d'archéologie de Beyrouth. Bibliothèque archéologique et historique,* Vol. XLV. Paris, 1953.

Strabo. *The Geography of Strabo.* Translated and edited by Horace Jones. Vols. I, VII, VIII. London: William Heinemann, 1923–30.

Strachan, R. H. *The Fourth Gospel.* London: Student Christian Movement Press, 1941.

Strathmann, Hermann. "μαρτυρεῖν," *Theologisches Wörterbuch zum neuen Testament.* Vol. IV. Herausgegeben von Gerhard Kittel. Stuttgart: W. Kohlhammer, 1942.

Streeter, Burnett Hillman. *The Primitive Church.* New York: The Macmillan Co., 1929.

Stumpf, Albrecht. "ζῆλος," *Theologisches Wörterbuch zum neuen Testament.* Vol. II. Herausgegeben von Gerhard Kittel. Stuttgart: W. Kohlhammer, 1935.

Styger, Paul. *Die römischen Katakomben.* Berlin: Otto v. Holten, 1933.

—— *Römische Märtyrergrüfte.* Berlin: Verlag für Kunst-wissenschaft, 1935.

—— "Gli Apostoli Pietro e Paolo ad Catacumbas sulla Via Appia," *Römische Quartalschrift,* XXIX (1915), 149–221.

—— "Scavi a San Sebastiano," *Römische Quartalschrift,* XXIX (1915), 73–110.

—— "Il Monumento apostolico a San Sebastiano sulla Via Appia," *Atti della Pontificia Accademia romana di Archeologia: Dissertazioni,* Second Series, XIII (1918), 3 ff.

Suetonius. Translated by J. C. Rolfe. 2 vols. London: William Heinemann, 1920.

Sullivan, K. "The Excavations under Saint Peter's," *Liturgical Arts*, XXVI (1958), 42–43.

Swete, H. B. *The Apocalypse of St. John*. London: Macmillan and Co., 1911.

Tacitus: The Annals. Translated by John Jackson. Vol. IV London: William Heinemann, 1937.

Tailliez, Frédéric. "Notes conjointes sur un passage fameux d'Eusèbe," *Orientalia Christiana Periodica*, IX (1943), 431–49.

Talmont, Louis. "L'apostolat de Saint Pierre à Rome devant la critique recente," *Revue Augustinienne*, XVII (1910), 329–36.

Testini, Pasquale. "Noterelle sulla 'Memoria Apostolorum' in Catacumbas," *Rivista di Archeologia cristiana*, XXX (1954), 209–31.

—— "Le 'Presunte' reliquie dell' Apostolo Pietro e la traslazione 'ad Catacumbas,' Actes du vᵉ Congrés internationale d'Archéologie chrétienne," *Studi di Antichità cristiana*. Vol. XXII. Vatican City, 1957.

The Theodosian Code. Translated by Clyde Pharr. Princeton: Princeton University Press, 1952.

De Theophania. Translated by Samuel Lee. Cambridge, England: Duncan and Malcolm, 1843.

Thesaurus Syriacus. Edited by R. Payne Smith. Oxford: Clarendon Press, 1879–1901.

Tisserant, Eugene. *Ascension d'Isaïe*. Paris: Letouzey et Ané, 1909.

Tolotti, Francesco. *Memorie degli Apostoli in Catacumbas* (Collezione "Amici delle Catacombe," XIX). Vatican City: Società "Amici delle Catacombe," 1953.

—— "Ricerche intorno alla Memoria Apostolorum," *Rivista di Archeologia cristiana*, XXII (1946), 7–62; XXIII (1947–48), 13–116.

Torp, Hjalmar. "The Vatican Excavations and the Cult of Saint Peter," *Acta Archaeologica*, XXIV (1953), 27–66.

Torrey, C. C. *Documents of the Primitive Church*. New York: Harper and Brothers, 1941.

Townsend, Gavin. "The Circus of Nero and the Vatican Excavations," *American Journal of Archeology*, LXII (1958), 216–18.

Toynbee, Jocelyn. "The Shrine of St. Peter and Its Setting," *Journal of Roman Studies*, XLIII (1953), 1–26.

—— A Review of Francesco Tolotti's *Memorie degli Apostoli in Catacumbas*, *The Antiquaries Journal*, XXXV (1955), 104–6.

—— A Review of Jérôme Carcopino's *De Pythagore aux Apôtres*, *Gnomon*, XXIX (1957), 261–70.

—— "The Vatican Excavations and the Tomb of St. Peter," *The Hibbert Journal*, LV (1957), 284–85.

—— An appraisal of T. Klauser's "Die römische Petrustradition, im Lichte der neuen Ausgrabungen unter der Peterskirche." *American Journal of Archeology*, LXII (1958), 126–29.

—— "Graffiti beneath St. Peter's. Prof. Guarducci's Interpretations," *The Dublin Review*, CCXXXIII (Autumn, 1959), 234–44.

Toynbee, Jocelyn, and John Ward Perkins. *The Shrine of St. Peter and the Vatican Excavations*. New York: Pantheon Books, 1957.

Tuker, M. A. R., and Hope Malleson. *Handbook to Christian and Ecclesiastical Rome*. London: Adam and Charles Black, 1900.

Turner, Cuthbert Hamilton. "The Papal Chronology of the Third Century," *Journal of Theological Studies*, XVII (1916), 338–52.

—— "The Early Episcopal Lists," *Journal of Theological Studies*, XVIII (1917), 103–34.

—— "I. St. Peter in the New Testament. II. St. Peter in the New Testament and the Early Church," *Theology*, XIII (1926), 66–78, 190–204.

Underhill, Francis. *Saint Peter*. New York: Longmans, Green and Co., 1938.

Vacchini, Francesco, "La Sua Tomba è stata trovata," *Ecclesia*, XI (1952), 7–13.

Valerii Maximi. Edited by Carolus Kempf. Leipzig: B. G. Teubneri, 1888.

Vallin, Pierre. "Le Culte des Apôtres Pierre et Paul 'ad Catacumbas," *Bulletin de Littérature Ecclésiastique*, LXV (1964), 258–79.

Van Cauwelaert, R. "L'intervention de l'Église de Rome à Corinthe vers l'an 96," *Revue d'histoire Ecclésiastique*, XXXI (1935), 267–306.

Van Deman, Esther Boise. "Methods of Determining the Date of Roman Concrete Monuments," *American Journal of Archeology*, Second Series, XVI (1912), 230–51.

Vassall-Phillips, O. R. "St. Paul and St. Peter," *The Month*, CLVII (1931), 436–42.

Vielliard, R. "Les Titres romains et les deux Éditions du *Liber Pontificalis*," *Rivista di Archeologia cristiana*, V (1928), 90–103.

Villiger, Johann Baptist. "Die Ausgrabungen unter der Peterskirche in Rom," *Theologie und Glaube*, Vol. XLII, No. 5 (1952), pp. 321–28.

Voelkl, Ludwig. "Vaticano," *Römische Quartalschrift*, XLVIII (1953), 244, 245.

Vogelsanger, Peter. "Petrusgrab und Papsttum," *Reformatio: Zeitschrift für evangelische, Kultur und Politik*, I (1952), 308–17.

Vogt, E. "Sepulcrum S. Petri," *Biblica*, XXXIII (1952), 165–68, 306–9.

von Gerkan, Armin. "Die Forschung nach dem Grab Petri," *Zeitschrift für neutestamentliche Wissenschaft*, XLIV (1952–53), 196–205. (The same article also appears in *Evangelisch-Lutherische Kirchenzeitung*, VI [1952], 379–82.)

—— "Kritische Studien zu den Ausgrabungen unter der Peterskirche in Rom," *Trierer Zeitschrift*, XXII (1954), 26–55.

—— "Zu den Problemen des Petrusgrabes," *Jahrbuch für Antike und Christentum*, I (1958), 79–93.

—— "Petrus in Vaticano et in Catacumbas," *Jahrbuch für Antike und Christentum*, V (1962), 23–32.

—— "Noch einmal Petrus in Vaticano et in catacumbas," *Jahrbuch für Antike und Christentum*, V (1962), 39–42.

Vouaux, Léon. *Les Actes de Pierre*. Paris: Libraire Letouzey et Ané, 1922.

Waal, Anton de. "La Platonia ossia il Sepolcro apostolico della Via Appia," *Atti della Pontificia Accademia romana di Archeologia: Dissertazioni*, Second Series, IV (1892), 141–63.

—— "Die Platonia ad Catacumbas," *Römische Quartalschrift*, IX (1895), 111–17.

—— "Zu Wilpert's Domus Petri," *Römische Quartalschrift*, XXVI (1912), 123–32.

—— "Gli Scavi nel Pavimento della Basilica di San Sebastiano sulla Via Appia," *Römische Quartalschrift*, XXIX (1915), 145–48.

Wand, A. C. "The Location of Constantine's Gold Cross," *Theological Studies*, II (1941), 84–88.

Wilpert, Josef. *Roma sotterranea, le Pitture delle Catacombe*. Rome: Descleé, Lefebre, 1903.

—— "Domus Petri," *Römische Quartalschrift*, XXVI (1912), 117–22.

—— "La Tomba di S. Pietro," *Rivista di Archeologia cristiana*, XIII (1936), 27–41.

Wilson, H. A. *The Gelasian Sacramentary*. Oxford: Clarendon Press, 1894.

Windisch, Hans. "Die katholischen Briefe," *Handbuch zum neuen Testament*. Vol. XV. Edited by Hans Lietzmann. Tübingen: J. C. B. Mohr (1930).

Winter, Michael M. *St. Peter and the Popes*, Baltimore, Md.: Helicon Press; London: Darton, Longman & Todd, Ltd., 1960.

Wohlenberg, D. S. "Der erste und zweite Petrusbriefe und der Judasbriefe," *Kommentar zum neuen Testament*. Vol. XV. Edited by Theodor Zahn. Leipzig: A. Deichertsche, 1923.

Zahn, Theodor. *Introduction to the New Testament*. Translation from the third German edition by Melancthon Jacobus *et al.* Vols. II, III. Edinburgh: T. & T. Clark, 1909.

Zeller, E. *La legende de Saint Pierre premier evêque de Rome*. Paris: Marchand, 1876.

—— "Der Märtyrertod des Petrus in der *Ascensio Jessiae*," *Zeitschrift für wissenschaftliche Theologie* (1896), pp. 558–68.

Zucchetti, Giuseppe. "L'Obelisco vaticano," *Ecclesia*, IX (1950), 523–26.

Index